P9-EGM-054

SOCIAL INEQUALITY

FORMS, CAUSES, AND CONSEQUENCES

FOURTH EDITION

CHARLES E. HURST

The College of Wooster

ALLYN AND BACON

Boston • London • Toronto • Sydney • Tokyo • Singapore

Series Editor: Sarah L. Kelbaugh
Editor in Chief, Social Sciences: Karen Hanson
Editorial Assistant: Lori Flickinger
Marketing Manager: Lisa Kimball
Editorial-Production Administrator: Annette Joseph
Editorial-Production Coordinator: Holly Crawford
Editorial-Production Service: Lynda Griffiths, TKM Productions
Photo Researcher: Katharine Cook
Composition Buyer: Linda Cox
Electronic Composition: Omegatype Typography, Inc.
Manufacturing Buyer: Julie McNeill
Cover Administrator: Linda Knowles

Copyright © 2001, 1998, 1995, 1992 by Allyn & Bacon
A Pearson Education Company
160 Gould Street
Needham Heights, MA 02494
Internet: www.abacon.com

All rights reserved. No part of the material protected by this copyright notice may be reproduced or utilized in any form or by any means, electronic or mechanical, including photocopying, recording, or by any information storage and retrieval system, without written permission from the copyright owner.

Between the time Website information is gathered and then published, it is not unusual for some sites to have closed. Also, the transcription of URLs can result in unintended typographical errors. The publisher would appreciate notification where these occur so that they may be corrected in subsequent editions. Thank you.

Library of Congress Cataloging-in-Publication Data

Hurst, Charles E.
    Social inequality : forms, causes, and consequences / Charles E. Hurst. — 4th ed.
        p.   cm.
    Includes bibliographical references and index.
    ISBN 0-205-31949-1
        1. Equality—United States.   2. United States—Social conditions.   I. Title.
    HN90.S6H87   2000
    305'.0973—dc21

                                                                99-089143

Printed in the United States of America

10 9 8 7 6 5 4 3 2 1   05 04 03 02 01 00

Cartoon credits: pp. 8 and 242: Cartoon by David Kordalski. p. 360: Chip Bok.
Photo credits: p. 22: Reprinted with permission of the *Akron Beacon Journal.* pp. 28 and 55: Sarah Brownlee. p. 38: Patrick G. Flanagan. pp. 46 and 322: UPI/Corbis-Bettmann. p. 67: Corbis-Bettmann. p. 92: AP/Wide World Photos. p. 102: Will Hart. p. 110: Robert Harbison. pp. 137, 258, and 332: Library of Congress. p. 225: From Etienne Esquirol's *Des Maladies Mentales,* 1938, courtesy of the National Library of Medicine. pp. 233 and 235: David C. Barnett. p. 371: Catherine H. Gledhill.

To Mary Ellen
with love always for who you are

CONTENTS

PART TWO
GENERAL EXPLANATIONS OF INEQUALITY

PREFACE

The last decade of the twentieth century witnessed an explosion of new technology, the beginnings of a third industrial revolution. Internet communication has created wider and more complex networks of contact throughout much of the world. Progress in technology has made possible advances in medicine and education. The United States is at the forefront of these expanding developments. Yet, it is still an open question as to who will be able to benefit fully from these changes. Some things change and others remain the same. Technology marches on, but many of our society's more fundamental and seemingly intractable problems remain intact. Widening gaps in wealth and income, continued racial and sexual discrimination, as well as persistent child poverty, hunger, and homelessness continue to tear at our social fabric. The number of billionaires has increased at a record pace, but about 36 million people are still poor. International competition, corporate outsourcing, and the quest for corporate efficiency have left increasing numbers of both white-collar and blue-collar employees unemployed or in new temporary positions. The latter are often called *contingent* positions because they lack the assumed security of many past jobs. Racial and ethnic tensions have resurfaced with an often brutal face as people try to assign blame for their threatened statuses and try to compete for a better life in a society in which the distant but strong glow of the American dream has dimmed. Women continue to push for greater equality in earnings and occupational opportunities. Gays and lesbians fight for respect and equal treatment even as they contribute to the political and economic strength of the nation.

Like earlier editions, this book is intended as an introduction to the study of social inequality. It is still based on the assumptions that (1) social inequality is multidimensional; (2) theoretical understanding is necessary to be successful in grappling with inequality's undesirable consequences; (3) couching a discussion of inequality in its broader historical and social structural context provides a fuller understanding of inequality's nature and role in society; and (4) an evenhanded approach covering the gamut of perspectives on inequality is most appropriate, especially for undergraduates being exposed to this material for the first time. My goal is to convey, simply but as compellingly as I can, a sense of the pervasiveness and extensiveness of social inequality, how it affects all of us, how it can be explained, and what is being done about it.

Following advice from students and colleagues, I have made numerous changes in this fourth edition that I hope will make coverage more complete, discussions clearer, and student engagement deeper. I have added new and updated old material, but I have continued to keep in mind that students are the book's principal audience. "Nutshells" and Critical Thinking questions remain. The core emphases on breadth of coverage, theoretical understanding, and current data in the text also remain, yet many significant changes distinguish this edition from earlier ones:

1. Given rapid and growing globalization, I have added a discussion of the relevance of the global economy and Internet technology for the shaping of social inequality in the United States.

2. Brief Web Connections conclude each chapter. These identify websites related to chapter topics and suggest exercises for students to broaden and deepen their understanding

of inequality issues and to provide them with additional sources on the changing profile of social inequality.

3. I have written a new chapter on sexual orientation since, in addition to women, gays and lesbians are also subject to the discrimination and prejudice that generally accompany assignment to a low-status level. In a general sense, this is an attempt to broaden and deepen understanding of the inequality that surrounds gender roles and sexual lifestyles.

4. While previous editions contained some material on affirmative action, I have supplemented this material and included in Chapter 16 a discussion of some of the central myths surrounding affirmative action. Suggestions for reform that address inequality rather than poverty have also been expanded in Chapter 16.

5. In light of the recent tragedies and notoriety involving high school lifestyles, I have incorporated an analysis of student cliques and lifestyles into the discussion on status groups in Chapter 3. The grouping of students into status groups along a hierarchy of prestige is nothing new. Believe it or not, these were even present when I went to high school. Students should find it easy to identify with this discussion.

6. Reviewers suggested that I provide more material on international differences in living conditions and life chances to Chapter 8. I have done that, adding material on differences in life expectancies, mortality rates, AIDS rates, sanitation, housing, and literacy. This affords a deeper understanding of inequality as being truly multidimensional.

7. In light of the fact that it has been several years since the 1996 welfare reforms were passed by the Congress, I have included a review of the highlights of current state welfare reform packages along with a discussion of follow-up studies designed to assess the effectiveness of these reforms.

8. A section on hate crimes is included in Chapter 12 to supplement the discussions of street and suite crime. This addition complements the new chapter on sexual orientation.

9. Finally, I have gone over the entire text, cutting out dated or unnecessary material and adding new commentaries and data where possible—for example, all the data on income and occupational distribution, earnings, and poverty are as current as possible.

After a brief introduction to some core issues in Chapter 1, *Social Inequality* is divided into four major parts. The chapters in Part One survey the *extent* of inequality along a variety of dimensions: economic, status, gender, sexual orientation, racial and ethnic, political, and comparative. Each also addresses *specific explanations* associated with a specific form of inequality. Not surprisingly, these theories draw on sociology, anthropology, political science, and economics, and include conservative, liberal, and more radical orientations. Part Two covers an in-depth discussion of *broad explanations* of inequality that have been espoused over time by many adherents. The first of the two chapters included in this section reviews the classical arguments of Marx, Weber, and Durkheim, whereas the second chapter analyzes and assesses more contemporary functional, reproduction, comparative, and labor-market theories. The chapters in Part Three demonstrate how inequality affects our personal lives as well as society. The *effects* of inequality reach inwardly into our most private mental and physical selves as well as outwardly into cultural and social conditions in society. Inequality's effects are pervasive. Finally, Part Four addresses *stability and change* in the system of social inequality. The extent of social mobility affects the relative stability of that system, as do its social-psychological and institutional underpinnings. Attempts to change and redress inequities in U.S. society are dealt with in the last two chapters. Historically, these attempts have included broad-based social movements and more specific governmental programs and reforms.

Although any shortcomings in the book are my own responsibility, any improvements in this edition are due in large part to the suggestions of colleagues, both anonymous and known, and to the students in my social inequality class at The College of Wooster. Sarah Kelbaugh at Allyn and Bacon was always there when I needed a question answered or a manuscript problem solved. I am grateful to those reviewers who read over and commented on the entire third edition, so that I could make the fourth one stronger. These include Tim Heaton, Brigham Young University; Melissa Latimer, West Virginia University; and Suzan Waller, University of Central Oklahoma. I kept their detailed reviews in front of me as I worked through this new edition and incorporated many changes that reflect their suggestions. Although no book can fully satisfy every reader, I have tried to make changes that correspond to the major and recurrent comments of reviewers. A few individuals made very helpful suggestions on specific parts of the new edition. I am especially indebted to my friends Heather Fitz Gibbon, Patrick Flanagan, and Barry Friedrichsen. I have also been aided by sporadic but incisive comments from colleagues using the book at other schools. Finally, and as always, I am deeply grateful to my wife, Mary Ellen, for her continued love, moral support, and help in preparing the final manuscript. She is one of the real heroes in my life. In an unequal world, she is without equal.

CHAPTER 1

AN INTRODUCTION TO THE STUDY OF SOCIAL INEQUALITY

It can be argued that the debate over social inequality formed the basis for the emergence of sociology as a modern discipline.
—Bryan S. Turner

Not too long ago, a student approached me to say how much she resented her wealthier acquaintances. What upset her was not merely the BMWs and Acuras some of the students drove, or the quality of their clothes, or their expensive computers, but the fact that they had not really earned these things; rather, they had been given to them by their parents. She herself had grown up with working-class parents who lived on a farm and who did not particularly value a seemingly nonpractical liberal arts education. She had been taught that one had to work for and earn the kinds of goodies other students had in abundance. This experience is not an isolated one. Over the years, knowing of my interest in social-class issues, numerous students have spoken to me about their discomfort of being at an elite liberal arts college where the fees are well above $25,000 per year. Some learn to accommodate themselves to their unusual and somewhat foreign situation, while others continue to wrestle with their marginality among students who are better off than they are, and some simply transfer to another school.

The same experience is felt by some faculty whose backgrounds are dissimilar from those of their colleagues and many of the students they teach. Recently, I interviewed faculty at several highly selective liberal arts colleges. Some expressed their lack of ease, even though they had been at their institutions for years. One, for example, who came from a background where his father had not graduated from high school and had worked in a factory, told me, "I have always felt a little bit of an outsider to the general social class here, certainly the students." He went on to say that he "felt sort of intimidated." Keep in mind that these feelings were expressed by a full professor with a Ph.D. in a natural science—not a person one would expect to have a shaky sense of self-confidence. The theme of not fitting in or being unsure of oneself occurred often among the faculty I interviewed whose class origins were below the middle. Consider your own situation. Imagine that you had come from a family of noticeably different wealth or from a different region or nationality, or that you were of a different race or sex. How would your experiences, perceptions, and opportunities be different?

Inequality is present and affects us at all stages of our lives. Think of your own experiences. Even when young, we hear people speak of others as being from the "wrong side of the tracks," as being not "our kind," as being "above" or "below" us. We hear about racism and sexism. As youths, we notice that because of the way others dress, where they live, and who their parents are, some are treated differently and have greater opportunities than others. We are also smart enough to see that there are class differences associated with different neighborhood elementary schools. If we are from a working-class family and attending an expensive college, we notice with wonder the BMWs, Jeeps, and racks of Canondale mountain bikes. We see the players in pick-up football games wearing Polo and Hilfiger shirts, showing little concern if their clothing gets ripped or stained. We know that there is a difference between those who shop at Kmart and those who frequent Saks or Lord & Taylor. If we are from a more fortunate class, we see corresponding differences—of those who do not dress or live as well as we. It is not hard to notice when driving through town that some neighborhoods are not as well maintained as others, evidenced by garbage strewn around the sidewalks or dirt yards.

The statistics confirming this inequality are extensive. In 1998, over 34 million people in the United States were poor by government standards, and almost 40 percent of these were children under 18 years of age. Hard work does not always lift the poor out of poverty, either. Some 5 million poor children live in homes in which at least one of the parents works full time all year. On the other hand, those at the very top of the economic ladder have done well. *Business Week* reported that in 1998, the average chief executive officer's (CEO's) compensation at a large company was 419 times that of the average factory worker. The 1998 average total pay of CEOs, including all kinds of compensation such as stock options, was $10.6 million ("Executive Pay" 1999). Many social, political, and economic forces are behind these statistics, and we will explore them later.

Also behind the statistics are the faces of real individuals whose lives have been drastically affected by those forces over which they have little immediate control. Consider the Schabows and the Bartelles, two hard-working couples caught on the treadmill of trying to keep up. Lawrence Schabow has worked as a truck driver for a firm that was bought out by a larger company that proceeded to cut wages and insurance benefits for its employees. In 1996, he earned 22 percent *less* in real terms than he did in 1983, and he had to pay for his own eye and dental insurance. Despite working full time, the family could not pay their debts and had to enter bankruptcy in 1992. Lawrence's own conclusion? "I'm supporting us and our three kids and going under more and more every week" (Bernstein 1996, p. 91).

Ernst and Anna Bartelle, both of whom are Mexican American, find the going tough as well, even though both of them work. They want the best for their children and they pay a psychological price for not being able to give it to them. Ernst confided, "And that's what hurts. The kids know it. In their minds, when the kids are gone, it's going to be, 'Oh, the parents were always scratching and scraping.' That's a hell of a legacy to leave them." In the past, Anna blamed Ernst for not being able to find a well-paying job. But now she feels that they have really been like hamsters on a wheel, running and working hard but getting nowhere (Schwarz and Volgy 1992, pp. 25–31).

Or consider Derrick White, a young African American living in an 850-square-foot apartment with his mother and five half-siblings in the Hurt Village housing project in Memphis (Kilborn 1993). Derrick's mother, one of 18 children born to a maid and sharecropper in a small Arkansas town, had worked full time until Derrick's birth, and is now working toward her high school degree. Presently, the family relies heavily on welfare for income. A quiet, unassuming person, Derrick graduated third among the boys in his high school, but has been in and out of college because of financial problems. He would like to be a doctor because he could then help people and make enough money to help his mom, his church, and his children when he has them. His mother supports his efforts and believes in pushing children to do their best. Derrick figures he can make it by "'getting people behind me' and playing by the rules."

The injurious impact of inequality is not confined to the working class and poor, however. In recent years, the effects of social and economic forces pushing people into different economic circumstances have been increasingly felt by those in the white-collar ranks as companies downsize to meet competition and maintain profits. Steven Holthausen, once a bank loan officer, is now a tourist guide because his job was eliminated in 1990. Since then, his wife has left him and his children avoid him, blaming him for his economic decline. He feels he has lost respect in the community. While part of his anger is directed at himself, he also blames the company and the government for his predicament. "The anger that I feel right now is that I lost both my family and my job. That is not where I wanted to be at this point in my life" (Uchitelle and Kleinfield 1996). Unfortunately, Steven's story is not unique. We have all seen the lists of 1990s layoffs prominently laid out in newspapers: 50,000 at Sears Roebuck, 123,000 at AT&T, almost 19,000 at Delta Air Lines, nearly 17,000 at Eastman Kodak, 11,000 at Tenneco, and so on. Many of the 36 million jobs eliminated from 1979 to 1993 involved white-collar workers.

The streamlining and downsizing of businesses have left millions of experienced, specialized workers with temporary part-time jobs or without jobs, and frequently the immediate response is like that of Edoardo Leoncavallo, a middle-aged recently unemployed architect who knows the family problems that result from downward mobility: "I think my wife initially felt resentment. I think she felt, Why can't you bring home the bacon?" (Labich 1993, p. 42).

At the same time, advances in computer and information technologies have created opportunities for others to become phenomenally rich. Five years ago, few people had heard of Jeffrey Bezos. Yet, in 1999, at age 35 and the moving force behind Amazon.Com, an Internet bookseller whose stock has skyrocketed, Bezo's wealth is estimated to be over $10 billion (Brown et al. 1999).

SOME CONTROVERSIAL ISSUES OF SUBSTANCE

Inequality and its effects are all around us. Consider the breadth of inequality's impact one is likely to see during a lifetime involving differences in possessions, places, wealth, experiences, bodies, races, genders, and power. The extensiveness of it is almost overwhelming. And yet, there is a great deal of controversy about social inequalities. Are social inequalities inevitable, especially in a capitalist society that stresses competition and individual success? Why do some have more than others? Is this natural or unnatural? Are Steven and the Bartelles right in having doubts about their own abilities and then turning blame on themselves if they do not succeed? Does hard work always pay off or are the positions that people occupy due largely to factors having little to do with personal motivation and effort? Is Derrick right in placing such importance on his own efforts or is he likely to be disappointed? Can inequality be lessened or not? Are economic and other resources becoming more or less equally distributed in the United States? Is inequality really a social problem? Is it desirable or not? Do we really have classes in the United States or merely individuals and families who happen to have different amounts of scarce resources? Can equality in political power exist even if economic resources are distributed unequally? Or does the Golden Rule operate—those with the gold rule? These are among the most intriguing and consequential of the questions that have been raised in the study of social inequality. We now examine some of these in more detail.

Is Inequality Inevitable?

Perhaps the most basic issue relates to the inevitability of inequality. It is important to clarify that reference is being made here to *institutionalized* rather than *individual* inequality (i.e., structured inequality between categories of individuals that are systematically created, reproduced, legitimated by sets of ideas, and relatively stable). We would not be studying this phenomenon if it was not a prominent feature of contemporary society with significant consequences. To ask whether it is inevitable is to address discussions of its origins (i.e., whether it is caused by natural or artificial factors). If social inequality is directly linked to conditions inherent in the nature of groups of individuals or society, then little might be expected to eliminate it. On the other hand, if such inequality arises because of the conscious, intentional, and freely willed actions of individuals or the structures they create in society, then perhaps it can be altered.

One side argues that inequality is always going to be present because of personal differences between individuals. If there is an open society and if people vary in their talents and motivations, then this would suggest that inequality is inevitable, a simple fact of society. "Some inequalities come about as a result of unavoidable biological inequalities of physical skill, mental capacity, and traits of personality" argued Cauthen (1987, p. 8) in his treatise on equality. Some early philosophers also argued that there are "natural" differences between individuals, and some people, in fact, still maintain that there are differences of this type separating the sexes, resulting in the inevitability of inequality. Aristotle took the position that "the male is by nature superior, the female, inferior; and the one rules, and the other is ruled" (in Kriesberg 1979, p. 12). More recently, Goldberg (1973, p. 133) argued that male dominance and higher achievement are probably inevitable because of the biological differences that he says exist between males and females. An unbroken thread running through several of the vignettes at the beginning of the chapter is the belief that it is differences in individuals that account for inequality between persons. These and other explanations of inequality will be discussed in detail later.

Other theorists have argued that inequality is inevitable because as long as certain kinds of tasks are more necessary for the survival of the society than others, and as long as those able to perform those tasks are rare, social inequality of rewards between individuals is needed to motivate the best people to perform the most difficult tasks. Under these conditions, the argument goes, inequality cannot be eradicated without endangering the society.

On the other side of the fence are those who argue that economic inequality is largely the by-product of a system's structure and not the result of major differences in individual or group talents,

characteristics, and motivations. Rousseau, for example, linked the origins of inequality to the creation of private property (Dahrendorf 1970, p. 10). It is the characteristics of the political economy and the firms and labor markets within it that are primary determinants of differences in income and wealth. Where a person works and in what industry have a major effect on income. Certainly, the job changes resulting from downsizing would suggest this. Essentially, then, this argument states that it is not human nature and individual differences but rather structural conditions that determine where an individual winds up on the ladder of economic inequality. Discrimination is another of those conditions.

> The theories that say…that women are "naturally" disadvantaged are of use to those who want to preserve and strengthen the dominant political and economic interests…. Contrary to the claims of biological determinists, studies of the contributions that biological factors make to human behavior can at most give only very limited information about the origins of present differences in human behavior and probably no information about the origins of present social structures. (Lowe and Hubbard 1983, pp. 55–56)

Clearly, both Steven Holthausen and the Bartelles suspect that their situations may be at least partially determined by forces beyond their control. If the conditions that generate social inequality are artificial creations of human actions, then they can be changed, and economic inequality is not inevitable, nor is it necessarily beneficial for the society and all its members. We will examine this controversy more thoroughly in later chapters.

Is Inequality Increasing or Lessening?

Another issue revolves around whether socioeconomic differences between classes, races, and the sexes are increasing or decreasing. One position is that the United States is largely a middle-class society and that government exerts pressure to limit the growth of the upper class's wealth, while at the same time it aids the lower classes through various social programs. The result is a *structural* tendency for most groups to move toward the middle—a class system with an ever-increasing bulge in the middle. This argument is related to the classlessness position in that if, ultimately, the pressure results in a largely middle-class society or middle mass, then in effect there is virtually only one large class. In *cultural* terms, this argument says that all classes are moving in the direction of the same values, and specifically, that lower classes adopt the values of those above them. This has been particularly stressed in some discussions of the working class, which, it is said, takes on the values of the middle class as its economic fortunes improve.

Another version of this homogenizing scenario suggests that race may be becoming less important as a determinant of life chances and that the differences between the races are diminishing. In fact, it is suggested that class differences *within* racial groups may be more significant than those existing *between* such groups. Similarly, as women have moved increasingly into the labor market, their status has moved closer to that of men, and many argue that women have made great strides in reducing the socioeconomic differences between themselves and men.

In sharp contrast to these images of decreasing differences and merging groups, others have argued that polarization is occurring with respect to the social classes, with the gap between the top and bottom increasing. They cite the number of poor, homeless, and an "underclass" as evidence for this trend, along with changes in governmental tax and poverty policies. In essence, they are saying that the rich are getting richer and the poor poorer. The same general kind of argument has been made regarding race and sex, stating that not only have race and sex continued to be important determinants of life chances but also there has been little reduction in the extent of differences that exist between the races and sexes in the United States. We will examine these issues closely in the next and succeeding chapters. If what is happening to Steven Holthausen and the salaries of chief executive officers is fairly typical of what happens to many as the economy shifts,

then perhaps the gap is increasing between the top and the bottom. On the other hand, if African Americans and women are breaking through the walls of discrimination and moving up, then perhaps some of the gaps are closing. We shall see.

Equality or Inequality: Desirable or Undesirable?

A variety of studies have asked Americans how they feel about equality and inequality, and it is clear that they are ambivalent in their feelings. In some ways, they are attracted to equality; in other ways, they view inequality as justified.

Part of the problem here is that people think about different things when they think about inequality, and people feel differently about the various kinds of equality/inequality. Moreover, there are numerous inequalities/equalities; thus, the meaning of equality/inequality is not self-evident. "Trying to think clearly about equality," wrote Cauthen (1987), "is indeed like being tossed naked into a tangled thicket in the midst of a briar patch" (p. 2). For example, Bryan Turner (1986) cited four basic kinds of equality: (1) equality pertaining to all as basic human beings—that is, the notion that basically we are all the same and equally worthy as persons; (2) equality of opportunity— the idea that access to valued ends is open to all; (3) equality of condition—that is, that all start from the same position; and (4) equality of results or outcome, or equality of income. The latter is the most radical of the four and the one most likely to incite controversy.

Studies suggest that most Americans are against limiting the amount of income an individual can make, but at the same time they feel that many in high-paying occupations receive more than they deserve (Kluegel and Smith 1986). Americans feel quite differently about equality of opportunity than they do about egalitarianism, and groups feel differently about the fairness of the system. A study of over 2,700 leaders in various areas, for example, showed that they feel any fair distribution of goods should be based on equality of *opportunity* rather than equality of *result*. At the same time, however, African American and feminist leaders are much less likely to consider the free enterprise system fair, and are more likely to consider poverty to be caused by problems in the system rather than by deficiencies in the individual (Verba and Orren 1985). We will examine the tangle of American beliefs about inequality and its fairness more fully in Chapter 14.

Are There Classes in the United States?

The economic differences that exist between families and individuals can be easily recognized, but does that mean that social classes exist in the United States? There is much to discourage the belief in classes. The value system stresses individualism, liberty, and equality. The belief in individualism and liberty would work against the development of stably reproduced social classes in the United States. Following these values, it is inconsistent to have group inequalities in which a person's fate is largely determined by the group to which he or she belongs, nor is it legitimate to have individual liberty curtailed by the application of structural constraints (e.g., laws, admission requirements) to some groups and not others. Finally, the value of equality—that we are all one people, that, underneath, U.S. citizens are all "common folk" without formal titles (e.g., duke, lord)—helps to reinforce the basic notion that all Americans are equal.

In addition to some central U.S. values, other conditions moderate the belief in the existence of classes. First of all, as we will see later, there is a great deal of disagreement about the definition of *social class*. This lack of agreement in conceptualization makes it more difficult for there to be agreement on the existence of classes. Second, the lack of belief is further strengthened by the fact that in contrast to race and sex, there are far fewer reliable and clear-cut physical clues to class position. Walking down the street, it is much easier to tell accurately if someone is Black or White and male or female than it is to tell what class he or she is in. Class is often invisible, and therefore we seem to be less often confronted by it. People do not always wear their class positions on their sleeves, so to speak. Think about it: Can you reliably and accurately tell the class positions of your classmates simply by their appearances?

Third, this very invisibility makes it much easier to create and manipulate ideas about the existence of classes in society. It is much easier to say that classes simply do not exist. Finally, the increasing concern for privacy and personal security in U.S. society, which isolates people from each other, enhances the belief in the absence of classes. It is hard to recognize classes and the predicaments of others if we live in shells. In this view, individual differences in wealth may exist, but basically Americans are all the same and equally worthy, and classes based on group or categorical differences do not exist. Any individual differences in wealth would be viewed as a continuum along which all individuals and families could be located. Here, the image of a system of inequality is one of a tall but narrow ladder. Discrete, wide, separate layers would not be a part of this perspective.

In fact, some social theorists have argued that the term *social class* has no relevance for the United States, at least in its Marxian definition. Social classes, as unified class-conscious groups with their own lifestyles and political beliefs, do not apply to the United States in this view, whereas they may still fully apply to European countries that have a tradition of class conflict. Frequently, part of this position is the conviction that there are differences in lifestyle and status between different occupational groups, but these differences are not class based. Much of the traditional research in the field of inequality, in fact, has focused on social lifestyle differences between groups rather than on economic-class differences. The focus of research is, of course, conditioned by the historical context in which it occurs, the cultural milieu, and the events of the times. As we shall see, this is clearly the case in U.S. research on social inequality.

One position, then, is that social classes as full-fledged groups antagonistically related to each other do not fit the U.S. condition today. Others suggest, however, that fairly distinct classes exist at the extremes of the inequality hierarchy but not in the middle, which is considered largely a mass of relatively indistinguishable categories of people. A third position is that distinct classes have always existed and continue to exist in the United States, and that *class* conflict has not been absent from its history and continues to this day. Distinct disparities in the incomes of those in different occupational categories would appear to reinforce the notion that classes exist in the United States.

Capitalism versus Democracy

Do economic and political inequality necessarily go together? The *economic* system of capitalism has been linked to the *political* system of democracy in both a positive and a negative manner (Almond 1991). It has been viewed as a determinant as well as an enemy of democracy. Can capitalism and democracy effectively coexist? Pure capitalism demands that markets be open and free and that individuals be able to freely pursue their economic goals, competing with others within the broad framework of the U.S. legal system. Capitalism's ideal conditions assume *equality of opportunity,* regardless of sex, race, or any other categorical characteristic. Presumably, individual talents and motivations are the prime determinants of how far a person goes in the system. This is how many would explain the high executive salaries noted previously. "My view of executive compensation is like all compensation, it's market driven. The company pays what it has to pay to recruit and retain a person.... A person is worth what the market is willing to pay for him" said Charles Peck, an analyst for The Conference Board (in Gladstone 1988, p. 4). A system like this presumably would result in the best people being in the highest positions, with the consequence being an efficiently run economy. But if this type of competitive capitalism operates in the United States, then economic inequality is unavoidable, since the talents and motivations of individuals and supply and demand for them vary. There is a potential for economic concentration

under these circumstances, with a few having much while many may have little.

Alongside this capitalistic economic system exists a political democracy in which everyone is supposed to have a vote in the running of the government. One person, one vote is the rule. *Equality of result* is expected in the political arena in the sense that power should be equally distributed. The question is: Can equality of political power and inequality in economic standing exist at the same time? Or does economic power lead to inordinate, unequal political power, thereby making a mockery of political equality? Can open economic capitalism and political democracy coexist? John Adams, one of the Founding Fathers of the United States, expressed concern that "the balance of power in a society accompanies the balance of property and land.... If the multitude is possessed of the balance of real estate, the multitude will have the balance of power and, in that case, the multitude will take care of the liberty, virtue and interest of the multitude in all acts of government (Adams 1969, pp. 376–377). Bryan Turner wrote, "Modern capitalism is fractured by the contradictory processes of inequality in the marketplace and political inequality at the level of state politics. There is an inevitable contradiction between economic class and the politics of citizenship" (B. Turner 1986, p. 24). How do individuals who lack economic resources react politically to this situation? Does the contradiction generate resistance? Is it possible to have a society that is both capitalistic and democratic?

Conservatives and radicals generally take different positions on each of the issues we have been discussing. Conservatives tend to praise the virtues of open capitalism and emphasize its benefits for the individual, rather than see the internal contradictions between capitalism and democracy. Radicals, on the other hand, view unbridled capitalism as destructive of human beings and stress the interlinkage between economic and political power. Conservatives also tend to consider social inequality to be inevitable, if not necessary and desirable, and perceive the United States as being largely classless, seeing the similarities among Americans as being more fundamental than the differences. In sharp contrast, radicals conclude that inequality is neither inevitable nor desirable, that the United States is a class society, and that basic social, economic, and political conditions create deep divisions within the population.

ISSUES OF METHODOLOGY

In addition to the preceding substantive controversies, there are also important methodological issues that must be considered in the study of inequality, most of which you will encounter as you read through the following chapters. How these questions are handled by scholars heavily affects the conclusions they draw about the nature and extent of social inequality. These issues frequently involve questions about definitions and measurement of concepts, levels of analysis, and the relative impacts of race, class, sex, and gender on individual lives.

Definitional Problems

One of the most fundamental questions involves the measurement of social class and poverty. As noted later, social class has been defined in different ways, using different indices. Some conceptualize given social classes as being characterized by particular levels of income, education, and occupational prestige, whereas others view class as having to do primarily with ownership and exploitation, or with class consciousness. Still others focus on lifestyle as the critical factor that distinguishes social classes. These different definitions result in different measures of social-class

Social scientists often have called different aspects of inequality by different names. There is always danger that we may mistake one part of inequality for all of it.

position. Hollingshead's Two-Factor Index of Social Position, for example, involves objectively rating a person from 1 to 7 on occupational and educational scales (Hollingshead and Redlich 1958). Wright's measure of social class, in sharp contrast, uses exploitation as its defining characteristic, and consequently separates different types of exploitation that individuals use or are exposed to while they work (cf., e.g., Wright and Cho 1992).

As in the case of social class, *poverty* has also been defined and measured in different ways, as you will see in Chapter 16. Some argue that being poor means more than not having money—it also means a lack of status and power. Even when money is used as the measure of poverty, there is disagreement about whether it should be gross or net income, whether it should include income from government programs, whether it should be current or long-term income, and so on. Other methodological issues arise when examining additional dimensions of social inequality. How to measure discrimination when discussing racial or gender inequality, how to measure the openness of a society using its mobility rates, how to measure political power, and how to gauge the comparability of situations when discussing how the degree of social inequality in the United States stacks up against that found in other countries—all are issues of significance and difficulty.

Why are these differences in measurement and definition so professionally and practically important? Professionally, varying definitions and measures make comparability of results difficult and raise problems of communication between scholars supposedly studying the same phenomenon. Practically, these different perspectives are significant and involve heated discussion among policymakers because how such things as openness, discrimination, poverty, and class are measured affects how egalitarian or inegalitarian the United States is seen to be. The measure of poverty affects how much poverty exists, how big a problem it is, and how much, if anything, needs to be done about it. The definition and measurement

of poverty, therefore, is a political hot potato because so much rides on which approach is accepted at the time.

There is also some controversy surrounding the usage of the terms *Black* and *African American,* and often confusion between *gender* and *sex.* Both *Black* and *African American* will be used as terms throughout the book. When speaking of the group in general terms, or in those situations when issues of heritage and/or cultural identity are paramount, *African American* will be used. But when discussing income, wealth, and especially poverty, the term *Black* will be used because inequalities in those areas are based on color or race. Thus, the tables in Chapter 2, for example, will use the U.S. Census categories of Black and White, but in such cases, the reference to Black is the same racial group as African American.

With respect to the discussion of women, the trend in terminology has been to use the term *gender* rather than *sex* when discussing differences and inequalities between men and women. However, they mean different things. The former reflects the images, roles, and behaviors society assigns to men and women; the latter is a direct reference to biology. Thus, the terms *sex* and *gender* will both be used in the text. When the focus is on inequalities between males and females as sexes (e.g., income and poverty differences), the term *sex* will be used. When the focus is on social definitions or roles, often socially ranked and culturally assigned to males or females, *gender* will be used. For example, occupations are often "gendered" (i.e., associated with or considered most appropriate for either men or women). One would think that it is indisputable that there are only two sexes. But even that is open to discussion, as the question and reply in Nutshell 1.1 indicate. This suggests that definitions are always socially constructed.

In addition to the definitional issues swirling around the latter sets of concepts, there is also a dilemma involving their interrelationship. Can one effectively separate the independent effects of race, class, sex, and gender on the individual?

Although each is a distinct variable, all are inextricably intermixed in the lives of actual individuals. Persons simultaneously occupy positions on each of these, and, in real life, they are deeply interconnected. We must recognize both their separateness and their interconnectedness when considering their roles in people's lives.

Levels of Analysis

The study of social inequality is concerned with both individuals and groups, personal positions as well as structural arrangements. Thus, analysis proceeds on several levels. For example, we are interested in how an individual's class-related characteristics affect the probability of that person being arrested, but we are also interested in how the structure of inequality itself affects the crime rate for the society as a whole. We are interested in the process by which individuals attain higher or lower status positions, but we are also interested in how class structures shift in society. We will look not only at how an individual's race or sex affects his or her income but also at how institutionalized discrimination affects the overall structure of inequality between the races and sexes.

Although the level of analysis that focuses on the individual is distinct from that which examines inequality on the broader group or structural level, conditions on each level affect the other. For example, the structure of inequality sets limits on what an individual can do, and conversely, individual actions can affect the structure of inequality, as we will see in Chapter 15. Many of the chapters to follow contain discussion of these important methodological issues.

ORGANIZATION OF THE BOOK

The text is divided into four major parts. Part One addresses the extent of inequality in its various forms. Chapters 2 and 3 concentrate on relating the extensive economic and social-status inequality in the United States, while Chapters 4 and 5 focus on inequalities related to gender, sex, and

---

NUTSHELL 1.1 _____

Is It Time to Rethink How Many Sexes There Are?

MARILYN VOS SAVANT

**I've read that we should think of people as consisting of five sexes: male heterosexual, female heterosexual, male homosexual, female homosexual and bisexual. What do you think about this?
—Robert, Midland, Mich.**

Five? How can it be an odd number? If we're going to define people like this, it would have to be "male bisexual" and "female bisexual." But this doesn't make much sense to me either. After all, why stop there? What about people who don't like to do *anything*? We'd have to add "male asexual" and "female asexual." And what about people who are fonder of *themselves* than anyone else? Add "male autosexual" and "female autosexual." (I can think of plenty others that I don't even want to list.)

There are also people whose chromosomal makeup is somewhere between male (XY) and female (XX). For example, some can be XXY, XXXY or XXXXY, or even XO. There are even XYs who are apparently females, and XXs who are apparently males.

In my opinion, there are men and there are women—no matter how they're constructed or what they do—and that's that. I can't imagine why anyone would campaign for more sexes. Just *two* has given us more than enough trouble.

Source: Parade Magazine, August 4, 1996, p. 6. Reprinted with permission from *Parade,* copyright © 1996.

---

sexual orientation. Chapters 6 and 7, respectively, turn attention to inequality between racial/ethnic groups and to inequality in political power. Finally, Chapter 8 puts the extent of economic, gender, and racial inequality into broader perspective by looking at how inequality in the United States compares to that found in other countries. It also examines inequality between countries and the explanations for it.

Several of the chapters in Part One include *specific* explanations of given forms of inequality. Part Two presents the major *general* explanations given for social inequality, with Chapter 9 including discussions of Marx's, Weber's, and Durkheim's classical perspectives on inequality. Chapter 10 analyzes more contemporary explanations, ranging from functionalist, to conflict, to labor-market theories of inequality.

Having discussed the extent and explanations of inequality in earlier sections, Part Three demonstrates the pervasive consequences of inequality for individuals and society. Physical and mental health, hunger, homelessness, and the intimate relationships within families are all subject to the influences of individual positions in the hierarchy of social inequality. These personal effects are the focus of Chapter 11. The long arm of inequality reaches far into personal and private worlds, but its effects also extend into the wider society as well. In Chapter 12, the effects of inequality on crime and collective protest are explored. Specifically, the effects of socioeconomic position, race, and sex and gender on criminal justice are examined, ranging from the chances of being arrested to the likelihood of being given a long sentence. Street crimes, white-collar crimes, and hate crimes are each discussed. Inequality also has played a role in generating high crime rates and in fomenting unrest. A focus on worker strikes as one form of such protest is presented.

Part Four of the book examines what has been happening to the system of inequality and what is being done about it. Chapter 13 asks whether there is a great deal of mobility in U.S. society. Do rags-to-riches stories provide a typical picture of the careers of most Americans? How does the United States compare with other countries in its rate of mobility? Is it more open than others? Have African Americans and women become more upwardly mobile in recent years? What determines how far up people go in the occupational hierarchy? Chapter 14 discusses the thorny issue of the equity of inequality. What do Americans think about their system inequality? Is it fair? What is being done about it? This is the subject of Chapters 15 and 16. What kinds of movements and policies exist to deal with inequality and poverty and how effective are they? Are there any better ways to address the problem of poverty? These comprise some of the central questions addressed in Part Four.

Each chapter ends with a short set of questions addressing some critical issues raised by the chapter. They are aimed at forcing you to come to grips with central problems in inequality, often by looking at inequality in your own life. *Web Connections* suggest various websites where you can get more information and use as bases for course exercises. These should broaden and deepen understanding of inequality. Many chapters also contain a brief *Nutshell* from the popular press. Each deals with an issue of inequality and can serve as a point of classroom discussion. Finally, a Glossary of Basic Terms follows the last chapter.

The lines separating the social sciences are often vague, the result being that discussions in the book often will draw on the work of economists, anthropologists, as well as sociologists, and others. In addition, there is material from other countries. These inclusions, hopefully, result in a more thorough and well-rounded perspective on the structure and process of social inequality.

CRITICAL THINKING

1. Try to think of a personal relationship you have with someone who is unequal to you in some way, and yet the inequality appears to have few negative effects on you or your relationship. What characteristics lessen the impact of the inequality in this relationship? Discuss some lessons from this relationship that might be used to diminish the negative effects of inequality in society as a whole.

2. Is social inequality a problem that demands the full attention of society or is it merely a personal trouble of those living below the middle class? Explain your answer.

3. What forms of inequality or social ranking exist in U.S. society and which are, or are becoming, the most prominent? Which forms most affect you personally?

WEB CONNECTIONS

A great deal of information on the Internet relates to issues of social inequality, but not all the information is equally accurate, current, or reliable. Before one accepts and uses information off the World Wide Web, Paula Hammett (1999) has suggested that several questions be asked about the information before accepting it. Among these are: (1) What is its source of authority? Is it reputable? (2) What is the site's purpose? Are the data aimed at a specific audience? (3) Is there evidence to suggest the accuracy of the information? Can the information be verified? (4) How up-to-date is the information? Are there any indications of the currency of the data? (5) Does the website betray a bias or ideological slant of some kind? Is it promoting a particular message? These questions should be kept in mind when browsing the Internet or carrying out the Web exercises suggested at the end of each of the following chapters.

CHAPTER 2

ECONOMIC INEQUALITY

The American economy is changing. It is becoming more polarized—
income inequality is increasing.
—Katherine S. Newman

In the next several chapters, we will be considering several forms of inequality: economic, status, gender, racial, and political. In this chapter, we examine economic inequality in the form of social class and income/wealth differences. *Social class* has been defined in a variety of ways, and conceptualizations especially vary between more conservative traditional and radical writers.

In recent years, there has been a continuing debate about whether classes really exist in the United States. The conclusions on this issue have hinged heavily on how the concept of *class* has been defined. Traditionally, U.S. researchers have defined social class statistically in terms of occupational status, education, and/or income. Individuals or families that fall in the same category on these dimensions are then said to be in the same social class. Generally, persons receive a score based on their placement on these variables; in essence, social class is thus determined by a statistical score. Since these scores are continuous, the class hierarchy is frequently viewed as a continuum where the boundaries between classes are not always clear and distinct. Classes may merge imperceptibly into one another and, as a result, boundary determination becomes an important problem.

Another characteristic of this approach is that the dimensions used to measure social class are not all purely economic in nature. Occupational status is essentially a measure of the prestige of an occupation—that is, it reflects the subjective judgment of individuals about an occupation. Education is also a noneconomic phenomenon. The result is that this measure of social class is not only multidimensional but it also mixes economic with social dimensions of inequality. Consequently, this measure is often referred to as *socioeconomic status*.

Finally, this measure does not assume any kind of necessary relationship between the classes. There is no assumption, for example, that the upper and working classes are in conflict with each other. Classes are merely the result of scores on a series of socioeconomic dimensions. In sum, the traditional, more conservative measure in the United States assumes that the structure of social class, or socioeconomic status, is (1) a continuum of inequality between classes, (2) partly the result of subjective judgments as well as objective conditions, (3) multidimensional, and (4) nonconflictual in nature.

The following are two examples of definitions of *class* that use this approach. Rossides defined a social class as being "made up of families and unrelated individuals who share similar benefits across the three dimensions of class, prestige, and power" (1976, p. 23). Similarly, Gilbert and

Kahl defined social class as "a large group of families...approximately equal in rank to each other and clearly differentiated from other families.... The various stratification variables tend to converge and jell; they form a pattern, and it is this pattern that creates social classes" (1993, p. 16). In other words, these authors said that individuals and families who are ranked similarly on several dimensions—income, occupation, and power—are in the same social class.

Generally, radical or Marxian sociologists have in mind a conceptualization of class that is quite different, and they object to the mixing of economics, social status, and other socioeconomic variables. This merging of a variety of factors, or using class to describe noneconomic hierarchies, the argument goes, dilutes what Marx considered to be the core meaning of social class. We will later examine in detail his concept of class, but essentially, Marx believed class was basically an economic phenomenon and was defined by an individual's position in the social relations of production, by control over the physical means (property) and social means (labor power) of production. In other words, class is not defined by income or occupation but rather by ownership/control in the system of production. In this view, introducing other socioeconomic variables, such as prestige or occupational status, only distorts the meaning of social class. Thus, in the Marxian definition, class is much less multidimensional in nature. Moreover, the crucial differences between the social classes are qualitative in nature—that is, the class system is not a continuous hierarchy. The boundaries between the classes are discrete and clear. Finally, classes in this view are defined by the exploitation that exists between them and by the interconnection of the functions of each class. This means that a given class is defined by its relationship to another class. Workers are members of the working class, for example, *because* of the nature of their relationship to capital and capitalists. Different classes perform distinct but interrelated functions in capitalist society.

As we have seen, the basic Marxian definition of class is "first of all a place in the system" (Ollman 1987, p. 62). This "place" simply may refer to ownership or nonownership or it may refer to a variety of *structural* conditions that define an individual's place in the system of production.

Some Marxian social scientists, however, argue that class consciousness or a similar sense of belongingness and organized opposition must also be present for *social* classes to be present—that is, individuals must identify with each other and understand their real relationship to other classes and act on that knowledge. Ollman stated flatly that the concept of class has both subjective and objective dimensions, the subjective element being a sense of unity that develops as a class emerges. People "tend to acquire over time other common characteristics as regards...lifestyle, political consciousness and organization that become, in turn, further evidence for membership in their particular class and subsidiary criteria for determining when to use the class label. Here, class is a quality that is attached to people" (Ollman 1987, p. 64). In this approach, people become a real *social* class when they acquire a common culture and political awareness. In addition to occupying the same location or position in relation to the means of production, then, people in the same social class "share the distinctive traditions common to their social position" (Szymanski 1978, p. 26). This common identity, especially when it involves awareness of common exploitation and engagement in class struggle, Marx suggested, is what welds an aggregate of people into a social class, or a "class-for-itself" (Bottomore 1966).

It should be clear at this point that even among Marxists there is lack of agreement on the exact definition and measurement of social class. Marx never gave an explicit, clear-cut definition of class. Moreover, he suggested various definitions and different numbers and types of social classes at different points in his writing. Nevertheless, his approach and that of contemporary Marxian analysts are clearly different from those discussed earlier who define class in broader socioeconomic terms. In sum, Marxists generally view classes as (1) discrete rather than continuous, (2) real rather than statistical creations,

(3) economic in nature, and (4) conflictual in their relations. In contrast, traditional conservative approaches define classes as existing along a continuous hierarchy, largely statistically created, and being multidimensional and nonconflictual in their relationships.

If you were to consider each of these conceptualizations of social class, how would your perception of U.S. class structure change as you went from one to another? Certainly, the definition a person has of something affects what he or she sees. This is no less true of class perceptions.

TECHNOLOGY AND THE SHAPING OF THE U.S. CLASS STRUCTURE

The class structure of any society is shaped by the political, cultural, economic, and technological context in which it is embedded. *Politically,* changes in rules and resources governing labor/management conflict, including unionization of workers, affect class conditions and relationships. Government trade and immigration policies, poverty programs, tax laws, and restrictions on business help determine the size and composition of classes, the extent of income and wealth differences, and the channels for moving up and down the class ladder. *Culturally,* broad-based values about democracy, equality, and justice can serve to temper the extent of social inequality, whereas the presence of prejudice, stereotypes, and derogatory ideologies about different groups can perpetuate such inequality. Finally, *economic* and *technological* developments have become increasingly significant for the changing composition of classes and for shifts in the distribution of individuals among classes. These developments need to be emphasized.

In recent years, technological developments have sped the integration of national economies into a global network. What happens to steelworkers in Ohio, textile employees in New York, and electronic-component workers across the country is directly tied to the international context within which the U.S. economy operates. The ties created between nations make each more vulnerable to economic and political shifts in other countries. Like a giant web, pressure on any part has reverberations throughout the system. Economic chaos in Russia, the economic union of European countries signaled by the new Euro-currency, and attempts by Latin American nations to better integrate their economies, all have economic repercussions for the United States.

The demand for goods produced by U.S. employees fluctuates with economic and political changes in other countries. For example, the disappearance of almost 170,000 U.S. manufacturing jobs in recent years is linked to economic problems experienced in Asian markets and the subsequent decline in prices for goods and reduction of U.S. exports to those countries. As economic crises occurred in Asian markets, their currencies were devalued, prices of their goods dropped, and importation of these goods into the United States became more attractive. Conversely, the higher cost of U.S. electronic and industrial equipment made them less attractive to economically strapped buyers in Asia, forcing a downturn in these exports to Asian countries. To compete successfully in world markets, many U.S. manufacturers had to reduce prices of their goods. Increases in cheaper imports, declines in U.S. exports, and reductions in prices have led to increases in unemployment in manufacturing (Slater and Suawser 1998; Goodman and Considine 1999).

Downsizing, lean production, and the exportation of jobs to cheaper foreign labor markets have been primary ways used by U.S. manufacturers to reduce costs and respond to foreign competition. *Successful* penetration of U.S. firms into foreign countries may mean higher profits for some, but it also spells lower incomes for many workers, white-collar and blue-collar alike. Higher unemployment means lower incomes for those affected, in part because it means lower pressures for increased wages. Not surprisingly, job loss and fear of job loss dampen appeals for wage increases, as does the weakness of U.S. labor's power (Aaronson and Sullivan 1998; Volgy, Schwarz, and Imwalle 1996). *Unsuccessful* foreign penetration, on the other hand, means fewer exports for U.S. firms, lower profits, and, very likely, lower stock prices. The latter means declines in the wealth of those who own these stocks. Thus, individuals throughout the entire class system are affected by international economic events, but not in the same ways.

The interconnectedness of the world economy has been intensified by progress in the technology of communication networks and information systems, which has brought together larger networks of individuals and organizations around the globe. This technology also has repercussions for the occupational structure. Increased computer usage in all kinds of organizations has provided the impetus for increases in jobs for systems analysts, software programmers, and computer technicians. Between 1996 and 2006, for example, employment of computer scientists, computer engineers, and systems analysts is expected to more than double to almost 2,000,000 workers. The number of temporary workers who are hired out to provide expertise in these fields to client companies is also expected to increase by 123 percent during this period (U.S. Department of Labor 1998; Melchionno 1999).

In addition to their effects on occupational distribution, advances in computer technology and the rapid growth of the Internet have also created greater possibilities for flexible work patterns and new forms of economic organizations. Because the technology allows dispersion of workers across space, even across countries, work groups are being formed in cyberspace, resulting in the creation of "virtual organizations" (Crandall and Wallace 1998). The Internet technology has opened up scores of opportunities for individuals who are adept in it. New companies made possible by the powerful computer technologies have arisen overnight and their stocks have rocketed so suddenly that their youthful creators have become millionaires in a very short time. eBay, Amazon.com, eTrade, and similar companies have made their management very wealthy on paper. More individuals have become billionaires since 1985 in the United States than in its entire previous history, and technical knowledge and opportunity have provided the bases for their wealth (Thurow 1999).

Employment and unemployment patterns are being dramatically affected by computer technology and the Internet. The freedom from restrictions of space and time that the Internet provides means that the line between home and work can easily become blurred. Employees can stay at home and still be employed in computer tasks. Even though the success rates of such businesses is low and self-employment accounted for less than 1 percent of all job growth in the United States in the 1990s, enterprising employees can start their own businesses and become entrepreneurs. Workers who are interested in moving, but wish to remain employees, are not limited in their job searches by local newspaper advertisements. Rather, they can search the Web for employment in a wide variety of geographic areas. Conversely, because of new communication technologies, employers can hire qualified individuals who live in very diverse locations. Knowledge and skills in new computer technologies have become a critical avenue for success. These possibilities hold the potential to complicate the processes of status attainment and diversify the compositions of given classes.

Moreover, new technology has made corporations and their workers less loyal to each other. It has created employment for some, unemployment for others; higher profits for some, and lower incomes for others. All this means that some will benefit from the ongoing technological revolution while others will remain onlookers, lacking access to and/or participation in it. A recent national survey found that households with incomes of at least $75,000 are 20 times more likely than those with lower incomes to have Internet access, and the gap has grown over the last few years. Similar discrepancies exist for individuals at different levels of education, and between individuals who live in rural and urban areas (National Telecommunications and Information Administration 1999).

Race is also involved. Historically, for example, Blacks have frequently been left behind in times of technological progress. Not surprisingly then, "blacks have traditionally been poorly educated...and deprived of the sorts of opportunities that create the vision necessary for technological ambition.... Not channeled to follow the largely technological possibilities for success in this society, black folkways have instead embraced the sort of magical thinking that is encouraged by the media and corporations whose sole interest in blacks is as consumers" (Walton 1999, pp. 17–18). Instead of encouraging education and the development of technical knowledge, these folkways have identified uniqueness of individual talent, as in sports or popular music, as avenues of attainment. But these folkways are reactions to real living conditions. Recent research suggests that less than one-third of Blacks own a personal computer, compared to just under one-half of Whites. Racial differences in ownership and usage are especially great in lower-income groups with differences declining or disappearing with increasing income and education (Hoffman and Novak 1998). Since computer skills and related access are important bases for attainment in the knowledge professions, to be left out is to be relegated to a "cyberghetto" separating the technological haves from the have-nots (McKissack 1998).

STRUCTURE OF THE U.S. CLASS SYSTEM

Some portrayals of class structure use sets of very diverse criteria, following closely the socioeconomic definition of class discussed earlier, whereas others try to be more faithful to Marxian criteria in outlining their perspectives. Neither of these approaches is inherently better than the other, and each focuses on criteria that have been found to have separate effects on individuals' life conditions. Each approach attempts to identify meaningful breaks in the class system. In the following sections, we will examine images of the class system based on both the socioeconomic and Marxian perspectives.

Socioeconomic Images of Class Structure

Two of the most famous socioeconomic measures of social class are Warner's Index of Status Characteristics and Hollingshead's Index of Social Position. With his index, Warner hoped to provide educators and others with a simple yet accurate

means of detecting an individual's class position. This is the way it worked. An individual would obtain a total score on the index, which was made up of scores from four separate subscales: one each on occupation, dwelling area, house type, and source of income (which may or may not be from the individual's occupation). Then the individuals could be placed in given classes based on their scores. When using this index, there is no necessary or basic reason why certain ranges of scores on the index are significant indicators of membership in a particular social class. "We are not told of any cluster or group of the various score values...which would lead one to conclude that there were 'natural breaks' in the series or that certain score values, for some reason, belong together'" (Cuber and Kenkel 1954, p. 127). Moreover, given the fact that Warner developed this measure while studying particular small communities almost half a century ago, one has to be careful in assuming that it is equally applicable today and in every setting.

Hollingshead developed similar types of measures of social class, one of which was a two-factor index that involved using an occupational prestige scale and an education scale. The occupational hierarchy ranges from higher executive/major professional positions to unskilled workers, while the seven-level educational scale goes from graduate professional training to less than junior high school. In computing the total score on this index, occupation is weighted more heavily than education. Like Warner's technique, Hollingshead's has been used as a quick and relatively easy way to uncover an individual's class position, but also like it, has been subjected to some criticism. Two criticisms are that it (1) dilutes the economic component of class by incorporating education and (2) introduces age as a confounding factor since age and education are correlated with each other (Haug 1972).

Using the socioeconomic criteria of income, education, and occupation, Gilbert and Kahl (1993) proposed that the United States contains six major classes. A condensed version of their model is presented here. Be aware that the family incomes mentioned are for 1990.

Class name (percent of households)

1. *Capitalist Class* (1 percent): Graduates of high-ranking universities who are in top-level executive positions or are heirs who have an income in excess of $750,000 mainly from assets.
2. *Upper Middle Class* (14 percent): Individuals with at least a college degree who are in higher professional or managerial positions or owners of medium-sized businesses who have incomes of at least $70,000.
3. *Middle Class* (30 percent): Individuals who have high school degrees and maybe some college who are in lower managerial or white-collar, or high-skill, high-pay blue-collar occupations who make about $40,000 a year.
4. *Working Class* (30 percent): Persons with high school degrees who are in lower-level white-collar (e.g., clerical, sales workers) or blue-collar positions (e.g., operatives) whose incomes are about $25,000 per year.
5. *Working Poor* (13–15 percent): Those with some high school who are service workers, or are in the lowest paid blue-collar and clerical positions who have incomes below $20,000.
6. *Underclass* (10–12 percent): Individuals with at best some high school education who work part time, are unemployed, or are on welfare, and who have incomes under $13,000.

In surveying different models of U.S. class structure that use several kinds of socioeconomic criteria, there are some remarkable *similarities* as well as differences between them. These models usually see the structure as being composed of five to seven classes, rather than as a dichotomy or trichotomy. Also, the proportion of the population said to be in each class in each model is very similar. Generally, the working and middle classes, in which the majority of the population is placed, are considered to be about equal in size, and the upper class is generally said to be around 1 percent. Then, depending on whether employed as well as unemployed are included in the lower class, its percentage can range from 10 to 25 percent.

Some of the most significant *differences* in traditional models center on the criteria used to place individuals in various classes. One notable difference lies in the distinctions made about the lower class. Some researchers simply include all those who are poor, while others draw a line between those who are poor but work and those who are chronically unemployed and poor for long periods of time. The term *underclass* is frequently used to refer to the latter group. There is some debate about the actual size of the underclass; of course, the proposed size depends on the definition given to it. A conference of experts on the issue agreed on the definition of the *underclass* as "poor people who live in a neighborhood or census tract with higher rates of unemployment, crime, and welfare dependency" (McFate 1987, p. 11). By this definition, the underclass would include 5 to 10 percent of the population.

Another difference among the models of class structure concerns distinctions between particular kinds of white-collar and blue-collar occupations. Traditionally, blue-collar and white-collar categories were distinguished on the basis of whether the occupation involved manual or nonmanual work. (Manual work was generally viewed as requiring primarily physical and routine rather than mental and intricate skills/tasks.) Recently, however, the lines distinguishing the nature of blue- and white-collar jobs have become blurred. The routine nature of much low-level white-collar work has encouraged some analysts to place individuals who do this kind of work into the working class, and to place those who do complex, high-skill, well-paying blue-collar work into the middle class. As technological change occurs, and some physical labor by humans is replaced by machines, the character of the working class changes correspondingly.

The question of the relative importance of the manual/nonmanual and level-of-complexity criteria is the subject of some debate and has become focused in the debate about the *proletarianization* of some white-collar work and the *embourgeoisement* of some blue-collar work. Briefly, the proletarianization argument states that a significant and increasing number of white-collar jobs are routine and boring, demand little skill, and involve little worker control. Qualitatively, this makes them no different from many blue-collar jobs. Some have described those who occupy these positions as a "new working class," especially as the economy advances and becomes more automated. Generally, radicals tend to view the U.S. class structure in a manner consistent with the proletarianization thesis.

In contrast, the embourgeoisement thesis, embraced more often by those with a more conservative bent, proposes that complex, high-paying blue-collar jobs take on many of the sociocultural characteristics of the white-collar middle class. As society moves into a postindustrial phase and its labor force becomes more saturated with white-collar service positions, the size of the blue-collar work force shrinks. Most people become middle class in their standards of living and lifestyles. While blue-collar workers' job situations may be different from lower white-collar positions, many in the higher blue-collar ranks, argued Mayer and Buckley (1970), have a lifestyle that "resembles that of the lower-middle class much more closely than that of the poorer semi-skilled and unskilled manual laborers.... Away from the job, they cannot be distinguished from the lower-middle-class white-collar men" (p. 94).

Are working-class individuals moving closer to the middle class in terms of their lifestyles and values as the embourgeoisement thesis suggests, or are many of those in lower white-collar positions being relegated to the working class because of the nature of their work? What does the evidence suggest? It is mixed. Some find that the traditional distinctions between middle (white-collar) and working (blue-collar) classes remain based on differences in status and authority (e.g., Kerbo 1983). It has even been suggested that if proletarianization does exist in some white-collar positions, the people in them can and frequently do move out of them, making proletarianization less consequential for them (Crompton and Jones 1984).

Although several past studies have found that clerical positions have become deskilled (e.g.,

Crompton and Jones 1984), others have found a distinct trend toward *deproletarianization*. There has been an increase in the proportion of the labor force who are managers, experts, or supervisors, providing more support for the postindustrial theories than the Marxist thesis of proletarianization. Wright and Martin (1987) proposed that these results may mean merely that capitalism has internationalized itself and has shifted more proletarianized occupations into Third World countries. Thus, the proletarianization issue is still unsettled.

Marxian Measures and Images of Class Structure

Perhaps the most sophisticated recent attempt to analyze the class structure of the United States in Marxian terms comes from Erik Wright. Since the mid-1970s, Wright has written extensively about class measurement and structure, refining and altering his scheme along the way. True to the Marxian perspective, Wright (1977) defined *classes* as "common positions within [the] social relations of production." His early depictions used four principal questions to define class position within these social relations: (1) Is one an owner or self-employed? (2) Does one have employees? (3) Does one have subordinates on the job? and (4) Is one an employee? In essence, these criteria boil down to issues of ownership, control, and authority.

In his continuing attempts to refine his work, Wright revised his Marxian conception of class structure. At the heart of Marx's conception of class is a view that stresses the relational, antagonistic, and exploitative relationship between property owners and nonowners. Accordingly, Wright's most recent characterization of U.S. class structure uses exploitation as the defining element (Wright and Cho 1992; Western and Wright 1994). Classes and class locations are distinguished by an individual's ability to exploit or be exploited on the basis of (1) property, (2) organizational authority, or (3) expertise or skill.

Combining these three criteria, Wright identified several class "locations" within this structure of class relationships. The most elemental distinction involves those who have property from those who do not (owners vs. nonowners). Among *owners*, Wright has separated capitalists who employ others (employers) from those who do not (petty bourgeoisie). Application of the other two criteria of class location, authority and expertise, result in distinctions among *employees*, which create a number of class locations. Considering the criterion of bureaucratic authority, there are those who have it and those who do not (managers and nonmanagers). Individuals are considered managers if they are involved in policy decisions and are in a position to impose sanctions on others. Employees also differ in level of skill or expertise, which is the third criterion of class position. There are (1) managers and professionals who are experts, (2) workers and managers who are not experts, and (3) semiprofessionals (such as those in technical jobs) who are in between. In this scheme, the owners might be considered the capitalist class and the workers compose the working class. The remaining groups among employees (managers, professionals, semiprofessionals) might be viewed as the middle class because they have characteristics of both those above and below them. In a real sense, as Wright has put it, these employees occupy "contradictory" locations because not only are they exploited as employees but they also exploit other employees because of their authority and/or expertise assets. Frequently, this group of employees is referred to as a "new" middle class because of its relatively recent growth within capitalism. Figure 2.1 graphically depicts Wright's class structure.

The figure gives a rather static, broad view of the class structure and how persons might be located within it. But Wright has pointed out that class position also depends on the relationship a person has with others in his or her family—relationships that may link the individual to different classes. In other words, a person's own position is "mediated" by the position of others. For example, two individuals may both be profes-

FIGURE 2.1   Wright's Class Structure

OWNERS (approximately 15 percent)
(are self-employed in the system of production)

includes

(1) employers, (2) petty bourgeoisie

EMPLOYEES IN CONTRADICTORY (MIDDLE) LOCATIONS
(approximately 45 percent)
(have expertise and/or authority but are not owners)

includes

(3) manager/experts, (4) other managers, (5) professionals, (6) semiprofessionals

WORKERS (approximately 40 percent)

includes

(7) those who are in nonowner/nonexpert/nonmanagerial positions

---

sionals, but one lives in a family made up primarily of workers while the other lives in a family in which all the adults are professionals. These varying sets of relationships connect each of these professionals to the class structure in different ways.

In addition, two individuals may be in the same class at a given time, but one is located on a clear and recognized career path that will take that person to a higher position (e.g., being on the "fast track" to an executive position at a corporation) while the other person is in a dead-end job. This "temporal" aspect of class position means that to define class location fully, one must take into account the span of the broader career trajectory in which the current position is embedded. The addition of the concepts of mediated and temporal class position makes Wright's characterization of class structure more complex as well as realistic. Several critics have raised questions about Wright's new measure of class position. Meiksins (1988) argued that it is not necessarily true that those with skills or credentials exploit those below them. This is an empirical issue and cannot simply be settled by conceptual fiat.

Some Generalizations.   As you have seen, all analysts of U.S. class structure wrestle with recurrent issues of where to place given sets of individuals within the class structure. Most prominent among these issues are (1) whether to place lower white-collar positions (i.e., routine clerical, service, sales occupations) within the middle or working class; (2) whether to place high-level managers within the middle or upper class, or in a separate category such as the corporate class; (3) how and where to incorporate the rising number of "knowledge" workers or professionals within the class structure; and (4) whether to include the poor and/or unemployed among the working class or to consider them a separate lower class or underclass. As the nation's economy experiences downsizing and similar corporate moves, another increasingly relevant issue will be to figure out how temporary, floating, and new entrepreneurs fit into the U.S. class structure.

In reviewing both the multidimensional socioeconomic and Marxian models, a few generalizations may be made about U.S. class structure. First, there appears to be general agreement across all these models that the upper or capitalist class makes up only a very small percentage of the population, about 1 to 2 percent. Second, most of these schemes suggest that the working class comprises at least close to half of the population. Third, estimates of the lower class or underclass range from approximately 5 to 12 percent. Finally, most of these models place lower-level white-collar occupations in the working class rather than in the middle class. This is consistent with the perceptions of Americans in general surveys.

INCOME INEQUALITY

Income has frequently been used as a measure of class position, and as such, its distribution can provide clues about trends within the U.S. class structure. *Money income,* as defined by the Bureau of the Census, includes money from virtually all sources, including wages or salaries, social security, welfare, pensions, and others. There are some advantages to using *total money income* when assessing the extent of economic inequality. In the first place, it is certainly more immediately quantifiable than many other measures, such as real estate. Second, income is highly valued in U.S. society and serves as a base on which people are evaluated by others. Third, income inequalities saturate and are reflected in a number of other economically related areas. Unemployment, inflation, farm and food prices, rent control, women's liberation, racism, and welfare are all areas that involve income-differential issues. In your own case, think about the number of ways that income is implicated in different areas of your life. Income, then, at least at first glance, would appear to be a more than adequate measure of economic inequality.

However, when interpreting the following statistics, several factors should be kept in mind. First, income is only a partial measure of a family's or

Changes in the economy, including corporate streamlining and downsizing, have strained relationships between unions and workers on the one hand, and corporate management on the other. They have also weakened the economic position of workers, as suggested by this photo showing union workers in July 1996 marching on the headquarters of Bridgestone/Firestone Inc. to demand an equitable contract.

individual's economic well-being. It does not include the value of stocks, real estate, or other noncash economic assets, and if it is *current* income, it does not take into account the income trajectory an individual may be on if, for example, he or she is just beginning in a lucrative career. Second, some of the estimates of income are based on pooled findings from several government studies that are not always identical in methodology or measures of income. Finally, and most significantly, the Bureau of the Census contends that there is an underreporting of income, with some sources of income being more likely to be reported than others. Tax filers tend to underreport their incomes on their income tax forms, and not all persons are required to file income tax returns. Independent estimates suggest that incomes from government benefit programs and

property income are among those most likely to be underestimated (U.S. Bureau of the Census, August 1992b).

As the tables in this chapter will demonstrate, the extent of income inequality can be shown in a variety of ways. Table 2.1 presents information on how U.S. households are distributed among different income categories. The top and bottom lines indicate that although the percentage of families with incomes below $15,000 has declined slightly over time (from 22.7 percent in 1967 to 19.1 percent in 1997), the percentage of those with incomes of at least $100,000 went up much more during that same time. However, the percentage of those in the $25,000–$49,999 categories have generally declined. The shifts in this table would appear to suggest that income inequality has lessened since 1967. But we need to

TABLE 2.1   Percent Distribution of Households by Income Level: 1967–1997

INCOME	1967	1977	1987	1997
Under $15,000	22.7	20.6	19.6	19.1
$15,000–24,999	16.2	15.7	14.6	14.9
$25,000–34,999	17.3	14.3	13.5	13.3
$35,000–49,999	21.9	19.1	17.4	16.3
$50,000–74,999	14.9	19.0	18.6	18.1
$75,000–99,999	4.3	6.8	8.8	9.0
$100,000 and over	2.8	4.5	7.4	9.4
Median income	$31,583	$34,467	$36,820	$37,005

Source: U.S. Bureau of the Census, *Money Income in the United States: 1997.*
Current Pop. Reports, Series P60, No. 200, September 1998, p. B3.

Note: Incomes displayed are in 1997 consumer-price-index adjusted dollars.

reserve that judgment until we explore the matter further.

One way in which income inequality shows up clearly is when comparisons are made between racial and ethnic groups. Almost 32 percent of Black and almost 28 percent of Hispanic households had incomes below $15,000 in 1997, compared to just over 17 percent of White households. On the other end of the income scale, over 10 percent of White households had incomes of at least $100,000 in 1997, yet only 3–4 percent of Black and Hispanic households did (U.S. Bureau of the Census, September 1998b). As Figure 2.2 shows, there are clear differences in the median incomes

MEDIAN INCOME

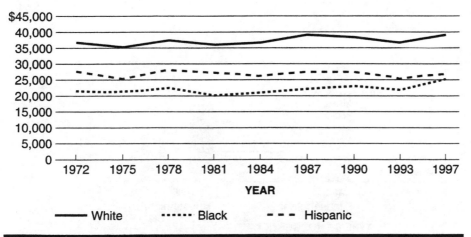

FIGURE 2.2   Median Household Incomes by Race and Hispanic Origin: 1972–1997

Source: U.S. Bureau of the Census, *Money Income in the United States: 1997.* Current Pop. Reports, Series P60, No. 200, September 1998, pp. B3, B4.

Note: Incomes displayed are in 1997 consumer-price-index adjusted dollars.

of these households, and these differences have persisted over time. As we will see in many cases, Hispanics generally fall in between Blacks and Whites on income and wealth.

Incomes also vary between household types. As might be expected, households with married couples are generally better off than those headed by only males or females. This is the case among Whites, Blacks, and Hispanics, but as Figure 2.3 demonstrates, Blacks and Hispanics are worse off than Whites in each type of household. Female-headed households have the lowest incomes among each racial and ethnic group. Overall, such households have only 45 percent of the income of married-couple families.

IS THE MIDDLE CLASS SHRINKING?

The decline in the percentage of families in the $25,000–$49,999 categories is one indication that the middle class may be shrinking. Of course,

one's conclusion about such shrinking depends heavily on the income measures used and the definition given to the *middle class*. These variations in measurement constitute the primary reason for the controversy surrounding economic fortunes of the middle class.

Most of the analyses on the middle-class issue do indicate a shrinking in the size of the middle-income categories. Horrigan and Haugen (1988) reexamined this issue, using family income and two ways of comparing changes in family income distributions over time. They were interested in examining any changes that may have occurred between 1969 and 1986. Regardless of the method used, they found that the middle was being reduced, but whether only the top or both the top and bottom were increasing in size depended on the method used in making comparisons over time. Part of the increase of families in higher earnings categories is due to the increase in two-earner families, especially with the increase of women

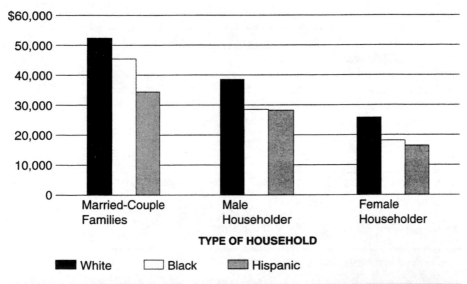

MEDIAN INCOME

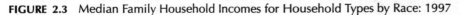

FIGURE 2.3 Median Family Household Incomes for Household Types by Race: 1997

Source: U.S. Bureau of the Census, *Money Income in the United States: 1997.* Current Pop. Reports, Series P60, No. 200, September 1998, pp. 2–4.

into the labor force on a full-time basis. The shriveling of the middle class continued into the 1990s, in part due to declines in upward mobility from the bottom (Gottschalk in Bernstein 1996, p. 90).

The conclusion that the middle is shrinking is also based on current trends in earnings, the major source of middle-class income. Median wages and salaries have declined over the last two decades. The earnings of those in the bottom 60 percent declined, whereas earnings in the top quintiles rose. The declines were especially prominent among noncollege workers; since 1987, however, the wages of college graduates and white-collar employees have also been declining (Mishel and Burtless 1995). This is one indication of the growing polarization in wages and reduction in the size of the middle class. The reasons that have been suggested for these wage trends are many: technological shifts, growing competition and the corresponding emphasis on being "lean and mean," deregulation, declines in unionization, free trade, immigration, and continuing trade deficits. Although some at the top have clearly benefited from these trends, not everyone has. As the article in Nutshell 2.1 indicates, lagging wages is still a problem for average workers.

Writing in 1993, Katherine Newman observed that recent "estimates suggest that if our present trajectories continue, fewer than half of all Americans will be in the middle class by the year 2000.... By the end of the 1980s, only six out of ten Americans were middle class—*a 20 percent decline in barely a dozen years*" (Newman 1993, pp. 43–44). Traditionally, much of the middle class has been composed of white-collar workers, and this group has been among the primary victims of recent shifts in the economy. Wider gaps in earnings have occurred, in part, because of the economic misfortunes encountered by middle-class workers, many of whom have found themselves unemployed because of downsizing and later needing to take jobs that pay less. Worker layoffs increased 39 percent during the 1990–1995 period, and, more often than not, the jobs workers found to replace their old ones paid less. The U.S.

NUTSHELL 2.1_____

Report: Wages Lagging Despite Economic Rally

MARTIN CRUTSINGER
ASSOCIATED PRESS

Washington—Americans are suffering from a long-term erosion in wages, deteriorating job quality and greater insecurity, despite improvements in the overall economy, the Economic Policy Institute said in a report Saturday.

In a 402-page study titled "The State of Working America," economists at the liberal-oriented institute surveyed wage data to determine how workers are faring in what is now the sixth year of economic recovery since the 1990–91 recession.

The report concludes that the wage situation that has plagued America since the mid-1970s has gotten worse in the 1990s.

"The changes in the economy have been all pain, no gain for most workers. The economy is clearly in transition but it is far from certain that it is headed to a better place," wrote the authors, economists Lawrence Misehl, Jared Bernstein and John Schmitt.

They reported that average hourly earnings have lost ground, standing in 1995 nearly 3 percent below where they were in 1989, after adjusting for inflation.

And median family incomes also have been weak, standing 5.4 percent below the 1989 level. For 1994, the most recent year for which family income data is available, the median, or midpoint, for family incomes was $39,881, compared with $42,049 in 1989, after adjusting for inflation.

The report notes that while it is normal for incomes to drop during a recession as the unemployment rate rises, the 1990s have been marked by continued weakness.

Source: Atlanta Constitution, September 1, 1996, p. A3. Reprinted with permission of Associated Press.

Census Bureau reported that the average weekly wages and salaries of those who left a job and then reentered the work force during 1990–1992 fell from $529 to $423 (a decrease of 20 percent).

PERCENT OF INCOME

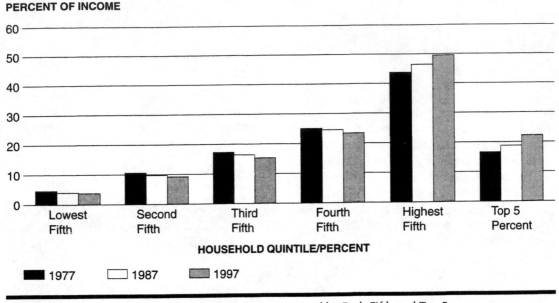

FIGURE 2.4   Percentage Share of Aggregate Income Received by Each Fifth and Top 5 Percent of Households: 1977, 1987, 1997

Source: U.S. Bureau of the Census, *Money Income in the United States: 1997.* Current Pop. Reports, Series P60, No. 200, September 1998, p. B6.

Another clue to the existence of the declining middle class lies in the changes that have occurred in the distribution of income among sections of the population. The median income among households generally declined during the 1990s, signaling an increase in those households with less than average incomes. Figure 2.4 confirms the decline in income shares going to those below the top 20 percent. As the figure indicates, the percentage of all income going to the bottom 80 percent of the population has declined since 1977, whereas that going to the top 20 percent increased from 43.6 percent in 1977 to over 49 percent in 1997. The top 5 percent alone holds almost 22 percent of all income. The gap in incomes between those in the top and bottom households has also increased since 1977. In 1997, the mean income of those in the top 20 percent was almost 14 times that found in the bottom quintile ($122,764 vs. $8,872) (U.S. Bureau of the Census, September 1998b, p. xi).

Finally, trends in the *index of income concentration*—which measures the extent of discrepancy between the *actual* distribution of income and a *hypothetical* situation where each quintile of the population receives the same percentage of income—also indicate increasing concentration of income in the United States. The index has a value range of 0 to 1; 0 indicates complete equality and 1 indicates complete inequality. In 1967, the index stood at .399; by 1997, it had risen to .459.

Consistent with the recent trend of growing income inequality, Table 2.2 indicates that the poverty rates have generally increased since 1977. In 1997, about 36 million persons, or 13.3 percent of the whole U.S. population, were defined as poor by government standards. This contrasts with 11.6 percent in 1977, when almost 25 million were poor. To be classified as poor in 1997, an average family of four had to have a *gross* income below $16,400. The income threshold that defines poverty varies

TABLE 2.2 Poverty Rates by Race, Age, and Family Status: 1977–1997

	POVERTY RATE (% IN POVERTY)		
	1977	*1987*	*1997*
All persons	11.6	13.4	13.3
Under 18 years old	16.2	20.3	19.9
18 to 64 years old	8.8	10.6	10.9
65 and older	14.1	12.5	10.5
Whites	8.9	10.4	11.0
Blacks	31.3	32.4	26.5
Hispanics	22.4	28.0	27.1
Married-couple families	5.3	5.8	5.2
Female-headed families	31.7	34.2	31.6
Male-headed families	11.1	12.0	13.0

Source: U.S. Bureau of the Census, *Poverty in the United States: 1997.* Current Pop. Reports, Series P60, No. 201, September 1998, pp. C2–C14.

with the size of the family, with smaller families having lower thresholds. Table 2.2 shows that Hispanics and Blacks have poverty rates that are almost three times those of Whites. Persons under 18 years of age have poverty rates almost twice those in the 18 to 64 age group, with more than one in five children (11 million) in the United States being classified as poor in 1997. The rate of poverty among children has generally increased significantly since 1974. In 1997, children under age 18 composed 40 percent of the entire poor population, and children under age 6 were particularly likely to be poor. (Almost 22 percent of children under age 6 living in families were classified as poor in 1997). Young children living in families with a female householder and no husband present were even more likely to be poor, with about 55 percent living in poverty. Female-headed families have continued to possess poverty rates that are over six times those of married-couple families.

Within the poor population, some people are poorer than others. Some have incomes that are very near the poverty threshold, whereas the incomes of others fall well below that poverty line.

How far one's income falls below the poverty line is referred to as the *income deficit.* The average income deficit among poor families was $6,602 in 1997. This means that the average poor family's income was over $6,000 *below* the poverty threshold. The income deficit was higher for Black and Hispanic families, families headed by females, and families with two or more children. Forty-one percent had incomes that were under 50 percent of their poverty thresholds (U.S. Bureau of the Census, September 1998c).

In 1992, there were a record number of billionaires in the United States, but as we have seen, the poverty rate has also increased. When we review the tables in this chapter, it is clear that there has been a rise in income inequality in recent years. How can this be explained? A variety of long-term factors seem to have been at work. Among them are the following:

1. Declines in earnings growth, a rise in the proportion of workers with low earnings, and resultant rises in earnings differences between low-skilled and higher-skilled workers
2. Shifts in the economy from production of goods to services, which contain wider variations in salaries and wages
3. Shifts in the demands for high- and less-skilled workers, in part creating more temporary positions with few benefits
4. Changes in the age structure of the population and labor force (e.g., influx of the baby-boom generation into labor market) and in the composition of households (e.g., rise in single-parent families)
5. An influx of poorly educated immigrants into the work force and the rising use of less-expensive foreign labor
6. Declining unionization and power of unions
7. Industrial streamlining, reengineering, and downsizing
8. Governmental policies such as tax reform and cuts in programs for the needy (Levy and Murnane 1992; U.S. Bureau of the Census, March 1992; Grubb and Wilson 1992; Hershey 1993)

WEALTH INEQUALITY
IN THE UNITED STATES

Although extensive income inequality exists in the United States, there is even greater wealth inequality, and it is growing. In 1993, the median net worth or wealth of the 20 percent highest in income was $118,996, whereas that of the lowest was $4,249 (U.S. Bureau of the Census, 1996). Over one-fourth of those in the latter category had zero or negative wealth. This is of higher significance than the inequality in *income* because *wealth* is a more complete measure of a family's economic power, since it consists of the value of all the family's assets minus its debts. Wealth includes the value of homes, automobiles, businesses, savings, and investments.

One last point should be made about wealth and the implications it has for an individual's eco-nomic ability. Although the amount of personal wealth gives a fuller picture of an individual's or family's economic position, even it does not fully suggest the fact that the wealthy also have at their disposal a greater number of economic tools that serve to enhance their economic opportunities and market situation. For example, ownership of a great deal of stock in a corporation that is inter-locked or directly connected with other corporations may give an individual indirect influence over the economic behavior of the latter organizations. Like poverty, wealth has economic implications beyond the actual size of the holdings. Economic opportunities are at least in part a function of the economic tools a person has at his or her disposal.

The methodology used to uncover the distribution of wealth is not as exact as one would desire. "Thus, the 'general' shape of the distribution

It is common to associate poverty with the inner city, but rural poverty is also high. In 1992, nonmetropolitan areas in the South had a poverty rate of almost 21 percent, and several of the states encompassing rural Appalachia have rates well above the national average. This photo of a now largely abandoned home was taken in Knox County, Kentucky.

of wealth...[has] been known for some time," wrote James Smith (1987), "but because our methodologies have been too crude and too narrow, we have failed to advance much beyond our understanding of 20 years ago.... None of these methods is adequate for estimating the total distribution of wealth" (pp. 72, 82). The cost of developing new methods and the comfort of using old ones are two of the reasons old methods persist.

Some of the difficulties associated with present methods are clear. Information about wealth is difficult to obtain. Virtually all data about it come from various field surveys and administrative records. Often, individuals are hesitant to be interviewed, and this is especially true of the wealthy who, for several reasons, may be sensitive about their wealth. "As a rule," stated Allen (1987), who has conducted an extensive analysis of the country's richest families, "the members of wealthy capitalist families refuse to divulge even the most rudimentary details of their wealth.... In order to maintain their anonymity, the members of corporate rich families typically refuse to disclose even basic biographical information about themselves" (pp. 26–27). What is requested of individuals in surveys and what is given are frequently not the same (J. D. Smith 1987).

Social scientists, in general, have produced hundreds of studies of the poor and poverty, even the middle class, but good broad-based information about the wealthy and wealth concentration has always been and remains difficult to find. Why this has been the case remains an interesting political question (Pessen 1973; Turner and Starnes 1976). Another problem with wealth data is that cash and personal items such as jewelry and art are often undervalued. To complicate these matters, researchers use different units of analysis in discussing the distribution of wealth. Sometimes the unit used is the individual, while in others the family or consumer unit is the basis of analysis. Keeping these difficulties in mind, we can now turn to the estimates on changes in the

distribution of wealth over time in the United States.

Wealth Concentration before the Civil War

If ever there was a time when equality was present, it surely must have been when the United States was first being established. When this nation was being politically formed, many left their European homelands because of oppression of one kind or another to escape to the "land of the free," where the streets were thought to be paved with gold. The Founding Fathers, using "the voice of justice," forged a document that not only enumerated the offenses committed against the then new American people but also demanded freedom and equality for all. While some, such as Alexander Hamilton and Thomas Jefferson, argued about whether the government should or should not take a strictly egalitarian form, many believed the period was an "era of the common man" (Pessen 1973). The Founders recognized the belief that "all men are created equal" and later devised a constitution that had among its objectives to "establish justice." Wealth inequality may exist today, but the virgin past was surely free from such a condition. In his famous visit to the United States, de Tocqueville (1969) was surprised by the "equality of conditions" that seemed to prevail in the youthful country. And although he believed wealth was certainly present, no one group held a monopoly on it. Indeed, de Tocqueville believed that wealth moved about quite a bit in the country.

Recent studies have simply not borne out these beliefs. Social historians, poring over probate records, tax forms, and old census documents, have found a decidedly different America than one might have expected. The studies of wealth distribution in the early United States consistently point to the fact that wealth inequality was a clear and constant condition during this period. This was especially true for the period between the Revolution and the Civil War, a time in which inequality was on the rise.

Before the Revolution, however, the increases in inequality do not appear to have been as great or as consistent, but differences in wealth were quite noticeable. Studies in Philadelphia and Chester County, Pennsylvania; Boston and Salem, Massachusetts; and Hartford and rural Connecticut point not only to evident variations in wealth among people, but in some cases to increasing differences as time passed (Pessen 1973). In the Chester County study, for example, the richest 10 percent possessed almost one-quarter of all wealth in the early 1700s. In the next century, their portion climbed to 38 percent. Before 1660, the wealthiest 5 percent in Salem held 20 percent of the wealth, and in 1681, they held about half of it. The same kind of trends are present for Boston, but for others, such as Hartford, fluctuations are the rule (Lemon and Nash 1968; Koch 1969; Main 1976). Consequently, uniform evidence about a trend toward increasing inequality before 1776 does not exist. However, especially after 1776, the trend toward increasing inequality is present everywhere.

The years after the Revolution did not produce more equality. In his studies of cities in New England, the Middle Atlantic, the South, and the Midwest, Sturm (1977) found some sobering results for believers in the "romantic hypothesis." Even though these cities may not represent the America of the time, Sturm felt that "major characteristics and trends can be indicated because the sample was drawn from important regions and segments of the population which were crucially involved in development of the national economy" (p. 24). Using probate data, he found distinct and increasing inequality in estate wealth for the period from 1800 to 1850. During this time, per capita holdings of the very wealthy had gone up about 60 percent (Sturm 1977). An examination by Pessen for this period in Brooklyn and Boston likewise confirms the general trend toward inequality. In Brooklyn in 1810, 1 percent of the population held 22 percent of the private wealth, and in 1840, 1 percent owned 42 percent (Pessen 1973, p. 36). Figures for Boston and New York duplicate these findings.

Concentration of wealth in the nineteenth century appears to have peaked during the period from 1850 to 1870. Soltow found that while wealth inequality remained fairly constant during this period, it was also very high. Using census data on real and personal estate holdings among free adult males, he found that in 1860, the top 1 percent owned almost 30 percent and the top 10 percent owned about 73 percent of estate wealth, again demonstrating a strong degree of wealth concentration. During the period from 1850 to 1870, "there very definitely was an elite upper group in America in terms of control of economic resources" (Soltow 1975, p. 180). A small percentage had great wealth, but large numbers had little, if any. In 1850, over half of free adult males owned no land even though it was quite cheap. Nor did the situation change much in the years following 1850 (p. 175).

Given the period, as one might expect, a person was more likely to be an owner of real estate if that person was native born, older, and a farmer (Soltow 1975). In 1860, there were an estimated 41 millionaires, 545 in 1870, and 5,904 in 1922. But if one uses constant 1922 dollars, the real estimate for 1870 would be between 1,800 and 2,600.

The main conclusion from all these data is that at least from the mid-eighteenth to the mid-nineteenth centuries, wealth concentration was high and tended to increase during that period. Little is known about the extent of concentration during 1870 to 1922 "except that it was lower after the Civil War than before and lower in 1922 than it was to become by 1929" (Lindert and Williamson 1976, p. 31).

Wealth Concentration in the Contemporary United States

In 1929, it is estimated that the richest 1 percent owned almost 43 percent of all wealth, apparently the greatest concentration at the top in U.S. history. The proportion held by the top 1 percent generally declined after the 1929 stock market

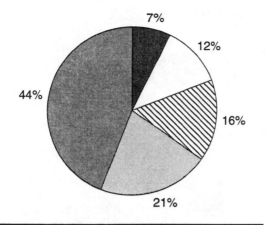

7%

12%

44%

16%

21%

FIGURE 2.5 Distribution of Net Worth by Household Income Quintile: 1993

Source: U.S. Bureau of the Census, *Asset Ownership of Households: 1993.* [Online]. <http://www.census.gov/hhes/www/wealth/wlth93b.html>

crash through World War II, and then remained relatively stable until the early 1970s. During the first half of the 1970s, the proportion of wealth going to the top 1 percent declined, but then began to rise significantly during the late 1970s and continued through the 1990s (Nasar 1992; Wolff 1992).

As Figure 2.5 shows, in 1993, the 20 percent at the bottom of the income ladder possessed only 7 percent of the net wealth in the United States. In sharp contrast, the top 20 percent owned 44 percent of the wealth. Most of the gains in the amount of wealth during the late 1980s and early 1990s benefited those at the top. Government data suggest that in the latter portion of the 1980s, 99 percent of the gains in wealth went to the top 20 percent, and the richest 1 percent got 62 percent. Only 1 percent of the gains went to the bottom 80 percent of the population. Estimates suggest that this trend has continued (Wolff 1995).

The reasons for the increasing concentration of wealth in recent years is related to the differences in the types of wealth held by various income groups. That is, their assets are distributed differently. Those on the top are more likely to

have much of their wealth in stocks, bonds, and related kinds of investments, whereas those with much less wealth are likely to have their wealth in savings accounts and home ownership (see Figure 2.6). Stocks did very well during the late 1980s and the 1990s, and those who had invested profited handsomely. Tax policies and increasing income inequality in the 1980s and 1990s also disproportionately benefited those at the top.

The large amounts of wealth owned by a very small percentage of the population makes one curious about where the wealth comes from and who the wealthy are. Historically, family and inheritance have been major sources of wealth among the corporate rich in the United States. Only a minority obtained their initial wealth through entrepreneurship or personal saving. Although these are important sources for some, "in terms of sheer numbers of people, most of the corporate rich in America are inheritors" (Allen 1987, p. 4). Gift and estate laws have done little to stem the flow of inherited wealth to subsequent generations. Wealth is kept in the family, and this is one reason why the extended family is such an important institution among the rich. The social, cultural, and economic capital passed on to children helps them maintain and even increase their wealth. The odds of the children of wealthy parents keeping their wealth is probably about 3 to 1 (Currie and Skolnick 1988, p. 106). In addition to inheritance, however, technology innovation is becoming a more prevalent source of wealth, as suggested earlier.

What characteristics are related to the amount of wealth one has? Certainly race and ethnicity are factors that are involved. As Table 2.3 demonstrates, Blacks and Hispanics generally have significantly less wealth than Whites, and are more likely to have no wealth at all. In 1993, Whites had 10 times as much wealth, on average, as Blacks and Hispanics. Family type is also linked to wealth, with married-couple households having over 4 times the wealth of female-headed households. Not surprisingly, wealth is also positively related to having more education, being older, and being in a professional, managerial, or

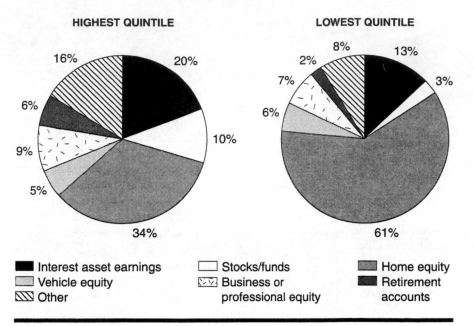

FIGURE 2.6   Distribution of Asset Types in Lowest and Highest Income Quintiles: 1991

Source: U.S. Bureau of the Census, *Asset Ownership of Households: 1993.* [Online].
<http://www. census.gov/ftp/pub/hhes/www/wealth.html>

self-employed occupation (Kennickell and Starr-McCluer 1994).

Studies of the richest people in the United States further clarify the characteristics of the

TABLE 2.3   Median Net Worth by Race, Hispanic Origin of Householder, and Type of Household: 1993

TYPE OF HOUSEHOLDER	MEDIAN NET WORTH
White	$45,740
Black	4,418
Hispanic	4,656
Type of Household	
Married-couple	61,905
Male-householder	13,500
Female-householder	13,294

Source: U.S. Bureau of the Census, *Asset Ownership of Households: 1993.* [Online]. <http://www.census.gov/ftp/pub/hhes/wealth/wlth93.html>

wealthy. Table 2.4 lists the top 20 richest individuals and families in the United States in 1999. Several characteristics jump out immediately. All are men. Most have derived their wealth from extensive activities in crucial areas of the economy (e.g., stocks, technology, communications). The majority are under 60 years of age, and some have gained their wealth over a short period of time. The list suggests the importance of new technologies and their development as a source of wealth.

The number of U.S. millionaires is expected to grow significantly over the next few years. In 1996, about 3.5 million U.S. households had wealth in the $1,000,000 category, and by 2005 that number is expected to increase to 5.6 million households. In addition to being men and under 60 years of age, the majority of millionaires work and are self-employed. Only about 20 percent are retired. Most have college degrees and just over one-third have advanced degrees (Stanley and Danko 1996).

TABLE 2.4   Richest 20 Individuals in the United States and Principal Source of Wealth: 1999

NAME	AMOUNT OF WEALTH (IN BILLIONS)	SOURCE OF WEALTH
William H. Gates III	$90	Computer software
Warren E. Buffett	$36	Investments
Paul Allen	$30	Cable, interactive investments
Steven Ballmer	$19.5	Computer software
Philip Anschutz	$16.5	Oil, railroad, telecommunications
Michael Dell	$16.5	Computers
S. Robson Walton	$15.8	Merchant retailing
John Kluge	$10.5	Communications
Jeffrey Bezos	$10.1	Internet business
Larry Ellison	$ 9.5	Computer software
Sumner Redstone	$ 8.7	Entertainment
Charles Schwab	$ 8.7	Stock brokerage
Pierre Omidyar	$ 7.8	Internet auction
Ted Turner	$ 7.8	Media
Kirk Kerkorian	$ 7.3	Auto and entertainment
Rupert Murdoch	$ 7.2	Media
Philip Knight	$ 5.8	Sports fashion
Gary Winnick	$ 5.1	Telecommunications
Micky Arison	$ 5.0	Cruise ships

Source: Based on Brown et al. 1999, pp. 206–208.

SUMMARY

This chapter has reviewed information on various types of economic inequality. Social class has been defined in several ways, most importantly in socioeconomic terms as a multidimensional phenomenon and in Marxian terms as a strictly economic concept. While there are some notable similarities in the perceptions of class structure in the United States using different measures, there are some significant issues that are, as yet, unsettled. Among these are the question of the placement of lower white-collar workers, the issue of the shrinking middle class, and the question of proletarianization/embourgeoisement.

Examination of income inequality reveals that the degree of inequality appears to have increased in recent years, with females and Blacks lagging behind White males in income, even when occupation and other factors are controlled. The poverty rate also increased in the early 1990s, but since the mid-1990s, it has declined.

Finally, wealth inequality in the United States is even greater than income inequality, and data suggest that the top ½ percent is receiving an even greater percentage of the total net wealth today than 25 years ago, while the bottom 90 percent's share has decreased. In sum, this chapter indicates that economic inequality continues to exist along a variety of economic dimensions. But inequality has more than an economic component. In everyday life, invidious distinctions often are made between individuals on the basis of other factors, resulting in a social ranking because of differences in education, lifestyle, and other social characteristics. It is to these social-status aspects of inequality that we now turn our attention.

CRITICAL THINKING

1. Are income and wealth all that need to be considered in determining the economic well-being of individuals? Is there anything else that goes into it? Explain your answers.

2. Consider the jobs you have held. What factors do you think led to your being employed and affected the earnings you received?

3. How well acquainted are you with people in economic classes different from your own?

   How would you characterize your relationships with those in different classes? To what extent does a person's class position insulate him or her from others?

4. What do you think economic and technological conditions will be like 10 years from now? How will it affect your chances of moving up or down in wealth?

WEB CONNECTIONS

Information on wealth and income inequality is available from several sources on the Internet. The Bureau of the Census has collected such data for decades. Examine the changes in income inequality that have taken place in the United States since the 1940s. Are the rich getting richer, and the poor poorer? Look at the report located at the following site and report your conclusions (you will need Adobe Acrobat to read the report):

http://www.census.gov/hhes/www/img/p60-191.pdf

CHAPTER 3

STATUS INEQUALITY

At high tide in the afternoon I watched his guests diving from the tower of his raft, or taking the sun on the hot sand of his beach while his two motor-boats slit the waters of the Sound, drawing aquaplanes over cataracts of foam.
—F. Scott Fitzgerald

Social status is largely about lifestyle and social characteristics. The previous chapter discussed the various types of *economic* inequality present in U.S. society—namely, class, income, and wealth inequality. But the ranking system is more complicated than that, and experiences in everyday life tell us that invidious distinctions are made between individuals on grounds other than economics. People often are evaluated and ranked on the basis of their education, religion, possession of "culture," type of occupation, and even their speech patterns and clothing styles. Think about how students are evaluated by their peers. In addition to gender and race/ethnicity, fraternity/sorority membership, academic major, athletic status, the regions of the country they are from, and even the dormitories in which they live serve as criteria for status rankings. In each case, these serve as systematic bases for high or low prestige. Even though some may not feel that there are distinct classes, there is widespread agreement that social rankings of this type proliferate in the United States.

Evidence presented in the last chapter supports the existence of *economic* classes, and there is no doubt that inequality includes *social* dimensions as well. More often than not, we notice these social distinctions in our contacts with others; that

is, they become most salient when we interact with individuals whose characteristics and lifestyles differ from our own. Research suggests that we often rank people differently depending on those characteristics and lifestyles. Indeed, the term *social stratification* suggests that alongside economic inequality we have a system of status inequality, and often these two forms are intertwined with each other, as we shall see. Quite often, for example, an individual's economic position will affect his or her social position. In this chapter, we will examine the nature of this status dimension of inequality.

THE THEORY OF SOCIAL STATUS

Social status refers to an individual's ranking with respect to some socially important characteristic; thus, some people are thought to be low in social status, while others are high on this scale. Max Weber, the great German sociologist, stressed the importance of distinguishing between (economic) class and (social) status inequality, while at the same time he pointed out that they could be empirically related to each other, as when social *status* is dependent on *class* position. Weber viewed a person's *status situation* as "every typical component of the life fate of men that is determined by a specific, positive or negative social estimation of *honor*. This honor may be connected with any quality shared by a plurality" (Gerth and Mills 1962, p. 187). This means that individuals are or are not given homage and respect because they possess or lack some characteristic the community considers honorable or dishonorable. That quality is social rather than economic in nature; for example, one's family name, the street where one lives, the kind and degree of education one possesses, or one's race or gender all may elicit such honor or dishonor. Weber argued that this "claim to positive or negative privilege with respect to social prestige" may be based on (1) a "mode of living," (2) "a formal process of education which may consist in empirical or rational training and the acquisition of the corresponding modes of life," and/or (3) "the prestige of birth, or of an occupation" (Weber 1964, p. 428).

Whereas economic position can be determined by essentially *objective* measures—for example, amount of money, ownership, and so on—social status is the result of a *subjective* appraisal of people by others in the community. In this appraisal, individuals or groups are compared with each other and ranked on the basis of some characteristic or quality thought to be of significance in the society. In other words, status ranking derives from opinions of others, opinions based on a community value system. A plurality or group of individuals who share some prestige-relevant characteristic, such as living in a particular area of town or being a member of the same kind of club, may occupy a clear place in the social-ranking system of a community and thereby form a social stratum. Weber argued that "status groups are normally communities" in the sense that there is greater cohesiveness among individuals in the same status position, whereas " 'classes' are not communities; they merely represent possible, and frequent, bases for communal action" (Gerth and Mills 1962, pp. 181, 186).

Status groups that are ranked in a certain place on a community's social hierarchy are characterized by (1) a set of conventions and tradi-

tions, or lifestyle; (2) a tendency to marry within their own ranks; (3) an emphasis on interacting intimately—for example, eating only with others in the same group; (4) frequent monopolization of economic opportunities; and (5) emphasis on ownership of certain types of possessions rather than others (Weber 1964). All of these serve to set a group off from others. Wearing team jackets or particular types of clothes, associating with only particular kinds of people, and participating in an initiation process when becoming a member of a group are all signals that social status is operating. Status groups are characterized by particular styles of life that set them off from other groups. They are frequently founded in occupations. Jazz musicians, construction workers, and college professors, for example, often are known by the particular lifestyles associated with their professions.

To be an accepted member of a status group, a person is expected to follow the normative lifestyle of the group and to have "restrictions on 'social' intercourse" (Weber 1964, p. 187). This means that he or she is expected to associate intimately with only similar kinds of people. Consider what might happen if a person in a distinct status group steps out of line by violating the expected customs of the group. A good example is provided by *Frasier*, the well-known TV comedy. The principal players are two snooty psychologists who are brothers and their father, who is a retired police officer and has a set of tastes and values entirely different from that of his sons. Their lifestyles, manners of speaking, and friendships differ markedly from each other. Beer, homespun and earthy language, and flannel shirts characterize the father, whereas fine wines, expensive European suits, and an arrogant professional demeanor characterize the sons' lifestyles. Not surprisingly, their eating habits are quite different, as well. In one hilarious episode, the sons condescend to go to dinner with their father at one of his favorite haunts, a rustic steak house. The sons, of course, do not fit in and violate the customs associated with those who frequent such places. Although the effects are funny, they are also sobering as they show what happens when status groups clash and expected norms are violated.

A group tries to set itself apart from other status groups, especially those that might contaminate the purity of the group. Status groups try to distance themselves from others by a variety of methods. To distinguish themselves from outsiders, members of a status group may wear certain kinds of clothes or hairdos, or belong to exclusive clubs. An extreme instance of this process exists when individuals of a particular status group agree to marry only among themselves (i.e., to practice endogamy) and to chastise or shun anyone who marries outside the group. Lewis Lapham recalled his own experiences in this regard: "At college I knew several boys whose mothers discouraged their sons' acquaintance with anybody who lived in towns not adequately represented in the Social Register. If a boy didn't come from Grosse Pointe or Burlingame or Fairfield County, then his place of origin was listed under the heading *terra incognita*" (1988, p. 160). After all, status honor rests on "distance and exclusiveness." Moreover, "exclusion" is a primary mechanism by which those in powerful status groups keep others from gaining power (Parkin 1979). Residential segregation, to the degree that it is voluntary on the part of a high-status group, might also be an example of an attempt at such separation. Or men may attempt to keep their corporate positions exclusive by preventing women from moving to the top of the ladder. From these examples, it should be apparent that in addition to occupation, status may be based on racial/ethnic or gender qualities possessed by individuals, depending on the values of the particular society.

The various conventions, rules, traditions, and rituals of a particular status group help to sustain it over time. Thus, it is not surprising that there are attempts to enforce them within the group. Status groups are the "bearers of all 'conventions'...all 'stylization' of life either originates in status groups or is at least conserved by them" (Gerth and Mills 1962, p. 191).

So far, we have seen that status groups are (1) associated with different estimations of social honor, (2) based on a variety of socially relevant characteristics such as occupation or ethnicity, and (3) tend toward closure—that is, toward restrictions on contact with those outside the group. In addition, if fully developed, membership in a specific status group may allow an individual to monopolize certain material commodities (e.g., costumes, food, arms, artwork). For example, a community may feel that it is appropriate for only a particular group to be the owner or protector of certain goods.

Weber contended that status groups tend to monopolize particular types of economic opportunities and acquisitions, while at the same time they discourage the possession of other kinds. For example, a status group whose honor or prestige is based on its class position may allow its members to acquire fancy homes in particular neighborhoods, but it may be considered bad form to spend money acquiring a new bowling ball or a gaudy automobile. In societies where there is extreme *social* stratification, this monopolization may be legalized. The *social* privileges of a group are based on their economic and political power. It follows from this view that status groups are "phenomena of the distribution of power within a community" (Gerth and Mills 1962, p. 181).

When social and economic conditions in a community are stable, Weber argued, stratification by status becomes dominant, and after status has been "lived in" for a while, status privileges can become legal privileges. Moreover, status becomes of central importance in societies where the economy is monopolistically controlled and is of a religious or liturgical character. The setting is also one where the needs of groups are based on a feudalistic or patrimonial arrangement, and one that is dominated by "conventional rules of conduct" (Weber 1964, p. 429). In the United States, these conditions are frequently found in small towns where the same kin groups have lived for generations, where relationships are based on family name, and where social connections are important.

When legalization of status privileges occurs, a society may be on the road toward a full-fledged caste system. According to Weber, the extreme of

What kinds of institutions people can or cannot get into depend heavily on whether they meet the requirements of entrance, which in many cases include the magnitude of their economic resources. In both of these cases, membership exclusivity is stressed, even though in each case it appeals to a different level of clientele.

a caste system developing out of a status system happens only when the "underlying differences... are held to be 'ethnic'" in nature (Gerth and Mills 1962, p. 189). There is a clear hint that supposedly inherent and even biological distinctions are being considered here. Race is a basis for defer-

ence/honor, or its opposite, because "it is thought to represent the possession of some quality inherent in the ethnic aggregate and shared by all its members." This "essential quality" is "manifested in...external features such as colour, hair form, physiognomy and physique" (Shils 1970, p. 428).

Indeed, there is evidence that ranking does take place on the basis of such external features (Lasswell 1965). The existence of varying degrees of social distance between various ethnic groups in the United States provides ample evidence of such a ranking system. In this instance, various ethnic status groups that may have been horizontally related are converted into a set of hierarchically arranged groups, those on the top being the most pure and those on the bottom being impure, contaminating, or even untouchable. The latter "pariah" groups may be tolerated only because of economic necessity; that is, the lower castes may perform necessary but dishonorable, dirty, and onerous work. For example, lower castes may be the only groups ritualistically permitted to collect garbage or dead carcasses from the street.

In sum, according to Weber (1964), ideal-typical caste systems are characterized by (1) classification into a caste on the basis of some ascribed characteristic such as race, ethnicity, or lineage, and as such it is hereditary; (2) immobility within the system; (3) endogamy and restricted social intercourse; and (4) typically prescribed ranges of occupations associated with each caste. Under a caste system, consequently, the relationships among various status groups have been shaped into a ranking system of superordination and subordination. As we shall see later, some scholars have argued that caste relations exist between the sexes and races in the United States. Others, however, have suggested that the changing, open society is qualitatively different from a society such as India, for example, to which the application of the caste system is most often made.

When ranking does occur among status groups, *deference* is expected to be shown toward those in more prestigious or honored groups. Deference "entails an attribute of superiority (or inferiority).... It is an attribution of merit (or of defect); it is an assessment which attributes worthiness (or unworthiness)" (Shils 1970, p. 421). Like Weber, Shils stressed that deference and status are of a different quality than economic phenomena such as class and wealth. "Deference-position—esteem, prestige or status—does belong to a differ-

ent order of events in comparison with events like occupation distribution, income and wealth distribution, etc. It belongs to the realm of values; it is the outcome of evaluative judgments regarding positions in the distribution of 'objective' characteristics" (p. 436).

The act of showing deference to persons in higher status positions manifests itself in various presentational rituals that essentially indicate to them how they are being regarded. The ways by which individuals greet and compliment others, as well as similar behaviors of homage, are examples of deferential behavior (Goffman 1959, 1967). For example, students are often concerned with how they should address me: should it be "Professor," "Doctor," "Mister," or simply "Chuck"? Some clearly feel uneasy using the latter form of address because they think it suggests a lack of respect or deference.

When a person of lower status approaches one of a higher rank, the interaction may take on a formalistic, ritualistic nature on the surface. That is, in the public setting, each party plays the role that is expected from persons representing each status group. But in private, feelings may be quite the opposite. That private aspect of life is frequently considered more inviolate for those in higher statuses than for those at the bottom, whose privacy/personal space may be more justifiably violated according to social norms. Because of the greater honor given them, the private lives of those in high statuses are more likely to be respected.

While those in lower statuses are presenting themselves in ways that demonstrate respect and deference for those at the top, the latter can use their resources to present themselves in ways that elicit and justify such respect. They typically have the resources and motivation to appear impressive, and so manage situations to obtain the responses they desire. Through their *demeanor,* individuals of higher status can suggest that they are worthy of such deference. Demeanor is "that element of the individual's ceremonial behavior typically conveyed through deportment, dress, and bearing, which serves to express to those in his immediate presence that he is a person of certain desirable or undesirable qualities" (Goffman 1967, p. 77).

Deference behavior between individuals in differently ranked status groups can be based on a variety of criteria. An individual may be considered entitled to such behavior from others because of occupation and race or ethnicity, as we have already suggested, but also on the bases of level and type of education, gender, lifestyle, political or corporate power or one's nearness to it, family name or kinship network, income, and amount and type of wealth. Service work on behalf of a community or society and formal titles also can serve as grounds for status honor in some locations. All these factors are deference relevant because they are linked with basic values and/or issues in the society. A region or area can also be the basis of deference because it is thought to be associated with a particular occupational role (e.g., Appalachia with coal mining, Manhattan with the stock market, etc.), with the exercise of power in a society, or with some other valued criterion (e.g., New England with quality education).

BASES OF STATUS IN THE UNITED STATES

As suggested earlier, the esteem in which a person is held in the United States can be founded on a variety of factors. Several of the more prominent bases will be discussed here, starting with the traditionally acknowledged criteria of occupation, education, lifestyle, and wealth. Less noticed, but also bases of status, physical appearance and place also are analyzed. A brief comment is also made on race and gender as bases for status.

Occupation

Occupational role, of course, is frequently associated with both social class and social status, but the most commonly used measures of occupational ranking tap the prestige/esteem dimension rather than the economic one. Occupation is a basis for deference and honor not only because of its association with valued goals (income, power, etc.) but also because there are often lifestyles as-

sociated with particular roles—lifestyles that receive different degrees of honor. Plumbers and professors clearly are accorded different levels of honor because of what people associate with each of these occupations.

A good analysis of a particular occupation as being the basis of status is given in Bensman's (1972) discussion of professional musicians. He argued that musicians form a "status community" in that they adhere to a particular and somewhat unique set of values that shapes their lifestyles. The institutions, behaviors, and practices that organize and comprise their lives, in turn, are based on those core values. Insiders are clearly separated from outsiders. There are regularized interactions and rituals that help keep the community cohesive. When the musicians get together informally, they perform, discuss music, or attend concerts, all of which increase their allegiance to the community's values.

In addition to having its own subcultural values, the music community is internally stratified according to a number of musically relevant criteria. Rank is affected by (1) the instrument one plays; (2) one's role in the community (conductor, performer, critic, etc.); (3) whether one is a soloist, accompanist, or in an orchestra or small group; (4) assessed skill; (5) extent of recording contracts and size of fees; and (6) affiliation with a particular school, conservatory, teacher, or type of music (Bensman 1972). Thus, for those close to the community, there is an understanding that diverse internal divisions exist within what may appear to the outsider to be a homogeneous community.

We can, of course, conceive of other occupational groups forming status communities. In fact, each of us is a member of several such communities and organizations in which our particular status may vary. Social rankings are at least implicit within and between many churches, civic associations (e.g, Rotary Club, Lion's Club), and social organizations (e.g., country clubs, square-dance groups). The existence of a large number of such status communities made up of individuals who have positions in several of them creates an image of a societal prestige/status system that is extremely complex. However, some of these status communities may be more central and important than others and, therefore, may have more of an impact on one's status position in the society.

Generally, status communities based on occupation are socially relevant and prominent. Over the years, there have been several attempts to rank occupations according to prestige or status. Early efforts to measure occupational status suffered from the fact that they generally were based on inadequate samples of respondents, were of a subjective nature, and contained prestige differences within the general occupational categories that were often almost as great as those between such categories (see Counts 1925; Edwards 1943; Smith 1943). It is also difficult to arrange these occupations along a single dimension using one criterion. Although it may seem obvious that skilled blue-collar work would rank above semi-skilled in prestige, it is not at all clear why professionals should rank above proprietors using the same dimension of skill.

Several attempts were later made to perfect an occupational status ranking, the most influential being the North-Hatt scale developed in the mid-1940s. It differed from the earlier scales in that a much wider range of occupation types was considered, and it relied less on the creator's judgment of rankings. The prestige rankings obtained were based on a 1947 survey of 2,920 individuals who were asked to classify the *general standing* of each of 90 occupations. No mention was made of prestige. The five-point evaluations ranged from "excellent," "good," and "average" to "somewhat below average," and "poor." The most frequently cited reasons for awarding a given occupation an excellent standing, in order of decreasing frequency, were that it paid well (18 percent), served humanity (16 percent), required a lot of previous training and investment (14 percent), and had a high level of prestige associated with it (14 percent).

The reliability and accuracy of the North-Hatt scale, which was heavily used in the past, have been called into question because it (1) was constructed using a nonrepresentative sample of re-

spondents; (2) ignored occupations traditionally held by women; (3) assumed knowledge by respondents of the occupations and consensus on the bases for evaluating each occupation; (4) was based on inconsistent instructions to respondents and variations in rationales for the ranking of specific occupations; and (5) consisted of both narrowly and broadly defined occupations (Reiss 1961, Chapters 2–3). However, a replication of the study in 1963 yielded very similar rankings for the 88 distinct occupation types (Hodge, Siegel, and Rossi 1964). The rankings appear to be stable over time. There appear to be fairly consistent feelings among Americans in general about the prestige ranking of occupations, a ranking that has not changed significantly since World War II.

Later, using the knowledge that occupational prestige was highly correlated with income and education, Duncan (1961) was able to develop an equation to estimate the prestige scores of all occupations. From these, a socioeconomic index (SEI) was developed for all occupations.

Education

In addition to occupational role, *education* has been a basis of prestige and honor. Level of education is supposed to be related to the level of knowledge and skill one has in a particular field. In addition to that, however, education also prepares one for a particular status group and ensures the continuation of status groups. The type of education as well as the place where it is received are bases for prestige. A degree from an Ivy League school such as Yale or Harvard, or a small private school such as Amherst or Smith is quite prestigious compared to a degree from a local community college. The elitism and degree of selectivity associated with a school is linked to the level of prestige accorded to it. Think about the differences in the students you might know who graduate from each type of school. Schools like to pride themselves on the kinds of students they produce. Different types of schools instill different sets of values and outlooks in their students, thereby encouraging the development of different cultural groups.

The cultural/status effects of education have been analyzed in depth. Bourdieu suggested that higher education helps to reproduce the class structure by functioning to reinforce the value and status differences between the classes (1977a). It does this by honoring the *cultural capital* held by those in the higher classes. This capital—which consists of a group's cultural values, experience, knowledge, and skills—is passed on from one generation to the next. In organizing itself around the linguistic and cultural competence of the upper classes, higher education ensures that members of the upper classes are successful in school. This legitimates the class inequality that results because, on the surface, it appears that the inequality is largely the result of individual performance in a meritocratic, open educational system. That is, the language used, the cultural knowledge expected for success in school, and the values and behaviors honored are those of the upper class. In short, in the words of one interpreter, "The school serves as the trading post where socially valued cultural capital is parleyed into superior academic performance. Academic performance is then turned back into economic capital by the acquisition of superior jobs" (MacLeod 1987, p. 12). The experiences in school and in the workplace of those in the working and lower classes, coupled with the general outlook and specific attitudes they have acquired because of their class milieu, lead them to believe that they cannot succeed in school, thus lowering their aspirations to do so (ibid.). The result is stratification within the educational system, which then reinforces the class stratification in the wider society.

One of the principal functions of education is to prepare students for the cultural status groups they will be entering after graduation (Collins 1971). In his biting satire at the beginning of the twentieth century, Thorstein Veblen observed that elite schools of higher learning had as their primary purpose "the preparation of the youth of the priestly and the leisure classes...for the consumption of goods, material and immaterial, according to a conventionally accepted, reputable scope and method." The "reputable seminaries of learning" are conservative and tend to stress the importance of the classics rather than practical and directly serviceable knowledge. The classics, according to Veblen, "serve the decorative ends of leisure-class learning better than any other body of knowledge, and hence they are an effective means of reputability" (Veblen 1953, pp. 239, 256). Similarly, authors of a more recent empirical study of elite prep schools observed that "curriculum is the nursery of culture and the classical curriculum is the cradle of high culture" (Cookson and Persell 1985, p. 74). But they also observed, in sharp contrast to Veblen's emphasis on the nonfunctional learning of the "leisure" class, that the education is deadly serious.

Analysis of the history of U.S. boarding schools supports the conclusion that they were developed to help the established upper class isolate and reaffirm its cultural characteristics. Initially, the founders hoped that these schools would help separate their cultural group from the new wealth developing in industry and from the increasing amounts of lower-class immigration. This suggests again the strong impetus toward social closure among the old rich. But the need for financial support of these schools necessitated taking in some of the sons of individuals who had become recently wealthy from industrial, manufacturing, or other enterprises in the latter part of the nineteenth century (Levine 1980). These *nouveaux riches,* consequently, infiltrated the boarding schools even though the established patrician families winced because the former were often seen as lacking in manners and polish. One of these new-wealth parents, Phillip Armour, once described his occupation as converting "bristles, blood, and the inside and outside of pigs and bullocks into revenue" (ibid., p. 83). This kind of comment is hardly the type that would have won over persons from the established old-wealth families.

While stressing the rigor and difficulty of attainment within them, studies of elite prep schools confirm the importance of cultural capital and the role of these schools in perpetuating the class system. A large part of the education for students in these status seminaries involves learning how to hide or mask their wealth, to acquire "taste," and to prepare themselves to be "soldiers for their class"—that is, to occupy and carry out the responsibilities of their class (Cookson and Persell 1985). As Shils (1970) observed, some schools are thought of as more important than others, and "those educated in them acquire more of a charismatically infused culture" (p. 426). The rules of eating, sleeping, and playing together along with peer expectations and formal discipline help forge cohesiveness at the same time that the classical curriculum, the emphasis on dialogue and discussion, and extracurricular activities such as sports encourage the development of specific values. The formal and informal curricula of these schools are designed to make sure that these results occur. Even the architecture of the school and demeanor of the headmaster or headmistress conspire to create an atmosphere in which such learning and value development can take place. "The cultural capital that prep school students accumulate in boarding schools is a treasure trove of skills and status symbols that can be used in later life" (Cookson and Persell 1985, p. 30).

For their students, elite prep schools also serve as a major linchpin between parental class position and obtaining positions of power in the wider society. These students tend to get into the better colleges and universities and, ultimately, to obtain positions of influence in the leading political, cultural, legal, and corporate institutions of society. Earlier studies of prep school graduates reinforce the conclusion that these students need to go on to the "right" Harvard, Yale, or Princeton; that is, they have to get into the appropriate clubs and societies at these universities, and to do this a student has to come from the "right" boarding school. Upon graduating from the university, these students can take up their memberships in the most exclusive city clubs and become established in a high-status Wall Street law or brokerage firm. This process, covering the youths from their teen years through their attainment of an occupation, helps ensure the exclusivity of this high-status group. A not insignificant reason for this attainment relates to the networks of relationships and values developed during the prep school years. The Cookson-Persell study confirms that going to the so-called right schools helps instill those values and aids movement into those positions most highly honored in U.S. society. In this manner, prep schools help to reproduce the values

Even the classical architecture and spacious, finely manicured grounds of prestigious prep schools conspire to create a feeling of tradition and specialness among their students.

and positions necessary for the legitimation and maintenance of the class structure. In prep schools, class and status intersect.

School and Lifestyle

Status inequalities between groups can be found in a variety of school levels. Unambiguous categorization of individuals according to appearance, behaviors, values, and attitudes develops early in childhood. Social cliques and categories have been found even among elementary-school children, as well as in junior and senior high schools. Initial analyses of recent school killings by students suggest the significance of popularity, social isolation, and social labeling for self-esteem, identity, and conflict between groups of students. While certainly not the only factor in these incidents, attachment of a student to a social category or clique has real consequences in the school setting. Self-esteem and identity appear to be linked to the status of one's "crowd" in school (Adler and Adler 1998; Brown and Lohr 1987).

The students responsible for the deaths at Columbine High School in Colorado were linked to a category of students called the Trenchcoat Mafia. But social clusters at different schools go by many names: jocks, burnouts, preppies, trendies, leading crowd, nerds, brainiacs, goths, wannabees, earth queens, stickup boys, geeks, freaks, grits, punks. People with similar interests, backgrounds, or accomplishments join together to separate themselves from others and to solidify their identities and sense of membership at school. Belonging to a clique or category is a way of avoiding social isolation. It is also a means of ranking different kinds of individuals.

Although membership can be unstable and rankings within each of them can shift, these social clusters have many of the properties of status groups (cf., Adler and Adler 1998; Eder 1995; Cairns and Cairns 1994; Kinney 1993; Eckert 1989). As such, they represent a type of status inequality. Among these qualities is *group ranking* in terms of popularity and prestige at school. A second feature following from this are explicit at-

tempts to attract certain youths while keeping others out (i.e., *attempts at maintaining boundaries* between insiders and outsiders). Being mean, picking on outsiders, and "putting them down" are techniques to keep outsiders at arm's length. Careful recruitment and monitoring of behavior and attitudes are common ways of ensuring insider loyalty once in a group. "Cliques' boundary maintenance makes them exclusive....The dynamics of inclusion lures members into cliques, while the dynamic of exclusion keeps them there" (Adler and Adler 1998, p. 72). People outside the cliques are thought of as different. "You don't even date outside of your clique. It's like a kind of racism," a senior high school girl observes (Brett 1999, p. A6).

A third status feature of these groups is a *lifestyle* that is perceived to be distinctive. A large part of the unique lifestyles among student groupings is suggested by the clothing and adornments they wear. Students labeled as "goths" tend to wear black clothes, whereas more mainstream "jocks" wear Polo or J. Crew. Tattoos, jewelry, and hairstyle also symbolize given social categories at school. As part of the distinctive lifestyles, involvement in school activities, musical tastes, and language also systematically vary. Fourth, *exclusive places or locations* tend to be associated with different social clusters. Given lunch tables are "owned" by clusters, as are places where students socially hang out. Finally, *stigmatization and avoidance of social contamination* is also found within these school groups. Because of recurrent jockeying for status within groups, individuals pick on each other and single out some for intense ostracism. Avoidance with outsiders antagonistic to the group is also enforced. Paradoxically, meanness to others is a way of maintaining popularity because it avoids the problems of being thought of as "stuck-up" or "supernice." Being stuck-up reduces popularity while being supernice to everyone reduces one's rank and distinctiveness (Merten 1997).

The cool relationships between members of different social clusters at school broadly reflect their different lifestyles. Lifestyle itself can be a principal source of status honor for adults as well, because the manner in which one lives is a concrete demonstration of one's social and cultural values. In essence, it is a symbol representing what one stands for. Such lifestyles are generally internally consistent (i.e., they contain behavior or style arrangements that go together by common agreement in the community or that are found frequently enough to be considered normative). Just as rap music is not likely to be found in a yuppie's CD collection, one does not mix general stylistic elements. Stylistic unity, then, becomes the basis of lifestyle (Sobel 1983a).

Individual lifestyles that stress (1) the accumulation of prestigious possessions; (2) the "high life" of travel, exclusive luxuries, and social activity; or (3) home maintenance, or (4) family-oriented activities tend to be associated with distinctive socioeconomic and geographic groups (Sobel 1983a). In his witty book titled *Class,* Fussell (1983) related the many ways in which classes differ in lifestyle, including the kinds of furniture they buy, vacation spots they choose, and even the way they shop through catalogues.

Wealth

As the preceding example implies, having a particular amount and type of *wealth* and/or *income* also can be a basis for status. Since each class may form its own status group, it should not be surprising that sociologists have found that certain lifestyles and values are found in each class.

For example, a number of scholars have focused on the status honor of the upper class. The use of inherited wealth, family lineage, club membership, quality of education, and general lifestyle as criteria for membership into the established upper class helps maintain the exclusivity of that class. We have already seen how early boarding schools functioned in this regard. Practicing endogamy within the class helps determine who can get into "Society." Maintaining a closed circle in the face of an ostensibly open democratic society demands that there be mechanisms present to keep just anyone from getting into the circle.

E. Digby Baltzell, a member of the upper class himself, insisted that "there exists one metropolitan upper class with a common cultural tradition, consciousness of kind and 'we' feeling of solidarity which tends to be national in scope." This upper class has been buttressed historically by institutions that serve its members, such as boarding schools, select eastern universities and colleges, and the Episcopal Church (Baltzell 1958; see also Domhoff 1971; Ostrander 1984). The upper class as a status group practices a particular kind of lifestyle with particular kinds of rules associated with it. Specifically, children are expected to be well bred, with manners and a sense of their importance in society. Boarding schools are a principal source of this training, but family ties are also central. Keeping the family line intact and marrying the right kind of person is important. Marriages are not made as facilely as might be the case in other social classes. But some restricted social activities, such as debutante balls and fox hunts, which once were prominent elements in the lifestyle of the upper class, have declined in recent years. Acceptable occupations include financier, lawyer, business executive, physician, art collector, museum director, and even architect. Membership in exclusive metropolitan social clubs, often composed only of males, is also important if an individual is to be part of the upper-class status community. Living in an exclusive residence separate from middle-class and other neighborhoods and maintaining a second summer home are also means by which separation from outsiders is preserved.

Upper-class families tend to be patriarchal, but even the female spouse may be a member of a private social club. Frequently, she is expected to be involved in charitable activities and other social events. There is a division of labor between the sexes in these families. Evidence suggests that members of this upper-status group are concerned with maintaining their separation from others, even in death. Their burial customs and sites tend to be different from those of lesser mortals (Kephart 1950). A historical analysis of cemeteries in the United States noted the long-term attempts

Every status group has some entrance rules. One social mechanism by which the entrance into "high society" is monitored has been debutante balls, in which young women are formally introduced into society. One hundred nine women were introduced into society at the Annual Debutante Cotillion and Christmas Ball held at the Waldorf-Astoria Hotel in New York in 1957.

by the middle and upper classes to segregate themselves physically in burial sites from those of a more lowly status, and to freely use monuments and mausoleums to proclaim their status. In recent years, mausoleums and monuments have again increased in popularity. Advertisements for these tout these structures as symbols of prestige that will remind viewers of how much success was attained during one's lifetime (Sloane 1991). As these characteristics indicate, "members of the upper class not only have *more,* they have *different*" (Domhoff 1971, p. 91).

Weber thought that status groups are ranked according to their patterns of consumption as manifested in their lifestyles (cited in Gerth and Mills 1962, p. 193). Many possessions have a level of prestige that differs drastically with their actual monetary value. For example, consider the relative prestige of a new Chevy pickup and an older Jaguar coupe, both of which may cost the same amount. It is not so much the economic value per se of the consumed goods that is important, but

rather the fact that these goods, especially if owned by a higher-ranking status group, serve as symbols of worth and ability. It becomes a matter of self-respect and honor to conspicuously display such goods, not merely to "keep up with the Joneses" but to surpass them if possible (Veblen 1953).

Veblen's Theory of the Leisure Class.   The linkage of class position to status is most clearly seen in the arguments of Thorstein Veblen, an early American sociologist and economist who grew up in rural Wisconsin and Minnesota. His discussion of status applies most directly to the periods up to the early part of the twentieth century. Writing his most important work around the turn of the twentieth century, Veblen contended that manual labor had become defined as dishonorable and undignified, not becoming to one who wished to be considered of high social status. On the other hand, he argued that nonproductive labor, such as that of being a business executive, increased the probability of owning great amounts of property, which in turn, increased one's status honor. Owning property had become, in Veblen's view, the equivalent of possessing honor. In order to show this honor and property to others, one then had to engage in ostentatious displays of wealth and status—namely, various forms of what he called "conspicuous consumption." This display served as a symbol of one's worth and ability.

Women were really the first type of private property owned by men. During an early historical period of "predatory, barbarism," according to Veblen, the major class distinction was between men and women. While women did all the essential, productive labor, men engaged most often in honorific hunting and various types of exploit and plunder, eager to produce trophies for themselves. This is the period in which industrious, productive labor came to be defined as dishonorable and dirty, whereas the kind of activities in which men engaged were considered to be honorable and praiseworthy. In a manner of speaking, men's work allowed them to avoid getting their hands dirty. In order to show their worth, men led a life of conspicuous leisure. It was an indication that one is not doing ignoble labor (i.e., working). Time was consumed nonproductively. It became a sign of the decency of one's life. Men competed with each other in demonstrating their worth by the accumulation of various possessions and trophies, so that they could make an invidious comparison of themselves with others. By *invidious,* Veblen meant "a comparison of persons with a view to rating and grading them in respect of relative worth or value—in an aesthetic or moral sense.... An invidious comparison is a process of valuation of persons in respect of worth" (Veblen 1953, p. 40).

In the civilized state of industrial society—a quasi-peaceable barbarian stage according to Veblen—the cultivation of manners and decorum are a central part of this leisure-class lifestyle. In modern times, the distinction between industry and business parallels the earlier difference between female and male labor. Modern-day businesspeople are industrial society's predatory class, whereas those directly involved in industrial work are those who are doing the productive labor.

Veblen argued that the modern leisure class of the industrial era not only engaged in conspicuous consumption and leisure but also in conspicuous waste. Women, for example, had become, in Veblen's view, not only the "property" of men but also an ornament with which men could display their wealth and power. Women took on a ceremonial function with the rise of the Industrial Revolution and were expected not to engage in industrious, productive work. Rather, in their behavior and appearance, women were to symbolize the status of their husbands. Men, even those in business, could satisfy their "instinct of workmanship" (i.e., the feeling needed by everyone that one is doing something useful), but women were essentially servants of the household head who were expected to be well bred and to use their time cultivating their beauty. Women were in charge of the household—the so-called woman's sphere—and were expected to engage in conspicuous leisure and consumption, since their behavior reflected the status of the men who owned them. In their dress, they were expected to be especially wasteful; that is, their dresses were to be nonfunctional waste material. "Special pains should be taken in the construction of women's dress, to impress upon the beholder the fact (often indeed a fiction) that the wearer does not and cannot habitually engage in useful work.... [It is] the woman's function in an especial degree to put in evidence her household's ability to pay" (Veblen 1953, p. 126).

As suggested earlier, conspicuous consumption and waste not only occurred in the area of dress but also in the cultivation of beauty. Indeed, during the nineteenth century, and largely as a by-product of the Industrial Revolution, the "cult of true womanhood" demanded that a respectable woman refrain from useful work, to be "fragile, idle, pure...submissive and subservient to her husband and to domestic needs. Her worth was based on her decorative value, a quality that embraced her beauty, her character, and her temperament" (Fox and Hesse-Biber 1984, p. 19).

We can summarize Veblen's ideas by indicating that he felt that people's worth and honor, in modern times, were linked to their ability to pay—that is, their wealth and possessions. The more a person can display such resources, the greater the respect attributed to him or her. This leads to an ostentatious show for others in a desire to impress and to a competition to outdo others in such display. Such display covers a wide range of possessions, even such things as better-groomed lawns, ownership of prize horses, and conspicuous dress. Everyone tries to battle in this competition, according to Veblen, but the leisure/business class is most successful.

Since Veblen, there have been other analyses of the lifestyle of the upper class. As noted earlier, status often rests on class position, and high-class position makes it possible for individuals to pursue desired lifestyles. Brooks (1979) argued that Veblen's ideas must be updated because the lower classes do not revere the upper class as in Veblen's day, nor is leisure strictly the province of the upper class today. More often, people engage in "parody display" of honored status symbols. Just as in a literary parody, people poke fun at possessions that, in the past, have commanded great respect. He views this parody as the result of a mixture of admiration and ridicule by the lower classes. But still he finds that competitive display and conspicuous consumption are alive and well in U.S society. Speech, clothing, and membership in exclusive clubs, for example, continue to be used in making invidious comparisons. Using beautiful women as ornamentation or as trophies also continues today. " 'Beauty' is a currency system like the gold standard. Like any economy, it is determined by politics, and in the modern age in the West it is the last, best belief system that keeps male dominance intact" (Wolf 1991, p. 12). By encouraging women to spend a lot of time on how they look and act as they attempt to meet culturally enforced standards, the "beauty myth" weakens their ability to fully develop their mental, political, and economic potential (Wolf 1991).

Physical Appearance and Status

Clearly, physical appearance can provide clues to and is often a basis for social status. In this regard,

in other chapters, we will focus in detail on race and gender as bases for inequality. Along with these variables, physical beauty also serves as a basis for granting status. Fussell (1983) suggested that even one's weight and profile suggest a class position. Beauty, of course, is in the eyes of the beholder, but what the beholder sees and how it is interpreted are shaped by culture's values. Beauty is a social construction, and in U.S. society it has significance. To realize its importance, one need only look at the media to see how it is used to sell everything from automobile transmissions to cologne. It implies that those who possess it have other qualities as well. Research has suggested that individuals who are considered physically attractive also are considered to have happier marriages, have better mental health, and be more confident and likeable than those who are considered unattractive. They also are thought to be more attentive when being interviewed, to be better performers in the classroom, and to deserve more room on the street (Webster and Driskell 1983).

A study by Webster and Driskell, conducted among college students who examined photographs of males and females, indicated that people who are labeled as beautiful are considered to be "better at situations in general, things that count in this world, most tasks, and abstract ability" (1983, p. 158). It is also considered more desirable to be beautiful than to be unattractive. Many, especially younger White women, are deeply conscious of their body shape and weight and have negative feelings about them (Cash and Henry 1995). The widespread use by women of elective plastic surgery, liposuction, and cosmetics that promise to make them look younger suggests the importance of appearance in their lives. Eating disorders, such as bulimia and anorexia, are also attempts to make one look thinner and more attractive in present-day society.

Status on other grounds, such as wealth and income, also can affect the way we see the attractiveness of an individual. The physical appearance, clothes, and behavioral styles of a person who has wealth may be seen as being more attractive because of his or her wealth, and what is considered attractive may be determined by those who have wealth. As Lewis Lapham acidly stated,

In a rich man's culture, art is what sells and its price determines its worth. If the diamond bought at Tiffany's sparkles more brilliantly than a diamond of equal weight and size bought for $758 on West Forty-seventh Street, then even bad novels by Norman Mailer or Joseph Heller or E. L. Doctorow become masterpieces by virtue of the prices paid for the paperback and movie rights. Once an author or an artist has demonstrated his or her ability to earn money, he or she acquires, as if by court order, a reputation for genius. (1988, p. 67)

Similarly, one acquires status because of an attractive appearance, and such an appearance is considered attractive because of one's wealth. The same appearance on a person of another class might very well be interpreted differently.

Of course, the definitions of beauty and other status symbols vary with societies and over time within the same society. The beauty of the human figure portrayed in a Rubens painting is not the same ideal of beauty seen today in the clothing ads of Calvin Klein or Ralph Lauren. Especially in open and democratic societies, the salience and ranking of status symbols waxes and wanes. In one year, having a particular characteristic or possession may result in great status honor or prestige, but a few years later, that same possession may be of little social importance, while another has ascended to a position of high prestige.

One of the tasks of those who rank highly is to ensure that they maintain their status. However, over time, others in an open society may be able to obtain the objects once held only by those on top. This devalues their worth in the eyes of the higher status group. Mills (1951) argued that, in the middle of the twentieth century, the middle-class, white-collar workers were in a "status panic" because "every basis on which the prestige claims of the bulk of the white-collar employees have historically rested has been declining in firmness and stability" (p. 249). In terms of wages, unemployment rates, education, political power, and ethnicity, Mills felt that the middle class was losing its higher status relative to the working class. This

leads to the erosion of status honor for those in the middle class, because "if everybody belongs to the fraternity, nobody gets any prestige from belonging" (p. 249). In order to maintain an edge in prestige, individuals try to increase their status within their own group, purchase as many possessions as possible that serve as status badges, and, finally, to temporarily raise their status by living extravagantly on the weekend (pp. 254–258).

In large and impersonal urban settings where individuals do not know each other personally, displays of status symbols are more common indicators informing strangers *who* their owners really are (Form and Stone 1957). It does not take long to pick up on the social meaning of what we put on our bodies. Even the smallest, seemingly insignificant adornment can suggest status. Pharoah, one of two Chicago elementary-school African Americans studied intensively in *There Are No Children Here,* was eager to have a pair of glasses, even if he didn't need them, because "he suggested, if he wore glasses, his teachers would choose him more often to run errands or to answer questions. They would, at the very least…make him look smarter" (Kotlowitz 1991, p. 62). There is no question that what we wear sends signals about our status.

It has been well established that one of the most often-used status symbols in urban settings concerns fashions in clothing. Veblen (1953) observed that at the turn of the twentieth century, clothing was particularly well suited to being a status symbol since "our apparel is always in evidence and affords an indication of our pecuniary standing to all observers at the first glance" (p. 119).

A study at Michigan State University considered "the degree to which clothing is used as a guide in identifying the role and status of unknown persons" and "the various shades of meaning attached to clothing in particular social situations" (Rosencranz 1962, p. 18). When asked to evaluate individuals in pictures shown to them, characters in the pictures who were dressed more formally than others were accorded a higher status, whereas other inappropriately attired individuals were viewed as being of a lower status. Dressing in a manner that was foreign to U.S. culture or considered inappropriate for the gender of the person resulted in a kind of negative sanction. A man dressed in a skirt in one of the pictures, for example, was described as being "dressed like a foreigner" or, in particular, "a Chinaman."

Undoubtedly, how we dress affects the attitudes and behavior of others with respect to us (Kaiser 1985). "Clothing itself is the beginning and end of human display, touching on one side the skin of the person and reaching out on the other to announce to all what the person inside the skin is or wishes to be" (Brooks 1979, p. 201). Clothing takes on a moral character in that people assume that your dress indicates something about the kind of person you are. "A cheap coat makes a cheap man," observed Veblen. The appearance of secondhand clothing stores in Washington, DC, which cater to the not-quite affluent, for example, testifies to the importance people place on trying to make an impression. Originally expensive suits can be purchased for a low price. Noted one customer: "It pays to shop in a place like this in a town like Washington where clothes are a big part of how you are perceived" (Barringer 1990, p. 10). Such concerns start early, with parents tramping off to buy Baby Gap, Baby Dior, and Baby Ralph Lauren designer clothing.

Some research suggests that clothing frequently brings out status-related reactions. Alison Lurie suggested a number of ways in which clothing can be used to give an impression of high status. She labeled these "conspicuous" addition, division, multiplication, and labeling. Conspicuous addition refers to the technique of layering clothes—that is, wearing several kinds of clothing over each other, even though it is not functionally necessary. Scarves and vests, for example, when worn ornamentally, would be a demonstration of conspicuous addition and an example of what Veblen called conspicuous waste. Conspicuous division and multiplication are different forms of the technique of wearing a wide variety of different types of clothing, especially for separate occasions. The point here is that, to indicate high status, a person does not want to wear the same piece of clothing twice consecutively and does want to wear different kinds of clothes for evening, dinner, casual, and other sorts of situations.

"Life itself has been turned into a series of fashionable games, each of which…demands a different costume—or, in this case, a different set of costumes.… The more different looks a woman can assume, the more fascinating she is supposed to be: personality itself has become an adjunct of Conspicuous Waste" (Lurie 1987, p. 129). "The constant wearing of new and different garments is most effective when those you wish to impress see you constantly—ideally every day. It is also more effective if these people are relative strangers" (p. 127). The latter comment reinforces the notion mentioned earlier that it is in large cities that these symbols become most significant as emblems of status.

A good example of conspicuous multiplication is found in the inner city of Harlem where status among youths is related to the number and kinds of sneakers worn ("The Well Heeled" 1988). One's status is indicated by the use of different sneakers for different occasions and activities. "A man's got to have style, or he's half a man," explained one youth named Mr. Washington. "The fact is, in the inner city you are what you wear—on your feet" (ibid., p. A1). One has to be careful not to wear the wrong brand or style of sneakers in the wrong place or on the wrong occasion. There are regions, sections of cities, even streets, that are closely identified with particular brands of shoes. "In Boston, there are Nike streets …and Adidas streets…and woe to anyone caught wearing the wrong brand on the wrong street" (ibid., p. A6). Shoes are used not only to identify one's status but also one's turf. Some youths are willing to sell drugs to keep themselves in shoes, some of which cost over $100 a pair. The youth quoted earlier, Mr. Washington, owns 150 pairs of sneakers. This recalls Veblen's comment that even those without the resources will go to great lengths, even murder, to practice such "conspicuous consumption." Status seeking is not a game only among the well-to-do.

Finally, a fourth form of clothing technique mentioned by Lurie, conspicuous labeling, is a way of ensuring that the knowledgeable would be able to distinguish the high-status piece of clothing from an imitation. Otherwise, a status crisis could occur for those who wish to use clothing as a status symbol, since several brand names of clothing may look virtually identical. Labeling on the outside, rather than the inside, of a garment is an obvious way of advertising your status to those around you.

Place and Status

Think for a moment of the United States as a large geographical grid on which different groups travel and reside in particular places. If you could see this grid from above, what would it look like? Social patterns of enclaves, segregation, inclusion, and exclusion would become evident. In the past few years, space and place have been increasingly recognized as being related to social status. Recently, Daphne Spain has even argued that space is used to acknowledge and reinforce inequalities between men and women. Earlier in U.S. history, the lower status of women was used to keep them out of college, and later to relegate them to separate women's colleges. At work, women's workplaces are most often open spaces characterized by a lack of doors and walls (e.g., as in a secretarial pool), in sharp contrast to the privacy found in the closed-door higher-status jobs of men. Finally, at home, different spaces and entrances are often assigned to men and women, especially in nonindustrial societies and in nineteenth-century United States (Spain 1992).

Where people live is also associated with their status. Regionally, for example, high concentrations of the upper class reside in New England, Florida, and California, whereas few upper class live in heartland states such as North and South Dakota, Iowa, Kansas, Oklahoma, West Virginia, Indiana, and Arkansas (Higley 1995). The United States has neighborhood clusters, many of which are clearly and intentionally connected with specific groups occupying different status levels. The elegant mansions of the so-called blue blood estates neighborhoods of places such as Beverly Hills and Scarsdale hold those at the top of the status ladder, while the public assistance neighborhoods of West Philadelphia and Watts are disproportionately dwelling places of African American and single-parent families. Public housing has also become increasingly occupied by female-headed families, and contains disproportionate numbers of elderly and children (Spain 1993). Throughout the status ladder are found neighborhoods known as "young suburbia," "middle America," "shotguns and pick-ups" and "sharecroppers." Each of these has its own core values and lifestyle. That these distinct cultural pockets exist should not be surprising: "People seek compatible neighbors who share their family status, income, employment patterns and values" (Weiss 1988).

We must not forget, however, that living in a particular community or neighborhood is not always the result of free choice. Resources and status help dictate where one lives. Constraint also enters the picture when people try to keep undesirables out of their neighborhoods through mortgage-loan practices, building restrictions, and zoning procedures. Increasingly, one can find new housing developments for the affluent and cultured that are surrounded by walls and maintained by armed guards at secured entrances. Often, these communities are planned and monitored by electronic surveillance devices, and constitute another, perhaps more blatant, form of segregated neighborhood. Mike Davis offered Los Angeles as a good example of "where the defense of luxury lifestyles is translated into a proliferation of new repressions in space and movement, undergirded by the ubiquitous 'armed response.'" He saw this approach to living as "a master narrative in the emerging built environment of the 1990s" (Davis 1992c, p. 223). As noted earlier in this chapter, Weber made a point of identifying exclusionary tactics as devices used by higher status groups to keep their position intact. Privacy and security, and, most importantly, seclusion from undesirables, mark these "walled communities" (Schneider 1992). Turf wars are not only perpetrated by those at the bottom of the status system but also by those at its pinnacle. The control of physical space is one reflection of status inequalities in our society. Nutshell 3.1 is a good illustration how class and social status frequently intermix. Class is a frequent basis for lifestyle, and status is characterized by attempts at exclusion.

Region and the Case of Appalachia. On a broader scale, not only do neighborhoods and communities conjure up different perceptions and evaluations but so do regions. There are stereotypes and lifestyles, for example, that have been attributed to Californians, New Englanders, the Old South, the New South, Midwesterners, and Appalachians. Regions can be and have been the basis for status grouping and ranking, even though the cultural, social, and sometimes even topographical homogeneity attributed to these set-apart places is usually mythical rather than factual. Nevertheless, some of these regions, perhaps most notably Appalachia, have been identified as constituting not only a separate subculture but also a status group that has been consciously ranked as being low in prestige. Let us explore Appalachia as an example of status based on region.

A discussion of Appalachia helps us in at least two ways. First, it allows us to examine economic inequality within a region sometimes described as a colony for more powerful economic interests. Second, it allows us to examine the cultural mystique and folklore associated with a section of the country that has often been thought to be out of touch with the mainstream of U.S. society and its culture. Associated in the public mind with mountain men, the region has been portrayed as being inaccessible and isolated. As such, it has been viewed in the popular press and mind as constituting a separate and often homogenous culture. It is principally the latter that we wish to investigate in this section. Does Appalachia constitute a separate subculture and, if so, how is it viewed in terms of social status? What is the origin of this subculture, and how is it linked with the economic inequality that prevails in the region?

As a strip in the eastern part of the United States, Appalachia covers an area involving parts of 13 states, bordered on the north by southern New York state; on the south by parts of Mississippi, Alabama, and Georgia; on the west by the eastern sections of Kentucky and Tennessee; and on the east by the western portions of Pennsylvania, Virginia, and the Carolinas. It includes all of West Virginia. Most of the discussion of Appalachia as a subculture, however, is based on material from southern Appalachia (northern Georgia, Alabama, North and South Carolina, and parts of Tennessee and Virginia), whereas discussions of the coal industry focus on central Appalachia (Kentucky, West Virginia, southwestern Virginia, and eastern Tennessee). Northern Appalachia is composed of parts of New York, Pennsylvania, Maryland, Ohio, and West Virginia. In their 1985 report, the Appalachian Regional Commission (1985) argued that "Appalachia existed for generations as a region apart, isolated physically and culturally by its impenetrable mountains" (p. 7). In his visit to Appalachian communities in 1999, President Clinton suggested that their isolation and neglect by outsiders had left them behind while the rest of the country prospered.

The Development of Appalachia. As with many developing countries, the economic development of the region has been uneven, and the contrast between rural Appalachia and its industrial areas can be dramatic (Carawan and Carawan 1975, p. ix). Outside timber, mining, and manufacturing interests were gaining increasing access to and ownership of much of the land and other natural resources in the region. Coal was becoming a major industry, and without understanding all the implications, many residents "sold their land and/or mineral rights for pennies an acre to 'outsiders.'... Appalachians became not the entrepreneurs but the labourers" (Appalachian Regional Commission 1985, p. 8). The "patterns of corporate exploitation were established that continue to dominate the resource utilization today" (Beaver 1984, p. 82). John Tiller, a former miner from Trammel, Virginia, described Appalachia as a colony: "It has all the earmarks—the absentee landlords; nothing built of permanence. You can look at the whole

Apartments in Falls Gain Supporters

Community Group Including Religious Organizations Backs Plan to Build Controversial Housing Complex

CAROL BILICZKY
BEACON JOURNAL STAFF WRITER

Cuyahoga Falls—A fledgling community group is trying to force this suburban city to accept a housing project for working-class families.

Working Families for Affordable Housing on Friday unveiled a campaign to help a Columbus-area developer build a 72-unit apartment complex in an upscale neighborhood on the city's northeast side.

That's on top of other efforts already in place—the two lawsuits that the nonprofit Buckeye Community Hope Foundation has filed to force the city to give it a building permit, and a complaint by Akron's Fair Housing Advocates Association that has landed before the Ohio Civil Rights Commission.

"Our group stands for an inclusive Falls," said Tom Allio of the Catholic Commission, which organized the coalition of eight organizations, including the Akron-area Association of Churches, the American Friends Service Committee and the National Association for the Advancement of Colored People. "The opponents are running your basic 'not in my backyard' campaign."

The nonprofit developer touched off a firestorm of complaints last spring when it sought to build the $4.1 million Pleasant Meadow Lane, west of Wyoga Lake Road and north of East Bath Road. The land was zoned multifamily.

The problem is neighbors in 400 nearby condominiums selling for $140,000 each and 120 existing and planned single-family homes costing $200,000.

They formed a citizens group called Preservation of Voters Rights and circulated petitions to get the Pleasant Meadows issue on November's ballot, complaining that the apartments would burden Woodbridge schools and that the city wasn't planning well.

Buckeye Community responded in kind, seeking an injunction in Summit County Common Pleas Court to stop the vote. The vote was upheld, so the developer appealed to the 9th District Court of appeals.

No one from Preservation of Voters Rights seems willing to talk to the media now, but Mayor Don Robart defends their grass-roots campaign.

"No one is saying that we shouldn't accept our fair share of low- and moderate-income housing," Robart said. "All we're saying is that the mayor and council ought to have some impact on where they go.

"The way the system goes, these guys can come in and plop down. I think that's wrong."

Buckeye Community would use federal tax credits to go after a certain market niche ranging from single people making as little as $18,000 yearly to families of six making as much as $30,000 a year.

Rents would be relatively low—$357 for a two-bedroom unit and $451 for a three-bedroom one, $200 below median rents in the Falls, according to Buckeye Community.

These are "working families who are trying to get over the initial threshold while at the beginning of their careers, when they're most likely to have children," said Lynn M. Clark of the Fair Housing Contact Service in Akron, which is part of Buckeye Community's complaint in U.S. District Court alleging discrimination.

"Here we have people saying, 'You are not going to be given this opportunity.'"

Time is short for the developer: It needs to get the complex built by November 1997, or it forfeits $3 million in federal tax credits over 10 years and $625,000 in grants, Executive Director Gil Barno said.

"Voters are going to decide if a site plan they've never seen conforms to a zoning code they've never read," he objected.

Working Families for Affordable Housing is organizing an informational campaign at churches and community groups, and assembling a list of Falls residents who want the 16 flats and 56 townhouses.

Source: Akron Beacon Journal, August 26, 1996, pp. C1 and C4. Reprinted with permission of the *Akron Beacon Journal.*

area—the poor roads, the poor schools, the lack of facilities—and realize that there's no solutions" (Carawan and Carawan 1975, p. 26). Hundreds of thousands of acres have been stripped for their lumber and coal resources by absentee owners, individuals who live outside the region but take its resources.

Thus, the region is wealthy in resources, but the native people have been relatively poor. During the late 1950s and early 1960s, about one-third of the families in the area lived below the official poverty level, unemployment was about 40 percent higher than in the rest of the nation, and net migration from the region was over 2,000,000 (Appalachian Regional Commission 1985, p. 13). In the 1990s, rural Appalachia continued to have higher poverty rates and a higher percentage of working poor than the national average (U.S. Bureau of the Census, April 1996; Duncan 1992). In many parts of Appalachia, the percentage of persons who had graduated from high school was much lower than the national average, and one in four rural dwellings were considered to have fundamental structural weaknesses. The 1960 presidential election brought many of these problems into the public eye for the first time. In the early 1980s, in many Appalachian counties, less than one-third of the people had a high school education. Almost as many (30 percent) adults in the *entire* region and almost half of the unemployed were functionally illiterate (Darling 1984).

Resource ownership in Appalachia has been very concentrated. Around 1980, over half of the land was owned by 1 percent of local residents working together with absentee owners, government, and corporations. This means that 99 percent of the local people controlled less than half of the land. Some of the largest owners were and still are multinational corporations. While the 1970s brought some economic growth to the region, the early 1980s brought renewed economic decline fueled by worldwide recession and foreign competition. Coal, oil, electricity, and steel industries all suffered setbacks. Between 1980 and 1983, Appalachia lost more than 500,000 jobs (Appala-

chian Regional Commission 1985, p. 77). Gaventa (1980) argued that the 1980s brought an intensified attempt to recolonize Appalachia because of the belief in some circles that if the United States drew energy resources from within the nation, the country would be less dependent on foreign sources for coal and other minerals. As we will see in a later chapter, the whole process of economic dependence and exploitation of Appalachia fits a general Marxian explanation of the dynamics of economic inequality.

The events and conditions just noted brought attention to the region, and media presentations helped form the images and conclusions outsiders developed about Appalachia. They even helped shape the perceptions of Appalachians about their region. Since the turn of the twentieth century, when major changes in the economy and ownership had already begun, the image portrayed of Appalachian culture has been one of stagnation and backwardness attributed in large part to the supposed physical isolation of the region.

But in his study of a central Appalachian valley, Gaventa (1980, 1984) argued that the proliferation of the cultural model of Appalachia as being backward, uncivilized, and so on was a creation that helped justify the exploitation (development) of that region by outside interests. The presence of excess investment capital and an ideology that encouraged development of undeveloped rural areas led to the purchase and control of Appalachian property by outside investors. Part of the justification of this easy appropriation of resources was couched in the specious argument that the inhabitants were quiescent and backward simpletons. Gaventa pointed out that the image of Appalachians was molded to fit and justify the exploitation that occurred. While those in his study were not ostensibly aggressive in defending themselves against the domination of outside financial interests, Gaventa demonstrated that this reaction suggesting passiveness and apathy was really a rational response to their condition of powerlessness. Repeated defeats, the greater resource power of outside forces, the construction of various bar-

Strip mining, which leaves noticeable scars on the landscape, has been common in Appalachia. This photo was taken in Whitley County, southeastern Kentucky.

riers, and the perpetuation of myths and stereotypes about the Appalachian people all have conspired to create less rebellion, even though extensive grievances and discontent on a variety of issues lie just below the surface.

The Subculture of Appalachia. Following the Civil War, Appalachia was "discovered" by journalists and others who viewed it as an off-beat place with unfamiliar vegetation inhabited by a people with odd customs. As one popular article of the day described it, Appalachia was "A Strange Land and Peculiar People" (cited in Beaver 1984, p. 86). A variety of values have been associated with Appalachians, many of them negative in nature. "The Appalachian is fatalistic," wrote Lewis (1974), "while mainstream Americans believe they can control their environment and their lives. The Appalachian is impulsive, personalistic and individualistic while mainstream Americans are rational, organized, can handle impersonal role relationships and have a social consciousness" (p. 222). Individualism, a love of and dependence on family and an attachment to home, a belief in personal liberty and independence, fatalism and resignation, a belief in the essential equality of all individuals, a disdain for and suspicion of formal education, and the centrality of personal religion all have been characteristics frequently associated with Appalachians (cf., e.g., Erikson 1976; Batteau 1984; W. H. Turner 1986; Vogeler 1975).

As was indicated earlier in this chapter, the social status given to another person or group is a subjective process, one in which the group is portrayed as having a specific lifestyle and set of beliefs that distinguish it from surrounding groups. In most groups, there is more heterogeneity than is suspected by outsiders, but it is the latter's perceptions, whether based on fact or not, that govern their reaction to the group. The fact is that despite the stereotypical view often taken of it,

Appalachia is a region with varied resources, differentiated geography, and people with varied ethnic backgrounds.

Alongside the negative image of Appalachia as a stagnant and backward region, another more patronizing image exists. This interpretation fosters the view of Appalachia as an area of great natural beauty being despoiled by greedy economic interests. Unsullied nature and the rugged individualism of mountain men are integral components of this perspective of Appalachia as an innocent victim (Batteau 1984). In this view, the mountains take on a mystical, romantic quality.

A problem with such subcultural descriptions—especially of an area that has been said to be socially, culturally, and physically shut off from the rest of the country—is that they tend to become caricatures overtime, ignoring internal differences within the region and changes that have occurred in its relationship with other parts of the world. These subcultural characteristics also have been interpreted as the principal causes for the unusually high rates of poverty found in Appalachia. This constitutes a form of blaming the victim, however, since evidence suggests that it has not been primarily subcultural values or isolation but rather the nature of a region's ties to the outside that have exacerbated and perpetuated the high poverty rate. Numerous scholars, many from the region, have labeled Appalachia as a rich land with poor people, poor because their resources have been exploited by outsiders (cf., e.g., Eller 1982; Gaventa 1980; Caudill 1962).

Even though Appalachia is a heterogeneous area, where many lead urban and middle-class lives, few have questioned the traditional stereotype associated with the Appalachian. Too often, images of an Appalachian character (1) are derived primarily from descriptions of adult *males,* (2) ignore the fact that many of the characteristics are shared by other Americans, and (3) minimize or deny the inconsistencies and differences found within Appalachian culture (Erikson 1976, pp. 75–78). With respect to the latter, for example, the African American ethnographer William Turner (1986)

suggested that many Blacks in Appalachia do not share the values and beliefs of their White neighbors. Rather than being fatalistic, traditional, and so forth, they are attracted to materialism and individual achievement and do not identify psychologically as strongly with the land and the region as White Appalachians do.

Despite the fact that changes have occurred in the region, many traditional values have become weakened, and many Appalachians are becoming integrated culturally and socially into the wider society, stereotypes still abound. Old images die hard deaths. Berger has cautioned that "myths are potent enough to survive evidence; they are not disarmed by understanding. Once myths gain currency…they become real and fiction as self-fulfilling prophecies" (cited in Billings 1974, p. 322).

The image of Appalachia as being composed of backward, fundamentalistic, individualistic mountaineers has lowered the status prestige of this region for most Americans. In the late 1960s, "in some popular and scholarly circles Appalachia was second only to Black America as a repository for social pathos" (W. H. Turner 1986, p. 279). Appalachia occupies "the lowest rung in [our] socio-economic ladder" (Coreil and Marshall 1982). Data collected in interviews with long-term rural Kentuckians suggested that a large majority of them feel that Appalachians are given "much less respect than other Americans." Many also believed that Appalachians experience greater occupational, educational, legal, and income inequality than other Americans. They also were inclined to view the inequality involving Appalachians as being separate from racial and class inequality, suggesting that they identify themselves as a separate group when it comes to the problems of inequality (Smith and Bylund 1983).

How do the elements of this discussion of Appalachia relate to our earlier conclusion that status can be based on region? Let us review the core factors that determine status and status-group ranking. We noted that status honor/prestige is subjectively given by a community to another person or group.

This perception, in turn, depends on the characteristics attributed to the person or group and on how valued these characteristics are in mainstream culture. Status honor can be based on (1) lifestyle, (2) extent of empirical/rational formal education, (3) family genealogy, and/or (4) occupation, according to Weber (1964). We also said that a distinct lifestyle and isolation from outsiders characterize status groups. Weber further argued that individuals in similar status situations tend to form cohesive communities. This cohesiveness is reaffirmed and maintained through intimate associations among themselves and by their wariness of and distance from outsiders. Status groups also are characterized by some uniqueness in their acquisitions; that is, their possessions may be exclusively associated with members of the group. Finally, higher status groups try to avoid contaminating contact with lower status groups, since they represent "impure" qualities and, in the extreme case, may be considered pariah groups.

The evidence we have reviewed strongly suggests that most Americans have a fairly coherent conception of Appalachians as a group and that they perceive them as having distinctive values and behaviors. Moreover, this subculture is more often than not portrayed in negative terms; that is, it is attributed with low-status honor. As Bensman stated, all status communities make claims for prestige, but "the validation of that claim, however, is based less on the claim itself than on the ability and willingness of others to experience and evaluate favorably the activities, characteristics, and institutions buttressing the claim" (Bensman 1972, p. 126). As we pointed out earlier, status honor/prestige is subjectively and willingly given.

This subculture of Appalachians is thought to have a unique lifestyle, according to the traditional conception, that includes a denigration of formal education, a genealogy composed of so-called common folk, and traditional occupations that are usually blue collar or agricultural in nature. None of these characteristics enhances the status honor accorded Appalachians. The mountain people frequently have been portrayed as being physically,

socially, and culturally isolated from the outside world, and conversely, as having close relationships among themselves, especially within families. The qualities assessed as different by the standards of the dominant culture help justify the ridicule and romanticism rained upon mountaineers and "hillbillies" by outside urbanites. In correspondence with the romantic view of mountain culture, some of the artifacts associated with this culture, such as musical styles and instruments, have been viewed as being unique and worthy of preservation, especially by intellectual outsiders. In sum, what exists in Appalachia is an interesting confluence of economic, colony, and status factors that must be understood within their historical context. Most importantly, our traditional image of Appalachians, while not consistent with much empirical evidence, has encouraged us to label Appalachians as a separate status group having low prestige.

Gender, Sexual Orientation, and Race as Bases for Status

There is no question that individuals of different races and genders are ranked unequally in U.S. society. Both Blacks and women have been thought of as separate status groups and, in some cases, even separate castes. Do Blacks and women constitute status groups that are distinct from those of Whites and males? Does it make sense to view them as being members of a caste? Does the concern for contact with homosexuals suggest that they, too, occupy a castelike position? Does this model help us understand and explain the situation of these groups better than other models? A fuller discussion of this matter will take place in Chapters 4, 5, and 6, but we should briefly address this general issue since we are dealing with the various bases of status in this chapter.

Weber (1964) argued that, ultimately, the caste system is based on ethnicity, and that is also legally sanctioned. Movement between castes is restricted, endogamy is expected, and traditional occupations are associated with each caste. On the surface, at least, there would appear to be a parallel between this description and a system in which ranking is based either on sex or race, both ascriptive characteristics. Some U.S. laws, in the past especially, have restricted areas or behaviors on the basis of sex and race, and race mixing and homosexuality have been frowned upon. One's attitudes toward Blacks and homosexuals can be partially attributed to the purity/impurity dimension associated with caste systems. The concerns for social distance, racial purity as typified by White supremacist and other extremist groups, and various forms of segregation suggest that purity/impurity is a fundamental dimension of races and homosexuals as status groups.

Although these comments on purity do not apply directly to an understanding of women and homosexuals in U.S. society, it is clear that assumptions about the basic characteristics of these groups, and associating these with specific types of skills, are relevant to explaining the socioeconomic predicament of women and homosexuals today. Clearly, the histories of women, homosexuals, and Blacks in the United States have been different, and thus it would be a mistake to assume that the same model can be used in the same manner to understand all of them. Blacks, for example, have never been expected to refrain from manual work or even participation in the labor market, whereas the nineteenth-century cult of true womanhood expected this of middle-class,

respectable women. We will pursue similarities and differences between these groups in Chapters 4, 5, and 6.

SUMMARY

This chapter has addressed the topic of social status, a form of inequality that is analytically separate from economic inequality, even though it is frequently based on an individual's economic resources. Status also can be based on occupation, education, lifestyle, physical appearance, region, race, gender, and sexual orientation. The prestige of our occupation, the kind of education we receive, the lifestyles we pursue, and the way we appear in public are each badges of status. They affect how others perceive us and how they treat us. In their extreme, status groups can be legally sanctioned and exclusive. Veblen was acutely aware of the invidious comparisons that groups made with each other in the early 1900s, and these continue today. Even the labels attached to various places and regions of the country suggest that they have implications for social status. We examined Appalachia in depth because differences in economic and political power and social status all converge in this region. By analyzing it, one can see several forms of inequality at work all at once. In the next three chapters, attention is turned to gender, sexual orientation, and race/ethnicity as additional bases of status.

CRITICAL THINKING

1. Discuss the new forms or bases of status developing in the United States. What are they and how important are they? Will they replace status based on older grounds? Explain your answer.

2. On what bases do you rank others? In what status groups do you belong?

3. How do space and distance become involved in relationships between unequals? What kinds of factors might cause alterations in space and distance?

4. What explains the continued stereotyping of Appalachians and what might change these perceptions?

WEB CONNECTIONS

As this chapter demonstrated, there are a number of widely held stereotypes about Appalachia. Although it is not the only region to have been stereotyped, those associated with it have been most damaging, resulting in the poor image many have of this region. To help dispel images you may have of Appalachia, go to East Tennessee State University's website containing the archives of Appalachia. These contain visual images and in-formation on music, geography, industry, and several types of data. The photo site is at:

http://cass.etsu.edu/archives/photoapp.htm

CHAPTER 4

SEX AND GENDER INEQUALITY

It is their [women's] differential role in the reproduction of labor power that lies at the root of their oppression in class society.
—Lise Vogel

I believe that not only must the hierarchical nature of the division of labor between the sexes be eliminated, but the very division of labor between the sexes itself must be eliminated if women are to attain equal social status with men and if women and men are to attain the full development of their human potential.
—Heidi Hartmann

Race and sex are ascribed statuses in the sense that people have no control over whether they are Black or White, male or female. However, although each is a biological condition, race and sex also are given particular meaning within the context of a culture's values and beliefs, which in turn may be based on dominant economic and political arrangements. What is immediately significant about race and sex, therefore, is not the biological differences in themselves, but the fact that these biological characteristics are socially defined and have meanings attached to them. These interpretations often result in races and sexes being hierarchically arranged in society.

In Chapter 6, we will pursue an analysis of racial inequality and demonstrate how race, gender, sex, and economic inequality are intertwined. In this chapter, we will be surveying the forms and extent of gender inequality, as well as explanations for it. We begin with a brief overview of the historical condition of women in U.S. society.

THE STATUS OF WOMEN IN THE EARLY UNITED STATES

What has it meant to be a woman in the United States? When I was growing up in the 1940s, my parents had a traditional arrangement—my mother was a homemaker and my father "brought home the bacon." Earlier, however, my mother had worked in a hosiery factory. Throughout our nation's history, women have consistently contributed to the economy while still maintaining a family.

In our own agricultural preindustrial colonial society, women were directly involved in a variety of ways in production. On the one hand, their work contributed significantly to the prosperity of the society, but on the other hand, the nature of the labor was more often than not based on gender (Chafe 1977; Blau 1978; Marshall and Paulin 1987). The cultural norms of that time, as well as for following periods, dictated that first and foremost, women should be good wives and mothers;

but, in fact, women were involved in the economy and often had difficult lives. They were involved in raising stock, weaving, gardening, and even running businesses. While some women took over for their deceased or disabled husbands, most of the unmarried and widowed women went on the market as hired domestic workers (Marshall and Paulin 1987).

Although there is some debate about the actual diversity of employment undertaken by women during this period, they made valuable contributions to the local economies, but were deprived of many of the political-legal, economic, and personal rights accorded men. They were attached to their families in a literal way, dependent on and subservient to their husbands (Matthaei 1982). A woman's identity was defined by her relationship to her husband and children. Moreover, wife beating was fairly common at this time. "The husband had the right to chastise his wife physically, and he had exclusive rights to any property she might have owned as a single woman, to her dower, and to any wages and property that might come to her while she was his wife. In short, like slave or servant women, married women whether rich or poor were legal non-entities" (Foner 1979, p. 11). Thus, the idealized life of the female as someone removed from the harsh realities of economic life was strongly inconsistent with the actual circumstances of her life.

Through their economic activities, women helped to contribute to the development of the first significant *industrial* organizations in the United States. The first textile factories, built around 1800 in Rhode Island and Massachusetts, recruited unmarried women from the farms of New England.

Despite the promises of a proper place to work, conditions at these early factories left much to be desired. Even though Lowell, Massachusetts, among the most famous early textile mills, was considered an advanced factory for its time, women worked an average of 13 hours a day, 73 hours a week, including 8 hours on Saturday (Dublin 1979). Working conditions were stifling. Windows in the plant were nailed shut and the air

was periodically sprayed with water to keep it humid enough so that the cotton threads would not break. The vapors from whale-oil lamps and floating lint made the air in the shop quite oppressive (Eisler 1977). The Lowell Corporation paid women mill workers $1.85 to $3.00 per week, depending on abilities, from which $1.25 was deducted for board. Female workers were paid only half of what men were paid, even though they made up approximately 75 percent of the workers at Lowell (Eisler 1977). Neighboring states exhibited similar sex differences in wages (Marshall and Paulin 1987).

Jobs in these early plants were also sex segregated. Men held all supervisory positions as well as jobs in the mill yard, watch force, and repair shop; women were restricted to particular jobs operating equipment such as the looms and dressing machines. The immediate reasons given for this segregation concerned differences in the skills developed and monopolized by men and women over the years, perceived physical strength and dangers associated with various jobs, and the general cultural values prescribing particular roles for men and women (Dublin 1979). Men also were concerned about the entrance of women into the labor market because they felt that it would have a depressing effect on their wages. They fought to keep women out of the craft unions that later developed. Women held strikes in the 1830s and 1840s to protest reductions in wages, speed-ups in work pace, and working hours (Dublin 1979).

In 1900, just over 20 percent (5,000,000) of all U.S. women 15 years of age or older were employed as breadwinners, but only 15 percent of native White females were, compared to 43 percent of Black females and 25 percent of White females with at least one foreign-born parent (U.S. Dept. of Commerce and Labor 1911, p. 262). Many young women 10 to 15 years of age also worked outside the home. In 1900, almost 6 percent of White, native-born females did so, compared to over 30 percent of non-White females 10 to 15 years old (pp. 256–259). From the end of the Civil War, the percentage of females in the work force had increased (U.S. Dept. of Labor 1947, p. 34).

At the turn of the twentieth century, women made up a disproportionate number of workers in several occupations. For example, in 1900, they constituted 80 to 90 percent of all boarding and lodging housekeepers, servants, waiters, and paper box makers and over 90 percent of all housekeepers and stewards, nurses and midwives, dress makers, milliners, and seamstresses. Men, on the other hand, dominated agricultural, common labor, bookkeeping, clerk/copyist, watch and shoemaker, printer, dye works, and photography positions (U.S. Census Office 1903, Plate 90). Perhaps surprisingly, women composed over 70 percent of the teachers and professors in colleges and over 50 percent of teachers of music, and men made up the majority of artists and teachers of art (ibid.). Black females, however, were more likely to be wage earners than either native- or foreign-born White females.

Those who were "native White of native parents" dominated the higher status professions, with over 50 percent of college teachers and clergy and about 75 percent of lawyers and physicians coming from this group. In contrast, they made up less than 30 percent of those in servant, tailoring, laundering, and textile mill working positions (U.S. Census Office 1903, Plate 88).

PRESENT OCCUPATIONAL AND ECONOMIC CONDITIONS FOR WOMEN

The influx of women into the labor force has continued in recent years. Over the last several decades, the percentage of women in the civilian labor force has increased dramatically, while the percentage of men 16 years of age and older in the labor force has consistently declined. In 1965, for example, just over 39 percent of women were in the labor force, compared to 59 percent in 1995. In contrast, the involvement of men slid from 81 percent in 1965 to 75 percent in 1995 (U.S. Dept. of Labor, January 1996). The labor-force participation of women is expected to increase well into the 21st century. Women made up 41 percent of the full-time, year-round labor force in 1997, compared to only 29 percent in 1967.

Among the most important factors behind the increased participation of women in the labor force are the shift toward a service and information-based economy, increased possibilities for flexibility in work scheduling, lower marital stability, and a greater need for dual-earner families (Gerson 1998; Presser 1998). In most cases, the income brought into households by women is a necessity, and makes a major difference in the incomes of families. The median incomes of married-couple families with wives in the labor force is almost $25,000 higher than families in which the wife is not in paid employment, and the gap has grown in the last 50 years (U.S. Bureau of the Census, 1998c).

The greater commitment of women to employment has resulted in a continuing struggle to balance home and work responsibilities. The related stresses are greater for women because of traditional gender-role expectations regarding women's responsibilities to families. Most employed married men and women agree that it is the woman who ends up being most responsible for cooking, cleaning, shopping, and child care. If a child is ill, it is the employed mother rather than the father who is most likely to miss work because of it (Galinsky and Bond 1996). Due to their traditional role as caregivers, "women in the middle" are often expected not only to take care of their children but also an elderly parent as well. And as the U.S. population ages, the need and responsibility for elder care is likely to intensify (Singleton 1998). Opting for contingency or part-time employment, having fewer children, and choosing a nonstandard work schedule are some of the ways women juggle home and work responsibilities (Gerson 1998; Raabe 1998; Presser 1998). More often than not, it is the mother who makes the compromise at work and who feels that she is not doing as well as she could in either family or work. Under these conditions, neither family life nor work is fully satisfying (Galinsky and Bond 1996). Until a better integration of home and work conditions is reached, stress will remain high for the majority of employed mothers.

Occupation and Sex and Gender

The gender inequities involved in balancing home and employment is just one area of the inequalities between employed men and women. Inequalities also extend to the nature of employment. To identify occupational inequalities between men and women in their work experiences, however, it is important to examine how they are distributed (1) across broad occupational categories, (2) among specific occupations, and (3) among specific occupations within specific organizational contexts. The resulting inequality varies in each of these cases.

Despite this rise in labor-force participation by women, occupational distinctions between the sexes remain within *broad occupational* groupings. The analysis of broad occupational categories suggests some recent decline in overall sex segregation, but most of it has been in middle-level white-collar rather than in blue-collar positions, and the major declines have been restricted

to a few occupations (Beller 1984). Much of this trend has been due to the decline of some traditionally male occupations in the labor force, such as agricultural, unskilled, and self-employment occupations (Blau and Ferber 1986). Figure 4.1 presents current information on the distribution of men and women over broad occupational categories. In general, women tend to be concentrated in white-collar and service occupations, while men are more spread out among white-collar and blue-collar positions.

Although this suggests some gender differences in occupation, as we examine more *detailed occupational* categories, the nature and extent of occupational segregation becomes clearer. A decline in occupational segregation has occurred in broad occupational categories, largely because of shifts in technology and organizational structures. But despite these general improvements, women still are found disproportionately in particular kinds of occupations. For example, women have increasingly moved into the ranks of managerial

PERCENT IN OCCUPATION

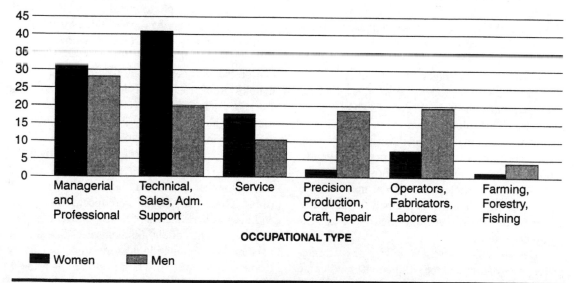

FIGURE 4.1 Occupational Distribution of Employed Civilians Age 16 and Older by Sex: 1998

Source: U.S. Department of Labor, *Employment and Earnings.* January 1999, p. 177.

and professional occupations, but they tend to be concentrated among sex-typed occupations, such as teaching and nursing, and hold only a small percentage of positions as computer specialists, scientists, and engineers. Similarly, a man and woman may both be in sales, but the woman is much more likely to be in clothing sales, while the man is involved in the selling of stocks and bonds. Craft occupations (carpentry, electrical contractors) is another group of occupations in which women continue to be severely underrepresented (Herz and Wootton 1996).

One of the most male-centered institutions has been the military. Recently, however, there may have been a slight move away from the almost total domination of males in combat-related roles. The government has ordered that women be allowed to be combat pilots in the military. Although there have been some older veterans who have objected to this development, first responses suggest that the majority of current pilots appear to be supportive. As one male officer stated, "We have this common experience, this bond. You get unit cohesion by going through something hard together, and you get that whether you go through it with men or with women.... What you do in a combat role in a cockpit doesn't require great strength. You don't need to be Arnold Schwarzenegger to be an effective naval aviator" (Rohter 1993, p. A12).

The military has been one institution where sex roles have been well defined. The recent Supreme Court ruling (described in Nutshell 4.1) requiring that the Virginia Military Institute (VMI) must admit women has not been unanimously embraced by alumni or those at the Institute. Since the article was written, however, the board of VMI voted 9 to 8 to open the school to women. Are all-male and all-female schools sexist by definition?

Despite small movement toward sex desegregation, many aspects of the occupational profiles are quite similar to those that existed in earlier years. In 1940, almost all of the servants, stenographers/secretaries, housekeepers, and nurses were women, and they comprised over half of the teachers (not

elsewhere classified), apparel and accessories operators, waitresses, and bookkeepers. As far back as 1870, women dominated in servant, clothing, certain kinds of teaching, and nursing occupations (cf. U.S. Dept. of Labor 1947, p. 52).

Table 4.1 suggests that this sex-typing has continued. As one glances over the lists, it is easy to see that the positions in which women dominate tend to be those that demand "feminine" or "motherly" characteristics. Being able to work directly with people and to take care of others are qualities that are required in these occupations. In contrast, the list of positions that contains virtually all men are characterized by a different set of qualities; they are manual or require certain physical attributes, often contain an element of danger, involve work with a product rather than a person, and demand technical or scientific skill. In essence, these occupations are distinguished by their "feminine" or "masculine" character.

Many of the occupations dominated by women also do not have the protections afforded other positions. For example, nannies and maids often suffer long hours, low pay, few legal protections, and physical harassment. "Nannies are among the most exploited workers in the country. There are almost no legal protections for this relatively new, mostly female class of workers that is more than 350,000 strong. Nor are there even social pressures to keep employers from subjecting nannies to abuses—from low wages and long work weeks to sexual harassment and physical violence." They are a "dirty little secret in middle- and upper-middle-class America" (Lipman 1993, p. Al). Said one nanny of the family for which she worked, "Their cats were treated better than I was." Another confessed, "I was like a slave" (ibid.). Often these nannies are recent immigrants and are left dependent on their employers for fair treatment. Maids often find themselves in a similar position of exploitation and dependence. Mary Romero, a sociologist who has served as a maid, suggests reforms involving higher wages, Social security benefits, unionization, and, above all, the elimination of the idea that household work should be done primarily by women (Romero 1992).

NUTSHELL **4.1**

Virginia Military Institute Must Admit Women

School Will Lose Its Funding If It Doesn't Comply, Supreme Court Says; 7–1 Ruling Also Affects The Citadel

LAURIE ASSEO
ASSOCIATED PRESS

Washington—Virginia Military Institute must admit women or give up its state funding, the Supreme Court said yesterday in a decision that shattered the school's 157-year males-only tradition and added muscle to protections against sex discrimination.

The 7–1 ruling also will affect The Citadel, South Carolina's state-run military school, which has a similar all-male policy and alternative program for women.

Noting that VMI aims to produce citizen-soldiers, Justice Ruth Bader Ginsburg wrote for the court, "Surely that goal is great enough to accommodate women."

A separate, unequal program for females offered by Virginia at Mary Baldwin College, a private women's school in Staunton, Va., relies on stereotypes about women and does not provide an equal education, she added.

At the school, cadet Nick Latsios saw nothing good in the decision.

"We're no longer VMI," he lamented, wearing a shirt with the slogan "Better Dead Than Co-Ed." "Now we're just any old school," he said.

The college's governing Board of Visitors will meet next month to "address the future of VMI," said board President William Berry.

Among the options that have been widely discussed is to privatize the institution, he said.

Dejected but philosophic, Superintendent Josiah Bunting said, "We have argued the case for single-gender instruction at VMI nobly, carefully, and I think we made our point as well as it could be made. We fought the good fight."

Justice Antonin Scalia, who attended a military-style high school in New York City, was the lone dissenter.

"I do not think any of us, women included, will be better off for its destruction," Scalia said, adding that the ruling could cut off all government support for single-sex education.

Justice Clarence Thomas, whose son, Jamal, attends VMI, did not participate in the case.

The court bolstered protection against sex discrimination by saying there must be an "exceedingly persuasive justification" for any government action based on gender.

But the justices stopped short of saying sex-discrimination cases must be judged by the same strict legal standard used in race-bias cases.

The ruling left open the possibility that some separate and truly equal educational programs could be approved. But the court made clear no such alternative could be created for VMI, which has the nation's largest per-student endowment.

VMI, founded in 1839 in Lexington, Va., and The Citadel in Charleston, S.C., are the nation's only all-male, state-supported military colleges.

Shannon Faulkner was admitted to The Citadel under court order last year but dropped out days later, citing stress and isolation.

Source: Akron Beacon Journal, June 27, 1996, p. A4. Reprinted with permission of Associated Press.

When we move on to examine specific occupations *within specific organizational contexts* in the private economy, occupational segregation again becomes magnified. Not only are women spread among fewer occupations than men, but within the same occupation, they are employed in different kinds of organizations and economic sectors, tend to have less authority in the same occupation and have different job titles, and make less money in their jobs than men do.

A survey of 264 companies in 1989 revealed that only one out of eight of their board members

TABLE 4.1 Sample of Occupations in Which Women Represented Over 90 Percent or Under 5 percent of Employed Labor Force: 1998

OVER 90%	UNDER 5%
Kindergarten teachers	Protective-service guards
Registered nurses	Airline pilots
Hairdressers/cosmetologists	Firefighters
Dental hygienists	Pest control
Licensed practical nurses	Vehicle mechanics
Secretaries	Industrial machine repair
Speech therapists	Construction supervisors
Receptionists	Office machine repairers
Bookkeepers	Tool and die makers
Child care workers	Furnace operators
Dental assistants	Railroad conductors
Childhood teachers' assistants	Service station operators
Billing and calculating machine operators	Crane operators
Typists	Brickmasons
Cleaners and servants	Timber cutting/logging

Source: U.S. Department of Labor, *Employment and Earnings.* January 1999, pp. 178–83.

was a woman (Ries and Stone 1993). However, the number of businesses owned by women has increased significantly since the 1970s, and so have their revenues. In 1998, the top 500 women-run firms in the United States collected over $80 billion in revenue. The revenue of the largest of these in 1998, an automotive firm (JM Family Enterprises), exceeded $6 billion. An additional 16 of these businesses had revenues of at least $1 billion each ("The Top 500 Women-Owned Businesses" 1999). Fewer than 25 percent of women workers are in manufacturing firms employing over 50 persons, while about 50 percent of those in nonmanufacturing firms work in organizations having fewer than 50 employees (Bielby and Baron 1984). Part of this overrepresentation in small firms is due to the fact that women are more likely to be found in the peripheral rather than the core sector of the economy. The peripheral sector is largely made up of small, less stable, local, nonunionized organizations lacking a clear career ladder, while the core consists of the larger, stable, multimarket, unionized organizations with career systems. These differences between men

and women exist even when experience, education, and other factors are taken into account (Coverdill 1988). Factors that are characteristic of each of these sectors, moreover, appear to contribute to differences in unemployment rates and earnings levels between the sexes (Bibb and Form 1977; Coverdill 1988; Beck, Horan, and Tolbert 1980). Given the organizations in which they tend to find jobs, it should not be surprising that women are more likely than men to be in occupations with short career ladders and, therefore, have comparatively flat career trajectories.

Women have been underrepresented in higher posts even in those institutions that have publicly indicated a concern for equality and fairness. In higher education, for example, women are more likely than men to be employed at less prestigious institutions and at nonresearch universities. They are less likely to be found at the full-professor level or to be among the tenured faculty. Even when men and women are equally productive, they are likely to be in different ranks (Long and Fox 1995). Women are also much less likely to be found in leadership positions of unions. Even in

Sometimes, under critical conditions, women have been able to and encouraged to assume so-called masculine jobs. While men were off fighting World War II, women frequently held important and physically demanding jobs in factories. Most were displaced when men returned home.

occupational areas where they dominate (e.g., elementary education and social work), they are often not in the decision-making positions of principals or department heads. And, as Kanter's research in corporations demonstrates, when women are put in unusual positions of authority, they are watched closely and under great pressure to perform because they are seen as "tokens" (1977b).

Our discussion thus far has focused on jobs in the private sector of the economy. When it comes to *public*-sector jobs, occupational mobility has been greater for women, but less than it was in the 1960s and 1970s. Women have increased their share of local governmental positions, with most of these jobs being in social service and health/ welfare areas, suggesting tasks and abilities that have traditionally been associated with women

rather than men. A slightly larger percentage of women than men work in the public sector. In 1995, about 15 percent of roughly 65 million employed women were working in governmental positions (U.S. Dept. of Labor 1996).

Accounting for Occupational Sex Segregation.
What are the reasons behind the sex segregation in the occupations just discussed? Some have suggested that differences in education and skills, experience, and career aspirations may account for women moving into particular kinds of jobs, but recent evidence suggests that individual factors such as these do not fully account for differences in occupations and earnings between the sexes (e.g., Blau 1984, England et al. 1988). Gender-role socialization appears to have affected choice of occupation, but differences based on such socialization have declined in recent years. Younger women now plan for more continuous lifetime employment (England and Farkas 1986). Those who argue that gender-role socialization is an important source of sex segregation also overestimate the incompatibility of home and employment responsibilities.

One should keep in mind that the free choice of an occupation takes place within a structure with particular characteristics. In a broad sense, employment is limited by shifts in the types of jobs on the market and by the supply of and demand for qualified workers. This context also includes cultural values into which both employers and employees have been socialized and a historical record, both of which encourage the employment of men and women into certain kinds of occupations. Consequently, the choices women make about jobs and their work at home are conditioned by broader labor-market discrimination in the first place. This means that labor-market opportunities affect the role and amount of time spent in home labor by men and women. If women spend more time in the home than men because of fewer opportunities open to them in the market, it seems questionable, at best, to argue that it is their free choice alone that determines the amount of time spent in accumulating experience and education which in turn affects their occupational positions (Blau 1984, pp. 124–125).

Among the more prominent barriers that have prevented women from obtaining more well-paying occupations are:

1. Less access to training and apprenticeship programs
2. Appointment to perceived gender-related tasks ("light" work)
3. Nonbureaucratized, patrimonial relationships with males in authority positions
4. Less access to information about job openings
5. Less fully developed job and contact network
6. Seniority systems that limit women
7. Protective laws inhibiting women from pursuing certain positions and restricting the number of hours and time of day they could work
8. Disproportionate representation of women in lower ranking or smaller industries, firms, and markets
9. Stereotyping, discrimination, and the consequent crowding of women into certain kinds of positions
10. Lack of internal mobility ladder for many so-called female occupations within organizations (i.e., dead-end or flat-career jobs) (cf. Roos and Reskin 1984).

Some factors do appear, however, to contribute to a decline in occupational sex segregation. Among these are the development of new forms of work resulting from broad economic changes and white-collar service employment of an unspecialized nature. On the other hand, it has been suggested that the large size and increased specialization in the core sector, along with the presence of a union and manual work, appear to have fostered greater sex segregation (Bielby and Baron 1984). Greater formalization—that is, increased presence of written rules, tasks, procedures, and so on—has been linked to sex segregation, but also to the greater hiring of women. In a review of research on the kinds of organizations that hire women and Blacks, Szafran (1982) concluded that greater formalization, centralization of deci-

sion making, and a large number of secondary occupations in an organization lead to a greater proportion of women being hired.

Earnings and Sex

As in occupational distribution, there are also significant earning differences between men and women. The gap in median earnings between men and women has been declining since the late 1970s. In 1979, women who worked full time made about 63 percent of what men did, but in 1998, women earned about 76 percent as much as men (U.S. Dept. of Labor, January 1999). However, this decline may be due more to decreases in the earnings of men, in general, than it is to real improvement for women. Another reason is the rise of women from low earnings positions into higher, but not the highest, earnings categories (Bernhardt, Morris, and Handcock 1995).

The earnings ratio still varies between occupations, and in all of the broad occupational categories, men have higher earnings (see Table 4.2). The discrepancies are most pronounced in the technical, sales, precision, and craft categories, and least different among farming and similar occupations where median earnings are low in general. The differences between earnings persist even when educational level is taken into account. At every educational level among full-time, year-round workers, men have higher average earnings than women (U.S. Dept. of Labor, April 1999).

Differences in human capital (experience, skills) may continue to account partly for the earnings gap. But differences in work effort or work interruptions, or attachment to labor force, which can take one away from the job, are not major variables in explaining sex earnings differences (Bielby and Bielby 1988). Even census data indicate clearly that differences in earnings persist even when work interruptions are taken into account. Women earn less than men even when their tenure on the current job is the same (U.S. Bureau of the Census, August 1987, Tables D and F). In sum, differences in work interruptions and work effort do not appear to be major factors in ac-

TABLE 4.2   Median Weekly Earnings of Full-Time Workers Age 16 and Older, by Occupational Category and Sex, Annual Averages: 1998

OCCUPATIONAL CATEGORY	MEDIAN EARNINGS		RATIO OF WOMEN'S TO MEN'S EARNINGS
	Men	Women	
Managerial and prof.	$905	$655	.72
Technical, sales, adm. support	606	419	.69
Service occupations	389	296	.76
Precision production, craft, and repair	587	408	.70
Operators, fabricators, and laborers	456	327	.72
Farming, forestry, and fishing	307	272	.89
Median earnings for all workers	598	456	.76

Source: U.S. Department of Labor, *Employment and Earnings.* January 1999, pp. 213–218.

counting for the earnings differential between men and women.

One structural factor that is clearly important is the distribution among and concentration of men and women in occupational categories. Occupations that are culturally defined as appropriate for women and in which there is a high proportion of women tend to have lower earnings attached to them regardless of who occupies them. Jobs of comparable worth do not have equivalent earnings because of the sex compositions (England and Far kas 1986; Treiman, Hartmann, and Roos 1984). For example, faculty in nursing, library science, and social work positions, all of which contain a high percentage of women, have significantly lower salaries than faculty in male-dominated departments such as engineering, physics, and dentistry (Bellas 1994).

Within occupational categories, women are less likely to be in positions of authority and to be given distinct kinds of tasks—factors that also influence earnings (Parcel and Mueller 1983; Wright and Perrone 1977; Blau 1984). The crowding of women into specific kinds of jobs, of course, increases the supply of women and could thereby reduce the wages associated with those occupations and jobs (Bergmann 1974). Evidence also suggests that female-dominant jobs yield lower earnings, even when men are in those jobs. "Net of human capital, skill demands, and working conditions, those who work in occupations with more females earn less" (England et al. 1988; U.S. Bureau of the Census, August 1987). These jobs frequently have shorter career ladders, which may further affect long-range earnings. Consequently, in addition to differences in characteristics between individuals, occupational, job, and organizational factors play significant roles in explaining earnings discrepancies.

Related to the occupational clustering of women and relegation to positions of lower authority are more subtle stereotypical beliefs about women that also lower their earnings. These include the perception that a woman's earnings are not as important to a family as those of a man, and that she is more committed to her family than to her job. Also involved is "that women sell themselves cheap—and companies know it.... Women tend to be more reluctant than men to talk money" (Krotz 1999, p. 47). This behavior, in turn, may be related to their socialization into the traditional feminine gender role.

Finally, a smaller percentage of employed women than employed men belong to unions, and union members consistently have had higher median earnings than nonunion workers. In 1998, the median weekly earnings of full-time union workers was $659, compared to $499 for non-union employees. In that same year, only about 11 percent of employed women were members, compared to 16 percent of men (U.S. Dept. of Labor, January 1999). Part of the reason for women's lower union membership rates relates to their lower percentage in occupations such as protective service and precision craft, where a significant proportion of employees are union members.

MICROINEQUITIES IN THE TREATMENT OF WOMEN

Beyond the occupational and earnings differentials just discussed, there are other forms of inequalities experienced by women. Sexual harassment on the job is one of the areas that demonstrates this inequitable treatment. As Nutshell 4.2 reveals, such harassment can be both serious and costly. While forms of inequity relating to occupation and earnings have been in the public eye for years, micro-inequities between the genders permeate the everyday world that we take for granted. "*Microinequities* refer collectively to ways in which individuals are either *singled out,* or *overlooked, ignored,* or *otherwise discounted* on the basis of unchangeable characteristics such as sex, race, or age" (Sandler 1986, p. 3). These microinequities generally take the form of different kinds of language, treatment, or behavior exhibited toward women on a regular basis. This brief section merely points to some inequities that appear in everyday language, communication, the media, and education.

NUTSHELL **4.2** _____

Ford to Pay $7.75 Million to Women

Company Also to Set Up Sensitivity Training in Lawsuit Settlement

ASSOCIATED PRESS

Chicago—Ford Motor Co. agreed to pay $7.75 million yesterday to as many as 900 women to settle complaints that they were groped and subjected to crude comments and graffiti at two Chicago-area plants.

The settlement also calls for sensitivity training by outside consultants at Ford plants across the nation at a cost estimated by the Equal Employment Opportunity Commission at $10 million. Ford said it did not know what the cost would be.

It was the fourth-largest sexual-harassment settlement in the history of the EEOC.

A record $34 million settlement involving almost identical allegations against Mitsubishi Motors Manufacturing of America Inc. received final approval in June. The alleged harassment took place at a plant in Normal, Ill.

The Ford "settlement demonstrates the EEOC's commitment to eradicate harassment from the workplaces of America," said the commission's chairwoman, Ida L. Castro.

Under the agreement, $7.75 million in damages would be split among an estimated 700 to 900 women who can show sexual harassment or sex discrimination at Ford plants in Chicago and suburban Chicago Heights.

How much each claimant receives will be decided by a three-member independent board to be set up under the settlement.

The board also will supervise efforts within the plants to root out sexual harassment and discrimination. Under the settlement, more women will also get management positions, and supervisors who see sexual harassment but do nothing will be ineligible for promotions and bonuses.

Source: Akron Beacon Journal, September 8, 1999, p. A11. Reprinted with permission of Associated Press.

As suggested, these inequities are often deeply rooted and seemingly unconscious. Growing up, we seldom sift through the reasons why we think the way we do. As young boys, we rarely think about the everyday difficulties of being a woman:

It was not my fate to become a woman, so it was easier for me to see the graces. I didn't see, then, what a prison a house could be, since houses seemed to me brighter, handsomer places than any factory. I did not realize—because such things were never spoken of—how often women suffered from men's bullying. Even then I could see how exhausting it was for a mother to cater all day to the needs of young children. But if I had been asked, as a boy, to choose between tending a baby and tending a machine, I think I would have chosen the baby.... So I was baffled when the women at college accused me and my sex of having cornered the world's pleasures. (Sanders 1993, p. 68)

Even as educated adults, we often find it difficult to identify with the deep unseen inequities. Reflecting on her work in Women's Studies, Peggy McIntosh observed that she had "met very few men who are truly distressed about systemic, unearned male advantage and conferred dominance.... Many men likewise think that Women's Studies do not bear on their own existences because they are not female; they do not see themselves as having gendered identities" (McIntosh 1988, p. 15). All these experiences and events give evidence to our lack of conscious recognition of many everyday inequities.

Microinequities of a subtle sort permeate our culture. In language, the generic term *man*, for example, has historically been meant to include both men and women. Yet when most people think visually of that term, they think of men rather than women. In other words, this term does not suggest all of humanity to most individuals, but rather men in particular (Richardson 1987; Martyna 1978). Similarly, the pronoun *he* when used in a generic sense is supposed to represent both males and females; yet it is often attached to various kinds of occupations in a way that perpetuates gender-typed career ambitions and expectations (Richardson

1987). For example, the pronoun *she* is often used when speaking of occupations in which a majority of persons are women. Nurses, elementary school teachers, and the like are almost always referred to as *she,* whereas mechanics, doctors, and mathematicians are usually spoken of in terms of *he.* Our own names, which are part of our identity, reflect gender inequities. Traditionally, women who marry have been expected to give up their surnames and take on that of their new husbands. Women who are named after their fathers frequently have names that are diminutive versions of their father's first names—for example, Georgina (after George), Paulette (after Paul), and so on. These names "are copies, not originals, and like so many other words applied to women, they can be diminishing" (Miller and Swift 1993, p. 79).

Even the styles of speaking and communication are often different between the genders, reflecting their social positions in society. For example, women's language tends to involve a greater use of qualifiers and to be less direct and forceful than men's language (Parlee 1979). Men also talk more than women, interrupt women more often than they do other men, and are more likely to initiate conversation on a topic that is then carried on by others (Bernard 1972; Zimmerman and West 1975; Eakins and Eakins 1978; Parlee 1979). People in an audience are also more likely to respond in depth to comments made by a man than by a woman, and to be more attentive to a speech by a male (Sandler 1986). It has been suggested that many of these differences are due to inequities in power rather than to the sex of the communicators. Research among undergraduates indicates that when individuals with different levels of formal authority communicate, subordinates are more supportive, cooperative, and speak less than leaders, regardless of the sex involved (Johnson 1994).

The images of women in the popular media similarly mirror the stereotypes we have of them (Andersen 1993). In music videos and commercials, women are most often displayed as sexual objects expected to be pleasing to the eye and satisfying to the opposite sex. Almost every year, someone does a survey on which colleges have the most beautiful women. The differences among various countries in the physical beauty of their women have also been commented upon, with the sex appeal of women in democratic, wealthy nations being greater than that of women in totalitarian, poorer countries ("Girl Watching" 1992).

In addition to how they are expected to appear physically, stereotypes of women's psyches are further perpetuated in the media. Muriel Cantor's survey of popular fiction indicated that despite women's increased movement into the economy and other changes, the dominant view of women remains. These images include the beliefs that (1) women's sexual relationships are the most important element of their lives, (2) women are subordinate to men whose work and choices are more important than theirs, and (3) women need romantic relationships to be happy and fulfilled (Cantor 1987). As in our earlier history, stereotypes and images have not kept pace with the reality of changes in women's social and economic lives. What is important about these media images of women's appropriate physical and psychological traits is that they help to lock women into traditional roles and reinforce their subservient position in society.

Within schools, sex and gender biases remain significant. In primary and secondary schools, females are more likely than males to be ignored by their teachers and get less attention and encouragement in math and science. Textbooks used are rarely authored by women. "Students sit in classrooms that, day in, day out, deliver the message that women's lives count for less than men's (cited in Chira 1992, p. A8). All of these treatments are part of the unofficial hidden curriculum of what schools teach their students.

Reports of sexual harassment in schools have also increased (Chira 1992, p. A8). An incident of the so-called Spur Posse in a California school illustrates the extent to which systematic harassment can go. A group of male high school athletes formed the group, in which status was measured by how many girls they could get into bed. Some "scored" into the 60s, and involved girls ranging

from 10 to 16 years of age. Some of the parents of the boys were not particularly concerned; one father even bragged about the virility of his sons ("Mixed Messages" 1993).

Inequity problems can even be found in colleges and universities, and the comparatively small numbers of women in top positions increase the chances of their being treated differently from men. A review survey by the Project on the Status and Education of Women reported that women are provided with fewer resources and less desirable offices, are not taken as seriously as male colleagues by students or male faculty, are considered less for their scholarly accomplishments than for their feminine characteristics, and are subject to a variety of forms of sexual harassment (Sandler 1986).

Sociologist Theda Skocpol also reflected on the significance of gender for her career. She noted that in 1984 she "was offered the Harvard tenured professorship that I am convinced would have been mine in 1981 if I had been 'Theodore' rather than 'Theda'" (Skocpol 1988, p. 155). She went on to comment that, in general, "ambitious women are still not accepted at the top and, no matter what their achievements, they still have to endure the worst personal insults and struggle without end against virtually insuperable obstacles to their having real power" (p. 156).

Traditionally appropriate gender roles are further reinforced by many college textbooks. A recent study of texts from several decades in the areas of human sexuality and marriage and the family concluded that traditional photographs of women's roles are dominant in them. Although the proportion of such images was higher in the 1970s, a large majority of images were still traditional in texts of the 1990s. This is especially disturbing since there was an increase in the number of photographs with women at their center (Low and Sherrard 1999).

These examples suggest the variety of problems that groups of lower status face in U.S. society. Benokraitis and Feagin (1986) summarized the kinds of subtle sex discrimination that exist. Some are intentional and others are not, but generally they occur on an informal basis. Among the types they cited are:

- Chivalry, which treats women in an overly protective manner and thereby encourages the image of them as nonadults
- Encouraging women to be ambitious and active but then creating blockages that make it difficult for them to perform effectively
- Forms of humor and suggestion, which on the surface may appear innocuous but are demeaning and embarrassing
- Treating women as objects—that is, as sex symbols or as status objects
- Devaluating the talents and abilities of women and focusing on stereotypical or superficial characteristics to honor them
- Overloading or overburdening women in their tasks or jobs under the guise of allowing them full participation or equality with men
- "Benevolent exploitation" in which women are exploited in an often unnoticed manner—that is, showcasing token women, using their talents and then not giving them appropriate credit
- Portraying dominant males as considerate and concerned with the welfare of women
- Socially and physically isolating women in professional settings

This list should serve as a reminder that sex discrimination can occur in several forms, not only in the formal institutional areas of occupation and earnings. The list also parallels the kinds of subtle discrimination that African Americans have experienced historically under paternalistic treatment of them as simple-minded children and tokens of their group.

GENERAL THEORIES OF SEX AND GENDER INEQUALITY

In addition to discussions of specific factors, such as those just reviewed, several types of general theories of sex inequality (i.e., inequality between males and females) have also been suggested. Be-

cause of the broad range of theories available, our discussion will be limited to theories that are more sociological or anthropological in nature. That is, the focus will be on explanations that emphasize the importance of social structure, ecology, or cultural contexts rather than biological or psychological elements. Biological explanations of sex inequality that suggest that basic genetic, hormonal, or physical differences determine sex inequality are inadequate for several reasons. Although there are some hormonal and physical differences between the sexes, they do not mandate that men will dominate women. These differences and any behaviors associated with them still have to be culturally and socially interpreted (i.e., gendered). For example, aggressiveness is related to domination only if it is interpreted in a particular way. In some societies, such behavior may be not only tolerated but also admired; in others, it may be considered deviant and those who engage in it may be assigned low status (Coontz and Henderson 1986).

Even in limiting this discussion to cultural and social explanations of sex inequality, only samples of each type of theory can be presented. Moreover, in some cases, such as in theories involving patriarchy and capitalism in their explanations, you should be aware that there are differences among specific theorists about details. The goal here is to present a general picture of the kinds of explanations that exist to account for sex inequality.

Largely for the sake of convenience, the theories on sex inequality are divided into four general categories: (1) cultural, (2) social-structural, (3) ecological, and (4) capitalist/patriarchal. This set of categories does not, of course, exhaust all the types of theories of sex inequality that have been developed, nor are they mutually exclusive. The categories in the list overlap to some degree, but they also serve to separate theories whose foci and thrusts differ from each other. One other point should be made. The theories discussed are principally concerned with addressing the *origins* rather than the *maintenance* of sex and race inequality. Theories involving socialization and the role of education in inequality, on the other hand, shed light on the maintenance of such inequality across generations.

Explanations of inequality between the sexes have been plagued by a number of difficulties (Mukhopadhyay and Higgins 1988; Schlegel 1977; Chafetz 1984):

1. It has become increasingly evident that discussions of women's status are often too broad. That is, women can be unequal or equal with men on a variety of dimensions, such as public power, prestige, type of work, education, and access to other services and goods that make life more enjoyable and meaningful. Moreover, the status of women on these dimensions is not identical across all cultures. How the genders and their appropriate roles are defined varies among cultures.

2. Some have attempted to develop a universal explanation of sex inequality, but because of the variation in cultural beliefs and settings, the development of such a generally applicable theory of sex inequality has been hampered. Without resorting to biological universals that distinguish men from women, it is difficult to identify other core factors that can explain the nuances and peculiarities of inequalities in different cultures. This is assuming that such a universal ahistorical theory is even possible let alone desirable.

3. Many of the data from ethnographic studies upon which explanations have been built were collected by anthropologists who were male and interpreted those cultures using a Euro-American gender model (Mukhopadhyay and Higgins 1988). One of the unfortunate biases with which we have approached other cultures is that we make judgments about women's status using our own measures of what is good, prestigious, and desirable. In essence, positions of the sexes are defined in terms different from those used by the groups in the cultures in question.

4. Several theories, especially earlier ones, have relied on simplistic dichotomies in trying to understand sex inequality. The dichotomies include nature and culture, natural and artificial, and private/domestic and public/social as being embodied in women and men, respectively, to name but a few.

Cultural Values, Sex, and Gender Inequality

When we speak of a person's *sex,* we ordinarily are referring to the biological status of being female or male. However, cultures assign different meanings to the definitions of *male* and *female.* To differentiate it from the term *sex,* the term *gender* frequently is used to denote the definitions and assignments that different groups and cultures associate with the sexes. In other words, *gender* is a "cultural construct" (Caplan 1987; see also Ortner and Whitehead 1981).

Cultures expect different attitudes and behaviors from members of each sex, but those expectations vary among cultures. In some cultures, what we consider so-called masculine behavior is expected of women, and in some cultures, men engage in what we would consider to be so-called feminine (i.e., effeminate in the U.S. value system) behavior. All this is to say that *sex* is a term used to describe a biological constant and *gender* is a term used to describe socially and culturally approved expectations, and these vary between societies. For example, we might argue that being a bouncer at a night club is quintessentially a male role; however, among the Dahomeyan of Africa, rulers used women as bodyguards because they considered women to be excellent fighters (Light, Keller, and Calhoun 1989). Among the Tchambuli of New Guinea, women were the dominant figures, the principal breadwinners, wore no jewelry, and kept their heads shaved. Margaret Mead's research uncovered some societies where both sexes were expected to be nurturant and gentle, and others where men and women were expected to be aggressive and arrogant (Mead 1963).

Thus, although women are members of the same sex and, are therefore, biologically the same across cultures, their gender roles may be markedly different and differentially ranked among those same cultures. One of the pitfalls of equating sex with gender has been to define the gender roles given to each sex as being natural, that by their nature men and women perform particular roles and have particular characteristics. The old phrase "men are men and women are women" captures this belief. In this view, there is a consistency between sex and gender that cannot or should not be changed. For example, in U.S. culture, "male homosexuality threatens male solidarity and superordination because some men take on what are thought of as female characteristics. Lesbianism is likewise seen as threatening to male superiority because the women who engage in it appear not to need men." We assume that there needs to be a "correct fit between sex, gender, and sexuality" (Caplan 1987, p. 2).

In eighteenth- and nineteenth-century Europe, it was common to associate women with nature. Women's nature was thought to reflect natural laws and their behavior to reflect a basic emotionalism and passion. Ortner (1974) has argued that because of women's reproductive role, they have been and still are viewed as being closer to nature than men, who, "lacking natural creative functions, must...assert [their] creativity externally, 'artificially,' through the medium of technology and symbols. In doing so [the man creates] relatively lasting, eternal, transcending objects, while the woman creates only perishables—human beings" (p. 75). Women are also seen as mediating between nature and culture, and men are seen as divorced from nature. Since nature is generally interpreted as being lower than culture and subject to the constraints of culture, Ortner argued, men are accorded more prestige and women less. While realizing that not all cultures neatly divide the sexes in terms of nature versus culture, Ortner said that most of the differences between the sexes are seen in dichotomous terms, nature/culture being one of them. Others of a similar kind involve the notion that women's activities and values are circumscribed by the domestic sphere or self-interests, whereas men's roles are in the public domain or for the social good. Since the public or social sphere of life encompasses the narrowly focused domestic sphere, higher value is attached to it (Ortner and Whitehead 1981, pp. 7–8).

The proposals that these dichotomies are central to the explanation of sex inequality have been severely criticized in recent years. Why are women necessarily seen as more natural than men when the procreative role of men and many of their other activities (eating, sleeping, etc.) are just as natural as those of women? Moreover, many of the forms taken by natural behaviors surrounding reproduction are limited by cultural constraints and are not, therefore, purely natural (MacCormack 1980).

While incorporating the element of cultural beliefs into her theory, Ortner appeared to ignore the structural constraints placed on behavior by the social and natural context of the society (Schlegel 1977). Not all cultures devalue what is natural, and the meaning of "natural" changes historically rather than remaining timeless and static as it appeared in Ortner's view (Coontz and Henderson 1986; Yanagisako and Collier 1987). Perhaps the most serious deficiency of the nature/culture dichotomy is that it simplifies the complex reality of diverse cultures. Research indicates that even where such a dichotomy can be derived, nature and culture may be defined in a manner different from western society, or males may be viewed as being closer to nature than females, or the dichotomy may not be associated with the sexes at all (Gillison 1980; Harris 1980; Strathern 1980).

The importance of Ortner's work is that it called attention to the significance of symbols and cultural constructs in understanding how individuals interpret the sexes and the relations between them. What distinguishes most of the theories discussed next from Ortner's view is that they emphasize the centrality of social structure in the process of inequality development between the sexes. Sex inequality is viewed as an outcome of particular kinds of social or economic structures, and not, therefore, historically universal.

Social-Structural Explanations

Several of the most significant social-structural theories highlight the importance of women's work activities and kinship structure in generating inequality between the sexes (e.g., Blumberg 1978, 1984; Chafetz 1988). They are usually cross-cultural in nature in that they propose to explain the degree of sex inequality in societies that are radically different in technology, size, culture, and so forth. Janet Saltzman Chafetz's explanation is a good example of a social structural theory.

Chafetz's Theory of Sex Stratification.   Chafetz argued that there has never been a situation where women dominated men on a systematic and long-term basis, so that societies vary "from near equality to radical inequality favoring males" (Chafetz 1988, p. 51). She has tried to explain the "degree of sex stratification" in a given society—that is, "the extent to which societal members are unequal in their access to the scarce values of their society" (Chafetz 1984, p. 4). These values include material goods and services, prestigious roles, political power, interpersonal decision making, freedom from unwanted constraints, and educational opportunities. In other words, Chafetz views stratification as multidimensional in nature. Moreover, some of these dimensions may vary independently of each other, causing women's positions to be high on some and lower on others.

Three of the factors most directly related to sex stratification, according to Chafetz, are (1) the nature of the work organization, (2) the type of kinship structure, and (3) the degrees of ideological and stereotyping support for sex inequality in the society. Of these, the most important is the work organization, which includes a number of specific elements (see Figure 4.2). Sex inequality will be high in a society when the following circumstances exist: (1) women do not contribute significantly to highly valued tasks, (2) women are easily replaced, (3) occupational tasks are sex-typed, (4) attention span is an important variable in a valued task, and (5) women do not have ownership and control over the means and products of their production.

The work organization itself is affected by several other independent variables, most of which are directly related to the level and type of technology in the society. Specifically, the more time women have to spend on child-rearing activities, the greater the distance between workplace and home, the more the need for physical strength and/or mobility, and the less emphasis that is

(1) Nature of Work Organization (sex division of labor; nature of work contribution; labor substitution; ownership/control of means of production

(2) Kinship Structure (descent; residence rules; sex division of labor in family)

(3) Degree of Ideological Support for and Degree of Gender Stereotyping

SEX STRATIFICATION

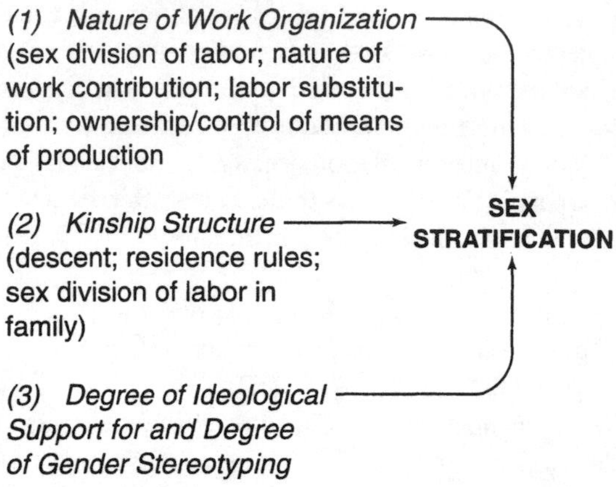

FIGURE 4.2   Factors Most Immediately Related to Sex Stratification

Source: Based on Chaftez 1984, pp. 10–22.

placed on subsistence rather than surplus production for exchange, the less women can be meaningfully involved in valued work tasks and, consequently, the higher the degree of sex stratification will be.

In addition to work organization factors, kinship structure also has an impact. When (1) married women live with or in the same places as their husbands' families (patrilocal), (2) a society traces lineage through the male line (patrilineal), and (3) there is a domestic division of labor based on sex, then inequality between the sexes will be high.

Finally, Chafetz included both the *degree of ideological/religious support* for sex stratification and the degree of *gender stereotyping* as factors that affect the acceptance of inequality between the sexes. For example, some societies may support the notion that "women's place is in the home" or that a wife must be submissive to her husband, while other societies may emphasize above all the belief in the worth and equality of all individuals as human beings. In addition, cultures usually contain stereotypes of male and female characteristics and appropriate behavior for each sex. According to Chafetz, these factors are more important for sustaining and justifying inequality than they are for generating it.

There have been conflicting reactions to Chafetz's argument. In a discussion of his view of how sociological theory should be structured, Gerhard Lenski praised Chafetz's model for being presented in a diagrammatic and essentially propositional form. Lenski believed that this makes the theory clearer and more amenable to empirical testing. In sharp contrast to the praise of Lenski, Pierre Van den Berghe was quite critical of Chafetz's formalistic approach to theory, which appears to be becoming more dominant in the field. In assessing her theory, he bluntly stated that "an exercise in loosely linking a grab bag of 'variables' does not constitute anything that a real scientist would recognize as a theory" (1985, p. 1350). However, this is an extreme reaction to what is a useful predictive model. It brings together variables that have been cited as important by others into a somewhat coherent and testable package. One variable minimized by Chafetz, considered central for Sanday's theory which is to be discussed next, is the role of cultural factors in explaining and maintaining sex stratification.

Ecological Explanations

The structural theories of Chafetz and others often rely on the cross-cultural evidence and ideas of anthropologists who have developed theories of sex inequality. The latters' theories usually focus on societies that are simpler in technology, whereas sociological theories usually emphasize complex industrial societies when trying to explain inequality (Chafetz 1988).

Sanday's Theory of Male Dominance. Peggy Sanday's theory is based on her analysis of information from over 150 societies, most of them not known to the average reader and many of them extinct. But they provide clues to the origins of male dominance. Sanday defined male dominance in terms of the "exclusion of women from political and economic decision-making" and "male aggression against women" (1981, p. 164). Her principal question addressed the origins of male dominance. Where does it come from? *The basic*

generating cause for male dominance relates to the nature of the environment in which a society operates. If that environment is one in which risk is great, danger is present, or resources are uncertain or in scarce supply, then the society is more vulnerable to male dominance over women. For example, when a society's ability to feed itself is dependent on hunting large migrating animals, its continuity is not as certain. This means that people's tie to the environment is more negative than positive under these circumstances. Survival is at risk. This contrasts with situations in which the immediate environment supplies abundant food without risk or uncertainty, as, for example, among the Mbuti, an African forest people.

These two different environments generate different stresses for the people exposed to them, their relationships to the environment are defined differently, and the general cultural orientations and consequent sex-role plans they develop also differ as a result (Sanday 1981). In other words, a group develops its sense of peoplehood and cultural orientations as responses to its environmental circumstances. When those circumstances involve risk, uncertainty, and so forth, as in the case of societies that rely heavily on the hunting of large animals, then there is a greater reliance on the aggression of men. These societies, in which animals must be killed, in which death and destruction predominate, develop what Sanday calls an "outer orientation" in their world view. "Men hunt animals, seek to kill other human beings, make weapons for these activities, and pursue power that is *out there*" (1981, p. 5). On the other side are societies whose environments produce abundantly and with certainty, cultures that rely on the surrounding plants for sustenance. Nature is viewed in a friendly manner, as freely satisfying human needs. In many cases where this situation is present, a basic affinity is seen between women and nature. As women produce, so does nature. Women are seen as being more in tune with nature and men are largely extraneous to this relationship. In these cultures, an inner orientation is dominant.

The cultural system that develops in a society not only contains scripts for the relationships between humans and the natural environment but also between the sexes. In societies in which the environment is potentially hostile, men spend much of their time in activities in the outer environment, outside the family, wrestling with forces beyond the family. In these kinds of societies, the ultimate source of power is believed to reside either in animals or in a supreme being of some kind who lives in a place beyond human beings. In these societies, because of their hunting activity, men are distant from their children and do not engage much in nurturing activity. The myths surrounding origins of the culture or world are imbued with masculine characteristics. The opposite is the case when a society, especially a technologically simple one, relies on plants in plentiful supply. Here, the earth supplies the food and men are close to their families and children. Growth and life are an inherent part of the culture. Like women, the earth provides and creates life. Tales of life origins have a feminine quality to them. Under both these circumstances, "the phrases 'man the animal' and 'mother earth' make a great deal of sense" (Sanday 1981, p. 73). There is a close connection between the economy of a society and the role of the sexes in myths and childrearing.

A strict sex-based division of labor is more likely when the society depends heavily on hunting as its means of subsistence, whereas a society that depends equally on hunting and gathering or inordinately on the latter for food is more likely to produce a division of labor that is sexually integrated. Cooperation rather than competition is likely to be emphasized. Females *achieve* power when a society has to depend on their economic activity for survival. This makes men more dependent on them. Women are *given* power when they are associated closely with nature and the society's continuity, as in the origin myths just mentioned (Sanday 1981, pp. 89 and 114).

With Western colonialism, women lost much of the higher status they held in traditional societies. The infusion of new weapons, new technologies, and the increased importance of aggression helped to redefine the roles of the sexes, with male activity becoming more highly valued. In many cases, the increased complexity of economic technology also led to the decline of women's status. In her survey of societies, Sanday concluded that "male dominance is associated with increasing technological complexity, an animal economy, sexual segregation in work, a symbolic orientation to the male creative principle, and stress" (1981, p. 171). Sex inequality is much more likely when the environment is unfavorable and unstable than when the opposite is the case.

To summarize Sanday's explanation, the nature of the surrounding environment gives shape to the economy and the stress in society and determines the relative worth of men's and women's behavior. Cultural orientations, myths, and sex-role plans develop that are consistent with these conditions. When environmental conditions create stress because they involve risk, danger, or uncertainty, greater reliance is placed on the economic efforts of men. An outer cultural orientation develops along with origin myths in which men dominate and create, sex-segregation of roles follows, ultimately leading to male dominance. Sanday's basic model is suggested in Figure 4.3.

Sanday's theory has been criticized for overemphasizing the role of the environment in determining cultural beliefs and for ignoring the internal sources of stress in society. It also does not take into account the fact that different cultures may react differently to similar environmental circumstances (Coontz and Henderson 1986). Additionally, her theory neglects the possibility that the difficulties men encounter in dealing with a harsh environment may strengthen them enough to dominate women directly.

Randall Collins has suggested, for example, that the form of the economic system and the habitability of the surrounding natural and political environments influence the extent to which warfare is an important element in the society. When the economic system is advanced enough and involves the protection of private property or settled territories, warfare is often part of a society's existence as it tries to defend itself against outside encroachment. Men are generally larger and stronger than women and are therefore more likely to control the fighting that occurs. In this kind of a potentially hostile environment, political alliances become important, and males use the exchange of females through marriage with surrounding groups as a means of establishing political, economic, and social ties. This control of females by males results in separate cultures and roles developing for each of the sexes (Collins 1971, 1986, 1988). In other words, the need for the mediation of the environment's impact on male domination through the intervening factors of cultural scripts and orientations may either not be necessary or the mediation may involve the operation of other variables like warfare.

The causal nature of the relationships outlined by Sanday also needs to be more fully examined (England and Dunn 1985). One would suspect, for example, that cultural orientation and beliefs would have an impact on the degree to which the environment is interpreted as being hostile or friendly. In other words, the environment may not only affect the culture, but the culture may affect the definition of the environment as well.

Capitalism, Patriarchy, and Sex Inequality

Generally, structural theorists, as well as many anthropologists, recognize the significance of broadly defined economic factors for sex inequality. Many point to the significance of labor, work organization, and family structure in shaping inequality. In a general way, then, their perspectives have been affected by Marxian thought as well as by perspectives that focus on the family structure and the sex/gender divisions within it. Some explanations, however, explicitly focus on the effects of capitalism and patriarchy on sex inequality. Figure 4.4 gives a basic model showing some of the alleged major impacts of capitalism/class on sex inequality.

Again, there are a large number of individuals who present such explanations (e.g., Sacks 1975; Leacock 1986; Vogel 1983). Some of them address the adequacy and insights of Engels's theory of the origins of sex inequality, so we will begin with an overview of his position.

Engels's Theory of Sex Inequality.   Frederick Engels contended that early in human history, people lived together communally and engaged in tasks together to produce goods principally for their own use. Since all resources were communally owned, individuals worked for the group as a whole. Separate nuclear families as we know them, as distinct productive units, did not exist. Rather than being wives within separate families, women were members of society and contributed

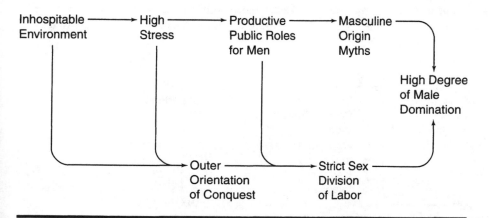

FIGURE 4.3   Sanday's Basic Model of the Genesis of Male Dominance

Source: Based on Sanday 1981, pp. 11–12, 64–75, 163–172ff.

fully and equally to society (Sacks 1975). Being a mother was a central role in those societies, according to Engels. Since all members of both sexes were involved in producing goods of direct value and use to their own communities, the work of both sexes was considered equally valuable. Women were full participants in the society. Although there was a division of labor based on sex, each sex was a master in its own sphere of work.

This situation changed, according to Engels, when certain material conditions changed. Specifically, the development of privately owned productive resources in the form of domesticated animals and land laid the groundwork for the differentiation of the sexes and the subordination of women to men. These resources appeared on a continuing basis when the technology and natural resources accessible to the group made possible the development of the abilities necessary to domesticate animals and make productive use of the land. Herding and the use of land made possible greater surpluses than were possible under mere hunting. Engels felt that once domestication and land use were stabilized and part of the society, then private ownership would also be stabilized. He also believed that men were the earliest owners of property (Sacks 1975).

Once private property was entrenched in society, economic and other divisions developed between individuals and families; that is, the *preclass* days were over. The extensive domestication of animals and land use made possible greater surpluses, allowing individuals to produce not only for themselves and their families but for others as well. Production for *exchange* began to become more dominant than production for *use* by the households themselves. With private property owned by men and the increase in production for exchange, the kind of work that dominated the lives of women changed, and with it their status in society (Sacks 1975; Leacock 1986). Because men now had property they could pass on to their children, men became more concerned about making sure they had children. This encouraged them to usurp more control in the nuclear monogamous family and the procreation process.

Consequently, women changed from being contributing adults equal to men to wards, wives, and daughters in a subordinate and increasingly domestic position. Their reproduction of children was now for producing heirs and workers for their own families rather than for producing another child for the societal group. Individual families and their economic statuses could then be preserved generation after generation. This domination of men over women in the nuclear family setting was, for Engels, the first instance of class domination and struggle in history. "In the family, he is the bourgeois; the wife represents the proletariat" (Engels 1973, p. 247). This class conflict is "a picture in miniature" of what appears later in the society as a whole (ibid.). Eventually, property owners joined together to defend their goods against those who owned nothing. This was the beginning of class society and class state (Sacks 1975, p. 217).

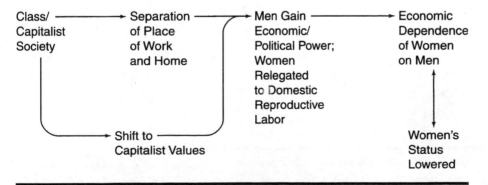

FIGURE 4.4   The Relationship of Class/Capitalism to Sex Inequality

Vogel's Reproduction Theory.   Lise Vogel reviewed and assessed Engels's analysis of women's oppression, but came to the conclusion that his theory was seriously flawed. For example, she said Engels does not clearly trace and explain the development of a separate domestic arena out of class or capitalist society. Also, he does not elaborate on the subordination of women in precapitalist class societies (Vogel 1983, p. 86). These problems led Vogel to attempt development of her own theory based on Marxian concepts.

Vogel began the development of her theoretical framework by reviewing several Marxian concepts: production, reproduction, and labor power. *Labor power* refers to the capacities, mental and physical, an individual exercises whenever he or she produces something of use. *Production* is a result of labor power. But every act of production is also an act of *reproduction,* since whatever is produced lays the basis for its being reproduced later.

Specifically, a society needs a labor force to continue to produce products, and this labor force, in turn, needs food to maintain itself. In other words, part of the reproduction process involves reproducing the laborers who are involved in the labor process. These workers must be maintained and, when necessary, replaced. Sex becomes a significant factor in the generational replacement of bearers of labor power, because it is only women who can perform this function. But regeneration or replenishment of the labor force does not have to occur within the family. Other sources—such as migration, enslavement, and the enlistment of nonworkers within the family—also may serve as potential sources of labor power.

In order for the capitalist system of production to continue, then, labor power must produce the conditions necessary for the constant renewal of the labor process. The labor needed to reproduce the workers and their replacement is *necessary* labor. For example, a certain minimum amount of labor is needed to provide basic subsistence to the workers and to produce new workers. Part of this necessary labor is done at the workplace and is paid for by wages, with which the worker can buy those necessities needed to reproduce himself or

herself and other nonworkers in the working class. Since it takes place in the social or public sphere, it is the *social* aspect of necessary labor. But as mentioned, biological reproduction and the rearing of children are also needed, and as such constitute a second *domestic* component of necessary labor. In addition to necessary labor, there is *surplus* labor. This is the labor time that is left over after socially necessary labor has been subtracted from the total labor time spent on the job. It provides the profit to the employer.

It is the unavoidable performance of the domestic component of necessary labor by women that creates a basic sex division of labor. But their involvement in reproduction creates a dilemma for capitalists and constitutes an internal contradiction in the capitalist system. On the one hand, this domestic labor reduces any time women could spend in the labor force producing profit for employers. So in the short run, capitalists suffer because of the smaller direct contribution of women to profit. On the other hand, if capitalism is going to continue over the long run, replacement and reproduction are necessary. So in these terms, capitalism benefits.

In order to benefit both ways, capitalists try to minimize the amount of necessary domestic time needed for reproduction in order to maximize the surplus value of labor, thereby increasing their profit. Thus, employers may allow maternity leaves for their female workers, but the leaves are kept short so as to maximize the work time of new mothers. At the same time, however, male workers try to get the best conditions and wages they can for themselves, their families, and their wives. This may mean more and better-quality domestic time for their wives. So while employers may be trying to enlist wives in the marketplace, husbands are trying to create conditions that will make it more possible for them to stay comfortably at home. In trying to resolve this contradiction, according to Vogel, what almost invariably occurs is the involvement of men in the labor force and the production of surplus labor and profit on the one hand, and the involvement of women in the reproduction of the labor force at home on the other. Accompanying this resolution is a male supremacy based on males as the laborers who produce the means of subsistence and receive a wage.

It is in capitalism that a distinct and strong division is accentuated between the arena in which surplus labor is carried out and that in which domestic labor is performed. In order to increase profit, separate factories in which workers are concentrated are needed that are socially and culturally isolated from the home. "Capitalism's drive to increase surplus…forces a severe spatial, temporal, and institutional separation between domestic labor and the capitalist production process…. Wage labor comes to have a character that is wholly distinct from the laborer's life away from the job" (Vogel 1983, p. 153). Men are clearly associated with the social, working sphere, whereas women are associated with the domestic sphere. This is a carryover from earlier class societies.

Of course, exceptions exist. Depending on the specific historical circumstances of a given society, either the importance of women's power of reproduction or their involvement in the labor force may be stressed. Migration and natural or other disasters may tip the scales in such a way that the participation of females in the work force is more important than their domestic labor. But the usual division of labor consists of men and women being associated with distinct spheres of labor. This clear division of labor, when accentuated in a situation of male supremacy, is the source for ideologies that serve to explain and maintain the sexual basis of the division of labor. Since this division of labor is so prominent and obvious, it comes to be viewed as natural even though it is rooted in the capitalist mode of production (Vogel 1983, p. 154).

As noted previously, according to Vogel, women's involvement in and relegation to domestic labor is the basic source of their subordination. In fact, she suggested that in advanced capitalist societies, sex sometimes is more important than class in determining differences between individuals. Men support women by working and receiving wages, and this gives them economic power over women. *It is the provision by men of means of subsistence to women during the childbearing*

period, and not the sex division of labor in itself, that forms the material basis for women's subordination in class society" (Vogel 1983, p. 147, emphasis added).

Since many of the immediate conflicts take place within the context of the family, it is easy to conclude that it is the sex division of labor within it that is at the source of the problems experienced by women. But Vogel reminds us again that it is the nature of the relationship of men and women to the capitalist system of production and women's role in reproducing it that is the basic cause. As long as capitalism remains unchanged, inequality between the sexes will continue. Figure 4.5 presents the core of Vogel's argument.

One of the problems with Vogel's theory is that she dated the beginning of women's oppression with the advent of class societies. Many would argue that male domination predated class society (Nicholson 1984). Vogel's theory also heavily stressed economic factors to the exclusion of cultural, psychological, and other possible contributors to male domination.

The Role of Patriarchy. Vogel acknowledged the division of labor and the inequality that exists between the sexes in capitalist society, but Sacks (1975) noted that in many nonclass societies the sexes were also unequal. This suggests strongly that sex inequality preceded capitalism and indeed is a form of domination distinct from class inequality.

In brief, many feminists argue that patriarchy not only preceded capitalism but also existed even in the earliest societies. The term *patriarchy* has been defined in a variety of ways, but basically it refers to a whole complex of structured interrelationships in which men dominate over women. It is a "system of sexual hierarchical relations" (Eisenstein 1981, p. 19). Just as capitalism is based on the relationship between capitalists and workers, so patriarchy is a system based on the unequal relationship of men and women (Phelps 1981). Because of its early appearance, patriarchy is considered by most radical feminists to be the most fundamental of all forms of social inequality, as one in which "men learn how to hold other human beings in contempt, to see them as nonhuman and to control them" (Lengermann and Niebrugge-Brantley 1988, p. 306).

In other words, in this view, sexism and the domination of women did not appear with class societies as some Marxists would have it; rather, it existed long before capitalism came on the historical scene. The roots of patriarchy have been tied to the reproductive function of women in society (Chafetz 1988; Eisenstein 1981; Phelps 1981; Firestone 1970). "On the basis of this capacity she has been excluded from other human activities and contained within a sphere defined as female" in Western society (Eisenstein 1981, p. 14). The division of labor between the sexes in this respect is ancient: "Where there is society, there is gender, and the gender division of labor is pervasive" (D. E. Smith 1987, p. 4). There was no primordial matriarchal society preceding class society. Table 4.3 suggests some of the basic elements tied to patriarchy and some of the forms it has taken under precapitalist and capitalist societies.

Once men dominate in areas outside the family and gain the economic and political resources attendant with those activities, they can use these resources to maintain patriarchy. The maintenance of patriarchy over generations is clearly in

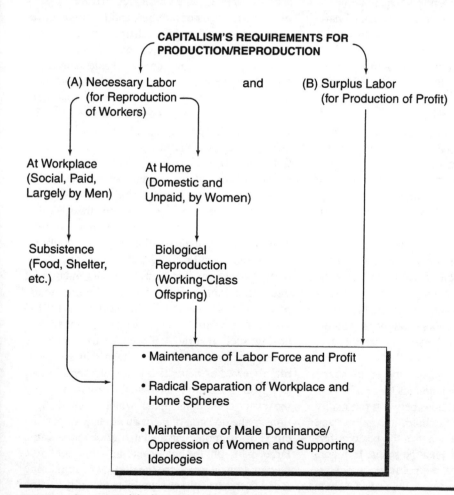

FIGURE 4.5   A Simplified Version of Vogel's Theory of Women's Oppression

TABLE 4.3   Patriarchy and Sex Inequality

GENERAL FEATURES OF PATRIARCHY	UNDER PRECAPITALIST SOCIETIES	UNDER CAPITALISM
1. Power, force of men 2. Control of outer resources by men 3. Separate work spheres 4. Division of labor based on sex 5. Reproductive capacity of women critical	Men engage in status-enhancing hunting; men control domesticated animals; women used as exchange, women purchased (bridewealth); men control military	Radical separation of home and work; women cheap labor for market, women largely confined to home, women economically dependent on men

the interests of men. Women serve the material interests of men by serving not only as sexual partners but also as potential laborers, childbearers, ornaments, and status enhancers.

The social institutions dominated by men, then, influence not only the shape of society and relations within it but also the cultural values and ideas that dominate in society. Thus, in present-day society, education and socialization agents instill those values consistent with patriarchal structure. Under capitalism, the culture consists largely of the ideas and values sanctioned by those in power—that is, men. This ruling ideology provides an official version of social reality, including beliefs about the real nature of men and women. Eventually, among women living under capitalism, a line of fault or disjuncture occurs between this official version of reality and how the system works and the concrete everyday experiences of women. But this experience is difficult to articulate because the symbols, language, and organization of thought in the society are those of men not women (D. E. Smith 1987).

The separation and inequality of men and women is reflected in dichotomies that go back to ancient times. The distinctions between rationality and passion, city and household, and public and private all derive from a belief in the basic differences and inequality between the sexes. In feudal and in capitalist societies, the public sphere is associated with the male, whereas the private sphere is the designated place for the female. In feudal

society, females were considered private property of the male heads of families, and in capitalist society, women are largely relegated to the private sphere of the family. In other words, although the economic system may change, basic patriarchal relationships remain intact and only change form.

One of the difficulties with patriarchal theories is that the original source of patriarchy is not always clearly spelled out. Sometimes it is associated with the differences in the reproductive function between the sexes, sometimes with the physical force of men over women, and other times its source is left undescribed. Collins (1988) argued that the basic problem with theories that propose patriarchy as the fundamental, original cause of sex inequality is that they are merely restating the question using a different label. That is, if "patriarchy" *refers* to male domination of one sort or another, then how can it be used to *explain* male domination? This seems to be too severe a criticism, given that many of those proposing such theories do attempt to locate the sources of patriarchy itself. Since that source is often viewed as being tied to the elemental function of reproduction, the task remains to identify the exact conditions under which such distinctions in the division of labor do *not* lead to patriarchy. For example, can socializing or spreading a large part of the child-rearing function free women to a degree from the destiny of remaining in the domestic sphere, thereby potentially raising their status in society?

Socialist-Feminist Theories of Sex Inequality.
In contrast to those who would opt for viewing either capitalism *or* patriarchy as the principal cause of women's subordination, there are those who see the two as complementary causes. Women's oppression by men cannot be reduced to a matter of class exploitation, according to these scholars. *Exploitation* of women, Eisenstein (1977) argued, exists when men and women are wage laborers. But women are also in a lower sexual hierarchy in their roles as mothers and housewives. "The study of women's oppression, then, must deal with both sexual and economic material conditions if one is to understand oppression rather than merely understand economic exploitation" (Eisenstein 1990, p. 124). As we will see, those who use an internal-colonialism model in explaining Black/White inequality in the United States make a similar argument about understanding racial oppression.

Eisenstein and Hartmann both emphasized the mutual reinforcement between capitalism and patriarchy. On the one hand, patriarchy supplies capitalism with generations of laborers it needs at minimal costs and with the techniques of control needed to keep oppressed women in their place. All the tasks carried out and raw materials worked on by housewives (e.g., children, husbands) are "future worker-commodities" (Secombe 1973, p. 19). In turn, capitalism reinforces patriarchy by only hiring women for certain low-paying positions, thereby encouraging job segregation, women's relegation to the domestic sphere, and their continued economic dependence on males.

> *Job segregation by sex, in my view, is the primary mechanism in capitalist society that maintains the superiority of men over women, because it enforces lower wages for women in the labor market. Low wages keep women dependent on men because they encourage women to marry. Married women must perform domestic chores for their husbands. Men benefit, then, from both higher wages and the domestic division of labor. (Hartmann 1990, pp. 147–148; see also Eisenstein 1990)*

The domestic division of labor is the linchpin that connects capitalism and patriarchy (Philipson

and Hansen 1990). Patriarchy defines the role of women as being in the home, whereas capitalism defines men's role as being in the wider economy and women's role as reproducer of workers in the economy. The division of labor, as it were, brings the private/domestic and public/economic spheres into contact. This has raised a number of questions about the nature of the relationship between the marketplace and the home.

One issue pits the obvious contributions of domestic work to the continuance of capitalism against the fact that domestic labor is basically unpaid low-status work outside the economy. If such work contributes to the economy by providing functioning laborers, why isn't it paid labor? Because it is not paid, it has lower status in a society in which the amount of money labor brings in is a measure of its status (Benston 1969).

A second issue concerns the basic character of domestic labor. In contrast to work in the marketplace, which is seen by some as being alienating and rationalistic, work in the home is sometimes seen as much less alienating and more leisurely (Vogel 1983; Sontag 1973). The home and family life are viewed as the areas in which love, warmth, spontaneity, cooperation, and fun have a central place. In sharp contrast, the public sphere of paid labor is interpreted as one where work is forced, competitive, and rational. It is, of course, questionable whether those who feel trapped in the home would describe it in the glowing terms just used. But part of our socialization is aimed at fostering the belief that these terms accurately describe family life in modern society.

A third issue among scholars relates to the effects of involvement in the marketplace on women. Engels viewed industrialization as providing women with a means of escape from the drudgery of housework and the oppression of domestic life. Work outside the home was interpreted as a liberating experience. However, if capitalism creates work that is fundamentally alienating, a legitimate question can be raised about how liberating and beneficial such an escape would be for women. Are they not just escaping into work that is also alienating and compounding their alienation by doing not only paid labor but unpaid domestic labor as well?

A final area concerns the family's role in socializing new members of society into a dominant set of values and ideas that perpetuate patriarchy and capitalism (Hartmann 1981). The traits attributed to the ideal male—competitiveness, rationality, coolness—are those valued in the marketplace, whereas those attributed to the ideal female under capitalism—emotionality, sentimentality, and so on—are those valued in the family. These are values that keep patriarchy and capitalism intact.

The last point demonstrates that the concerns with profit in capitalism and with social control in patriarchy are "inextricably connected" and "cannot be reduced to each other." Capitalism and patriarchy, being mutually reinforcing, become an "integral process" (Eisenstein 1990, p. 134). The conditions in the marketplace affect what goes on in the family in terms of production, reproduction and consumption; conversely, production, reproduction, and consumption in the family affect the production of commodities in the marketplace.

The centrality of the sexual division of labor in maintaining both patriarchy and capitalism has caused both Eisenstein and Hartmann to call for its elimination. Eisenstein argued forcefully that it is this division of labor that must be changed because it is the principal means by which men maintain control. It suggests that the roles and activities that divide men and women are rooted in nature (Eisenstein 1990, p. 140). Eisenstein stated that for conditions to change, women must organize and they can do so by becoming conscious of what they have in common with each other. They may differ in their ties to the marketplace, but their "commonality derives from the particular roles women share in patriarchy. From this commonality begins the feminist struggle" (ibid.). Similarly and even more pointedly, Hartmann believes that both men and women will be better off and more equal only when "we eradicate the socially imposed gender differences between us and, therefore, the very sexual division of labor itself" (1990, p. 170).

One of the great values of seeing capitalism and patriarchy as dual systems is that it encourages us to examine the interlinkage between class and sex in trying to understand the relative roles of men and women in society. Clearly, an individual's position in the general system of inequality is an outcome of the confluence of economic, sexual, and racial/ethnic factors. Understanding the nature of this intersection and its origins will provide us with a more comprehensive and exact explanation of sex inequality. There is no question that women, as a group, are in a unique position in contemporary society. Race, of course, also plays a role in determining the unique position of a group in society.

It is clear from the array of different explanations just presented that there is no agreement on the basic source(s) of sex inequality. It may be asked if there even is a basic set of causes; perhaps the causes vary from culture to culture. Coontz and Henderson (1986) may be right: "The search for origins will never be definitively settled" (p. 27).

SUMMARY

This chapter has documented the historical socioeconomic position of women in the United States. Despite having been consistently involved in the economy, women have generally held lower positions in it. Even in colonial times, women who worked received lower pay even though they made valuable economic contributions, and factory jobs were segregated on the basis of sex. By the beginning of this century, women already dominated certain occupations, although those of higher ethnic and class positions controlled most of the prestigious occupations. Gender roles culturally associated with women (e.g., homemaking, clerical work, etc.) generally are given lower status in our society, resulting in gender inequality. Occupational conditions today still reveal distinct inequalities between men and women. Women (1) are spread over a smaller range of occupations, (2) are less likely to be in positions of authority, (3) are more likely to work in smaller organizations in the peripheral sector of the economy, (4) are more likely to occupy positions with short career ladders, and (5) make less money than men even when they work full time, year round, and have comparable educational levels. A variety of microinequities involving language, popular media and stereotypes, and education also pervade relationships between men and women.

Attempts to account for the inequalities between the sexes suggest that differences in human capital, commitment to the labor force, work effort, and interruptions due to childbearing and rearing do not account substantially for the differences in earnings and occupational placement. The differential arrangement of women and men along the occupational hierarchy is, however, directly related to the discrepancy in earnings between the sexes, especially when we consider the differences in the characteristics of the jobs most often held by men and women.

Broader theories of sex inequality have also been advanced, and we focused on those that are more sociological or anthropological in nature. Among the factors that have been linked with sex inequality are: (1) the cultural association of women with nature and men with culture or society, (2) the position of women in the work organization of society, (3) the hostile or friendly character of the natural environment, (4) capitalism's requirements and women's role in necessary labor, and (5) early patriarchal structures. Women's roles in the domestic and economic public spheres appear to have direct consequences for their overall position in society. It seems reasonable to conclude that in our own society, the demands and expectations of capitalism and traditional or patriarchal views of what is appropriate for men and for women has affected the kinds of occupations and levels of earnings that each of these groups is likely to attain.

CRITICAL THINKING

1. Think about a specific occupation and its likely occupant (e.g., police officer, elementary school teacher, home builder). Does a specific sex come to mind? Why?

2. In your own life, how have sex and gender limited you or allowed you to act a certain way or get involved in particular kinds of ac-

tivities? What was it about your sex or gender that created this effect?

3. Which of the theories presented in the chapter most completely explains sex inequality in the United States? Why? Can you infer from any of the theories what might be done to reduce such inequality?

WEB CONNECTIONS

Employment discrimination and harassment can be based on several characteristics of individuals. Data from the U.S. Equal Employment Opportunity Commission show the extent of discrimination and harassment based on race, sex, and

religion. Which is most frequent? What changes have occurred since 1992? Answer these questions by seeing the site at:

http://www.eeoc.gov/stats/index.html

CHAPTER 5

SEXUAL ORIENTATION
AND INEQUALITY

The greatest debates and ethical dilemmas of our time are about drawing boundaries. This is because placing lines here or there has definite implications for how we treat each other and the world around us.
—Christena E. Nippert-Eng

In the previous chapter, we focused concern on sex and gender and discussed a variety of inequalities that exist between males and females as the two traditionally recognized sexes. In this chapter, we will examine status inequality that results from sexual orientation, principally the inequities associated with being gay or lesbian.

Historically, Western society has viewed sex, gender, and sexuality as dichotomous and interrelated. The conceptual sets of male/female, masculine/feminine, and heterosexuality/homosexuality have been thought to accurately and completely characterize sexual possibilities. Moreover, "normal" men are supposed to be masculine and women feminine and both are supposed to be heterosexual. Further dichotomies in social science, such as public/private, instrumental/expressive, and rational/emotional, have built on these typologies and helped reinforce their perceived legitimacy. The continued emphasis on these dichotomies as "natural" lends them a seemingly timeless and universal quality. Consequently, individuals who do not fit into these neat categories or do not behave in the culturally prescribed manner for their category have been thought of as deviant. Judeo-Christian dogma views normal, moral, and legitimate sex as

having a reproductive function and as belonging in monogamous marriages between men and women, and views same-sex relations as sinful and abnormal (Herdt 1997). Heterosexuality is generally conceived of as being normal, while homosexuality is defined as pathological. But traditional binary categories of sex and related genders are neither timeless, universal, or natural. They are social constructions found only in some societies during specific periods of time.

THE COMPLEXITY OF SEXUALITY
AND GENDER

The simplistic, traditional, either/or categories of male/female, masculine/feminine, and heterosexuality/homosexuality miss much of the variety of actual human experiences (Lorber 1996). While most Westerners think of man and woman as mutually exclusive categories, a number of countries around the world recognize more than two sexes, sexualities, and genders. For example, in traditional Navajo society, *berdaches* were persons who, anatomically, were men, but were considered to be in a third gender and "intersexed." They married individuals who were considered ordinary masculine men, and yet were not considered homosexual. In India, the *hijras,* while male at birth, define themselves as neither men nor women but as a third gender. They wear women's clothing and may marry men. Yet they are not stigmatized, but are thought to exemplify the time-honored Hindu belief that each person possesses both male and female elements. *Hijras* personify this dualism and the valued "ambiguity of in-between sexual categories" (Andersen 1997, pp. 21–22). Another illustration of the complexity of sexuality concerns individuals born biologically as hermaphrodites. At birth, they lack an enzyme that would allow them to develop male genitals and so they are initially defined as female, even though male features begin to develop later during puberty. These "manlike" women are placed in a third sex category (Herdt 1997).

The oversimplified dichotomy of male and female is further demonstrated in studies of *transgendered* individuals—that is, individuals who deviate from the traditional gender binaries of Western society and who sometimes define themselves as belonging to a third gender category (Gagne and Tewksbury 1998). These include individuals who wish to be women or men and who may or may not undergo surgery for sex reassignment. Men who are transsexuals may describe themselves as being heterosexual, bisexual, or lesbian. They are persons whose gender identity is not consistent with their anatomical characteristics. Ironically, a majority of these individuals do not challenge the idea that men should be masculine and women should be feminine. That is, they accept the traditional gender categories. However, they define themselves as women rather than men, and therefore adopt many of those roles and attitudes traditionally associated with women. Some argue that sexual identity involves a variety of elements and thus their combinations can result in multiple possible sexual identities. Among others, these elements include one's biological sex at birth, self-identity of gender, biological sex of partner, and the distribution of masculine and feminine traits in one's personality (Sedgwick 1998). The wide variety of self-identities, gender practices,

and even biological differences found in contemporary society have led a growing number of scholars to urge replacement of the traditional dichotomies of male/female and masculine/feminine with more complex classification systems of sexuality and gender (e.g., Lorber 1996; Andersen 1997; Herdt 1997).

In the discussion that follows, I will concentrate on *homosexual* groups. It appears that while knowledge of same-sex relations goes far back in history, the technical dichotomy of heterosexuality and homosexuality as we know it today is of nineteenth-century origin, that it "is a product of the transition to modernity.... This sexual transformation involved such factors as the institutionalization of bourgeois middle-class values, the secularization of social medicine and state discourse on sexuality, the individualized concept of desire and identity, and the premium placed on reproduction within the nuclear family" (Herdt 1997, p. 39). At that time, homosexuality was considered abnormal and a disease, a kind of degeneracy from the healthy condition of heterosexuality. In fact, up until the early 1970s, homosexuality was listed as a mental illness by the American Psychiatric Association (APA). Recent studies indicate that homosexuality *itself* is not a good predictor of mental illness. Child gender identity disorder and transsexualism are still formally listed as mental disorders by the American Psychiatric Association (Bailey 1996).

Despite evidence to the contrary, and even after its removal from its list as an illness by the APA, some psychoanalysts and Christian counselors continue to view homosexuality as a pathological condition (Gonsiorek 1996). In each of the traditional dichotomies of male/female, masculine/feminine, and heterosexual/homosexual, one category has been given higher social status in the United States over the other. In the case of the last, heterosexuality is valued and honored over homosexuality. Influential public figures such as Senate Majority Leader Trent Lott and professional football legend Reggie White, for example, have denounced homosexuality as immoral and avoidable. Lott has likened homosexuality to the addictions of alcoholism and kleptomania (Newport 1998).

PUBLIC OPINIONS ON HOMOSEXUALITY

The preceding comments suggest that there continues to be a deeply held view among some national figures that homosexuality is unnatural and unhealthy, if not immoral. When one adds to this the strong negative reaction to homosexuality by staunchly religious groups, it is not surprising that, up until the early decades of the twentieth century in the United States, gay networks tried to avoid harassment by keeping out of the public eye. In the mid-twentieth century, the anti-alien crusades of Senator Joseph McCarthy and FBI director J. Edgar Hoover as well as city police across the country continued to single out gays and lesbians as legitimate targets who were thought to undermine the heterosexual family as a cultural foundation. These attacks were viewed as legitimate because of the legal status of homosexuality. "Homosexual acts were illegal in most states under existing anti-sodomy statutes.... Furthermore, gays and lesbians were specifically excluded from laws and policies regulating fair employment practices, housing discrimination, rights of child custody, immigration, inheritance, security clearances, public accommodations, and police protection" (Button, Rienzo, and Wald 1997, p. 24).

Despite the appearance of a slight decline in the 1990s, national surveys of adults since the 1960s suggest that just under two-thirds of U.S. adults believe that homosexual relations are wrong. Somewhat smaller majorities believe that homosexuality is not "an acceptable alternative lifestyle" and is "morally wrong" (Yang 1997; Gallup 1997). Consequently, a solid majority does not think that marriages between homosexuals or their option to adopt children should be legalized. There are, however, some signs of improvement in attitudes toward homosexuals. A much smaller proportion of adults viewed themselves as being "very unsympathetic" toward homosexuals in the mid-1990s than in the mid-1980s, the percentage falling from 46 percent in 1983 to 16 percent in 1994. Acceptance of homosexuals in broad terms appears to have increased. But when homosexuality comes close to home, acceptance is much less likely. If told by a child that he or she was homosexual, a large majority of parents would be highly disturbed (ibid.).

Many adults may not like homosexuality, but that does not mean they advocate discrimination against homosexuals as a group. With respect to *specific* economic areas of civil rights, there does appear to be an increase in the percentage of those who would not exclude homosexuals from teaching, sales, medical, clerical, and political professions. In most cases, this includes a majority of those sampled. The public appears to be split on allowing gays and lesbians to serve in the military, but most recent polls suggest that close to a majority may be in favor of their participation. In general, over 75 percent of adults feel that homosexuals should have equal job and housing opportunities. At the same time, however, a majority contend that homosexuals, as opposed to women and racial minorities, should not be explicitly covered under *broad* civil rights laws (ibid.).

Not all subcategories of adults are equally likely to hold positive or negative attitudes about homosexuals, however. One should be cautious in drawing conclusions on this matter because most studies have involved either small, student, or nonrandom samples. There are also fewer studies of lesbians than gay men, perhaps suggesting a gender bias. Nevertheless, several research patterns emerge that suggest systematic variations in prejudice against homosexuality. Those who believe that it is something one is born with or cannot be changed are more sympathetic toward homosexuals than are those who view it as a chosen lifestyle (Button, Rienzo, and Wald 1997). Men appear to be more prejudiced against homosexuals than women on a variety of dimensions. They are more hostile (1) toward homosexuals as *individuals,* especially when this involves gays rather than lesbians; (2) toward homosexual *behavior;* and (3) toward *civil rights* for gays in traditionally masculine roles such as service in the military (Kite and Whitley 1998). In addition to gender, education is also related to homophobia, with more education being associated with lower degrees of prejudice. Within educational institutions, students in the arts and social sciences are more positive in their attitudes than are those majoring in business or science (Schellenberg et al. 1999). Among age groups, a greater proportion of those age 65 or older are prejudiced, compared to those under 30 years of age. This may be partially accounted for by the generally lower education and greater religious traditionalism among older adults. Not unexpectedly, political conservatism and right-wing authoritarianism have also been found to be linked to hostility toward homosexuality. "Right-wing authoritarians" are individuals who adhere to "the traditional family structure and feel threatened by liberalization and individuals who threaten their conventional values" (Haddock and Zanna 1998, p. 85). Relatedly, conservative religious groups have demonstrated their opposition to homosexuality by being in the forefront of battles against gay rights' policies around the country.

A recent survey of gay rights ordinances in 126 communities identified evangelical, charismatic churches as most likely to oppose gay-rights legislation (Button, Rienzo, and Wald 1997). This includes Black evangelical groups as well. Within the Black community, the heritage of seeking justice and supporting the underdog coexists with more conservative social attitudes which, in turn, are tied to fundamentalist religious beliefs. The result has been a wide variation in the attitudes of Blacks to homosexual issues. The survey also identified communities with gay-rights ordinances as being (1) larger and growing, with (2) higher average incomes and educational levels, (3) lower median age, and (4) greater proportions of Blacks and nonfamily households in the populations, than communities that do not have such legislation. The South is less likely to be supportive of homosexual rights than other regions. These results are consistent with those found in other surveys. Individuals with lower incomes and education, who are older and from the South and

rural areas are more likely to feel that homosexuality is morally evil (Newport 1998).

In most cases, these variables interact with others in individuals to either intensify or weaken antagonism toward homosexuals. Sherrod and Nardi's 1998 three-year study of 3,542 mock jurors in 15 states sought to identify characteristics of individuals who are most likely to be biased against persons who were either gay or lesbian. Using an established homophobia scale that tapped the extent of personal prejudice and beliefs about homosexual rights in a variety of areas, the researchers developed profiles of those most likely to be antihomosexual as jurors. They found that White and Latino males were the most homophobic, and Latina and White females the least. Black males and females were in the middle. Generally, the most important predictors of homophobia were found to be political conservatism and the absence of close homosexual friends. As Figure 5.1 shows, within each racial and gender group certain types of individuals were most likely to harbor such hostility.

The attitudes adults hold about homosexuals are at least moderately related to stereotypes held about them. These stereotypes include beliefs about gays' personality traits, behavior, and physical characteristics. Popular stereotypes of gays and lesbians suggest that negative reactions to them are due in part to the fact that they are seen as violating traditional gender rules about behavior and interests. The hostility toward men who violate masculine roles appears to be stronger than that toward women who violate feminine prescriptions (Kite and Whitley 1998). Stereotypes about gay men, for instance, suggest that they are viewed as being feminine, emotional, security-seeking, neat, interested in fine arts, creative, with high-pitched voices (see Simon 1998 for a summary). In her multimethod study among Rutgers University students, Stephanie Madon found that there are also subtypes within stereotypes of gay men. On the one hand, they are generally viewed as possessing some positive feminine personality traits (e.g., compassionate, gentle), while on the other hand, they are seen as violating masculine

Under a mass of balloons, 10,000 to 12,000 proponents of homosexual rights march down Beacon Street during the 11th annual "Gay and Lesbian Pride Day" in Boston.

roles (e.g., "walk like girls," "transvestites"). Of these two components, it is their violation of traditional masculine roles that is more strongly held in popular stereotypes, and it is this dimension of the stereotype that may be most clearly linked to prejudice against gay men (Madon 1997). Stereotypes about lesbians, like those of gay men, contain violations of traditional feminine roles in featuring many masculine traits. Lesbians are characterized as being independent and independently minded, open and loud, stubborn, and not being good for children.

Labeling an individual as having the traits of either of these stereotypes, and therefore as being automatically lesbian or gay, can have significant consequences. Consider the case of Sara Harb Quiroz, a permanent and employed U.S. resident

who, on her way back into Texas from Juarez, Mexico, was stopped by an immigration agent (Luibheid 1998). Evidence indicated that she was stopped because her appearance revealed several masculine characteristics. She wore pants and a shirt instead of a dress and her hair was cut "abnormally" short for a female. Ms. Quiroz may or may not have been a lesbian.

Since as late as 1990, lesbian immigrants could be refused entry into the United States, and conscious attempts were made by border agents to identify lesbians. They looked for visible cues to the individual's sexual preference. Lesbian immigrants were often aware of this kind of screening, so they dressed and prepared themselves physically so that they would not appear to violate traditional images of what a woman *should* look like. This is

FIGURE 5.1   Characteristics of Potential Jurors within Selected Groups Who Are
Most Homophobic

White men	No homosexual friends, traditional in values, actively religious, politically conservative, Protestant, from the South
Latino men	No homosexual friends, conservative, guided by religious values, military veterans
Black women	Actively religious, politically conservative, no close homosexual friends, do not read newspaper regularly
Black men	No close homosexual friends, conservative, traditional in values, do not read magazines regularly
Latina women	No close homosexual friends, guided by religious beliefs in daily life, married, conservative, traditional in values
White women	Politically conservative, religious in daily life, no close homosexual friends, live in South, traditional in values, attends religious services regularly, do not read newspaper regularly, have high school or less education, believe in fate

Source: Based on Sherrod and Nardi 1998, pp. 32–35.

known as "straightening up," which "includes practices like growing one's hair and nails, buying a dress, accessorizing, and donning makeup.... [The fact that one has to do this only] confirmed the 'bug'-like status of lesbians within the immigration system" (Luibheid 1998, pp. 485–486).

HOMOSEXUALS AS A STATUS GROUP

As the surveys just discussed indicate, homosexuals, like women and Blacks, form a status category with low prestige or social honor in the United States. As such, they possess all the core attributes of status groups. Most notably, they are subjectively viewed by others as sharing certain lifestyle characteristics while being qualitatively different from outsiders. Being gay or lesbian is associated with having certain kinds of occupations (e.g., hairdresser) and dress (high fashion, artsy) (Madon 1997). However, their differences are defined as even deeper. Recall that in his depiction of status groups, Max Weber argued that extreme status separation between groups is most likely if the differences that separate them are thought of as being "ethnic" in nature. Consistent with this conception, gay scholar Stephen Murray has referred to the homosexual community as a "quasi-ethnic group" (1996, p. 4). This suggests

that the differences must be viewed as fundamental, almost biological in nature, for castelike arrangements to develop between groups. Indeed, depending on the survey used, somewhere between one-third and one-half of U.S. adults currently believe that homosexuality is either biologically based or something with which one is born that cannot be changed (cf., e.g., Yang 1997; Newport 1998). In their fight for political legitimacy and equal rights, the earliest gay-rights organizations in the United States (e.g., the Mattachine Society) characterized "homosexuals as a sexual minority, similar to other ethnic and cultural minorities" (Button, Rienzo, and Wald 1997, p. 25). Those currently at the forefront of the gay-rights movement also "argue that homosexual orientation is a genetic condition like skin color or gender" (Newport 1998, p. 14).

The latter comment is quite revealing because in the case of each of the three principally involved groups implied in the statement (i.e., homosexuals, Blacks, women), fundamental values are at stake. Specifically, sexual orientation, race, and gender are each controversial and sensitive areas of conflict. They are touchstones for battles in the United States over basic values involving sexual behavior, racial superiority, and appropriate gender roles. Since these are important matters in

U.S. society, it should be expected that status boundaries should separate those who fall on different sides of these values.

In addition to being viewed as qualitatively different in lifestyle, being seen as a different "kind" of people, separated from the rest of society, and occupying a distinctive place on a hierarchy of social honor or prestige, a status group is also perceived as having an internal social cohesion that unites them. That is, they are seen as sticking together and being mutually supportive of each other. As with most status groups, outsiders lump them all together, even though there are sources of internal division, such as race, within the homosexual community. On the other hand, given that the crucial factor of sexual orientation is what divides them from and is the prime basis for conflict with outsiders, it is defense involving this factor that helps to unite them. Not only has this resulted in the creation of informal friendship networks among gays and lesbians, but also in the development of neighborhoods with high concentrations of homosexuals, separate institutions catering to a homosexual clientele, and political-rights organizations.

Finally, what further marks homosexuals as a negatively defined status group are fears of contamination and contact on the part of outsiders. Concerns about purity on the part of traditionalists and heterosexuals are indicative of concerted attempts to keep boundaries between heterosexuals and homosexuals intact. Publically known association by a heterosexual with homosexuals, especially of a personal kind, creates the risk that some of the ostracism held for homosexuals may "rub off" on the individual. The recent murder involving guests on Jenny Jones's television show is a good example of the stigmatization felt by a man who had been connected to a gay acquaintance. In front of live and national audiences, the gay guest professed his love for the man. The man later killed his gay friend because he felt "humiliated" by this profession of love (Turner 1999).

Fear of association is also suggested by polls that indicate that less than 10 percent of U.S. adults feel warmhearted about gays and lesbians and less than a one-third feel homosexual couples should be allowed to adopt children (Yang 1997). This is despite the fact that concerns that homosexuals are more likely than heterosexuals to be sexual predators on unsuspecting children or that children who are raised by gays or lesbians will be damaged or turn out to be homosexuals themselves are simply not supported by evidence (Andersen 1997). Still, these beliefs persist in part because they are consistent with prevailing stereotypes and help justify hostile treatment of homosexuals. In their campaigns, opponents of gay rights often use "lurid stereotypes of gays as child molesters, sources of disease, and an abomination in the eyes of God" (Button, Rienzo, and Wald 1997, p. 195). It is feared that unless gays and lesbians are held in check, traditional morality and family structure as foundations of our society will become contaminated and seriously weakened. In the eyes of these opponents, social, cultural, and moral purity must be maintained, and contamination avoided at all costs.

A SOCIOECONOMIC PROFILE OF HOMOSEXUALS

Like data on the wealthy, we do not know very much about the actual socioeconomic position, or even the number of homosexuals, because many still fear "coming out" and can remain hidden because of the generally lower visibility of sexual orientation compared to one's race and sex. This alone tells us a great deal about the stigma attached to being homosexual. Moreover, the measurements of homosexuality have varied wildly. Persons who have sex with others of the same gender do not necessarily define themselves as homosexuals, nor are individuals who have had a homosexual experience at one time or another necessarily thought of as homosexuals. The *invisibility* of homosexuals in society is a key feature differentiating this group from those based on gender and race. On one hand, it provides a group that the majority may attack without concern regarding damage to family and friends who are unknown members of the group. On the other hand, the invisibility of homosexuals prevents young gays and lesbians from finding local positive role models and supporters. The unique invisibility aspect of homosexuals as a group is revealed by reference to the military's "don't ask don't tell" Policy which, if applied to Blacks, would basically say it is acceptable to be Black and in the military as long as one does not identify oneself as such.

These problems of stigma, invisibility, and measurement make it difficult to agree on the size of the homosexual population. Some estimates have put the figure as high as 10 percent, but that is considered by some to be too high. A national survey of sexual practices suggested that about 2.4 percent of men and 1.3 percent of women (1) consider themselves homosexual or bisexual, (2) have same-sex partners, and (3) are attracted to homosexuality (Laumann et al. 1994). The percentage in the largest cities is much higher, however, closer to 11 percent. The proportions found in these cities are seven times greater than those found in rural areas (Herdt 1997). This may help account for the regional differences in prejudice against homosexuals discussed earlier. Education is also related to the incidence of homosexuality, with those in the college ranks being more likely than those with less education to have had homosexual experiences. This relationship is stronger for women than for men, however (Laumann et al. 1994).

Not only are estimates of the extent of homosexuality relatively scarce but there have also been very few attempts to assess the socioeconomic condition of gays and lesbians. Christopher Hewitt (1995) recently brought together much of the gay information on this issue drawn from national surveys, samples of gays, and obituaries. He also admitted that "available data are somewhat limited, and all surveys are probably biased by the unwillingness of some gays to disclose their sexual identity" (p. 462). Consequently, the data presented here should be interpreted as being estimates rather than exact figures.

The evidence cited by Hewitt indicates that gay men are more likely to be self-employed than other men and to be in the labor force, probably because of the greater likelihood that they are younger and single. With respect to the distribution among occupations of gay men, information from different sources reveals the same kinds of patterns. First, gay men are not as broadly distributed along the full range of occupations as are heterosexual men. Like minorities and women, they tend to be concentrated in a smaller number of occupations. Second, the concentration is especially great within white-collar occupations. A much greater proportion of gay men than heterosexual men are in white-collar, higher status jobs. Well over half of gay men are in managerial, administrative, "artistic-creative," or "nurturant" occupations, the latter category referring to traditionally female jobs in which a customer or client receives a face-to-face service of some kind. Under 10 percent are in blue-collar occupations. Third, within broad white-collar categories, there are concentrations of gay men in specific occupations. Although frequently based on small samples, it has been estimated that a disproportionate number of male artists, hairdressers, librarians, architects, entertainers, and fashion designers are gay. Although gay men are heavily overrepresented in these fields, they appear to be very underrepresented in quintessentially "male" occupations such as the military, business, law, and sports (Hewitt 1995). Again, this information must be treated with caution because of the problems of data collection noted earlier.

It has been suggested that concentrations of gay men in particular kinds of occupations are linked to several factors, including discrimination and networking. The hostility expressed by the military establishment to President Clinton's proposal that gays freely be allowed to enter the military suggests the homophobia involved in discrimination. In fact, despite this attempt by Clinton to lessen discrimination, there have been more gays coerced into leaving the military since the "don't ask, don't tell" policy was installed in 1994. In 1998, 1,145 members of the military were forced out of service, compared to 617 members in 1994 ("Bigotry in the Military" 1999). Networking and connections are important. As noted by Murray (1996):

In most places the prototypically masculine occupation of construction worker requires knowing someone to get him into the union or hired by a patron (foreman or employer) at a nonunionized site. Obtaining a position in what hairdressers consider a good salon similarly depends upon personal sponsorship from inside. In any field, there is routine insider trading of information about job vacancies and even secrecy about them. Therefore, any concentration...is likely to be replicated and reinforced over time. (p. 159)

Given that gay men are more likely to be in higher-prestige, white-collar positions than other men, it should not be surprising to find that their average incomes are also higher. Surveys suggest that gay males have incomes several thousand dollars higher than those of heterosexual males, including those who are White (Murray 1996).

Surveys reveal some broad similarities among gay men, but this does not mean that there are no significant internal differences in this population. One of the problems of being viewed as a separate status group is that outsiders tend to see everyone within that group as being essentially the same. This is the case for women, professors, Blacks, the Amish, and other status groups—including homosexuals. Yet, as in any large group, there are significant differences and conflicts among homosexuals. In addition to differences in attitudes toward and identification with homosexuality within the gay and lesbian communities, alienation often exists between those who consider themselves working class and those in higher-status occupations. Race has also been a divisive factor. Ethnic lesbian groups have formed as a reaction against the whiteness of established lesbian organizations and as a desire to celebrate distinct ethnic backgrounds. Generational differences in attitudes and lifestyle also appear to exist (Murray 1996). The fact that older lesbians and gay men grew up in and had to develop mechanisms to survive the significant difficulties of living in a society that has been broadly and actively hostile toward homosexuality may help account for the high degree of self-acceptance and satisfaction among them (Jacobson and Grossman 1996).

NEGATIVE CONSEQUENCES OF STIGMATIZATION

As an ostracized status group, homosexuals have historically experienced a wide variety of systematic stresses and obstacles in the United States, ranging from psychological difficulties, to personal physical attacks, to institutional and legal discrimination. While the eighteenth-century extreme reaction of legally putting persons to death because of their homosexuality no longer exists, physical victimization has been experienced at one time or another by almost all gay men and lesbians (Button, Rienzo, and Wald 1997). In this section, I will touch on three significant consequences of being homosexual: minority stress, family rights, and suicide. A brief discussion of hate crimes is included in Chapter 12.

Minority Stress

The stigma placed on homosexuality exposes gay men and lesbians to a wide array of stresses ranging from everyday microinequities, such as slurs and constant sensitivity to not be too obvious in one's identity, to problems in their families, religious practice, and the labor market. The stresses themselves, in turn, affect health and feelings of well-being, having been related, for instance, to recurrent headaches, depressive moods, and more serious psychological conditions. In the case of women and minorities who are homosexual, these stresses can be intensified because of their added status as gender and ethnic/racial minorities (DiPlacido 1998). The negative labeling of same-sex intimacy and the consequent uneasiness among some homosexuals about their own behavior and feelings can also lead to problems in developing and maintaining intimate relationships, and greater stress and adjustment problems in general (Meyer and Dean 1998).

During school years, when boys are dating, and are culturally expected to date girls, homosexual youths find themselves at a psychological and social disadvantage. These same expectations apply to everyone. A lesbian recalls from her youth:

"Love of women was never a possibility that I even realized could be. You loved your mother and your aunts, and you had girlfriends for a while. Someday, though, you would always meet a man" (quoted in Savin-Williams 1996, p. 170). A gay youth remembers experiencing a similar plight: "Throughout high school and college I had no way to meet people of the same sex and sexual orientation. These were more years of isolation and secrecy. I saw what other guys my age did, listened to what they said and how they felt. I was expected to be part of a world with which I had nothing in common" (ibid.). Gay youths may experience the stress of their family's bigotry because of their invisibility, unlike Black children whose status is obvious and generally the same as that of their parents and siblings. All of these consequences exist on the personal and interactional level, but stresses that result from the homosexual label exist on the institutional level as well.

In employment, up until the late 1960s, some occupations—such as those in law, education, medicine, and the military—were not open to homosexuals in most of the United States. Evidence suggests that one-third of gays have experienced discrimination in employment (Button, Rienzo, and Wald 1997). Even now, despite President Clinton's attempts to make the military more open for gay men, harassment and footdragging in making the institution more hospitable for gays continue. I have already discussed the hostility of some Christian religious groups toward homosexuality. It is viewed by them as a sin and abomination in the eyes of God. These beliefs serve to justify, and even encourage, hostility toward homosexuals. Interestingly, religious beliefs, such as the "curse of Ham," that were used to justify and encourage racism against Blacks in the past have diminished, leaving gays and lesbians as a religious target.

Marriage and the Family

Marriage protects couples both politically and economically. In addition to sanctioning parenting, legal recognition of the relationship between two individuals allows each of them to benefit from the other's social security and pension participation. Existing tax and probate rules similarly favor those whose relationships are sanctioned by the state. Such has not been the case with gay and lesbian couples because, up until the early 1980s, homosexual relationships were not recognized anywhere in the United States (Rubenstein 1996). The difficulties of not having legally recognized relationships were made much more apparent later in the 1980s, when same-sex couples ran into conflicts with hospital regulations and partner's families attempting to take care of partners who had serious health problems or were dying of AIDS. The case of Sharon Kowalski and Karen Thompson helped focus attention on and galvanize support for addressing the problems faced by these couples. Kowalski was left seriously disabled as a result of a major car accident, and her partner fought Kowalski's biological family for nine years so that she could be appointed legal guardian (ibid.).

Upon the death of a partner, a gay or lesbian person is also left vulnerable to attacks over estate issues by the decedent's family. Because they are not legally married, gay and lesbian individuals who are in a relationship cannot receive their partner's social security checks after the latter dies. Thus, experts suggest that these individuals need to put more care and money than usual into their retirement plans. "The tax code, the investment process, and the probate process is hostile to the retirement needs of gays and lesbians.... Retirement planning for gays is even more critical because they face so many obstacles. It's not uncommon for hostile blood relatives to launch—and win—nasty court battles over ownership of assets after death" ("Nest-Egg Planning" 1997, p. 84). Although "domestic partnerships" are recognized in some places and organizations, the battle for legal recognition of same-sex couples goes on (Rubenstein 1996).

Suicide

Homophobia, social isolation, self-blame, and other stresses can have dire outcomes for the individuals who are victims of these conditions. Reviews of research suggest that gay and lesbian youths are two to three times more likely to attempt suicide than their heterosexual counterparts. It has been fairly typical for studies of homosexual youths to cite suicide attempt rates of 20 to 40 percent (Savin-Williams and Cohen 1996; D'Augelli 1998). Adolescence has its own set of stressful events, and when adding homosexuality to these, its problems are intensified.

However, suicide attempt rates are not spread evenly over this minority population. Gays and lesbians most likely to attempt or seriously think about suicide tend to (1) be younger, (2) be victims of physical assault, (3) feel more confused about sexual identity, (4) have lower self-esteem, (5) have more family problems, and (6) recently "come out" or have been exposed as homosexual (ibid.). It has also been suggested that gays and lesbians who are members of a racial or ethnic minority may be more vulnerable to these problems because of the singular problems they face as both racial/ethnic and sexual minorities (Savin-Williams and Rodriguez 1993).

Despite the obvious need for various kinds of social support for these individuals, however, the seeking out and offering of such support is problematic because of the demeaned social status of gays and lesbians in U.S. society. Homosexual youths find themselves between a rock and a hard place. On the one hand, they may be willing to seek out individuals who might be able to help, but at the same time, they may be unwilling to risk rejection or reveal their problems because of the stigma attached to the homosexual label. Finally, the invisibility of the homosexual group presents a further barrier for youths who are seeking a support network or role model to guide them through a difficult period.

SUMMARY

This chapter has presented a brief overview of the inequities involved in being homosexual rather than heterosexual in sexual orientation. The concept of homosexuality has served to single out and stigmatize a group that does not fit dominant cultural ideas about appropriate sexual behavior and lifestyles. Although sympathy and opinions in specific areas of civil rights appear to have improved in recent years, significant proportions and subgroups within the United States continue to be hostile to homosexuality. Stereotypes for both gay men and lesbians continue, and they continue to be a minority with distinct status-group attributes, yet without the legal protections afforded other minority groups.

Because of the difficulties involved for homosexuals and the disregard in which they have been held, reliable and thorough statistics on this group are nonexistent. Estimates about the size of the homosexual population and its characteristics vary from study to study. Lack of knowledge about this community can only help to reinforce existing stereotypes about them. The consequences for individuals in this group are momentous. Few areas of their lives are left untouched; psychological, economic, social, legal, and health problems arise from their position as a stigmatized status group.

CRITICAL THINKING

1. What would be the social consequences if everyone accepted the belief that sexual variation is a continuum rather than a dichotomy (i.e., if we believed that there are many more than two sexes)?

2. How does the invisibility of being homosexual affect the homosexual individual and the status image of homosexuals as a group?

3. Specifically, what needs to change for homosexuals to be accommodated in U.S. society? Are homosexuals in the same position as other demeaned status groups based on race or ethnicity?

WEB CONNECTIONS

We know relatively little about gay and lesbian communities. The result is that stereotypes and misinformation flourish. To get a list of gay and lesbian groups in different states and on campuses, see:

http://www.ngltf.org/ngltflink.html

To learn more about faulty thinking on the alleged relationships between sexual orientation, mental health, and child molestation, review the information at the University of California, Davis site. Research by noted scholar Gregory Herek and others provide evidence that test homophobic thinking. How do these data break stereotypes? Find out at:

http://psychology.ucdavis.edu/rainbow/

CHAPTER 6

RACIAL AND ETHNIC INEQUALITY

The social problems of urban life in the United States are, in large measure, the problems of racial inequality.
—William Julius Wilson

The positions of women and minorities are often thought to have a lot in common. Certainly, both groups tend to be in lower socioeconomic positions than White males. Moreover, as mentioned in Chapter 4, race and sex have both been associated with biological differences that have been given social and cultural meanings. Both groups have also been referred to as castes vis-à-vis White males. But despite these broad and sometimes superficial similarities between racial minorities and women, there are distinct differences in their histories and socioeconomic conditions.

RACE, ETHNICITY, AND INEQUALITY IN THE UNITED STATES: A BRIEF HISTORY

The problems of race relations continue to simmer and frequently boil over into violence in the United States. The brutal murder in 1998 of James Byrd, Jr., who was dragged to his death behind a pickup truck driven by a White supremacist, is a disturbing reminder that Black Americans are still considered by some to be of a lesser status than Whites. "Color prejudice," which W. E. B. DuBois (1969) called the "problem of the twentieth century," threatens to become the "problem of the twenty-first century" as well. The unequal treatment of racial minorities in the United States goes back to the early years of colonization and even before to English views about African Americans.

Anglo-Saxon colonists' earliest contact with a visibly different group were with American Indians. Ideas and stereotypes of the "savage" had developed in the sixteenth and seventeenth centuries and provided colonists with a framework within which to interpret American Indians. Rather than color or racial distinction, religious and ethnocentric criteria were used initially to separate groups into superior and inferior categories. Specifically, distinctions were made between "Christians" and "heathens" and between "civilized" and "savage" (Fredrickson 1981). Clearly, the American Indians were placed in the heathen and savage categories. Thus, distinct attitudes about this group were entrenched by the time the American Revolution occurred.

Despite these beliefs, early relations between colonists and American Indians were frequently cooperative since both groups were interested in trade and barter. In fact, American Indians frequently had quite a bit of power when it came to bargaining because of their prowess in the fur trade (Lurie 1982). But this cooperation was short-lived. Relationships with the British became increasingly belligerent, since the British were farmers and interested in obtaining American Indian land, whereas the French were primarily traders (Garbarino 1976). The American Indians whose economy emphasized agriculture and who were located near the coast were the first to be overwhelmed by the colonists (Lurie 1982).

In order for the colonists to spread their civilization, land held by American Indians had to be obtained. Many of the latter resided in villages and cultivated crops in a manner not very different from the traditional European way. But arguments about the savage and heathen way of life of American Indians were used as devices to justify taking over this land. Many of the arguments were similar to those used to justify slavery (Farley 1988). The belief was that such action would rescue the earth from these savages and speed progress and Christianity (Fredrickson 1981). This is an early instance of a group using an ideology to justify the taking of economic resources from another.

In the period roughly between 1880 and 1930, over 65 percent of the 138 million acres that had been held by American Indians moved to White ownership (Carlson and Colburn 1972). By the last decade of the nineteenth century, most American Indians were on reservations where they were forbidden to practice their religions and their children were forced to go to boarding schools run by Whites where they had to speak English (Farley 1988). Much of the policy of this period was aimed at forcing American Indians to assimilate into the dominant White culture (Marden and Meyer 1973). Nevertheless, they were not allowed to vote since they were not considered citizens. The Constitution had never actively incorporated concerns for the rights of these groups, and it was not until the 1920s that American Indians were granted citizenship. Even as late as the 1920s and 1930s, there was a feeling among some influential individuals that American Indians were biologically inferior to White Anglo-Saxons (Carlson and Colburn 1972). The consequences of this poor treatment bore bitter fruit.

In the 1920s, the death rate of American Indians was actually greater than their birth rate, and in the 1960s, their life expectancy was still only 47 years old. The Termination Act of 1953 aimed at removing American Indian dependency from the federal government, but it did so by cutting back and eventually eliminating needed health, educational, and other services, which proved to be a disaster for these people (Schaefer 1988). While their numbers grew to about 1.9 million in 1990, American Indians at that time were considered the poorest group in the nation.

> American Indians have the highest infant-mortality rate, the shortest life span, the poorest housing, the poorest transportation, the lowest per-capita income, and the lowest level of education in the nation.... 40 percent of those on reservations lived below the poverty level.... No ethnic group in America has lower average income than the Indians. Suicide and alcoholism are epidemic. The rate of alcohol-related deaths among Indians is 5.6 times that of the general population. (Williams 1987, p. 29)

In 1990, family median income was lower and poverty rates higher among American Indians than those found among Whites or Blacks (U.S. Bureau of the Census 1998b). The reservation system, which is a kind of exile and permanent dependency, has only intensified these problems (Williams 1987).

In reviewing the history of their relationship with the dominant group, it is clear that several things contributed to the development of American Indians as a minority group—for example, (1) the nature of the initial contact between them and the latter group, (2) the battle over scarce and valuable resources such as land, (3) early ethnocentric and prejudicial attitudes, and (4) a discrepancy in the amount of power held by each group (O'Sullivan and Wilson 1988; Noel 1968). The competition between the groups was over resources, the seizure of American Indian land was justified by stereotypes and beliefs about "savages," and the greater power of the colonists served to solidify their ranking as a higher stratum.

Black/White Inequality in History

Land in early America was plentiful but greater labor power was needed to take full advantage of its resources. The absence of large numbers of willing free laborers led to attempts to obtain forced labor that could be justified on ideological or philosophical grounds. American Indians were difficult to subdue and were a potential major threat since they were familiar with the country-side and could put up fierce resistance. On the other hand, large-scale, prolonged use of inden-tured White servants was unrealistic because they were freed after a period of servitude. This made the importation of non-White slave labor attrac-tive. It created a large labor pool of workers who did not know the land, and it helped to elevate all Whites to a higher status (Fredrickson 1981). A major difference in the initial contacts, of course, was that whereas colonists conquered American Indians and annexed their land, in initial Black/White contact, it was a case of involuntary immi-gration (O'Sullivan and Wilson 1988).

Moreover, this treatment of African Ameri-cans could be justified on ideological grounds. Even before the English colonized America, they had a negative view of Blacks. "Blackness was synonymous with filth, foulness, and evil" (Feld-stein 1972, p. 13; see also Carlson and Colburn 1972). Many of the images that had been associ-ated with American Indians—viewing them as savages, animalistic, and so forth—were imposed on African Americans. It also has been argued that the un-Christian character and what was per-ceived as the uncivilized nature of African Ameri-cans may have been more significant in justifying their use as slaves than the fact that they were Black. But, late in the seventeenth century, there was a movement to make slaves of all those with a heathen *ancestry,* thus fostering the notion of *race* as a basis for slavery (Fredrickson 1981). The conviction that these were uncivilized heathens promoted the conclusion that African Americans were basically different from the colonists. Later, especially in the first half of the nineteenth cen-tury, a systematic argument about the *racial* infe-riority of Blacks developed, even though there was a general feeling about the inferiority of Blacks well before that time (Praeger 1987; Fredrickson 1971). Science often lent credence to

Two American Indian boys climb the bare branches of a small tree while playing in the yard of a home in an arid terrain.

such views by its insistence on the biological and genetic inequality of the races (Gossett 1963).

Given these views about Blacks, it is not sur-prising that the early colonies passed laws banning sexual mixing and intermarriage. Children of mixed parentage were considered Black (Fredrick-son 1981). Even though several thousand African Americans fought in the Continental Army, at the Constitutional Convention it was decided that a Black man was only three-fifths of a man. Al-though Thomas Jefferson is associated with the belief that "all men are created equal," he owned 180 slaves when he died and thought of Blacks as inferior to Whites: "I advance it therefore as a sus-picion only, that the Blacks, whether originally a distinct race, or made distinct by time and circumstances, are inferior to the Whites, in the endowments both of body and mind" (quoted in Feldstein 1972, pp. 52–53). Beliefs in the different endowments helped to justify slavery. After all, inhuman treatment could be tolerated if the members of a race were not considered fully human.

At the time of the first official census in 1790, the Black population was approximately 757,000 of whom almost 700,000 were slaves. The Black population grew to almost 4.5 million in 1860, of whom 89 percent were slaves. Between 1790 and 1860, about 90 percent of all Blacks in each census were slaves. Even though the slave trade was officially outlawed in 1808, it still flourished along the long east coast of the country (U.S. Bureau of the Census 1979; Schaefer 1988). In 1790, 23 percent of all families had slaves, while in 1850, 10 percent of families owned them. Most of these owned only a small number, the average being seven to nine slaves per family (U.S. Bureau of the Census 1979).

The system of inequality that developed between the races during the heyday of slavery up to the Civil War was essentially a caste system. Laws forbade Blacks to (1) intermarry with Whites, (2) vote, (3) testify against Whites in legal cases, (4) own firearms, (5) use abusive language against Whites, (6) own property unless permitted by a master, (7) leave the plantation without permission or disobey a curfew, (8) make a will or inherit property, and (9) have anyone teach them to read, write, or give them books (Blackwell 1985; Schaefer 1988; Fredrickson 1981; Elkins 1959; Franklin 1980).

The end of the Civil War, Emancipation, and Reconstruction did not end the misery for Blacks, and in fact, appear to have done little to change their caste relationship with Whites (Turner, Singleton, and Musick 1984). Legal, intellectual, economic, and population changes were occurring that provided support for continued discrimination against Blacks. The Jim Crow laws in the South and beliefs about the inferior nature of Blacks, along with increased labor competition from a continuously rising number of White immigrants from all parts of Europe, conspired to keep Blacks

in a lower socioeconomic position. Lynchings increased in the latter part of the nineteenth century. IQ tests, developed as early as the 1890s, were erroneously used to test native intelligence, and then used to demonstrate the intellectual inferiority of Blacks. This occurred even though some of the early inventors of such measures cautioned against using them for this purpose (Gossett 1963). Social Darwinism, an intellectual application of the notions of the "survival of the fittest" and "natural selection" to whole groups and societies, provided another basis to explain the differences in the accomplishments of the races (Turner, Singleton, and Musick 1984).

Racist feelings were fueled by several events during this period. The rising number of immigrants from Europe, especially eastern Europe, in the latter decades of the nineteenth century and the early twentieth century helped to create a fear on the part of some that the White race was in danger of being extinguished. The Eugenics Movement of the early twentieth century also argued that Blacks could not serve as builders of the country, but could only serve to threaten its progress (Carlson and Colburn 1972). World War I and the Russian Revolution of 1917 with its attendant "Red Scare" only helped to bolster a hatred for individuals of different nationalities and races. During and immediately after World War I, membership in the Ku Klux Klan grew dramatically (Johnson 1976). Black southern migration to the industrializing North during and after World War I resulted in severe clashes between Black and White workers, and in the years from 1917 to 1919, riots broke out in several cities (Brody 1980; Schaefer 1988). Protectionist nativist feelings ran high, and in the 1920s, legislation was passed that restricted immigration.

In the 1920s, anthropologist Franz Boas spoke out forcefully against the racially based theories being propagated at the time, and by the 1930s and 1940s, other important scientists joined him in attacking the idea that Blacks were inferior to Whites (Gossett 1963). Nazi racism also contributed to a reexamination of race domination in this country (Turner, Singleton, and Musick 1984). But discrimination continued, with Blacks still having problems within unions and industry. Blacks also were segregated within the military. Riots occurred during World War II, which further demonstrated that the United States still had a long way to go to bring about equity between the races. Increasing organization and political power of African Americans during the late 1940s and 1950s helped to bring about some legislative changes and, eventually, the Civil Rights movement.

RACIAL INEQUALITY TODAY

The preceding historical sketch reveals how extensive racial inequality has been in U.S. society. American Indians and African Americans were not, of course, the only minority groups to be treated unequally. Mexican Americans have been exploited for their land and labor. In the last half of the nineteenth century, Mexican Americans frequently had their land taken away by Anglos. Historically, the use of Mexican workers waxed and waned, depending on the demand for labor. They were used and then dispensed with when no longer needed. For example, early in the twentieth century, many Mexican immigrants came to the United States as agricultural laborers, only to be deported or repatriated after demand for their services declined. During World War II, Mexican workers were again imported, only to be sent back during the 1950s under "Operation Wetback" as expendable and undesirable. Illegal raids, threats, and expulsions have not been uncommon in our treatment of Mexicans, currently our largest immigrant group (Farley 1988; Schaefer 1988).

Asian Americans have also suffered the effects of stereotyping and unfair treatment. Near the end of the nineteenth century, Japanese immigrants took laboring jobs but were disliked by unions and other employees. They were lumped in with the Chinese as part of the "yellow peril," the fear that yellow races would overtake the White race. The events at Pearl Harbor, initiating the entry of the United States into World War II, exacerbated negative feelings toward Japanese Americans. Under Executive Order 9066, people on the West Coast with virtually any Japanese ancestry at all were rounded up and taken to way stations for removal to concentration camps. This was not done to either German or Italian Americans, even though the United States went to war against Germany and Italy as well as Japan. This strongly suggests a heavy influence of racism. The 113,000 Japanese sent to these camps without the benefit of trial could take only personal items, leaving behind and often losing most of their property. After the war, terrorism and bigotry against Japanese Americans continued, although no instances of espionage by them had ever been proven. Even while in the camps, they remained loyal to their adopted country. Today, when we examine the low rates of social problems among Japanese Americans, they appear to be model citizens. They also have achieved levels of earnings and education that are higher than those of Whites. But continued friction and trade difficulties between the United States and Japan is likely to keep ethnic prejudice simmering between these two nations.

We have focused on African Americans, then, not because they have been the only ethnic group treated unfairly and unequally, but because they constitute the largest ethnic minority in the United States (Marger 1997). Perhaps recent legislation, affirmative action, and economic expansion have contributed to a lessening of this inequality. How far have African Americans really come today? We now turn to an analysis of present-day racial inequality. Despite some clear advances, Blacks and Whites continue to have significantly different incomes, occupations, and earnings. In a variety of socioeconomic areas, there are conflicting trends, so that in some areas, Blacks have improved their positions relative to Whites, whereas in others, little or no progress has been made. On the one hand, if the emphasis is on comparing the situation of African Americans with what it was in the past, then undoubtedly improvements have occurred. In absolute terms, illiteracy among African Americans has declined drastically since the turn of the century, educational levels are up, and occupational upgrading has occurred. On the other hand, if we compare the situation of Blacks to Whites today, then there is still a great deal of inequality in the areas of earnings, income, and occupations.

Income, Earnings, and Race

Since the mid-1970s, the income gap between Black and White households has not changed much. In 1977, the median income of Black households was 59 percent that of White households, whereas in 1997, it was 64 percent of White households ($25,050 vs. $38,972). Over that period, the incomes of Hispanic households actually declined from 75 percent to 68 percent that of White households. In 1997, the median income of Hispanic households was $26,628. In addition to being behind Whites on median income, as we saw in Chapter 2, Hispanics and Blacks also have poverty levels about three times that of Whites, and they are poorer.

The mid-1980s showed only a small advance in the median household incomes of Blacks, which moved from $21,388 to $22,142 between 1977 and 1987. This was partially accounted for by the overall decline in the number with incomes between $15,000 and $75,000 (see Figure 6.1). Declines in median incomes and in middle-income categories, coupled with a rise in the percentage of those with incomes below $15,000, were also experienced by Hispanics. Concentrations in income distribution also increased within all major subpopulations during the 1977–1997 period. Increases in the total proportion of income went to the top 20 percent, and decreases in the percentages went to the middle 60 percent and bottom 20 percent (see Figure 6.2). In sum, although the incomes of Blacks and Hispanics relative to those of Whites have not changed significantly since the 1970s, the degree of income concentration within these groups has accelerated.

Given the differences in household incomes, it should not be surprising that there are also inequalities in the earnings of these groups, even when they work full time. Table 6.1 shows that the incomes of Blacks and Hispanics are lower than

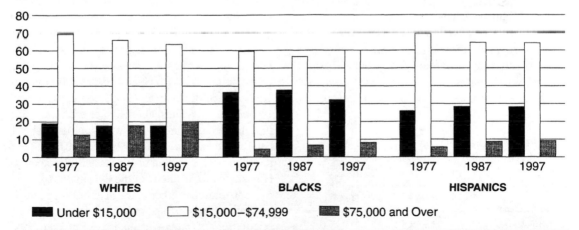

FIGURE 6.1   Percentage of Households with Income under $15,000, $15,000–74,999, $75,000 and Higher, by Race and Hispanic Origin: 1977–1997

Source: U.S. Bureau of the Census, *Money Income in the United States: 1997.*
Current Pop. Reports, Series P60, No. 200, September 1998, pp. B3, B4.

Note: Figures given in 1997 consumer-price-index adjusted dollars.

PERCENT

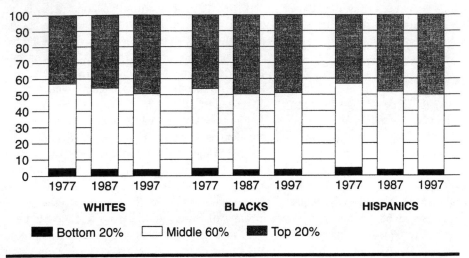

FIGURE 6.2 Percent Distribution of Total Incomes within White, Black, and Hispanic Populations: 1977–1997

Source: U.S. Bureau of the Census, *Money Income in the United States: 1997*. Current Pop. Reports, Series P60, No. 200, September 1998, pp. B6, B7.

Whites among both men and women. Several possible reasons have been suggested for these income gaps, such as differences in education, labor-force participation, occupations, and sizes of families. But even when these are taken into account, minorities still have lower incomes than Whites. In 1997, the income of Black males who worked full time, year-round was about 74 percent that of White males. The discrepancies among females are not as great. A higher percentage of

TABLE 6.1 Median Income of Full-Time, Year-Round Workers, by Race, Hispanic Origin, and Sex: 1997

	MALE	FEMALE
White	$36,118	$26,470
Black	$26,897	$22,764
Hispanic	$21,799	$19,676

Source: U.S. Bureau of the Census, *Money Income in the United States: 1997*. Current Pop. Reports, Series P60, No. 200, September 1998, pp. 28–29.

Black and Hispanic workers, especially women, are also poor.

Differences in earnings and income are one indication of the economic inequalities between minorities and Whites. Wealth differences are even greater, however. In 1993, the median net worth of Whites was $45,740, compared to $4,418 for Blacks and $4,656 for Hispanics, a ratio of 10 to 1. One-quarter of all Black and Hispanic householders had zero or negative wealth, compared to only 10 percent of Whites. On the other end of the continuum, about one-third of all White households had wealth assets worth at least $100,000, compared to only 8 percent of Blacks and 11 percent of Hispanics (U.S. Bureau of the Census 1996).

Historically, inheritance of family wealth, or lack of it, has been a significant factor in the "sedimentation of racial inequality.... Between 1987 and 2011 the baby boom generation stands to inherit approximately $7 trillion.... One-third of the worth of all estates will be divided by the richest 1 percent, each legatee receiving an average inheritance of $6 million" (Oliver and Shapiro 1995,

p. 6). Wealth inequality between Blacks and Whites has been perpetuated or "sedimented" since early in U.S. history, beginning with slavery, by governmental policies that prohibited Blacks from beginning certain kinds of businesses or entering particular markets, agencies such as the Federal Housing Authority which made loans and mortgages for Blacks more difficult to obtain, and the lack of opportunity to take advantage of the wealth-accumulation benefits of lower capital gains taxes, home mortgage deductions, and social security benefits. White mob violence has also weakened attempts to build up wealth that could be passed on to future generations. Consequently, 75 percent of Black children grow up in families with no wealth assets (Oliver and Shapiro 1995).

Occupation and Race

Part of the reason for the differences in income between racial and ethnic groups relates to differences in their occupational distributions. Examining broad occupational categories, we find that Blacks, Whites, and Hispanics are variously concentrated among them. There has been some occupational upgrading for Blacks in recent decades, however. A greater percentage of Blacks have moved into white-collar and blue-collar/manufacturing positions since World War II, and a smaller percentage are service and farm workers. For example, in 1940, 32 percent of employed Blacks were farm workers, but by 1970, that percentage had fallen to 3. In contrast, in 1940, only 6 percent of employed Blacks were white-collar workers, compared to 24 percent in 1970 and 44 percent in 1990.

These changes are largely a result of broader changes in the US. economy and polity. Principal among the changes that have reshaped the distribution of occupations among Blacks have been:

- The shift away from agriculture since 1900
- A decline in the centrality of unskilled work
- The movement toward a service-oriented economy

- The movement of industry out of central cities into suburbs, different regions of the country, or even different countries
- Attacks on unions, and the general weakening of the power of labor relative to corporate management
- "Retrenchment of civil rights enforcement" (Wacquant and Wilson 1989; see also Blau and Ferber 1986; Glasgow 1987)

Not only are these macrolevel shifts important for understanding the distribution of occupations among African Americans and Whites but they are also directly tied to unemployment and poverty levels, the *hyperghettoization* of the inner city, and the size of the underclass discussed in Chapter 2. The decline in basic blue-collar jobs, especially those requiring little formal education, and the mismatch between the location of jobs and Blacks have intensified the unemployment problems of inner-city Blacks (Lichter 1988; Kasarda 1989). These shifts in the economy, however, do not mean that race itself has become unimportant as a factor in accounting for occupational differences between Blacks and Whites. The relative significance of economic class and race will be discussed shortly.

Table 6.2 presents the current occupational distribution for Blacks and Whites of each sex using broad categories. While the greatest percentages of White males are in upper-white-collar and technical positions, Black males are most disproportionately represented in the operator/laborer category, and Black females in the technical and service categories. Black females are also less likely than their White counterparts to be in managerial/professional positions and more likely to be found in service occupations. But these general categories mask greater discrepancies among more detailed classifications of occupations. Data suggest that Black mobility has been much more restricted than that of Whites. Blacks do not become managers very often and have difficulty moving from the poor-paying, unstable jobs in the peripheral sector to the better paying positions in the core sector of the economy (Pomer 1986).

TABLE 6.2 Occupational Distribution of Employed Civilians Age 16 and Over, by Race and Sex: 1998 Annual Average

OCCUPATION	WHITE MALE	WHITE FEMALE	BLACK MALE	BLACK FEMALE
Managerial/professional	29.1%	32.6%	17.0%	23.2%
Technical/sales/adm. support	19.5	41.1	18.3	39.1
Service occupations	9.2	16.3	17.8	25.0
Precision prod./craft/repair	19.4	1.9	14.6	2.0
Operators/fabricators/laborers	18.5	6.8	30.1	10.4
Farming/forestry/fishing	4.3	1.2	2.2	0.3

Source: U.S. Department of Labor, *Employment and Earnings.* January 1999, p. 177.

As is evident in Table 6.3, Blacks are most underrepresented in certain high-level professional and upper-level skilled white- and blue-collar positions, and they are overrepresented in various private and governmental service and aide occupations. Those positions in which they are typically underrepresented are generally either unionized or require high levels of education. Their overrepresentation in certain public-sector jobs—such as postal service and correctional officers—has suggested to many that the government is a significant route to the middle class for Blacks. However, the economic benefits for Blacks of working for the government seem to have eroded in the 1980s and 1990s (Zipp 1994). Moreover, even when Blacks do gain high-level positions in the public economy, their positions are tenuous because of the volatility of political conditions (Collins 1993). Similar to Blacks, Hispanics are underrepresented in many white-collar positions and overrepresented in agricultural, service, and textile-related jobs.

Blacks and Whites also differ, like males and females generally, (1) on the authority they possess in their jobs, (2) on the specific kinds of organizations in which they are employed, and (3) in the economic sector in which they work. Similar to the situation for females, human-capital variables do not fully account for these discrepancies. Rather, structural factors, such as place of employment, along with discrimination, appear to be implicated in inequalities in the occupational structure.

MICROINEQUITIES IN THE TREATMENT OF RACIAL AND ETHNIC MINORITIES

Like women, racial and ethnic minorities have been subjected to a host of everyday indignities. Language, which reflects cultural values, helps to undergird the system of social inequality as it pertains to minorities, and yet because it is so much a part of our everyday lives, we seldom step back and look at it in any depth. The derogatory terms used to describe different ethnic and racial groups suggest the value placed on these groups, and reinforce this negative imagery when terms referring to these groups are used to describe some disliked or despised behavior (e.g., "an Indian giver," to "Jew down," to "gyp," to "nigger lip," etc.). Language is a powerful tool for shaping the attitudes toward and general beliefs about groups, and what makes it exceptionally influential is the fact that these terms are part of the matrix of everyday life and often used without intentional thought being given to their implications.

Embedded in this language are stereotypes of different racial and ethnic groups. Stereotypes, in turn, often have subtle yet negative effects on those affected. For example, a recent study of Atlanta employers found that many employers carry a negative stereotype of Black women as single mothers who are more concerned about their children than work, and are therefore generally late to work, lack education, and are not good role models for their children. These stereotypes, based on

TABLE 6.3   Sample of Specific Occupations in Which Blacks and Hispanics Are Significantly Over- and Underrepresented: 1998

BLACKS			
Underrepresented	*%*	*Overrepresented*	*%*
Geologists	0.3	Barbers	39.4
Farm operators and managers	1.3	Nurses aides/orderlies	34.0
Agricultural supervisors	1.6	Winding/twisting machine operator	30.7
Airline pilots	1.9	Correction officers	29.2
Veterinarians	1.9	Postal clerks	28.2
Speech therapists	1.9	Pressing machine operators	27.8
Tool and die makers	1.9	Telephone operators	26.8
Architects	2.0	Maids and housemen	26.7
Civil engineers	2.0	Taxicab drivers & chauffeurs	26.5
Authors	2.2	Concrete and terrazzo finishers	25.2

HISPANICS			
Underrepresented	*%*	*Overrepresented*	*%*
Underwriters	0.6	Graders/sorters (agriculture)	64.2
Occupational therapists	0.7	Farm workers	44.9
Farmers	0.8	Cleaners and servants	37.0
Chemical engineers	1.0	Pressing machine operators	35.2
Technical writers	1.2	Helpers, construction trades	33.3
Authors	1.3	Butchers/meatcutters	32.0
Biological scientists	1.5	Packaging/filling machine operator	30.8
Radiology technicians	2.0	Textile sewing machine operators	30.2
Dentists	2.0	Production helpers	29.3
Geologists	2.0	Insulation workers	27.5

Source: U.S. Department of Labor, *Employment and Earnings.* January 1999, pp. 178–183.

a lack of specific knowledge, affect the attitudes employers have toward prospective and current employees, and put Black women at a disadvantage (Kennelly 1999).

The media, especially movies and television, also have perpetuated stereotypes of African Americans learned in other contexts. Traditionally, African Americans and other non-White individuals have either been absent from the media or have been portrayed in negative terms—for example, the African American as lazy, slow thinking, and subservient, and the American Indian as savage and hostile (Marger 1997). Even the image of Asian Americans as a "model minority" (i.e., as educated, family oriented, and successful) glosses over educational and economic distinctions within the Asian American community, and recently has taken on a negative cast as others look for scapegoats for our economic difficulties. Instead of being viewed positively and as consistent with American values, the competitiveness displayed by some of these groups has been seen as a reason for the nation's problems. Just as competitive women are often seen as being unfeminine and aggressive, Blacks who are competitive are often considered pushy and uppity.

The belief in a competitive threat has been renewed in the recent controversies surrounding immigration to the United States, especially illegal immigration. Polls suggest that a significant proportion of U.S. adults have negative feelings about continued immigration (Gallup 1996; Andreas 1994). The conviction that such immigrants take away jobs from U.S. citizens and are a economic burden for which average citizens have to pay is a belief that goes back at least to the latter part of the nineteenth century, which also experienced an influx of "undesirable" immigrants. However, most evidence indicates that job raiding by immigrants does not occur to any significant degree, nor does immigration decrease wages for native employees (Waters and Eschbach 1995).

Further examination of the possible reasons for the strong negative reaction to immigrants, especially those who enter illegally, suggests that cultural differences are a root cause. Groups whose cultural values are more distant from those of immigrants are more likely to harbor hostile feelings about immigrants than those whose cultures are closer (Espenshade 1995). As was stressed in Chapter 3, insularity and security are core characteristics of status groups. Contamination from intruders is not taken likely and is to be avoided if possible. A desire to seal off national

borders from immigrants, to create a "Fortress America" is one reaction. Senator Alan Simpson represented this belief in his straightforward statement: "The first duty of a sovereign nation is to control its borders.... Uncontrolled immigration is one of the greatest threats to the future of this country" (quoted in Andreas 1994). No doubt these emotions are reinforced by the bombardment on TV showing Mexicans evading the border patrol and sneaking into the United States, seemingly bringing few skills or economic resources.

On other occasions, it is the absence of their presence in the media that indicates the status held by minorities. From the mid-1960s to the mid-1990s, there appeared to have been a small increase in the representation of African Americans on prime-time television programs, but a decrease in the presence of Hispanics. That presence, however, is not always positive. Most Blacks, for example, were in criminal or comedy roles (Schaefer 1996). A negative presence is also felt in media news reporting. A survey of how Blacks, Asian Americans, and Hispanics felt about news coverage about them revealed that although all these

Border patrol officers arrest a few illegal Mexican aliens in a parking lot in Nogales, Arizona. Such immigration has been a seething problem in the Southwest.

groups are more dissatisfied with such coverage than Whites, Blacks especially feel alienated from media coverage about them. Just under one-half believe that media reports about them actually *worsen* racial and ethnic relations, and a large majority contend that newspapers totally disregard their criticisms of coverage of them. Generally, Blacks are much more negative about media coverage than Hispanics or Asian Americans, but large majorities of each group feel that the quality of a story's report improves dramatically when a reporter from one's own ethnic group is used (McAneny 1994).

There are many additional, subtle, taken-for-granted advantages that are attached to the status of being White. In a thoughtful, reflective essay, Peggy McIntosh listed 46 conditions that she feels are connected primarily to the privilege of being White in our society, and that non-White individuals cannot take for granted. Among these, she included her being able to:

- Freely choose a place that she wants and can afford to live in
- Go shopping, feeling secure that she will not be harassed or followed
- See others of her race prevalently displayed in the media
- Be fairly sure that her voice will be heard even in a non-White group
- Rely on her skin color to protect her from being seen as financially unreliable
- Feel that her children will receive an education that acknowledges the contributions of her race and in which teachers treat her children fairly
- Talk with her mouth full and not have people put this down to her color
- Not worry about acknowledging the views of non-White people
- Consider a wide variety of options in her life without worrying about whether her race would be a factor in limiting them
- Select a service or public accommodation without considering whether she will be treated poorly because of her race

- Not worry about her "shape, bearing, or body odor" being seen as a reflection of her race
- Use a flesh-colored bandage and have it blend with her skin (McIntosh 1988)

THE INTERSECTION OF CLASS, RACE, SEX, AND GENDER

In the last few chapters, we have been examining the economic, racial, and gender dimensions of social inequality, and although they have been, to a large extent, treated separately, in the context of a *society* and in the lives of real *individuals,* these dimensions are interconnected. If we wish to understand how the dynamics and effects of each of these dimensions play out in actuality, we need to probe the nature of these interconnections at both the social/societal and individual levels. The significant meaning of these relationships can be uncovered by examining them at both levels.

When we speak of analyzing the interaction of class, race, and gender at the *social/societal level,* we are essentially considering each of these as separate variables that affect each other at the group or aggregate level. For example, consider the discussion of the relationship between the class measures of occupation and earnings on the one hand, and race on the other. The search for a statistical relationship among these variables can be carried out without ever addressing the psychological effects or experiences of individuals. We are concerned with effects at the level of the group or society.

The intersection of race and class can also be understood at the *level of individual experience.* Here, we are concerned with how race and class interact in the lives of individuals. How do people *experience* race and class in their lives? In their everyday lives, individuals accumulate *simultaneous* experiences as members of particular races, classes, *and* gender groups. A person is all of these things at the same time. The dimensions are not as readily separable. How do these elements interact *within* the individual? Consider a person who is Black, upper class, and male—a Black surgeon, for example. What is it like to be him? How do the effects of class and race and gender interact in his life? And, at the same time, what is it like to be poor, White, and female? To address these questions is to examine the intersection of race, class, and gender at the individual level.

There are many areas in which the connections among race, class, and gender have been examined. One obvious area of study is the effects of race and gender on class position. Another has been the relationship between race and gender-role expectations. A third has been the fascinating effects of class on race. Usually, we think of race as a biologically fixed category that cannot therefore be affected by class. But races are socially constructed, and how one identifies with a given race and is placed in a racial category can depend on one's class position. The Brazilian phenomenon of "whitening" provides a vivid example of this. Money can "whiten": "Thus, a dark-skinned man is considered mulatto or mestizo if he has status through education, family, or employment" (Jefferson 1993, p. 211). Brazil's racial classification system is extremely complex, involving over 100 terms to describe individuals on a Black-White continuum (ibid.). It is believed to be possible to "whiten" a family over generations not only through physical intermixing with whites but also through social advancement and retreat from Black culture (Wade 1993). The process of whitening forcefully drives home the fact of the social construction of races. Like class and gender, race, in a very real sense, is a product of social dynamics.

One of the most controversial and prominent discussions on the intersection of race and class involves arguments about the relative effects of race and class on the life chances of individuals. Scholars differ on which they think is most important. Around the turn of the twentieth century, W. E. B. DuBois suggested in his study of *The Philadelphia Negro* (1973) that not only racial discrimination but economic factors as well affected the everyday living conditions of Blacks. E. Franklin Frazier (1937) also suggested that both race and class play a role in determining what happens to Blacks, but finally felt that eco-

nomics may be more important than race, an opinion later shared by Oliver Cox. Cox viewed race relations in the United States as stemming from and continuously being conditioned by economic class relations. Racism exists as one of several devices used by capitalists to control, exploit, and keep workers down. As a result, it is rooted in economic conflict.

William Julius Wilson has argued that class has become more important than race in determining the life chances of Blacks today. This is because even though political and economic changes in society have opened up more potential opportunities for Blacks, these changes have also helped create urban joblessness. Blacks have been particularly affected, for example, by the shift from a manufacturing to a service economy, by the broadening split between low-wage and high-wage labor markets, and by the movement of industries out of the central cities (Wilson 1987; Bonacich 1985). "The net effect is a growing class division among Blacks, a situation, in other words, in which economic class has been elevated to a position of greater importance than race in determining individual Black opportunities for living conditions and personal life experiences" (Wilson 1982, pp. 399–400). Wilson has not argued that race is irrelevant today but he has said that historically racism has had a major effect on the lives of Blacks that continues today. However, this *historical* discrimination has a more significant impact on Blacks' lives today than does *contemporary* discrimination. Still, it is broader economic and political forces that are most immediately important for understanding events and behaviors within the Black community.

In examining the relationship between race and class, others have explored how race is used to create and maintain class positions. Capitalist owners exploit Blacks by using racism to create a pool of Black laborers whom they can hire for demeaning jobs at low wages, and White workers fight to keep Black workers out of their professions because of the fear of labor competition, thereby creating a split labor market (Bonacich 1985).

In sharp contrast to those like Wilson and assorted exploitation theorists, who stress the primacy of economic-class factors in explaining the socioeconomic condition of Blacks, others emphasize the greater and, in some cases, increasing significance of race in understanding the economic predicament of Blacks. They suggest that the gains that Blacks have made relative to Whites have been blown out of proportion (Willie 1979).

Analyses of national surveys done from 1972 to 1996 reveal the continuing influence of race on one's quality of life. Over this period, Blacks continued to score lower on measures of happiness, life satisfaction, and health, and were more mistrusting and anomic than Whites. "What is clear is that being black in U.S. society results in a lower quality of life than does being white. Also clear is the substantial degree of racial inequality in U.S. society...and the continuing experience of racism in the lives of African Americans.... The coexistence of these facts suggests that racial differences in quality of life are produced by racial inequality and the experiences it produces" (Hughes and Thomas 1998, p. 792).

Earlier studies by Myrdal (1944) and by Davis and colleagues (1941) also suggested that race was more important than class in explaining the living conditions of Blacks. The presence of Blacks in many white-collar, middle-class jobs masks the underlying and continuing significance of race for them. The growth of a Black middle class as evidence of real and lasting changes within the Black community is criticized by Collins (1983), who found that most Blacks in white-collar positions are in tenuous government positions and therefore are not a stable middle class (see also Hout 1986). Moreover, the fate of middle-class Blacks is still tied to that of poorer Blacks through (1) family connections and community living, (2) the need for voting blocs along racial lines, and (3) their middle-class government jobs whose clients are often poor Blacks (Omi and Winant 1986). These arguments suggest that class is not as important a factor in dividing the Black community as it has been made out to be by some class theorists.

Attempts have been made to find out how important people think race and class are in their lives. Studies with Black respondents indicate that while an increasing percentage of Blacks have identified themselves as middle class, there is not much evidence to support the notion that Blacks from different classes differ much in their opinions on social policies and programs (Cannon 1984; Welch and Combs 1985; Gilliam 1986). Moreover, Jackman and Jackman (1983) found that Blacks in the middle class feel closer to other Blacks and to those in lower classes than they do to others in their own class. So as Blacks climb the social-class ladder, their social class apparently does not become more significant than their race as a basis for identification. It is only when Jackman and Jackman examined the poor class that they found Blacks identifying as closely with their class as with their race.

While being in a particular class position does not automatically mean that Blacks will identify with others in that position, there is some evidence that race is an important predictor of class consciousness, with Blacks being more militantly class conscious than Whites (cf. Zingraff and Schulman 1984). Finally, as another indicator of the primacy of race, Blacks and women have views of the class system and the operation of equality of opportunity that are different from those of White males (Kluegel and Smith 1986).

One of the unfortunate consequences of the debate about the relative significance of race and class is that there is a temptation to ignore one while emphasizing the other. It is not necessarily the case that because one variable may increase in importance, another, by definition, must decline in significance. "The fallacy lies in the belief that an increase in the predictive power of one set of variables (class) requires a decrease in the predictive power of another set (race)" (Pettigrew 1985, p. 336). In this instance, race conditions class while class conditions what a member of any particular race can attain.

The same can be said regarding sex. Sex discrimination appears to be an important element in the continuance of occupational segregation, thereby affecting class position. At the same time, class and race divisions among women historically helped to determine the nature of their involvement in the labor market. Almquist (1984) found, for example, that some female minority groups have different occupational patterns than others. The patterns of Asian women approximate those of Anglo women, whereas those of American Indians are closer to the patterns found among African American and Hispanic women. Educational patterns also vary among these groups. "People's class position at birth, even for those of the dominant ethnic group, is an overarching factor in determining their eventual wealth, power, and prestige.... But for minorities, the chances of winding up at the bottom are much greater" (Marger 1997, p. 63). In essence, we can say that race, sex, and class are each important and often interact in their influence on the individual.

We saw that, historically, economic and racial factors interacted in the treatment of American Indians and African Americans. Economic motives played a role in driving American Indians from their land and developing African American slavery into an extensive labor force. At the same time, we found that class distinctions existed among African Americans and women that were important for understanding the differences in life conditions. We also found that racism as a fully developed ideology was used to legitimate and sustain the economic systems that were being constructed. In the same way, ideologies about the sexes and their proper roles have helped to keep occupational sex segregation intact. Economic as well as other conditions helped bring about the migration of Blacks to the North and the consequent form of the class structure within the Black population.

In contemporary times, Wright (1978) has shown in his studies that race as well as class, measured in largely Marxian terms, has an influence on income. Race plays a different role at different class levels. Among managers, Blacks receive less income return for their education than Whites, but Black supervisors and workers receive returns that are similar to those of Whites.

Ethnicity, race, and class background all play a role in determining earnings (cf. Hirschman and Kraly 1988). Blacks and women both earn less than White males, even when they have the same qualifications, but Black women are the worst off of these groups. Another study by Tienda and Lii (1987) indicated that the earnings of non-Whites, including African Americans, suffer when they are derived from participation in a labor market with a concentration of minorities, whereas the earnings of college-educated Whites benefit from association with such a labor market.

What is important to demonstrate, then, is how race, gender, and class interweave and coincide to influence the situations of groups and the lives of individuals within them. The data presented on incomes of full-time workers make it evident that race *and* gender have an influence on income, earnings, and the distribution of occupations. Blacks and Whites differ on each of the latter, but within each race males and females are differently situated with respect to income, earnings, and occupation. Census data clearly show that although Blacks and women, in general, have increased their representativeness in professional occupations, they continue to be severely underrepresented in professions dominated by males (Sokoloff 1988). Even though the proportion of male professionals declined, males continue to dominate certain high-ranking professions. In fact, their overrepresentation in these professions has increased. Black men are the next group most represented in these professions, followed by White women and Black women, respectively. These findings again suggest the complex interplay of race and gender that affects class position.

Attitude toward the feminist movement is another area that demonstrates the detailed interworking of race, gender, and class. Many African American women do not identify with the movement because they associate it with White, middle-class women, a group whose interests and needs differ in many ways from their own (cf. Davis 1981; hooks 1981; Reid 1984; King 1988). Historically, African American women have been suspicious of White women (Chafe 1977). Many view their class and race interests as separating them from the feminist movement that has developed in the United States. hooks (1981) wrote:

> We were disappointed and disillusioned when we discovered that White women in the movement had little knowledge of or concern for the problems of lower class and poor women or the particular problems of non-White women from all classes.... Black feminists found that sisterhood for most White women did not mean surrendering allegiance to race, class, and sexual preference.... It did not serve the interest of upper and middle class White feminists to discuss race and class (pp. 188, 190)

Some argue that the race-versus-gender stance suggested here is unfortunate because it hinders Black women from working against *both* racism and sexism (Reid 1984).

The influences of race, class, and sex on the life chances of an individual are multiplicative because they interact in complex and different ways depending on the specific sociohistorical and cultural context and the area of life chances in question (King 1988). In this sense, African American women are often in a situation of "multiple jeopardy" because of their racial, sexual, and class positions. It is inappropriate to lump Blacks and women into the same category because their current life experiences and past histories are unique, even though, in general terms, the two groups share some characteristics. For example, both (1) are readily physically distinguishable from White men, (2) have endured similar kinds of social control to keep them "in their place," and (3) are assigned characteristics of excessive emotionality and childlike qualities (Chafe 1977; Hacker 1951). But these somewhat superficial and broad similarities disguise what are more specific and deeper differences between the groups in terms of their concrete historical experiences, as our earlier historical summary of these groups indicates.

Moreover, whereas the races have been expected to restrict intimacy with each other, men and women have been expected to do the opposite. In this manner, Blacks have occupied a caste-like position while women have not (Keller 1987). Even more specifically, Black women are often left to fall between the cracks when discussions of Blacks (usually meaning Black men) and women (usually meaning White women) are carried out. The lesson here is that even though the histories of the sexes and races have been unique in many ways, the influences of race, sex, and class interweave when affecting individual lives.

THEORIES OF RACIAL AND ETHNIC INEQUALITY

As is the case for sex and gender inequality, there have been a variety of attempts to explain race inequality, ranging from biological to cultural and structural. Attempts to anchor an adequate explanation in biology have been widely criticized. The work of Herrnstein and Murray (1994) has elicited an avalanche of commentary, most of it negative. Basically, these scholars have argued first that an elite of highly intelligent people has developed that is increasingly separated from the rest of society, socially and economically. The high demands for intelligence and education in our sophisticated economy have funneled these elite into the high-paying, high-prestige occupations and left the rest of the population behind. The result is greater social inequality. The second part of their argument is that intelligence has been shown to be significantly linked to a wide array of social effects, including wages, poverty, school dropouts, crime, and having an illegitimate child. A highly controversial position follows this discussion in which Herrnstein and Murray suggested that racial groups vary on intelligence, that a large portion of intelligence is very likely genetically based, and that most of those at the bottom of the socioeconomic ladder are also those who score low on intelligence. The society stands to suffer since this group is also more likely than the more intelligent to have high fertility rates. In essence, their argument appears to be that intelligence has become more significant for the class placement of individuals, that intelligence has a strong genetic component, and that the United States is moving toward a more volatile class-stratified society based on intelligence in which classes are isolated from each other.

Briefly, Herrnstein and Murray's work has been criticized for, among other things, (1) its reliance on intelligence tests given later in life and whose results might thus reflect both genetic and environmental influences, (2) the omission of other significant factors that can affect socioeconomic outcomes (e.g., labor-market experience), and (3) the belief in the fixity and rigidity of genetic mechanisms and related social problems (Massey 1995; Nielsen 1995; Haynes 1995). Earlier research by the psychologist Arthur Jensen, who argued that there are significant differences between Blacks and Whites in native intelligence, also had been heavily criticized. But even if such differences could be demonstrated, their relevance for social and economic inequality between the races would still be problematic given the fact that numerous studies demonstrate that individual characteristics do not fully explain such inequality. Finally, the whole idea of racial differences in biology is based on the assumption that different races can be accurately, indisputably, and objectively identified.

The fact is that, like gender, race is largely a political and cultural creation rather than a biological one. Defining someone as Black who has only a small percentage of Black ancestry, as we have done in the United States, hopelessly blurs the biological distinctions between individuals. Mixed ancestry is widespread, making the delineation of discrete racial categories an impossible task. The mixing of ethnicity and race for political purposes, as in the concept of Aryan race, makes it clear that the concept itself is often merely an ideological weapon used to demonstrate superiority and justify unequal treatment. Moreover, some groups that we would define as members of a Black race are not considered so in other cultures. For example, many who live in Paris would be defined as Black by Americans but are not so defined by the French. Rather, they are identified according to their cultural background such as African, Brazilian, West Indian, or North American (van den Berghe 1967).

Even the U.S. Bureau of the Census has moved racial categories around, making it more obvious that race is a social rather than an immutable biological concept.

> *Groups such as Japanese Americans have moved from categories such as "non-White," "Oriental," or simple "Other" to recent inclusion as a specific "ethnic" group under the broader category of "Asian and Pacific Islanders."…Viewed as a whole, the census's racial classification reflects prevailing conceptions of race, establishes boundaries by which one's racial "identity" can be understood, determines the allocation of resources, and frames diverse political issues and conflicts. (Omi and Winant 1986, pp. 3–4)*

Race, then, like gender, is ultimately a social creation. It is significant because it receives a certain meaning and interpretation in society. It is this social dimension that makes race significant when discussing it in relation to inequality. This raises the important question of how race and race relations have been interpreted—that is, how they have been conceptualized. In the sections that follow, various interpretations of race relations and explanations for racial inequality will be presented. Most will focus on the United States even though they are frequently based on analyses developed for the characterization of intergroup relations in other countries such as India and Third World countries in general. The caste model is one of these.

The Caste Analysis of Race Relations

The application of the caste concept to race relations in the United States has not served to explain those relations as much as to describe them. It will be recalled from Chapter 3 that caste relations are generally argued to fall under the category of status relations; that is, caste structure is an extreme form of status inequality in that relationships between the groups involved are said to be fixed and supported by ideology and/or law. Membership in a particular caste is hereditary, mobility is virtually impossible, marriage within one's caste is mandated, and occupation is strongly related to caste position. These are the fundamental characteristics of a caste structure.

In *An American Dilemma,* Gunnar Myrdal described Black/White relations in the United States as constituting a caste system. Caste characteristics are largely a remnant from the slavery system and are to be distinguished from the class distinctions found within each racial caste (1944, pp. 221 and 667–668). One can move *within* one's caste but not *between* castes. "The boundary between Negro and White is not simply a class line which can be successfully crossed by education, integration into the national culture, and individual economic advancement. The boundary is fixed.... It is a bar erected with the intention or permanency...against the whole group" (p. 58). Like most caste theorists who followed him, Myrdal argued that a caste system was incompatible with the characteristics of democracy. The ultimate result of both existing alongside each other is not only a conflict in values but a "split in American personality," creating the "American dilemma."

The caste model has continued to be used in recent times (van den Berghe 1967; Berreman 1960, 1972; Willie 1979). Van den Berghe (1967) viewed race stratification as "an extreme case of status ascription making for rigid group membership," one that is comparable to the Hindu caste system and stratification by sex (p. 24). But he said that before the Civil War, race relations were *paternalistic* in nature, yet afterwards they could be described as being competitive. Under a paternalistic system of master and servant, the socially dominant group treats subordinate group members as if they were children with an "ideology of benevolent despotism." Members of both castes are expected to abide by a code of race relations in which appropriate behavior and position are expected by each group. In virtually all areas of life, there is a wide gap between the races and government is tyrannical. While conflict is present, the uneasy stability is maintained partly by the constant undercurrent of force, but also by the enforced complementarity and acquiescence of the subordinate group (van den Berghe 1967). This type of system, according to van den Berghe, is most likely to be found in complex agricultural systems, especially those that produce cash crops

on a large scale, such as in slave plantations. A paternalistic ideology also heavily informed our treatment of American Indians on nineteenth-century reservations (Farley 1988).

In contrast, a *competitive* system of race relations is more characteristic of industrial societies and developed abruptly in the United States after the Civil War, according to van den Berghe. Briefly, under this system, although caste relations remain, class positions within each caste become more elaborated and more important. In industrial societies, human-capital factors take precedence over race in determining position, and competition characterizes the relationship between African Americans and working-class Whites. Mobility is more likely, with the result that relationships between the races are more aggressive than accommodative. The stereotypes of African Americans change from being perceived as easy-going, immature children to that of an aggressive, "uppity," and dangerous people (van den Berghe 1967).

One of the implications of van den Berghe's description of the conditions under which caste or class predominates is that the former is more likely in a static agricultural society while the latter becomes more important with the advance of industrialization and industrialism. Caste is viewed as being associated with rural areas (e.g., the early twentieth-century South) and class with industrialization (e.g., the North). Frazier (1957) took a similar position when he said that the conflicts surrounding African Americans' status in the United States are symptomatic of the attempt to "force into the mold of a static agricultural society the dynamic economic and social relations which characterize an industrial urban society" (p. 268). The general image of the structure of race relations in a society in which a dominant agricultural economy is in the process of being supplanted by an ever-growing industrialism is one in which caste and class are both components, as described by Warner, Dollard and others (e.g., Willie 1979).

The caste model of U.S. race relations has come under severe attack from both conservative and more radical scholars. On the conservative side, there is the belief that race either is or is becoming largely irrelevant in modern industrial society. Position in the system of inequality is allegedly based on achieved rather than ascribed characteristics, and movement is based on results of an open contest between individuals rather than on the sponsorship of influential others. Critics have commented on the inappropriateness of comparing U.S. race relations with the Indian caste system, arguing that in contrast to the Indian situation, Black/White relations are (1) not stable, but changing; (2) characterized by mobility for Blacks; (3) conflictive and pathological; and (4) characterized by upward aspirations on the part of Blacks. Other significant differences between India and the United States, it is argued, are that whereas each caste in India is tied to a particular occupation, in the United States, Blacks are not relegated to a single type of occupation. Furthermore, the Indian caste system is legitimized through religion, but in the United States, racial inequality has been justified on the basis of biological or subcultural differences (Simpson and Yinger 1965; Cox 1942, 1948; Barrera 1979). Finally, as mentioned earlier, the caste model has been used more as a descriptive device than as an historical explanation of racial inequality.

Not all of the preceding criticisms are valid, however. There is evidence that as in the United States, the caste system in India has been challenged by those in the lower groups. There is no consensus on the part of all to see it as a legitimate system (Berreman 1960, 1972). Despite the Constitution in India guaranteeing certain rights and outlawing castes, caste relations still operate and contrast sharply with Constitutional provisions, creating an inconsistency between what is on paper and what really exists in society (Sivaramayya 1983). Similarly, in the United States, a distinction has been made between de jure and de facto segregation. In other words, this condition is not unlike the internal contradiction between the tenets of American democracy and the reality of racial inequality—what Myrdal called the "American dilemma." Moreover, as in the U.S. case where classes are divided by race, in India, the primordial loyalties of caste have weakened the unity of classes and prevented poorer classes from organiz-

ing (Chakravarti 1983, p. 170). What several of these comments suggest is that it is not acceptable to compare an *idealized* model of the Indian caste system with a *realistic* view of the U.S. race structure (Berreman 1960; Das and Acuff 1970).

Domination Theories of Race Relations

A variety of specific theories are included under this general category, but all of them incorporate the historically crucial role of power and/or domination in shaping racial inequality. Thus, they tend to be more dynamic and historically rooted than caste approaches. They do not anticipate the eventual automatic assimilation of minorities, nor do they emphasize the stability of the system of inequality or the active complicity of the minority group as is often suggested in caste analyses. Three of these approaches are (1) Noel's theory of ethnic stratification, (2) imperialist/colonial explanations, and (3) class-based explanations of racial inequality. Because of the focal role of power in each of these explanations, these theories are not incompatible and attempts have been made to synthesize them (Barrera 1979; Bonacich 1985).

Noel's Theory of Ethnic Stratification. Noel (1968) generated a broad theory of the origins of ethnic stratification which he then tested by applying it to the development of slavery in the United States. By ethnic stratification, he means "a system of stratification wherein some relatively fixed group membership (e.g., race, religion, or nationality) is utilized as a major criterion for assigning social positions with their attendant differential rewards" (p. 157). He begins with the assumption that before the possibility of such stratification even exists, there must be a period of prolonged contact between the groups involved. Whether or not contact results in stratification depends on the existence of (1) ethnocentrism, (2) competition, and (3) differential power. All three of these factors must be present for ethnic stratification to emerge.

Ethnocentrism, of course, refers to the belief that one's culture is the best, the center of the universe so to speak. All others are judged according to it. Cultures that are similar to one's own are ranked highly, and those that are radically different are looked down upon. Consequently, ethnocentrism fosters an in-group/out-group or us/them orientation toward others. Since people are so classified, double standards may be applied to the groups involved. What one expects of oneself may not be what is expected of others. It is important to note that each group is ethnocentric, thinking of the other in terms of mild or severe disdain. Each group measures the other in terms of its own values and beliefs, and of course, the other group is always found to be wanting to some degree. Each group also remains separate and autonomous from the other.

However, mere ethnocentrism is not enough to create ethnic stratification according to Noel. Groups can remain independent and relatively equal with a mutual and healthy respect for each other even though both are ethnocentric. Thus, it is also crucial that competition exists between the two or more groups in question. *Competition,* as defined by Noel, refers to the interaction between groups who are trying to attain "the same scarce goal." What is important about this interaction is that the goal is the same and that it is scarce. This could be competition over a prime neighborhood area or desirable jobs, for example. If the groups were after different goals, there would be no sense of competition and perhaps even lack of concern over the goals of the other group. If the goal is easily attainable and in abundant supply, there is no reason for one group to try to exploit or stratify the other. There is plenty for all.

If, on the other hand, the desired object or goal is actually or believed to be in scarce supply, then stratification may be seen as functional by each group. The intensity and terms of the competition along with the relative adaptive capacity of each group will affect the probability and form of ethnic stratification. Competition is more likely to be highly intense if there are many valuable, scarce goals that are shared by both groups, and will be less intense if those shared goals are few in number and relatively unimportant. The more intense the competition, the greater the likelihood of

ethnic stratification, other factors being equal. The terms of the competition concern the values, rules, and structural opportunities present in the setting. If competition is regulated by agreed-upon rules and some basic humane values are shared by the two groups, then ethnic stratification is far less likely to occur than if the competition is essentially a free-for-all and the groups had no values in common. Moreover, if there are few structural outlets in the form of opportunities, then competition is more likely to lead to stratification.

Finally, the adaptive capacity of a group relative to its competitor also has an impact on ethnic stratification. Basically, the group that has more cultural and other internal resources to call on when problems of adaptation and adjustment arise will be more likely to be able to dominate the other group. The chances of stratification occurring are lower when both groups are equal in their adaptive capabilities.

According to Noel, in addition to ethnocentrism and competition, a third variable, *differential power,* is also necessary for the emergence of ethnic stratification. "Highly ethnocentric groups involved in competition for vital objects will not generate ethnic stratification unless they are of such unequal power that one is able to impose its will upon the other" (Noel 1968, p. 112). Ethnic stratification simply will not appear in the absence of differential power. Once the greater power of one group is established, the more powerful group develops measures to subordinate and regulate the other group and to stabilize the current distribution of differential rewards.

In sum, Noel argued for an interactive model in that all three variables—ethnocentrism, competition with particular characteristics, and differential power—are needed to produce ethnic stratification. In applying this theory to the development of slavery in the early English colonies of the United States, Noel concluded that it adequately explains ethnic stratification. "Given ethnocentrism, the Negroes' lack of power, and the dynamic arena of competition in which they were located, their ultimate enslavement was inevitable" (Noel 1968, p. 117). Earlier, we saw how these factors also were implicated in the subjugation of American Indians.

In our early contacts with Mexican Americans throughout the Southwest, competition for land, accompanying racial/ethnic stereotyping, and imbalances in numbers and power contributed significantly to the inequality that developed between Whites and Chicanos (Farley 1988). Although Noel's theory does not identify all the specific historical and societal factors that might affect stratification in specific settings, his theory does identify in broad brush strokes three core factors that make it likely.

The next two theories, which also focus on differential power, have a great deal in common. The colonial model of race relations owes a significant amount to the Marxian class framework, and early architects of that model generally acknowledge their debt to Marx (e.g., Fanon 1963; Memmi 1965). In recent years, there has been a lot of cross-fertilization of both the colonial and class perspectives, with each using concepts from the other. But since the primary impetus that gave rise to each was not the same, they will be presented as if they are distinct approaches. However, their overlap in general orientation will become clear as each is discussed.

Internal Colonialism and Race Inequality. This approach to understanding the domination of Whites over Blacks in the United States is based on discussions and analyses of relationships between colonizing countries in the First World and those who have been colonized in the Third World. In this way, it bears a striking resemblance to world-system and dependency theories (to be discussed briefly in Chapter 8). The popularization of the internal-colonial perspective arose during the tumultuous 1960s when the War on Poverty, Civil Rights movement, and major urban racial confrontations were at their height. Militancy and discussions of "Black power" and "Black Nationalism" made the parallel between the Black predicament and that of other oppressed racial groups seem viable. In other words, the times were ripe for a colonial theory of U.S. race

relations. Fanon and Memmi, who wrote about colonial relationships in the Third World, had their writings adapted to the U.S. racial setting. Following them, a large number of scholars suggested and elaborated on what they felt was a basic parallelism between the dynamics in those relationships and those that occur in Black/White relations (cf. Carmichael and Hamilton 1967; Allen 1969; Blauner 1972).

One of the noted differences between classic colonial relationships and the internal-colonial relationship said to exist between Blacks and Whites in the United States is that the former generally involves groups from one territory invading and dominating the territory of another group, whereas in the latter case, both groups are from and occupy the same country. What can be said in response to this difference is that it is the character of the relationship rather than the factor of geography that defines a relationship as colonial (Bonacich 1980; Barrera 1979).

While acknowledging that the analogy is not perfect, Carmichael and Hamilton argued that Blacks in the United States "stand as colonial subjects in relation to the White society.... That colonial status operates in three areas—political, economic, social" (Carmichael and Hamilton 1967, pp. 5–6). *Politically,* while Blacks are technically just as free as Whites, Whites dominate the power structure of society, holding the most influential positions. Moreover, they exercise "indirect rule" by coopting and controlling selected influential Blacks to help maintain the Black community in a subordinate position. *Economically,* Blacks are more likely to be poor and unemployed and to pay exorbitant prices for shoddy goods. In this manner, the Black ghetto is sapped of its resources, which are transferred to the dominant part of society. *Socially,* Blacks are looked down on and demeaned in everyday contacts with Whites. Racial ideologies arguing their basic inferiority and presenting negative stereotypes help justify and maintain control over Blacks. This interpretation presents all Whites as benefiting from the colonial structure.

Perhaps the most often-cited architect of the colonial model of race relations in the United

States the sociologist Robert Blauner. Blauner argued that *assimilationist* theories, which view minority groups as being on a one-way road to blending into the rest of society, do not accurately characterize the historical conditions of African Americans because they draw a false analogy between the present situation of African Americans and that faced by White ethnic immigrants about a century ago. He pointed out that this analogy cannot hold up because the histories and circumstances of their arrival in the United States were qualitatively and highly different. Not only the slavery experience, but the nonvoluntary nature of their entrance into the country and the more permanent control of their lives by those outside their communities, distinguishes African Americans from earlier White-ethnic immigrant groups. African Americans are not merely the latest batch of immigrants who are waiting to be assimilated and upwardly mobile.

Although there are some differences between classic colonialism and internal colonialism, Blauner felt that they share several basic characteristics. First, the political domination and advanced technological level of the West was the basis for both slavery of African Americans and the colonization of many countries by Europe. Second, the economic and political superiority of the dominant group encourages a feeling of racial superiority used to justify the exploitation of the other group. In other words, since both types of colonialism have similar roots, Blauner said that they share "a common process of social oppression" (Blauner 1972, p. 84).

Blauner (1972) suggested that there are five basic characteristics in the colonization complex:

1. The dominant-subordinate relationship begins with forced, involuntary entry; that is, African Americans were brought here as slaves and ghettoes are controlled from the outside by the dominant group. White settlers also, of course, forceably took over American Indian lands.

2. The indigenous culture and social organization of the dominated group is altered, manipulated, or destroyed; that is, African American culture and institutions are undermined. Native American culture also has been subjugated.

3. Representatives of the dominant group control the subordinate group through their legal and government institutions; that is, White institutions control much of the lives of African Americans. The placement of American Indians on reservations also serves as an example of control by the dominant group.

4. Racism as an ideology is used to justify the oppression of the subordinated group; that is, Blacks and other racially or ethnically distinguishable groups are seen as biologically or otherwise inferior to Whites.

5. The colonizers and colonized occupy different positions in the labor structure and perform different roles; that is, by and large, African Americans are relegated to menial, nonprestigious jobs while Whites dominate in higher ranking positions. The dual-labor market characterizes the occupational positions of dominant and subordinate groups.

The listed characteristics suggest that the Black ghetto, instead of being isolated from the rest of society in some kind of autonomous culture of poverty, is in fact tied to White society by bonds of exploitation and dependency. The educational, political, economic, and legal institutions of the dominant society infiltrate and permeate the dominated colony. Then racism is used to maintain and justify the lower status of Blacks.

In addition to these structural characteristics, there are also cultural and psychological ramifications to the colonial relationship. In the colony, individuals cannot break through the racial-ethnic barrier. Colonized individuals can move up in class but cannot change their position of being colonized except through successful revolutionary movements that transform the structure of society. They may try to gain entrance into the larger society but "everything is mobilized so that the colonized cannot cross the doorstep, so that [they understand and admit] that this path is dead and assimilation is impossible" (Memmi 1965, p. 125).

In attempting to assimilate, colonized persons may initially admire and even adopt aspects of their oppressors, but when it is realized that full structural assimilation is not possible, they begin to reassert themselves in part through resurrecting old traditions and through the advocacy of violence. "Those who understand their fate become impatient and no longer tolerate colonization" (Memmi 1965, p. 120).

Most of these stages appear to apply to African Americans and their movements in the United States, although some of the protest behaviors of African Americans could be interpreted in ways other than through the colonial model (Omi and Winant 1986). Among the strengths of this model are its historical and comparative dimensions and the fact that it can account for a relatively large number of factors within a fairly straightforward theoretical framework (Barrera 1979). Among the weaknesses of the internal colonial model is one that Blauner recognized himself:

> When the colonial model is transferred from the overseas situation to the United States without substantial alteration, it tends to miss the total structure, the context of advanced industrial capitalism in which our racial arrangements are embedded—a context that produces group politics and social movements that differ markedly from the traditional colonial society.... It lacks a conception of American society as a total structure beyond the central significance that I attribute to racism. (1972, p. 13)

To effectively deal with this shortcoming, Blauner suggested that an adequate theory must incorporate elements dealing with characteristics of both colonialism and capitalism. Indeed, several of the attempts to develop a class-based theory of race inequality include references to both of these (e.g., Bonacich 1980; Hunter and Abraham 1987). Omi and Winant (1986) also pointed out that the internal-colonial model does not take into account class differences within the colonized (African American) group or relationships between minority groups. Despite these difficulties, the colonial model probably provides a more accurate analysis of Black/White relations in the

United States than either the assimilationist or caste perspective (Wilson 1970; Barrera 1979).

Class-Based Explanations of Race Inequality. Wilson (1970) has argued that economic and class dynamics are becoming more important for determining the life chances of Blacks. But well before Wilson developed his theory, others also argued that economic factors lie behind the inequality between Blacks and Whites in the United States. One of the most sophisticated class-based theories of race relations in the United States was developed by Oliver C. Cox in the late 1940s. Cox was very critical of the caste model presented earlier, arguing that the structural, cultural, and historical conditions in India were radically different from those characterizing U.S. Black/White relations. For example, he contended that a caste structure is ancient, nonconflictive, static, nonpathological. status oriented, and contains caste-fixed occupations. In contrast, he said, race relations and racism are relatively recent, conflictive, and pathological, do not usually involve narrow occupational restrictions, and are rooted in political-class conflict and capitalism (1942, 1945, 1948).

Cox viewed race relations and inequality in the United States as a product of economic exploitation. Forcibly bringing slaves to the United States was essentially a way of getting labor to exploit the natural resources of the country. Racial exploitation is only one form of the proletarianization of labor according to Cox. Racism as an ideology was not the root of exploitation; rather, it followed from it and was used to justify economic exploitation of Blacks. Racism, therefore, is a relatively recent phenomenon. Given its character and economic basis, "racial antagonism is essentially political-class conflict." Racial antagonism is used by employers to divide Black and White workers, and racial ghettos are maintained because they facilitate control over Blacks and perpetuate a self-defeating lifestyle. Blacks may want to assimilate but it is not in the interests of dominant Whites for them to do so (1948, 1976).

What is attractive about Cox's arguments is that he intermingled elements of racism, colonialism, class inequality, and capitalism in a comparative framework. Racial inequality is bound up with the development and expansion of European empires and the rise of capitalism and its labor needs. Trade is the lifeblood of international capitalism. The need to control potential markets and sources of raw materials strengthens the tendency of capitalism to colonize and exercise political control in the world economic system. Loans, raw materials, markets for manufactured goods, and imperialism each play a part in creating and fastening ties (chains) between dominant and subordinate nations in the worldwide capitalist system (Cox 1959, 1964). Race prejudice is then used to justify imperialism. Much of Cox's later writing anticipated many of the ideas associated with world-system and dependency theory.

One of the thorny areas of disagreement among class-based theorists of race relations concerns who benefits from racism and the nature of the relationship between Blacks and the White working class. From one point of view, racism is used by employers to drive a wedge between Whites and Blacks in the working class, and nationalism is used to divide members of the working class from different ethnic/racial groups in different countries. White workers come to view foreign workers who labor for low wages as unfair competitors, and their racism, which is ultimately rooted in the worldwide development of capitalism, is an attempt to protect their own jobs (Bonacich 1980). Although White or dominant workers may benefit from this racism in the short run, in the long run, the inequality within the working class creates divisions that weaken its collective power against employers. Employers exploit members of the minority for greater profits and money with which to pay the dominant working class. Accordingly, the principal beneficiaries of racism are employers rather than all Whites (Szymanski 1976; Reich 1977).

In general, having an ethnic/racial working class provides capitalism with a surplus army from which to draw poorly paid workers to perform jobs that are necessary but that no one in the dominant group wants to perform. But as the capitalist economy advances and the revolutionary potential of minority groups grows, many large employers begin to feel that the long-run costs of race inequality may be too high and that it should be eliminated (Baran and Sweezy 1966). One obvious cost of racism to employers is the loss of bright minority members to employers who could use them to increase productivity.

Edna Bonacich (1980) attempted to integrate and synthesize many of the arguments in class-based theories of race inequality. She began by commenting on the motivations for imperialism abroad. One important source for this movement is the desire to find more malleable and cheaper labor since the cost of labor rises as capitalism develops within a country. Wages rise because (1) the absorption of the entire labor supply into the expanding economy creates increased demand for it, (2) workers have a need for higher wages to purchase the increasing number of commodities produced in the economy, (3) large factories create social conditions conducive to the political organization and greater union power among workers, and (4) increased state support of workers cushions them and enables them to hold out for higher wages (see also Piven and Cloward 1982).

Because of these pressures for higher wages by domestic workers, then, employers look outside national boundaries for new sources of cheap labor. Pick up a piece of clothing from a well-known and expensive brand (e.g., Gant, Polo, etc.) and notice where the item has been sewn. The labels frequently cite places such as Honduras and the Dominican Republic. The public scandals dealing with the making of celebrity-endorsed clothing in Third World sweatshops is another example of attempts to profit through the use of low-wage workers. Wages are lower in less developed countries because of the existence of additional sources of subsistence (production for use) and a traditionally lower standard of living. Members of the domestic working class then see themselves as competing with cheap laborers in Third World countries, and may (1) react with nationalist and racist fervor against such groups or (2) see both themselves and other working-class groups from around the world as victims of capitalist development. Which of the two reactions is pursued by the domestic working class depends in part on the extent to which capitalists can control the colonized working class and manipulate the domestic working class, on how imminent the experience of competition with outside cheap labor is in the domestic working class, and on how proletarianized this class is itself (Bonacich 1980).

In terms of their relationship with upper-class elements in the host country, outside capitalists can try to use the native elite classes in the colonized countries for their own benefit as a sort of intermediary between themselves and the local labor force. This causes some of these elite to benefit in the short run from this arrangement while others lose by foreign capital's intervention into their country. Those who receive short-run gains will encourage native workers to work for outsiders for nationalist reasons, whereas those who are themselves immediately exploited will attempt to eliminate foreign intrusion into the home economy and press for the development of their own national industries.

The essential theme of Bonacich's argument is placing class and race dynamics in an international context and tracing racism and race inequality to the expansion of capitalism. It should be obvious by now that there are several similarities between the class and colony theories of race inequality. First, both have as central themes the notion of the exploitation (especially economic) of a lower group, African Americans, and/or the working class. Both perspectives view top and bottom positions in relational terms—that is, the position of one group is considered to be inextricably linked to that of the other group. Second, in both models, justifications (ideologies) are crucial for legitimating the power relationships that exist. But in both, the relationship is both "destructive and creative" (Memmi 1965). Third, both perspectives emphasize the polarization of society and the importance of rising consciousness among the exploited. In general theoretical terms, these basic congruences between internal colonial and class

theories outweigh their differences (Wilson 1970; Tabb 1970; Blauner 1972; Barrera 1979).

SUMMARY

Historical and contemporary evidence documents the inequality that has existed between Whites and various minority groups, including African Americans, American Indians, Asian Americans, and Hispanic Americans. The exploitation of African Americans for their labor and American Indians and Mexican Americans for their land were justified by racist ideologies, stereotypes, and the force of law. Like women, many minority groups have incomes and occupational statuses that are lower than those of Whites, while their poverty rates are higher. Differences in family compositions, educational levels, and labor-force participation do not fully account for these economic discrepancies. African Americans and other minorities also experience day-to-day microinequities, frequently of a type similar to those experienced by women. Biases in language, education, and the media constitute many of these, but there are many, such as those noted by McIntosh, that occur in a variety of settings.

A variety of theories have been developed to explain racial and ethnic inequality, ranging from the caste model to more radical internal-colonial and class explanations. In general, the latter are more sophisticated and focus on the centrality of differential power and economic domination in accounting for race inequality. As is the case with some gender inequality theories, several of these theories are couched in a comparative framework and intertwine class and economic processes in their explanation, which lends them some depth.

These theories and research evidence show how the variables discussed in the last several chapters—class, sex, and race—have been intertwined and influence each other. Debates in recent years have centered on the relative importance of race, sex, and class in producing these inequalities between groups. Some have argued for the primacy of one of these over others, but it seems clear that all affect the life chances through complex routes. Early racial and ethnic antagonisms helped to justify the economic exploitation of American Indians, Mexican Americans, and African Americans, and sexual stereotypes had the equivalent effect on women. At the same time, class differences within these groups created divisions that are sometimes hard to bridge. Sex and race also interact. For example, women of different races have different occupational and educational patterns. Race has been a source of division within the feminist movement, as well.

In addition to their lower economic status, racial and ethnic minorities and women also have had fewer political power resources. In the last four chapters, we have reviewed economic, status, racial and gender inequality. In the next chapter, we turn to a discussion of political power differences as a final form of inequality in the United States.

CRITICAL THINKING

1. What do you think lies at the root of racial and ethnic inequality? What social conditions or recent events are likely to intensify or lessen this inequality?

2. Will changes in the *class* positions of racial and ethnic minorities affect their position as *status* groups in the eyes of the majority? Why or why not?

3. What explains the content of stereotypes? How and why do stereotypes of groups change over time?

WEB CONNECTIONS

Segregation is still widespread in many major cities in the United States. A website for the Bureau of the Census allows one to see how racial and ethnic minorities are distributed in cities. Choose a major city, perhaps your hometown, and request the percentage of Black residents by census tract at the site below to visually see the distribution of races in the city. A map is produced that shows the location and degree of concentration of racial and/or ethnic minorities. Are your results surprising? Find out at:

http://www.census.gov/cgi-bin/gazetteer

CHAPTER 7

POLITICAL INEQUALITY

Every social act is an exercise of power, every social relationship is a power equation.
—Amos Hawley

The exercise of power and the experience of powerlessness are implicit in all the forms of inequality I have discussed so far. The relationships between wealthy and nonwealthy, men and women, gays and straights, and Blacks and Whites are frequently mediated by their relative power. *Power* also has a narrowly political meaning as well, relating to the varied involvement of individuals and groups in the making of public policy. Since there is debate about the extent of inequality in this critical area, this chapter will focus on political inequality. It will begin with a discussion of images of political power structure in the United States and then proceed to a review of the evidence that bears on those images.

PORTRAITS OF NATIONAL POWER STRUCTURE

In characterizing the political power structure of the United States, some argue that the majority are dependent on a minority, that a power elite or ruling class exists. Others believe the evidence supports a more pluralistic interpretation of the national power structure. Basically, the argument boils down to one over the extent of inequality in political power. Some argue that U.S. institutions and cultural values are such that they promote an elite structure, whereas others contend just the opposite.

Most of these theories can be listed under one of the following types: (1) pluralist, (2) power elite, or (3) ruling class. A brief description and critique of each of these approaches follows. The principal issue on which these approaches differ is the degree to which they see power as being concentrated in the United States. After the summaries of these perspectives, a survey of the empirical evidence that bears on them will be presented.

The Pluralist View

Basically, this widely accepted position argues that there are a number of competing groups and organizations that hold much of the power in the country, but no one of these groups holds power all of the time. There is no central or inner circle that dominates or coordinates the connections between these groups, since each is relatively autonomous and self-interested. Each group pursues issues that are of narrow interest to its organization; in those areas it can have influence, but in others it has little or no power. Generally, social inequality is "non-cumulative, i.e., most people have some power resources, and no single asset (such as money) confers excessive power" (Manley 1983, p. 369). Although there is some contact between organized groups, it tends to be inconsistent and deals with specific issues rather than broad orientations (Higley and Moore 1981). For example, conservative and liberal religious organizations may join together and have some power in their support of proposed policies revolving around rights of the fetus or unborn, but on other issues, they may differ or have no influence or interest. The shifting of power from group to group as issues fluctuate keeps power in a rough balance throughout the society. Individuals can exercise power in part by becoming members of these groups.

In sum, although the pluralist approach has spawned a number of specific theories, most share these core ideas:

1. Power is shared rather than concentrated among a variety of groups and individuals.
2. These groups are relatively autonomous of each other and become politically active primarily when political policies are at issue that directly affect their narrow interests.
3. The average citizen can be politically influential through membership in these groups and through voices of responsible journalists and intellectuals.
4. The consequences of items 1 through 3 is that there really is no single, permanent structure of power. Power is mercurial and its distribution is somewhat balanced by the existence of varied competing groups (Riesman 1950; Galbraith 1952, Dahl 1959; Rose 1968).

In these theories, one is given the impression of a society that, although made up of a variety of different groups and categories of people, is fundamentally based on *a system of values on which there is a widespread consensus.* In this society, each individual is rational and free, and his or her interests are taken into account in one way or another by those organizations such as government or corporations that might be seen as having greater power. Power and powerlessness do not appear to be problems. The sharing of power actually helps the society to function.

The pluralist image of power in the United States has been very popular in many quarters. Cunningham (1975–1976) explained much of its popularity by observing that it has something to

offer everyone. "On the one hand, pluralists offer their view as a tough, realistic perspective, one that gets down to the power-political guts of society; on the other hand, they paint a 'soft' picture of the community of happy Americans...able to get along...despite their differences" (p. 388). Since U.S. society is so complex, it is easy to think of cases where different groups were powerful in different situations and to believe that, in the final analysis, some competition exists. Rose (1968), in proposing his "multi-influence hypothesis," stated that this position portrays reality as much more complex than does elite theory. There is an "indefinitely large number of groups and categories" that exercise political influence and the result is that "power is...dispersed through the general population" (pp. 152 and 179).

A variant of the pluralist model was proposed by Keller (1969), who contended that the increasing complexity and differentiation in modern societies makes the existence of "coordinating elements" essential. To prevent this society from disintegrating because of all of its different parts, some groups must play a central role in keeping the parts together. These "strategic elites," as Keller calls them, perform this function and serve as the "guardians and creators of common purpose and...managers of collective aims and ambitions.... Whether or not an elite is counted as strategic depends not so much on its particular activities than on its scope, impact, and society-wide influence" (Keller 1969, p. 521). These elites have knowledge that is both expert and critical for the functioning of the entire society. Obviously, not all organized groups in the society qualify for this elite status. Included among the strategic elites are leaders in the political, economic, military, cultural, and recreational fields.

Since strategic elites are specialized, none of them dominates according to Keller, nor do these elites constitute a ruling class. Unfortunately, this theory is not very informative about the *degrees* of importance of each of the strategic elites; nor does it explain what happens when strategic elites, such as those in economic, political, and military domains, collide with each other. As just noted,

Keller did suggest that since each is specialized, none can dominate over the others. This conjures up a view of power as being balanced among these elites. Finally, what makes these groups strategic elites is their expert knowledge in critical areas. But a theory that stresses specialized knowledge as the important basis for power neglects the fact that ideology and outlooks frequently are the bases for advancement in power (Prewitt and Stone 1973, pp. 126–127).

Two of the principal architects of the pluralist position, Charles Lindblom (1977) and Robert Dahl (1982), have argued that corporate groups have become increasingly powerful and even more powerful than other groups in the competition for power. Dahl has suggested that what is needed to maintain pluralism is a changed civic consciousness to increase pressures for equity in the distribution of power and increased control of corporations by workers to decentralize power. The question, of course, is whether one could expect such workers to be more civic-minded than protective of their own narrow interests once they assume greater control of corporations. Lindblom and Dahl have been criticized for trying to maintain the viability of the pluralist model while at the same time acknowledging the inordinate power of corporations, which suggests that class and elite power are not equally distributed in the United States. This position, which Manley (1983) labels *Pluralism II,* "now tries to hold in balance severe criticisms of the system's performance, the need for major structural reforms, support for redistribution of wealth and income, and more government ownership of private enterprise, at the same time that it supports social pluralism as necessary for democracy, denies the special importance of class, reconfirms the inevitability and value of incremental change.... The problem...is that Pluralism II still defends many features of the system that perpetuate the social results it now deplores" (pp. 371–372). Nevertheless, some still hold the position that the power of corporations can still be incorporated into a pluralist or interest-group approach (Vogel 1987).

For over 40 years, pluralism has been roundly criticized (Bachrach and Baratz 1962; Mills 1956; Connolly 1969; Prewitt and Stone 1973; Cunningham 1975–1976). Social and historical events during the 1960s and 1970s helped develop a critical stance in all the social sciences, especially economics, political science, and sociology. The central criticisms of pluralism frequently reflect skepticism about the reality of democracy in society today and are based on an analysis of current events on the political scene. First, the issues of concern to many people frequently are not dealt with by the government. In large part, this occurs either because these individuals are not in positions to make their interests known or because their interests are of less concern than those of people who hold positions of economic and social power and whose values are represented and reflected in the government (Connolly 1969; Prewitt and Stone 1973).

Second, voluntary associations are no longer effective representatives of the average citizen since they have themselves become oligarchical in nature. In addition, individuals in positions of organizational power do not represent the average membership. These members do not have access to power (Presthus 1962; Kariel in Connolly 1969, p. 16). Finally, nondecisions and problems that never become publicly defined as issues must be examined. Pluralism examines issues but ignores "the values and biases that are built into the political system and that, for the student of power, give real meaning to those issues which do enter the political arena" (Bachrach and Baratz 1962, p. 950).

The Power-Elite View

The idea of a power elite differs drastically from pluralist conceptions and Keller's concept of strategic elites, but it is not the same as the ruling-class concept, which we will discuss shortly. Perhaps the most famous U.S. power-elite theory was developed by C. Wright Mills (1956). Because Mills's portrayal of the power elite has drawn an inordinate amount of attention in the years since it was written, and because it represents a prime example of a theory in opposition to the pluralist position, it is presented here in detail. Mills's essential argument is that power is centralized in a power elite. According to Mills, certain historical changes have brought about the development of a power elite. As the society has grown, institutions have become more complex, and national functions have become centralized in specific institutions—namely, the economic, military, and political institutions. Mills contended that with historical changes, the tasks in top positions in each of these institutions have become so similar that it is now possible for those at the top to interchange positions. Consequently, in addition to centralization in institutions, there has been an increasing coalescence, so much so that *three* separate political, military, and corporate elites are now *one* power elite made up of individuals in the highest positions in an interconnected set of institutions. "By the power elite, we refer to those political, economic, and military circles which as an intricate set of overlapping cliques share decisions having at least national consequences" (Mills 1956, p. 18). The nucleus of the power elite includes those who hold high positions in more than one of the three major institutions, as well as those, such as prestigious lawyers and financiers, who serve to knit the three institutions together (Mills 1956, pp. 288–289).

The persons within this structure have their power because of their positions. It is not their personal characteristics that make them powerful but their positions in the military, political, and economic institutions. Nevertheless, they do tend to come from the same kinds of economic, social, and educational backgrounds and do informally intermingle. Ultimately, however, it is their position that makes them powerful in national decision making.

Mills described the top part of the power structure as possessing a "higher immorality." What he was talking about is not personal immorality (i.e., one caused by a corrupt personality) but a structural immorality, in that because of the way society is organized and because of the way its institutions are structured, certain individuals can take advantage of others and their positions. It is similar to what has recently been called "structural corruption," a situation in which structural avenues are open in society that allow outside money to influence the political and intellectual stance of those in positions of power (Judis 1990). Part of the higher immorality is reflected in the fact that Mills believed that such characteristics as cynicism, personality selling, conformity, and mediocrity (all valuable in a society such as ours) have replaced values based on knowledge, skill, and independent thinking.

Some may feel that Congress is part of the power elite, but Mills did not agree. Rather, he referred to the Congress as a "semi-organized stalemate" made up of people who, since they have their eyes on reelection, are concerned largely with the fluctuating local issues of their constituencies back home. In other words, such groups as the farm bloc, labor unions, white-collar workers, and Congress really have little to do with decisions of national consequence. These groups, specifically Congress, make up a middle level of power in the United States. If the competition of groups in pluralism operates at all, it is at this level, as Congressional members exchange favors, make compromises, and balance each other out. Mills further believed that the wealthy and political officers who are entrenched in local interests will not become nationally important. As he stated, "to remain merely local is to fail" (1956, p. 39). Local society has, by and large, been swallowed up by the national system of power and prestige. This is in part due to increasing urbanization, increasing satellite status of smaller towns, improved transportation networks, and now the World Wide Web. Again, it has been changes in the structure of the society that have resulted in the appearance of a particular kind of power structure.

On the bottom of this pyramidal power structure are the large majority of people who are quickly developing into a mass society. Masses are characterized by the fact that they are always on the receiving end of opinions, cannot or do not effectively respond to opinions expressed in the mass media, and really have no outlet for effective action in society. Mass media, largely controlled by those on the top of the power structure, have only served to weaken communications between the top and the bottom of the structure. The media tell people what their experiences are or should be and stereotypes them. Education only serves to help people to "adjust" to a society that is very hierarchical in terms of power. Voluntary associations, although theoretically may be viewed as a link between the individual and the people at the top, do not perform this function because as they have grown, the individuals in them feel less powerful. Power is distant and inaccessible to average members.

Gusfield's (1962) neat summary of the central characteristics of mass society fits in nicely with Mills's description. In a mass society, there is a:

1. Weakening of primary and local associations
2. Strengthening of impersonal bureaucraticized relationships in large-scale organizations that have replaced smaller and more informal systems of loyalty and affiliations
3. Homogenization of the population and a leveling of conditions and ideologies that have reduced traditional authority systems characteristic of stratified communities
4. Lengthening of the chain of organizational authority, which makes local groups less viable and more amenable to control from above
5. Personality disintegration in the individual characterized by alienation, lack of commitment, and malaise (in addition to the structural disintegration indicated)

It should be pointed out that Mills was not saying that there is a conspiracy on the part of a small group of individuals to control political power in the United States. Rather, it has been a sequence of historical and structural events and changes, such as the growth in major institutions, that has led to the development of such a power structure. For example, the military is not powerful because it is conspiring against civilian popu-

lations, but it is in a position of power because the United States as a nation is now within an international military neighborhood, surrounded by allies and enemies. This means that what in the past may have been simply and purely political issues have now become largely military issues. Foreign aid is no longer just an economic or political issue but a military issue as well. In any case, it bears repeating that, for the most part, Mills felt that a series of structural and historical changes have brought about the power elite, not a conscious conspiracy on the part of a tightly knit group of corrupt individuals.

The *current* power elite is a relatively recent phenomenon which, in Mills's view, came into existence only after the New Deal in the 1940s and 1950s. Before that time, the power structure passed through several other epochs in which either no single institution or one of the three major institutions was dominant. Today, the hierarchy among these institutions is much less clear, and they are much more equal and intertwined.

Mills's power-elite theory has been criticized on several grounds, including the arguments that his terminology is vague and his selection of issues to test his theory is biased. He has also been faulted for choosing data that support his theory and ignoring contrary evidence. Third, some critics have attacked his conception of power, questioning his decision to use "position" as a measure of power and to see power as flowing only from the top down. Finally, some have branded his a conspiracy theory because of its emphasis on the interrelationships among institutional sectors and the similar backgrounds of those occupying high positions in them.

Despite these criticisms and others, however, Mills's analysis is not without its strengths. Among other points, Prewitt and Stone (1973, p. 90) mentioned that "whatever else it accomplished, *The Power Elite* raised the level of debate to a higher plane" since the author was the "first major analyst of American society" to observe that power relationships can vary with the issue at hand and to anchor his analysis in concrete and major institutions.

The Ruling-Class View

As we have seen, Mills's description of the power structure is one in which a group of individuals in high positions in core institutions dominate, while those at the bottom comprise an unorganized, ineffectual mass. They have little power and offer little active resistance. Rather, they are manipulated and educated in a manner that makes them almost willing subordinates in the society. The ruling-class view similarly proposes that a small group has inordinate political power in the society and that there are important interconnections between economic and political institutions. However, aside from these similarities, the ruling-class model differs from the power-elite model in several ways:

1. Rather than stressing several types of institutions as being involved in the elite, the ruling-class view emphasizes the dominance of the economic institution and position within it.

2. The ruling-class model often views the bottom of the power structure as being more active and effectual as a working class. It can organize and bring about change in the society. In the case of the power-elite model, the mass is largely passive in response to its position, whereas in the ruling-class model the working class can be class conscious and organized. Thus, the relationship between those on the top and those on the bottom is characterized more fully by conflict (Bottomore 1964).

3. The relationship between the upper class or bourgeoisie and political power is portrayed as being much tighter than is the case in Mills's power-elite theory where the upper class and celebrities are more tangential to the political process. In Mills's view, it is strictly *institutional position,* not *personal wealth,* that leads to political power.

G. William Domhoff's argument that the corporate rich and owners constitute a "dominant class" that largely controls the political process is perhaps the best representation of a ruling-class theory of U.S. politics. Briefly, Domhoff contends that a cohesive power elite dominates federal governmental affairs, and it is composed of those members of the upper class whose wealth is heavily concentrated in corporate holdings and who actively become involved in corporate affairs and political policy making (Domhoff 1998). Consequently, their power is based in both class position and corporate attachment. In addition, these individuals have similar backgrounds, often know each other, and have general political and economic interests in common. Because of the cohesiveness founded on these similarities, the upper class "is a *capitalist* class as well as a *social* class" (Domhoff 1998, p. 116, emphasis added). Although there may be internal disagreements over specific policies, there is wide agreement over the general direction that policy should take. The corporate-based elite dominate the political arena through its heavy influence on public opinion, participation in lobbying through its powerful interest groups, and involvement in policy formation through foundations, board room discussions, and various research groups.

In contrast to Mills's view of the power elite, Domhoff does not present a picture of power structure in which there is a mass society without voice and in which no group but the elite can have any power of consequence. Rather, he notes that unions and different liberal groups frequently conflict with the corporate rich, but that generally, it is the latter group that sets the parameters within which conflict occurs. Domhoff is quick to point out that, given the size, internal disagreements, and bases of the dominant class, his is not a conspiracy theory. Rather his argument focuses on providing evidence that there is "an upper class that is tightly interconnected with the corporate community...[and] that the social cohesion that develops among members of the upper class is another basis for the creation of policy agreements" (Domhoff 1998, p. 71).

DISTRIBUTION OF POLITICAL POWER

Each of the positions just discussed suggests a different distribution of power and political influence. But the data that bear on them must be examined before conclusions can be drawn about the concentration and dispersion of political power. The degree of power and political participation can be measured in a variety of ways, and each of these measures provides clues concerning the actual distribution of power.

Though some people feel they have little influence, perhaps they are wrong. To what extent are all individuals really politically influential in the United States? Does being a citizen mean by definition that a person is a participant? One means by which to assess the potential political impact of a group is through its history of participation in the political process. "Participation is a potent force; leaders respond to it. But they respond more to the participants than to those who do not participate" (Verba and Nie 1972, p. 336). A group obviously has to make its desires known if it is to have the possibility of gaining political power under the present system. "Party politicians are inclined to respond positively not to group *needs* but to group *demands,* and in political life as in economic life, *needs* do not become *marketable demands* until they are backed by 'buying power' or 'exchange power' because only then is it in the 'producer's' interest to respond" (Parenti 1970, p. 528; emphasis in original).

The recent campaign to reform health care in the United States provides a good example of varied lobby groups jockeying for position and battling to have their constituencies' interests represented in the final policy. Since health care involved about $950 billion in spending in 1994 and since it is an issue that touches everyone's life, it has attracted the attention of many interest groups. In a 12-month period covering parts of 1992 and 1993, the federal government's Health Care Reform Task Force met with almost 600 organizations. "Who is lobbying? Everyone: groups for children, the elderly, doctors, X-ray manufacturers, nurses and truckers" (Rubin 1993, p. 1081).

While the Congress will ultimately make a decision about health-care reform, other important interest groups outside government will affect how they vote. Among these are the following:

- Organized labor and consumer groups (e.g., AFL-CIO, Consumer's Union, Common Cause)

- Business lobby groups (e.g., National Leadership Coalition for Health Care Reform, Washington Business Group on Health, National Federation of Independent Business, Health Industry Manufacturers Association, pharmaceutical interests)
- Medical and professional groups (e.g., American Medical Association, American Hospital Association, American Association of American Medical Colleges, National Association of Psychiatric Health Systems, National Association of Social Workers)
- Insurance groups (e.g., Blue Cross and Blue Shield, Health Insurance Association)
- Senior citizens' groups (e.g., American Association of Retired Persons, Gray Panthers) (Oliver 1991; Rubin 1993; "Suddenly" 1992).

Each of these specific interest groups represents somewhat unique constituencies. The balance of power among them is currently in a state of flux as discussions of critical issues are carried out over who is to pay how much, what services and who should be covered, what kinds of cost controls should be made, and who should ultimately direct the field of health care. What groups dominate the shaping of policy in this area is shifting (Imershein, Rond, and Mathis 1992). The frenetic activity of these groups demonstrates their belief that it is group *demands rather than needs* that dictate influence in policy making: "The players in the debate on health-care reform realize that being at the table is critical" ("Suddenly" 1992, p. 37). The debate over Medicare during the 1996 presidential election indicates that health-care costs continue to be a source of controversy and political struggle.

Voting

A frequently used measure of participation in the political process is voting. Voting turnouts for national elections in this country are well below the 80 percent turnouts found in other industrial democratic nations. This lower voting rate is somewhat surprising, given the fact that evidence suggests

PERCENT VOTING

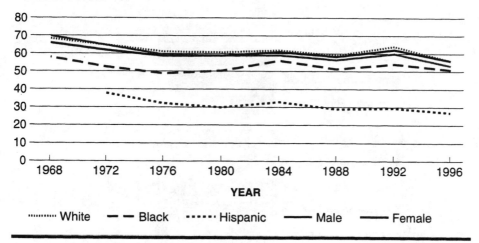

FIGURE 7.1 Percent of Voting-Age Population Who Reported Voting in Presidential Elections by Race, Hispanic Origin, and Sex: 1968–1996

Source: Lynne M. Casper and Loretta E. Bass, *Voting and Registration in the Election of 1996.* Current Pop. Reports, Series P20, No. 504, July 1998, p. 1.

that Americans tend to be more politically aware than adults in other similar countries. The party system's lack of close connection with many other social groups, along with voluntary registration, have weakened participation in the U.S. political process (Powell 1986).

Generally, there are clear relationships between selected social characteristics and voting behavior. Historically, Whites have been much more likely than African Americans or Hispanics to register and to vote in congressional and presidential elections. The data show that during the 1960s—the period of the Civil Rights movement, racial disorders, and War on Poverty—a greater percentage of African Americans voted in presidential elections than did in 1996. That percentage declined during the 1970s only to rise again to almost 56 percent in 1984, and then fall to 51 percent in 1996. African Americans are less likely to vote than Whites, and an even lower percentage of Hispanics vote. Generally, just under one-third of voting-age Hispanics vote in national elections (Casper and Bass 1998). The difference between the sexes has not been as great, and in fact, in the 1996 presidential election a slightly

higher percentage of women than men voted. Figure 7.1 shows the distribution of voting for these groups from the late 1960s to the 1996 presidential election.

Figure 7.2 presents the patterns for voting by education, occupational status, and family income. Again, these patterns vary by social characteristic. Those who have higher occupational statuses, incomes, and more education are more likely to vote. This pattern holds regardless of sex, race, or Hispanic origin.

Clearly, a large percentage of some groups do not participate much in the political process, even at this basic level. What Verba and Nie concluded in 1972 remains true today. Voting patterns reveal "a picture of low levels of citizen participation and concentration of political activity in the hands of a small portion of the citizens" (1972, pp. 26–27).

The principal reasons given by those who were registered but did not vote in the 1996 presidential election were the following: too busy or cannot get time off (22 percent), lack of interest (17 percent), illness or disability, (15 percent), and dislike of candidates (13 percent) (Casper and Bass 1998).

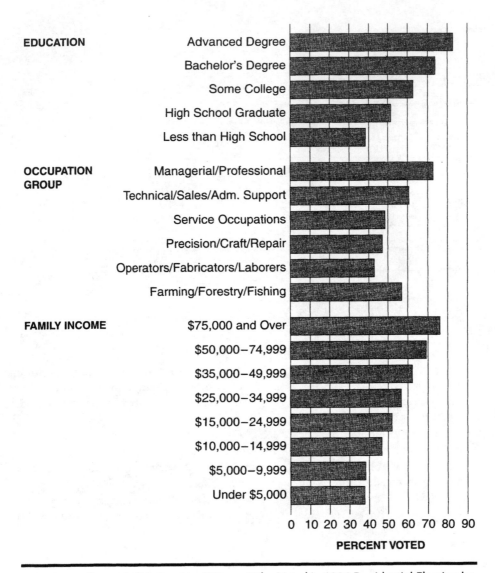

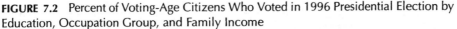

FIGURE 7.2 Percent of Voting-Age Citizens Who Voted in 1996 Presidential Election by Education, Occupation Group, and Family Income

Source: Lynne M. Casper and Loretta E. Bass, *Voting and Registration in the Election of 1996.* Current Pop. Reports, Series P20, No. 504, pp. 5–6.

If people did vote, would they be more politically powerful? Unfortunately, if past legislation is any guide, it does not appear that popular will is the kind of participation that has been significant in bringing about political changes. Rather, it has been the organized efforts of groups with resources that have been effective in the past (Prewitt and Stone 1973). Platitudes about popular control and the average citizen's importance simply have not held up (Parenti 1970; Prewitt and Stone 1973). Modes of participation other than voting have been more effective.

Some groups are, at best, only minimally involved in the political process. Those who are totally inactive have disproportionate numbers from low-income and low-education backgrounds, whereas "complete activists" have an overrepresentation of high-status individuals in their ranks (Verba and Nie 1972, pp. 97–99). The complete activists are individuals who participate in a variety of ways (voting, attending meetings, campaign contributions, contacting officials, etc.). Regardless of how it is measured, political inequality is present, and present to a large degree. Simply put, those who are better off vote more and are more involved.

Holding Political Office

Holding political office is another and more substantial means by which to wield political power. White males dominate political positions at the federal level. In terms of absolute figures, the number of Black elected officials has gone up dramatically since 1970. In 1997, there were 8,656 Black elected officials, compared to 1,469 in 1970. But Blacks still compose less than 2 percent of all elected officials, even though Blacks make up over 11 percent of the voting-age population. Under 1 percent of these positions are at the federal level. As a result of the 1998 elections, there were 39 Black members of House of Representatives, but none in the Senate. This compares to 19 Hispanic and 5 Asian-American/Pacific Islander members of the 106th House of Representatives. In 1999, the Senate contained 3 minority members (two Asian American/Pacific Islanders and one American Indian) (Pope 1999).

Among Blacks, the proportion of such officials who are males has declined in recent years, but Black male officials still outnumber Black female officials 2.1 to 1 (see Table 7.1). In 1999, 14 of the 39 Black House members were women. The same pattern exists for other minority groups. Only 5 of the 19 Hispanic House members and 1 of the 5 Asian/Pacific Islander members are women (Pope 1999).

Females, in general, are underrepresented in elected political positions. In 1997, women were

TABLE 7.1 Change in Number of Black Elected Officials and Ratio of Male-to-Female among Black Elected Officials: 1970–1997

YEAR	NUMBER	MALE-TO-FEMALE RATIO
1970	1,469	9.2
1975	3,503	5.7
1980	4,912	4.0
1985	6,056	3.4
1990	7,370	2.8
1993	8,015	2.4
1997	8,656	2.1

Source: David A. Bositis, *Black Elected Officials: A Joint Center for Political and Economic Studies, Statistical Summary 1993–1997.* Washington, DC.

32.5 percent of all elected officials, up from 10.9 percent in 1970. Most of these women do not have the seniority that even several Blacks in Congress possess. This is in part due to the fact that most Blacks in Congress are elected in districts with very large minority populations, whereas "women don't run from districts that are generally women" ("Record Number" 1988, p. 3294).

In addition to sex and race, other studies indicate that socioeconomic background also is tied to the likelihood of holding office. Matthews's (1954) study of the Eighty-first Congress in 1954 suggests that upper-class origin is linked to being a member of Congress. While 63 percent of the employed in 1890 were low-salaried workers, wage earners, servants, and farm laborers, only 4 percent of the senators in the Eighty-first Congress had fathers in any of those categories. As the cliché might put it, the Senate was largely made up of White Protestants, most of whom were born into middle- and upper-class families, and a majority of whom were lawyers. Matthews concluded that his and other findings suggest a class ranking of political office, with those from the higher classes occupying the highest political offices.

In both houses of 1999 Congress, 75 percent were businesspeople, bankers, or lawyers, and a large majority had advanced degrees. Only 12 percent were members of racial or ethnic minorities and only 13 percent were women (Pope 1999). The overrepresentation of individuals from higher-status backgrounds has clearly continued in the Congress.

Mintz (1975) and Freitag (1975) researched the class backgrounds of *all* cabinet officers during the period from 1897 to 1973 and found that there were strong ties to the upper class. A full 66 percent of these officers were from upper-class backgrounds and 90 percent had occupied a top corporate position before or after being appointed or had upper-class origins. The particular political party that happened to be in power at the time did not make much difference (Mintz 1975). Freitag's analysis supports Mills's conclusion that there is a clear connection between corporate and political elites and does not support Keller's and other pluralists' arguments about autonomous elites. His study, based on biographical information for all cabinet secretaries from McKinley to Nixon's first term, involving 358 cabinet positions, shows that *at least* 76 percent of cabinet members were tied to the corporate sector by being either corporate executives, officers, or corporate lawyers. Since President Truman's administration, this percent is even higher (86 percent under Eisenhower, 77 percent under Kennedy, 86 percent under Johnson, and 96 percent under Nixon) (Freitag 1975). Again, neither the political party in power nor the particular cabinet post make any difference in this relationship. Most of these individuals had connections with their corporations *before* taking office, but over 40 percent had such ties *before and after* appointment. Freitag concluded that the data do not prove that the corporate and governmental elite sectors are unified in terms of policies, but they do suggest that it is a "serious possibility" that the Cabinet may be accountable to large corporations. More recently, several members of Reagan's cabinet were found to be multimillionaires, and over 25 percent of the top 100 Reagan administrations officers had wealth of at least $1 million (Nader in Brownstein and Easton 1982).

Top federal officials are not likely to come from working-class or lower-class families. Presidents also tend to come from higher educational and occupational backgrounds, and certain ethnic backgrounds are overrepresented in these positions. For example, 20 of the first 36 presidents were of English background, 26 were college graduates, and 25 were lawyers (Kane 1974, pp. 343–344, 351). "If you aspire to political-elite status, it is advantageous to be white, well-educated, Protestant (and more specifically of Episcopalian or Presbyterian upbringing), native born and preferably British or Northern European extraction, and successful in a prestigious occupation" (Prewitt and Stone 1973, pp. 137–138).

Over the last two decades, Dye (1995) has documented the characteristics, backgrounds, and interconnections of the institutional elite in the United States. He included in his definition of elites all those who occupy positions of high authority in the governmental, media, educational, civic/cultural, military, financial, industrial, and legal institutions in the United States. Based on this definition, Dye concluded that there are 7,314 such positions. Taking all of the corporate, public-interest, and governmental elite together as a group, Dye estimated that about 30 percent come from upper-class origins, measured in terms of education and occupation of parent. However, while that class is disproportionately represented, the remaining 70 percent come from middle-class backgrounds. Ten percent of these institutional leaders are women and a much smaller percentage are African Americans (Dye 1995). Considering only the governmental elite—that is, those who occupy the top positions in the executive, legislative, and judicial branches—almost 75 percent have law or other advanced degrees. Over 40 percent are graduates of highly prestigious, private universities or colleges. Women and African Americans, as might be expected, are grossly underrepresented.

What is the meaning of these studies in terms of the perspectives on power presented earlier? If the essence of pluralism is the presence of a rough balance of power between constituencies with different interests, then these data clearly do not support the pluralist position. Some groups—most notably women, racial minorities, and working/

Although power-elite and ruling-class theories stress the significance of institutional position and social class as bases for power, gender has also separated those with more and less political power. Historically, women have been routinely kept out of the formal political process. It was not until August 26, 1920, that the Nineteenth Amendment was passed, giving women the right to vote.

lower-class members—are seldom found in offices of political power. To the extent that these offices are a principal means by which to gain and exercise political power, and that incumbents reflect and work for their own interests, then some groups have much less power than others.

INTERLINKAGE OF ECONOMIC AND POLITICAL POWER

Several of the studies discussed suggest that those with economic power are also more likely to be in positions of political power. It is important to know what the actual connection is between economic and political power in a society such as that of the United States, if only because it is widely considered to be a democracy in which every individual counts politically. As noted in Chapter 1,

there has been a long-standing concern for keeping economic power from contaminating the political arena and thereby keeping those who are wealthy from controlling the political process. Individuals still can contribute as much as they want for advertisements promoting a particular candidate, and there is no ceiling on how much candidates can spend on their own candidacies (Allen 1987). Moreover, political action committees (PACs) still can be created under various names to contribute to and campaign for chosen candidates and issues.

The studies discussed earlier show that office incumbents are most likely to come from high social classes. This class connection raises several questions about the relationship between economic and political power. First, does this connection necessarily mean that, as officeholders, incumbents will press only for policies that bene-fit their own classes? Second, are PACs and lob-bying groups so influential in the political process that it suggests dominance by one social class? Does money buy elections and votes? Third, and perhaps most important, is the upper class in gen-eral and its ruling "power elite" as united as Dom-hoff suggests? Each of these issues will be addressed in the following pages.

With respect to the first question, there are clear dangers in assuming that once in office, a person will automatically represent the interests of his or her class. Consider the following:

1. Although most of the elite are from wealthy backgrounds, not all wealthy individuals be-come members of the elite.
2. Not all of the wealthy who become members of the elite were born into or inherited their wealth. Some are more obviously self-made individuals, although they are wealthy. Those of poor backgrounds may certainly act differ-ently from those who inherited their wealth.
3. The values of the elite can change even though recruitment continues to be from the wealthy (Prewitt and Stone 1973, pp. 146–147).
4. Finally, internal conflicts and competition within the elite among those with different capital interests hinder unity on specific pol-icy content (Poulantzas 1973).

Despite these factors and the possible wide range of specific policies the elite may introduce, these differences are outweighed by the cohesiveness of broader agreements on how policies should be made and by concern for the preservation and pro-tection of U.S. values and institutions (Prewitt and Stone 1973, pp. 148–157).

Candidate Selection and Campaign Funding

Short of actual occupancy in a political office, an-other substantial manner in which an individual or organization can attempt to have political impact is through direct influence of officeholders. Two forms these attempts can take are the formation of interest groups and campaign contributions. Any mass of people thinking about organizing into an interest group must have access to resources nec-essary for effective mobilization in support of its interests. Presently, it is much easier for wealthy elites to mobilize political party support for their interests. Most consumers, for example, "find it hard or impossible to [organize] for obvious rea-sons—their large numbers, their lack of face-to-face contact or facilities for communicating with each other, and above all, the fact that people do not often think of themselves in the role of con-sumers" (Dolbeare and Edelman 1971, p. 343).

In the recent past, direct lobbying has been carried out by various groups with financial power. Since the 1960s, there has been a signifi-cant increase in the number and activity of interest groups, an increased centralization of their head-quarters in Washington, DC, a rise in the number of public-interest and single-issue interest groups, and more "formal penetration" on their part into governmental activities (Cigler and Loomis 1995). The number of political action committees has spiraled upward in recent years, going from 608 in 1974 to 3,844 in late 1997 (Salant 1998). Basically, PACs are interest groups that collect money from individuals sympathetic to their cause(s), and present it to desirable candidates. Many are worried about their influence because candidates rely heavily on money to run success-ful campaigns.

PACs represent many different interest groups. Corporations, labor, assorted trade, and nonconnected specific-issues groups are among the organizations with PACs, and each follows different strategies. For example, the National Ri-fle Association is frequently cited as a formidable interest group, having great influence on govern-mental policies involving gun control.

PACs vary in their approaches to elections and in deciding who will receive contributions. Some PACs support incumbents in office because they are primarily interested in obtaining access to officeholders, whereas others contribute to those who will increase the proportion of office-holders from a particular party. Finally, still others are "ideological" or "adversarial" and promote candidates who are on a particular side of an issue (Eismeier and Pollock 1986). Some are more likely to support challengers, but most PAC contributions appear to go to incumbents (Wilhite and Theilmann 1986; Stern 1988; Eismeier and Pollock 1986). Black candidates receive much less PAC support than Whites (Wilhite and Theilmann 1986).

Getting elected is very expensive. Spending for the 1996 general presidential election totaled $700,000,000, and congressional candidates during the same year spent $653,000,000 on their campaigns (Dougherty et al. 1997). The most expensive Senate race in 1996 cost the candidate almost $12,000,000 (Mark R. Warner of Virginia), and the most costly House race involved $5,578,000 (Newt Gingrich of Georgia) (Barone and Ujifusa 1997). In the 1996 elections, PACs contributed a total of almost $218,000,000 to Senate and House candidates, compared to just under $88,000,000 in the 1982 (Salant 1998). Table 7.2 lists the top 10 PAC contributors to the 1996 congressional elections and the amounts they spent.

The concern over the influence of PACs is based on the assumption that, *as a monolithic group,* contributors have disproportionate influence over federal policies. But it should be kept in mind that these groups vary widely in their specific interests and are not monolithic in this sense. In fact, the proliferation of these varying interest groups might be viewed as an indication of pluralism at work (Alexander 1992). At the same time, however, there is some question about whether the attention paid to *specific* interest groups will hinder the ability of governing officials to effectively address problems that affect the *general* interest of U.S. society (Cigler and Loomis, 1995).

In an attempt to limit and make known the sources of contributions, the Congress passed the Federal Election Campaign Act of 1971 to which amendments were added throughout the 1970s and later, but it is still questionable that such legislation affected the system of giving significantly. Political action committees, "bundlers" (fund-raisers who gather up numbers of $1,000 checks from

others), and the use of *state* party organizations to fund *federal* candidates have all reduced the effectiveness of the campaign reform laws. Enforcement is also lax, encouraging many wealthy givers to frequently exceed legal contribution limits (Abramson and Petzinger 1992a, 1992b). Some feel that the whole emphasis on trying to limit *individuals* is misplaced, that what needs changing is the *economic system,* because as it stands, the officeholders can do little else but support powerful economic interests. Individual officeholders do not have to consciously attempt to uphold the interests of these groups in order to do so (cf. Block 1977).

Regarding the issue of PACs and their impact, studies suggest that although PACs may increase an individual's access to given members of Congress, they do not systematically affect how these members vote. However, Senator Russell B. Long once said that "the distinction between a large campaign contribution and a bribe is almost a hairline's difference" (quoted in Stern 1988, p. 146). But in

TABLE 7.2   Top 10 PAC Contributors to 1996 Congressional Elections

GROUP	AMOUNT GIVEN
Teamsters Union	$2,606,140
American Federation of State, County, and Municipal Employees	$2,504,021
United Auto Workers	$2,467,319
Association of Trial Lawyers of America	$2,336,938
National Auto Dealers Association	$2,335,425
National Education Association	$2,326,830
American Medical Association	$2,321,197
National Association of Realtors	$2,099,683
Electrical Workers Union	$2,070,587
United Food & Commercial Workers Union	$2,030,795

Source: Federal PACs Directory 1998–1999. Congressional Quarterly. Washington, DC, 1998.

research on 20 labor-related issues in the U.S. House of Representatives, Jones and Keiser (1987) found that the amount of contributions from union-approved PACs was related to voting only on issues that had little media attention. In other words, the less visible the issue, the greater the effect of contributions on voting behavior.

A second analysis of 120 PACs connected to 10 different organizations examined the effect of PACs on the voting behavior of members of the House of Representatives and no significant influence on voting was found. However, these PACs and the organizations they represent can influence voting to the extent that they can influence the election process in the districts from which these congressional members originate (Grenzke 1989). It is not through the amount of the PAC contribution itself, but through other mechanisms that economically powerful groups can influence voting patterns.

RULING-CLASS UNITY

Pluralists argue that the upper class and corporate elite are not united, but these data indicate that although PACs with corporate affiliations may follow different general strategies, they rarely conflict with each other when it comes to specific races. This analysis of 243 PACs that made contributions of $25,000 or more revealed that while some PACs backed a candidate or incumbent for "ideological" reasons, others followed a more "pragmatic" course by backing the incumbent, assuming his or her reelection. This suggests an internal division within the corporate elite. However, on the level of the individual races there was a great deal of overlap between these types of PACs in terms of which candidate was supported. In almost 75 percent of the races, 90 percent of the corporate money went to only one of the two candidates. In other words, these corporate groups do not tend to conflict with each other when it comes to specific political races (Clawson, Neustadt, and Bearden 1986).

Several studies on PACs bear on Domhoff's argument about the unity of the ruling class,

which has been the subject of a recent controversy. Some view the corporate capitalist class as being divided along a variety of dimensions. Varying sizes of the work forces, differences in regions and in economic sectors (agricultural, manufacturing, etc.) with which organizations are identified, and competition and private property within capitalism make it inevitable to some that this class would be fragmented because of the different short-run specific interests within it (Offe 1973; Poulantzas 1973; Aldrich and Weiss 1981). In this view, the narrow interests of each corporation take precedence over the classwide interests of the corporate economy as a whole. This internal division weakens the power of the corporate class as a whole (for a review, see Useem 1984).

Mills and Domhoff's descriptions of the social backgrounds of the elite and the historical circumstances in which they rule suggest that they are unified. Domhoff described their common membership in and interaction at exclusive clubs, attendance at elite schools, and frequent listing on the Social Register, while Mills not only described their social-psychological similarities but also the concentration and coalescence that occurred among the major institutions involved in the power elite. Domhoff detailed some evidence of intermarriages, unique schooling, and leisure activities that point, he argued, to the existence of a cohesive upper class of which the public is conscious:

> *The corporate rich are drawn together by bonds of social cohesion as well as their common economic interests. This social cohesion is based in... common membership in specific social institutions and friendships based on social interactions within those institutions.... Social cohesion is important from a class-dominance perspective because the most socially cohesive groups are the ones that do best in arriving at consensus when dealing with a problem. (Domhoff 1998, p. 72)*

Ostrander's (1984) study of upper-class women suggests that they are highly conscious of their class and their responsibilities in maintaining their social-class position. In supporting their husbands' economic activities, and as members of voluntary associations and social clubs, upper-class women work to perpetuate their social class.

> *A central aim of upper-class women's community volunteer work, as they describe it, is to keep private control over community organizations. Private control comes to be identified as the control of their own class.... Their social life is the social life of a class, and their relations weave the fabric of upper-class life. As community volunteers, upper-class women work almost entirely as members of their class. They have little in common, here, with other women. (Ostrander 1984, pp. 148–149).*

Although there are tensions and individual disagreements within this group, as a whole they are united in defense of their class. This not only helps to maintain their class, but because it is male dominated, the subordinate position of these women within it (ibid.).

The studies cited focus on the unity of the upper class as a whole. Other studies reviewed earlier on political activity, however, also imply unification of the elite as a group, many of whom are not of upper-class background. In his study of elites, involving individuals from a variety of institutional areas, Dye (1995) also concluded that there is general unity of opinion among the elite, even though there is some evidence of rising factionalism within it.

> *It is our own judgment, based on our examination of available surveys of leadership opinion as well as public statements of top corporate and governmental executives, that consensus rather than competition characterizes elite opinion. Despite disagreements over specific policies and programs, most top leaders agree on the basic values and future directions of American society.... Disagreement among various sectors of national leaders... is confined to a relatively narrow set of issues—the size of governmental budgets, specific details of tax reform, and the adequacy of current defense spending. There is widespread agreement on the essential components of welfare-state capitalism. (p. 217)*

Verba and Orren's study of 2,762 leaders from various institutional areas in the late 1970s also suggests unity on *basic values*. They found that all types of leaders tend to agree, for example, that a fair distribution of economic resources is one in which everyone has equal opportunity to pursue legitimate goals. They do not feel that everyone should have an equal amount, however. This solidarity of opinion included African American, feminist, and labor leaders. However, when it comes to opinions on *specific* matters rather than *general* values, or to descriptions of actual rather than ideal situations, there is disagreement among these leaders. For example, only 9 percent of business leaders view poverty as the result of the workings of the economic system, whereas 86 percent of African American leaders and 76 percent of feminist leaders see it this way (Verba and Orren 1985, p. 74). Seider's (1974) content analysis of the speeches of big business executives also indicated that although there are differences among them on specifics, there is fundamental unity on beliefs supporting the capitalist economic system that are never challenged.

Even though he has concluded that the elite are generally united on basic values, Dye (1995) argued that a split has developed within the elite between those he labels the "sunbelt cowboys" and the "established yankees." As the labels suggest, the "cowboys" as a group are individualistic, conservative, and often from non-upper-class backgrounds. Their wealth has been recently acquired. In contrast, the "yankees" tend to be more liberal and have established family wealth. They have attended the best Ivy League schools and are also likely to have occupied high positions in prestigious corporate, financial, or legal institutions. Thus, as to the issue of how unified the elite or upper class is, it is important to indicate whether one is speaking of the *general* or *specific* level, in *ideal* or *real-situational* terms, and of *social background* or *behavioral* unity. In some ways, these groups appear unified and in others they do not; the results from attitudinal and positional studies on unity are clearly mixed and one can find statistics to support both positions.

Like Domhoff, Dye, and others, Useem has dissected the capitalist class and its unity in detail. His studies concern the structural texture of that class (cf. 1978, 1979, 1984). Useem defined the capitalist class as "those who own or manage major business firms and their immediate kin" (1980, p. 200). In one analysis, he studied 2,843 officers from 200 corporations that varied in size and sector. The officers also differed in the number of corporations to which they were tied through directorships. Generally, Useem found that members of the capitalist class are not equally powerful. Those from larger firms who were also directors at other corporations were significantly more likely to have served on advisory committees for government at the local, state, and federal levels. They were also more likely to participate in national business groups such as the Business Roundtable, Business Council, Council on Foreign Relations, National Association of Manufacturers, and U.S. Chamber of Commerce and to be involved in significant cultural organizations (elite university boards, art, and research organizations) (1980). Useem, however, did not find significant participation differences between major industrialists and financiers.

In other research, Useem directly addressed the issue of the political unity of what he calls the "inner circle" of business, looking at whether members of this group act on behalf of their own separate corporations or on behalf of the capitalist class as a whole. Useem drew his information and conclusions from a wide variety of data sources, including personal interviews and documentary and survey data. The inner circle he described is a network of leaders from large corporations who serve as top officers at more than one firm, who are politically active, and who serve the interests of the capitalist class as a whole rather than the narrow immediate interests of their individual companies. To be a member of the inner circle, it helps to (1) have been successful in a major corporation, (2) have multiple directorships, (3) have occupied a senior position, (4) be a member of business associations, and (5) have been a consultant or advisor to government. Members of the inner circle are more often members of the upper class than are other business leaders—that is, they are richer, have attended elite prep schools, and are in the Social Register (Useem 1984, pp. 65–69).

Useem viewed capitalism in the United States as having moved from (1) "family capitalism" in which individual upper-class families dominated corporate ownership, through (2) "managerial capitalism" in which managers began to replace the dominance of upper-class owners around the turn of the twentieth century, to (3) "institutional capitalism" in which networks of intercorporate ties characterize the core of capitalism. The increasing control of corporations by their managers rather than owners and the increased concentration and interlocking in the corporate sector during this century have helped lay the basis for the development of this powerful circle (Useem 1984).

Indeed, Dye's study of individuals in top institutional positions revealed that 4,000 to 5,000 individuals have formal control over 50 percent of the country's industrial, banking, communications, transportation, and utilities assets and over 66 percent of the nation's insurance assets. The top 100 of 200,000 industrial corporations control over 58 percent of the $1.6 trillion in industrial assets, the 50 biggest banks control almost two-thirds of all banking assets, and 50 insurance companies control over 80 percent of assets in their field (Dye 1995). Some 15 percent of the 7,314 institutional leaders studied by Dye occupied more than one top position (i.e., were interlockers) and a smaller percent held as many as six or more such positions. He viewed this "inner group" as cohesive for a number of reasons, and, like Useem, found that multiple corporate interlockers were more likely than single directors to participate in governmental and other major organizations.

In addition to these trends in the corporate sphere, the "inner circle" of corporate leaders Useem (1984) described also developed as a result of the disparate nature of the business community and the uncertain environment that exists for business in capitalist societies. That is, the inner circle unifies the interests of business as a class in a turbulent political and economic setting.

The development of this circle is not the result of a conscious conspiracy, but rather is largely the consequence of structural changes and characteristics of capitalist society. Those in the circle serve on several boards, making them sensitive to the interests of business as a whole—that is, to the "classwide" needs of business. The circle's political style is to adopt a "posture of compromise" and accommodation rather than to be directly confrontational on every specific issue. Its interests are in the general protection of capitalism as a whole, not in the interests of specific companies.

There are a number of ways in which this elite group of business leaders gets politically involved. One principal mechanism is through governmental ties. As Useem's and others' research indicated, for example, they are more likely to serve as cabinet officers. During Ronald Reagan's first term, Weinberger (Defense), Regan (Treasury), Baldridge (Commerce), Haig (State), and Pierce (Housing and Urban Development), as well as Smith (Attorney General) had all been multiple corporate directors. Like Dye and others, Useem also found that the inner-circle members play crucial political roles by directing nonprofit organizations, serving as political fund-raisers, endorsing candidates, giving larger campaign contributions, and influencing media content (Useem 1984, pp. 76–94).

This inner circle is much more politically active than business in general because its members occupy several important positions at once, which (1) creates cohesiveness among its members, (2) helps mobilize economic and other resources, and (3) provides a powerful platform from which to express political positions. Moreover, its members are also closely tied to the upper class, which increases the circle's influence (Useem 1984). In contrast to other research, Useem found that if members of the upper class are in the business elite, they are more likely than persons from other classes to get into the inner circle. In sum, characteristics of the U.S. political economy create opportunities for the interconnection of political and economic power.

The Structural Tie

A significant part of the reason for the tie between economic and political power lies in the interlocking between private and corporate wealth and political opportunity. It takes wealth, or at least access to wealth, to run a viable campaign for a major national political office. The connection between economic and political power may be deeper than this suggests, however, and may be based not on the characteristics of particular *individuals* but on the *structure and functioning* of the society.

The *structuralist* position suggests that given the structure of a capitalist society such as the United States, the government *must* act in a manner that supports the capitalist class and capitalism in general. This occurs regardless of who is in office. The political and economic institutions are so intertwined that the government, although it may be "relatively autonomous," is constrained to support and pass policies that maintain the capitalist economy. Even in the absence of direct influence by the ruling class, the state would find it difficult to carry out anticapitalist policies (Block 1977). It is the structural context in which the government is embedded that directs its policies most powerfully, rather than individuals who hold political office. "The functions of the state are broadly determined by the structures of state power" (Gold, Lo, and Wright 1975, p. 36). This does not mean that every policy will always benefit each individual corporation, but it does mean that in the long run the interests of capitalism in general will be served by these policies. Hicks, Friedland, and Johnson (1978), for example, found that the presence of corporations in general has a negative impact on government policies of redistribution to the poor, whereas the presence in a particular state of labor unions has a positive effect. According to structuralists, this wedding between economic interests and governmental policies exists for several reasons:

1. *The capitalist economy has developed in such a manner that increasing numbers of workers are together under one system.* This creates a greater possibility for working-class unity, which in turn can threaten the existing nature of the economy. The state works to prevent this worker unity from becoming too strong by endorsing policies that transform general political interests of the working class (e.g., control of the production system) into narrower economic ones (e.g., wages and vacation times) (Gold, Lo, and Wright 1975, pp. 36–37). Class antagonisms can endanger the state and, as a result, policies and ideologies are used to mask and reduce class struggle.

2. *The government helps to provide and regulate a labor force for hire through its provision of educational facilities and restrictive welfare policies.* Educational institutions exist to help prepare individuals to fit into their roles in the economy and class structure, whereas demeaning and meager governmental support through welfare programs helps to ensure that any surplus labor force will be eager to take any job at low wages (Bowles and Gintis 1976; Szymanski 1978; Piven and Cloward 1982).

3. *The state needs to maintain a certain level of economic activity if it is to survive; it needs revenue to run itself.* If capitalists do not invest, then government has problems. Consequently, policies are created to encourage investments and capital accumulation (Offe 1975). This takes place even though the state may not be made up of members of the ruling class. In fact, the state can function best to support capitalism in this view if its class character is hidden and it is seen as a legitimate classless state (Offe 1973).

4. *The state has to ensure the smooth running of the economy, because if it is not stable, the state will lose public support.* If the state pursues anticapitalist policies, business confidence will decrease; if that occurs, investments will decline and the economy as well as the government will be in danger. Consequently, it is in the state's own interest to pursue capitalist policies—that is, to act responsibly (Block 1977, p. 1519). "As long as the economic system provides an acceptable degree of security, growing material wealth, and opportunity...for the next generation, the average American does not ask who is running things or what goals are being pursued" (Fusfeld 1972, p. 2).

5. *The development of monopoly capitalism encourages the intrusion of the state into the economy, and thereby the state itself develops an interest in capital accumulation* (Gold, Lo, and Wright 1975, pp. 40–48; O'Connor 1973; Block 1977). One manner in which this occurs is through the creation of unemployment in part because of technological advances in the monopoly sector. The state then steps in to deal with the problem.

The preceding studies on campaign financing, holding office, and the capitalist economy indicate that both individuals and structural arrangements foster a relationship between economic and political power. Structural ties among institutions make it possible for some individuals to have access to positions of great power. According to some, however, one of the major problems with both these analyses is that they assume that all major policies are made within the government and, therefore, the focus of both approaches is on the state. In fact, it has been suggested, many major policies are created outside the government, principally by the actions of corporations. Industrial change, for example, to the extent that it can be considered a "policy," has largely been the result of actions by the private sector, not the government (Schwartz 1987).

SUMMARY

This chapter began with a brief discussion on the importance and difficulty of conceptualizing power. We then moved to an analysis of pluralist, elite, and ruling-class views of the national power structure, and the data that bear on the validity of each.

There are clear relationships between socioeconomic position and voting, holding political office, and other forms of political participation. Those closer to the bottom of the class hierarchy are less likely than those in the middle and upper classes to vote, be elected to office, and to be represented in powerful lobbying groups. Research indicates that those from higher socioeconomic levels, especially the upper class, are disproportionately represented in elite positions in a variety of institutional spheres.

Each of these measures is characteristic of an approach to understanding the relationship between economic resources and political power that traces the careers and institutional paths of *individuals* rather than focusing on the *structure* of the institutional network itself as a basis for such understanding. The structuralist approach, on the other hand, focuses on the systemic interrelationships between the economy and the state, suggesting that the government is inextricably tied to the capitalist economy and needs to support capitalism in order to maintain itself. This is independent of the particular individuals who may occupy office at the time. A number of the changes that have occurred in the political economy—such as increased concentration, interlocking between institutions, and the like—encourage greater centralization and unity of economic and political power. On balance, the data presented provide evidence of a greater concentration of political power than is suggested by pluralist theory.

CRITICAL THINKING

1. Are information technology and the World Wide Web creating new bases for power and domination? Is it the corporate rich who will claim these bases or are new, powerful groups being created by these technological developments? Discuss your answer.

2. Is the average citizen becoming more or less powerful in influencing governmental policy? Support your answer. Is political power becoming more or less centralized in the United States? Why?

3. How can economic and political power be separated to ensure the influence of all, regardless of wealth?

WEB CONNECTIONS

Historically, women and minorities have been underrepresented in elected political offices, especially at the federal level. Find out how many women got elected in 1998, and compare the states for variations in this gender gap. How did your home state do compared to others? See:

http://www.gendergap.com/elections.htm

CHAPTER 8

U.S. INEQUALITY IN COMPARATIVE PERSPECTIVE

The fact that rising earnings inequality occurred in other industrialized countries with different job creation experiences suggests that rising inequality may be related to more general phenomena occurring across nations.
—Gordon Green, John Coder, and Paul Ryscavage

Despite convergence in the labor market histories and qualifications of women and men, occupational distributions in many industrialized countries reveal large and persistent sex differences.
—Maria Charles

The last several chapters have discussed several forms of inequality in the United States. This chapter helps to put the extent of that inequality in comparative perspective by addressing the extent of economic, gender, and racial/ethnic inequality on the international scene. One might expect that the United States, as a democratic nation, would exhibit less inequality than most other countries, especially those which are less developed economically and less democratic politically.

As an industrial nation, the United States is generally thought of as having a *class* system, a relatively open system of inequality based primarily on economic holdings in which positions are largely attained rather than ascribed. This contrasts with *caste* and *estate* systems, which have been more characteristic of agrarian societies. A caste system is a closed status system of hierarchically arranged groups based on ascribed characteristics; it is ultimately legitimated by religion (e.g., Hinduism) and custom. India, to be discussed later in this chapter, has been characterized by its caste system. An estate system, as found in feudal Europe around the twelfth century, is a fairly rigid system based primarily on land ownership, and sanctioned by the state and religion (e.g., Catholic Church in medieval Europe). The clergy, nobility, and commoners made up the three major estates in early Europe. *Slavery,* a fourth system of inequality, is based on ownership of human beings. The permanence of one's position and relations between masters and slaves can vary, as it did in Brazil, the United States, and ancient Greece.

Although descriptions of these broad systems of inequality help put the U.S. system of inequality into a comparative framework, the main focus of this chapter will be on contemporary differences among countries, especially variations in economic inequality. International comparisons of economic inequality, although desirable, have been hazardous for a variety of reasons:

1. Survey data have usually been collected in different years in different countries.
2. Different measures of poverty have been used at various times. For example, some surveys have used an absolute measure, setting a particularly low threshold to define poverty, whereas others have recommended a more relative measure, defining poverty in terms of how a particular population segment compares to others in the society.
3. Families and households, which frequently are the unit of analysis in wealth and income analyses, are defined differently in different countries. For example, even within the Luxembourg Income Study, which is considered the best source for comparative income research, there are differences in the data sets between countries. Data from the Netherlands, for example, do not distinguish between households and families, whereas in Sweden, youths over age 18 who live with their parents are considered a separate family.
4. Differences in degrees of underreporting of economic resources exist between countries, and what is included in income and wealth also varies. For example, the United States includes trust funds in its determination of a family's wealth, but France does not (Kessler and Wolff 1991).

DIFFERENCES IN QUALITY OF LIFE

There are significant international inequalities on a wide variety of conditions that measure the quality of life for people. A group experiencing one of the worst qualities of life today are the Dinka tribe in southern Sudan. Thousands of Dinkas have been and continue to be enslaved by their more powerful northern Muslim neighbors in Sudan's civil war. The number of slaves is generally estimated to be about 20,000. "Their Muslim owners ...consider it a traditional right to enslave southerners.... The slaves have been put to work as cooks, maids, field hands, and concubines.... Many are fed and kept like cattle, often sleeping beside livestock that their owners consider far

more valuable. Like cattle, they are branded, sometimes just below the eye, with the Arabic name of their owner" (Miniter 1999, p. 64).

Specific differences in quality of life are especially noticeable when industrial and developing/underdeveloped countries are compared. For example, individuals in industrial countries had an average *life expectancy at birth* of over 74 years in 1995; those in developing countries averaged about 62 years. Even though it is lower than that in industrial countries, the latter is still an improvement over 46 years, which was the life expectancy in developing countries in 1960. In sub-Saharan Africa, the life expectancy is only 50 years, and in some parts of Africa, it is even lower because of the spread of HIV/AIDS (United Nations 1998).

Child mortality rates (i.e., the number of children under age 5 who die per 1,000 live births) also differ significantly between countries. The rate for developing countries is 6 times that found in industrial nations (95 vs. 16) (United Nations 1998). Variations in these rates are related to internal and external conditions that affect the level and rate of development in countries. Internally, economic growth, education, health-care service, women's status, and strength of central government are *directly* associated with *lower* child mortality rates, whereas externally, ties of dependency of a country to other nations (e.g., foreign investment and debt) are *indirectly* related to *higher* child mortality rates through their negative influence on women's status, economic growth, and other internal elements. Of all these, women's status appears to be the best predictor of child mortality rates (Shen and Williamson 1997).

In addition to the chances for life, extensive comparative inequalities also continue in living conditions. Ninety percent of those who become infected with HIV live in developing countries, one consequence of which was the 8.2 million orphaned children in 1997 who lost their parents to AIDS. Although HIV/AIDS rates are very high in many places in Africa (e.g., 40 percent of all adult deaths in rural Uganda are HIV/AIDS-related), India had the highest *number* of HIV victims in 1997 (2 to 3 million) (United Nations 1998).

© The Stock Market/Andrew Holbrooke

A grieving emaciated mother carries a dead or unconscious child through dirt streets during a famine in Africa. Images like these are not unusual in some African countries where natural disasters have reduced living conditions to a very low level.

Sanitation and consumption levels are also part of one's living conditions. About 60 percent of the 4.4 billion people living in developing countries lack sanitation, 25 percent lack decent housing, and 20 percent do not have access to effective health services. These figures compare to often negligible percentages for people in industrial countries (United Nations 1998). Gross inequalities in consumption of necessities also plague the poorest people on earth. "Globally, the 20% of the world's people in the highest-income countries account for 86% of total private consumption expenditures—the poorest 20% a minuscule 1.3%" (United Nations 1998, p. 2). In 1995, for example, the United States consumed 119 kilograms of meat per capita, compared to 3 kilograms in Bangladesh; spent $2,765 per capita on health care in 1990, compared to $3.00 (in U.S. dollars) spent per capita in Viet Nam; and used almost as much electrical energy in 1995 as all developing countries *combined* (United Nations 1998).

Finally, inequalities in access to knowledge and information continue. Adult literacy rates vary wildly among countries, ranging from an average of over 99 percent in the United States and industrialized countries to 14 percent in Niger, 38 percent in Pakistan, and 45 percent in Haiti (United Nations 1998). The importance of access to modern informational technology in an increasingly global economic network was discussed in Chapter 2, and the apparent worldwide discrepancies in access do not bode well for reductions in economic inequality between nations. In 1995, there were 328 computers per 1,000 individuals in the United States, whereas there were only about 7 per 1,000 in developing countries. Similar extreme discrepancies exist in Internet use, fax machines, and international telephone calls (ibid.). Table 8.1 shows how industrial countries compare with the least developed countries on several quality-of-life measures. For example, in industrial countries, adult literacy rates are about twice as high, life expectancy one-and-a-half times as high, and child mortality only one-tenth as high as rates in the least developed countries.

ECONOMIC INEQUALITY

Many of the inequalities just discussed are related to economic differences between countries. The way to consider how bad poverty levels and income inequality are in the United States is to compare them with what is found in other countries. Clearly, the rate of poverty is much higher in many other countries, especially considering the fact that poverty is measured in less generous terms in these countries.

Over 1 billion people in developing countries currently have incomes of less than $420 per year. Among developing countries, although poverty

TABLE 8.1 Ratios on Selected Measures of Quality of Life Comparing Industrial with Least Developed Countries

MEASURE	INDUSTRIAL/LEAST DEVELOPED
Adult literacy rate	2 to 1
Life expectancy	1.45 to 1
Child mortality rate	1 to 10.69
Doctors (per 100,000 people)	20.5 to 1
Dependency ratio[a]	0.57 to 1
Electricity consumption	211 to 1
Televisions	16 to 1
Human Development Index[b]	2.65 to 1

Source: Based on United Nations 1998.

Note: [a]*Dependency ratio* generally refers to the proportion of the population, usually very young or old, who are not in the labor force. [b]The *Human Development Index* is a composite measure that includes life expectancy, educational attainment, and adjusted income. A higher score on each element indicates higher human development.

rates in Asia have declined since 1985, those in the Middle East, North Africa, Latin America, the Caribbean, and sub-Saharan Africa have increased. Just under half of the people in the latter region are poor by the above standards (International Bank for Reconstruction and Development/ The World Bank 1992). In some sub-Saharan African countries such as Zaire, Sudan, Malawi, and Rwanda, at least 80 percent of the rural population is poor. In 1995, the per capita income in the U.S. was 89 times higher than that found in the least developed countries of the world (United Nations 1998).

The higher poverty levels in most nonindustrial countries might placate Americans, but when compared to other industrial countries, the poverty rate in the United States does not fare so well. Overall poverty rates and those for children, the elderly, and women are higher in the United States than in other industrial countries. Less adequate governmental programs and lower employment rates among women are two of the major reasons for these discrepancies (Smeeding 1992; Casper, McLanahan, and Garfinkel 1994).

With respect to income inequality, in most cases, the poorer a country, the greater is the income discrepancy between the richest and poorest 20 percent of the population. In about half of the developing countries, the income of the top 20 percent is at least 15 times that of the bottom 20 percent. For example, in Kenya in 1992, a so-called low-income country, the poorest 10 percent owned 1.2 percent of all income, compared to 47.7 percent being owned by the richest 10 percent. In contrast, the distribution in Denmark, a so-called high-income country, the poorest 10 percent possessed 3.6 percent of income, whereas the top 10 percent held 20.5 percent (United Nations 1998; The World Bank 1999).

Income distributions also differ among industrial nations, with the United States having among the highest concentrations of income. Table 8.2 presents the shares of income going to each income quintile in various industrial countries. Keep in mind that data were collected in different years from these countries. But among them, the United States has the highest degree of income inequality (gini = 40.1). In 1994, the poorest 20 percent owned only 4.8 percent of income, compared to over 45 percent for the top 20 percent. In contrast, in Norway, for example, the corresponding figures were 10 percent and 35.3 percent, respectively.

TABLE 8.2 Percentage Share of Income or Consumption among Population Quintiles in Selected Industrial Market Countries

COUNTRY	BOTTOM 20%	SECOND 20%	THIRD 20%	FOURTH 20%	TOP 20%	GINI INDEX[a]
Australia (1989)	7.0	12.2	16.6	23.3	40.9	33.7
Belgium (1992)	9.5	14.6	18.4	23.0	34.5	25.0
Canada (1994)	7.5	12.9	17.2	23.0	39.3	31.5
Denmark (1992)	9.6	14.9	18.3	22.7	34.5	24.7
Finland (1991)	10.0	14.2	17.6	22.3	35.8	25.6
France (1989)	7.2	12.7	17.1	22.8	40.1	32.7
Germany (1989)	9.0	13.5	17.5	22.9	37.1	28.1
Ireland (1987)	6.7	11.6	16.4	22.4	42.9	35.9
Italy (1991)	7.6	12.9	17.3	23.2	38.9	31.2
Netherlands (1991)	8.0	13.0	16.7	22.5	39.9	31.5
Norway (1991)	10.0	14.3	17.9	22.4	35.3	25.2
Spain (1990)	7.5	12.6	17.0	22.6	40.3	32.5
Sweden (1992)	9.6	14.5	18.1	23.2	34.5	25.0
Switzerland (1982)	7.4	11.6	15.6	21.9	43.5	36.1
United Kingdom (1986)	7.1	12.8	17.2	23.1	39.8	32.6
United States (1994)	4.8	10.5	16.0	23.5	45.2	40.1

Source: Adapted from The World Bank 1999, pp. 198–199.

Note: The dates in parentheses are the years in which data were collected. [a]The gini index measures the dispersion of income across the whole income distribution. The index ranges in score from 0 to 1.0, with 0 representing perfect *equality,* where each person or group gets an equal share, and with 1.0 representing perfect *inequality,* where one person or group owns all the income. In other words, the higher the index score, the higher the inequality. Gini scores were multiplied by 100.

Industrialized countries also differ in earnings distributions. When compared to Australia, Canada, Sweden, and West Germany in the 1980s, the United States had the most unequal distribution regardless of the method used to measure earnings inequality (Green, Coder, and Ryscavage 1992). The lowest 10 percent of men, ages 25 to 54, working full time, year-round, received 3 percent of all earnings in the United States, compared to a next low of 3.4 percent in Canada and a high of 5.9 percent in Sweden. On the other end of the scale, the top 10 percent of earners received a high of 23.3 percent of all earnings in the United States, while in Canada they received 20.7 percent and in West Germany 18.9 percent.

The greater income and earnings inequalities in the United States, compared to other industrial countries, coupled with the fact that inequalities increased in most of these during the 1980s, sug-gest that there may be underlying mechanisms common to industrial countries that are creating pressures for greater inequality, but that are accentuated in the United States. Among the possibilities are rises in the demands for various high-tech skills and declines in others. New communication technologies have also opened up new sources for wealth and income attainment for those with access to and skills in them. Organizational streamlining has also left many unemployed or demoted and others wealthier than before (Green, Coder, and Ryscavage 1992). These changes in technology create an impetus for growing inequality.

In addition to differences in data collection, a wide variety of factors will affect the distribution of income and wealth in a country, and therefore help account for the differences between countries: (1) Demographic factors (e.g., particular age structure, family composition, and marital dissolution rates) of a country, along with its (2) economic conditions (e.g., inflation, productivity, employment patterns, growth rates), and (3) tax and inheritance laws, all affect the distribution of economic resources. For example, Japan's income distribution tends to be fairly equal compared to many other countries. Part of the reason for this is its highly progressive personal income tax system. Those earning over $160,000 (defined in terms of U.S. dollars) are taxed at the rate of 65 percent. Divorce is also much less frequent in Japan than in the United States, and divorce is a major cause in the rise of poverty rates among poor single-parent families and children. On the other hand, the proportion of the elderly population in Japan is increasing, and this will likely increase the concentration of income and wealth there as economic resources are inherited and spread among smaller numbers of offspring (Bauer and Mason 1992).

There appears to be a curvilinear relationship between development and income inequality. Early in development, inequality is low, but then it increases along with development, and eventually declines while the country continues to develop. This trend is related to shifts in the economy, population size, and educational levels of countries. Inequality, at first, increases and then decreases as (1) the industrial sector grows and eventually becomes the primary source of employment, (2) the rate of population growth increases and then decreases, and (3) educational levels increase (Nielsen and Alderson 1995). While also finding evidence of these trends, Stack and Zimmerman's (1982) study of 43 countries found, nevertheless, that the level of development was not related to the share of income received by the bottom 20 percent of the population. In other words, the trend toward greater equality in developed nations applies only to the top 80 percent. "Development does not result in the redistribution of income to low income groups" (p. 355).

A poor industrial base, high population growth rates, and low levels of education in countries foster income inequality within countries and help to maintain the gap between developed and underdeveloped nations. The income gap between the richest and poorest of the world's population has increased over the last several decades, increasing income concentration worldwide. In 1960, the 20 percent richest countries had an income that was 30 times that of the poorest 20 percent, but by 1995, that gap had increased to 82 times. *In 1997, it was estimated that the total wealth of the richest 225 people in the world was over $1 trillion, which equaled the combined income of the poorest 47 percent (2.5 billion people)* (United Nations 1998).

Changes in the global income gap partly reflect trends in the former Soviet Union as well as in other less developed countries. In many of the East and Central European countries, economic conditions have worsened since the collapse of the USSR, creating real difficulties within as well as increased discrepancies between them. These countries' economic profiles approximate those of developing countries. At least in the short run, per capita income has fallen in Central Europe and the former USSR, whereas unemployment has gone up and consumer prices have risen dramatically (Hauchler and Kennedy 1994). These developments further promote the large economic gaps that exist among countries. How can we account for these gaps?

A number of theories discussed in this chapter, most notably the dependency and world system perspectives, suggest that inequality is often accelerated by relationships between countries. As Nutshell 8.1 makes clear, the gap in wealth has increased, with wealth becoming more concentrated internationally.

Explaining International Inequality

Think about how you would account for the difference in wealth between two people. You might say it could be just a matter of time before one catches up with the other. Or it could be that the poorer individual does not have enough motivation or the right values to allow accumulation of wealth. Or it could be that the two people are differentially constrained by structures or circumstances beyond their control. One happens to be in

NUTSHELL 8.1 _____

Wealth Concentrating, UN Says

Some Asian Growth Rates Are Called Unprecedented

COLUM LYNCH
GLOBE CORRESPONDENT

United Nations—The world's 358 billionaires have amassed more assets than the combined gross domestic product of countries with nearly half of the world's people, according to a United Nations report scheduled to be released this week.

As part of an overall trend in the concentration of wealth, the report found that since 1980, 15 countries, mostly in Asia, have enjoyed rates of economic growth higher than any recorded in 200 years of industrialization, according to the UN's Human Development Report.

But the fortunes of the few have largely eluded poor nations, bringing diminishing job opportunities, falling wages and a rate of economic decline throughout much of the developing world that surpasses levels faced by the industrialized world during the Great Depression of the 1930s.

Some 1.6 billion people in 89 countries, mostly in Africa, are worse off economically today than they were 10 years ago. Since 1960, the income gap between industrialized nations and poor countries has tripled, according to the report.

"The world has become more economically polarized, both between countries and within countries," said James Gustave Speth, administrator of the UN Development Program, which published the report. "If present trends continue, economic disparities between industrial and developing nations will move from inequitable to inhuman."

Although the United States has maintained steady economic growth, high standards of living

and sustained job growth in recent decades, the gap in wages between the nation's richest and poorest citizens has been widening, according to the report. Between 1975 and 1990, the richest 1 percent of the population increased its share of the wealth from 20 percent to 36 percent.

"In the United States, and to a lesser extent in some nations of the European Union, the inequality of income and wealth seems to be increasing," Robert M. Solow, an economist and Nobel laureate, wrote in the report.

The report, which measures a nation's quality of life on the basis of an individual's life expectancy, access to education and purchasing power, found that Canada, followed by the United States, Japan and the Netherlands, has the highest standard of living in the world. At the bottom of the ladder were African countries like Somalia, Niger and Sierra Leone.

Richard Jolly, the report's principal author, said that economic growth is essential to improving the lot of the world's poorest nations. However, he warned that economic expansion without sufficient investment in social welfare programs is a prescription for disaster. In Ghana, as in many parts of Africa, the economy grew (by 4.8 percent between 1986 and 1991) while employment fell (by 13 percent).

Jolly appealed to policy makers to follow the example of many Asian governments that have invested the profits of economic expansion into education.

Source: The Boston Globe, July 16, 1996, p. A10. Reprinted with permission of Colum Lynch.

---

a better situation than the other, allowing for the accumulation of wealth.

The explanations given for the inequality that exists between nations parallel these same reasons. There are (1) evolutionary/stage, (2) psychological/value, and (3) dependency/world-system theo-

ries of international inequality. Broadly speaking, *evolutionary* or *stage explanations* contend that development results from movement up through a set of stages brought about by processes at work within the society. For example, Rostow (1960) suggested that societies go through five major stages in their movement to development: (1) traditional stage, (2) preconditions for takeoff, (3) the takeoff, (4) the drive to maturity, and (5) the age of mass consumption. In each stage, certain events must occur in order for a society to move on to the next phase of development. Clearly, the fifth stage is modeled after the United States. A cruder version of this approach is found in earlier evolutionary theories that portray development as an almost automatic and universal process that comes with increasing population and progressive integration within the society. Leaving aside the ideological issues surrounding this approach to development, Rostow's theory, like others in this school of thought, has been heavily criticized as being ahistorical and weak in its consideration of how the ties between countries affect underdevelopment.

The second type of theory stresses that in order for development to occur, a particular set of *values* has to be present in a significant proportion of the population. Psychologist McClelland (1961), for example, stressed the importance of need for achievement as a value in individuals, and sociologists Inkeles and Smith (1974) argued for the importance of a number of values if development of a "modern man" is to occur. Among the characteristics of the modern person they list are a readiness for new experience, a democratic orientation, a belief in human efficacy, a faith in science and technology, and a disposition to form and hold opinions. Traditional values such as superstition, ethnocentrism, fatalism, norms of pride, dignity, and modesty are viewed as cultural barriers to development (Foster 1973). In these theories, the importance of structure and history for development pales next to the significance of personality and values.

Both of these sets of theories assume that there is a fundamental conflict between tradition and modernity, that one is the enemy of the other, and that the gap between them must be bridged if development is to occur. The final set of theories suggests that the degree of development of a country is tied to its position in the system of inequality in the world economy. These theories developed largely as alternatives to the kinds of modernization theories just discussed. More specifically, advocates of the *dependency theory* contend that the principal reason some countries are underdeveloped is because they are minor players in the world market and are linked to major nations through ties of exploitation. Large, powerful nations drain less powerful countries of their resources, establish markets for their own finished products in these countries, penetrate their economies with multinational corporations, and largely determine the terms of trade and pricing in the world economy. This leaves weaker, less prosperous countries in a state of seemingly permanent underdevelopment. For example, one advocate of this position, Andre Frank (1969), refers to this dependency condition as one in which underdevelopment is developed.

More recently, there has been a great deal of interest in *world-system theory*. Wallerstein (1974, 1979) is largely credited with initiating this discussion, but earlier thinkers had already considered the idea (Hunter and Abraham 1987; Chiot and Hall 1982). Similar to dependency theory, the world-system approach views the world economy as an interdependent system in which countries play different roles and are in different economic positions. In effect, there is a geographic and functional division of labor among all of the countries. Dominance in this world economy is established through state control and legislation, economic penetration of other countries, and a lowering of a country's dependence on external markets.

Capitalism is the driving economic force that has gradually enveloped most of the world, vastly increasing the commodities for sale on the world market, and creating a large international working class. Since many of those in the working class of underdeveloped countries are non-Whites, the inequality that results takes on racial overtones. An overlapping of racial and economic inequality occurs with a vast majority of those in underdeveloped countries being both working class and members of a racial minority. Recall our discussion of a class theory of race relations in Chapter 6. The most important nations in this world economic system, the *core* nations, own most of the capital, whereas the less developed or *peripheral* nations provide raw materials and labor for the development of finished commodities. Having developed historically because of (1) protective trade policies, (2) conquest, and (3) economic support from the state, core nations siphon off resources and capital from peripheral nations, many of which are or have been colonies.

The dependency that appears between core and peripheral nations goes through several stages. In the first phase of dependency, core nations return to sell finished products to the peripheral nation, discouraging the development of local, indigenous manufacturers. The ultimate result of this is a spiral of deepening dependency on core nations and the progressive underdevelopment of the peripheral country. In the second phase, peripheral nations borrow capital from foreign banks and transnational corporations to build capital-intensive factories that produce goods for the local market. To create these factories, heavy machinery must be purchased from core sources. This keeps dependence alive as more capital flows from the periphery to the core. In a third phase of tighter economic ties between the core and the periphery, the low labor costs in peripheral countries attract transnational corporations that use the labor power in less developed nations to assemble products for export to developed nations. The lower labor costs, weaker unions, fewer environmental restrictions, and beneficial tax packages from host governments make movement into peripheral countries attractive to many corporations. Pharmaceuticals, electronic equipment, and clothes have been among the products created (Ward 1993). As a form of dependency, foreign investment has been found to be a drag on economic growth in many countries (Shen and Williamson 1997).

The relations between core and peripheral nations have become the topic of often heated debate. One example of that controversy is reflected in discussions over the North American Free Trade Agreement (NAFTA), which phases in free and open trade relations between Canada, Mexico, and the United States. Some of the controversy over this agreement has been due to its alleged impact on the environment, but there are also several economic issues that relate to the inequality between and within the nations involved. On a broad international level, some have argued approvingly that the pact would open up an area of free trade between different countries, allowing for open competition. Others have countered, however, that regional pacts of this kind only make free trade on a global level more difficult to attain. The supposed result is that the region would flourish while those outside the agreement would find it as difficult as ever to crack into the markets of the pact nations. "Regional trade agreements are discriminatory," wrote one critic of NAFTA, "as they distort trade and divert investment, but they also unleash a new dynamic on the part of outsiders: the only thing worse than a regional bloc is being on the outside of one looking in" (Aho 1993, p. 24). With respect to relations between the nations in the pact, supporters saw all three nations benefiting through open competition and the creation of more jobs in each country. The scenario for inequality suggested here is that working-class people within every country involved would benefit from the creation of jobs, resulting in less poverty and a higher standard of living. At the same time, however, given the shift to a trade surplus from increased involvement in Mexico, the pact raised the specter of a more powerful nation progressing at the expense of the less powerful. If this is the case, economic inequality between the countries would increase.

NAFTA went into effect on January 1, 1994. At the beginning of the twenty-first century, its effects are still being assessed and stirring controversy. Thus far, it appears that the impact has not been as extreme as either defenders or opponents had expected. Writing in 1999, John Robey concluded that "it may well be that both the supporters and opponents of NAFTA are overstating their cases," but that the impact on the U.S. economy in general will be less than that on the Mexican economy (1999, pp. 122–123). On the positive side, some have suggested that increased cooperation among workers' organizations has been instigated, and that shopping along the border by Mexicans has helped maintain at least 1,000,000 U.S. jobs (Carr 1999; Brown 1997). Other U.S. critics have argued, however, that the U.S. economy has been damaged by NAFTA, which created a multibillion-dollar trade deficit between the United States and Mexico in 1998 and left "over 200,000 U.S. workers certified as NAFTA casualties under just one narrow government program," many of these workers in "high-paying manufacturing jobs" (*Public Citizen* 1999, p. 3).

Not unexpectedly, the geographic area that has so far generated the greatest amount of concern is the border region between Mexico and the United States. On the one hand, it is the place where U.S. and Mexican cultures most directly confront and mix with each other. On the other hand, it is also the location of several thousand manufacturing plants *(maquiladoras),* a profileration that was not fully anticipated because it was believed by some that the opening of free trade between the United States and Mexico would not make it any more profitable for companies to locate along the border (Robey 1999). This concentration of industry has exacerbated existing environmental, crime, safety, and immigration problems, and has underlined variations in the standards between participating countries and the need for Canada, Mexico, and the United States to reach some compatibility on the issues (Brown 1997; Atkinson 1998).

The discussion of NAFTA is used here primarily to show how economic relations might impinge on inequality processes between and within countries. Does freedom of trade help to reduce inequality or increase it? Is it economically beneficial to workers in some countries but not others? Do regional trade agreements of this type foster greater economic inequality between blocs of nations? Will open competition between different ethnic and racial groups fuel greater intergroup hostility or will it usher in a deeper respect and tolerance of group differences? Either way, there are implications for the state of economic inequality.

In sum, the essence of the world-system perspective emphasizes the importance of the struc-ture of the world economy and a nation's position in it as an explanation of development/underdevelopment. Despite these studies, world-system theory has been open to criticism. Most importantly, Brenner (1977) suggested that, in some cases, the general backwardness of a society can lead to its dependent position rather than viceversa. The theory has also been attacked for not fully considering the active role of women in the economies of the world and the effects that world-system development has on gender inequality (Ward 1993). (For further critiques, see Chase-Dunn 1975; Rubinson 1976; Bornschier and Ballmer-Cao 1979; Sullivan 1983; Stack and Zimmerman 1982.)

As suggested earlier, it is not my task here to give a full assessment of each of these approaches as they bear on development. However, in recent years, the dependency/world-system perspective has been linked by many to the degree of income inequality in a country, and studies have been conducted testing the general hypothesis that the degree of dependency is directly related to the extent of income inequality. Similarly, it also has been argued that a greater level of economic development is associated with lower income inequality. Let us look at each of these propositions.

Dependence and Economic Inequality. Non-core nations are tied to core nations by a dependent relationship. Their economies, labor markets, levels of development, and political structures are partially shaped by the direct and indirect influence of core nations. This dependent position also helps produce greater income inequality within these nations, in part through its creation of uneven development within these economies.

A variety of studies using various measures of economic dependency indicate that greater dependency produces greater income inequality within the dependent country. More specifically, multinational corporate penetration, foreign debt dependency, and export patterns of concentration all have been found to be positively linked with income inequality (Kuznets 1963; Lenski 1966; Jackman 1975; Bornschier and Ballmer-Cao

1979; Stack and Zimmerman 1982). This relationship has been found even when the country's level of development has been taken into consideration in the analysis. In essence, these studies suggested that both level of development and dependency in the world economy have independent effects on income inequality.

A link also has been found between the level of economic development and dependency on the one hand, and the extent of political democracy on the other. Bollen's (1983) analysis of 100 nations revealed that political democracy, as measured by the degree of popular sovereignty and the presence of certain political liberties, is hindered by lower levels of development and greater dependency. Muller (1988), in turn, found that political democracy is related to the degree of the income inequality. His study of about 50 countries revealed that the more stable and longer the democratic tradition in a country, the less income inequality there tends to be. Conversely, when income inequality continues for a number of years, political democracy is undermined. These relationships persist even when a country's level of development is considered (Jackman 1975; Stack and Zimmerman 1982; cf. Rubinson and Quinlan 1977; Weede 1982; Muller 1988).

In sum, the proposed relationship is illustrated in Figure 8.1. There appears to be a network of relationships between dependency, level of development, political democracy, and income inequality. Of these, the relationship between political democracy and income inequality is the least settled. Some have found little or no relationship between these two factors, while others have found the predicted relationship (Brenner 1977).

GENDER INEQUALITY

The discussion of the world-system perspective noted that the role of women is usually not considered in that approach. How do international development processes affect the status of women in societies? It appears that the increased foreign investment and the introduction of cash crops and advanced manufacturing has the effect of weakening their economic position vis-à-vis men in their countries. Ward's (1993) study of 126 countries revealed that increased involvement in the world system lowered women's shares of the labor force, agricultural sector, and industrial sector of the economy.

Women's status is related not only to the level of involvement in the world economic system but also to the type of economy in the society. Women have always participated in the economies of countries. This has certainly been the case in hunting and gathering societies, which have been among the most egalitarian, in part because of (1) the lack of a large surplus, (2) the nomadic nature of life, (3) the minimal presence of private property, and (4) the absence of distinct specialized institutions. Structured classes are not present even though there are differences in prestige based on age, sex, and personal skills. In these societies, the division of labor is organized on the basis of age and sex. Although women are not primarily engaged in the more honorific adventure of hunting, they often have been responsible for foraging. More often than not, the economic activities of women contribute more to the daily diet than the animals brought in by hunters. Hunting by males, however, generally carries greater prestige because (1) it involves an element of challenge and excitement, (2) meat has more value than vegetables, and (3) it can be shared with the entire group rather than just the immediate family. The risk involved in hunting, the lower mobility of women due to reproduc-

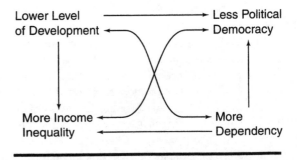

FIGURE 8.1 Macroprocesses and Income Inequality

tive and nursing obligations, and differences in physical strength are possible reasons for the domination of hunting activities by men.

In hunting and gathering societies, the degree of inequality between the sexes is much less than is found, for example, in agricultural societies. Generally, where women contribute heavily to the economy, there is less inequality between the sexes, and in hunting and gathering societies, gathering has provided the bulk of the diet in the majority of cases. Among the !Kung in Africa, for example, women are very important economically, and there is a great degree of equality between the sexes (Sanderson 1988). In some societies of this type, however, males are still distinctly higher in prestige and power. In several Australian groups—the Tiwi, for example—men are dominant and use their daughters through a betrothal system to establish economic and political ties. A greater number of wives is an economic asset because it means not only more food but also a wider network of support. However, even here, women traditionally contribute more food than men because of their gathering activities (Hart and Pilling 1966).

In horticultural societies, the status of women varies with the form of kinship descent and the specific society in question. In societies where lineage is traced through the female line and land is owned matrilineally, women tend to have higher status than in societies where lineage and ownership are linked with males (Martin and Voorhies 1975). Among the Yanomamo, on the other hand, which is a distinctly masculine society but one that relies heavily on garden-grown crops, women are held in low esteem. Female children are given household chores before males are, and women have little prestige and power. Female children are promised to others in marriage at an early age, with little consideration of their own wishes. Once married, women are expected to cater to the desires of their husbands, and a husband can beat his wife ferociously for any infraction, however minor (Chagnon 1977). In stark contrast, Iroquois women held positions of high prestige within their society (Brown 1975).

The status of women within horticultural societies is mixed, but it is low in agrarian societies. The invention of the plow, argued Joan Huber, affected gender stratification because (1) wherever it was introduced, it was controlled by men; (2) it made land the primary source of wealth; and (3) it made life more sedentary than in horticultural societies where periodic moving was mandatory because of soil depletion. The sedentary nature of life meant that the number of potential inheritors of land had to be controlled, and this translated into greater constraints on the behavior of women (Huber 1989). As men gained greater control over production of food, the status of women fell, and a clearer distinction developed between the familial and economic spheres, or between the domestic (inside) and public (outside) areas of life. The outside life—which entails meaningful involvement and influence in religious, economic, political, and educational institutions—was male dominated, whereas the more intimate inside sphere was more fully the province of women (Martin and Voorhies 1975). To maintain this fundamental separation, women's behavior was strictly limited, and social and ideological beliefs supported appropriate roles for each of the sexes.

Current Comparisons across Countries

The review in Chapter 4 on gender inequality in the United States showed that women are generally below men in their earnings, income, and occupational statuses, and the families that they head are more likely to be poor. Clearly, such inequality is not restricted to the United States.

There are great variations between countries in the quality of life experienced by women. In its analysis of gender inequality in 163 countries, a recent United Nations study took into account women's (1) life expectancies, (2) educational attainment, and (3) incomes in its measure of gender-related development. Results showed that, *compared to men,* women are worst off in Oman, Saudi Arabia, Iran, Syrian Arab Republic, Algeria, Libya, and the United Arab Emirates. But in no society are women as well off as men. The country with the least gender inequality is Armenia, followed by Latvia, Slovakia, Sri Lanka, Kazakhstan, Czech Republic, Bulgaria, and Poland. This list of countries show that less gender inequality is not directly related to a country's income. Keep in mind that the "gender-related development index" used by the United Nations merely measures the *relative disparity* between men and women on the above three variables; it does not directly tap the level of quality of life in an *absolute* sense. In *absolute* terms, women are best off in Canada, Norway, Sweden, Iceland, Finland, United States, France, New Zealand, Australia, and Denmark, respectively. In terms of women's opportunities to participate fully in the economic and political life of a country, Sweden, Norway, and Denmark rank highest. The United States is 11th among 102 countries. Most of the top-20 on this measure are industrial countries (United Nations 1998).

Across the world, a significant proportion of women are active in the economy. In 1995, women 15 years of age or older made up 41 percent of the world's labor force. The rate for industrial countries was slightly higher (44 percent) (United Nations 1998). Many of the countries in which women make up at least 45 percent are in eastern Europe. Conversely, Muslim nations in the Middle East, sub-Saharan Africa, and South Asia dominate those economies in which women make up a significantly smaller proportion of the labor force (Neft and Levine 1997). In addition to their involvement in the formal economy, women throughout the world also spend significantly more time than men on unpaid housework. In industrial countries, women spend at least 30 hours per week on housework, compared to 10 to 15 hours for men. In developing countries, the figures are 31 to 42 hours and 5 to 15 hours, respectively. Despite their heavy participation in both paid and unpaid work, however, women's unemployment rates tend to be higher in most countries (United Nations 1995).

As in the United States, the world's employed women are unevenly distributed across occupational categories. About half of them are

in various services (e.g., retail, restaurants, communications, insurance, personal services, etc.) and over one-third are involved in agricultural work. The rest are in manufacturing (Neft and Levine 1997). Overall, women are heavily represented in professional, technical, clerical, and service positions. By and large, these patterns follow those found in the United States. In Europe, Latin America, and the Caribbean, women occupy about half of all professional and technical positions and about two-thirds of clerical and service jobs (United Nations 1995).

With respect to distributions among specific occupations, some countries have few female-dominated positions, while others are overwhelmingly occupied by females. For example, in Malaysia, 81 percent of women are in positions in which less than half the workers are women, whereas in Finland, 68 percent of women work in jobs in which 70 percent of the employees are women. Most countries, however, appear to have several occupations in which women dominate. As we saw in Chapter 4, the United States is among these. As a representative illustration, women make up at least 97 percent of:

- Chimney sweeps in Austria
- Nurses in Bulgaria and Japan
- Child day-care workers in Finland
- Secretaries in France and Sweden
- Maids in Luxumbourg
- Cashiers in Poland
- Kindergarten teachers in Bahrain
- Sewing maching operators in Cyprus
- Housekeepers in Malaysia (United Nations 1995)

These patterns, as well, follow those generally found in the United States.

Although women are concentrated in some positions, they are underrepresented in others. Women are most underrepresented in administration, managerial, production, and transport occupations. Underrepresentation applies to positions of political importance, as well. In 1997, only about 9 percent of parliamentary seats in developing nations were occupied by women. About 15 percent of such positions were held by women in industrial countries (United Nations 1998).

When compared to those in European countries and Canada, U.S. women are much less likely to be in national legislative positions. In 1990, for example, 38 percent of such positions were held by women in Sweden, yet only 5 percent of comparable positions were occupied by women in the United States. However, worldwide, most women who hold positions of leadership in government are in areas traditionally and stereotypically associated with women (e.g., education, culture, and social welfare) (United Nations 1991).

Among industrial countries, the gender gap in authority in the private economy appears to be lower in the United States than in many other countries. A recent study of employed individuals in Canada, the United Kingdom, Australia, Sweden, Norway, Japan, and the United States revealed that the gap was smallest in the United States and Australia, whereas Japan showed the widest difference in male and female authority. These differences persisted even after differences in characteristics in workplaces, jobs, and individual characteristics were taken into account (Wright, Baxter, and Birkelund 1995).

As in the United States, the expected attitudes and behavior of women in their occupations reflect cultural values. Kanter (1977a) found that U.S. women in corporations were often expected to perform the social duties of a wife or servant, even though their job descriptions did not specify these as part of their work. But these expectations are consistent with beliefs about women's general roles and place in society. The same is the case in other societies.

Jeannie Lo's fascinating study of "office ladies" (OLs) and factory women in a Japanese company reveals similar expectations. Office ladies are expected to "carry out their 'domestic' responsibilities: they serve tea to their superiors (the men in the office), keep themselves presentable and feminine, and do the cleaning" (Lo 1990, p. 100). These ladies are careful to maintain the delicate network of relationships ("shigarami")

underlying the work system, and expect to leave their jobs and marry before the age of 30. Female factory workers find their work more physically exhausting, but do not put up with as much harassment on the job as OLs do. Women's pay is low, even for those in senior worker positions. They work to save money for their dowries and quit to marry. "Marriage is the ticket out of suffering and hard work" (Lo, p. 101). The patrimonial system is further evidenced in the dormitories which provide living quarters for workers who live far from home. As residents, like those in early American factories, female workers "are expected to act like 'obedient daughters,' do housekeeping, and observe strict rules on curfews, morality, and general tidiness" (p. 102). In addressing his mostly female employees, the president of an apparel company, Azumi, reiterated the message that women should follow traditional paths:

> *Azumi is a company founded with the grand purpose of making women beautiful, but beauty is not only a matter of form. A splendid heart and beautiful spirit are even more important.... [In the past], as fitting complements to such splendid women, there were great men. However, when the women changed the men began to fall as well. Men no longer have strength. There are few manly men nowadays and I feel that is the result of this kind of [modern] woman. (quoted in Smith 1987, p. 8)*

A memorandum from another large Japanese firm similarly warned those responsible for hiring new employees to "be wary of young women who wear glasses, are very short, speak in loud voices, have been divorced, or are daughters of college professors" (Smith 1987, p. 17). Clearly, nontraditional women are viewed as sources of trouble.

Earnings is another area in which gender inequality is prominent. In none of the 50 countries in which men's and women's earnings have been analyzed are women's earnings equal to those of men. Unfortunately, these studies focus on earnings from manufacturing or nonagricultural occupations. Since many women work in agricultural jobs, especially in developing nations, the picture given of wage discrepancies between the genders in these studies is, at best, incomplete. Those countries in which women receive earnings that are at least 85 percent of what men receive include Norway, Sweden, and Australia among industrial nations, and Tanzania, Vietnam, Sri Lanka, Colombia, Kenya, and Turkey, among developing countries. As noted in Chapter 4, U.S. women earn about 75 percent of what men do, which puts the United States near the middle in earnings differences between men and women. Among industrial countries, the United States lags behind Australia, Norway, Sweden, France, New Zealand, Denmark, Finland, Netherlands, Germany, Belgium, Italy, Portugal, Greece, Austria, and Poland in gender earnings equality. Among the nations with the greatest earnings inequality are Russia, Bangladesh, Japan, and Guam, where women's earnings equal no more than half those of men (Neft and Levine 1997; United Nations 1995). In sum, women's involvement in the economy, occupation segregation by sex, and lower authority for women are common around the world, but when compared to many other industrial countries, earnings differences between men and women are higher in the United States.

RACIAL/ETHNIC INEQUALITY

Having surveyed conditions for women in various countries, we turn now to a brief overview of racial and ethnic inequality in selected countries. Race and ethnic problems exist in all parts of the globe, from South Africa to the Middle East, through Central Europe, and into Asia and Japan. In this brief discussion, we will touch on only a few of these areas.

South Africa

Since the early 1990s, South Africa's government has attempted to move the country in the direction of greater racial equality. The accepted presence and power of the African National Congress and Nelson Mandela's election have helped solidify determination to create better lives for all of the nation's citizens. At this point, the future re-

mains open and serious internal hostilities must be resolved if progress toward racial equity is to continue.

One problem is that old habits die hard, for while apartheid has been officially outlawed, many of its remnants remain in everyday intercourse (Marger 1997). Until very recently, apartheid dominated economic, social, cultural, and political life in South Africa. For that reason, apartheid represented a situation of extreme racial inequality, which contrasts with the much more fluid racial relations present today. The dominance of Whites, who today are outnumbered by Blacks six to one, was rooted in the seventeenth- and eighteenth-century European conquest and colonization of the region. The process of increasing encroachment and control by Dutch and other White settlers as they moved into the country was not unlike that which occurred in the United States when early settlers pushed American Indians off their lands (Farley 1988).

Basically, South Africa had a caste system in which skin color was the criterion used to distinguish caste membership. The system was backed up by law and a government dominated by Afrikaners (Dutch descendants), right-wing Whites who felt they had a manifest destiny and biblical right to South Africa. There were four official castes, with Whites (Afrikaners and English) on top, followed by Coloureds, Asians, and Africans. However, since the latter three are non-White, they are usually lumped together, making the caste system essentially a White/non-White dichotomy (Marger 1997). Apartheid was a system of segregation that kept Blacks and Whites separate. Blacks were required to live in certain areas and lacked formal political rights. As earlier in the American South with its Jim Crow laws, Blacks and Whites had their own facilities so that contact between the races could be minimized. On the job, Whites typically earned more than 15 times what Blacks earned (Schaefer 1988). Under apartheid, the poorest 40 percent of the population, who were mostly Black, lived in conditions that were far below those of the richest 20 percent (mostly White). For example, in 1993, households for the poorest were much more crowded, only about one-fifth lived in households with electricity, about one-quarter had inside water, and less than one-fifth had a toilet in the house (United Nations 1998).

Current attempts to destroy vestiges of apartheid have been met with resistance by White extremist groups in South Africa, most of which are composed of Afrikaners. Those who have benefited from apartheid are feeling more desperate as pressure for Black involvement in Nelson Mandela's government grows. Said one White extremist: "Now the Boer (an earlier name for Afrikaner) really feels his back [is] up against the wall" (Ransdell 1993, p. 43). Whites possess critical economic skills and still control central positions in the economy. To be successful, Mandela's government must negotiate a balancing act between obtaining cooperation from Whites and improving conditions for Blacks who expect nothing else (Marger 1997).

Social class has also been implicated in South African struggles in that many of those who heavily profited from the White government and the system of segregation have been working-class Whites whose race gave them an advantage in getting jobs. These groups make up the majority of membership in extremist groups. A small cadre of religious fundamentalists have also organized themselves to defend apartheid (Rarsdell 1993).

It is clear that, as in the case of early U.S. colonists' justification for severe treatment of slaves and Americans Indians, defenders of racial inequality in South Africa had much to gain politically and economically from the apartheid system. The elements of Noel's theory of race inequality—competition for resources, ethnocentrism, and unequal power—still lurk in South Africa. As we head into the twenty-first century, serious discrepancies continue to exist between the races in South Africa. The life expectancy of Whites is still 14 years longer than that for Blacks, and when compared to that of Blacks, human development in general is twice as high among Whites (United Nations 1998).

Canada and Great Britain

South Africa is only the most glaring example of racial inequality. Even industrial Western countries that we normally consider to be free and democratic have their own versions of racial/ethnic inequality. Canada and Great Britain are two examples. Canada's ethnic composition has been described as a "vertical mosaic" (Porter 1965) made up of three elements: (1) English- versus French-speaking groups; (2) Native Aboriginal persons, or "First Nations" as they preferred to be called; and (3) other ethnic groups that are neither French nor English. The latter "visible minority," as they have been officially designated, consists of Black, Chinese, Japanese, Indo-Pakistan, Middle Eastern, Asian, and other culturally different individuals. In 1986, there were over 1,500,000 persons who were members of visible minorities, and about half as many who were classified as Aboriginal (Richmond 1990).

The main reason for referring to this mosaic of cultural groups as "vertical" is that there is a clear ranking system among them. Historically, English-speaking Whites have been the dominant group, monopolizing high-level economic and political positions. In recent years, French-speaking Whites have made some headway, but differences remain. Those at the top of businesses and other large financial firms are still most likely to be English or American. But institutional leadership appears to be becoming more ethnically diverse as economic conditions have improved. Still, some groups are much worse off than others. As in the United States, Native or Aboriginal people have the worst life chances. They rank lowest on scales of education, housing, occupational status, and income, and have disproportionately high rates of suicide, poor health, and functional illiteracy. For instance, the unemployment rates of Inuit men are more than 3 times those of other Canadian men (United Nations 1998).

As in other developed countries whose natives feel economically insecure because of recent recessions and high unemployment, immigration has been used as a tool of protection and for screening appropriate and desirable new residents in Canada. In recent years, the largest group of immigrants has been from Asia (48 percent in 1989), Hong Kong being the single-most important source. Europe is the next most prolific source (27 percent), with the rest being scattered among other continents and regions. Care has been taken in the last few years to encourage business immigrants and discourage other kinds of workers. The restrictions placed on immigration in Canada, as elsewhere, have been compared to apartheid in South Africa. "Restrictive immigration policies implicitly label non-White immigrants as less desirable and provide a spurious legitimation for racist attitudes. Immigrants themselves are seen as a 'problem' and policies are then directed toward exclusion" (Richmond 1990, p. 158). Richmond has referred to the use of immigration to exclude others as "global apartheid" (1990). The use of policy to maintain control over economic restrictions and to limit competition, together with labeling certain groups as "undesirables," again echoes Noel's point about the roles of power, competition, and ethnocentrism in generating racial and ethnic inequality.

Great Britain has similarly used immigration to restrict the entrance of certain ethnic minorities that it views as a threat to societal harmony. Recent estimates show that about 5 percent of the British population consists of ethnic minorities, the majority of whom have Indo-Pakistani or West Indian origins. As in Canada, employment rates, educational levels, and housing quality are lower for these groups than for other British residents.

Historically, race relations in Britain have been much more violent than in Canada, although instances of ethnic violence have occurred in the latter country as well. England experienced race riots following World War I and into the 1980s in Brixton, Bristol, Liverpool, and other British cities. Racism is often blatant. Observed one minority resident: "Liverpool is a very racist city.... Racism? It means shopkeepers don't even place the change in your hand, but throw it down on the counter" (Seabrook 1992, p. 16). In both Canada and Britain, the police have been viewed by mi-

norities as agents and protectors of the dominant group. But rather than being a solution, the use of police underlines the questions being raised about social, economic, political, and other inequalities that persist in those societies (Richmond 1990; Schaefer 1988).

Japan

Japan provides an interesting variation on racial and ethnic inequality. About 4 percent of Japan's population are treated as minorities and are discriminated against. Among these are Okinawans, Koreans, Ainu, and a group called the *burakumin* ("hamlet people"). In contrast to most minority groups elsewhere, the roughly 3 million burakumin are physically indistinguishable from other Japanese. Thus, they are sometimes called an "invisible race" (DeVos and Wagatsuma 1966). The only way to really know that a person is a burakumin is to know where he or she lives (DeVos and Wetherall 1983).

Historically, the roots of the burakumin go back to feudal times of 400 years ago. At that time, a rigid system of stratification prevailed, consisting of four clear strata (warrior, farmer, artisan, and merchant). The burakumin formed an outcaste group outside this system. Similar to outcastes in India, these people were viewed as being ritually unclean because their work involved touching the dead or animals. Their occupations included grave digging, butchery, leather tanning, and so on. They were forced to live in certain areas. Consequently, knowing where one lived provided a strong clue to his or her identity. Even in recent years, individuals with such a heritage have been systematically discriminated against socially and economically. In fact, at one point, their villages were not even shown on maps, reinforcing their invisibility and the custom of not recognizing them (Rowley 1990).

The burakumin still live in their own communities. In 1986, there were about 6,000 buraku districts, containing about 3 million people (Takagi 1991). Attempts have been made to legally ban discrimination against the burakumin, and some improvements have been made in their living conditions, but serious problems remain. Prejudice based on feelings of disgust and fear is still prevalent and carries over into everyday concerns. As late as the mid-1980s, companies actively discriminated against burakumin. Procuring secretly created lists of buraku residential areas, and then comparing applicants' addresses against those lists, company interviewers have been able to screen out burakumin as employees (Takagi 1991). There continue to be significant problems in securing good employment. Some argue that burakumin are three to four times more likely to have physical problems because of being forced by discrimination into brute manual work (Rowley 1990). The mean buraku family income is only 60 percent of Japan's average (Guest 1992).

In addition, it is still difficult for burakumin to marry freely. There are detective agencies that specialize in researching backgrounds of potential mates to see if they have a "degraded" heritage. Relatives routinely and actively oppose the marriage to another with a burakumin heritage, and if the marriage is carried out, social ties with the couple are usually cut. In some cases, when a buraku residence has been uncovered, even suicide has resulted.

Since one's physical appearance does not betray buraku membership, one dilemma for those from buraku communities is in deciding whether to freely and openly admit one's heritage. For a young person, this can be a difficult problem, similar to that felt by anyone having a serious stigma. Hiromi is a young Japanese woman who chose to hide her heritage (i.e., she decided to try to pass as a member of the majority) while her sister took the opposite route to fight the discrimination openly. It is easy to understand Hiromi's choice when listening to one of her non-buraku friends: "I would never marry a burakumin.... It's not that I'm prejudiced or anything. But just think what my family would say if I went and did a thing like that." "I know what you mean," said another, "burakumin are different. Most of them can't even read" (Guest 1992, p. 28). Conversations of this kind help to provide explanations

and legitimation for the continuing plight of the burakumin in Japan.

India

The caste system in India provides an example of an extreme case of status stratification. But rather than being simply a system of social inequality, it is also a hierarchical system in which castes are mutually dependent—a "harmony unifying diversity," to use Lannoy's description (1975, p. 138). Thus, castes are a source of integration as well as inequality. One's position in a caste is most often determined by birth and, and at least theoretically, cannot be altered. This gives the basis for position an "ethnic" quality in that birthright is taken into account. The legitimation of the caste system is rooted the earliest of Hindu texts in which the four "varnas" are described. A hymn in the *Rig Veda,* an ancient religious script, describes society as a body in which the Brahmans represent its head, the Kshatriyas its arms, the Vaishyas its trunk, and the Sudras, the feet. As in any organism, all the parts need to work together for the whole system to function properly. Kolenda (1978) has commented that although some Western social scientists view the caste system as basically exploitative of those at the bottom, others see it as a system that includes and functions for all. The latter analysts regard the exploitative view as being too narrow and even ethnocentric.

At the top of the varna system, the Brahmans are considered the most pure. They are engaged in teaching as priests, giving sacrifices, and receiving gifts. Brahmans have privileges not open to the members of other castes in classical Hinduism. Theoretically, Brahmans cannot be fined or beaten, for example. Because of their duties and abilities, Brahmans can transmit the sacred and religious element to the king, through whom it then radiates out into the rest of society. The whole caste hierarchy is infused with religious beliefs that tie the various castes together.

As is the case with Brahmans, every other varna is associated with specific duties and tasks (the dharma of the caste). The Kshatriyas, below the Brahmans, are associated with political and top military positions; that is, they function to protect society. The distinction between Kshatriyas and Brahmans is essentially between religious and political functions. The Vaishyas make up the next varna and earn their living from the land as farmers or in grazing livestock or in commerce and usury. Members of these first three varnas are said to be "twice born" in that adolescent boys undergo a particular initiation ceremony when they are just beginning to study the sacred religious texts. The task of the Sudras, the last of the four varnas, is simply to serve those above them. There is a qualitative difference between the Sudras and the three varnas above them. Unlike the other three, the Sudras do not "participate in initiation, second birth, or the religious life in general" (Dumont 1970, p. 67). In most areas of the country, Sudras compose the majority of the populations and are associated with a large number of specific occupations involving physical labor and service for those in the top three classes (Milner 1994). A fifth stratum, the Untouchables, are left out of the formal classification system entirely. In a ritual sense, they are outside the caste system.

The four major varnas make up the classic hierarchical system of Indian society. But the real, concrete system of castes (jati) is actually more complex. Any given village may have had a few or large number of castes, and these may vary in nature from village to village. There also may be kinship or other ties between similar castes in different villages. In other words, in everyday life, the operating caste system is very complicated. However, most Indians still associate specific castes in a village with one of the four varnas. In this way, the latter form a sort of "all-India caste system" (Kolenda 1978, p. 94).

Dumont described an actual caste system as a situation in which "the society is divided into a large number of permanent groups which are at once specialised, hierarchised, and separated (in matter of marriage, food, physical contact) in relation to each other" (Dumont and Pocock 1961, pp. 34–35). Summarizing a number of social-

anthropological studies, Kolenda (1978) distilled what she considers to be the core features of the local caste system in India:

1. It operates as a system only in a confined locality and may consist of a few or many more specific, mutually exclusive castes.
2. A dominant caste or family usually has economic and political control in the area. Its dominance is based on control of land and force.
3. Each caste has an occupational specialty associated with it and offers its services to members of other castes in exchange for food, services, or other products (the jajmani system). This exchange system performs not only an economic function but also serves to keep the higher castes pure, allowing those in the bottom castes to absorb pollution.
4. Castes are ranked according to pollution and purity.
5. Each caste segment tends to live in its own area. Untouchables are isolated from the rest of the village, either living in a separate setting altogether or on the edge of a given village.
6. The caste is an endogamous descent group, and the local contingent of a caste are usually kin related.
7. Efforts to improve caste rank are made by the lower ranks. These include emulating the Brahman lifestyle (Sanskritization) and eliminating certain polluting customs. Mobility is also attempted through (a) arguments that the low rank of one's caste is really the result of a historical error or having really been deprived of one's rightful place, (b) allusions to having been the descendant of a great or high-ranking person or caste, and (c) gaining wealth, allowing a caste to change its name and live an honored lifestyle.
8. Disputes within a village are settled either by a council or by an elder in the dominant caste.

It should be evident that the basic element of separation pervades the system (in associations with others, marriage, and residence). This fundamental trait should not be surprising. In our earlier discussion of Weber's concept of status group, we noted the importance of social distance and exclusivity. The separation underlying the castes is based on religious and ritualistic notions of purity and pollution. The term *caste,* in fact, comes from the Latin root word *castus,* which means pure (Lannoy 1975). Formally, the caste hierarchy contains the purest castes at the top and the most polluted at the bottom. One must remain ritualistically pure if one is to perform religious duties effectively, and contamination from the outside environment as well as pollutants from the inside (bodily waste) can endanger the purity of the body. One must avoid proximity to the contaminant, because prolonged closeness can mean permanent pollution if the contaminant is strong enough. It can then be passed on through one's children. In other words, pollution can be hereditary, even though there are both permanent and temporary types of pollution. Castes associated with polluting jobs (e.g., leather workers, barbers, sweepers, funeral workers—all occupations that involve working with body parts, excrement, or dead organisms) have permanent pollution. Temporary pollution, on the other hand, can be overcome with various rituals of purification. Everyone is exposed to potential contaminants every day because all people eat, go to the bathroom, have sexual relations, and so forth—all activities that bring them into contact with impurity.

Rules determine from whom one can receive food or water without becoming polluted. Thus, commensality, eating only with members of one's own caste, encourages the maintenance of purity. Certain foods are believed to be more open to contamination than others or are associated with certain castes. With respect to the latter, for example, some foods are believed to promote lightness and purity, whereas others supposedly encourage physical strength and passion. There is a concern for maintaining bodily purity because it is believed that spiritual development requires purity through the avoidance of impure relationships and

objects, including not only food but also clothing and homes (Lannoy 1975, pp. 145–152). Thus, in this ritual sense, strangers and foreigners are major sources of pollution for the strict caste member. Certainly notions of racial purity underlaid many of the justifications for racial inequality early in U.S. society.

There is increasing evidence that the Indian caste system is not the monolithic, simple system it is sometimes portrayed to be. For example, educated, westernized Indians are less likely to believe in the purity/pollution theory (Lannoy 1975, p. 148). As suggested earlier, there is also some evidence that even in India, there are avenues of social mobility. To move up, for example, some lower-caste persons have started their own religious movements, while others have married upward. By gaining political power or mobilizing, a group can also raise (or lower) its caste rank, and some individuals can increase their statuses because of increased economic resources (Kumar 1982; Das and Acuff 1970; Berreman 1960). But these are movements to change one's position *within* the system, not revolutions *against* the system (Kolenda 1978). Moreover, the actual caste system is made up of many subcastes, often varying from region to region. In other words, as we have seen, some have suggested that the manner in which a caste system works in theory is not the same as it works in reality.

In 1975, Richard Lannoy wrote that the caste system is still "the most distinctive feature of Indian culture; it has remained the bedrock of the social structure from ancient times to the present day" (p. 137). Nineteen years later, Murray Milner, Jr., agrees: "In sum, while the caste system has undergone great changes over the long period of its existence, it has been relatively stable compared to most human institutions" (1994, p. 56). Hindu religious beliefs have helped to maintain the stability of stratification in India. Most notably, the emphasis on dharma, karma, and reincarnation have encouraged believers to abide by the status quo. Individuals have been expected to follow the duties of their castes (dharma). They also have been taught to believe that their present behavior has a direct causal linkage with what happens to them in their next lives (karma). However, there is evidence that the caste system, although still operative, may be weakening in the face of changes in technology, urbanization, and education; economic and political systems that are increasingly international and competitive in nature also put tradition at risk (Kolenda 1978). These may be creating permanent fissures within the caste system, but at the same time, the new formal democracy and constitution have not meant the erasure of real caste inequalities in the Indian system (Sivaramayya 1983).

SUMMARY

This chapter has provided a comparative context into which to place the degree of economic, gender, and racial/ethnic inequality in the United States. When making comparisons across countries, one has to be careful because of differences in data collection. Nevertheless, some general conclusions were reached. On the international scene, we noted that poorer countries have both higher rates of poverty and economic inequality than the United States. The United States generally fares well when compared to poorer countries, but when compared to other developed industrial countries, the United States has one of the highest rates of poverty, especially for children and the elderly, and one of the highest rates of economic inequality. Japan has among the lowest degrees of inequality. The reasons for differences of this sort include variations in population composition, economic conditions, government programs, and tax and inheritance laws.

Explanations for economic inequality between nations include those that stress the importance of psychological, cultural, and world-economic conditions. Dependency and world-system theories are the most recent and emphasize the nature of the interrelationship among countries in the world economy. The basic argument is that through trade, assistance, internationally sponsored attempts at development, and economic penetration by transnational corporations, underdeveloped, peripheral countries enter into an ever-deepening relationship of dependency with powerful core nations, weakening their chances of development.

Gender inequality also varies across types of societies. Generally, such inequality is usually less in hunting and gathering than in agricultural societies. Across the world, women have been and are heavily involved in economies, and in fact their involvement has increased while that of men has decreased in recent years. When their housework is taken into account, with few exceptions, women work more hours per week than men. Despite women's extensive economic activity, occupational segregation and differences in authority by sex exist in virtually all countries. Stereotypes of gender-appropriate work and behavior can also be found among other industrial countries. However, the United States does not compare favorably on sex-earnings differentials to many other industrial nations such as Australia, Sweden, Norway, and Canada.

Racial/ethnic inequality is also found elsewhere. Although a worldwide survey of such conditions was not possible here, a brief description of predicaments in South Africa, Canada, Great Britain, Japan, and India demonstrated that racial and ethnic inequality exist in all parts of the globe. Although they were not discussed, the Middle East and Central Europe are also regions that are currently undergoing significant ethnic strife. South Africa's apartheid system had been the most glaring international example of racial inequality. Analyses of Canada and Great Britain show how countries have used immigration policies to control shifts in the racial composition of populations. Japan's burakumin provide an interesting case of low caste status involving a group thought to be qualitatively different from the rest of the population. Finally, India's caste system has served as a frequently cited examplar of a rigid status system that has resisted radical change. For this reason, it was described in detail. Although systems of inequality vary drastically throughout the world, that in the United States is extensive enough to produce a variety of personal and social effects. The next two chapters examine those impacts.

CRITICAL THINKING

1. Why are the women in so many other industrial countries better off economically than they are in the United States? What can be done to improve conditions in the United States?

2. Is it inevitable that the economic gap between developing and developed nations will increase? If yes, why? If no, what has to change to reduce the gap?

3. What are the connections between racial inequality within different countries and the income gap between them? Do increased income gaps intensify racial inequalities? Explain your answer.

WEB CONNECTIONS

The United Nations provides a wealth of information on socioeconomic conditions in countries across the world. This includes the site for the United Nations Development Fund for Women, which displays variations among women in health, education and literacy, age distribution, economic activity, and participation in government. Compare the differences in the conditions for women across continents and nations by exploring the following two websites:

http://www.undp.org/unifem/

http://www.un.org/womenwatch/world/index.html

CHAPTER 9

CLASSICAL EXPLANATIONS
OF INEQUALITY

*Quote from a rich man: Being poor is a matter of their own choice. Some
people would rather live in Harlem than Fifth Avenue.*
—Joan Huber and William H. Form

*Quote from a poor man: The rich? Got to be a certain amount of crook in
'em or they wouldn't be rich.*
—Joan Huber and William H. Form

The discussions throughout Part One make it clear
that multidimensional inequality is extensive in the
United States, and, in a number of ways, is becoming even more pronounced and disconcerting for
many. The widespread nature of social inequality
makes explaining it all the more important. Several
previous chapters have offered specific explanations tailored for understanding particular forms of
inequality. This chapter examines the broad classical explanations of Marx, Weber, and Durkheim,
from which many modern thinkers have drawn.
Karl Marx is discussed first because virtually all of
his central ideas were formulated before any of the
others and because subsequent theories are often
viewed as reactions to Marx's own work.

KARL MARX (1818–1883)

Few social scientists have had as great a political
and economic impact as Karl Marx. His perspectives on society have been used by social scientists
and ideologues, and his influence on modern sociology, and even society, has been pervasive. The
ideas of all scholars are in large part shaped by the

historical events and life situations they experience. This appears clearly in the case of Marx, as
well as Weber. Karl Marx was born on May 5,
1818, in the city of Trier, Prussia (now part of Germany). His family was of Jewish background and
provided a bourgeois setting for Marx in his youth.
His father and a neighbor, Ludwig von Westphalen, introduced him to the thinkers of the Enlightenment. Ludwig von Westphalen in particular
became an intellectual companion with whom
Marx discussed philosophy and literature. Marx
later married von Westphalen's daughter, Jenny.

While studying at the universities of Bonn and
Berlin, Marx became a friend of a group known as
the Young Hegelians. Although Hegel was dead,
his ideas survived as an intellectual force at Berlin.
The Young Hegelians helped to convert Marx from
the study of law to the study of philosophy. The increasing radicalism of his ideas encouraged his de-
parture for Paris in late 1843. It was in Paris, a
center of invigorating intellectual activity, that
Marx began his close association and collaboration
with Frederick Engels, the son of a manufacturer
who acquainted Marx more fully with the real con-

ditions of the working class. Marx's writing again caused his expulsion, and he moved from Paris to Brussels in 1845. By then, Marx already considered himself a socialist and revolutionary. He had aligned himself with several workers' organizations, and in 1848 he and Engels produced the *Manifesto of the Communist Party.*

After some moving around, Marx left in 1849 for London, where he stayed for most of the remainder of his life. It was there that he produced most of his major writing. During his stay, his life and that of his family were marked with poverty, which was relieved only by his occasional employment as a European correspondent for the *New York Daily Tribune* and periodic help from his friend, Engels. He became a leader of the International, a radical movement made up of individuals from several European countries, and in 1867 published the first volume of his monumental *Capital.* In the last decade of his life, Marx was already an honored figure among socialists and was able to live somewhat more comfortably than in his earlier years in London. He died on March 14, 1883, only one year after the death of his elder daughter and two years after the death of his wife, Jenny (Coser 1971).

Despite the familiarity of Karl Marx's name to most, many of his ideas are still not properly understood by numerous students. Two of these are especially relevant to his statements concerning class relations. First, Marx did not believe that everything is determined by the economic structure, that all other institutions are merely reflections of the economic system and are without causal influence. Although Marx considered the economic aspect the "ultimately determining element in history" and the "main principle," he did not think it was the only determining one. In a personal letter, while admitting that he and Marx had probably contributed to the confusion on this point, Engels put the matter succinctly: "The economic situation is the basis, but the various elements of the superstructure...also exercise their influence upon the course of the historical struggles and in many cases preponderate in determining their *form.* There is an interaction of all these elements in which, amid all the endless host of accidents...the economic movement finally asserts itself as necessary" (Marx and Engels 1970, vol. 2, p. 487, emphasis in original). Thus, political, religious, and cultural factors play a role, though the "ultimately decisive" one is economic.

A second misconception is that Marx argued that only two classes exist in any society. On the contrary, Marx was aware of the diversity of classes that can exist at any one time, as well as the factions that can be present within a given class. His discussions in *The Class Struggles in France* and in the third volume of *Capital* make this abundantly clear. We will explore further comments on Marx's ideas after a discussion of the core elements of his theory.

Marx's Conception of Class

According to Marx, the earliest societies were classless, being based on a "common ownership of land" (Marx and Engels 1969, vol. 1, pp. 108– 109). But all known subsequent societies have been class societies, and the engine of change in history has been class struggle. Private property spurs the development of classes. Although societies change and the specific names given to the various classes may change, the presence of dominant and subordinate classes remains. The particular form that relations take between the classes depends on the historical epoch and the existing economic mode of production. The mode of production refers to the particular type of economic system in operation, such as feudalism, capitalism, and so on. Within every mode of production are (1) means of production and (2) social relations of production. The *means of production* refers to the tools, machines, and other resources used in production, whereas the *social relations of production* refers to the property and power relationships among individuals in the economic system. Marx contended that up to his time there had been four major "epochs in the economic transformation of society" (1969, vol. 1, p. 504). These were the Asiatic, ancient, feudal, and capitalist modes of production. Our primary focus is on the last of these.

Generally, classes are defined by their relationship to the means of production. Hence, in the capitalist mode of production, "by bourgeoisie is meant the class of modern capitalists, owners of the means of social production and employers of wage-labour. By proletariat, the class of modern wage-labourers who, having no means of production of their own, are reduced to selling labour-power in order to live" (Marx and Engels 1969, vol. 1, p. 108). But when specific treatment is given, Marx's definition of class appears loose, and a variety of criteria are used differentially in different places. A full-fledged class that satisfied the criteria suggested by Marx would be one that possessed:

1. A distinct relationship to and role in the mode of production (in terms of ownership of means of production, employment of wage labor, and economic interests).
2. A clear consciousness of its existence as a unified class with objective interests that are hostile to those of other classes.
3. An organization of the class into a political party aimed at representing and fighting for its interests.
4. A distinct set of cultural values and a separate style of life (Ollman 1968).

"The owners of mere labour-power, the owners of capital, and the landowners, whose respective sources of income are wages, profit, and rent of land...form the three great classes of modern society based on the capitalist mode of production" (Bottomore and Rubel 1956, p. 178). Other transition classes exist, such as the petty bourgeoisie and small land-owning peasants, but these would disappear as capitalism inexorably reached its peak as a mode of production. Marx believed that in his day of the "two great hostile camps," the "two great classes" that were being polarized were the bourgeoisie and the proletariat (1969, vol. 1, p. 109). However, his use of such terms as "strata," "gradation," "middle classes," and "dominated classes" makes it clear that Marx was aware of the complexity that can characterize a concrete system of inequality. What is also apparent is that mere occupation or source of income is not the criterion used by Marx to define a class. Each class has within it a hierarchy of strata. Thus, within the proletariat, for example, individuals vary by specific occupation and income.

Because of the classes' different relationships to private property, (i.e., owners vs. nonowners), conflict is inherent in class society. Class antagonism is built into the very structure of society. Marx's theory is one of class struggle. The existence of a given class always assumes the existence of another hostile class. "'Who is the enemy?' is a question that can be asked whenever Marx uses 'class'" (Ollman 1968, p. 578). When the economic bases for classes are eliminated, they will disappear since the proletariat will be without the enemy, the capitalist.

In the process of class struggle, however, the proletariat develops from an incoherent mass (a class in itself) into a more organized and unified political force (a class for itself). The conditions that bring about this change are discussed in detail later.

Maintenance of Class Structure

The system of inequality—class positions, the given relations of production, and the profits of capitalists—is maintained and protected by a variety of mechanisms. The state, of course, is the ultimate arbitrator and represents "the form in which the individuals of a ruling class assert their common interests" (Bottomore and Rubel 1956, p. 223). "The executive of the modern State is but a committee for managing the common affairs of the whole bourgeoisie" (Marx and Engels 1969, vol. 1, pp. 110–111). The state has used its force and legislation to maintain capitalist class relations (Marx 1967, pp. 734–741). Struggles that do occur within the state are always class struggles.

A second mechanism used to maintain class relations is ideology, and the dominant ideology supports and legitimizes the position of the capitalist. "The ideas of the ruling class are in every epoch the ruling ideas: i.e., the class which is the ruling *material* force of society is at the same time its ruling *intellectual* force." Just as the ruling class has control over "material production," so too does it control "mental production," and the form these ideas take is clear: "The ruling ideas are nothing more than the ideal expression of the dominant material relationships" (Marx and Engels 1969, vol. 1, p. 47, emphasis in original). Of course, the ideas generated can and have been mentally separated in their association with the dominant class and hence can appear as eternal laws (such as the "free market") or rules generated by all of the society. Members of the ruling class have themselves believed that. The ideas that support class relations are frequently promoted by bourgeois intellectuals who are often nothing more than "hired prize-fighters" for capitalism (Marx 1967, p. 15). Religion as an ideological institution similarly helps maintain the class system by preventing labor from seeing its real situation.

A third factor serving to bolster the set of economic relations is much less obvious than the two just mentioned. The capitalist structure itself strengthens its seeming inevitability by creating a working class that because of custom and training comes to view "the conditions of that mode of production as self-evident laws of Nature" (Marx 1967, p. 737). The condition of workers freely hiring themselves out to capitalists who freely employ them to work in factories run for maximum efficiency makes capitalism appear as an entirely natural process and creates a dependency of workers on it that makes it difficult for them to resist or rebel. As Miliband wrote, "The capitalist mode of production...veils and mystifies the exploitative nature of its 'relations of production' by making them appear as a matter of free, unfettered, and equal exchange" (1977, p. 45).

Development of Capitalism

The meaning and utility of Marx's central concepts bearing on inequality are embedded in his analysis of historical changes in the mode of production. To fully understand Marx's concept of class, one cannot legitimately remove it from his theory of capitalism but must view it in the context of capitalist development.

Several factors aid in bringing about early forms of capitalism. One of these is the accumulation of capital by some individuals. Increased trade and the opening up of the New World fueled the accumulation of capital. When feudal serf groups were broken up in the fifteenth and sixteenth centuries, "great masses of men [were] suddenly and forcibly torn from their means of subsistence, and hurled as free and 'unattached' proletarians on the labour market" (Marx 1967, p. 716). The direct motivations behind these expropriations of land were most often economic and political in nature. Larger tracts of land then became owned by fewer individuals. By the end of the sixteenth century, England had a group of rich capitalist farmers (Marx 1967, p. 744). The forcible expropriation of all this land through various means "made the soil part and parcel of capital, and created for the town industries the necessary supply of a 'free' and outlawed proletariat" (Marx 1967, p. 733).

The newly developing capitalism required a stable labor force, but it could not possibly absorb all those thrown off the land. Many became "beggars, robbers, vagabonds." Laws were then passed against such individuals and against laborers who tried to organize. Capitalists found it necessary to use legislation to mold these workers into a compliant but disciplined labor force (Marx 1967, pp. 737–742).

Moreover, the means of production they brought with them, which had been scattered in individual homes (spindles, looms, etc.), could then be brought together under one capitalist's roof. And the raw materials freed up by the expropriation of this population provided a fuller basis for the production of goods by capitalists. The need of these individuals to work as employees who manufactured goods owned by capitalists rather than by themselves meant that, as a group, they became a mass market to which such goods could be sold. The products that the worker would have developed at home as a means of subsistence became commodities of the capitalist. In sum, freed labor power, raw materials, means of production, and a new market became available to capitalism as a result of the removal of part of the agricultural population from the land.

Capitalists then did all they could, including resorting to force, to speed up the fuller development of capitalism in "hothouse fashion." "Force is the midwife of every old society pregnant with a new one" (Marx 1967, p. 751). The increasing prominence of the colonial system in the seventeenth and eighteenth centuries aided capitalist development by providing slave labor power, raw materials, and markets. Systems of trade protection and taxes further strengthened capitalism, as did the increasing use of children and women in the factories. Capital and its accumulation, then, were not attained by owners through careful saving and hard work, according to Marx, but rather came into the world "dripping from head to foot, from every pore, with blood and dirt" (Marx 1967, p. 760).

As capitalism develops, in Marx's view, larger capitalists swallow up the smaller ones; centralization occurs and with it the increasing inclusion of a broader and broader circle of peoples in the world market. Capitalism takes on an international character. The problem of creating a secure, collective labor force in the new colonies, where land is available and where potential laborers might otherwise labor for themselves through their acquisition of such land, is dealt with by placing artificially high prices on the land, which then means that the laborer has to work longer to earn the wages needed to buy the land. The money obtained from the purchase of land can then be used to bring more laborers to the colonies to keep the labor supply full (Marx 1967, pp. 771–772).

As centralization of capitalism grows, so does the misery and manipulation of the working class. But this misery is not without consequence, because the capitalist system of production serves as a crucible that perfects the discipline and unification of the expanding working class. Eventually, the control of capital by the few hinders the production system and speeds the dissolution of capitalism. "Centralization of the means of production

and socialization of labour at last reach a point where they become incompatible with their capitalist integument. This integument is burst asunder. The expropriators are expropriated" (Marx 1967, p. 763). Individual private property had been taken by the capitalists; now capitalistic property is expropriated by the masses. It becomes socialized property.

Stages of Capitalism.   According to Marx, capitalism as a mode of production has gone through three principal stages: (1) cooperation, (2) manufacture, and (3) modern (machine) industry.

Cooperation.   Capitalism begins when a large number of laborers are employed in one place working together to produce a given product. "A greater number of laborers, working together, at the same time, in one place…in order to produce the same sort of commodity under the mastership of one capitalist, constitutes, both historically and logically, the starting point of capitalist production" (Marx 1967, p. 322). It is when workers are thus brought together that "the collective power of the masses" for the individual capitalist can be realized. Workers become more productive and efficient under these conditions, resulting in greater profit for the capitalist. This and each successive change in the mode of production are motivated by the desire to increase the surplus value of labor power and, therefore, the level of profit.

Manufacture.   "While simple cooperation leaves the mode of working by the individual for the most part unchanged, manufacture…converts the laborer into a crippled monstrosity, by forcing his detail dexterity at the expense of a world of productive capabilities and instincts" (Marx 1967, p. 360). The period of manufacture begins in the sixteenth century and extends to the last part of the eighteenth century. Its characteristic is a strict and detailed division of labor among workers who have been brought together to cooperate in the production of the capitalists' products. Everyone has a specific function to perform; no one carries out all the tasks. Thus, with this change there no longer exists a group of independent artisans co-operating, but rather a group of individuals performing minute tasks dependent on each other. "Its final form is invariably the same—a productive mechanism whose parts are human beings" (Marx 1967, p. 338).

Weber's later description of work under rationalized capitalism is strikingly similar, as we shall see. In manufacture, each person performs the same task over and over again until the job becomes routine and the laborer becomes a mere mechanism, but efficiency and perfection in production become reality. Skills that had been learned in apprenticeship become less necessary, and manufacture creates a set of unskilled laborers. The collective laborer, when organized in this fashion, increases production, and as a result, increases the surplus value of his labor power to the capitalist. The profit for the capitalist goes up, and conditions for him could not be better. Larger manufacturing factories develop different departments that produce different products, with each having its own division of labor: To further speed production and the growth of profits, some workshops produce the new tools of labor—machines.

For the laborers, however, conditions worsen. Under the capitalist mode, their labor is no longer their own, because to increase capital, each worker must be "made poor in productive powers" (Marx 1967, p. 361). They become unfit to produce independently, and their labor power becomes productive only within the factory. They need the factory. Working on minute operations rather than whole products, they become "a never failing instrument," "a mere fragment of his own body...a mere appendage" (Marx 1967, pp. 349, 360). And the constant regularity and monotony of the task "disturbs the intensity and flow of a man's animal spirits, which find recreation and delight in mere change of activity" (Marx 1967, p. 341).

In essence, the workers become alienated from their own labor. The work being done (1) is not an end in itself but a *means* to an end, (2) is not voluntary but *forced,* (3) is not part of human nature (i.e., it is *external*), (4) is not work for the workers but for *someone else,* and (5) is *not spontaneous.* The object of their labor does not belong

to the workers even though they have put a part of themselves into it. Rather, the product "becomes an object, takes on its own existence...exists outside him, independently, and alien to him, and... stands opposed to him as an autonomous power" (Bottomore and Rubel 1956, p. 170). As appendages, workers become alienated from themselves, each other, and nature.

Under manufacturing, therefore, capitalists prosper as workers' conditions deteriorate, and the real nature of capitalism as a mode of production becomes clear. Capitalists prosper because laborers suffer. The two classes are not merely different levels but are inextricably interlinked in the capitalist mode. People and their labor power become commodities, things of use value to the capitalist, who owns and controls the instruments of production, the raw materials—everything. The laborers, in turn, have nothing but their own labor power to sell, and even that becomes twisted into a form suitable for maximum production.

Modern (Machine) Industry. Like other forms of capitalist production, the development and use of machines are aimed at reducing the cost of commodity production for the capitalist by reducing the part of the day when the worker is working for himself or herself, and increasing that part when he or she is working for the capitalist. That is, it is a way of increasing surplus value for labor. "The machine...supersedes the workman" (Marx 1967, p. 376). In modern industry, machines are organized into a division of labor similar to that which existed among laborers during the manufacture period. Since machines replace labor power, physical strength becomes less important, and capitalists seek to hire children and women. The result is a decrease in the value of the man's labor power, and a concomitant increase in the general exploitation of the family overall. When the value of the workman's labor power vanishes, laborers flood the market and reduce the price of labor power. Supply then outweighs demand for labor. In effect, machines are a means of controlling the collective laborer. "It is the most powerful weapon for repressing strikes, those periodic revolts of the working class against the autocracy of capital" (Marx 1967, pp. 435–436).

With the advance of machines, production becomes more and more centralized, forcing many small bourgeoisie who cannot compete or find little use for their skills into the proletariat (Bottomore and Rubel 1956, p. 188).

Crises in Capitalism and Class Struggle. The increased competition for profit among capitalists generates crises at both the top and bottom of the class structure, ultimately leading to the polarization of large capitalists and the massive class of the proletariat. The initial result of the introduction of machinery is to increase profit, but problems arise. Employees are thrown out of work or work for low wages because they are not in demand. The proletariat increases in number and becomes more concentrated, and life conditions among members become equalized at a level of bare subsistence.

Competition among capitalists produces commercial crises, an "epidemic of over-production" which in turn leads to increased concentration of capital, since many go bankrupt (Marx and Engels 1969, vol. 1, p. 114). Overproduction serves as an indication that the forces of production have become too strong for the property relations by which they are controlled ("fettered"). The capitalist responds by destroying productive forces and by trying to find new markets, but these solutions are, at best, stopgap measures and crises recur, each more serious than the previous. "Modern bourgeois society…is like the sorcerer, who is no longer able to control the powers of the nether world whom he has called up by his spells" (Marx and Engels 1969, vol. 1, p. 113). The means of production that the bourgeoisie originally brought into existence to benefit their own position and that permitted them to supplant feudalism now become the means that destroy them.

Bourgeois society becomes the stage for the impending class struggle between the capitalist and the collective laborer, between the bourgeoisie and the proletariat. As capitalism improved from simple cooperation through modern industry, the bourgeoisie became more powerful and entrenched, their ideology and ideas became dominant, and the organization of the state more evidently reflected their power. But so, too, did the proletariat develop as a class with the progress of capitalism. Initially, struggle against the bourgeoisie takes the form of individual protests, then protests by larger groups—not against the relations of production, but against the forces of production: Workers smash tools, machines, and so forth in order to maintain their status as workers. At this point, they are still just a mass rather than an organized whole. But as conditions for them worsen—that is, as they become increasingly massed together on an equal basis in a minute division of labor under conditions of extreme alienation and emiseration—and as their livelihood becomes more uncertain, their actions become more those of a united class and less those characteristic of individuals competing among themselves. The conditions under which the proletariat labor forge it into a class.

During the struggle that has its roots in the domination of the means of production and appropriation of its products (i.e., in a peculiar set of property relations), the proletariat becomes honed as a class, and the struggle takes on a greater political character. Ironically, the bourgeoisie has created the conditions that develop the class that revolts against it. As the decisive hour approaches, and the class and crisis nature of the society becomes increasingly evident, those in the bourgeoisie who see what is happening on the historical level also join the working class (Bottomore and Rubel 1956, pp. 184–188).

Marx argued that a given social order is not replaced until all the forces of production that can be produced under it have been developed, and new relations of production (i.e., new social orders) do not appear until the material basis for their existence has been formed in the old society. This is essentially what happens, according to Marx, when revolution occurs. Revolutions do not take place until the material conditions for their appearance are present. The mode of production shapes all other aspects of social life, and "at a certain stage of their development, the material productive forces of society come in conflict with existing relations of production…. From forms of development of the productive forces these relations turn into their fetters" (Marx and Engels 1969, vol. 1, pp. 503–504).

With proletarian revolution, the bases for the class system are removed and the proletariat is emancipated. In the interim, between the capitalist and classless society, a "dictatorship of the proletariat" exists, paving the way for a communistic society and the beginning of truly human rather than class history. Figure 9.1 summarizes some of the key elements of Marx's model that we have been discussing on the last several pages.

Some Comments on Marx

There are few areas in social science that have not had to confront the work of Marx. The sheer number of analyses and critiques of Marx's theory of class struggle and capitalism is voluminous (e.g.,

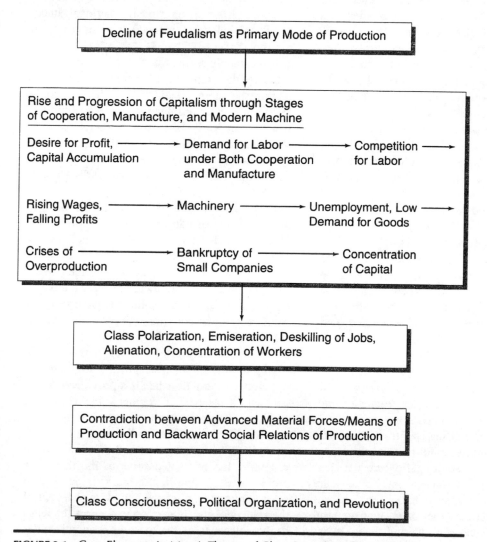

FIGURE 9.1   Core Elements in Marx's Theory of Class Struggle within Capitalism

Bottomore 1966; Dahrendorf 1959; Mills 1962; Giddens 1973; Miliband 1977). Consequently, only a few of the recurrent comments and criticisms about that theory are presented here.

Marx's theory has had a significant impact not only on the contemporary analysis of class structures but on the orientation taken in the study of society in general. Marx's approach allows us to see at once the simultaneous existence of organization and conflict and their historical roots. In this sense, Marx's theory is a comprehensive one, in many ways unparalleled in social science. Individual actions and emotions, such as alienation, organizations, and class structure, are analyzed against the backdrop of societal settings and historical change. Marx was aware of their mutual interaction and should not be considered as a simple economic determinist. His impact radiated beyond social science to philosophy and the study of morals and to the political arena. That his work continues to generate not only discussions but explanations and analyses built on his own is a tribute to the continued cogency and relevance of his theory.

Marx's theory of class is based to a large extent on the work of others, notably Saint-Simon, and Marx was well aware of his debt to others: "And now as to myself, no credit is due to me for discovering the existence of classes in modern society or the struggle between them. Long before me bourgeois historians had described the historical development of this class struggle and bourgeois economists the economic anatomy of the classes" (Marx and Engels 1969, vol. 1, p. 528).

Still, his conception of class is often vague and inconsistent, though the main thrust of his criteria—relationship to means of production, employment of labor, and class consciousness—is clear. His description of the classless society and the problems associated with the dictatorship of the proletariat as an interim period are not clear and precise. The state and bureaucracy in what are called communist societies have certainly not withered away. On the other hand, it is doubtful that Marx, who believed in uniting theory, practice, and human needs to help bring about a more humane society, would have considered these societies to be the kind he had in mind. Nevertheless, that these societies have turned out as they have suggests a basic flaw in Marx's view of how and why societies become structured as they do. Some have traced this fault to Marx's perspective on human nature which, they argue, is overly optimistic and does not consider the selfishness of people. "The most monumental error in Marx's thought" wrote Lopreato and Hazelrigg (1972), "is his failure to accept the fact...that man is by nature a fallible and 'sinful' animal" (pp. 40–41). Moreover, Marx appears to have "seriously underrated" the ability of individuals to adjust to inequality (Duke 1976, p. 34).

It certainly seems true that Marx also underestimated the strength of nationalism as a force inhibiting the international union of classes, and the "right to self determination" is something on which many early Marxists could not disagree. Miliband observed that "'nationalism' has proved a much more enduring and therefore a much more difficult problem to confront than early Marxists thought likely" (1977, p. 105).

Another criticism that has some validity is that the extent of pauperization and polarization of classes that Marx expected has not, as yet, come about. How much one makes of this comment depends heavily on the time frame one selects, because certainly there are indications that the extent of relative economic inequality has not declined and that corporate concentration has increased over the last 75 years. Capitalism has proved exceptionally resourceful in maintaining itself and forestalling widespread revolution. Being able to internationalize has provided capitalism with a mechanism for obtaining wider and wider markets and, therefore, has put off a crisis caused by its internal contradictions. The capitalist state, in being reformist and offering welfare programs, has alleviated some of its immediate problems. But, according to Marxists, reformism serves only to disguise the real class character of the state, and concrete reforms support the long-run maintenance of the existing economic order and are meant to solve only immediate problems rather than fundamental underlying ones (cf. Piven and Cloward 1971). Moreover, Miliband contended, "capitalism, however many and varied the reforms it can assimilate, is unable to do without exploitation, oppression, and dehumanization" (1977, p. 39).

Marx thought that the members of the working class would be the "gravediggers of capitalism," But, to use Giddens's colorful phrasing, "the grave remains undug, a century later; and its prospective incumbent, if no longer in the first flush of youth, does not seem seriously threatened by imminent demise" (Giddens 1982, p. 63). But the fact that the working class has not revolted is not conclusive proof of the inadequacy of Marx's theory or that capitalism is not a class society. This is because an effective class society, as Marx argued, can have a number of economic, political, and ideological characteristics that encourage false consciousness and minimize the chances for revolt by workers. Sooner or later (and he believed sooner), however, Marx thought that workers would become aware of their situation and act accordingly.

Although Marx's main predictions have not turned out exactly as he thought, many of the phenomena that he foresaw do exist to a degree. As we have seen in an earlier chapter, there has been a consistent trend toward more concentration of corporate power. There is also quite a bit of wealth inequality and there are business fluctuations, ups and downs, that capitalism follows. Moreover, every capitalist society has "class-based, working-class politics" to a certain degree (Collins 1988).

A final criticism is that Marx defined the concept of property too narrowly and misread its role (Dahrendorf 1959). To Dahrendorf, authority is a broader concept than property, and it is really authority that is the basis of class position. "Dahrendorf would have us believe that Marx, *of all people,* did not understand that property relations refer most fundamentally to power and domination with respect to the production of resources" (Hazelrigg 1972, p. 480). Dahrendorf's criticism on this count is weak; it is hard and erroneous to

imagine that Marx was not aware of the importance of control of property as well as sheer ownership or of their separation. In *Capital,* discussing the organization of capitalism, he wrote: "The joint-stock companies in general...have a tendency to separate the function of management more and more from the ownership of capital, whether it be self owned or borrowed" (Bottomore and Rubel 1956, p. 153).

Despite the criticisms that have been leveled against Marx's theory of class and class struggle, some of which are ill-founded, the theory has much to offer as an approach to the analysis of class structure. Moreover, to use Marx's propositions in his general theory of capitalism as predictions about concrete capitalist societies without reference to a specific historical society is a mistake. The exact operation of a society depends on a variety of factors other than the abstract characteristics of capitalism (Giddens 1973, p. 37). Reissman's advice still holds: "Marx should be read today with understanding rather than with misplaced pedantic precision" (Reissman 1959, p. 44).

MAX WEBER (1864–1920)

Many of those who immediately followed Marx in time, and especially the major social theorists of the period, were engaged in a "debate with Marx's ghost" (Zeitlin 1968). Among those most evidently aware of Marx's work and some of its shortcomings was Max Weber.

Weber is often considered to be the greatest sociologist who ever lived. His "shadow falls long over the intellectual life of our era," wrote Mitzman (1971, p. 3). Much of what he contributed to social science still remains intact and even those of his ideas that have proven weak or been discarded still provide a foundation from which further analysis can begin. Indeed, it is difficult to imagine what sociology would have been like without his influence. Like Marx and other great theorists, whose specific theories fit into a coherent whole, Weber's formulations regarding inequality must be considered in the context of his broader theory of the rationalization of the modern world. We will examine what Weber had to say about inequality, how U.S. sociologists have interpreted his work in this area, and if and how he added to Marx's own analysis of class structure.

Max Weber's life was quite different from Marx's, but like Marx's, his life experiences were clearly related to propositions about society that he developed. Weber was born in Erfurt, Germany, in 1864, 16 years after the publication of *Communist Manifesto* and three years before the publication of the first volume of *Capital*. His family was upper middle class. His father was a fun-loving conformist who disliked and feared upsetting existing political arrangements. In sharp contrast, Weber's mother was an extremely religious person of Calvinist persuasion, who often suffered the abuses of her much less moralistic husband, a fact that later became central in Max's repudiation of his father.

Despite its drawbacks for Weber, his parents' home was the site of frequent and diverse intellectual discussions featuring many of the well-known academicians of the day. So from the beginning, Max was exposed to a potpourri of ideas. Though he was a sickly child, he was very bright, becoming familiar with the writings of a variety of philosophers before setting off at the age of 18 for the University of Heidelberg, where he studied law, medieval history, economics, and philosophy. At age 19, Weber left for Strasbourg to put in his military service. It was there that he developed a lifelong and deep friendship with his uncle Hermann Baumgarten, a historian, and his wife, who was a devout Protestant and was effective in putting her religious fervor into action. Consequently, Weber developed a greater respect for those religious virtues found in his mother and less of a regard for the worldly and cowardly qualities of his father.

A year later, he returned to live with his parents and to study at the University of Berlin, where he wrote his dissertation on medieval business. Carrying on a very disciplined and rigid life, he served as a barrister in the Berlin court system and as an instructor at the university and wrote several works on agrarian history and agricultural laborers. These investigations included discussions of the social and cultural effects of commercialization and the role of ideas in economic behavior.

After getting married and serving at the age of only 30 as a full professor of economics at the University of Freiburg, Weber and his wife, Marianne, left for Heidelberg, where he took a professorship, became more politically involved, and quickly developed a close circle of intellectual friends. During this period, Weber suffered a severe emotional breakdown and was able to do little of anything, even reading. He was only 33 years old at the time, and it was a number of years before his energy was restored. The breakdown may have been precipitated by a harsh confrontation with his father, very shortly after which the father died.

In the early 1900s, Weber's health was restored, and it was between this time and his death that Weber produced most of the works for which he is best known. He became enmeshed in German politics, volunteered for service during World War I, but later became disillusioned by it and the German government's incompetence. Weber, unlike Marx, was accepted in polite society and was not a political radical, but he was generally a liberal and participated in the writing of the Weimar Constitution. There were many occasions when he fought bigotry and close-mindedness. Weber died of pneumonia on June 14, 1920, his broad knowledge leaving an unmistakable mark on social theory (Coser 1971; Mitzman 1971).

Rationalization of the World

Much of what Weber wrote had an undeniable unified theme. His discussions of bureaucracy, the Protestant Ethic, authority, and even class, status, and party fit into his overall concern for social change and the direction in which he thought the western world was moving. Thus, as is the case with Marx and many of the other nineteenth-century theorists, Weber's work on stratification must be understood in the context of his general perspective.

In contrast to Marx, who believed that capitalism and its accompanying denigration of the human spirit were necessary conditions that would eventually lead to a communistic, more humane society, Weber contended that alienation, impersonality, bureaucracy, and, in general, rationalization would be permanent societal features. Weber agreed with Marx that modern modes of technology have dehumanizing effects, but he contended that bureaucracy and alienation are not temporary or peculiar to a passing period, but rather are at the core of the disenchanted world. What the future promised in Weber's view was not a wonderful free society where people are reunited to themselves and nature, but rather an "iron cage"; what we have to look forward to is not "summer's bloom," but rather a "polar night of icy darkness and hardness." Bureaucratization and technical rationality are not likely to decrease but to increase under socialism.

A bureaucracy is characterized by its impersonality, hierarchy of rational-legal authority, written system of rules, clear division of labor, and career system. According to Weber, it is technically more perfect than other methods of organization and is the most efficient. "Precision, speed, unambiguity, knowledge of the files, continuity, discretion, unity, strict subordination, reduction of friction and of material and personal costs—these are raised to the optimum point in the strictly bureaucratic administration" (Gerth and Mills 1962, p. 214). Bureaucracy is the perfectly rational system. Business is carried out "without regard for persons," under "calculable rules." The lack of regard for persons is a central characteristic of all purely economic transactions. Since status honor and prestige are based on who the person is, the domination of the bureaucratic organization and a free market mean "the leveling of status 'honor'" and "the universal domination of the 'class situation'" (Gerth and Mills 1962, p. 215). The leveling of status strengthens the rule of bureaucracy by weakening status as a basis for position and encouraging the equal treatment of all regardless of background.

Capitalism and bureaucracy support each other; bureaucracy hastened the destruction of feudal, patrimonial organizations and local privileges. Whereas feudalism was characterized by

ties of personal loyalty and was grounded in small local communities, bureaucracy denies or destroys personal loyalty and demands loyalty to position and thereby equalizing individuals. Capitalist production requires it. Conversely, capitalism can supply the money needed to develop bureaucracy in its most rational form (Roth and Wittich 1968, p. 224). Bureaucracy and capitalism are characteristics of the contemporary modern society.

Bureaucracy and capitalism increase the prevalence of authority based on rational-legal, as opposed to charismatic or traditional, grounds. In the rational-legal form, authority is based on the acceptance of rules regarding the right to issue commands as they apply to formal position in the organization. Authority is attached to the office, not the person; it is impersonal.

Putting all of this together, we see that capitalism and the secularized Protestant Ethic, class, bureaucracy, and rational-legal authority are mutually supportive and are integral parts of the increasingly rationalized modern society that Weber saw emerging. They stand in stark contrast to feudalism, the personalism of status honor, tradition and charisma, and premodern forms of organization. An adequate understanding of Weber's perspective on class and status, their relationship, and their distinction can be obtained only if his broader theory of historical development and its associated concepts are incorporated in the analysis. Wrenching them out of this context distorts the meaning of what he had to say about inequality. Keeping Weber's broader theory in mind, we turn to discussion of his more specific ideas on inequality.

Tripartite Nature of Inequality

Weber argued that power can take a variety of forms. "Power," in general, refers to "the chance of a man or of a number of men to realize their own will in a communal action even against the resistance of others who are participating in the action" (Gerth and Mills 1962, p. 180). A person's power can be shown in the *social order* through his or her status, in the *economic order* through his or her class, and in the *political order* through his or her party. Thus, class, status, and party are each aspects of the distribution of power within a community. For example, if we think about an individual's chances of realizing his or her own will against someone else, it is reasonable to believe that the person's social prestige, class position, and membership in a political group will have an effect on these chances.

Social order refers to the arrangement of social honor (prestige) within a society. Different status groups (e.g., professors, construction workers) occupy different places along the prestige continuum. *Economic order,* in turn, refers to the general distribution of economic goods and services (e.g., owners and nonowners)—that is, to the arrangement of classes within a society. Finally, *political order* relates to the distribution of power among groups (parties) to influence communal decisions. Weber's general scheme for inequality is presented graphically in Figure 9.2.

Although these are presented as three distinct and separate orders, it is a mistake to see them strictly as such. All of them are manifestations of the distribution of power and can and usually do influence each other, often in a quite predictable manner. The inclusion of the social and political dimensions are ordinarily seen as a "rounding out" of the economic determinism of Marx (Gerth and Mills 1962, p. 47). But, as already pointed out, Marx was not a simple economic determinist; he viewed causal relationships in a more complex

fashion. Moreover, Weber's own writing suggested that he did not view the three dimensions as being equal in salience in capitalist society. Parkin (1971) persuasively argued that neo-Weberians have stressed the independence of these dimensions of stratification and thereby ignored, where Weber did not, the systematic relationship between the dimensions of inequality. Weber did not fully develop his political dimension, and the economic factor, as we shall see, outweighs the status element in the capitalist system of inequality. But at this point, it is necessary to examine each of Weber's three dimensions in greater detail.

Class.   More so than Marx, Weber deliberately set out a number of formal definitions for his concepts (Roth and Wittich 1968). But Weber acknowledged his debt to Marx: "Whoever does not admit that he could not perform the most important parts of his own work without the work that those two [Marx and Nietzsche] have done swindles himself and others" (Mitzman 1971, p. 182). Weber's own conception of class parallels Marx's in several ways. Class, at its core, is an economic concept; it is the position of individuals in the market that determines their class position. And it is how one is situated in the marketplace that directly affects one's life chances, "a common condition for the individual's fate" (Miller 1963, pp. 44–45). Just as Marx indicated that capital begins when capitalist and laborer meet freely in

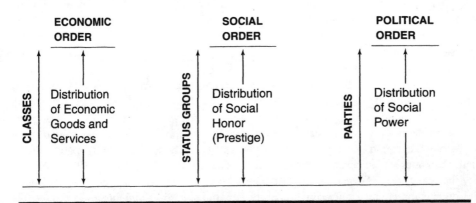

FIGURE 9.2   Weber's View of the General Distribution of Power

the market, when the laborer is free to sell his or her labor and form a relationship with the capitalist, Weber pointed out that persons are members of a class only if they have "the chance of using goods or services *for themselves* on the market" (Miller 1963, p. 45, emphasis added). Consequently, slaves are not members of classes.

Weber distinguished three types of classes: property classes, commercial (acquisition) classes, and social classes. Individuals belong to the same class if they are in the same "class situation," which refers to the probability of individuals obtaining goods, position, and satisfactions in life, "a probability which derives from the relative control over goods and skills and from their income-producing uses within a given economic order" (Roth and Wittich 1968, p. 302).

Property classes are "primarily determined by property differences." There are those who monopolize costly foods and status privileges, such as education, and those who control the bulk of wealth, capital, and sales in the society. Such classes usually are composed of "rentiers," who get income from a number of sources, including people, land, factories, and bank securities. Those who are not privileged are those who are unfree or are paupers. Weber stressed the distinction between the top and bottom classes but did mention that in each set of classes there are "middle classes" (Roth and Wittich 1968, pp. 302–303).

Weber is not clear, but he does not appear to make a complete separation between property and commercial classes. Rather, he has a broad conception of property in terms of ownership, and it is "'property' and 'lack of property'" that are "the basic categories of *all* class situations" (Miller 1963, p. 44, emphasis added). These general categories in turn can be broken down "according to the kind of property that is *usable for returns;* and, on the other hand, according to the kind of *services* that can be offered in the market" (Miller 1963, p. 44, emphasis added). In a manner of speaking, one can own and dispose of property as well as skills and services.

Commercial-class position is determined by "the marketability of goods and services," in other words, by the opportunity to exploit the market (Roth and Wittich 1968, p. 302). Commercial classes, then, are determined by the skills and occupational characteristics members bring into the market. Hence, those who are privileged in this regard may monopolize management and exercise influence over government political policies that affect their interests. Merchants, industrial and agricultural employers, bankers, ship owners, professionals, and workers who have cornered certain skills are examples of the entrepreneurs who are members of privileged commercial classes. In contrast, those who are unprivileged are usually laborers (skilled, semiskilled, and unskilled) (Roth and Wittich 1968, p. 304). Again, there are middle classes, but these are treated more as residual categories when compared with the other classes.

Social classes make up all class situations "within which individual and generational mobility is easy and typical" (Roth and Wittich 1968, p. 302). That is, a social-class structure is one in which there is fluidity and movement of individuals between class situations. Upward mobility is most likely, however, between adjacent classes. Examples of such social classes are the "working class as a whole," "the petty bourgeoisie," "the propertyless intelligentsia and specialists," and "the class privileged through property and education" (Roth and Wittich 1968, p. 305).

Class Consciousness and Class Struggle.   According to Weber, classes of whatever kind need not be class conscious as Marx conceived them; they are not necessarily unified "communities." Class organization can occur in any one of these three types of classes, but class consciousness and class (communal) action are likely only under certain conditions. Weber argued that just because there are different property classes, for example, does not mean that they will necessarily engage in class struggle, although they may when circumstances are right. And when struggles do occur, they may not be over a basic change in the entire economy but may be more superficially over the distribution of wealth.

Class-conscious action is most likely if, first, "the connections between the causes and consequences of the 'class situation'" are transparent, or clear. If individuals can plainly see that there is a connection between the structure of the economic system and what happens to them in terms of life chances, class action is more likely. Weber believed this had happened among the proletariat. A second condition for class unification exists if there is an immediate opponent on whom the class can focus. Hence, workers will react against their immediate employers rather than those who are more distantly and perhaps even more profitably involved (such as stockholders). Third, class organization is also more likely if large numbers of individuals are in the same class position. The increasing growth of the proletariat would increase the chances of class action by them. Fourth, if all of the individuals are in one place and therefore are easier to organize, class unity is more probable. Finally, if the goals they have are directed and interpreted by a group of intelligentsia who are actually outside their class, class organization is more likely (Henderson and Parsons 1947, pp. 427–428; Roth and Wittich 1968, p. 304; Miller 1963, p. 46). These are not inconsistent with the conditions that Marx thought would forge a mass of individuals in the same class situation into a "class for itself." However, Weber cautions us about the belief that fully developed classes are never wrong—that is, "falsely conscious"—about their own interests. They can be.

Class struggles have changed in content throughout history, according to Weber. The focus of conflict has altered from struggles over debt and credit in antiquity, to struggles over the availability of consumer goods and their prices in the market during the Middle Ages, to struggles over the price of labor in the modern world. Historically, class struggles begin when a credit market exists in which debtors pay high and often increasing rates of interest to the wealthy, who monopolize the credits (Miller 1963, pp. 45, 48). But in each case, by definition, the struggle is of an economic character.

Status. Standing in theoretical opposition to the market principle of class, which "knows no personal distinctions" and "knows nothing of 'honor,'" is the principle of status. Traditionally, status groups are ranked in terms of the "*consumption* of goods as represented by special 'styles of life,'" whereas classes are determined by their relations to the production system and acquisition of goods (Miller 1963, p. 56, emphasis in original).

In addition, then, to being ranked in terms of market situation, individuals can be ranked on the basis of honor or prestige. A person's "status situation" consists of all aspects of his or her "life fate" determined by a "social estimation of honor" (Miller 1963, pp. 49, 54). Status groups are based on a particular style of life, formal education, and/or inherited or occupational prestige. Certain groups may lay claim to (or, in other words, may usurp) a certain level of honor because of their hereditary background or family tree (such as "First Families of Virginia"), because of their peculiar lifestyle (such as liberal arts professors, perhaps), or because of their power. The existence of status groups most often shows itself in the form of (1) endogamy or a restricted pattern of social intercourse, (2) sharing of food and other benefits within groups, (3) status conventions or traditions, and (4) monopolistic acquisition of certain economic opportunities or the avoidance of certain kinds of acquisitions. Thus, because of their formal education and occupational prestige, liberal arts professors might tend to socialize only among themselves and might have certain unwritten rules about how a member of the group should act or what kinds of goods and services are suitable for use in the status group and what kinds are not. The conventions associated with the status group control the kind of lifestyle allowable (Roth and Wittich 1968, pp. 305–306). It is clear that some of the bases of class and status may concern the same factor, such as occupation. However, their characteristics mean that status groups are usually cohesive communities. They tend toward closure—that is, restriction of their memberships (Collins 1988; Grabb 1984).

The stability of status groups is linked to political and economic conditions in a society and is one way in which the latter two aspects of inequality are related to the social dimension. The likelihood of a conventionally recognized status group developing into a *"legal privilege,* positive or negative, is easily traveled as soon as a certain stratification of the *social order* has in fact been 'lived in' and has achieved stability *by virtue* of a stable distribution of *economic power"* (Miller 1963, p. 51, emphasis added). Weber is saying that status groups can be legalized and, therefore, become bases for political power differences when they have been around for some time and are buttressed by parallel differences in the distribution of economic resources. A belief in the long-run consistency between economic and social power is clear in his writing.

Where such stability exists, *caste groups* develop. Castes become supported by ritual (e.g., of purity), convention, and law. Separate castes may even develop their own religious beliefs. Usually, the status structure approaches this extreme form only when the fundamental differences between the groups are considered ethnic in nature (e.g., Jews). Caste is more than just simple ethnic segregation. The latter still permits each group in question to consider its own values (honor) to be high, but a caste system arranges these groups hierarchically, allotting one more honor than the rest. Any sense of dignity a lower caste group might have would derive from its belief in a *future* beyond present conditions in which it would have an elevated status. In contrast, the privileged caste groups can and do derive their own sense of dignity from their *present and/or past* situation (Miller 1963, pp. 51–52, emphasis added).

Weber stressed that class, status, and political power can be reciprocally related, with each affecting the others. Status can influence and even determine class (Roth and Wittich 1968, p. 306). However, his writing emphasized the effect of class on status in capitalist society. "Property as such is not always recognized as a status qualification, but in the long run it is, and with extraordinary regularity" (Miller 1963, p. 49).

Frequently, the richest person has the greatest prestige, and those in similar economic situations normally socialize with each other rather than with persons from different classes. Equality of status among individuals in unequal classes can "in the long run become quite precarious" (Miller 1963, p. 49). Weber observed that although race, political power, and class have all been bases for status in the past, "today the class situation is by far the predominant factor, for of course the possibility of a style of life expected for members of a status group is usually conditioned economically" (Miller 1963, p. 53).

Despite the controlling importance of the class factor, Weber emphasized that status and class are not necessarily connected. Individuals who are low in class position can be high in prestige and vice versa. Analytically, status is opposed "to a distinction of power which is regulated exclusively through the market" (Miller 1963, p. 54). If individuals who were high in class automatically received high status, "the status order would be threatened at its very root" (Miller 1963, p. 55). Groups who base their high status on their lifestyle rather than crass property are likely to feel threatened when the basis for honor shifts to the economic order.

Weber said very little about the conditions under which stratification by class or status predominate. In fact, his whole definitional classification of class and status is too brief. Parkin (1971, Chapter 1) argued that there was greater justification for seeing class and status as distinct and separate orders in the Middle Ages than is the case today, when status seems increasingly to be based on occupational and economic considerations. Weber maintained that "when the bases of the acquisition and distribution of goods are relatively stable, stratification by status is favored" (Miller 1963, p. 56). If a status order is entrenched by virtue of a monopolization of certain goods by particular groups, then the free-market principle is hindered; it cannot operate. Under these conditions, "the power of naked property per se, which gives its stamp to 'class formation,' is pushed into the background." But "every technological repercussion and economic transformation threatens stratification by status and pushes class situation into the foreground" (Miller 1963, pp. 55–56). In contrast to commercial-class societies, which ordinarily operate in market-oriented economies, status societies are economically organized around religious, feudal, and patrimonial factors (Roth and Wittich 1968, p. 306). In capitalist societies, classes play a more important role than status (Giddens 1973).

Parties.   Political power generally is considered to be a third dimension of inequality included by Weber, though some interpret Weber to be saying that class, status, and party are each different forces around which the distribution of power can be organized (Giddens 1973). Although Weber's entire specific treatment of class and status is brief, vague, and sometimes even ambiguous and confusing, his treatment of parties is even briefer.

Parties are associations that aim at securing "power within an organization [or the state] for its leaders in order to attain ideal or material advantages for its active members" (Roth and Wittich 1968, p. 284). Thus, Weber is not referring narrowly to what we think of as political parties (such as the Democrats) but to political groups more broadly conceived. Instead of parties being an outgrowth of class struggle, they can represent status groups, classes, or merely their own members and may use a variety of means to attain power. Since parties aim at such goals as getting their programs developed or accepted and getting positions of influence within organizations, it is clear that they operate only within a rational order within which these goals are possible to attain and only when there is a struggle for power. Parties themselves, however, can be organized around a charismatic or traditional leader as well as being structured in a rational way with formal positions to which members are elected. Formally recognized political parties are not the only kind that exist; parties also can be organized around religious issues or those that concern the traditional rights of a leader in an organization (Roth and Wittich 1968, pp. 285–286).

Marx and Weber

Weber's theory of stratification has traditionally been hailed in U.S. sociology as a major improvement over the supposed narrowness of Marxian theory. Why is this so? To some extent, it reflects the nature of U.S. sociology and the interpretation of Weber by U.S. sociologists. The vagueness in parts of Weber's treatment has encouraged multiple interpretations of what he said on the subject of inequality and the unintentional shaping of what he said to fit the peculiar characteristics of one version of sociology. U.S. sociology has tended to focus on the individual and has, until very recently, tended to ignore the role of the market in generating and perpetuating inequality. Weber's incorporation of noneconomic (status, party) and more general economic elements (such as market situation) is more appealing to a sociology rooted in a society that has been antiradical and staunch in the belief that individuals can distinguish themselves in a variety of ways other than economic.

Despite superficial measures such as income and occupational status, until recently U.S. sociologists have generally neglected the development of measures of Marx's concept of class and an adequate measure of Weber's market situation. Part of the reason for this appears to lie in the fact that many sociologists have an ideological dislike of purely economic and especially Marxian theory, and that Weber's multidimensional theory offers a more complete portrait of social inequality than does Marx's.

It is very easy to exaggerate the differences between these two men. Lopreato and Hazelrigg (1972, p. 90), in fact, argued that Weber added little to what was at least already implicit in Marx's theory. For example, certainly the assignment of prestige (honor) to given positions can be viewed as one way in which the dominant ideology maintains the class system.

There are two basic similarities between Marx and Weber. First, both argued that capitalist society is a class society. Capitalism is characterized by laborers and capitalists meeting freely in the market; it creates a large pool of dehumanized workers of all types and it broadens the market. Second, even though Weber talked about status and party as well as class, he argued that in a rationalized market society, such as capitalism, class becomes predominant, and there is a "leveling of status honor." This distinct separation of status honor from the market principle and property is most characteristic of traditional or premodern societies (Parkin 1971, p. 38). Thus, on the importance of class in capitalist society, Marx and Weber appear to agree.

In light of these core similarities, a good argument can be made that many U.S. sociologists have accepted Weber because they have trivialized his ideas by latching onto the multidimensional aspect of his theory and minimizing the systematic nature of the relationship between those dimensions. Their interpretation of Weber is that class, status, and party are separate, independent dimensions along which each individual can be ranked. By abstracting these concepts while ignoring their systematic interrelationship and the historical context in which they are embedded, Weber's theory becomes seriously distorted.

Of course, there are some basic differences between Marx and Weber. As mentioned earlier, Marx had a more optimistic view of the long-term future than Weber, who believed society would become increasingly rationalized and bureaucratized even under socialism, because bureaucracy once established was virtually "escape proof" (Grabb 1984). Socialism would only intensify the bureaucratic characteristics of the state. Thus, future society would not see the removal of alienation and impersonality but rather their enhancement. A second major difference between the theorists is that because Weber was concerned with status and party and defined class generally in terms of market situation, the system of inequality contained within it many more groups than are suggested by a class society in which only a few groups dominate. Market situation, for example, if defined broadly enough and in detail, could ultimately mean that each individual is in a distinct class position, meaning that there are as many classes as there are persons. Perhaps the greatest weakness in Weber's discussion is the brevity and ambiguity in his treatment of class, status, and party.

EMILE DURKHEIM (1858–1917)

In contrast to the theorists we have discussed, Emile Durkheim was not principally concerned with social equality. Rather, his emphases were establishing sociology as a scientific discipline, uncovering the sources and forms of integration and moral authority, and tracking and understanding the place of individualism in modern industrial society (Giddens 1978). Most of his works revolve around issues of integration and cohesiveness— that is, the question of order in society. Although liberal and reformist in outlook, Durkheim was a central founder of the functionalist school of thought in sociology, which views society as a social system tending toward equilibrium. The organic analogy of society is clear in his writing. Despite his preoccupations with questions of order and the evolutionary growth of societies, however, Durkheim had something to say about social inequality, and it is for that reason that this brief discussion is included here.

Emile Durkheim was born in 1858 in Alsace-Lorraine into a Jewish family, which expected him to become a rabbi. Later, as a young man, he turned away from religion and became an agnostic, even though his study of the "elementary forms of religious life" is one of his major works. Durkheim was a terrific student in his early youth, but was not entirely happy with the lack of scientific and moral emphases at the normal school he attended (Coser 1971). Later, he was to become a highly successful teacher at the high school and university levels.

Durkheim wanted to study a subject that would directly address issues of moral and practical guidance for society, and he wanted to use a scientific approach in the analysis of issues. He turned to sociology as the discipline of choice and, to the disdain of many colleagues, became an imperialistic advocate of sociology rather than the other social sciences (Giddens 1978). It is not surprising that topics related to order, development, and the relationship between the individual and the society would run as a common thread through Durkheim's body of work because of conditions in French society at the time. The early years of the Third Republic in France, when Durkheim was a young man, were filled with instability and conflicts between the political right and left. While events calmed down briefly in the late 1800s, conditions were shaken again by the Dreyfus affair in which a Jewish officer was wrongly accused and convicted of selling sensitive information to Germans. The affair pitted right against left again. At the same time these political events were occurring, France was moving toward more industrialism and a socialist movement was developing. In sum, French society was not experiencing complete stability; it was a time of change.

Durkheim was a defender of Dreyfus and became actively involved in public affairs, including aiding in the restructuring of the university system and helping early in the World War I effort by completing articles attacking Nationalist German writing (Coser 1971). Durkheim's major sociological works did not begin to appear until the end of the nineteenth century. *The Division of Labor,* the source we will be concerned with here, was completed in 1893, followed by *The Rules of Sociological Method* in 1895 and *Suicide* in 1897. Later, in 1912, he finished *The Elementary Forms of Religious Life.* Durkheim died in 1917 at the age of 59.

Durkheim and Inequality

In *The Division of Labor,* Durkheim developed his theory of the movement of society from "mechanical" to "organic" solidarity. A society based on mechanical solidarity is homogeneous, with a simple division of labor, and based on the similarity of the individuals in it. There is a strong collective conscience that serves as a principal source of moral cohesion. The individual ego is not prominent in this kind of society. In sharp contrast, societies organized around the organic form of solidarity are characterized by differences and interdependence in their division of labor. This specialization, along with the increased individualism, can threaten the cohesiveness and stability of society. Corporate groups, according to Durkheim, are to serve as means for integrating individuals in this kind of society. They stand midway, as it were, between the state and individual.

In a fully developed organic society, characterized by individualism, equal opportunity, specialization, and interdependence, inequality is to be expected because at this point in evolution it should be based on differences in the internal abilities of individuals. A "normal" division of labor is based on these internal differences between individuals, including differences between men and women. Differences in the division of labor between men and women should persist, but other differences, including classes, based on external qualities (e.g., race, inheritance) should decline and eventually disappear. As society evolves, differential rewards should, because of equal opportunity, directly reflect *individual* differences in abilities and differences in the social value of occupations. In short, Durkheim believed that as time moved on, modern society would be characterized by social inequalities between individuals based on their inner abilities rather than external characteristics. He believed that such internal differences existed between the sexes, and thus justified social inequalities between men and women, but he also argued that class and racial inequalities would diminish. Although there is some ambiguity in his treatment, this is Durkheim's primary position (Lehmann 1995).

Until this point in evolution is reached, however, the division of labor can take on "abnormal" forms that prevent its appropriate and efficient functioning. Durkheim argued that this occurs when individuals' positions in it are forced or determined without moral regulation. Individuals must recognize the rights of others in the division of labor and their duties to society as well as to themselves. Each person must have the opportunity to occupy the position that fits his or her abilities (Grabb 1984). When these conditions are not present, abnormal forms of the division of labor develop. Two of these are the *anomic* and *forced* forms of the division of labor.

In the first type, relations between people in the workplace are not governed by a generally agreed upon set of values and beliefs. Two of the developments that divided people were the split between "masters and workers" in which the organization is privately owned by the masters and the arrival of large-scale industry in which workers were each given very narrow and different functions to perform. Both of these factors served to drive a wedge between employers and workers. With large industries, "the worker is more completely separated from the employer." And "at the same time that specialization becomes greater, revolts become more frequent" (Durkheim 1933, p. 355). In smaller industries, in contrast, there is "a relative harmony between worker and employer. It is only in large-scale industry that these relations are in a sickly state" (p. 356). Large industry develops as markets grow and encompass groups not in immediate contact with each other. Producers and consumers become increasingly separated from each other. "The producer can no longer embrace the market in a glance, nor even in thought. He can no longer see its limits, since it is, so to speak, limitless. Accordingly, production becomes unbridled and unregulated" (p. 370). That is, a condition of anomie or normlessness exists. Economic crises develop but industry grows as markets grow.

With the growth of industry and an increasingly minute division of labor, the individual worker becomes more "alienated," to use a Marxian term. Like Marx, Durkheim concluded that the worker becomes a "machine," performing mind-numbing, routine, repetitive labor without any sense of the significance of his or her role in the labor process.

Every day he repeats the same movements with monotonous regularity, but without being interested in them, and without understanding them. He is no longer anything but a living cell of a living organism which unceasingly vibrates with neighboring cells,...He is no longer anything but an inert piece of machinery, only an external force set going which always moves in the same direction

and in the same way.... One cannot remain indifferent to such debasement of human nature. (Durkheim 1933, p. 371)

Although this description may sound intriguingly Marxist, Durkheim's view of the division of labor in modern society was quite different from that of Marx. Because of its nature, Durkheim viewed the division of labor as a central basis for integration in modern industrial society. It is only in certain abnormal forms that it becomes a problem. But basically, a complex division of labor is a necessity in *industrial* society. It is expected that as societies develop they become increasingly complex. In contrast, Marx viewed the division of labor as a source of basic problems in *capitalist* society. Class conflict was over fundamental issues in the property and social relationships involved in the division of labor. For Durkheim, class conflict was a surface symptom of an anomic state in which the employers and workers conflicted because of the absence of a common, agreed on set of moral rules. The problems of the modern society are not due to contradictions withn capitalism, "but derive from the strains inherent in the transition from mechanical to organic solidarity" (Giddens 1978, p. 36). Marx sees regulation in capitalist society as stifling human initiative, whereas Durkheim sees moral regulation as necessary for individual liberty and happiness.

However, the mere presence of rules is not enough to prevent problems in the division of labor because "sometimes the rules themselves are the cause of evil. This is what occurs in class-wars" (Durkheim 1933, p. 374). The problem here is that the rules governing the division of labor do not create a correspondence between individual talents or interests and work functions. The result is that the division of labor creates dissatisfaction and pain instead of integration and cohesiveness. "This is because the distribution of social functions on which [the class structure] rests does not respond, or rather no longer responds, to the distribution of natural talents" (p. 375). When the rules regulating the division of labor no longer correspond to the distribution of true talents among individuals, then the organization of labor becomes *forced*. (This is the forced division of labor referred to earlier.) Durkheim felt that inequalities that were not based on "internal" differences between individuals were unjust. "External" inequality, which is based on inheritance or membership in some biological group, must be eliminated, according to Durkheim, because it threatens the solidarity of society. Superiority that results from differences in the resources of individuals is unjust. "In other words, there cannot be rich and poor at birth without there being unjust contracts" (p. 384). The sense of injustice associated with the significance of external inequalities becomes greater as labor becomes more separated from employers and the collective conscience becomes weaker.

Despite his realization of the injustices suffered by workers in the division of labor, Durkheim was not an advocate of class revolution. As mentioned, he did not feel that there is anything inherently wrong with a complex division of labor and, consequently, only reformist change was needed to eliminate the problems associated with it. Durkheim felt that complete revolution would destroy the delicate and complex membrane that made up society. "I am quite aware when people speak of destroying existing societies, they intend to reconstruct them. But these are the fantasies of children. One cannot in this way rebuild collective life: once our social organization is destroyed, centuries of history will be required to build another" (quoted in Fenton 1984, p. 31). Durkheim felt that deep, lasting change would take place gradually and through ameliorative reform rather than through drastic conflict. In this way, he also differed from Marx. Nor did he feel that the state was an instrument of oppression, but rather felt it could serve as an instrument of reform for a better society (Giddens 1978). However, like Marx and in contrast to Weber, he had an optimistic view of future society. Fundamental class conflicts would be minimized once problems in the division of labor could be ironed out with appropriate policies and moral regulations over time.

SUMMARY

It was mentioned at the outset of the chapter that a thorough understanding of what Marx, Weber, and Durkheim had to say about inequality depends on seeing and analyzing that work in the context of their broader theories and perspectives on society and human beings. Too often, as a reflection of our specialization and departmentalization, we wrench out only those segments of an individual's theory in which we have an immediate interest. This is not the way in which these theories were developed, and so taking them out of context can lead to distortions and, at best, only superficial understanding. Consequently, the specific observations made by these individuals on inequality should be couched in the broader frameworks of their overall perspectives and life experiences. Hopefully, this leads to a fuller comprehension of what each of the given theorists was trying to convey.

It is clear from the discussion in this chapter that theorists differed significantly in their views on human nature, the forms that inequality could take, and the bases and future of inequality. Weber saw human beings as self-seeking, whereas Marx viewed them in more selfless terms. Durkheim felt that individuals required regulation and guidance. Marx focused on economic classes, as did Durkheim in *The Division of Labor*, while Weber examined economic classes as well as status groups, and to some extent, parties. Marx sought the source of inequality in an individual's relationship to the means of production, whereas Weber saw inequality arising from a number of sources, including market situation, lifestyle, and decision-making power. Durkheim argued that although inequality continued to be based on biological and inheritance factors, he assumed that eventually in organic society most social inequality would be founded solely on individual differences in abilities. Weber and Durkheim did not see inequality as disappearing in the future, but Marx was more optimistic on this point.

Marx and Weber agreed that classes, class struggle, or both are significant elements in societ-

TABLE 9.1   Summary of Basic Ideas on Inequality from Classical Theorists

		THEORIST'S VIEWS ON INEQUALITY			
THEORIST	MAJOR CONCERN	Forms	Causes	Inevitability	Future
Marx	Classes in capitalist society	Historical class structures	Private property	No	Revolution and classless society
Weber	Dimensions of inequality and shifts in their prominence	Class, status, party	Market situation; granting of status honor; political power	Yes	Rationalization of society and growing salience of class
Durkheim	Abnormal forms of division of labor	Masters and workers	Anomic and forced divisions of labor	Mixed	Decline of class conflict in industrial society

ies. Weber and Marx both felt that capitalism has dehumanizing effects and is class structured and that class is a predominant factor in modern society. Their conceptions of the effects of class anticipated many of the specific effects discussed in later chapters on life chances, crime, and protest. Similar conditions for class consciousness and protest were outlined by Marx and Weber.

Table 9.1 highlights the central features of the main theorists covered in this chapter. The theories of Marx, Weber, and Durkheim were presented here because their perspectives have helped to shape modern social science. Their impact has not always been obvious, but it has been pervasive.

CRITICAL THINKING

1. How important is one's economic position compared to other criteria (e.g., race, gender, lifestyle) in determining ranking in a community?

2. Is a classless society possible or even approachable? If so, what problems, if any, would arise from the classlessness? If no, why not?

3. Capitalism or at least modern industry plays an important role in classical theories of inequality. Do you agree? Why? What features appear to be most closely linked to the creation of inequality? How could capitalism be altered to change the class/status system of the United States?

WEB CONNECTIONS

Marx, Weber, and Durkheim were among the giants of sociology during its classical period. To find out more about them, and to read interviews that Marx and Engels had with various media representatives, go to the Marx/Engels Archive, which also contains information on writers who

followed in their footsteps. Comparisons of Marx with Weber and Durkheim can also be carried out by browsing and reading in these two websites:

http://csf.colorado.edu/psn/marx/

http://www.geocities.com/CollegePark/Quad/5889/

CHAPTER 10

MODERN EXPLANATIONS
OF INEQUALITY

Social inequality is thus an unconsciously evolved device by which societies insure that the most important positions are conscientiously filled by the most qualified persons.
—Kingsley Davis and Wilbert E. Moore

[The poor] are also separated from the non-poor in the positive sense that they have economic value where they are and hence that there are groups interested, not only in resisting the elimination of poverty, but in actively seeking its perpetuation.
—Michael J. Piori

This chapter consists of a discussion of some of the more recent explanations of social inequality. One of the earliest and most controversial of these theories is the one developed by Davis and Moore. These scholars provide a functionalist perspective on inequality, a perspective that is generally interpreted as being conservative when compared to those developed by conflict-oriented or radical theorists. The functionalist theory of inequality is presented in detail because it occupied an important place in discussions and controversies concerning the origins of inequality, and because the general framework of functionalism dominated social thought in the United States for several decades.

Social reproduction theories are fairly recent conflict, largely Marxian, models aimed at furthering understanding of the mechanisms that keep inequality intact over time. Lenski's theory, in turn, is an overt attempt to combine both conservative/functionalist and radical/conflict assumptions and propositions into a coherent theory of social stratification.

Finally, economic labor-market theories of inequality have, in a broad way, mirrored conservative and radical perspectives in sociology. Yet they are distinct enough to warrant separate discussion. Thus, the analysis of Lenski's synthetic theory is followed by a presentation of various versions of labor-market theory as they pertain to inequality. This includes a discussion of more recent radical models.

This chapter is not an exhaustive treatment of all contemporary theories of inequality. The work of Erik Wright, for example, a prominent American Marxist scholar, is not discussed in this chapter. Wright's principal publications have been concerned with the Marxian conceptualization and measurement of class and their application to understanding the shape of class structure in capitalist societies. As a result, his view of the class concept and class structure were reviewed in

Chapter 2, along with other perspectives on class structure.

FUNCTIONALIST THEORY OF STRATIFICATION

The arguments of Durkheim that inequality will be based primarily on differences in internal talents and the division of labor is echoed in the 1945 theory of Kingsley Davis and Wilbert Moore. Few theories of stratification have called forth the attention and criticism that the Davis-Moore theory has received.

Like Durkheim's theory, Davis and Moore's theory is based on a functionalist framework. The functional perspective views societies as social systems that have certain basic problems to solve or functions that have to be performed if the society is to survive. One of these problems concerns the motivation of society's members; if that motivation is absent, a society will not survive (Aberle et al. 1950, p. 103). If a society is to continue, important tasks must be specifically delineated and some means for their assignment and accomplishment created; for a society, "activities necessary to its survival must be worked out in predictable, determinate ways, or else apathy or the war of each against all must prevail" (p. 105). And since certain goods of value are scarce (property, wealth, etc.), "some system of differential allocation of the scarce values of a society is essential" (p. 106). The result of this differential allocation (stratification) must be viewed as being legitimate and "accepted by most of the members—at least by the important ones—of a society if stability is to be attained" (ibid.). Many functional prerequisites are assumed to be necessary for the survival of a society, but it is the assumption of the necessity of stratification that concerns us here.

The most celebrated and damned theory of stratification using the functionalist perspective was formulated by Davis and Moore in 1945. Their ideas are quite simple to grasp and, on the surface, may appear to be common-sensical and even self-evident. One should keep in mind that the kind of thinking that is represented in their theory dominated sociology throughout the 1950s and much of the 1960s in the United States. Let us take a closer look at their reasoning.

Davis and Moore indicated at the outset of their argument what they were trying to do:

1. "To explain in functional terms, the universal necessity which calls forth stratification in any social system."
2. To explain why positions, not persons, are differentially ranked in the system of rewards in any society (Davis and Moore 1945, p. 242).

Assuming that structure is at least minimally divided into different statuses and roles (i.e., a division of labor), Davis and Moore began by arguing that every society has to have some means to place its members in the social structure. A critical issue is the problem of motivating individuals to occupy certain statuses (full-time occupations) and to make sure that they are motivated to adequately perform the roles once they occupy those positions. Since some tasks are more onerous, more important for the society, and more difficult to perform, a system of rewards (inducements) is needed to make certain that these tasks are performed by the most capable individuals. "The rewards and their distribution become a part of the social order, and thus give rise to stratification" (1945, p. 243). Like Durkheim's view of the ideal industrial society, Davis and Moore assumed that the society will run smoothly because the distribution of rewards to individuals will reflect the "internal inequalities" of their skills and capabilities.

Every society has a variety of rewards that it can use: (1) those "that contribute to sustenance and comfort" (money, goods of different kinds), (2) those related to "humor and diversion" (vacations, leisure plans), and (3) those that enhance "self-respect and ego expansion" (psychological rewards, promotion). Consequently, Davis and Moore are not simply talking about the distribution and system of economic rewards but all kinds of inducements that can promote motivation to perform tasks in the society. Not all positions have equal rewards attached to them, of course, and since that is the case, "the society must be stratified because that is precisely what stratification means. Social inequality is thus an unconsciously evolved device by which societies ensure that the most important positions are conscientiously filled by the most qualified persons" (1945, p. 243). According to this approach, since every society has tasks that are differentially important to its survival, every society is stratified.

Davis and Moore specified two criteria that determine the amount of rewards that accrue to given positions: (1) functional importance of the task and (2) the "scarcity of personnel" capable of performing the task, or the amount of training required (1945, pp. 243–244). Together these determine the rank of a given position in the system of rewards—that is, in the stratification system. Consequently, "a position does not bring power and privilege because it draws a high income. Rather it draws a high income because it is functionally important and the available personnel is for one reason or another scarce" (pp. 246–247). The exact contribution of each of these criteria, singly and in combination, to the level of rewards is not spelled out, so one can only guess as to how rewards would be affected if one of these criteria ranked high but the other low on a given position (Abrahamson 1973).

Davis and Moore implied that a third and more radical factor also is involved in determining an *individual's* (as opposed to a position's) rank and reward: economic power or control over resources. They recognized that having a great deal of money can give an individual an advantage in seeking a higher position. Power and prestige can be based on ownership, and "one kind of ownership of production goods consists in rights over the labor of others.... Naturally this kind of ownership has the greatest significance for stratification because it necessarily entails an unequal relationship" (1945, p. 247). These comments are repeated in Davis's revised version of the theory. Kemper (1976) stated that it is remarkable that, given all the critics of the theory, none seems to have noticed that economic power also is considered a cause of distribution in the reward system by Davis and Moore. Clearly, however, it takes a secondary place alongside functional importance and training or talent, especially since it is more clearly a determinant of why *individuals,* and not *positions,* are distributed as they are in a reward system.

Societies differ in their stratification systems because they contain different conditions that affect either one or both of the principal determinants of ranking—that is, either functional importance or scarcity. The stage of cultural development and their situation with respect to other societies vary between societies, causing different tasks to be more important in one society than in another, and in personnel being more scarce for certain tasks than for others.

Figure 10.1 outlines the essential argument of the Davis-Moore thesis. Davis and Moore concluded their presentation by noting several di-

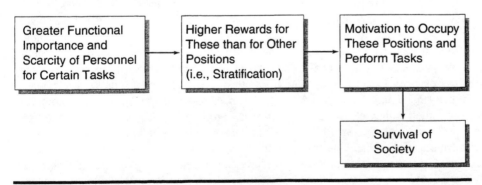

FIGURE 10.1   The Davis-Moore Theory of Stratification

mensions along which stratification systems in different countries can vary. Among others, these include how fine the gradations are between ranks (specialization), the degree of social distance from the top to the bottom, the extent of mobility in the system, and the extent to which classes are clearly delineated in the society. What could be more logical? Certain tasks are more important than others, and some are more difficult to carry out. In order to make sure they are performed, more rewards are attached to them. Thus, people are motivated to perform them, and the society continues to function.

Critique of the Functionalist Theory of Stratification

The functionalist theory and the Davis-Moore article, in particular, have precipitated a storm of criticism and counterattacks. The vehemence with which some of the arguments are made and the tenacity with which this debate has held on for almost five decades suggests that a number of fundamental issues are involved. Of the host of criticisms that have been made of the theory, I will focus on three: (1) the issue of the differential functional importance of positions, (2) the question of whether the functionalists are addressing themselves to real societies, and (3) the neglect of the dysfunctions of stratification.

Differential Functional Importance. A central problem of the Davis-Moore theory is how to establish the *functional necessity* of a task for a society. Davis and Moore acknowledged that it is difficult to define functional necessity, but they suggested two indicators of importance: (1) "the degree to which a position is functionally *unique*"—that is, there are no functional alternatives to the position, and (2) "the degree to which other positions are *dependent* on the one in question" (Davis and Moore 1945, p. 244, emphasis added).

It is not clear whether Davis and Moore are speaking of the evaluation of positions as being differentially important or of positions being dif-

ferentially important by some more objective standard. In the 1945 version, the indicators for measuring functional importance suggested that they are speaking of functional importance in an objective sense. But in a later statement, Davis (1948–1949) suggests that it is the *subjective evaluation* of a role's importance that is the significant determinant of its functional importance. And, of course, if this is the case, about whose evaluation is he speaking—all of society or a select few? Moore (1970) also took a more subjective position later when he noted the importance of evaluating performance, qualities, and achievement in determining rewards. The bottom line is that their criteria for defining *functional importance* are not clear nor are their attempts to measure it adequate (Huaco 1963).

An interesting attempt at escape from the difficulty of measuring functional importance is to substitute the concept of supply and demand in its place (Grandjean 1975). The two determinants mentioned by Davis and Moore, scarcity of talent and functional importance, are comparable in many ways to supply and effective demand, respectively. That is, the smaller the supply, the greater the scarcity of talent, and the greater the demand, the greater the evaluated importance of a position. Studies attempting to test the functionalist hypotheses have not been very successful, either because of difficulties in measuring functional importance or because the results have not been entirely supportive of the theory (Lopreato and Lewis 1963; Abrahamson 1973). Until better measures of functional importance are developed, or until the concept is recast in other terms, the exact role of functional importance in generating differential rewards will have to await more thorough testing.

The Issue of Dealing with Real Societies. One of the principal criticisms of the functional perspective is that it deals with highly abstract social systems (utopias) yet ignores the operation of real societies (Dahrendorf 1958a). As it applies here, the criticism means that if stratification of rewards is the means by which a society ensures that the most qualified people fill the most important positions, then it is crucial that there be free flow of talent throughout the society. But, in fact, as Tumin (1953) made plain, this is not the case in real societies. People in the lower strata usually have restricted opportunities, the society is not freely competitive, and people probably are not taking full advantage of the talent they may have. The roles of conflict and lack of opportunity must be considered when trying to understand the socioeconomic arrangement of real societies (Dahrendorf 1958a), and although Davis and Moore did mention the roles of power and wealth in determining and maintaining positions, they did not stress these as major determinants.

One way by which Davis and Moore tried to handle the criticism that some are hindered from attaining a high position was by reiterating that the theory is about *positions,* not the mobility of *people.* However, even given this insistence on their part, people do, in fact, become important in the theory because of Davis and Moore's belief that "it does make a great deal of difference who gets into which positions, not only because some positions are inherently more agreeable than others but also because some require special talents or training and some have more importance than others" (1945, p. 367). Concerns over motivation and scarcity of talent necessarily implicate people in the theory.

Neglect of the Dysfunctions of Stratification.
Tumin (1953) was the first major critic to point out that stratification can have numerous dysfunctions for society and the individual, a point ignored in the original Davis-Moore argument. Among the dysfunctions he noted are that stratification (1) inhibits the discovery of talent, (2) limits the extent to which productive resources can be expanded, (3) provides those at the top with the power to rationalize and justify their high position, (4) weakens the self-images among those at the bottom and thereby hinders their psychological development, (5) can create hostility and disintegration if it is not fully accepted by all in society, (6) may make some feel that they are not

full participants in the society and, therefore, (7) may make some feel less loyal to the society, and (8) may also make some less motivated to participate in the society.

It is somewhat surprising that the original argument by Davis and Moore would neglect the question of dysfunctions, given their comments about power and wealth affecting the reward system. But, on the other hand, Tumin does not indicate that a condition of full equality may generate problems of its own, such as lack of motivation and feelings of inequity. Wrong (1959), in fact, has indicated that many critics of the Davis-Moore theory point to the dysfunctions of stratification and the role of power and so forth in determining rank, but they neglect the dysfunctional effects of equality of opportunity. In a society where individuals can freely move up on the basis of their talent, would not the failures then suffer even more acutely, knowing that they and not the system are to blame for their low position in the system of rewards?

In addition those just mentioned, the Davis-Moore theory is also plagued by other problems surrounding the clarity of their subject matter. Some have even argued that the theory has nothing to do with stratification (Buckley 1958). For instance, Davis used the terms *class, stratification, system of differential rewards,* and *social inequality* interchangeably. As an example of the resulting confusion, Davis said that although "no society is 'classless,' that is, unstratified," in small primitive communities "no class strata appear...but even here [there is] an incipient stratification" (1948–1949, p. 366). There also appears to be some disagreement between the authors as to whether stratification is inevitable (cf. Davis 1953; Moore 1970). Finally, Davis has defended the importance of viewing the family rather than the individual as the basic unit of stratification. "This is because one of the family's main functions is the ascription of status....Between members of the same family class antagonisms are felt to be inappropriate. This is why all wives do not constitute a social class opposed to all husbands" (1953, p. 364). Davis went on to indicate that the wife is certainly "closer to her husband in loyalty and interest" than to other women and "closer to her social class than to the feminine sex as a whole." However, whether this is the case is a matter for empirical testing, not for theoretical fiat. Evidence will be presented in other chapters that demonstrates that men and women have different social positions, even in the family.

SOCIAL REPRODUCTION THEORY

During the mid- and late fifties, the functionalist perspective came under a barrage of criticism in sociology. Social reproduction theories are generally built on a conflict model of society and are often aligned with Marxian views on inequality. But rather than focusing on the explanation of the *original appearance* of inequality, these theories focus on outlining the process by which the social class structure is *maintained*. Specifically, they are concerned with the question of how the class structure reproduces itself generation after generation. As MacLeod (1987) stated, "Social reproduction theory explains how societal institutions perpetuate (or reproduce) the social relationships and attitudes needed to sustain the existing relations of production in a capitalist society" (p. 9).

Thus, even though they are concerned with the reproduction of inequality over time, these theories are in sharp contrast to those that emphasize a culture-of-poverty approach—that is, blaming the perpetuation of inequality on the values and other characteristics of poor individuals and their families. Case studies of such individuals make this point unequivocally. "The view that the problem resides almost exclusively with the children and their families, and that some sort of cultural injection is needed to compensate for what they are missing, is not only intellectually bankrupt but also has contributed to the widespread popular notion that the plight of poor whites and minorities is entirely their own fault" (MacLeod 1987, p. 99). Of the families she studied, Rubin (1976) wrote:

These families reproduce themselves not because they are somehow deficient or their culture aberrant, but because there are no alternatives for most of their children. Indeed, it may be the singular tri-

umph of this industrial society...that not only do we socialize people to their appropriate roles and stations, but that the process by which this occurs is so subtle that it is internalized and passed from parents to children by adults who honestly believe they are acting out of choices they have made in their own lifetime. (p. 211)

Needless to say, there are a number of specific theories of reproduction, but only a couple will be summarized here to leave you with the basic outlines of this approach to understanding inequality. Reproduction theories variously focus on the role(s) of (1) institutions, (2) culture, and/or (3) the individual in the perpetuation of social inequality. Following is a summary of these foci and the central catalysts for each in the inequality-reproduction process:

Levels of Analysis	Catalysts of Reproduction
Macro- and microstructure	Opportunities and barriers
Societal and group culture	Hegemonic values
Individual	Action and reaction

Institutions as social structures create avenues of and barriers to achievement. Societal and subcultural values encourage or discourage attitudes and behaviors that affect achievement. Finally, even though individuals may share values, they may enact them in different ways. Moreover, since each individual's situation is at least a little different, his or her immediate values that are grounded in this situation may also differ, and thus so may the individual's actions/reactions. Examples of arguments that stress each of these follow.

The role of institutions is stressed by Oliver and Shapiro (1995) in their historical analysis of racial wealth inequality across generations. As reviewed in Chapter 6, governmental agencies and programs have often created opportunities for wealth accumulation for some but not for others. Since degree of access to opportunities allows or prevents the growth of wealth for current and future generations, institutional conditions encourage the cementing and, in some cases, the increasing of economic gaps between racial groups.

Education is another institution prominently displayed in some reproduction theories. Drawing upon Marx's work, Bowles and Gintis's theory addresses how the educational system helps to reproduce class relationships in capitalist society. The educational institution has been studied and considered as an avenue to upward mobility and a means for developing the human personality, but, according to Bowles and Gintis, education has not been seen as an institution to perpetuate the capitalist or class system in U.S. society. However, even early in its development, education was a means "to help preserve and extend the capitalist order. The function of the school system was to accommodate workers to its most rapid possible development.... Since its inception in the United States, the public-school system has been seen as a method of disciplining children in the interest of producing a properly subordinate adult population" (Bowles and Gintis 1976, pp. 29 and 37). A higher level of education for most people has not reduced economic inequality, nor has it developed their full creativity. Its structure rewards those who conform to its rules and obey authority.

As in the workplace, obedience to authority and rules is expected. There is a correspondence, Bowles and Gintis argued, between the structure of educational institutions and the workplace. Specifically, there is a similarity between the two spheres in (1) the nature of their authority structures, (2) the student's lack of control over his or her classes and the workers' lack of control over the work process, (3) the role of grades and other rewards (e.g., colored stars on papers in grade schools) and the role of wages as extrinsic motivators in the workplace, (4) ostensibly free competition among students and similar competition among workers, and (5) the specialization and tracking of courses in school and the narrow functional specialization and career paths in the workplace (Bowles and Gintis 1976; MacLeod 1987). These correspondences between the school and workplace reflect a parallelism between them.

In going through the educational process, consequently, individuals are prepared for their respective roles in the economy. In performing this function, "schools are constrained to justify and reproduce inequality rather than correct it" (Bowles and Gintis 1976, p. 102). By providing a setting in which success appears to depend solely on the individual and his or her talent and effort, schools give the appearance of rewarding those who are most meritorious. The school rewards certain attitudes and behaviors and penalizes others. It rewards those who act and think in a manner that will serve them in the jobs they will perform in the division of labor. Not all who go to school will move on to higher white-collar professional jobs; many will perform the tasks of blue-collar work. As I noted in an earlier discussion of prep schools, education prepares each class differently, depending on the roles they will play when they collectively leave school. This means not only teaching the appropriate skills but also inculcating the appropriate values and demeanor for each class. Schools in different class neighborhoods differ in their organization and value structure.

Parents from different classes and school administrators expect different characteristics from schools. For example, parents from the middle class expect a more open school structure in which autonomy and creativity are valued. This reflects their image of what is needed in middle-class jobs. In contrast, working-class parents know from their job experiences that obedience and discipline are important. This is reflected in the organization and value structure of schools that are made up primarily of working-class students (Bowles and Gintis 1976, pp. 131–134). As Rubin (1976) found in her study of the working and middle classes, "for the working-class parent, school is a place where teachers are expected to be tough disciplinarians; where children are expected to behave respectfully and to be punished if they do not; and where one mark of that respect is that they are sent to school neatly dressed in their 'good' clothes and expected to stay that way through the day" (p. 126).

In contrast, the professional middle-class parent expects school "to be relatively loose, free, and fun; to encourage initiative, innovativeness, creativity, and spontaneity; and to provide a place where children…will learn social and interpersonal skills" (Rubin 1976, p. 126). In this view, students are perceived as empty vessels that must be filled up with appropriate knowledge and attitudes. To use Freire's (1986) colorful phrase, this is the "banking concept of education" in which teachers and students are seen as being on opposite sides. The teacher is the actor and the student is the object that is acted upon.

This one-way form of education serves the interests of those in the dominant group. It is not liberating to those who receive it. Instead, it serves "to minimize or annul the students' creative power and to stimulate their credulity [which in turn] serves the interests of the oppressors, who care neither to have the world revealed nor to see it transformed" (Freire 1986, p. 60). It launches a "cultural invasion" in which "those who are invaded come to see their reality with the outlook of the invaders rather than their own; for the more they mimic the invaders, the more stable the position of the latter becomes" (Freire 1986, p. 151). The educational experience, then, reproduces different workers for the economy and the social relationships upon which the economy is based.

In sum, schools are not only interested in producing appropriate laborers for the economy but they also serve the long-term goal of perpetuating the institutions and social relationships that will ensure the continued profitability of capitalism. An educational system accomplishes these goals in four ways:

1. It provides some of the skills needed to perform jobs for each class adequately. Curriculum tracking channels individuals from different classes into appropriate courses.
2. Through its structure and curriculum, the educational system helps to justify and legitimate the economic and occupational inequality present in society. It fosters a belief that individuals wind up in different positions solely because of differences in merit.
3. It encourages the development and internalization of attitudes and self-concepts appro-

priate to the economic roles individuals will perform. Those who conform to prized values (e.g., those of the upper or middle class) are rewarded, while those who do not are negatively labeled.
4. Through the creation of justified status distinctions within the school, education helps to reinforce a taken-for-granted acceptance of social stratification in the wider society (Bowles and Gintis 1976).

MacLeod (1987) has criticized the Bowles-Gintis theory as being too crude and mechanistic because it views individuals as simply outputs of capitalism and the educational system. It does not give adequate attention to the possible individual differences in reactions to structures that constrain the person. Nor does it take into account cultural or subcultural variations in values and lifestyles that may shape unique adaptations to structural barriers. Giroux has similarly criticized Bowles and Gintis for ignoring the active element in the individual within the structural framework of the school and economy. People *experience* the authority structure of the school and its teachers and they react to them, sometimes through acceptance and sometimes through resistance. In Bowles and Gintis's theory, "the subject gets dissolved under the weight of structural constraints that appear to form both the personality and the workplace" (Giroux 1983, p. 85). The complexity of school life, the varied ways and levels in which structural constraints operate and curricula are taught in varied school sites is reduced, in Bowles and Gintis's approach, to "a homogeneous image of working-class life fashioned solely by the logic of domination" (ibid.).

A more culturally oriented theory of class reproduction is suggested by the work of Pierre Bourdieu. In this perspective, culture is a mediating element between class structure/interests and everyday life and behavior. By appearing to be objective and a source of knowledge, schools that produce successful and failing students can justify the inequality that follows. Since schools represent the interests of the dominant culture,

Bourdieu argued, they value the cultural capital of the dominant class more than that of the lower classes. *Cultural capital* refers to all the sets of beliefs, practices, ways of thinking, knowledge, and skills passed on from one class's generation to the next. Schools, especially those in higher education, espouse the cultural capital that is most characteristic of the privileged classes, thereby denigrating that which is characteristic of the working and lower classes (Bourdieu 1977a, 1977b). Since this occurs in the objective setting of the school, those in the latter classes who do not do well in classes develop an attitude in which they blame themselves and "actively participate in their own subjugation" (Giroux 1983, p. 89).

Generally, Bourdieu has suggested that individuals compete within different "fields" in a struggle for economic, cultural, and social capital. These fields constitute networks of relationships among positions (Bourdieu and Wacquant 1992). As a result of these struggles, individuals come to occupy different classes that vary in the amounts and forms of their economic, social, and cultural capital. Research does indeed indicate that variations in capital are reflected in positional arrangements within fields (Anheier, Gerhards, and Romo 1995). Respectively, some possess great amounts of wealth, extensive social networks, and fancy tastes and lifestyles, whereas others do not, and they can use these resources to justify their possession of capital. The presence or absence of these resources form a large part of the social context in which individuals live, and these objective conditions give rise to particular tastes, lifestyles, and ways of looking at the world. The upper class possesses a "taste of liberty and luxury," whereas the lower has "popular taste." "Distance from necessity" permeates the taste of the upper class, meaning that it is less directly functional and practical compared to that of the lower class.

An individual's *habitus,* or system of stable dispositions to view the world in a particular way, is a direct product of the person's structural situation; in fact, it is the psychological embodiment of the objective conditions in which one lives. Thus, different life conditions give rise to different forms of habitus and those exposed to the same conditions will develop the same habitus (Bourdieu 1990). The habitus, in turn, has a direct, constraining effect on the social action of individuals, which, coming full circle, contributes to reproducing the social structure. Figure 10.2 gives a rough outline of Bourdieu's model. For example, an adolescent who lives within a structure with poor job opportunities as evidenced by the experiences of his or her parents will develop a view that the chances of success are slight and that school makes no difference. This leads to behavior that accommodates him or her to a menial job, which in turn reinforces the existing job opportunity structure. Nothing changes.

Such an image of reproduction of social structure does not lend itself to reconstructing the social order, nor does it acknowledge the possibility of resistance or rebellion on the part of dominated groups (Giroux 1983). In Bourdieu's theory, the prospect of radically altering the educational institution or the system, in general, seems dim, indeed (MacLeod 1987). MacLeod believes that while Bourdieu has incorporated an important cultural element into his theory of reproduction, a necessary corrective to the structural-correspondence theory of Bowles and Gintis, his theory is still too

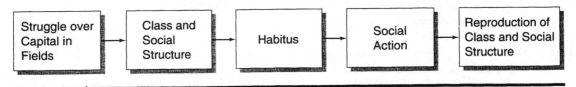

FIGURE 10.2 A General Model of Bourdieu's Explanation of Social Reproduction

deterministic. To have an adequate theory, "we must appreciate both the importance and the relative autonomy of the cultural level at which individuals, alone or in concert with others, wrest meaning out of the flux of their lives" (MacLeod 1987, p. 139). Too often, as well, class reproduction theories have ignored the separately lived experiences of women and minority groups, an omission that can seriously limit the theories' ability to understand the habitus of these individuals.

The theories reviewed so far suggest mechanisms discussed by Marx and Weber and further codified by Tilly (1998) as fundamental for the reproduction of "durable inequality." These are the mechanisms of (1) exploitation, (2) opportunity hoarding, (3) emulation, and (4) adaptation. Groups in economic and political positions of dominance *exploit* their positions for their own and at the cost of others' benefits. Politicians, for example, make laws that benefit themselves but punish others, and capitalists take advantage of the labor power of workers without extending to them the full benefit of their work. Dominant groups also keep others from seeing and taking advantage of *opportunities* for upward mobility through rules of exclusion and closure. This allows them to monopolize chances for maintaining their high class position. Effective, traditional perspectives and bases of inequality are then copied or *emulated* in organizations, thereby reinforcing their existence. Means that are effective in controlling workers in the economy, for example, spread to schools and other institutions. Finally, as Marx suggested much earlier, people get used to and learn to *adapt* to existing inequalities, further perpetuating them. They take them as a given and organize rules and behaviors around them.

MacLeod's (1987) case study of the conditions and behavior among two groups of adolescent males in a public housing development reveals much about the process by which social positions are reproduced. The "Brothers" are a Black group and the "Hallway Hangers" are White. Over time, the adolescents in these groups develop lower aspirations about their futures. MacLeod's research vividly demonstrates the

specific and sometimes different factors that produce these leveled aspirations. Among the Brothers, for example, there is some evidence that success is possible when they look at the occupations of their siblings. Their parents also believe that conditions have gotten better for Blacks, and thus they encourage their children in their school work. They have been exposed to tenement living for a shorter time, on average, than the Hallway Hangers, and they are antagonistic to the views of the latter group that regards the Blacks with disdain. These conditions lead the Brothers to accept the dominant achievement ideology that opportunity exists and success is possible with the proper effort. What ultimately leads the members of this group to lower their aspirations is a combination of the devaluing of their cultural capital by school officials, lower teacher expectations, tracking, discrimination, and their own self-blame. The school's treatment of them leads to relatively poor performance, and since they subscribe to the achievement ideology which says that it is the individual's own characteristics and efforts that determine how far he or she can get, poor performance leads to self-blame. The combination of self-blame and poor performance results in a lowering of expectations and aspirations. Figure 10.3 outlines the basic processes present in the development of leveled aspirations among the Brothers.

In contrast to the Brothers, the Hallway Hangers do not subscribe to the achievement ideology even though they are White. The conditions of their lives are such that they see little evidence for its validity. Their parents and siblings have not done well even though they are White; their parents believe things are stacked against them; they have lived (or been trapped) in the tenements longer than the Brothers and have a longer history of welfare. They have not seen that education produces many successes in their immediate surroundings. These conditions have bred a feeling of cynicism about the achievement ideology. Their own subculture exerts peer pressure that encourages the rejection of raised aspirations. These experiences and feelings lead to leveled aspirations and a negative attitude toward school. The

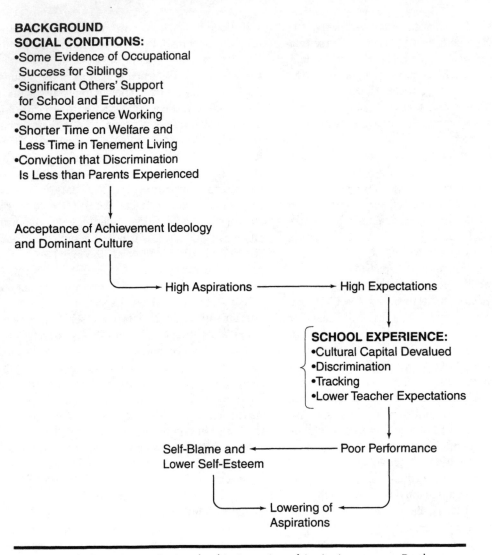

BACKGROUND
SOCIAL CONDITIONS:
• Some Evidence of Occupational
  Success for Siblings
• Significant Others' Support
  for School and Education
• Some Experience Working
• Shorter Time on Welfare and
  Less Time in Tenement Living
• Conviction that Discrimination
  Is Less than Parents Experienced

Acceptance of Achievement Ideology
and Dominant Culture

High Aspirations ──────→ High Expectations

SCHOOL EXPERIENCE:
• Cultural Capital Devalued
• Discrimination
• Tracking
• Lower Teacher Expectations

Self-Blame and ←────── Poor Performance
Lower Self-Esteem

Lowering of ←── Aspirations

FIGURE 10.3   Basic Dynamics Involved in Lowering of Aspirations among Brothers
Source: Based on MacLeod 1987, pp. 42ff.

latter, in turn, results in poorly rated performance and tracking, which reinforce the leveled aspirations and results in a negative evaluation of them from others. The lowered self-esteem that derives from this negative evaluation leads these adolescents to turn to their own subculture with its own values. But it provides only an imperfect haven from the shame of failure in school, an area highly valued in the wider society. MacLeod (1987)

stated that "the mechanisms of social reproduction" are "well hidden," and thus these adolescents partially blame themselves for their predicament. The Hallway Hangers also resort to racism as a convenient scapegoat. Neither of these interpretations by them, however, results in a full and accurate understanding of their situation or to a radical consciousness on the part of the Hangers. In the last analysis, the conditions that perpetuate their lower class position are repeated. The basic process leading to leveled aspirations among the Hallway Hangers is laid out in Figure 10.4.

GERHARD LENSKI'S SYNTHESIS

In 1966, Gerhard Lenski published a much heralded synthesis of the functionalist (conservative) and conflict (radical) traditions in the study of inequality. Lenski selected assumptions from both traditions and tried to build an explanation of inequality based on them. Rather than simply focusing on the fact of inequality, Lenski was concerned with the question of how scarce resources come to be distributed as they are—that is, with the *process* of inequality.

He based his theory on several postulates, which he took as givens:

1. Humans are social by nature and therefore live with others as members of society. Cooperative behavior is essential for survival.

2. Unselfish behavior occurs most often when only minor issues are involved. When important decisions are at stake and there is a conflict of interests, individuals virtually always make decisions that benefit themselves rather than others.

3. Most of the items of value that individuals strive for are in short supply, especially given the fact that a fixed satiation point does not exist for many of them (such as money and status). Thus, they are always in demand.

4. From the preceding postulates, it follows that there will be "*a struggle for rewards...in every human society*" (Lenski 1966, pp. 31–32, emphasis in original).

5. Humans are "unequally endowed by nature" with the tools needed to be successful in the struggle for rewards.

6. Humans are powerfully influenced by habit and custom, giving stability to the distribution system.

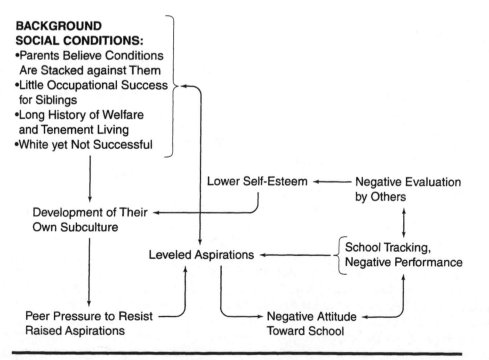

BACKGROUND SOCIAL CONDITIONS:
• Parents Believe Conditions Are Stacked against Them
• Little Occupational Success for Siblings
• Long History of Welfare and Tenement Living
• White yet Not Successful

Lower Self-Esteem ← Negative Evaluation by Others

Development of Their Own Subculture ←

Leveled Aspirations ← School Tracking, Negative Performance

Peer Pressure to Resist Raised Aspirations → Negative Attitude Toward School

FIGURE 10.4   Basic Dynamics Involved in Leveled Aspirations among Hallway Hangers
Source: Based on MacLeod 1987, pp. 23ff.

In addition to these postulates, Lenski argued that humans are basically goal seeking in their behavior. Their fundamental goal is survival, followed by health, self-respect (prestige), comfort, salvation, and affection. Money, office, and education as *instrumental goals* help individuals obtain their *fundamental goals*. And resources of whatever kind an individual starts out with at birth or gains from society help him or her to attain those instrumental goals.

Starting → Instrumental → Fundamental
resources   goals   goals

Societies, like individuals, are also self-seeking units whose primary goals are "the minimization of the rate of internal political change" and "the maximization of production and the resources on which production depends" (Lenski 1966, p. 42). The system of distribution in a society reflects both societal and individual needs.

Principles and Structure of Distribution Systems

Using principally his postulates about human nature, especially the first two, Lenski generated his "first law of distribution." Since humans are selfishly motivated but also need others in order to satisfy their principal goal of survival, "men will share the product of their labors to the extent required to insure the survival and continued productivity of those others whose actions are necessary or beneficial to themselves" (the law of need) (Lenski 1966, p. 44).

But after that minimum is so distributed to ensure survival, what of the goods and services left over? If we assume that they are in short supply, as in the third postulate, and that there will be struggles for their possession (the fourth postulate), then the "second law of distribution" is "that power will determine the distribution of nearly all of the surplus possessed by a society" (the law of power) (Lenski 1966, p. 44). Power, following Weber, is "the probability of persons or groups carrying out their will even when opposed by others" (ibid.). Privileges then are primarily a result of power, and prestige is largely a function of both.

Lenski went on to argue that the conditions of the first law of distribution must be satisfied before power, the determinant specified in the second law, becomes operative as a determinant of the distribution of goods and services. Hence, in societies where goods and services are extremely scarce, as in hunting and gathering societies, distribution is based largely on the processes specified in the first law. It is only when, because of changes in technology, a surplus develops that a greater and greater proportion of the goods and services are distributed on the basis of power. As a consequence, the nature of distribution will vary with the level of technology in societies.

Of course, other factors affect the specific character of distribution in any given society, but they are secondary to the technological factor. They include peculiarities in the physical environment, the proportion of the male population who participate in the military, and the specific variations in the technologies that may exist even among societies at the same level of technology. Distribution systems also may vary because of political conditions in a society.

As technology advances, power becomes a more important determinant in the distribution process. Power as coercion and power as right defined by law, public opinion, and propaganda can create and protect the system of inequality that has developed. The law can be phrased to protect those who make it and to punish those who are outside the ruling elite. But, argued Lenski, the shift from the rule of might to the rule of law means a greater decentralization of power, since alternate centers of power can proliferate as long as they stay within the law. In advanced industrial societies, some types of power become shared, such as political rights and education (Milner 1987). Lenski said that under might, the elite need not worry about what the average citizen thinks, but under the rule of law, there is at least the pretense that no one is above the law; therefore, the elite cannot do fully as it pleases. "Thus, even though the laws promulgated by a new elite may be heavily slanted to favor themselves, there are limits beyond which this cannot be carried if they wish to gain the benefits of the rule of right" (Lenski 1966, p. 55). Under the rule of law, power becomes institutionalized, legitimated, and can be based on position or ownership of property.

In addition to describing the *process* of distribution, Lenski discussed the *structure* of distribution systems. This structure is composed of *power classes,* power that can be manifested as force or as institutionalized power (based on property or position). The distribution of individuals into prestige and privilege classes is largely determined by their power-class positions. Hence, Lenski said that the focus should be on the latter. In essence, he said that there are three major hierarchies in distribution systems: privilege classes, prestige classes, and power classes. It is the last that is the most fundamental. Nevertheless, stratification is essentially multidimensional, especially in modern industrial societies.

In reality, since individuals vary quite widely in their prestige, privileges, and power, the stratification hierarchies are also best viewed as continua rather than sets of distinct classes with clear boundaries. These classes need not be class conscious in a Marxian sense, although members of the same class share interests that may or may not result in conflict with other classes.

We can now see that to Lenski, the distribution system of a society taken as a whole consists of a number of analytically separate class hierarchies. Each of the separate class systems can vary in (1) its overall *importance* in the distribution of power, (2) its internal *complexity,* (3) its *span*—that is, the range from the top to the bottom, (4) its *shape*—that is, the distribution of power, privilege, or prestige within it, (5) the degree of *mobility* in the system, (6) the amount of *hostility* that exists between classes, and (7) the degree to which the positions in the class structure are *institutionalized*—that is, stabilized on some basis. Individuals can vary in their position within each of the class systems; that is, their rankings can be consistent or inconsistent across each of the hierarchies.

To test his general theory of inequality, Lenski examined inequality in societies at different technological levels, ranging from simple hunting and gathering societies, to horticultural and agricultural societies, to mature industrial so-

cieties. Generally, Lenski found, as expected, that the degree of inequality increases along with advances in technology until the advanced industrial stage is reached. At this point, there is a "significant reversal in the age-old evolutionary trend toward ever increasing inequality" (Lenski 1966, p. 308). As two examples of this trend, Lenski noted that there is less extreme income inequality in industrial than in agrarian societies and that the government is more responsive to the needs of those who are outside the political elite. This reversal obviously flies in the face of his observation that inequality varies directly with the size of the surplus (p. 85).

To explain the shift, Lenski cited a number of causes for the trend toward greater equality:

1. Because of the greater complexity of knowledge in the modern world, there is a greater need to delegate power and authority.

2. The vastly greater productivity of industrial society allows greater concessions to those in the lower classes without a necessary concomitant decrease in absolute gains for those in higher classes. In industrial societies, more often than not, the struggle between those at the top and those at the bottom has benefited those on the bottom, leading to less political, economic, and social inequality (Lenski and Lenski 1982).

3. The creation of effective birth control methods has resulted in a tighter labor supply and therefore greater bargaining power for the working class.

4. The greater amount of knowledge and accompanying specialization result in individuals becoming experts and therefore less dispensable in the labor force. Advanced technology has upgraded the occupational structure by creating more white-collar jobs resulting in more upward mobility. "Nearly every industrial society has eliminated the excess of downward mobility" (p. 337).

5. More widespread education and higher levels of living have made it easier to participate in the political process, thereby strengthening the democratic nature of political institutions. "The rise and spread of *the new democratic ideology*" has made those in political power more vulnerable to pressure from the majority (Lenski 1966, p. 317, emphasis in original). The state is believed to belong to the people. Thus, Lenski links political democracy with less inequality.

All of these factors have contributed to a reversal of the trend toward greater inequality.

Assessment of Lenski

Lenski's synthesis is multilayered in the sense that there is a broad basic theory, stressing technology, which then leads to more specific layers involving levels of societies and analyses within each of them. He also incorporated consideration of human nature and physical-environmental factors into his theory. Unfortunately, his attempt suffers from several serious weaknesses. He argued that the distribution of rewards, especially in advanced societies, is based primarily on power, but his perspective on power leaves something to be desired. He defined *power* in Weberian terms as "the probability of persons or groups carrying out their will even when opposed by others," but in a concrete setting, what does this mean? Power, as Lenski admitted, can refer to force as well as to institutionalized power; the latter can be based on position or property. But the crux of the matter still is how property and position themselves are distributed. To say that power is based on property and position and that property and position are based on power would not be too illuminating. Power, in Lenski's hands, still remains a much too vague and broad concept to serve as a viable foundation for the explanation of inequalities in privilege and prestige.

His treatment of the concept of class is also disturbing in two basic ways. First, he argued that the stratification system of industrial societies is fundamentally multidimensional, since classes refer to aggregates of individuals who are similar in their power, privilege, or prestige. Since each of these three can take a variety of forms, there are numerous class systems: occupational classes, property classes, political classes, educational classes, racial classes, religious classes, age classes, sex classes, and ethnic classes. Earlier in his argument,

Lenski stated that privileges and prestige were largely based on power, but by presenting a long list of separate class systems, he is watering down the historical meaning of the term *class* and underestimating the systematic interrelationships among power, privilege, and prestige.

The second way in which he weakens the concept of class in his analysis is by defining caste and estate as classes of a particular type. He defined both of them in terms of class and by so doing ignores the historical and societal uniqueness of these systems. In essence, the term *class* is used to cover too much, and when spread so broadly it comes close to being meaningless.

One of the strengths of Lenski's theory is its application to a variety of cultures. By reviewing situations in different types of societies, Lenski tried to demonstrate how inequality changes through time as the levels of technology in societies change. But by taking such a broad evolutionary sweep, he underplays the uniqueness of particular societies and their history. A cross-cultural view is not the same as an historically specific one. His postulation of universal propositions about human nature and societies forces a neglect of crucial differences in the cultures and histories of societies. Fallers (1966) complained that Lenski has not given enough weight to variations in values and cultures in understanding differences in stratification. He "assumes that the ends of action are objectively given and universal" (p. 718). Moreover, so much attention to stages or levels of evolution leads to an underemphasis on the interdependence of societies on different levels and an explanation of international stratification based on dependency relations and exploitation.

Finally, some comments ought to be made about Lenski's view on industrial society and its progress toward equality. His conclusions about the extent of equality in such societies, even the United States, about which he cites data to support his claims, can leave one too optimistic. Data on income and wealth in the United States, we have seen in Chapter 2, still indicate a high and stable degree of inequality. In fact, there is evidence that earnings inequality has increased in recent years.

Lenski's optimism flows largely from the fact that he is comparing industrial with agrarian societies. But by doing so, he is led into the conclusion that U.S. society is more democratic and equalitarian than it actually is.

Despite these shortcomings, Lenski's theory is one of the most detailed and carefully developed in recent decades. His work has led to numerous areas of inquiry. Most notable among these is research on the interrelationship of economic development, political democracy, and income inequality and attempts at developing general theories of stratification and societal evolution.

LABOR-MARKET THEORIES OF INCOME AND EARNINGS DISTRIBUTION

All of the theories addressed thus far in this and the previous chapter are macroscopic in nature. They focus on the issue of inequality on a very general level, often trying to generate principles of inequality that apply cross-culturally, through historical periods, or both. Since these theorists often dealt with such questions on a global level, it is sometimes difficult to see the intricacies of the process of inequality in concrete societies and thus even more difficult to derive specific policies for dealing with the inequality issue.

In recent years, a set of economic theories regarding income and earnings inequality has been crystallizing, some of which are based on rather old explanations of the working of the marketplace, while others are quite different. The treatment that follows is general and aimed at drawing out the core elements of the approaches. Consequently, specific theorists using a given approach may differ on specific elements in the approach. What is immediately appealing about these theories is that they put some meat and teeth into explanations by making the detailed process of inequality more testable. Whereas it might be extremely difficult to satisfactorily test a theory of inequality based on the distribution of sentiments or the functional necessity of inequality, it is possible, for example, to see what the effects of various kinds of human capital investment, such

as education and training, are on an individual's earnings.

Most of the theories presented here are principally concerned with explaining poverty and unemployment, but they can easily be used as explanations of the extent of inequality. Each of them focuses on one or another aspect of the labor market in generating inequality.

Neoclassical Labor-Market Theory

This theory is based on several important assumptions: (1) A relatively free and open market exists in which individuals compete for position. (2) Position in that market depends heavily on the individual's efforts, abilities, experience, training, or "human capital." (3) There are automatic mechanisms that operate in the marketplace to ensure that imbalances between one's input (human capital) and one's rewards (wages) are corrected in a way to restore balance.

The ideology of individualism argues that a person should be rewarded to the extent that he or she contributes to the society. In a society in which free competition exists, persons who contribute equal resources in the society receive a wage commensurate with their contributions. The more resources one offers and the greater one's value to any potential employer, the greater the demand for one's services and the higher the wages (Leftwich 1977; Thurow 1969). Thus, factors such as one's education, training, skills, and intelligence are productivity components that are crucial in explaining an individual's wages. These are the elements that must be changed if one's wages are to change (Thurow 1969, p. 26). An extreme version of this argument would assume that individuals are free to choose the amounts of their human capital investments such as education, training, and so on, as well as their occupations. Thus, African Americans and women might be considered to have lower and relatively nonchanging levels of income because they have invested less in education and have less or interrupted work experience (Gordon 1972; Mincer and Polachek 1974). The ultimate result is "that you take out what you put in" (Okun 1975, p. 41). Of course, as we have seen, it often does not work that way.

In addition to one's resources, the demand for one's skills is also important and that demand depends on conditions in the marketplace. Demand for individuals, and therefore their wages, depends on the type of skills they possess and how talented they are at using them. In sum, it is the combination of supply and demand in the market and one's resources (human capital investments) that determine one's wages in the open marketplace (Cain 1976).

If an imbalance develops between what the individuals contribute and the wages they receive, then supply and demand forces are set in motion to restore equilibrium in the market. If the wage is less than is due, the supply becomes smaller, and in the long run the demand for the smaller supply becomes greater. For example, if the perceived crisis in the quality of education in the United States results in the public's raising its view of teachers' contribution to the society, we might expect an upward pressure on their salaries. If greater demand for quality teachers occurs, there should be an increase in the wages employers are willing to pay these workers. In this way, equilibrium is restored. If the opposite occurs—that is, individuals are paid too much for the resource(s) they offer—a large supply of potential workers will appear, too large for the demand for them in the market. In order to ensure getting jobs, they will lower the wages for which they are willing to work. With the lower wages, employment expands, thus leading to a clearing of the labor market and a balancing between supply and demand. Again, equilibrium is restored (Leftwich 1977, p. 76). So, in addition to assuming a competitive market, this approach assumes that automatic mechanisms operate in the market to regulate it toward equilibrium. This tendency toward equilibrium, according to some critics, implies that there is a basic harmony between employers and employees (Gordon 1972, p. 33). Figure 10.5 summarizes the basic elements in the neoclassical explanation of earnings inequality.

Open competitive market
+
Differential free investment in personal human capital
+
Differential supply of and demand for positions
↓
Earnings inequality

FIGURE 10.5   Basic Elements in the Generation of Earnings Inequality According to Neoclassical Theory

If one accepts this argument, then what must be done to reduce earnings inequities is to attack the problems of human capital investment and the choices and returns associated with such investment. Thus, solutions might stress more education and training opportunities as well as accurate and appropriate assessment of individuals' skills and economic payoffs for those skills.

The pure neoclassical model has some distinct limitations, two of which are noted here. First, it is more concerned with wage differentials than with occupational differences and thus is less equipped to deal with sex segregation, for example (Blau and Jusenius 1976). Second, it presents an image of a U.S. economy that is freely competitive and tending toward equilibrium. Like the scarcity and functional-importance factors of the Davis and Moore theory of inequality, this model argues that the level of one's human capital (i.e., how scarce one's talents are) and the demand for them in the market (i.e., their functional necessity) largely determine differences in earnings. Like the kind of society conjured up in the functional approach, Dahrendorf would consider the open, largely conflict-free society of neoclassical theory to be a utopia. The nature of this imaginary society is explored more fully in Chapter 13, since this kind of society provides the assumed social framework within which status attainment processes operate. It should be mentioned that most economists are aware that the real marketplace does not operate without flaws and imperfections, and that discrimination does limit the opportunities of some in the market.

Dual-Labor Market Thesis

It has become increasingly obvious to some in recent years that explanations of income and earnings distribution that rely on images of the free market and investments in human capital as the primary or sole factors in understanding economic inequalities are inadequate. Critics of the orthodox view say that the market simply does not work the way that pure traditionalists say it does. Rather, the major reasons for inequality lie deep within the workings and cleavages of the capitalist economy.

A number of observations about continuing difficulties in the market have made many analysts skeptical about the orthodox approach and its potential effectiveness in reducing inequality. Among those observations are (1) the continuation of poverty; (2) continued income inequality; (3) the ineffectiveness of educational and training programs in reducing inequality; (4) the use of education as a screening device by employers to procure only culturally acceptable rather than qualified individuals; (5) discrimination against minorities in the labor market; (6) the power of labor unions, employer monopolies, and government intervention to weaken the competitive market; (7) bad attitudes toward work that result from the market itself and not outside the market; and (8) extensive alienation among workers, suggesting that the competitive, equilibrating economy is not working as smoothly as the orthodox model suggests (Cain 1976).

In the face of these alleged anomalies in the economy, some have tried to devise alternate explanations for continued poverty and income inequality. One of the more prominent of these is the dual-labor market approach. Briefly, this thesis consists of four basic elements or assumptions: (1) the private economy is split into two major sectors; (2) the labor market is similarly divided into two parts; (3) mobility, earnings, and other outcomes for workers are contingent on place in the labor market; and (4) a systematic relationship

exists between race/ethnicity, gender, and position in the labor market (Hodson and Kaufman 1982).

On observing labor-market processes in the ghetto, a number of economists have come to the conclusion that two markets operating by different rules exist. The poor are members of a separate market that is largely outside the central economy and as such do not participate in the effects of increases in demand, since those demands usually refer only to certain types of occupations. Researchers have found that the kinds of characteristics usually considered as qualifications (such as education) often seem to have little connection with the type of job the person occupies. In effect, some jobs are "race typed" (Reich, Gordon, and Edwards 1977, p. 109). The range of jobs available to minority members, in spite of their qualifications, seems to be quite narrow, and consequently many prefer not to work. In other words, they turn down jobs that are not consistent with their qualifications.

As a result of these observations, more attention has been focused on the kinds of jobs these individuals are actually offered and perform. The tasks seem to be menial, not intellectually demanding, with poor working conditions and low wages. They are isolated and have no internal structures or career system. In other words, they appear to be qualitatively distinct from other kinds of jobs in the market.

Because of the poor nature of the work, workers in this secondary market often quit their jobs, which only encourages the belief that these jobs are unstable, and that performing these types of jobs to the exclusion of others encourages instability in the habits of the workers themselves. This *secondary labor market,* as it has come to be known, is set off from the *primary labor market* in which jobs are characterized by stability, high wages, good working conditions, greater degree of internal job structure, and unionization (Gordon 1972, pp. 43–48).

Within firms in the primary sector, there is an *internal labor market* in which individuals from the outside may enter only at selected points. For example, an outsider may get a job at the bottom of a career ladder in an industrial firm because all other jobs higher up the ladder are being filled from within the firm through promotion. These latter jobs are, in effect, protected from outside competition, resulting in a segmentation of the market into competitive and noncompetitive jobs (Doeringer and Piori 1971). Since the skills taught to employees are frequently important, necessary for higher status jobs, and specific to the firm, there will be an attempt by the firm to keep these employees, since training new ones would be costly to the firm. In this protected environment, employees can then work up from the bottom toward the top. In this setting, employees can more easily find security and a lifetime career. Unions also favor the resulting stability for employees, and the employers similarly benefit from retaining trained employees. Given the career system, workers and employers dealing in the primary labor market are less concerned with the perfect balance between earnings and productivity *at a given time* than they are with equity over the long run (Doeringer and Piori 1971).

By and large, the primary labor market—with its stability, unionization, career systems, and high wages—is limited to a certain sector of the private economy, sometimes called the *core* or *monopoly sector,* whereas the secondary market exists primarily within the *peripheral* or *competitive sector* of the private economy. In the monopoly sector, firms tend to be large, capital intensive, with high productivity per worker, and to possess large, often national and international markets. Examples of firms in this sector would be those in the automobile, railroad, steel, electric, and airlines industries. On the other hand, firms within the competitive sector are much smaller, more labor intensive, with low productivity per worker, more local in their markets, and not in control of any stable product market (O'Connor 1973, pp. 13–16). Examples of firms in this sector would be local restaurants, gas stations, grocery stores, garages, and clothing stores.

Despite the fact that conditions are generally worse for the workers in the secondary market and

competitive sector, the tasks performed, though often irregular, are needed in the economy. Consequently, an effort was made historically to stabilize this market and sector; employers worked toward creating a separate market for these workers and these kinds of jobs. Some kinds of workers are in that sector even though they may have the characteristics that would qualify them for work in the primary market. Blacks and women, for example, are usually disproportionately found in the secondary market because of statistical discrimination and other reasons (Gordon 1972, pp. 46–47). Secondary workers were then left with little alternative but to work as part of the secondary labor market in the competitive sector.

The movement toward separate markets has been strengthened by (1) the desirability of retaining individuals who have been carefully trained in large established firms, (2) the presence of unions in some and not other industries, and (3) federal legislation. The trends toward greater job specificity, more on-the-job training in the primary job sector, and the power of custom within given firms have tended to increase the structuring of the internal labor markets within the primary job sector, setting it off more from the unstructured, noncareer patterned secondary job sector (Doeringer and Piori, 1971).

Dual-Labor Market and Income Inequality.

The existence of segmentation in the U.S. economy, especially in the form of a dual-labor market, helps to perpetuate income inequality and poverty. Generally, there is little intermarket mobility. The market in which individuals are presently working is generally the one in which they began (Gordon 1972, p. 50). Blacks and women are disproportionately found in the lower wage, secondary market and generally do not move up much over their careers. Wolf (1976) found that women have relatively flat career occupational statuses. She observed that occupations are sex segregated and "we speculate that, at least for most women, these 'women's jobs' are not stepping stones to other more prestigious occupations" (p. 20). Sell and Johnson (1977) also found a great deal of stability in occupational distribution among women across age groups, suggesting that when women leave the labor force, they often reenter the same types of jobs. They also found that changes in the occupational distribution were slight at best during the period from 1960 to 1970 (pp. 10–12). Wolf's research further indicates that contrary to what might be expected, it is not the interruptions in employment ("career contingencies") that primarily account for the occupational attainment of women. Rather, as we observed in an earlier chapter, women simply do not get the same kinds of jobs as men, even when their qualifications are similar.

Figure 10.6 brings together several of the core elements of the dual-labor market argument on the factors that produce earnings inequality. Notice that in sharp contrast with the neoclassical explanation that stresses the characteristics of *persons,* the dual-labor market theory focuses on the importance of *impersonal* labor markets and economic sectors in producing inequality.

Being in either the secondary or primary labor market has an initial impact on an individual's wages. As already mentioned, jobs in the secondary market generally have lower wages than those associated with the primary market. But once in either the secondary or primary market, the determinants of earnings vary. In the primary market, earnings are affected by seniority and whether a person is in a career job hierarchy. O'Connor (1973) stressed that in the monopoly sector, wages and prices are not primarily determined by market forces; prices are largely administered since the corporations in this sector usually have considerable market power. With respect to wages, when the demand for labor is low and the supply is large, monopoly industries, because of their attractiveness to workers, can choose from the oversupply at the going rate. In this way, they have an advantage over competitive industries. When labor is in demand, union power, pattern bargaining, and productivity have major impacts on wages and wage movements. But many of the wage increases in the monopoly sector do not trickle down to workers in the competitive sector, which results in a further bifurcation of the working class (O'Connor 1973, pp. 19–22).

In the competitive sector—that is, for most of those in the secondary labor market—wages are largely determined by market forces. Since the workers in this market are generally considered homogeneous in nature and have little, if any, union power, their wages are primarily the product of supply and demand forces. If the supply of labor is particularly small and the demand consequently high, their earnings are likely to go up because they will work more. Thus, the differences in earnings among those in the secondary labor market are probably due more to differences in the hours worked than to other factors. But because of the homogeneous nature of the work force in this market, wage differences are not likely to be great (Gordon 1972, pp. 50–51).

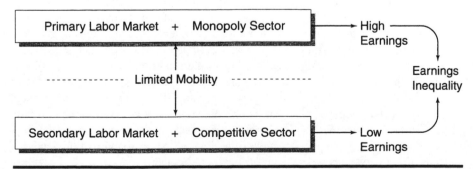

FIGURE 10.6   The Effect of the Dual Private Economy on Earnings

Moreover, in the competitive sector, the raging competition among firms and the poorer and more unstable economic environment in which they operate often mean that they are less able to raise wages compared with the large firms in the monopoly sector that are relatively free from the extremes of competition (Bluestone 1977).

Osterman's (1975) analysis of a national sample of male workers bears out the hypothesis that the determinants of earnings vary with the labor market in question. His results indeed show that earnings in the secondary market are tied significantly to the numbers of hours worked, with neither experience, race, nor education being important. This supports the view that workers in this market are seen as being interchangeable. In the higher-ranking jobs in the primary market, education, age, and hours worked are important, whereas in the lower tier in the primary market, education is important although less so than in the higher jobs. Age and hours worked are also significant for the lower-ranking jobs in the primary market, as is race. In sum, the human capital argument seems much more viable in the primary than in the secondary market. Osterman's conclusion is that "an individual's income is greatly affected by the segment of the labor market in which the individual works" (1975, p. 21).

In applying the dual-market theory to poverty, the central conclusion is that many individuals are poor not because they are unemployed or do not participate in the economy but because of the way in which they participate in the economy. Not only are they *excluded* from certain kinds of activities and organizations, they are *included* in the economic structure at particular places because "they have economic value where they are and hence …there are groups interested, not only in resisting the elimination of poverty, but in actively seeking its perpetuation" (Piori 1977, pp. 95–96).

Radical Perspective. Many of the notions of dual-market theory have found their way into a radical denunciation of orthodox theory. Basically, the radical argument is that capitalists have found it beneficial to segment the labor market

and to stratify the working class so as to prevent its unification and to stabilize the labor market. In this view, if we are to understand the creation of poverty and a particular income distribution, we must understand the historical development and conditions that underlay such distributions.

During the late nineteenth century, the U.S. labor force was becoming increasingly homogeneous and proletarianized; having been herded into factories, the separate craft talents became merged into a mass of semiskilled jobs. The potential threat of a unified working class, especially given the increasing evidence of their militancy, had to be met by employers. To deal with this problem, argued Reich and associates (1977), employers actively promoted labor-market segmentation in order to effectively split up what might otherwise have been a unified work force.

If employers could successfully stratify the working class, it would not only splinter its unity but also, if it could be legitimized, ensure that less desirable (secondary) jobs could be filled. As the clusters of workers were separated from each other, each would develop his or her own habits and lifestyles consistent with the kinds of jobs performed. The result would be stability in the labor market for the capitalist class. "To the extent that employers could accomplish this stratification, it became more likely that blue-collar workers would accept their poorer working conditions (relative to those of white-collar workers) because they did not have the necessary credentials and education to move on to jobs with better opportunities" (Gordon 1972, p. 73).

The rise of monopoly capitalism and of large corporations necessitated the existence of a stable labor force. New techniques of division and control were developed to restructure and stabilize relationships within industries (Edwards 1979). The rigid bureaucratic organization of firms served this purpose admirably. The clear and minute division of labor and hierarchy of authority associated with this form of organization encouraged the development of an internal labor structure of the kind discussed earlier. Education increasingly became a means of justifying division of the workers, since it became a regularized credential for obtaining certain jobs (Reich, Gordon, and Edwards 1977, p. 111). Those most readily looked down on by unions and the public—namely, women, Blacks, and youth—could more easily be used to fill less desirable jobs. Stereotypes and dislikes of these groups were used to further segment the labor market (ibid.).

Alongside the conscious efforts of employers to segment the labor market were systemic forces that furthered the segmentation. Racism was and is used to strengthen the hold of employers by weakening the bargaining power of the working class. The result is lower incomes for both Blacks and the White working class and higher profits for the capitalists (Reich, Gordon, and Edwards 1977, p. 185). Evidence does suggest that White workers do not gain from racism against Blacks but lose while capitalists gain; even income inequality between white capitalists and workers is increased when racism is present (Reich, Gordon, and Edwards 1977; Szymanski 1976). Racism also benefits capitalists by preventing or at least forestalling the unification of Black and White workers into strong and more broadly based unions. Research on the period between World War I and the New Deal indicates that employers fought White worker gains by using available Blacks as strikebreakers and in place of White workers. This served to help split the working class along racial lines (Bonacich 1976).

As different industrial organizations grew, historically, they advanced at different rates, and a fundamental division developed between them. In one sector were the large, monopoly, capital intensive, technologically advanced, high-profit, and growth industries, whereas in the other were the more competitive, smaller, lower profit, more labor-intensive organizations. The large organizations required a stable labor force, given their continuous and ongoing production. This sector could not handle, to its benefit, those areas where the work was seasonal or otherwise erratic. Production of those goods and services in which the demand was unstable demanded a certain kind of labor and was subcontracted or exported to the smaller more competitive firms. Thus, each sector demanded and evolved specific kinds of labor forces—namely, the primary and secondary labor markets—just as the dual-labor market thesis suggested (Reich, Gordon, and Edwards 1977, p. 111). The overall result of this segmentation process has been the segmentation of the economy into monopoly and competitive sectors, segmentation of primary and secondary markets, segmentation within the primary sector into routine and creative jobs, and segmentation by race and sex (pp. 108–109).

The existence of segmentation of various types in the labor force has been widely accepted, although the dimensions along which that segmentation takes place have not always been agreed on (Osterman 1975). Results reported in Chapters 4 and 6 show Black/White and male/female differences in occupational allocation. Blacks are still underrepresented in the high-reward occupations that involved the exercise of authority, domination by Whites, and/or equal-status contact with customers. But they are overrepresented in lower status occupations even though some improvement has apparently occurred in recent years.

Gordon (1972, p. 78) suggested that employers will continue to find it beneficial to fill secondary-market jobs with members of minority groups since (1) they are easily distinguishable physically and have been discriminated against before; (2) more than other groups, they have become more resigned to such jobs; and (3) they are least likely to identify with nonminority groups and unite with them against the capitalists. Such segmentation certainly appears to perform certain functions for capitalists. Reich and associates (1977) outlined three of these:

1. *It divides the workers and thus prevents unified movements against employers.*
2. *It establishes qualitative breaks across job hierarchies through the creation of different sets of criteria for access, thereby discouraging mobility aspirations among workers.*
3. *The division of workers legitimizes the differences in authority between superior and subordinate position holders. (p. 112)*

Assessment of Labor-Market Theories

In assessing these labor-market theories, it is clear that there are inadequacies in the orthodox explanations, but given the lack of a fully embellished theoretical system by radical theorists, it is not clear how powerful their explanations of occupational and income inequality really are. In fact, perhaps the most valuable contribution of the dual-labor-market approach to understanding economic inequality is its emphasis on a textured economy and labor market—that is, on its insistence that these are not homogeneous in nature and that this texture affects rewards for workers (Hodson and Kaufman 1982). The orthodox approach is most likely to be acceptable when it incorporates some of the elements of dual-labor-market theory and information about imperfections in the market. Some evidence appears to support radical arguments, as was indicated in our discussion, whereas other critics (e.g., Cain 1976) do not see it as being able to replace orthodox theory. The support for the viability of the radical perspective is clearly split.

Dual-market theory has its evident weaknesses. Within broad sectors, there is a large variety of firms. How are differences among them to be explained? For example, the dual-market theory does not explain differences and sex segregation within each market and differentiation within the female sector (Blau and Jusenius 1976, p. 197). Moreover, within each sector of the economy, there are firms that cater to both the primary and secondary labor markets. Evidence suggests that the tight link assumed by the approach between the primary labor market and core sector on the one hand, and the secondary labor market and peripheral sector on the other, is much looser than suggested by the model. Moreover, the assumption that African Americans and women are concentrated in the peripheral sector is also questionable (Hodson and Kaufman 1982; Kaufman and Daymont 1981; Wallace and Kalleberg 1981). The theory has also been said to be largely of a descriptive rather than explanatory nature, and its concepts to have been improperly measured (Hodson and Kaufman 1982). Finally, splitting the private economy into two parts results in too coarse an image of the real economy within which there are continuous variations among organizations along a variety of dimensions (Baron and Bielby 1984, Hodson 1984).

Splitting the economy and labor market into dichotomous sections ignores changes occurring *within* the national and *between* international economies. As U.S. corporations increasingly enter a world market involving highly competitive adversaries who may also enter the U.S. market, they have reacted by downsizing and streamlining, which has meant lower job stability for many employees. In a sense, what may have been a monopoly sector becomes more competitive, and those employed in those organizations become more vulnerable to fluctuations in economies. In essence, the primary job market takes on some of the characteristics traditionally associated with the secondary market: lower wages, lower job stability, and less unionization. This blurs the distinctions between monopoly/competitive sectors and primary/secondary markets. Further blurring the distinctions in dual markets and sectors is the fact that given firms can contain core *and* peripheral, primary *and* secondary characteristics (Parcel and Sickmeier 1988). In addition, the recent influx of small, entrepreneurial firms into the economy also makes a dual-market perspective appear to be too crude to capture the richer and changing texture of the U.S. economy. Despite weaknesses, however, the dual-market and radical perspectives have properly forced us to address the role of market and economy variations in generating inequality.

SUMMARY

The focus in this and the previous chapter has been on general explanations of inequality. Each of the theories covered views the concept of inequality in a different way and is suggestive of different measures of it. Nevertheless, all of them are concerned with the distribution of scarce resources in society, principally political power, economic power, or both. One of the primary values in looking at the classic theorists is that each of them suggests different ways of viewing inequality and makes us sensitive to different aspects of it.

Several of the theories covered in this and the previous chapter have basic elements in common. Most generally, one can see the influence of Marxian thought in social reproduction theory and radical labor-market theory. On the more conservative side, Durkheim's functionalist tradition has been carried through most fully in neoclassical economic theory and the Davis-Moore theory. Lenski's synthesis, in contrast, intentionally includes elements from both radical and conservative traditions.

All of these theories organize the phenomenon in diverse ways and evoke different images of how the society is to be seen. Some of these, such as the functionalist and labor-market theories, assume a society that is largely free, competitive, and lacking in organized constraints and conflict, while others, most notably social reproduction and dual-labor-market theories, view society as consisting of constraining structures and systemic conflict between groups. Because this is so, each of the theories provides us with alternative tools and concepts with which to approach the study of inequality; together, they anticipate the kinds of questions and issues that significantly can be raised about inequality. Each of the theories covered has been primarily concerned with answering the question: How do we explain the existence of inequality, the shape that it takes, and its perpetuation? Indirectly, several devote some attention to a second question of how given individuals become placed in positions in the system of inequality.

CRITICAL THINKING

1. What is wrong with an argument that simply says that rewards, in fact, reflect one's skills and credentials as well as the importance of one's job?

2. If our actions and behaviors serve largely to reproduce the conditions in which we live, how can change in inequality ever occur?

3. Imagine yourself in a full-time occupation. What factors would account for your income, and how well do these fit in with the theories that have been discussed thus far?

WEB CONNECTIONS

The following website contains a list of articles published in *Sociological Research Online*. Many of these are of a theoretical nature. As suggested in this chapter, Pierre Bourdieu is one of the most in- fluential social-reproduction theorists. Articles that use his theories can be found at this European site:

http://www.socresonline.org.uk/archive.html

CHAPTER 11

THE IMPACT OF INEQUALITY ON PERSONAL LIFE CHANCES

It is the most elemental economic fact that the way in which the disposition over material property is distributed among a plurality of people, meeting competitively in the market for the purpose of exchange, in itself creates specific life chances.
—Max Weber

"I am a single mother of two children ages 4 and 5.... I work full-time making $5.50 per hour, living week-to-week, paycheck-to-paycheck, and then barely making it. In April [1993], I brought home $691.55. Out of that has to come $360 for rent, all utilities included; $235 for babysitter (and that's at $1.50 an hour, which is way below the going rate). That leaves me with only $96 a month for gas, car maintenance, food, medical attention, clothing, etc. How is someone like myself supposed to be able to pay the premiums for medical insurance, car insurance, renters' insurance and still be able to live, all on this $96? How? I don't." (Noland 1993)

There wouldn't be much point in studying inequality if it had few implications for people. Inequality is an important subject because, ultimately, its existence affects the day-to-day lives of people. The social positions that individuals find themselves in help to determine who they are, what they think and do, and where they are going. Close your eyes for a moment and imagine yourself as a very poor or extremely wealthy person. What do you see? As a person in either position, how do you feel about life in general and yourself in particular? How do you view the future and your prospects? How do you account for the position you're in?

Most basically, social inequality affects the life chances of individuals. In this chapter, we will focus on the relationship of inequality to *personal* life chances: physical and mental health, personality, and relationships and abuse in the family. In Chapter 12, the emphasis will be on two of the many *social* effects of inequality—crime and collective unrest.

The studies reviewed here do not measure social class in any one way, but rather in variable ways in terms of education, occupation, income, and/or racial-ethnic status. Consequently, results are not always strictly comparable because different measures have been used; however, rough comparisons can be made because of the interrelatedness of the measures used. As often as possible, I make note of the kinds of measures used so you can take this into account in your own assessment of findings.

BASIC LIFE CHANCES: PHYSICAL HEALTH

There is nothing more basic to life than physical health, and it is evident that individuals rate their own health status differently, depending on their race and income. Generally, Blacks, and Hispanics are more likely than other groups to rate their own health as only fair or poor, and in all groups, it is those with lower incomes who are most likely to assess their health as fair or poor. Individuals with the lowest income are 5 to 7 times as likely as those in the highest income bracket to view their health as fair or poor (see Figure 11.1). Interestingly, this self-assessment is a good predictor of a person's actual health, and indeed, individuals in lower-status categories are worse off on virtually all fundamental health measures (National Center for Health Statistics 1998).

The life expectancies at birth of Blacks and Whites, males and females, have varied historically, and these differences are expected to continue in the twenty-first century. In 1996, average life expectancy for all Americans was about 76 years, which is comparable to that found in the United Kingdom and France, but slightly lower than the life expectancies in Italy, Canada, and the Netherlands. The life expectancy of Whites was over 6 years longer than that of Blacks, and within each racial group, those with lower incomes lived

a shorter time. A middle-aged White man with an income of at least $25,000, for example, can expect to live 6 to 7 years longer than a similar man with an income of under $10,000. Generally, women live longer than men, but the life expectancy of Black women is closer to that of White men than to White women (National Center for Health Statistics 1998).

Differences in mortality rates parallel the discrepancies in life expectancies, and the differences between socioeconomic groups are especially strong among *urban* residents (Hayward, Pienta, and McLaughlin 1997). Mortality rates related to chronic diseases such as heart disease, lung cancer, and diabetes are significantly higher in lower education and income groups, as are the risk factors associated with them, such as smoking, exercise, and lead poisoning. Black females have higher death rates for breast cancer than White females, but within both races, those in the poorest social class have the shortest survival period (Bassett and Krieger 1986). Deaths from communicable diseases and injuries are also higher for lower

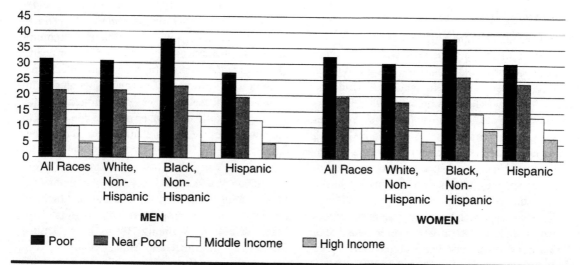

FIGURE 11.1   Percent of Adults Age 18 and Older with Self-Assessed Health as Fair or Poor by Sex, Family Income, Race, and Hispanic Origin: 1995

Source: Health, United States, 1998 with Socioeconomic Status and Health Chartbook (Hyattsville, MD: National Center for Health Statistics, 1998), p. 154.

socioeconomic status individuals. For example, among men, the 1995 death rate from chronic diseases was 2.5 higher for those with less than a high school education than the rate for those with at least a high school education. A similar discrepancy exists among women. The male death rate from injuries was 3.4 times higher in the lower education group (National Center for Health Statistics 1998).

Socioeconomic status differences in mortality rates extend to children, as well. Overall, these rates are about twice those found in Japan and are 40 percent higher than Canadian rates. Infant mortality rates (deaths per 1,000 live births) are significantly higher for Blacks than for Whites and, within both groups, for those with lower education. For example, among Blacks, the rate is 17.0 for those with less than 12 years of education, compared to 11.3 for those with a college education. Among Whites, the rates are 7.6 and 4.2, respectively. In 1995, the rate for college-educated Blacks approached that found among lower-educated Whites 10 years earlier (National Center for Health Statistics 1998).

Health Conditions

Differences in health still exist between the classes in the United States, as well as in other industrial countries such as England and France (Susser, Hopper, and Richman 1983; Hollingsworth 1981; d'Houtaud and Field 1984; Cockerham et al. 1986). Those with lower incomes generally report more acute conditions and a greater number of days being restricted and confined to bed because of such conditions. In contrast to acute ones, chronic conditions are health problems that continue over a long period of time, and they, too, appear to have greater consequences for those with lower status or incomes. The rate of AIDS among Black men was over 6 times higher than that found among White men in 1997, and 19 times higher among Black women than among White women. In 1995, poor persons were approximately 3 times as likely as those with higher incomes to be limited in activities due to chronic conditions. Poor individuals over 65 years of age

were less able to carry out routine personal care than those with middle or high incomes. Hypertension, diabetes, and heavy alcohol consumption are all higher among lower-income groups (National Center for Health Statistics 1998). Reports at a recent national medical conference also revealed higher stress and higher risks for cardiovascular disease, arthritis, and a large number of infectious diseases among those in lower-income categories (Goode 1999).

The findings of a recent study of almost 7,000 adults over a 15-year period show that the health of Blacks deteriorates more rapidly than that of Whites over time, and that Blacks more often than Whites increasingly view their health as poorer as they get older (Ferraro and Farmer 1996). By both objective and subjective standards, the health of Blacks declines more dramatically with age. Proportionately, Blacks lose about twice as many years of life before age 65 as Whites because of chronic conditions.

These findings make it clear that health is related to *individual* socioeconomic status. But what is also interesting is that the health of individuals also appears to be related to the socioeconomic status of the *community* as a whole and to the degree of income inequality in a *society,* independent of the effects of one's *individual* status. Communities with lower average incomes and higher unemployment rates report higher rates of chronic conditions (Robert 1998), and societies with greater income inequality have poorer health status among individuals. The latter may be due in part to the lower investment in education as well as higher distrust and frustration found in societies with greater inequality (Kawachi and Kennedy 1999). Frustration as a factor in health may be manifested in the finding that greater income and occupational inequality in a metropolitan area is related to higher suicide rates among Blacks in the United States (Burr, Hartman, and Matteson 1999). Keep in mind that the effects of inequality just discussed are independent of those found for differences in socioeconomic status among individuals.

In sum, there have been and continues to be distinct gaps in the health statuses of Blacks and Whites and between those in different socioeconomic groups, and the gap appears to have widened in recent years. This widening reflects not only health gains for those in higher-ranking groups but also simultaneous declines in the health status in lower status groups. The recent increase in economic inequality, which has already been documented, is a major force behind the growing discrepancies in health status. Economic inequalities appear to be causally related to differences in mortality rates *among* countries and to discrepancies in health statuses among groups *within* countries (Williams and Collins 1995).

Gender is also related to differences in health, but we know less about the factors related to women's health because most medical research has focused on men (Andersen 1997). Although men have higher mortality rates, women have higher rates of disability, of acute conditions such as respiratory, infective, and digestive problems, and of most chronic conditions. AIDS is an exception. In 1997, the AIDS rate was about four times higher among males than among females over 12 years of age (National Center for Health Statistics 1998). Women over the age of 70 are more likely than older men to report difficulty in their daily activities. Their rates of acute conditions are typically 20 to 30 percent higher than those of men. Among chronic conditions, the rates for *nonfatal* varieties are especially higher for women. These include various disgestive problems, anemias, arthritis, migraine headaches, urinary infections, and varicose veins. The rates for fatal chronic conditions are higher for men. Verbrugge (1999) suggested that important reasons for these gender discrepancies are differences in risks associated with work and leisure, consistent health care, lifestyles and role behaviors of men and women, and the fact that women are more likely to report symptoms and pursue medical help. Women tend to engage in healthier lifestyles and seek more preventive care than men. Women are also more attentive to their bodies and therefore more sensitive to symptoms. They take more continuous care of their health problems than men do. Finally, women are better at reporting minor health problems and this might help minimize the seriousness of those problems later in life and help account for their higher life ex-

pectancy. Traditionally in U.S. society, men are supposed to be "strong and silent." But this may work against them. Biological differences are also involved, but are probably less important than other factors. It is expected that gender differences in health will diminish in the twenty-first century as gender differences in exposure to risk factors also diminish (Verbrugge 1999).

Variations in health-related lifestyles also extend to different income groups. Although the *concern* for physical appearance, healthy diet, and alcohol consumption may not vary among income groups, there is evidence that those with lower incomes and education, and in lower-skilled occupations, are less likely to practice healthy lifestyles. That is, they are generally more likely to smoke and less likely to exercise regularly or wear a seat belt. Overall, lower socioeconomic groups are also less likely to be vaccinated or get regular checkups (Weiss and Lonnquist 1994).

Employment conditions also appear to affect the differential health statuses of men and women. Even when their initial health is the same, women become healthier and have fewer physical limitations the longer and more continuously they are employed than women who are either intermittently employed or not in the labor force. Those who are recently nonemployed are the least healthy (Anson and Anson 1987; Pavalko and Smith 1999). Increases in earnings are also positively related to health, but the effects of increases in *spousal* earnings appears to be different for men and women. A national longitudinal study suggests that, among married couples, an increase in wives' earnings raises the chances of husbands dying, whereas the reverse was found for wives when husbands' earnings increase (McDonough et al. 1999). These results suggest that health can be negatively affected when traditional gender roles such as the male as the "breadwinner" have been violated (i.e., when wives begin to obtain earnings which are higher, perhaps higher than those of their husbands). In addition, the nature of the employment and social support for it affect perceived health. More enriching work, coupled with support by colleagues and spouses, is related to better health (Hibbard and Pope 1987).

Use of Health Services

Given the differences in health conditions between groups, one would expect parallel differences in the use of physicians, hospitals, and other health facilities. Indeed, low-income adults who have a health problem were two to three times as likely as high-income adults not to have had contact with a physician or dentist in 1994–95, and are less likely than higher-income persons to have a regular source of care. A similar relationship exists among children. Only about two-thirds of poor children have been fully vaccinated, compared to three-fourths of the nonpoor. Preventive care among adults also varies with social class. In 1993–94, middle-aged, high-income women were about 70 percent more likely than their poor counterparts to have gotten a mammography in the previous two years. At about the same time, almost one-third of poor adults indicated an "unmet need for health care," compared to only 7 percent of high-income adults. Part of the consequence of the lower rates of preventive care among the poor are greater numbers of emergency-room visits and higher rates of hospitalizations that could have been avoided with preventive care (National Center for Health Statistics 1998).

A significant reason for the lack of regular health care among the poor is that they are less likely to have health insurance, and as a result, have to pay more out-of-pocket expenses for their health services. In 1998, over 44 million people in the United States did not have any health insurance. Over 11 million of these were children. Hispanic and Black children were more likely than White children to be covered by Medicaid. Generally, people who work are more likely to be insured than those who do not, but ironically, among the poor, those who work are *less* likely to be insured. This is just one of the problems faced by the working poor. Overall, almost one-third of the poor did not have any health insurance, not even Medicaid. As income declines, the probability of not having any insurance increases. Over 25 percent of those with incomes below $25,000 in 1998 had no insurance, compared to 8 percent of those in the $75,000-or-more bracket. Over one-third of

Hispanics, 22 percent of Blacks, and 15 percent of Whites lacked health insurance in 1998 (U.S. Bureau of the Census, October 1999). Lack of insurance means more of the health costs have to be borne by private individuals. It has been estimated that, in 1997, low-income elderly Medicare beneficiaries spent about *half* of their own incomes on health care (Gross et al. 1999).

What we have seen so far is that those in lower socioeconomic positions experience greater health problems, but are less likely to have insurance, and consequently have to pay a greater proportion of their meager incomes for their own health care (see Figure 11.2). This is an obvious instance where inequality directly impacts life chances. Lack of insurance, however, is not the only factor affecting differences in use of health services. In his survey of various models of service use, Shortell (1984) concluded that "generally, need for care is the best predictor of differences in use, although the availability of a regular source of care, insurance coverage, and sociodemographic characteristics such as age are also associated with various patterns of use" (p. 83). Some have further contended that the values and characteristics of the poor themselves contribute to a reluctance to use medical services. "The poor are…less aware of the concepts and practices of scientific medicine, and differences in many beliefs and values make communication between patient and practitioner difficult" (Herman 1972, p. 12). The greater number of work days lost and physical contacts by lower-income individuals may be related to their interpretation of symptoms and determinants of health. They are more likely than those in the higher-income categories to feel that given symptoms require a physician visit and to feel that the quality of their health is primarily affected by factors beyond their control (Cockerham et al. 1986).

Suggesting that personal values and motivation are central in getting good health care, an article in *Parade* (Downs 1996) encouraged people to choose to "Take Charge of Your Health" and featured a celebrity and his wife who were invited by the magazine to undergo a thorough checkup at the famed Mayo Clinic in Rochester, Minnesota.

Unfortunately, *being able* to take charge of one's health is a more complicated matter involving barriers linked to race, income, and gender. In addition to values and beliefs, usage of facilities appears to be related to the perceived quality of care an individual receives, and often those who are less well off will not use a service because of this problem (Dutton 1978). Quality of care is a problem for many U.S. citizens, however. Polls suggest that almost half of all Americans are dissatisfied with the quality of health care, three-quarters are not happy with the availability and cost of health care, and almost two-thirds feel that Congress should reform the health-care system (Gallup 1994).

A 1986 national survey of over 10,000 persons revealed that access to health-care services is worse for Blacks regardless of income, that they are less likely to pursue needed medical care, that they were more dissatisfied than Whites with their care by doctors and in hospitals, and that they are more likely to believe that their stays in hospitals

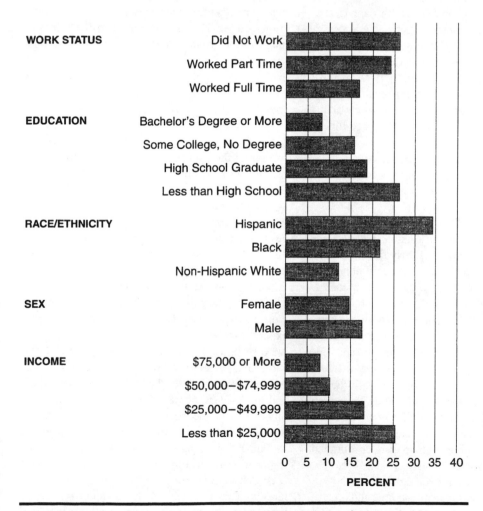

FIGURE 11.2   Percent of Persons Who Lacked Health Insurance, by Household Income, Sex, Race, Hispanic Origin, Education, and Work Status: 1997

Source: U.S. Bureau of the Census, *Health Insurance Coverage: 1997.* Current Pop. Reports, Series P60, No. 202, September 1998, pp. 2–3.

are too short. The small number of minority physicians, the low ratios of doctors to population in minority communities, the fact that Blacks are more likely to live in states with low Medicaid benefits, and the greater percentage of Blacks than Whites who have no health insurance are some of the possible reasons for the poorer access to health services for Blacks. Higher percentages of Blacks than Whites also are less satisfied with the attention given them by physicians and the level of seriousness with which their illnesses are taken by professionals (Blendon et al. 1989).

Differential treatment in health care is also affected by sex and gender. "When a woman seeks medical care from a physician, there are seventy-eight chances out of one hundred that the person she sees will be a man" (Andersen 1997, p. 216). Doctors tend to bring in their expectations about gender roles and behaviors into their beliefs about health and illness. Male doctors often see illness and complaints among women as having a psychological rather than physiological origin. This suggests that women are not taken as seriously as men who come in with health problems (Andersen 1993).

The negative image of women's bodies and sexist beliefs about women's nature have a long history. In the nineteenth and early twentieth centuries, the female body was considered abnormal compared to the male body. Pregnancies, menstruation, menopause, and similar natural biological events were considered conditions to be "treated" and physicians generally thought that it was in women's nature to be sick (Ehrenreich and English 1981; Rothman 1984). The ovaries and uterus were thought by male physicians to be the absolute core of the female body. Thus, the womb often was viewed as the source for many ailments suffered by women (Ehrenreich and English 1981). At the same time, women were encouraged to develop their "maternal instincts" and were not believed to have a sex drive as strong as men.

Because of their greater economic and organizational resources, male obstetricians successfully competed against midwives in the delivery of children, enabling them to gain control of a whole area

of women's lives (Wertz and Wertz 1981). A captive group of female patients not only provided fees at a time when the number of clientele was dwindling but also their bodies provided "teaching material" for budding male physicians (Rothman 1984, pp. 72–73). Many of these attitudes still survive. An analysis of 27 general gynecology textbooks published since 1943 in the United States revealed that at least 50 percent of them emphasize that women are "destined to reproduce, nurture, and keep their husbands happy" (Scully and Bart 1981, p. 350). Many of these same texts also stress that women's primary interest in sex is for "procreation" rather than "recreation" and that most females are "frigid." The authors of this study concluded: "Gynecologists, our society's official experts on women, think of themselves as the woman's friend. With friends like that, who needs enemies?" (Scully and Bart 1981, p. 354).

Class differences also have surfaced in the images of women's health and bodies. Historically, women of the upper class were thought to be more "civilized" and refined than those in the working and lower classes. As a result, they were thought of as more fragile and vulnerable, more susceptible to various maladies. Ehrenreich and English suggested that much of their sickness may have been due to the "sexuo-economic" relationship in their marriages (1981). Essentially, these women were viewed as providing sexual and reproductive services in exchange for economic support from their working husbands. The ill-fitting, heavy clothes expected to be worn by "ladies" of the upper class were responsible, in fact, for many of the illness symptoms experienced by these women. But as a consequence of these "health" problems, middle- and upper-class women became a "client caste" to physicians, while poor women received virtually no medical attention. African American, American Indian, and working-class women were seen as being hearty of constitution in contrast to their upper-class counterparts and, therefore, in need of less attention. This stereotype provided a convenient rationale for giving medical care to those who had the financial resources to pay for it (Ehrenreich and English 1981; Wertz and Wertz 1981).

Even today, those with lower statuses receive poorer health services. One reason is that obstacles of different kinds prevent or at least hinder the use of appropriate medical facilities. Clinics may be difficult to get to for certain groups or may be overcrowded (or both). Costs may be too high for those without health insurance, and they are less than half as likely as those with insurance to see a physician (Zaldivar 1993a). It has been shown that if barriers such as these are eliminated, individuals take advantage of important health services regardless of class. Research has demonstrated, for instance, that Black individuals in lower socioeconomic groups often take advantage of free health services to a disproportionate degree, especially when their honor and self-worth are respected (Slesinger, Tessler, and Mechanic 1975). This may be related to the previously mentioned greater worry over symptoms among lower-income groups.

HEALTH-CARE COSTS AND INEQUALITY

Health-care costs undoubtedly have an effect on the extent to which individuals pursue preventive and other health-care services. In 1996, Americans spent $1,035 billion on health care, which amounts to almost $3,800 per person—higher than costs found in any other industrialized country. Health-care expenditures ate up about 21 percent of the federal budget ($351 billion) and 14 percent of state and local governmental budgets ($132 billion). A greater share of the gross domestic product (13.6 percent) went to health care in the United States than in any other major industrialized nation. Most others spent 7 to 10 percent on health care (National Center for Health Statistics 1998). Medical costs continued to increase throughout the 1990s, even though the *rate* of increase slowed.

Obviously, obtaining health care is an expensive proposition. Rising health-care costs are a matter of great concern, and the reasons for the rise are various, relating in part to (1) changes in the size, sex, and age distribution of the population; (2) increased use of facilities; (3) advances

in technology; (4) increases in third-party payments; (5) inflation; (6) changes in the frequency and types of illnesses; (7) malpractice insurance and litigation expenses; and (8) increases in the numbers of diagnostic tests being given. It also appears that changes in hospital administrations can affect costs. Nutshell 11.1 relates the costs associated with for-profit health facilities.

Possessing health insurance can buffer the personal cost of health care, but insurance is expensive, even when employers make a contribution for employee coverage. In 1994, employees at small companies still personally paid out $160 per month for coverage, whereas at larger companies, the cost was lower but still over $100 per month. Costs are prohibitive for employers as well, as they bear part of the cost of health insurance. Consequently, the proportion of employers who provide health insurance coverage has declined in recent years. This has been especially true for smaller companies and has especially affected retirees. In 1993, only 61 percent of the working-age population in the United States had insurance through their employers (Davis 1997).

The increased costs of health care take their toll on everyone, but especially groups that are less well off and more vulnerable. Like small businesses, small rural hospitals find it more difficult than larger ones to digest the costs of those who cannot pay or whose costs are not fully picked up by insurance. In 1988, 81 community hospitals were forced to close, due in part to inadequate payments from Medicaid and Medicare programs, the loss of physicians, and area economic problems. Most of these were small hospitals (Society for Hospital Social Work Directors 1989). Teaching hospitals also suffer because they are more likely than others to take in patients with long-term problems. One analysis recently labeled such hospitals "an endangered species" (Schwartz, Newhouse, and Williams 1985). Poor individuals, of course, suffer because if they cannot pay, they may be dumped by a given hospital. It is estimated that hospitals dump about 250,000 persons a year for financial, not medical, reasons (Ansberry 1988, p. A1). Obviously, the problem of costs is a vicious one in

NUTSHELL 11.1 _____

Medicare Spending Rises
with For-Profit Hospitals

U.S. Study Contradicts Idea That
Such Facilities Manage Costs Better

ASSOCIATED PRESS

For-profit hospitals drive up the cost of all health care for Medicare patients in their communities, a study has found, contradicting arguments that they manage costs and services more efficiently than nonprofit hospitals do.

Medicare spending in communities served only by for-profit hospitals grew faster from 1989 to 1995 than spending did in areas served by nonprofits or a mix of both, according to researchers from the U.S. Department of Veterans Affairs and Dartmouth College.

The study, published in today's New England Journal of Medicine, looked at 3,436 hospital service areas, some in rural areas with only one hospital and others in cities where residents could choose among half a dozen or more.

The authors of the study said Medicare spending grew nearly 50 percent faster in communities where hospitals converted from nonprofit to for-profit ownership.

The study found that average annual Medicare spending in communities served by nonprofits was $3,554 per elderly resident in 1989, compared with $4,006 in areas served by for-profits, a gap of $452.

Mixed areas fell in between.

By 1995, the gap had grown to $732: Average Medicare spending per person in nonprofit areas was $4,440 a year, compared with $5,172 in for-profit areas.

Of the nation's 5,507 hospitals, 797 are investor-owned, and the rate of conversion from nonprofit to for-profit status is increasing.

One way that for-profit hospitals increase their Medicare reimbursements is by aggressively referring patients to nursing homes, rehabilitation centers and home medical agencies they own, said Dr. Steffie Woolhandler, a Harvard Medical School professor who co-wrote an accompanying editorial.

Source: Akron Beacon Journal, August 5, 1999, p. A8. Reprinted with permission of Associated Press.

which a host of interrelated causes and consequences are tangled.

One proposal to deal with the issue of high health-care costs is the health maintenance organization (HMO). The number of people enrolled in HMOs has risen rapidly over the last 25 years, going from about 6 million in 1976 to almost 67 million in 1997. In 1997, over 25 percent of the U.S. population was enrolled in HMOs (National Center for Health Statistics 1998). Basically, HMOs provide a variety of care services to individuals for a fixed monthly premium, and there appears to be general agreement that HMO costs are lower than those for more conventional plans, but the exact reasons are not clear (Wolinsky 1980; Luft 1983; Welch 1985). Keeping costs lower and

maintaining profits for HMOs have had implications for both government and the individual. Attempts by the federal government to keep medical costs down have allegedly resulted in the exiting of HMOs from markets serving senior citizens because of supposed underpayment to HMOs by the government. The first half of 1999 alone left 250,000 seniors needing to look elsewhere for some medical coverage in 2000 (Shinkman 1999).

The implications of HMOs for individuals goes even deeper. Because the costs are lower, there is some fear that the individuals who join and stay in HMOs will tend to be those who are sicker than most others. The result will be at least a two-tier health system—the traditional "fee-for-service" system in which individuals choose their own doctors and are covered by private health insurance, and a second system of "prepaid" health groups that for a flat fee offer a certain range of health-care services. The healthier, wealthier individuals will gravitate toward the former, while the latter will attract those who are worse off in terms of both health status and income. Under these conditions, there is some concern that the quality of care in the latter will be adversely affected. If costs continue to spiral upward, short of national health insurance, there is some belief that a lower tier of minimal health services will be financed by the government for the poor and older persons—a system that is not likely to attract the highest quality of professionals (Thurow 1985). The ultimate result of these processes would be unequal health care, meaning worse care for the poor and others who cannot afford quality services.

Is it the case that HMO enrollees are indeed lower in income and poorer in health than those who enroll in more traditional health plans? There is a lot of research on this topic of adverse selection bias. The results tend to be mixed (Luft 1983; Greenlick 1984; Freeborn and Pope 1982; Garfinkel et al. 1986). The weight of the evidence since 1980 points in the direction of a favorable rather than an adverse selection bias. That is, HMO members are less likely to have had established ties with physicians, more likely to use preventive services, and show greater health concern than those in more traditional plans (Wilensky and Rossiter 1986). The bulk of the evidence also shows that HMO members have lower hospitalization rates than those in more conventional health plans (Luft 1983) but may have higher prospective health-care costs, as would be the case with young families (cf. Berki 1980; Luft 1983; Schuttinga, Falik, and Steinwald 1985).

Data on the socioeconomic characteristics of HMO members are also mixed, with some studies showing a greater probability of members to be from financially vulnerable groups, while other research demonstrates the opposite (cf. Wolinsky 1980; Buchanan and Cretin 1986; Freeborn and Pope 1982). At this point, then, one cannot say unequivocally that HMOs contain a disproportionate number of poor, sick individuals.

BASIC LIFE CHANCES: PSYCHOLOGICAL HEALTH

Consider for a moment how important physical health is in anyone's life. It affects one's chances in employment, social activities, travel, and relationships with others. Psychological health is also a basic element in contributing to a meaningful life, but are the chances for such health evenly distributed among groups in U.S. society? Recent estimates are that about 8.2 million, or about 5 percent of the adult population, suffer mental and emotional problems that "seriously interfered with the ability to work or attend school or to manage day-to-day activities" (Willis et al. 1998). Women, unmarried, unemployed, and poor individuals are overrepresented in this population

In 1988, approximately 2 million persons were admitted to inpatient mental health facilities in the United States. Over 75 percent of them were White. In addition, the poor are two and one-half times as likely as the nonpoor to have a "serious mental illness" (Manderscheid and Sonnenschein 1992). In terms of placement in 1980, African Americans were more likely to be admitted to state and county psychiatric facilities than to any other facility, and minority group members had higher rates of admissions to such facilities than nonminority groups. For all major groups, males had higher admissions than females to state and county psychiatric and veteran's facilities, but for private and nonfederal general hospitals, admissions rates for each sex were similar. Males and Blacks were more likely than females or Whites to be *involuntarily* admitted to state and county mental hospitals, and most of these involved a criminal commitment (Manderscheid and Barrett 1987).

In terms of diagnoses for the admittants, schizophrenia was a more frequent diagnosis for Blacks than for Whites, with over 50 percent of the former in state and county mental hospitals being so labeled. In fact, in every setting, schizophrenia was the most frequently entered diagnosis for Blacks, whereas the dominance of a particular diagnosis for Whites varied with the type of psychiatric facility. Schizophrenia was the most frequently given diagnosis for Whites in county and state mental hospitals, but in private psychiatric and nonfederal general hospitals, affective disorders were the most prominent type of diagnosis (Manderscheid and Barrett 1987). These refer largely to emotional disorders such as manic depression.

Some research suggests that there is a relationship between race, sex, socioeconomic status, and diagnosis. A study by Loring and Powell (1988) aimed at finding out whether the psychiatrist's or client's race or sex influenced the diagnosis given to the client, even though the symptoms presented in each case vignette did not vary. The authors presented a stratified random sample of 290 psychiatrists with two case studies each, in which the sex and race were either disclosed or not. The point was to see whether these doctors would evaluate the client simply on the basis of symptoms classified in a standard manner by the *Diagnostic and Statistical Manual* (*DSM-III*) used by clinicians. Some interesting patterns emerged in the research. The authors found the following:

1. White male psychiatrists were more likely to classify a given case in the general schizophrenia category if it involved a White male than if the client were Black or female.
2. Black male and female psychiatrists followed a similar pattern; that is, they were more likely to present the general schizophrenic diagnosis to clients who were of the *same* sex and race as the psychiatrist.
3. Black psychiatrists tended to give the least serious diagnoses to White male patients, and male psychiatrists did not label any White males as having paranoid schizophrenia. In contrast, this was the most frequently given diagnosis for Black male clients by every type of psychiatrist.
4. Male psychiatrists tended to diagnose female clients as having depression disorders, but female psychiatrists shied away from this label.

What these and other results show is that when psychiatrists are not given either the sex or race of the case they are examining, there is widespread agreement among them on the diagnosis. But when such information is provided, if the sex and race are

the same as the psychiatrist who is doing the diagnosing, then the diagnosis is basically the same as that which would have been given had no information on sex and race been provided. In other words, the diagnoses appear to be more "objective." In contrast, in those cases where sex and/or gender of client and psychiatrist differ, diagnoses appear more subjective. For example, male psychiatrists, on the whole, are inclined to perceive females as having depressive disorders and to assign White females to the histrionic category, even when the case study itself gives little evidence of such a disorder. It seems that the stereotype of women being emotional is carried over into these diagnoses. Similarly, the diagnoses of Black males also appear to be affected by stereotypical views. Black males are more likely to be considered as being violent, suspicious, or dangerous, even when their clinical characteristics are the same as those of Whites. Psychiatrists of *both* races tend to give such diagnoses, suggesting internalization of these stereotypes to some extent by both types of psychiatrists. If these biases enter into diagnoses, then official rates of such illnesses for different groups may not accurately reflect the incidence of these disorders among the different sex and racial groups (Loring and Powell 1988).

Stereotyping and labeling the mentally ill according to traditional gender and racial roles is nothing new, however. In the seventeenth and early eighteenth centuries, the artistic and scientific images of the mad were decidedly male in nature, depicting someone who was "aggressive," "muscular," "seminude," and "raving," with "uncivilized animality." By the first half of the nineteenth century, the image of madness had changed to a feminine one: "antisocial, violent, unruly, and oversexed.... The figure of the sexually aggressive madwoman effectively displaced the previously more common figure of the raving male lunatic" (Kromm 1994, pp. 507–508, 530–531). In part, this shift reflected concerns about the increasing political involvement of women in Europe after the French Revolution. This imagery served to control women's power (Kromm 1994).

Other research has found that whether an individual is admitted voluntarily or involuntarily into

From Etienne Esquirol's *Des Maladies Mentales,* 1838, courtesy of the National Library of Medicine.

Early in the nineteenth century, the image of the insane person as female and feminine became established, reflecting concerns about the rising political force of women after the French Revolution.

a state hospital is also related in part to his or her socioeconomic status as well as to the severity of the disorder. Briefly put, individuals from lower socioeconomic levels are more likely to be involuntarily admitted when the disorder is not obvious or severe—that is, when there is room for various interpretations of symptoms (Rushing 1978). Schizophrenia, which is more frequently diagnosed among African Americans, is also a disorder in which individual interpretation by the caregiver plays a large role. It has been labeled as an "open concept" and "fuzzy natural category" (quoted in Gottesman, McGuffin, and Farmer 1987, p. 41).

Similarly, diagnoses of "personality disorders"—which display ambiguous symptoms, are more difficult to identify objectively, and are therefore open to interpretation—show sex biases associated with traditional female roles (Dixon, Gordon, and Khomusi 1995).

The relationship between race, gender, and socioeconomic factors, on the one hand, and mental illness/psychological distress, on the other, has been studied extensively. Several classic studies examined the relationship between social class and mental illness, and each of them raised questions and issues that have continued in the field and found relationships that have since been reconfirmed. These studies found that lower socioeconomic groups had higher rates of mental illness, but each study suffered from methodological problems that have yet to be fully resolved (Faris and Dunham 1939; Hollingshead and Redlich 1958; Srole et al. 1962). These studies used different measures of socioeconomic status and mental illness, different kinds of samples, and cross-sectional rather than longitudinal designs. The latter would have allowed researchers to more carefully dissect the nature of the relationship between status and mental illness by looking at it over time. As it was, the cross-sectional design obtaining data at one point in time did not enable them to provide irrefutable evidence about the causal direction of the relationship. That is, the question remains: Is there something about being in a lower socioeconomic status that causes mental illness (social causation), or does being mentally ill cause one to fall ("drift") into a lower socioeconomic status (social selection or "drift")?

As noted, this question has not yet been fully resolved. Evidence seems clear that there is a significant relationship between lower status and mental illness, but debate continues as to why that is so. A logical argument has been made for each side of the debate. On the one hand, social-causation advocates contend that high stress, lack of adequate resources, and lack of occupational control—all of which are more characteristic of the lower socioeconomic strata—generate conditions favorable to the onset of mental illness. On the other hand, social-selection or "drift" proponents argue that mental illness makes upward status attainment or even maintenance of one's status difficult (Miech et al. 1999).

Current Status of Evidence

A number of studies have confirmed the relationships between socioeconomic status, race, or gender and psychological difficulties. In 1975, Dohrenwend summarized the findings of a large number of studies conducted since 1900 that examined the relationship between class and the prevalence of mental disorders:

1. About 85 percent of the studies found that the highest rates are in the lowest SES group.
2. This relationship is intensified when urban rather than rural groups are considered.
3. This relationship is "consistent for schizophrenia and personality disorders but not for neurosis or manic-depressive psychosis."
4. The exact reason for the relationship is not clear. That is, the relative roles of class, genetics, and disorder in explaining this relationship have not yet been determined.

Using information from over 2,000 Floridians, Ulbrich and her colleagues (1989) found that race and socioeconomic status interact in their effect on psychological distress symptoms. Specifically, in the lower categories of occupational status, Blacks show greater distress symptoms than Whites, whereas in the middle categories, the differences are reduced, and in the higher-ranking occupations, the racial differences are reversed with Whites showing a higher rate of symptoms. The authors also found that within the lowest occupational category, Blacks are exposed to more economic problems than Whites, but these differences do not exist on other occupational levels. "Undesirable life events"—such as deaths, divorces, being fired, and so on—create greater distress only for Blacks in lower socioeconomic positions, but on the other hand, they react less strongly than their White counterparts to economic problems even though they are more exposed to them. Perhaps this is related to the strong kinship ties among the Black families.

Other studies also have found a link between low occupational status or unemployment and psychological problems (cf. Link, Dohrenwend, and Skodol 1986; Brown and Gary 1988). It has been found that educational, income, and occupational level all have independent effects on feelings of psychological distress, but that the relative importance of each depends on the sex and employment status of the respondent. Among working men, for instance, income is the most important predictor of distress, whereas among women in the labor force and homemakers, education is the most significant (Kessler 1982).

In a word, the relationship between lower socioeconomic status and psychological distress, each measured in a variety of ways, has been repeatedly verified in research. However, most of this research does little to clarify the answer to the social-causation/social-selection question. There have been some attempts to test the validity of the drift hypothesis among individuals with specific disorders. Turner and Wagenfeld (1967) studied its presence among schizophrenics. Taking a random sample of 214 patients, they found that a certain percentage of them grew up in low-status families. This would support the social causation thesis. On the other hand, it did not account for the very large proportion of schizophrenics they found in that status. Comparing that group with a large sample of the general population, Turner and Wagenfeld discovered that a much smaller proportion of schizophrenics were upwardly mobile relative to their parents and that a large percentage were downwardly mobile when compared with the general sample. But within their own careers, the large majority did not move at all, suggesting that although some drift is present, it is not an adequate explanation of the low occupational positions of these schizophrenics. Rather, it appears that these individuals simply are not likely to attain high position and disproportionately move downward compared with their parents. In this respect, the social causation thesis does not appear to account significantly for the social class/schizophrenia relationship.

In contrast, however, some longitudinal data do suggest that conditions associated with low status do affect the likelihood of experiencing psychological disorders (cf. Wheaton 1978; Turner and Gartrell 1978; Dooley and Catalano 1980; Link, Dohrenwend, and Skodol 1986). Kohn (1976a) tried to summarize the argument about causation of schizophrenia:

1. Class is related to schizophrenia, but researchers are not sure why this is so.
2. Genetics plays a causal role, but researchers do not know in what manner.
3. Stress also seems to be involved.

Implicit is the argument that no single factor accounts for the illness. Rather, Kohn argued, the conditions for life in the lower class make individuals less able to effectively cope with stress. Together with genetic vulnerability and great stress, the probability of schizophrenia increases. The curved dashed lines in Figure 11.3 serve to indicate that Kohn's primary concern is to show the causal connections between class, genetic conditions, and stress, on the one hand, and schizophrenia on the other. He is less concerned about the interrelationships among the first three variables.

As is suggested by the disagreement in findings, the nature of the relationship between socioeconomic status and mental illness has been difficult to untangle. It may very well be that the relationship is reciprocal; the conditions associated with a social-class position affect one's health, and conversely, one's health status affects how far one can go socioeconomically.

The latest evidence does suggest that the relationship is more complex than originally thought. Specific types of mental disorder may be related to specific measures of socioeconomic status differently, and some may not be related at all to status position. A recent longitudinal study of young adults who had been studied from birth to age 21 again found the inverse relationship between mental disorder and lower educational attainment, but the nature of the relationship varied with the type of illness: "We found that the relation between mental disorders and SES is unique for every disorder examined in this study" (Miech et al. 1999). In fact, the study yielded results that supported every possible form of interpretation. First, in support of the social-selection or drift hypothesis, researchers found that having attention deficit disorder negatively affected one's educational attainment. Second, on the other hand and in support of social causation, they found that low socioeconomic status affected anxiety. Third, they found that the relationship between antisocial disorder and lower socioeconomic status involves *both* social-selection and social-causation processes. Finally, in the case of a depression disorder, they found no relationship between SES

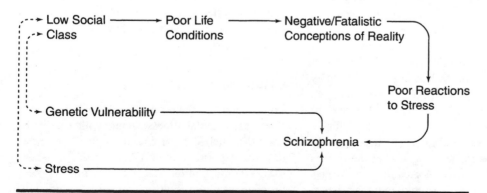

FIGURE 11.3   Melvin L. Kohn's Model of Schizophrenia Etiology

Source: Based on Kohn 1976, pp. 177–180.

and mental illness. This study used data from New Zealand, and in addition to the complexity issues raised by the results, the question remains whether its results can even be generalized to the United States (ibid.). The Gordian-knot relationship of low socioeconomic status and mental illness still has to be disentangled.

Gender and Distress.   It already has been suggested that sex is related to the *diagnosis* of mental illness. In fact, women do experience, not just report, greater psychological distress than men (Kessler and McRae 1983; Mirowsky and Ross 1995). Clinically defined major depression has been found to be two to three times as likely among women than among men, although the gap between them may be narrowing because of the recent increase in depression among young men. These trends have been found not only for the United States but for Sweden, Germany, Canada, and New Zealand as well, but not for Korea or Puerto Rico or among Mexican Americans (Klerman and Weissman 1989).

It also has been discovered in analyses of data from five general population surveys that psychological distress among women is more likely to be affected by some undesirable incidents affecting someone close to them than is the case among men. But women are not *generally* more vulnerable than men to all types of undesirable events. Among the possible contributors to these trends in depression are changes in women's roles and alterations in occupational patterns for men and women (Kessler and McLeod 1984).

It appears that a greater breadth of roles for women may have healthy results. There is evidence that individuals with multiple roles display a greater sense of psychological well-being, and that loss of roles is related to increased feelings of distress. People with multiple roles—for example, employed, married, and parents—tend to have better health than those with none of these roles (Verbrugge 1983). Sociologically, this makes sense since roles provide people with their identities. "The greater the number of identities held, the stronger one's sense of meaningful, guided existence. The more identities, the more 'existential security,' so to speak. A sense of meaningful existence and purposeful, ordered behavior are crucial to psychological health" (Thoits 1983, p. 175).

On the other hand, involvement and responsibility in *too many* areas can increase a person's feeling of loss of personal control and thereby increase stress and depression symptoms (Rosenfield 1989; Cleary and Mechanic 1983). Another factor probably contributing to the greater distress felt by housewives is their little power in the home compared to their employed husbands (Steil 1984). Employment brings power in the family, and distress may be a function of both lack of power and lack of multiple roles outside the family.

Obviously, some conditions and life events may help prepare and strengthen individuals for stressful conditions. Middle-class women who were in or approaching young adulthood during the Great Depression and who suffered serious economic loss because of it, today are less likely to feel helpless and are more assertive and in control of their lives than middle-class women who did not experience such losses. Working-class women, on the other hand, who entered the Depression with fewer resources to begin with and experienced serious reductions in economic resources, feel less assertive and have a greater sense of being victimized (Elder and Liker 1982). What this suggests is that life's obstacles are more easily overcome and can even have long-term beneficial effects when those experiencing them have had ample resources on which to build a strong life originally.

Well-Being, Choice, and Control

The frequently found relationship between lower status and mental illness, along with the likelihood that such status is causally related to illness, raises the question about what it might be about lower socioeconomic status that would increase the chances of psychological distress for individuals. There is an old saying that some people look at the world through rose-colored glasses. Everything is bright and rosy. It is much easier, of course, to have this sunny outlook if you are sitting in a comfortable position. Unfortunately, ideas about ignorance being bliss and the poor being content in their misery are simply not borne out in research. Not surprisingly, compared with Whites and those in higher statuses, Blacks and those in lower socioeconomic positions are less satisfied with their personal lives, housing, incomes, jobs, free time, and standard of living. They also tend to be less satisfied with the way things are going in the country as a whole (Gallup 1985, 1988).

Results suggest that the relationship between race and feelings of well-being have not changed significantly in recent years (Hughes and Thomas 1998). It also appears that both race and SES have independent effects on such feelings (Hughes and Thomas 1998; Redmond 1988). In addition, gender appears to be related to feelings of well-being, with men showing a slightly stronger sense of well-being (Haring, Stock, and Okun 1984). However, gender is not more important than social class in explaining well-being. Analyzing data from 556 sources and using income, occupational status, or a composite measure of socioeconomic status, Haring and her associates found that there is a positive relationship between each of these measures and well-being, and that men have a slightly higher sense of well-being than women, but that gender accounts for little of the variation in feelings of well-being. When men and women are analyzed separately, social-class measures still predict well-being within each group. While women are worse off than men on a variety of *objective* conditions, these conditions are not directly translatable into similar negative *feelings* (Haring, Stock, and Okun 1984). Race and sex interact in their effects on well-being. One national study found Black females to have the lowest sense of well-being among the race and sex groups (Redmond 1988).

The greater feelings of distress found in the lower socioeconomic groups have been linked to greater feelings of vulnerability, powerlessness, and alienation. Those with lower incomes and lower status occupations are more likely to feel this way, while those in higher positions have a greater feeling of mastery and control (Mirowsky and Ross 1983; Wheaton 1980). This was seen earlier in the relationship between SES and personal control over health. Women, those in lower status jobs, and those who are unemployed have less of a sense of control over their lives (Mirowsky and Ross 1983; Wheaton 1980; Kohn and Schooler 1982; Pearlin et al. 1981). Individuals with a sense of powerlessness have feelings of little control over their lives, believing that they cannot master or determine the paths that life will take. Rather, the belief is that factors outside the individual—fate or "society," for example—determine what happens to them and that there is little they can do to change that.

In sum, feelings of self-mastery and control over one's life appear to be an important set of mediating influences on mental health. Those in low socioeconomic positions generally have a greater sense than those in higher statuses that their lives are controlled by factors beyond their immediate control. These feelings, in turn, are related to greater depression and less overall satisfaction with life (Lachman and Weaver 1998). The importance of mastery over one's life for mental health is further implied by findings that show that job restructuring and increased job demands, over which individuals have little control, increase depressive feelings and lower a sense of life satisfaction (Tausig and Fenwick 1999). Of course, those with few resources are lacking in the choices available to others. In a critical sense, lacking a sense of power and control is about lacking choices. The luxury of considering choices is not available for one who is scrambling merely to stay alive or to have a little bit of comfort.

Consider, for example, that Michele Hazard, a working mother from Kalamazoo, Michigan, with two children and mounting bills for health, child care, car insurance, and housing, has had to move six times between working and AFDC, a government welfare program. She explained, "The way the system is built, we have no choice. If you need help to get through a month, you're either on AFDC or you're working, there's no happy medium" (Pierini 1992, p. C1).

Several decades ago, Cohen and Hodges proposed that lower blue-collar class values are formed as an adaptation to the concrete conditions under which these individuals live. Their study in California of 2,600 male family heads indicated that those in the lower class have a perhaps realistic but nevertheless pessimistic view of their lives. "In his view, nothing is certain; in all probability things, however, will turn out badly as they generally have in the past" (Cohen and Hodges 1963, p. 322). Kohn's (1969) judgment likewise confirmed this conclusion. While members of the upper class are likely to feel that one's life can be shaped and directed by the individual, "the essence of lower class position is the belief that one is at the mercy of forces and people beyond one's control, often beyond one's understanding" (pp. 189, 192).

A young electrician apprentice summarized this feeling well: "See, I feel like I'm being held back, like I'm not on top of things.... I don't know what you would call it, maybe sort of powerless, but it's a feeling not about any one thing that's gone wrong" (Sennett and Cobb 1973, p. 34). Falling from their comfortable upper-middle-class life, Kerry Russo reflected on the predicament of her newly unemployed husband: "I look at a successful businessman going through this absolute torture. I can hold him. I can tell him it's going to be okay. But it's out of my hands. And that's the frightening part, how little control we have over our lives.... It used to be that if you followed the rules, you'd be fine. That doesn't apply anymore. They've changed the rules" (Safran 1992, p. 115).

Despite the belief that one has little control, Americans have traditionally been brought up to believe in individualism (i.e., the belief that individuals are responsible for their own fates). Imagine how you would feel if you, on the one hand, believed in individualism and, on the other hand, had little opportunity to improve your situation. The personal consequences of being caught in this vise are, in part, psychological. This combination of different amounts of opportunities for classes

and an ingrained belief in individual responsibility creates the conditions for self-damaging feelings and doubts among those who are not economically successful on the one hand, and feelings of self-confidence and entitlement among those living in successful families on the other. Sennett and Cobb's (1973) moving study of Boston working-class men and their families who sense a lack of control revealed the corrosive psychological effects that the combination of individualism and varying success has on individuals.

Individualism encourages the desire to excel, and some do excel while others do not. Those who *do* attain positions develop feelings of competence and freedom, while those who *do not* develop feelings of guilt and suspicions of their own inadequacy. For those at the top, individualism reinforces their belief in the deservedness of their position and abilities and reaffirms their high self-worth, while for those at the bottom, individualism has the doubly damaging effect of confirming the deservedness of their lowly position and reinforcing in their minds that they do not have what it takes. Figure 11.4 summarizes this process.

The lack of control experienced by those below the middle has been linked to their occupational experiences. Those who do repetitive work of little complexity and are closely supervised are more likely to sense a lack of power over their own lives (Blauner 1964). Most jobs of those in the working and lower classes are characterized by a lack of self-direction, which further leads to a feeling of powerlessness (Kohn 1976b). Roger Swardson spent some time working as a telephone representative for a mail-order catalog firm. He took calls from potential customers who wished to order catalog items. He described people who work like he did as being "fastened like barnacles to the bottom of the computer revolution. Soldering tiny leads on circuit boards. Plugging data into terminals. All sorts of things that tend to share one characteristic: repetition.... I head down a double row of 20 stalls where the backsides of seated people stick out like the rumps of Guernsey cows.... I find an open stall, adjust the chair height, get my headset on, and log onto the phone

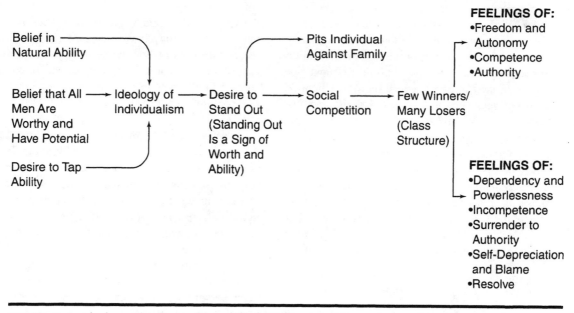

FIGURE 11.4   Ideology, Class Inequality, and Their Effects on Self-Perceptions among Men of Different Classes

Source: Based on Sennett and Cobb 1973.

and computer systems, using my password. An orange light on my console indicates that there are callers on hold....I swing right into it. 'Good morning. Welcome to Wireless. My name is Roger. How can I help you?'" His accommodation to this work is "a detachment that comes out now and then as rage or despair" (Swardson 1993, pp. 88–90, 93). William Thompson worked on the assembly line in a large beef-processing plant and also found the monotony and lack of control difficult. "The assembly line worker became a part of the assembly line. The assembly line is not a tool used by the worker, but a machine which controls him/her" (Thompson 1991, p. 230). To cope with these conditions, workers daydreamed, fooled around, and occasionally engaged in sabotage.

Education is often seen as a way to gain control over one's life, to gain autonomy and choices. Indeed, those with lower educations are more likely to feel more vulnerable and less in control of their lives (Umberson 1993). The working-class respondents in Sennett and Cobb's (1973) study

realize the potential of education to give their children independence in their lives, but they also suspect that educated people can get away with things that the average person cannot, and that education drives a wedge between less-educated parents and their children. Thus, education becomes a double-edged sword, serving to grant independence but also creating a seemingly permanent breach in understanding between generations. Richard Rodriguez, who went from knowing little English to earning a Ph.D. and becoming a successful writer and professor, described how he and his family drifted further apart: "Years passed. Silence grew thicker, less penetrable" (1982, p. 190).

To summarize, the objective conditions under which these groups live help to produce particular sets of beliefs. These, in turn, affect levels of distress and the ability of individuals to cope with that distress. If individuals are vulnerable and believe that they can do little to change conditions, then they tend to be more distressed, and their feelings of powerlessness discourage the development of coping devices to deal with the distress (Wheaton 1980, 1983). It has been found that lower status persons react more severely to stressful situations, such as physical health problems, death, and divorce (Kessler and Cleary 1980; Turner and Noh 1983). In their research review on the relationship between socioeconomic status, beliefs, and distress, Mirowsky and Ross (1986) concluded that "people in lower socioeconomic positions have a triple burden: They have more problems to deal with; their personal histories are likely to have left them with a deep sense of powerlessness; and that sense of powerlessness discourages them from marshalling whatever energy and resources they do have in order to solve their problems. The result for many is a multiplication of despair" (p. 30).

BASIC LIFE CHANCES: FOOD AND SHELTER

The research on physical and psychological health just discussed clearly shows that economic, racial, and gender inequality are deeply implicated in the chances of individuals for a healthy life. It does not warrant belaboring that food and shelter, like health, are basic to a decent life, and it is the poor who are disproportionately found among the hungry and homeless. On the international level, poor nutrition is widespread within the countries listed as "low income" by the World Bank. Moreover, within those countries, the poorest and least educated suffer the most from malnutrition, and when food is scarce, it is not evenly distributed among family members. The young and females are most likely to suffer in these conditions. Poverty, inequality, the level of economic development, and hunger are closely related.

Because of controversies over the definition of *hunger* and the lack of a *consistent national* attempt to assess the magnitude of the problem, there is little agreement on the extent of the problem in the United States. Estimates suggest that anywhere from 8 to 43 million people are hungry (Eisinger 1996). Some of the most accepted studies to measure the hunger problem have examined the demand on emergency food providers, such as soup kitchens and charitable food programs. Re-

sults from the early and mid-1990s indicate that the demand for food from these sources is not only great but may have increased (ibid.). Most recent estimates of how widespread food insufficiency and food insecurity are put the figure at about 10 million people. When including those at risk for hunger, the estimates are as high as 43 million (ibid.).

The problem of hunger, of course, is linked to the issue of good health. The Physician Task Force has argued that inadequate diet has an impact on the health of pregnant women and on the children to whom they give birth. Higher infant mortality rates, low birth weight, slower or deficient brain growth, poorer resistance to infection, and general stunting and anemia are among the conditions related to poor nutrition among children. Other negative effects are found among older persons who are chronically hungry. Many of the health problems among older people—for example, hypertension and weakening of the bone structure (osteoporosis)—require careful attention to quality and quantity of diet, and hunger worsens these maladies (Physician Task Force 1985).

The poor also contribute disproportionately to the ranks of the homeless. Along with the increased attention given hunger in recent years, there also has been more media emphasis on the problem of homelessness in the affluent United States. Most studies of homelessness have been done on the local or state level—such as in Los Angeles, Chicago, and Ohio (Redburn and Buss 1986; Ropers 1988; Rossi and Wright 1989). One of the many problems in studying the homeless problem concerns the definition of *homelessness,* and studies vary in this matter. For example, Rossi and Wright made a distinction between "the literally homeless" and "precariously, or marginally, housed persons" (1989, p. 134). The former, upon which they focused in their study, are those who have no access to housing of any sort, "and who would be homeless by any conceivable definition of the term" (ibid.). Even when a definition is decided on, it is difficult to find out how many are homeless in an area. "Counting the homeless is a social scientist's nightmare." It is difficult because

Hunger has become an increasingly serious problem worldwide and in the United States. In 1992, demands for emergency food assistance in the United States went up by about 25 percent over the previous year. In that same year, an estimated 700 million people worldwide were chronically malnourished, and in the United States an estimated 20 to 30 million people were hungry. Of the latter, 5.5 million were children under 12 years of age. Just over one-third of homeless persons report eating only one meal or less per day (Select Committee on Hunger 1992).

of the relative "invisibility" of the homeless, hostility among them, the mixing of poverty and homelessness, the frequent movement of the homeless from place to place, and the existence of multiple causes that make it difficult to find them (Redburn and Buss 1986, p. 16).

Consequently, national surveys yield wildly different appraisals on the extent of homelessness in the United States, with estimates ranging from several hundred thousand to several million. Estimates based on single counts at a given time ("point-in-time counts") tend to be lower than estimates based on counts of those who are homeless sometime during a period of time ("period prevalence counts") (National Coalition for the Homeless, February 1999). For example, in 1990, the Bureau of the Census carried out a "point-in-time," one-night "shelter and street night" count of persons located in places typically frequented

by the homeless. Almost 179,000 were found in emergency shelters for the homeless, and another 50,000 were found in various street locations. Several hundred thousand could easily be added to this count if one incorporates the numbers of those living in campgrounds, shelters for abused women, and other noninstitutionalized group quarters (U.S. Bureau of the Census, November 1992). In contrast, a study carried out in 1994 estimated that 12 million adults had been homeless at some point in their lives, and that 6.6 million had been homeless sometime between 1989 and 1994 (Link et al. 1995).

The homeless population has become much more heterogeneous since the 1970s. Studies conducted since the mid-1980s indicate that greater percentages of the homeless population are members of families and minorities, and are children (Rossi 1989; U.S. Conference of Mayors 1998).

The U.S. Conference of Mayors' 1998 study of homelessness in 30 cities revealed that 38 percent of the urban homeless were families, 25 percent were under 18 years of age, and 49 percent were African American. Although the majority of single homeless persons are male, most adults in homeless families are female. The average education of the homeless adult is not significantly differenct from the average for the general population, and 20 to 25 percent are employed (Shinn and Weitzman 1996; U.S. Conference of Mayors 1998). The profiles of the homeless vary with the setting, however. For example, Whites make up a much greater proportion of the homeless in rural areas, as do American Indians and migrant laborers (National Coalition for the Homeless, February 1999).

Although estimates vary, the homeless population also contains significant minorities with mental or addictive disorders. An estimated 20 to 25 percent of single adults who are homeless suffer from some kind of chronic mental illness, with a smaller percent of adults in families having this problem. Homeless children are also more likely than other poor children to have mental or emotional problems. Finally, single homeless adults are also more likely than those in families to have drug-related problems (Shinn and Weitzman 1996; National Coalition for the Homeless, February 1999).

What is it like to be homeless? Here are glimpses into the lives of three individuals:

> In New York, Frank, a thirty-four-year-old former warehouseman with an "anxiety and nervousness problem," is fearful of being attacked during the night. He sleeps on his side because otherwise, he says, "I be a flat target."...
>
> In Houston, Rosa, a forty-two-year-old homeless woman, considers her options. To arrive early to get in line for the free 10:30 meal at the soup kitchen means only an hour or so wait. On the other hand, arriving close to noon will result in no wait at all, but it means going without food for an additional hour and a half....
>
> In Detroit, Arch has always been single and a working man for most of his thirty-three adult years. "I don't have no friends. I really haven't in a long time," he says while his eyes scan the rem-

> nants of neighborhood tenement buildings that are ninety years old. "I sometimes hear them saying that I've got the v's, y'know, the lines on the back of your neck. It's supposed to mean that you don't have much time...." (Sweeney 1993, pp. 1–3)

These vignettes suggest the unique set of stresses faced by the homeless. Homeless persons suffer greater emotional pressures than those encountered by the housed poor. They have higher levels of depression and are more likely to avoid active confrontation of problems than other members of the poor population (Banyard and Graham-Bermann 1998). Again, the relationship between health and socioeconomic status appears reciprocal. Mental disorder may precipitate homelessness, and homelessness generally intensifies psychological distress. Adding to this distress is the distinct stigma placed on the homeless by the public. National research indicates that the homelessness stigma is over and above the stigma placed on being poor. One supported explanation for the stigma is that the homeless "are viewed as dirty, smelly, lice-ridden, or diseased," resulting in a desire on the part of the public to keep from being contaminated by them (Phelan et al. 1997, p. 333). A recent national telephone survey found that almost two-thirds of respondents felt that "the presence of homeless people threatens the quality of life in America's cities, hurts local businesses, spoils parks for families and children, and makes neighborhoods worse" (Link et al. 1996, p. 145). In the same study, a majority also believed that the homeless were either dangerous, potentially violent, or threatening. Although the public does not fully blame homeless individuals for their plight, these perceptions of the homeless mark them as a negatively evaluated status group, as defined in Chapter 3.

A number of other factors have been linked to the rise in homelessness. Primary among these are the lack of unskilled or semiskilled jobs available and lack of affordable housing. Changes in the economy have brought about a decline in low-skilled jobs, making employment a significant problem for many of the homeless. Not being able to afford housing is another source of the problem. The higher cost of housing is due in large

There has been a significant rise in the amount of homelessness in recent years.

part to declines in the building of affordable private homes and in public housing. This has left a larger poor population competing for smaller numbers of affordable residences. This increased demand has pushed rents up (Koegel, Burnam, and Baumohl 1996).

The homelessness problem is thus exacerbated by the high cost of what is available. There is evidence that the poor are paying more for their housing. Almost two-thirds of the poor pay more than half of their income for shelter. In sharp contrast, only 8 percent of the nonpoor pay that high a proportion of their incomes for housing. Federal data indicate that whereas in the late 1970s, there were many more low-cost housing units available than there were poor needing them, by 1985, that situation was reversed. Immediate causes for this situation include an increase in the number of poor households, a decline in their average incomes, and an increase in the level of rents (Dionne 1989). "Never before in postwar American history have so many poor people competed for so few affordable dwelling units" (Wright and Lam 1987, p. 49). The destruction or conversion of housing units for other purposes, along with gentrification, have worsened the problem.

Other factors, then, beyond the characteristics of the homeless themselves, also have contributed to the homeless problem. Deinstitutionalization of those with mental problems, the recession of the early 1980s, the declining value of public assistance benefits, no-fault divorces and increasing numbers of no-children rental rules, the net migration to metropolitan areas, and tighter governmental rules about disabilities have all had an effect on this problem (Hope and Young 1986; Wright and Lam 1987; Carliner 1987; Hoch 1987). Thus, many of the elements that affect the extent of homelessness are "macroprocesses" related to the government and market economy (Rossi and Wright 1989). And it is the poor who are especially vulnerable to shifts in these processes. "As long as the distribution of shelter security remains tied to income and social class the poor will bear the burden of going homeless" (Hoch 1987, p. 29).

FAMILY RELATIONSHIPS AND VIOLENCE

We have been examining the effects inequality has on the intimate lives of people, their health, their chances for the material necessities of life, and their feelings about themselves and their everyday living conditions. This section continues that theme by analyzing the effects of inequality on family structure and relationships. First, we look at family stability and how it varies by class and race, and then we look inside the family at the important problems of wife and child abuse.

Family Stability

Traditionally, Black families and those with parents of low education and/or unstable income and employment have had higher divorce rates than higher status White families (Teachman, Polonko, and Scanzoni 1987). Two-parent homes with children contain parents who are significantly more likely to be high school graduates, be employed, and have incomes above the poverty level than those in which only one parent is present. A greater percentage of Black and poor two-parent families break up within two years (Taeuber 1996).

A variety of reasons have been offered to explain the higher rate of divorce among lower status groups. It may be that since tradition is stronger in the higher classes, divorce is considered less of a viable alternative and a messier solution to marital problems. For those in the lower classes, on the other hand, it may be a viable alternative. The wider access of those in the upper status to a variety of alternative activities and opportunities may serve to defuse difficulties in the home by turning attention away from them. Finally, the strains, economic and otherwise, on the lower class are greater overall than in the higher classes, making the probability of a long-lasting deep marital relationship less likely.

The actual reasons given by individuals for divorce vary by SES. Lower status couples appear more likely to give "physical abuse" as a reason for their divorces than middle-class couples. Wives of lower status families more often complained about problems of money, drinking, and abuse, whereas those in middle-status groups more often expressed anger over absence of love, fidelity, and consideration (Levinger 1966). These findings suggest that different levels of needs are not being satisfied in each case. In lower status

families, almost by definition, such physical needs as food and shelter are less likely to be met because of higher unemployment, lower income, and the like. It is not surprising that financial complaints would occur more frequently at these levels than at higher ones. Conversely, at higher status levels, the motivators are more psychological in nature. Physical needs can be much more easily met, and thus such needs as love become more central and problematic. It should be mentioned that the grounds legally allowed for divorce do not always correspond to the real underlying causes for divorce (Adams 1975).

Inequality itself, not just low status, apparently can generate stress within the family, especially between husband and wife. Pearlin (1975) found that differences in the status backgrounds of the spouses can create problems in the marriage. Individuals who marry down and consider status important experience much greater stress than equal-status mates or those individuals who marry persons of higher status. His study of 2,300 spouses in urbanized Chicago indicated that this particular form of status inequality leads to breakdowns in reciprocity, affection and communication exchange, and value consensus, which in turn lead to stress. On the other hand, women who are full participants in the labor force and who make high earnings are more likely to divorce than those who are economically dependent on their husbands (Teachman, Polonko, and Scanzoni 1987). This suggests that, under certain conditions, an equalization of statuses and economic power between husband and wife can make divorce a realistic alternative.

Child and Wife Abuse

The preceding discussion indicates that family problems are related to socioeconomic position. This relationship extends to the areas of child and wife abuse, as well. Over the last two decades, there has been a marked increase in the number of reported cases of child abuse and neglect in the United States, rising on average about 9 percent a year since 1980. In 1992, just under 3,000,000 children were reported as abuse/neglect cases to Child Protective Services agencies. Most of the victims are White, but a disproportionate number (about 25 percent) are Black. A majority of maltreatment victims are female (Schmittroth 1994). The accuracy and stability of these rate statistics, however, have been extensively criticized (Starr 1988; Hampton 1987; Faller and Ziefert 1981). Most of the data, for example, show that lower socioeconomic status groups have a higher rate of child and wife abuse than higher status groups (cf. Gil 1971; Garbarino 1976; Biller and Solomon 1986). But the assumptions about abuse that are drawn from these conclusions can be dangerous. Lystad has proposed that upper status persons are more likely to get help from private physicians than lower status persons who are more likely to wind up at a state or county hospital, which has to report the abuse (1975). Moreover, a whole host of individual characteristics, relationship variables, and social-cultural factors have been linked to abuse, with socioeconomic factors being only one of these (cf. Van Hasselt et al. 1988). "While poverty may well be fertile ground for abuse or neglect tendencies to mature, a great deal of variability exists within the poverty population. Ignoring these demographic, ethnic, and functional variations may well lead to faulty conclusions regarding the underlying causes of maltreatment and the most effective interventions" (Daro 1988, p. 65).

What constitutes "abuse" is also open to question. For example, the percentage of those who feel that a "good, hard spanking" is sometimes necessary for disciplining children has declined in recent years, suggesting that a higher percentage would now consider such action to be abuse (Gallup 1995).

Despite these considerations, research has repeatedly found an inverse relationship between lower socioeconomic status and child abuse. Such status, of course, is connected with other factors related to abuse—for example, slightly larger families, unemployment, poorer health and housing, social isolation, and lack of a support network. Lower educational and occupational attainment

are among the other stressors related to child abuse (Biller and Solomon 1986). However, poverty is not a necessary cause of abuse, nor is abuse confined to the lower class. Moreover, most poor parents do not abuse their children (Faller and Ziefert 1981; Gelles and Cornell 1985).

The factors associated with abuse suggest that the *social contacts* in which persons of lower SES operate are a major source of child abuse (Gil 1975). Thus, parents guilty of child abuse should not be seen as sadists who alone are responsible for their conduct. A "subculture of violence" argument that focuses complete blame on the abuser is misplaced (Erlanger 1974; Giovannoni and Billingsley 1970; Gil 1971, 1975). Rather, the conditions in which individuals live and their lack of meaningful ties to the larger society contribute to stresses that in turn activate abuse. Furthermore, a culture that itself supports familial violence through its reluctance to interfere in the relationship between parents and children and that actively supports competitions in which only the "qualified" survive while many others "lose" contributes to the generation and widespread prevalence of child abuse (Gil 1971, 1975; Giovannoni and Billingsley 1970).

Most of the studies mentioned here specifically point to the fact that abusive or neglectful parents (or both) are frequently cut off from connections to institutions that might help them. In his report on child abuse in 58 New York counties in 1973, Garbarino (1976) concluded that "such appears to be a major feature of the human ecology of child abuse/maltreatment: economically depressed mothers, often alone in the role of parent, attempting to cope in isolation without adequate facilities and resources for their children" (p. 183). The stresses placed on mothers in poverty seem to be especially important, including the relative and absolute deprivations of "demeaning and debilitating social statuses" (Lystad 1975). Unemployment, overcrowding, dilapidated housing, low incomes, and the frequent presence of only one parent create further pressures and frustrations. Given these conditions, one has to be careful where to point the finger of blame. Gil (1975), in fact, has proposed a very broad definition of child abuse in this regard. He refers to it as "inflicted gaps or deficits between circumstances of living which would facilitate the optimal development of children, *irrespective of the sources or agents of the deficit*" (pp. 346–347, emphasis added). He rightly suggested child abuse can take place on the institutional and societal level as well as in the family.

Consistent relationships between race and likelihood of abuse have not been found. But among abusing families, those that are African American tend to be poorer and female headed, with younger parents who have less education and are more likely to be unemployed (Hampton 1987). Some studies have found that a greater proportion of child abusers are women, but these studies often do not control for family type. Within families where both spouses are present, men are more often the abusers. In female-headed families, which are more likely to be poor and subject to many stresses, females of course are more often the perpetrators. But when men are present, men are more often abusive (Gelles and Cornell 1985; Biller and Solomon 1986). Younger children and children in larger families are more vulnerable to abuse.

The effects of abuse carry over into adulthood, especially for women. A greater proportion of women who were abused as children experience depression, low self-esteem, and a higher chance for alcoholism (Banyard 1999; Langeland and Hartgers 1998). Some may even experience abuse as wives. Statistics on wife battering suffer from many of the same problems as those on child abuse. A low estimate is that at least 1.8 million wives were severely assaulted by their husbands in 1985. Considering that these figures do not include mild forms of violence or date or nonmarried partner violence, and that the average abused wife is abused three times a year, it is likely that the amount of abuse against women is much higher than these figures suggest (Straus and Gelles 1990; Gelles and Cornell 1990).

Many, if not most, incidents of wife battering, however, never come to the attention of authorities.

Even confidential reports underestimate the extent of the problem because of the embarrassment and sensitivity of the problem, the belief on the part of some that a certain amount of violence is "normal" and even acceptable, and because many who are abused look for help outside official channels, such as from other couples (Margolin, Sibner, and Gleberman 1988). Finding agreement on what constitutes wife abuse also has been difficult, and definitions vary from state to state.

As is the case in child abuse, a large number of factors have been found to be related to wife abuse. Black women are victims of abuse more often than White women, but this may be due in part to the fact that they are more likely to report it and a confounding of race with income and other socioeconomic factors (Casanave and Straus 1979; Hampton 1987; Stark and Flitcraft 1988). Most studies, including those done on a national level, have found an inverse relationship between social class and wife abuse. Part of the difference between the classes may be due to the reporting issues on the statistics discussed earlier. Unemployment of the husband also has been found to be related to greater probability of abuse. Men who work part time or are unemployed have rates of abuse that are about twice as high as those for husbands who are fully employed (Gelles and Cornell 1990). On a more general level, neighborhoods that contain populations with lower educations, lower incomes, poorer housing, and higher unemployment and welfare rates have been found to have higher rates of spousal abuse (Miles-Doan 1998).

Some evidence also shows that the degree of status inconsistency between spouses may be related to wife abuse. Specifically, wives whose educational and occupational statuses are higher than those of their husbands' may be at greater risk than wives whose statuses are consistent with those of their husbands (Hotaling and Sugarman 1984; Stark and Flitcraft 1988). Moreover, there is some evidence that working wives whose earnings approach or equal those of their working husbands are also at greater risk for abuse by their husbands. This suggests that when the breadwinner role of the husband is jeopardized, the probability for abuse may be greater because his domestic control is at stake. In this context, child abuse as a way of controlling the wife is also more likely (McCloskey 1996). Domestic violence also seems to be related to the balance of power within families, with democratic, egalitarian families having the lowest rates of violence (Gelles and Cornell 1990).

The preceding discussion indicates that social inequality is implicated in wife abuse. It has been suggested by theorists of patriarchy that as long as a society's values and institutions support male dominance over women, then wife abuse will continue, because such behavior is a manifestation of the greater power and status of men. The institution of the "ideal" family with its male "head," and other legal, economic, political, and social institutions help to maintain the power of men over women. Moreover, women and men are socialized to believe in and accept the inequality between them (Dobash and Dobash 1979; Bersani and Chen 1988). This patriarchy theory of abuse has been criticized for not considering the influence of a number of other factors in domestic violence and by focusing primarily on spouse abuse while ignoring child abuse (Bersani and Chen 1988).

If patriarchy is an important element in the explanation of wife abuse, then one should expect to find that in those societies where women have higher statuses there will be less abuse than in those where women are completely dominated by men. Reports from a study done on 90 small and peasant societies from all over the world indicate that wife beating is the kind of family violence found most often, occurring in almost 85 percent of these societies. It occurs in over 50 percent of the homes in almost half of these societies, but seldom or never in only about 16 percent (Levinson 1988). Evidence from this study suggests that an economic version of the patriarchy theory may be viable. Abuse is more frequent where men are in full authority in the family and control wealth and labor than in societies where women are in control in the household and can acquire wealth and property on their own (Levinson 1988). Interestingly, other research indicates that wife abuse may be re-

lated in a curvilinear manner to status, with women being most likely to be victims in places where they occupy either the lowest *or* highest status (Yllo 1983, 1984).

SUMMARY

This chapter has focused on a variety of areas concerning personal life chances in different racial, gender, and SES groups. It appears clear that the latter factors are related to physical and mental health in several ways. Moreover, these groups also tend to use health services in different ways, to contact doctors and dentists at different rates, and to differ in the likelihood of possessing health insurance and taking preventive health measures. Inequality also is related to the problems of hunger and homelessness. Finally, it affects family stability and the probability of family violence. Table 11.1 summarizes the relationships that have been explored in this chapter.

Two points should be made about the research conducted on these relationships. First, frequently different measures of SES have been used in studies on the same issue, and, for the sake of convenience, the term *social class* has been used in this chapter as if it were synonymous with SES measures. Second, although significant relationships have been found between race, gender, and SES, on the one hand, and health, on the other hand, I do not want to suggest that these are the only variables or always the most important variables in explaining variations. Rather, the question of interest has been whether inequality in its various forms plays any role in producing various personal life chances. It seems apparent that it does. Indirectly, the organization of a competitive capitalist society and, more directly, the system of inequality that it creates, results in individuals and families being placed in different positions regarding access to and possibilities of gaining the "good things" in life. At the same time, the lack of economic power of some individuals affects relationships at home. Unemployed housewives are more likely to experience various symptoms of distress, and families in which there is a clear imbalance of power between

TABLE 11.1 Summary of the Relationships Found between Gender, Race, Socioeconomic Status, and Life Chances

CONDITION	GENDER	RACE	SOCIOECONOMIC STATUS
Self-assessments of their health	X	X	X
Life expectancies	X	X	
Acute and chronic conditions	X		X
Life-threatening conditions	X		
Frequent physician and dentist visits	X	X	X
Mortality rates		X	X
Hospital visits and stays	X	X	X
Evaluations of health care	X	X	
Diagnosed with depressive or histrionic mental disorders	X		
Dental or health insurance		X	X
Feelings of control over their lives	X	X	X
Feelings of well-being and/or life satisfaction	X	X	X
Divorce		X	X
More difficult access to health care		X	X
Diagnosed with paranoid schizophrenia (males)		X	
Work days lost due to illness			X
Mental illness and distress			X
Family abuse			X

parents are more likely than egalitarian families to contain domestic violence. In many ways, then, the effects of inequality reach inside the intimate lives of families and individuals. In Chapter 12, we turn from these personal effects of inequality to more societywide effects—crime and collective unrest.

CRITICAL THINKING

1. How do you think your gender, race, and socioeconomic position have affected your path through life thus far?

2. To what extent should individuals be held responsible for their health and actions if these are shaped by their opportunities and circumstances?

3. What can be done to alleviate the negative effects of inequality on people's lives?

WEB CONNECTIONS

The University of Michigan's Documents Center is a wonderful source of information, and includes data on basic life chances. For example, it provides information on the number of people with mental illness, life expectancy, top hospitals by locale, effects of welfare reform on loss of health insurance, and health insurance ownership by resident's state and socioeconomic characteristics. How does your state compare with others? Visit:

http://www.lib.umich.edu/libhome/
Documents.center/sthealth.html/#healthcare

CHAPTER 12

CRIME, PROTEST, AND INEQUALITY

The frustrated expectation of equality has been a major factor in all major revolutionary upheavals since Luther posted his Ninety-five Theses on the Wittenberg church door. Indeed, since long before that.
—James Davies

As you know from the previous chapter, various forms of inequality deeply affect the lives of individuals. But as you will see in this chapter, inequality also helps create problems for society as a whole, such as crime and social unrest.

INEQUALITY AND CRIME

The likelihood of individuals committing crime has been linked to their social-class position, and on a broader level, the extent and nature of inequality in a society have been causally connected to its crime rate. More specifically, inequality has been related to the nature and collection of crime statistics, the likelihood of arrest, the social production of crime, and sentencing. In other words, its effect appears to contaminate most phases of the criminal justice process.

The Inadequacy of Crime Statistics

Unfortunately, discussions about the relationship between inequality and crime are mired in disagreements about the definition of *crime* and the varying statistics about it. Controversy about what constitutes crime and how criminals are detected and arrested make definitive conclusions about this relationship difficult.

Clearly, labels applied to persons and actions have an impact on what behaviors are defined as criminal, how much laws are enforced, and how the behavior of individuals is interpreted. Because of this, the definition of "the crime problem" is a social construction, and the definitions given by some groups may be favored over those of others. Perhaps you consider the crime problem to consist mainly of street crimes such as rape, robbery, murder, and the like, but others may feel that the real crime problem is found in white-collar crime that costs billions of dollars every year and yet receives little attention in the popular press. In the small city in which I live, it is now illegal to "cruise" the downtown in the evenings, a pastime previously engaged in by many youths. What defines *cruising* is rather arbitrary, however. *Loitering* is another rather vaguely defined illegal act. The more one examines various "crimes," the more it becomes evident that they are defined into existence.

Similarly, once laws and crimes are defined, their enforcement is also uneven. This selective enforcement is a means for ensuring that groups are kept in their respective places.

Unequal administration of the law is functional because it keeps the status arrangements of society from being disrupted. When, for example, a drunk

241

appears in public, police often react differently in terms of his social status. If he is lower class, he has a good chance of being arrested. If he is upper or middle class, he will more likely be driven home. Middle- and upper-class people, who control the administration of justice, want these laws enforced only against a certain segment of the population. (Reid 1988, p. 36)

Several scholars have suggested that the police are biased against those in the lower class and, thus, are more likely to arrest them than individuals in higher classes who commit the same offenses (Turk 1969; Quinney 1970). In sum, these and similar observations should make us wary in drawing conclusions about crime because statistics about it have several shortcomings.

Even self-report studies have potential biases built into them: (1) respondents may misunderstand the question or understand it differently; (2) persons may wish to shock or impress the in-

terviewer; and, perhaps most important, (3) respondents, especially adults, may be unwilling to admit the commission of a crime (see Tittle and Villemez 1977). Self-report studies, in which respondents indicate whether they have committed certain illegal acts, have been criticized for (1) being less valid for some classes than others, (2) containing primarily trivial criminal acts and excluding more serious crimes, (3) focusing on single sites or areas that are class-homogenous, (4) focusing on continuous socioeconomic status scores rather than discrete classes as measures that are relevant to the commission of crime, and (5) excluding school dropouts and absentees from surveys, thereby minimizing the probability of finding a class effect (Kleck 1982).

Unfortunately, except for some self-report studies, for the most part, all we have are the official statistics on which most studies have been based. We must keep both statistical inadequacies and possible shortcomings in mind when drawing conclusions about the relationship between crime rates and socioeconomic status.

Our discussion of the relationship between inequality and crime/delinquency in sections of this chapter covers "street," "suite," and hate crimes. Included are discussions of several phases of the criminal justice process, starting with arrests and the commission of crime and ending with sentencing.

Street Crime and Inequality

Crime rates are ordinarily determined by using the FBI's Crime Index, which includes both property crimes (burglary, larceny-theft, motor vehicle theft, arson) and violent crimes (murder, forcible rape, robbery, and aggravated assault). One of the problems with this list of "street" crimes is that it does not include any serious, very costly white-collar, corporate, or "suite" crimes as they are sometimes called. Since the latter are largely crimes perpetrated by middle- or upper-class individuals, it would be a mistake to look only at the Index crimes to reach a conclusion about the relationship between race, sex, socio-

A lot of evidence suggests that the scales of justice may be tilted against the more powerless of our society.

economic status, and crime. To do so would bias the conclusion against individuals in lower social and economic rankings.

Another point to keep in mind when examining crime and delinquency rates is the manner in which arrests are sometimes made. Whether or not individuals have encounters with police or are arrested appears to be related to the socioeconomic status of the persons involved. Police generally have particular images of delinquents, stereotypes that result in lower-class persons being arrested more often (Sampson 1986). In essence, police have certain expectations of the criminal behavior of youths, and these images lead them to monitor and arrest youths in the lower class more often, regardless of the frequency of their actual criminal behavior (Irwin 1985). Similarly, in studies comparing Black and White youths, there is evidence of police stereotypes that results in biases against Blacks. Accounts given by police indicate that they develop negative stereotypes of Blacks in the course of their work (Waegel 1984).

The negative perceptions of lower-class youths by police lead the latter to label whole neighborhoods as being contaminated because they are made up of individuals who are considered undesirable (Irwin 1985; Sampson 1986). The result is that the general socioeconomic status of a neighborhood can influence the attention paid to it and its inhabitants by authorities. A study by Sampson (1986), using data from the Seattle Youth Study, found that the number of contacts and reports by police is strongly and inversely related to the neighborhood's general SES, independent of the actual extent of criminal and delinquent behavior in the area. He concluded that "for the bulk of offenses typically committed by juveniles (e.g., larceny, fighting, vandalism, burglary, drug violations) official police records and referrals to court are structured not simply by the act itself but by socioeconomic and situational context (e.g., delinquency of friends) as well, a process which may in turn amplify the effect of prior record in later decisions concerning official delinquents" (1986, p. 884).

All of this research strongly suggests that the ecological area and perceptions of law officials affect the relationship between official rates of crime/delinquency and social class. These additional limitations of official statistics should be kept in mind when viewing the information in Table 12.1, which presents the arrest distributions for Index crimes by race and sex of those arrested. In 1997, there were 1,910,953 arrests made for such crimes, and 75 percent of those arrested were males. The highest arrest rate for females was for larceny-theft (35 percent). In recent years, the arrest rates for women have increased. While the majority of those arrested in 1997, with the exception of robbery and murder, were Whites, Blacks were disproportionately represented in the arrest rates for all Index crimes. In fact, the majority arrested for robbery and murder were Blacks, and 40 percent of all those arrested for forcible rape were Blacks. In total, 41 percent of all those arrested for violent crimes and 32 percent of those arrested for property crimes were Black. A small percentage of arrests, generally 2 to 3 percent, involve American Indians, Alaskan Natives, Asians, or Pacific Islanders.

Social Class and the Commission of Crime

The statistics just presented suggest strongly that Blacks and males are more likely to commit crimes than their counterparts, and that the differences in arrest rates are too large to believe otherwise (LaFree 1995). However, as you will see in the next section, the differences in rates between Blacks and Whites are not due primarily to cultural differences between these groups, but to differences in the structural contexts in which they live. That is to say that the causes of Black crime are similar to the causes of crime by any group, but Blacks are exposed more forcefully and thoroughly to social contexts that encourage criminal behavior. Much of this context involves elements related to inequality such as poverty, economic discrepancies, social isolation, poor jobs, and unemployment.

In contrast to the apparently clear relationships between race, sex, and crime, the relationship

TABLE 12.1 Arrests by Index Offense Charged, Estimated Distributions by Sex and
Race: 1997

	PERSONS ARRESTED				
OFFENSE CHARGED	% Male	% Female	% White	% Black	% Other[a]
Murder and nonnegligent manslaughter	90	10	42	56	2
Forcible rape	99	1	58	40	2
Robbery	90	10	41	57	2
Aggravated assault	81	19	61	37	2
Burglary	88	12	68	30	2
Larceny-theft	65	35	65	32	3
Motor-vehicle theft	85	15	58	39	3
Arson	85	15	73	25	2
Violent crime[b]	84	16	57	41	2
Property crime[c]	71	29	65	32	3
Total Crime Index	75	26	63	35	3
Total Index arrests = 1,910,953					

Source: Uniform Crime Reports for the United States 1997 (Washington, DC: Federal Bureau of Investigation, 1998).

Note: Totals may not add up to 100% because of rounding.
[a]American Indian, Alaskan Native, Asian, or Pacific Islander.
[b]Violent crimes are murder, forcible rape, robbery, and aggravated assault.
[c]Property crimes are burglary, larceny-theft, motor-vehicle theft, and arson.

between social class and crime/delinquency has been a source of great controversy. Certainly there are theories that suggest that the definition of crime, the enforcement of laws, and the judicial and sentencing procedures work against the lower classes, which are reflected in higher crime rates and more severe sentencing for those groups.

Overviews of studies done on the relationship between social class/socioeconomic status and crime/delinquency have not been consistent. Tittle and his colleagues (1978) concluded after their review of 35 studies that the relationship between social status and official crime rates is only weak and that the relationship of status to self-reported crime is nonexistent. They argue that "class and criminality are not now, and probably never were related, at least not during the recent past" (p. 652). However, another review of over 100

studies by Braithwaite (1981) reached the opposite conclusion—that is, that there is quite a bit of support for the inverse relationship between class and crime.

A large part of the explanation for discrepancies in findings, on this relationship appears to relate to the measures used for social class and crime (Kleck 1981). Virtually all of the studies in recent years have used occupational prestige, income, or educational hierarchies as measures of class, rather than Marxian measures (e.g., ownership, control over labor, etc.). Hagan and his colleagues (1985, 1987) suggested that differences in power ought to be more fully incorporated into studies of class and crime. This is especially relevant for studies purporting to understand the relationship between gender and crime. When one considers that power differences frequently separate men and women in families and may be directly linked to the probability of white-collar crime, the request for other measures of class seems more than reasonable.

To test their ideas about the importance of power differences in producing common delinquency, Hagan and his associates (1985, 1987) collected data from students in Toronto and used a measure of authority and ownership to determine the position of men and women in the households. The common delinquent acts included less serious behaviors such as minor theft, fighting, minor vandalism, and the like. The authors hypothesized that in families in which wives and daughters have little power, there is less freedom and risk taking on the part of women. Hence, they will be significantly less likely than the sons to commit delinquent acts. It is in these types of families that gender differences in delinquency will be most pronounced. On the other hand, in those in which females have some freedom and can take risks, there will be little difference between the sexes in their delinquency rates. Analyses by Hagan and his colleagues supported these hypotheses and also revealed that the gender differences in delinquency declined as one went down the class hierarchy. Gender differences were largest in the employer class. A large part of the reason for this gender difference seems to be that sons in this class have greater power relative to their mothers and are not taking as great a risk in being punished as are daughters. In other words, the authors pointed out again that gender differences in delinquency are linked to power differences in the family, which in turn are a reflection of power differences in the workplace.

The Structure of Inequality and the Social Production of Crime

When it comes to the commission of crime, an analysis of its relationship to inequality involves more than just examining the connection between the statuses of individuals and the commission of crime. At the social-structural level, or macrolevel, the system of inequality itself may be related to the generation of crime rates. This section examines this possibility as it appears in theory and research.

The generation of crime and varying crime rates appears to be intimately connected to the organization and culture of U.S. society. Homicide and incarceration rates in the United States are higher than those of any other industrialized nation. "In short, at all social levels, America is organized for crime" (Messner and Rosenfeld 1994, p. 6). Our capitalistic emphases on individual competition and economic success at almost any cost in the context of a system in which rewards are unequally divided encourages ventures outside the law, especially because economic success is so frequently used as a measure of a person's worth (Messner and Rosenfeld 1994; Gordon 1973). Gordon theorized that crime in this institutional context becomes a rational response to the manner in which society is organized.

Indeed, a great deal of research indicates that structural features related to economic inequality are significantly linked to the creation of street crime, and of course it is generally members of minorities and the lower classes that are most likely to experience life on the lower rungs of the economic ladder. At the social level, poverty rates, economic deprivation, income inequality, unemployment, and employment in unstable jobs have all been found to be positively related to crime rates (e.g., Blau and Blau 1982; Williams 1984; Williams and Flewelling 1988; Crutchfield 1995; Kposowa, Breault, and Harrison 1995).

Ehrlich's 1973 analysis of the FBI Crime Index in different states in 1940, 1950, and 1960 found a strong relationship between the degree of income inequality in a state and its property crime rate. Unemployment rates also have been found to be related to property crime rates. Extensive reviews of studies suggest strongly that unemployment and property crime are positively related (Devine, Sheley, and Smith 1988; Chiricos 1987). These studies rely heavily on official rather than self-reported statistics. In a longitudinal study, Cantor and Land (1985) examined rates for seven Index crimes from 1946 to 1982. Their results are valuable because they indicate that unemployment can have both positive and negative effects on crime, depending on the particular crime in question. Specifically, unemployment can have a dampening effect on the crime rate because it means in part that the opportunity to be a victim of a property or violent crime is lower. When people are unemployed, they are at home, among friends and relatives, "guarding" property more often. This means that they are less likely to be victims of crimes by a stranger. On the other hand, unemployment has a positive effect on criminal motivation, thereby increasing the probability of crime, especially property crime.

At the individual level, employment has been found to be related to a lower probability of committing a crime. An experimental study of over 2,000 ex-offenders in Texas and Georgia revealed that those who were given employment were less likely to commit a crime after being released than those who were not given employment (Berk, Lenihan, and Rossi 1980). Moreover, those who were given some money in the form of transfer payments, which in effect reduced their poverty, were less likely to commit a crime. The latter suggests that there may be a trade-off between unemployment/poverty and crime. Among African American teenagers, employment and criminal behavior do appear to be used as substitutes. Both are viewed as income-producing activities. African American teenagers who are employed engage in fewer criminal behaviors and vice versa. Involvement in criminal activity, in turn, results in less employment (Good and Pirog-Good 1987; Freeman 1989). Not only unemployment itself, but the quality of employment can have an effect on property crime rates. Among young adults, those with poor-paying jobs having bad hours are more likely to be arrested for property crimes (Allan and Steffensmeier 1989). Having a criminal record, in turn, affects the chances of being employed over the long run (Thornberry and Christenson 1984).

In addition to property crime, violent crime is also related to inequality of different types. Gender inequality, for example, has been linked to homicide rates in developed countries. Child homicide rates are higher in developed countries in which there is (1) high female labor-force participation but (2) little child support for them and (3) low female status in the society (Fiala and LaFree 1988). This combination creates greater economic stress that heightens the likelihood for child abuse and homicide. Nations that provide more public assistance to mothers in the form of family allowances or social security programs have lower rates of such homicide. It has been argued elsewhere that not alleviating this kind of stress among women in families increases child abuse and is part of the reason why the United States has a higher rate of abuse than many other developed countries (Kamerman 1980; Zigler and Muenchow 1983).

The Blau and Blau (1982) study of inequality and violent crime rates in metropolitan areas used official crime statistics from the largest 125 metropolitan areas in the United States to find out if the crime rates varied with the extent of socioeconomic inequality in the area. Theoretically, they reasoned that in a democracy, inequalities based on skill or other achieved qualities are perceived as justifiable, while those based on ascribed characteristics such as race or sex are not. When a nominal or horizontal trait like race is closely connected to the vertical structure of economic inequality, racial and class differences become consolidated, and conflict between groups results in the society. One result of this situation is higher violent crime rates. Their findings bear out this theory. Economic inequality generally, and racial socioeconomic inequality in particular, is related to the production of violent crimes. Areas with greater inequality have higher crime rates. Inequality, rather than racial composition of an area, is principally related to violent crime rates.

Messner's (1989) cross-national study of homicide rates supports the Blau and Blau theory, as well. Messner predicted that countries with greater ascribed economic inequality in the form of discrimination would have higher homicide rates. While his measures of discrimination are rather crude, the analysis of data from 52 nation-states confirms this hypothesis and, in fact, demonstrates that inequality in the form of economic discrimination is more strongly related to homicide rates than is the extent of overall income inequality. This suggests that the *form* of inequality may be more important than its *extent* in accounting for homicide rates.

A reanalysis of the Blau data by Williams (1984) suggested that poverty may indeed also be related to homicide rates, especially in areas outside the South. This supports the findings of other studies (e.g., Danziger and Wheeler 1975; Messner 1980; Loftin and Hill 1974; Williams and Flewelling 1988). As Williams and Flewelling stated, "It is reasonable to assume that when people live under conditions of extreme scarcity, the struggle for survival is intensified. Such conditions are often accompanied by a host of agitating psychological manifestations, ranging from a deep sense of powerlessness and brutalization to anger, anxiety, and alienation. Such manifestations can provoke physical aggression in conflict situations" (1988, p. 423).

Given this proposal, let us consider the situation of Blacks living in the interior of a city. Residential segregation is extensive in U.S. society and has not declined in recent years. Over 80 percent of Blacks would have to move for society to be fully integrated. The vast majority live in cities, not suburbs, and are isolated from Whites since most live in neighborhoods that are largely Black. Thus, what exists is a concentration of the Black population in ghettos, the city as having "a black core surrounded by a white ring" (Massey and Denton 1993, p. 67). Many Blacks are "hypersegregated"—a term used by Massey and Denton to describe a living situation in which Blacks are not only heavily concentrated in given areas and isolated from Whites but also clustered and concentrated in limited areas and centralized in the center of the city (1993).

Such residential segregation itself is largely a result of inequality processes. Early in the twentieth century, Blacks moved in large numbers from the South to the North, frequently recruited by employers who were fighting unions and who wished to use Blacks as strikebreakers. This only intensified racist feelings among Whites. Fear by Whites led to "restrictive covenants" in neighborhoods and blockbusting by real estate dealers who hoped to profit from the Black migration. Later, movement of industry out of cities and increasingly poor opportunities for stable employment impoverished these areas. These developments led to the consequent concentration of Blacks into isolated, packed, poor neighborhoods or ghettos.

What is important about such segregation is that it "is not a neutral fact;...Because of racial segregation, a significant share of black America is condemned to experience a social environment where poverty and joblessness are the norm, where a majority of children are born out of wedlock, where most families are on welfare, where educational failure prevails, and where social and physical deterioration abound. Through prolonged exposure to such an environment, black chances for social and economic success are drastically reduced." And just as importantly, its effect is structural: "Residential segregation lies beyond the ability of any individual to change; it constrains black life chances irrespective of personal traits, individual motivations, or private achievements" (Massey and Denton 1993, pp. 2–3). Figure 12.1 captures much of the context in which ghetto residents live and the factors that have created it.

The concentration of poverty and unemployment in these isolated and highly dense areas of cities has led to a stable underclass, the collapse of effective institutions (family disorganization, poor housing, poor employment opportunities), and the development of cultural adaptations that undermine mainstream values. There is little to bind individuals to the community. Consequently, social controls to minimize crime are not in place; neither institutions nor cultural values are effective in controlling crime in this context. Segregation and Black isolation from Whites are highly and directly related to higher rates of violence (Olzak, Shanahan, and McEneaney 1996; Shihadeh and

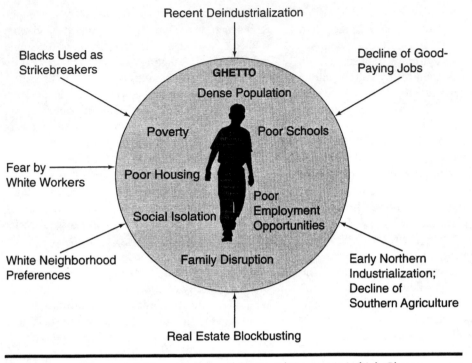

FIGURE 12.1   Causes and Characteristics of the Social Context in Which Ghetto Residents Live

Source: Based on Massey and Denton 1993.

Flynn 1996). This setting results in fewer opportunities and less attachment of Blacks to the wider society and its values. Higher crime rates follow, as do victimization rates, and since it is Blacks who are concentrated in these areas, it is their rates that spiral upward. Generally, victimization rates for property and violent crimes are higher among Blacks (see Table 12.2). The victimization rate for murder is especially high among young Black males. The rate among Black males 18 to 24 years of age, for example, is 10 times higher than it is among White males of the same age (Maguire and Pastore 1995).

What is clear in the research done is that the causes of crime and victimization among Blacks are not unique. Any individual exposed to this environment over time is vulnerable to criminal behavior and victimization (Sampson and Wilson 1995; Kposowa, Breault, and Harrison 1995).

Thus, to understand differences in crime and victimization rates between rich and poor, Blacks and Whites, we need to appreciate the social context that generates such differences. And, as you have seen, this is a context largely created by and resulting in multidimensional inequality.

All of these results suggest that changes in the structures of capitalism and inequality would result in changes in crime rates. Danziger and Wheeler's (1975) research suggested that income distribution affects crime rates and that reduced inequality is related to reduced crime rates. They contend, as others have, that inequality generates crime both of the street and suite variety. They concluded from their analysis of 57 large metropolitan areas that "levels of criminal activity are responsive to changes in the distribution of income…a one percent reduction in…inequality was shown to reduce crime to a larger extent than

TABLE 12.2 Rates of Victimization in Violent and Property Crimes, by Race and Sex: 1993

	WHITE	BLACK	MALE	FEMALE
Violent Crimes (per 1,000 persons 12 and older)	50	66	61	42
Rape/Sexual assault	2	3	0	4
Robbery	5	13	8	4
Assault	42	51	52	34
Purse snatching/Pocket picking	2	6	2	3
Murder/Nonnegligent homicide (per 100,000)	5	38	15	4
Property Crimes (per 1,000 households)	315	369		
Household burglary	57	86		
Motor-vehicle theft	17	34		
Other theft	241	250		

Source: Kathleen Maguire and Ann L. Pastore (Eds.), *Sourcebook of Criminal Justice Statistics— 1994* in U.S. Department of Justice, Bureau of Justice Statistics (Washington, DC: U.S. Government Printing Office, 1995), pp. 231–232, 240, 339–340.

Note: Rates rounded off to nearest whole number.

a one percent increase in deterrence" (1975, pp. 126–127).

Inequality and Criminal Sentencing

Once arrested for commission of a serious crime, Blacks, those with lower educations, and those from the lower class are more likely to have a court decision made against them, to be labeled as criminal, and/or given more severe punishments than their counterparts (Chiricos, Jackson, and Waldo 1972; Chambliss 1969). The issue of sentencing goes to the heart of questions about the fairness of the criminal justice system. We have seen that inequality is related to crime at the individual level and to crime rates at the structural level. Next, we ask if, once arrested and convicted of a crime, individuals in different socioeconomic positions are likely to receive similar sentences. Do the populations of correctional facilities represent a cross-section of the American public? Does an individual's position in the system of inequality affect length or type of sentence, even when the crime and criminal record

are taken into account? Certainly, the information in Table 12.3 implies that social class, race, and sex do make a difference.

Table 12.3 presents a profile of those found in U.S. jails and state prisons. As the table indicates, in 1996, almost 9 out of 10 jail inmates were male and a majority were White. The population of state prisons is disproportionately male, Black, and poorly educated, and almost one-third had been unemployed prior to being arrested. Blacks and Hispanics are also overrepresented in federal prisons, as well.

How does one account for the disproportionate numbers of lower-ranking groups in correctional facilities? If these groups have higher crime rates, then one might expect to find them overrepresented in jails and prisons. However, given the issues concerning (1) the definition and creation of crime statistics, (2) the studies of arrest suggesting some bias against lower status groups, and (3) the inconsistency in many studies on the relationship between race, class, and crime, there is reason to be at least minimally suspicious of the conclusion that higher crime rates are the only or

TABLE 12.3 Percent Distribution of Jail Inmates (1996) and State Prison Inmates (1991)

	JAIL INMATES (1996)	PRISON INMATES (1991)
Male	89	95
Female	11	6
White	56	49
Black	43	47
Other	2	4
Less than 12 years education		41
12 years or more education		59
Prearrest Employment		
Employed		67
Not employed, looking		16
Not employed, not looking		16

Source: U.S. Bureau of the Census, *Statistical Abstract of the United States 1995 and 1998* (Washington, DC: U.S. Government Printing Office), p. 217.

even the primary reason for the strong connection between status and being incarcerated.

With respect to gender bias, recent studies are more mixed in their results than earlier ones that suggested a paternalistic or chivalric reaction to female offenders. Nagel and Weitzman's (1971) often-cited study of national data concerning over 11,000 criminal cases revealed that while the poor and Blacks received less favorable treatment than well-off Whites, women were treated more leniently. They were less likely to be held in jail before the trial and to be sentenced to prison. The analysis focused on the crimes of grand larceny and assault. A study by Curran (1983) in Florida supported the leniency argument. She found that at the sentencing stage of the criminal process women received lighter sentences even when relevant legal (e.g., prior arrests, etc.) and other nonlegal factors (race, age, occupational status) were taken into account. Other studies, however, have suggested that the courts have become less chivalrous in their behavior toward women, and that if the criminal act for which a woman is ar-

rested is considered a "manly" crime, she may receive a longer sentence than a man (Simon and Sharma 1979; Kruttschnitt and Green 1984).

Whether a judge is male or female also affects the probability of incarceration and length of sentence. In contrast to the image of women as more lenient, female judges tend to be harsher in their sentencing. They are more likely than male judges to incarcerate an offender and for a longer period of time. Judges of both genders are less likely to incarcerate White, older, and female offenders, but this is especially the case for female judges. Female judges are significantly more likely than their male counterparts to give longer sentences to Black repeat offenders. In other words, offender characteristics affect the decisions of women on the bench more so than those of male judges (Steffensmeier and Hebert 1999).

The studies just discussed suggest that Blacks receive harsher sentences than Whites for the same property crimes. Table 12.4 shows the differences in sentences served by different groups *released for the first time* from prison. In other words, this table does not include repeat offenders who have been released. Overall, there is only a slight difference in the median number of months served by Black and White first-releases. When specific crimes are considered, however, differences appear in some cases, with Black males serving significantly more time than White males for homicide, rape, and kidnapping. Historically, Blacks have been heavily overrepresented on death row, along with others with low socioeconomic status (U.S. Department of Justice 1976, pp. 2–3). Of the 455 rapists who were put to death between 1930 and 1975, 405 were Black; of the convicted murderers, 49 percent were Black. No executions were recorded for the period from 1968 to 1975, but between 1977 and 1993, 39 percent of the 224 executed were Black (U.S. Bureau of the Census 1996). Forty-two percent of those in prison under a death sentence in 1995 were Black (Maguire and Pastore 1997).

Suggestive as these statistics are, however, they do not constitute conclusive evidence that Blacks or those in poorer circumstances are more

TABLE 12.4   Median Number of Months Served by First Releases from State Prisons in 36 States, by Crime, Race, and Sex: 1992

	WHITE MALES	BLACK MALES	WHITE FEMALES	BLACK FEMALES
All Crimes	13	14	10	10
Violent Crimes	23	26	20	19
Homicide	38	56	34	39
Kidnapping	25	36	25	51
Rape	42	55	44	45
Other sexual assault	25	22	24	26
Robbery	26	28	18	18
Assault	15	16	16	13
Other violent crimes	14	19	11	13
Property Crimes	11	11	8	7
Burglary	14	16	11	11
Larceny-theft	9	9	8	7
Motor-vehicle theft	11	11	8	5
Arson	17	21	15	12
Fraud	10	9	8	7
Drug Crimes	13	12	10	10

Source: Kathleen Maguire and Ann L. Pastore (Eds.), *Sourcebook of Criminal Justice Statistics—1994* in U.S. Department of Justice, Bureau of Justice Statistics (Washington, DC: U.S. Government Printing Office, 1995), p. 556.

harshly sentenced than those in higher ranking groups. The findings from research on this issue are mixed. A number of studies lend support to the belief that those in lower statuses receive more severe sentences (Bedau 1964; Judson et al. 1969; Nagel 1969; Thornberry 1973). But some do not. Investigations in some cities have shown that race is not important in court disposition (e.g., Burke and Turk 1975; Clarke and Koch 1976).

Chiricos and Waldo (1975) criticized the methodology, operational definitions, and the small number of offenses considered in prior studies of severity of sentence. Most of them, for example, utilize only gross categories to measure status, a dichotomy to measure severity of punishment (such as death penalty or not; probation or not), and do not control for the effects of other potentially influential factors such as prior record and other pertinent demographic variables. Chiri-

cos and Waldo (1975) attempted to overcome these shortcomings in their study of all felon inmates in three states in the late 1960s and very early 1970s. Using a measure of SES tapping income, occupation, and education, measuring sentence in terms of number of months sentenced, and considering 17 different offenses, the authors found little support for the thesis that lower SES is related to more severe punishment. However, they did not include those convicted of first-degree murder because "virtually all penalties received are life or death sentences" (p. 758). And, since the sample includes only those in prison and not those on probation, the full relationship between status and sentencing is not examined. Chiricos and Waldo readily admitted that "the present research must be regarded as but a partial test" of the proposition that those in the lowest status categories receive the most lengthy penalties (ibid.).

Research carried out in other parts of the country reveal that discrimination is indeed operative. National research on a variety of crimes has found that Black defendants who have no previous record receive stiffer sentences even when the type of offense and other factors are taken into account (Tiffany, Avichai, and Peters 1975). Another study of almost 900 sexual assault cases between 1970 and 1975 in a large Midwestern city confirmed that Black men who assault White women (1) have more serious charges leveled against them, (2) receive more severe sentences, (3) are more likely to have their offenses listed as felonies, (4) receive sentences that are executed, and (5) are more likely to be sent to a state penitentiary than those convicted of other kinds of rape (LaFree 1980). These relationships were found even when controls for past record, age, and other factors were taken into account.

Finally, in their study of all recorded offenders who were sentenced in a western state, Hall and Simkus (1975) found that American Indians were more likely than Whites to be put in prison. This is despite controlling for differences in background characteristics and type of offense.

Although Hall and Simkus's results indicated that ethnicity does not account for much of the variation in sentencing, being American Indian was significantly related to it. Their results tentatively suggested that the lack of power and stereotyping of American Indians do not explain the differences in the sentencing, but rather the interviews with judges imply that a defendant's attitude in the courtroom and the report of the probation officer are significant in determining the type of sentence given. Hall and Simkus proposed a circular process: The lower status individual knows his or her group receives more severe sentences, which in turn leads to a poorer attitude in court, which then leads to a prison term.

Like the research on rape mentioned earlier, evidence from a study of capital murder in South Carolina also strongly suggests that the race of the victim plays a role in determining whether the defendant is given the death sentence. *Capital murder* refers to homicides that are committed in conjunction with another serious felony, such as rape, burglary, kidnapping, or robbery. The information from 300 homicides shows that, when other relevant factors are controlled, homicides involving White victims result in death penalties being given significantly more often than when victims are Black. This discrepancy in penalty was found to be especially operant when there were fewer aggravating circumstances associated with the murders. The relationship becomes much weaker when multiple felonies are associated with the homicides (Paternoster 1984). Otherwise, Blacks were found to be given the death penalty more often than Whites regardless of number of victims or offenders, sex, age, or acquaintanceship of victim involved in the crime. Racial biases of this type have been found in other studies of homicide disposition (e.g., Radelet 1981; San Marco 1979).

Kleck (1981) stated that in some cases Blacks receive more lenient sentences than Whites for the same crimes. He cited as possible reasons for this that (1) most involve Black victims who are devalued and considered less important; (2) White paternalism toward Blacks is present; (3) White guilt about Blacks is present; and/or (4) Blacks are perceived as being less responsible for their crimes since they are exposed to more pressures beyond their control than Whites.

In addition to gender and race, income also has been found to be related to sentencing in some studies. Even when such factors as the type of offense and previous criminal record are controlled, income appears to affect whether or not a defendant receives a prison sentence, with lower-income persons getting more severe sentences. Clarke and Koch (1976) argued that such persons have less of a chance for pretrial release on bail and for a private rather than a court-appointed attorney, and this may explain why income is related to severity of sentence for burglary and larceny, which their study examined.

Suite Crime and Inequality

All the adult crimes discussed thus far involve those listed on the FBI's Crime Index. White-collar or "suite" crimes are not part of the FBI's Crime Index, which raises further questions about equity in the treatment of types of crime generally associated with different segments of the population. Generally, though not always, white-collar crime refers to crimes committed by white-collar persons in the course of their occupations. It is the latter part of the definition that is critical; thus, blue-collar workers who steal or defraud in the course of their jobs might be considered guilty of similar crimes, but ordinarily the focus has been on those in the higher status occupations. The classic definition and usual usage of the term are given by Edwin Sutherland: "A crime committed by a person of respectability and high social status in the course of his occupation" (1949, p. 2).

Edelhertz (1970, p. 12) suggested that several ingredients are found in most white-collar crimes:

1. Intent to commit a nonlegal act
2. Concealment of the real intent of the act
3. Reliance on the ignorance or laxness (or both) of the victim
4. Compliance of the victims in what they think is the real nature of the behavior
5. Hiding the crime by making the victim think he or she has not been exploited
6. Making plans for those few who realize they have been victimized in the event they try to retaliate

Since the crime occurs in the context of a job, white-collar crime usually involves violation of trust. Thus, such acts as misadvertising, price fixing, credit card abuse, computer fraud, and other kinds of duplicities and misrepresentations are a large part of white-collar crime.

White-collar crime, including corporate crime, is costly for economic and social reasons. Price fixing, monopoly violations, price gouging, deceptive advertising, and fraud cost an estimated $200 billion per year—a cost larger than that of all other crime types combined (Simon and Eitzen 1993). Estimates for the ultimate cost of the savings-and-loan scandal of several years ago, which Americans had to pay for, ranged from $500 billion to $1.4 trillion, "more money

than American street criminals steal in 4,000 years" (Simon and Eitzen 1993, p. 2). But in addition to the economic costs, depending on the type of crime, white-collar crime also has detrimental effects on the health of individuals and their trust in institutions.

Generally, individual white-collar crimes involve many more than one victim. When safety-code violations or price fixing occur, for example, many are harmed or seriously injured. In fact, although one ordinarily does not think of white-collar crime as violent, "there is considerable evidence that so-called 'nonviolent' white-collar criminals kill and maim more people each year in the United States than do violent street criminals" (Messner and Rosenfeld 1994, p. 32). This includes 100,000 who die from job-related illnesses and 30,000 who are killed by unsafe products every year (ibid.). An additional heavy cost of white-collar crime is the erosion of faith in social institutions that occurs when such crime takes place. Trust is a basis of solidarity and when it is damaged, society as a whole suffers. Thus, the damage resulting from white-collar crime radiates from the immediate victims to include many more.

Corporate crime appears to be extensive. A survey of 1,043 large corporations searched for evidence of bribery, fraud, illegal political contributions, tax evasion, and antitrust violations (Ross 1980). The examination revealed that 11 percent of them were guilty of at least one violation. In terms of domestic violations, there were 98 cases of antitrust violations and smaller numbers of the other crimes.

One case of criminal fraud involved the investment giant E. F. Hutton. It was found that individuals in the company were taking advantage of funds available before checks were cleared at the banks. This is parallel to an individual writing checks on money that has been deposited but not yet registered in an account. Essentially, E. F. Hutton employees intentionally did this for a period of about one and one-half years. In effect, E. F. Hutton was getting the free use of money on which it earned interest. The government determined that about two dozen employees were involved in the fraud, but no one was prosecuted. Instead, the company was ordered to pay $2,750,000 in fines and costs (Barlow 1987). Numerous other corporate crimes have occurred in a variety of other fields: computers, credit cards, health, repairs, sales promotions, advertising, drugs, real estate, and securities.

In early 1990, Michael Milken pleaded guilty to six felonies concerning securities fraud. In return for his cooperation and plea, more than 90 charges pending against him were dropped by federal prosecutors. These charges included allegations of racketeering and insider trading in the stock market.

In sharp contrast to many past cases of white-collar abuse, Milken was sentenced to 10 years in prison. The judge and U.S. attorney for the case cited abuse of his talents and leadership position as well as deterrence as justifications for the sentence (Fatsis 1990). Milken was released after serving 2 years of a 10-year sentence. He spent one month in a halfway house and the last month of his sentence under government supervision at his home. His sentence was reduced from 10 to 2 years because of his cooperation in an insider-trading investigation by the government. In addition to his sentence, he paid over $1 billion in fines and was required to put in 5,400 hours of community service over a three-year period. Lest one consider the fine to be exorbitant, one should also consider the fact that Milken made over $1 billion in the four years between 1983 and 1987 ("Sniping" 1990, p. 48). Milken was viewed by many as the epitome of abusive practices on Wall Street during the 1980s.

But white-collar crime is not a new phenomenon. A study of white-collar crime during World War II by Marshall Clinard (1946), a sociologist who held an important position in the Office of Price Administration (OPA) at the time, uncovered well over 300,000 violations of the price and rationing rules of the OPA in 1944 alone. In the vast majority of cases, only warnings, dismissals, or minor reprimands were used as punishments. In 1961, a major antitrust violation was taken to court involving General Electric and Westinghouse. Behind closed doors, using hidden codes and meetings, the conspirators negotiated with each other, deciding how the market should be divided among themselves. "A low price would be established, and the remainder of the companies would bid at approximately equivalent, though higher levels" (Geis, 1967, p. 122). A newspaper account recorded by Geis described the high-status defendants as they appeared in court as "middle-class men in Ivy League suits—typical businessmen in appearance, men who would never be taken for lawbreakers" (p. 117). One defendant's lawyer called the government's recommendation of a jail sentence "cold blooded" and said that the government did not realize what would happen to "this fine man" if he were put in jail in which there were "common criminals who had been convicted of embezzlement and other serious crimes" (pp. 117–118). One of the witnesses referred to his actions as "illegal...but not criminal." Milken's lawyer similarly described his client's behavior as "deviations from an otherwise admirable life" and asked for a sentence of community service instead of prison (Fatsis 1990, p. 113).

Most white-collar criminals, it appears, do not really think of themselves as criminals but as just trying to advance or gain promotions. The public's reactions have been mixed at best since many of these acts exhibit a cleverness and ingenuity that Americans prize. Moreover, most Americans do not directly experience the crime as is the case in robbery, rape, or other crimes against the person or private household. Corporate officials who commit corporate crimes are also usually subject to civil rather than to criminal law, and such violations are handled by agencies rather than by the criminal courts. This is because "corporations" have not, traditionally, been considered "persons" who commit criminal acts with "intent" (Reid 1988).

The manner in which white-collar crime is treated—namely, the special kind of legislation, the special kind of enforcement groups used, and the usual minimal types of punishment meted out—indicate that white-collar crime is treated differently than street crime in the U.S. justice system, even though its cost to victims is much greater. Geis (1974) stated the point bluntly: "Upperworld crime portrays the manner in which power is exercised in our society. A review of upperworld violations and the manner in which they are prosecuted and punished tells who is able to control what in American society and the extent to which such control is effective" (p. 114).

Some systematic studies have been done of the relationship between individuals' characteristics and their punishment for white-collar crimes. Wheeler and associates' (1982) study of several white-collar crimes over a three-year period in seven federal districts suggests that socioeconomic status is positively related to being incarcerated and to the length of sentence given those convicted of these crimes. The crimes included in the study were eight federal crimes: "antitrust offenses, securities and exchange fraud, postal and wire fraud, false claims and statements, credit and lending institution fraud, bank embezzlement, IRS fraud, and bribery" (Wheeler, Weisburd, and Bode 1982, p. 642). Paradoxically, the authors found that not only were those with occupations of higher prestige more likely to be imprisoned and given longer sentences but the same was also true for those with less impeccable past lives. They suggested that a "paradox of leniency and severity" runs through a judge's decisions on these matters, impeccability and SES pulling in opposite directions. Other factors, of course, also were found to be related to imprisonment, such as the severity and scope of the crime and the sex of the offender. Men were much more likely to be sent to prison than women, but it is not the role of motherhood that accounts for the differences in treatment. Rather, the authors suggested, "the answer lies deep in the history of sex-role relationships in American society.... There is something about the specter of women behind the bars and walls of the prison that leads many judges to a kind of protective paternalism" (p. 656). In making their decisions, judges consider (1) the seriousness of the crime, (2) the "blameworthiness" of the criminal, (3) the category of the offense and the district in which it is committed, and (4) the offender's sex.

Following up on Wheeler and colleagues' model of sentencing, Benson and Walker (1988) studied sentencing for a sample of white-collar criminals in one federal court over a 10-year period. Basically, the crimes examined were the same as those in the previous study, with the addition of embezzlement by a public employee. In contrast to the Wheeler study, Benson and Walker found that SES and impeccability had little to do with the decision to send an offender to prison. They also found that non-Whites were more likely than Whites to be imprisoned even after SES was taken into account. With respect to length of sentence, the researchers found that SES was not related to it, but that being non-White and scoring high in impeccability were related to longer sentences. In essence, most of their results contradict those of Wheeler and associates. They attribute much of this variation to differences in the distribution of crimes among the sample, the differences in the districts studied, and perhaps different values among judges in large urban settings, and those in smaller rural areas. They suggested, in sum, that contextual factors may affect the findings in different studies. The districts studied in the Wheeler and associates research "have larger caseloads, are more urbanized, and are more racially mixed than most federal districts" (Benson and Walker 1988, p. 301). They included the Atlanta, Los Angeles, Dallas, Manhattan and the Bronx, Chicago, and Seattle areas. In contrast, the Benson and Walker study was based on one district in a midwestern state.

What makes such white-collar crime possible? The widespread availability of sophisticated computer systems has made possible a wide variety of fraudulent acts. Moreover, U.S. society stresses the goodness of competition, success, and getting ahead, which nurture such activities. After all, free enterprise and the right to make a profit are part of the "American Way." Society encourages the clever fellow who can "pull the wool" over someone else's eyes (Schur 1969). And no one likes to admit that he or she has been duped or defrauded (read as "stupid"). Most of those caught do not even consider themselves criminal, even though their acts are clearly illegal and should be treated as crimes (Clinard 1946; Geis 1974).

With respect to corporate crime, a capitalist society in which corporations must successfully compete to survive creates pressures to violate the law. The uncertainties in the social, political, and economic environments in which corporate profits must be obtained make success problematic (Box 1983). Corporations, like other large organizations, try to control their environments in order to create a level of certainty in their operations, and they have become powerful actors in their own right (Thompson 1967; Coleman 1982). One of the means to create predictability in the resource and consumer markets is to behave in an illegal manner. When legitimate means to obtaining organizational goals are either difficult to use or unavailable, pressure exists to obtain legitimate goals such as profit by illegitimate means (Sherman 1987). This argument suggests that capitalism itself helps to generate corporate and other white-collar crimes.

Hate Crimes and Inequality

Social conditions also affect the extent of crime committed against members of demeaned status groups. *Hate crimes* are those "committed against a person, property, or society which is motivated, in whole or in part, by the offender's bias against a race, religion, disability [mental or physical], sexual orientation, or ethnicity/national origin" (U.S. Department of Justice 1998, p. 59). What distinguishes hate crimes from others, then, is the motivation behind the criminal act. Otherwise, they include the same crimes that compose the FBI's Crime Index. Even though the preceding definition does not include sex as a basis for hate crime, many of the rapes and other assaults against women might also be reasonably included as hate crimes.

A systematic attempt to assess the number of hate crimes began in 1990 with the passage of the Hate Crime Statistics Act. In 1997, a total of 8,049 incidents of hate crime were reported, involving 10,255 victims. Most of these were crimes against persons, with about 30 percent be-

ing crimes against property. Almost two-thirds were committed by Whites. Sixty percent of the incidents were motivated by racial bias, 15 percent by religious bias, 14 percent by biases against sexual orientation, and 11 percent by biases against particular ethnic or nationality groups. Extreme concerns about racial and ethnic purity, continued immigration, job competition, residential infiltration, and the sanctity of marriage and Christianity most often lie behind these biases. Target groups are viewed as threats to the living standards of these hate groups, which see their own way of life as under seige from contaminating elements. The extent to which given groups are victims of hate crimes is given in Table 12.5.

Biases against particular groups are longstanding. As we saw in Chapter 6, abusive acts against Blacks were permitted during slavery, and the creation of the Ku Klux Klan (KKK) after the Civil War helped keep racist fires burning. Current White separatist groups in the United States include the various segments of the KKK, neo-Nazi and Skinhead groups, and some extreme Christian groups such as Christian Identity and the Christian Defense League. Estimates in the mid-1990s put the number of members and supporters of these groups at 200,000 (Dobratz and Shanks-Meile 1997).

One of more recent publicized instances of a racial hate crime was committed on June 7, 1998, against 49-year-old James Byrd, Jr., a Black man, in Jasper, Texas. Byrd was picked up, beaten, chained to the bumper of a pickup truck, and dragged three miles until his head, shoulder, and other body parts were severed from each other. Showing no remorse and only contempt for his victim and his family, John William King, a White supremacist and one of three White men arrested for the murder, was sentenced to death (Lyman 1999).

A second publicized case, involving a gay man, occurred the fall of 1998. Matthew Shepard, a 21-year-old gay college student, was kidnapped, robbed, beaten, and tied to a fence in Laramie, Wyoming. Shepard died from his ordeal less than a week later (Brooke 1998). Like racism, prejudice against homosexuals has deep historical

TABLE 12.5   Number of Incidents and Victims of Hate Crimes by Bias Motivation: 1997

MOTIVATION	NO. OF INCIDENTS	NO. OF VICTIMS
Race	4,710	6,084
Anti-White	993	1,293
Anti-Black	3,120	3,951
Anti-Asian/Pacific Islander	347	466
Other	250	374
Religion	1,385	1,586
Anti-Jewish	1,087	1,247
Other	298	339
Sexual Orientation	1,102	1,401
Anti-male homosexual	760	927
Anti-female homosexual	188	236
Anti-homosexual	133	214
Other	21	24
Ethnicity/National Origin	836	1,132
Anti-Hispanic	491	649
Other	345	483
Disability	12	12
Anti-physical	9	9
Anti-mental	3	3
Multiple-Bias Incidents	4	40
Totals	8,049	10,255

Source: Uniform Crime Reports for the United States 1997 (Washington, DC: Federal Bureau of Investigation, 1998), p. 60.

Note: The "victim" can be a person, institution, or society.

roots, principally highlighted by laws against sodomy, which were in place as early as the 1600s in the United States, and which required the death penalty or severe mutilation as punishment. In 1997, 21 states still had sodomy laws, and, until recently, human rights laws did not specifically protect gays and lesbians, which allowed continued discrimination against homosexuals in jobs, housing, and public facilities (Button, Rienzo, and Wald 1997; Herek and Berrill 1992; American Civil Liberties Union 1997). Among other elements, feelings of superiority and concerns about

relative deprivation demonstrate the role of inequality in the production of hate crimes.

INEQUALITY AND COLLECTIVE UNREST

Crime rates are only one social phenomenon related to inequality. Strikes and social movements are also reactions to inequality. While inequality is not the only factor precipitating these forms of collective unrest, inequality helps to nurture comparisons and discontent, and affects the success or failure of such collective actions. The history of the United States is replete with examples of deprived groups that have become conscious of their conditions and have acted to try to change them. On the other hand, the class consciousness of a collection of individuals is itself shaped by specific historical, cultural, and social-structural conditions. This section will focus on an analysis of strikes and the conditions that give rise to them. We will also briefly detail the social-structural conditions associated with collective actions by "underdog" groups in U.S. society.

Workers, Unions, and Strikes

Working-class consciousness is measured in part by the collective organization of workers. This collective power, in turn, affects the economic benefits workers receive. Historically, the earnings of union members have been higher than those of nonunion workers. When unions have been well established, they have had a significant effect on wages, independent of the effects of supply and demand in the market. When unions have not been institutionalized in a particular economic sector or period, wages have been more vulnerable to fluctuations in the economy (Rubin 1986). In 1997, the median weekly earnings of union members was $640, compared to $478 for nonunion workers (U.S. Department of Labor, January 1999). The discrepancy in wages is especially clear in occupations below the professional level.

Despite the benefits of union affiliation for many workers, only a small percentage of workers are union members. In the late 1940s, about

The *Ku Klux Klan marches during a demonstration on a street in front of the Capitol building Rotunda in Washington, DC. The Klan and similar groups have been implicated in hate crimes against minority groups.*

one-third of all nonagricultural employees belonged to unions. In contrast, in 1997, only about 14 percent of the employed wage and salary workers in the United States were members. While the vast majority are White, a larger percentage of Blacks than Whites are members (18 versus 14 percent) (ibid.). The latter is probably related to differences in the occupational distribution between Blacks and Whites. In general, workers in blue-collar, machine, transportation operator, and laborer positions, along with those in protective service work and professional specialties, are the most unionized. Overall, unions appear to be becoming less important as representatives for labor, which may be a sign that the traditional understanding between labor and management to collectively bargain peacefully through unions has been disintegrating (Rubin 1986).

In addition to unionization, strikes sometimes are used as a measure of the degree of class militancy among workers. Strikes are part of the "class struggle American style" (Rubin 1986). But since 1980, when there were 187 strikes involving at least 1,000 workers each, the number has declined dramatically, along with the power of unions. In 1997, there were only such 29 work stoppages (strikes). In the years immediately following World War II, there were many more strikes. The numbers of workers involved in strikes have also declined significantly. Figure 12.2 shows the number of work stoppages involving 1,000 or more workers over the period 1947 through October 1998.

Along with the general decline in the number of strikes has come a decline in the numbers of workers involved in them. In 1947, 1,629,000

NUMBER OF STOPPAGES

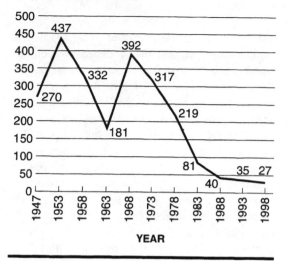

YEAR

FIGURE 12.2   Number of Work Stoppages Involving 1,000 or More Workers: 1947–1998

Source: U.S. Department of Labor, Bureau of Labor Statistics, *Compensation and Working Conditions* (Washington, DC: Office of Compensation and Working Conditions, Winter 1998), p. 70.

workers struck; but in 1997, only 339,000 were involved in strikes. Since the late 1970s, unions have not been in a position of political or economic strength. Following earlier arguments, it is not surprising that the number of strikes has declined. Almost all strikes have involved members of unions, with the AFL-CIO (American Federation of Labor/Congress of Industrial Organizations) affiliates accounting for well over half of all workers involved. The largest work stoppage in 1995, between General Motors and the United Automobile Workers (UAW), lasted only three days and involved 38,000 workers. Two other large stoppages involved Boeing Company and the International Association of Machinists, and retail grocery chains in California and the United Food and Commercial Workers. These included 33,000 and 32,000 workers, respectively (Cimini 1996).

The reasons for strikes vary, of course, and specific causes change as shifts occur in the economy. In the mid-1990s, the major bargaining issues

between labor and management reflected concerns about health care, stable employment, and the stagnation of worker incomes relative to those of upper management. Consequently, the major efforts by unions and workers involve attempts to increase wages, maintain health-care coverage, optimize job security, and strengthen training programs (Wasilewski 1996). You will notice that these issues reflect attempts by workers to improve their position *within* capitalism rather than efforts to radically reform capitalism itself. "Workers have used neither their strikes nor their unions to question capitalism itself" (Rubin 1986, p. 619).

Most observers agree that the U.S. working class and most of its unions have been concerned with improving the market situation of workers rather than with changing capitalism (e.g., Perlman 1923; Giddens 1973). This contrasts sharply with the historical situation in some European countries, notably France and Italy, where labor has been linked with more radical political movements.

That this reformist perspective is a permanent one for U.S. workers (not necessarily unions), however, should be questioned because several developments in the economy may serve to invigorate the moribund labor movement:

1. Extensive downsizing in recent years, along with instability of employment and growing income differences between rank-and-file workers and management

2. The elimination of much middle management and increased polarization within the labor force, and the downward movement of lower nonmanual workers into the working class

3. Awareness on the part of many young workers that "most work in our society is deadening and much of it unnecessary" (Aronowitz 1973, p. 261)

4. The decline in union power coupled with reductions in traditional worker benefits such as health care and the 40-hour work week

5. Foreign ownership/control of corporations located in the United States employing U.S. workers, and the use of foreign workers by U.S. corporations

The bitterness of many recent labor/management conflicts recalls those of the 1910s and 1920s when workers were struggling to increase their power. In recent decades, with the decline of union influence, workers again appear to be trying to flex their muscles. A recent case in point of union militancy involved the strike by workers at the Japanese-owned Bridgestone/Firestone Tire Company in which workers striking in part against attempts to install 12-hour work shifts were permanently replaced by others (see photo in Chapter 2). United Steelworkers' president George Becker viewed the strike as a virtual call to arms for labor and put the matter in historic terms: "This fight is not simply about our differences with Bridgestone/Firestone.... So much is at stake. It's not just the future of the Bridgestone/Firestone workers. It's not just the future of the labor movement. It's the dignity and future of the United States of America" (Gamboa 1996, p. B2). As U.S. corporations expand, increase their involvement abroad, and at the same time try to hold costs down, it is not likely that labor/management conflict will significantly decline in the near future.

Historically, union leaders, union workers, and nonunion workers often clashed with each other. Early unions frequently did not want to include all kinds of workers within their ranks, especially workers who were unskilled, Black, or female. This split between unionized and nonunionized workers highlights what many consider to be a central characteristic of the U.S. economy—namely, a dual-labor market. In addition, conservatism and accommodative policies by union leaders often put them at odds with their own union members. Historically, unions had to act as intermediaries between labor and management and head off disruption; consequently, unions, industry, and government had entered into an alliance (Piven and Cloward 1977, pp. 159–167). There were times when unions were contented, while workers were not. But in assessing the overall significance of union for workers, however, Piven and Cloward concluded that American workers have still been better off with than without

them "because unions still lead strikes; they still use some disruptive leverage" (p. 174).

The findings that most strikes involve unions and that unionization is related to higher worker compensation suggest that collective actions by workers and their success depend in large part on the collective power of labor. Simply put, the greater the power of labor, the less vulnerable it is and the more likely it is to strike and be successful. Thus, the success of labor is intricately tied to its position in the wider power structure of the production process. Perrone (1983) proposed a new measure of positional power that takes into account the location of workers in the production process. If the workers' performance significantly affects all phases of the production process, then workers are in a pivotal position and thus have great power. In this sense, they are indispensable to the success of the overall production process. Evidence from the period from 1963 to 1977 suggests that power in this sense has an important and positive effect on (1) unionization, (2) striking or labor militancy, and (3) wages (Wallace, Griffin, and Rubin 1989). Power provides opportunity for collective action and increases the likelihood of its success through the provision of resources necessary for a successful battle. In essence, the structure of power in a society or industry helps determine the amount of collective protest by groups within it. Historical studies of the determinants of strikes confirm the importance of economic and political structural factors.

Inequality and the Occurrence of Strikes.
What kinds of economic and political conditions promote strikes? Do conditions of severe inequality enhance or dampen the chances for worker strikes? Before unions were well established, strikes and other uprisings frequently occurred, many involving demands for rights to organize. But initially the worker protests of the Depression era grew out of the economic and related strains of the Depression. High unemployment rates and a drastic drop in wages caused agitation among the ranks of workers, and accompanying political instability and attempts by the government to im-

prove the economic situation served to legitimize worker unrest (Piven and Cloward 1977, p. 172). The latter point is significant because it suggests that the possible gains for labor during these periods were greater because of unstable political conditions. It afforded the workers a chance to show their dissent in their voting, as they did in the national elections of the early 1930s.

Snyder (1975) proposed that in a setting such as that which existed before the 1930s, where unions are not well institutionalized, have erratic and small memberships, and are considered an illegitimate interest group, strikes are more likely to focus on political rather than economic goals. Indeed, many of the strikes during this period emphasized labor's right to organize and labor's attempts to gain more influence in industry and society. Initially, this political tact took the form of voting for Roosevelt, "a president of 'the forgotten man,'" and his consequent election confirmed in workers' minds the justness of their cause (Piven and Cloward 1977, pp. 110 and 113). Labor legislation increased the confidence of workers, and from 1935 through 1937, strikes increased, often again involving demands for union recognition (p. 133). With their focus on a *political* agenda in the pre–World War II period, it does not seem that laborers carefully took into account the short-run *economic* costs and benefits of their strikes (Snyder 1975, p. 268).

Snyder (1975) argued that during this period, a government sympathetic to labor abetted labor's demands. He found, in fact, that in the United States during 1900 to 1948, the percentage of Democrats in Congress and the party of the president were positively related to the number of strikes occurring. Strikes are more likely to be successful when supported by the government. Before the Depression, strikes were often crushed by the state (Piven and Cloward 1977, pp. 102–104). Strikes also increased when union membership increased or when new unionization was discouraged by employers, established mainstream unions, or a wavering government.

All this suggests that under conditions of a lack of political and economic power, labor will protest for greater organization and political power, and that once it has unions and a sympathetic government behind it, institutionalized strikes are more probable. Under these conditions of political stability and organizational power, the costs of strikes to labor become lower, and the probability of strikes becomes more responsive to short-run economic changes affecting workers, such as unemployment rates and wage trends.

When labor is in demand and unemployment is low, the risks involved in a strike to entrenched labor are low, and strikes over wage changes are more likely (Piven and Cloward 1977, p. 98). Thus, Snyder (1975) found that although political and organizational factors were significant predictors of strikes during 1900 to 1948, after 1948, economic factors were more important.

For the period from 1949 to 1977, however, Kaufman found that only unemployment rates and price inflation were related to the number of strikes (1982). Other single political events or legislation are not, nor is union membership or the particular political party in power. In sum, like Snyder, Kaufman concluded that while economic factors were important predictors of strikes for the entire period, political conditions were relevant only in the pre-1948 period. Since then, economic issues have become the major factor in strike activity. He argued that inflation and unemployment affect the relative bargaining power of labor and management. Other research suggests that the lower the vulnerability of labor and the greater the vulnerability of the firm involved, the higher the probability of strikes. This again emphasizes the crucial role of the structure of power in determining strikes. Tracy (1986) found that smaller firms with more unpredictable profits and with more educated workers who are in demand are more likely to have strikes than firms that are larger and more powerful and who have a larger labor pool from which to draw.

In sum, economic and political arrangements are intricately related to strikes and worker protests. During the late 1920s and 1930s, when economic conditions were bad and the organizational power of workers was low, but political and organizational power were anticipated, strikes were likely to occur. Once the economic and political power of organized labor was established after World War II, strikes were more likely to be successful and, accordingly, the occurrence of strikes has become less responsive to changes in political officeholders and more attuned to fluctuations in wages and other short-run economic trends.

The growth of unions, the organizational power of labor, and the integration of organized labor into the U.S. political economy have similarly affected the form that strikes have taken, generally making them more institutionalized and less violent. The specific shape taken by strikes also depends on industry, plant, and union characteristics. Britt and Galle (1974) analyzed data from the Bureaus of the Census and Labor Statistics to look at the "structural antecedents of the shape of strikes" in the United States. The study led to several conclusions:

1. Larger industries are more likely to have short but more frequent strikes.
2. The more workers in an industry, the more strikes "would be expected by chance alone" (Britt and Galle 1974, p. 648).
3. Unionization and union size are both related to more frequent strikes, but unionization is related to broader and shorter strikes.
4. Concentration of workers (as measured by plant size) was related to fewer strikes during 1968 to 1970, but concentration is related to broader and shorter strikes (as measured by number of workers involved and number of work stoppages).

In essence, the context for potential strikes is important not only in determining whether they will take place but also in influencing the shape they will take.

EXPLANATIONS OF COLLECTIVE PROTEST

It is perhaps inevitable that inequality would be a significant spur for social protest. As you have seen from previous studies of strikes, however, deprivation alone does not produce protest. And as in understanding the generation of crime, the more concrete structural aspects of inequality and the social context that affects the probability of protest also have to be considered.

Structural Shaping of Disorders and the Role of Inequality

The research on strikes has clearly indicated the importance of structural characteristics in the economy and society for the frequency and shape of strikes. Deprivation and/or position in a deprived group are not enough to produce collective action, nor may they even be the most significant predictors of such disorders. Even when frustrations do exist, as they usually and consistently do for deprived groups, one must still explain how individual frustrations develop into collective protests (Snyder and Tilly 1974, p. 612). In fact, relative deprivation theory, as it applies to the generation of social movements, has been severely criticized for its psychological emphasis and vagueness. (Gurney and Tierney 1982).

Collective protest depends in large part on conditions that affect the mobilization possibilities of a group and on political conditions in the wider society. "The occasions when protest is possible among the poor, the forms that it must take, and the impact it can have are all delimited by the social structure in ways which usually diminish its extent and diminish its force" (Piven and Cloward 1977, p. 3).

The immediate characteristics and requirements for collective protest are clear: (1) the system being attacked has lost legitimacy in the eyes of the protestors, (2) individuals begin to feel more acutely that they have rights, and (3) they begin to think that their desperate, deprived situation is no longer inevitable but can be changed. Groups of people then collectively defy laws and arrangements that undergird established institutions (Piven and Cloward 1977, pp. 3–5). It is clear, for example, that from the point of view of the several minority groups that participated in the 1992 Los Angeles riot, the political system had lost its legitimacy. A lack of faith in the police and local political regimes was articulated by different minorities. Korean Americans, whose stores were looted, felt that neither the police nor the National Guard would protect them, and some felt that the media had systematically ignored African American prejudice against Asians, and only recognized White prejudice against African Americans (Awanohara and Hoon 1992; Iyer 1992). Political corruption also poisoned the feeling that government represented the people at large (Davis 1992b). Finally, the Rodney King verdict, in which some police were acquitted for the alleged beating of an African American motorist, only helped to cement belief in the illegitimacy of the entire legal system, and served as a reminder of the violation of minority rights. The lack of educational and occupational opportunities, which are supposed to be available to all Americans, intensified the sense of violation.

These political, educational, and occupational deficiencies in the structure of the community nurtured feelings of extreme frustration and illegitimacy, which, in turn, led to violence. The deficiencies were the "severe maladjustment" of which violence was the symptom (Coser 1967). The lack of opportunities may be related to segregation and the isolation of Blacks from Whites, both of which are related to urban violence. Violence serves as a final means for calling attention to the severe unequities that exist in a community. The critical issue is what and how conditions in the wider society, especially those relating to the system of political and economic inequality, affect these characteristics in such a way as to enhance the probability of collective disorder.

At least seven elements pertaining to structural conditions have been related to the frequency and form of protest. The first of these is the existence of severe concentrated inequality and wrenching changes in the society. Severe inequalities in the form of social isolation from Whites, and, paradoxically, increases in desegregation, have both been found to be predictors of the 154 race riots during the 1960–1993 period, which included primarily Black participants. Segregation appears to be a major contributor to urban vio-

lence and may be "the key for understanding race relations in America" (Olzak, Shanahan, and McEneaney 1996, p. 608). The transformation of institutions in a society leads to a clash between old and newly developing rules and frameworks for everyday behavior. Under these conditions, political leaders are more vulnerable, and new opportunities to protest can easily surface, especially if the dislocations are severe and last long enough. Dislocations, then, can create both deprivation and opportunities to protest. Among the basic transformations that would most readily have implications for protest would be drastic fluctuations in the business cycle; shifts in the nature of technology, such as the continued trend toward automation and sophisticated technology; and basic changes in the content of the labor market, such as the influx of women into the market.

Certainly basic and major economic and social changes have taken place in the Los Angeles area in recent decades. Among the *economic* changes are (1) an influx of 400,000 immigrants who work for low wages in southeast Los Angeles County; (2) a decline of at least 40,000 good-paying manufacturing jobs in the area, and a total of 75,000 jobs in general during the 1975–1985 period; (3) an unemployment rate that runs as high as 50 percent in parts of south central Los Angeles; (4) an erosion of the city's tax base as employers and middle-class and White workers move to the suburbs; and (5) a growing gulf between the rich and the poor. These economic downturns have exacerbated social problems arising from the changing composition of the local population. The *social* issues include (1) an interracial and interethnic hostility involving Korean Americans, Hispanics, Whites, African Americans, and other recent immigrants, each of whom is not always similarly situated economically; (2) poor, crowded housing but high rents; and (3) poor-quality education. It appears that while those involved in the 1992 Los Angeles riot were from several ethnic groups, the separation and hostility between them has not been diminished by their common involvement. While they all have economic problems, race remains a divisive force (Davis, 1992a, 1992b; "Economic Crisis" 1992; Meyerson 1992).

> *The Chicano organization NEWS From America blames Central American immigrants for joining the riot; certain black leaders, jealous of the economic success of the Asian community and the coming political success of the Latinos (by sheer weight of numbers), lash out at both; many Koreans conceal a raging anti-black animus behind a wafer-thin veneer of peace rhetoric. Neither multiracial rioting nor multiracial riot defense seems to have loosened the stranglehold that separatism exerts within L.A.'s communities of color. (Meyerson 1992, p. 24)*

This description suggests that the animosity is at least partially rooted in the economic and political inequality that is perceived to exist between these groups. Both racism and classism divide the population there, "and it may be futile to try to pinpoint where racism ends and classism begins" (Segal 1992, p. 47).

A second societal condition for protest is related to the first. The ideology of the state and its agents can and usually tries to symbolically lighten the burden of deprivation or encourages the belief that the individual is responsible for his or her own fate, not the system against which reaction might otherwise take place (Segal 1992, pp. 6–7). A maintaining ideology is essential: "The willingness of mass publics to follow, to sacrifice, to accept their roles is the basic necessity for every political regime. Without a following there are no leaders." Such sacrifice and willingness to be loyal are legitimized by policy rationales, such as those that appeal to national security and similar symbols (Edelman 1977, p. 5). Severe dislocations can shake adherence to ideologies, and the latter are necessary to maintain peace in the system as it stands. The role of ideology in maintaining inequality is discussed further in Chapter 14.

The third condition relates directly to the power of the state and political inequality in the society and concerns the power and likely use of repression in dampening unrest. Repression is most likely to be used when the central institu-tions of the society are being attacked and when concessions have been made, but some continue to protest. Repression raises the cost of protest for those with grievances and thus lowers the odds for successful protest. Snyder and Tilly's (1972) analysis of collective violence in France from 1830 to 1960 found evidence that some measures of the government's repressive action were negatively related to the extent of collective violence.

The fourth structural factor is the power of the government to create opportunities and grant concessions. By doing these, government can defuse protest. One of the first responses of a government to protest is in some way to co-opt leaders or channel protest into legitimate routes. If legitimate opportunities are available, protest, if it occurs, is not likely to be violent. Violence is usually a last resort and involves a great many risks for the group (Coser 1967; Piven and Cloward 1977, p. 19). Government can create opportunities by developing acceptable and responsible programs to deal with grievances, and thereby, in effect, reshape the stated demands of the group. In this way, the government can weaken public support of the continued protest and present itself as "a benevolent and responsive government that answers grievances and solves problems" (Piven and Cloward 1977, p. 34). Then when protest dies down, concessions can be safely diluted or taken away; concessions that are not withdrawn can often be made to serve powerful groups as historically has often been the case with unions (p. 35). "Protestors win...what historical circumstances has already made ready to be conceded" (p. 36).

The structure of opportunities also affects the tactics protestors must use and the duration of protest. When protestors devise tactics to attain their goals that are then counteracted by successful tactics by the other side, protest is neutralized unless protestors create new tactics and approaches to continue the protest. The life of a movement depends on the ability of its members to constantly develop innovative tactics against those in power. Analysis of the Civil Rights movement during the years 1955 to 1970 demonstrates this process (McAdam 1983). In other words, the maintenance of protest depends on the power structure and opportunities in the social setting.

The fifth condition is connected to the fourth and concerns the political position of government vis-à-vis the aggrieved group. If the government is suspected of being supportive or actually does actively support potential protestors, protest is more likely. Jenkins and Perrow (1977) found in their historical study of farm worker movements that some were successful while others failed because of changes in political circumstances in the society. Their success in the late 1960s and early 1970s was heavily due to the fact that government was not solidly against them, and liberals united with workers in publicly denouncing agribusiness. Success requires tolerance or support from those in power or a lack of unity among those who would discourage protest.

The resources of the group gleaned from inside and outside constitute a sixth way in which outside social and economic circumstances affect protest. In discussing strikes, Korpi (1974) suggested that their probability and likelihood of success increase with the strength of resources a group possesses. Relative deprivation may intensify the wish for change, but strikes are more likely if a group has ample power resources from which to draw. These resources can come from individuals or be collective in nature. Coalition formation, for example, can serve as a type of collective resource that can strengthen the position of a discontented group. Since deprivation is usually constantly present for many groups, it is external resources that are needed to organize them and create viable protest. "Disorders do not arise from disorganized anomic masses, but from groups organizationally able to defend and advance their interests" (Jenkins and Perrow 1977, p. 250).

Finally, the shape of protest is influenced by the structure, function, and ideology of the institutions in which protesting groups are immediately located. They determine the composition of groups that will protest, the avenues of protest, and the terms in which demands are phrased. Students protested war in Vietnam while in college and did so by symbolically attacking the system through their assaults on college administration offices and company interviewers. Factory workers protest through strikes; the unemployed cannot go on strike because they are outside the institution. It is the institutions in which the people are immediately involved that help shape protest. "People cannot defy institutions to which they have no access, and to which they make no contribution" (Piven and Cloward 1977, p. 23).

To sum up, in a number of ways the probability and form of protest are determined by political and economic factors other than feelings of deprivation and powerlessness. Several of those previously listed clearly implicate the system of inequality in the likelihood of protest. For example, the factors of resource availability and likelihood of repression reflect to a large degree the extent of economic and political inequality in society.

SUMMARY

Inequality can affect behavior and social events in several ways. At the outset it was stated that not only individual position in the system of inequality but the system as a whole can have such effects, and in this chapter concern was expressed for both aspects. We looked at the relationship between class, race, sex, and crime rates, as well as the relationship between capitalism/inequality and crime rates in general, and found that in each case inequality is implicated in the generation of crime. Official statistics reveal a relationship between being Black and of low income and the probability of being arrested. The bulk of the studies on sentencing suggests a bias against groups of lower socioeconomic standing. This is especially borne out in cases of rape and homicide when the victim is White. A variety of data, then, raise questions about the fairness of the criminal justice system. The definition of the crime problem in terms of FBI Index crimes, which do not include white-collar crimes, and the special treatment given to white-collar crime, the frequent discovery that SES is related to likelihood of arrests, official reporting of crimes, and type of punishment strongly suggest that justice is not evenly meted out in U.S.

society. Moreover, the findings of a relationship between income inequality and property crime rates further suggest that inequality helps produce crime and that reductions in inequality may produce reductions in property crime. Hate crimes, motivated by biases against particular demeaned status groups, also reflect the social inequalities perceived by different clusters of people.

If inequality and deprivation are clear and severe enough, they also can foment collective protest. Deprivation, however, is insufficient to produce such protest. The lower class often has been found to be more willing to use violence or see it as necessary for progress, but feeling a need to be violent and actually engaging in protest are two different things. Wider structural conditions also must be considered when explaining protest. Studies of the riots and strikes during the 1960s suggest that the structure of inequality affects the social factors that generate collective protest. The power to mobilize resources, to avoid repression from official sources, to gain concessions, to successfully counter the tactics of those in power, and to discredit official ideology all depend heavily on power arrangements in the society at large.

CRITICAL THINKING

1. What must be done to change the living conditions in ghettos that help generate crime?

2. This chapter emphasized the importance of the social context and conditions for crime and protest. What newly appearing characteristics of current society are likely to have effects on the extent and nature of social inequality? What characteristics are likely to alter the negative effects of inequality on individuals and society?

3. What conditions in society and culture affect fluctuations in the rate of hate crimes?

WEB CONNECTIONS

Race and sex are both correlated with crime in one or several ways. The Bureau of Justice Statistics regularly collects information on crime, offenders, victims, and various components of the justice system. What are the trends in homocide victims and offenders by gender and race? What racial and gender patterns exist among offenders who were executed or sentenced to death? Go to:

http://www.ojp.usdoj.gov/bjs

CHAPTER 13

TRENDS IN MOBILITY AND STATUS ATTAINMENT

OPENNESS IN U.S. SOCIETY

We found scant evidence that the system of occupational inheritance is growing more rigid.
—Elton G. Jackson and Harry J. Crockett, Jr.

There is no indication of increasing rigidity in the class structure.
—Peter M. Blau and Otis Dudley Duncan

The strata are becoming more rigid; the holes in the sieve are becoming smaller. Status is crystallizing.
—J. O. Hertzler

Children in U.S. society often are told that if they work hard enough and want something badly enough, they will obtain it. The achievement of desired goals depends on the effort individuals are willing to expend. The opportunities are there to be grasped if a person has the aspirations and perseverance required to take advantage of them. The United States as a storied land of opportunity and freedom is chronicled in many myths and fables about how the individual, no matter how humble and lowly, can succeed. The traditional belief has been that ours is a very fluid society in which individuals frequently rise and fall on hierarchies of inequality.

U.S. society is one in which achievement is believed to take precedence over ascription. Mobility is seen as resulting from a "contest" with others rather than from "sponsorship" by the powerful. The importance that has been placed on ed-

ucation not only by the public but also by social scientists in their theories of achievement suggests the significance that is attributed to individual effort in the attainment of socioeconomic rewards.

In light of these values concerning the individual and achievement, it is not surprising that a central question raised in the study of inequality has concerned the extent to which the United States has been and continues to be an open society. One important aspect to examine in any system of inequality is its characteristic patterns of mobility.

QUESTIONS CONCERNING OPENNESS

Any conclusions about the openness of a society depend on how the question is posed. Openness has meant different things to different researchers, and the concern for openness has been expressed and studied in a variety of ways. Consequently, it is possible to approach the issue of openness with several different and specific questions:

1. In terms of sheer amount, how much mobility has there been and is there now in the United States? How does the United States compare with other countries on mobility?

2. What is the nature of the mobility that has occurred? Is it more often long-distance or short-range mobility?

3. What have been the trends in intergenerational inheritance? Are individuals more or less likely to have the same occupations as their parents?

4. What has been the pattern of mobility as it pertains to the recruitment and dispersion of individuals into particular occupational strata? When individuals in a given strata do move, into which strata are they most and least likely to move?

5. What role does socioeconomic background play in determining an individual's present status, and has this role changed significantly over time?

6. What conditions in the economic, social, and cultural structures affect the chances for and levels of attainment by individuals?

Each of these questions poses a separate issue, but all of them are relevant to the general question of how open U.S. society is, and each of them has been addressed in research. The first four questions have been the concern of traditional mobility studies, whereas the last two have been a main focus of status-attainment research. We will review both of these areas in later sections, but first we need to clarify some basic definitions and methods in the study of mobility.

STUDY OF MOBILITY

Definition of Terms

Sorokin distinguished between horizontal and vertical mobility. *Horizontal mobility* refers to movement into another role or place that does not involve a change in an individual's position in the system of inequality. For example, an individual might change from one occupation to another, even though both occupations yield essentially the same incomes, status, and authority. Our concern here is with vertical rather than horizontal mobility. *Vertical mobility* refers to "any change in the occupational, economic or political status of individuals which leads to a change in their social position" (Sorokin 1959, p. 414). Of course, that change can be upward or downward. Most sociologists have focused on the extent of upward rather than downward mobility in the United States, even though some feel the latter is a better indicator of the openness of a society.

A study of mobility also can focus on the movement of groups or individuals. Whole categories of individuals can and have sometimes changed positions or created new groups of positions (e.g., occupations may come into existence causing a shift in the positions of other groups). Most often, however, studies of mobility have concentrated on the individual and his or her movement up or down an occupational hierarchy.

Sorokin also pointed out that mobility can vary in its *intensiveness*. This refers to the amount of vertical distance traversed in the mobility that occurs. Another way of putting this is to say that social mobility can be short or long range—that is, it can take place over small as well as large distances. The *generality* of mobility, in Sorokin's terms, concerns the number of persons who are involved in the mobility. For example, it has been suggested that only a limited number of African Americans have moved up in recent decades, with many being left behind as an underclass. A final distinction is made between *intra*generational and *inter*generational mobility. The former refers to movement that occurs to individuals during their own careers and thus deals with the effects of their own efforts and experiences since the time of their first social position. Intergenerational mobility, on the other hand, deals with changes in social position that have occurred between generations, comparing the parent's position with that of the offspring in some way. Consequently, the study of intergenerational mobility directly addresses the issue of inheritance of position.

TABLE 13.1 Mobility from Father's (or Other Family Head's) Occupation to Current Occupation: U.S. Men in the Experienced Civilian Labor Force Aged 20 to 64 in 1962 and 1973

YEAR AND FATHER'S OCCUPATION	SON'S CURRENT OCCUPATION					TOTAL (%)	FATHER'S PERCENTAGE TOTALS
	Upper White Collar (%)	Lower White Collar (%)	Upper Manual (%)	Lower Manual (%)	Farm (%)		
1962							
Upper white collar	53.8	17.6	12.5	14.8	1.3	100.0	16.5
Lower white collar	45.6	20.0	14.4	18.3	1.7	100.0	7.6
Upper manual	28.1	13.4	27.8	29.5	1.2	100.0	19.0
Lower manual	20.3	12.3	21.6	43.8	2.0	100.0	27.5
Farm	15.6	7.0	19.2	36.1	22.2	100.0	29.4
Son's percentage totals	27.8	12.4	20.0	32.1	7.7	100.0	100.0
1973							
Upper white collar	52.0	16.0	13.8	17.1	1.1	100.0	18.2
Lower white collar	42.3	19.7	15.3	21.9	0.8	100.0	9.0
Upper manual	29.4	13.0	27.4	29.0	1.1	100.0	20.5
Lower manual	22.5	12.0	23.7	40.8	1.0	100.0	29.7
Farm	17.5	7.8	22.7	37.2	14.8	100.0	22.6
Son's percentage totals	29.9	12.7	21.7	31.5	4.1	100.0	100.0

Source: Adapted from Featherman 1977, Table 2. The basic source of information about this study is from Featherman and Hauser 1978.

Note: Data are from March 1962 and March 1973 Current Population Surveys and Occupational Changes in a Generation Surveys. Occupation groups are upper white collar: professional and kindred workers and managers, officials and proprietors, except farm; lower white collar: sales, clerical, and kindred workers; upper manual: craftsmen, foremen, and kindred workers; lower manual: operatives and kindred workers, service workers, and laborers, except farm; farm: farmers and farm managers, farm laborers, and foremen.

Open societies generally have been considered to be those in which a maximum amount of mobility takes place and, more crucially, those in which individuals in different strata can move without being encumbered or aided by the status of their parents. In other words, the most open societies are thought to be those in which there is no relationship between the status of the parents and that of the offspring. Independence exists between these two statuses in the sense that individuals from any socioeconomic background can move into any other positions depending solely on their achievements (Goldhamer 1968). *Closed societies,* of course, are of the opposite kind. Little mobility occurs and position in the system of inequality is entirely dependent on the position in which an individual was born. The caste system of India approached a closed system of inequality.

Issues and Tools

The standard tool used to detect the extent and nature of mobility between two generations is the mobility table (sometimes called a *transition matrix*).

These tables show how the percentages of offspring from given occupational origins distribute themselves in the occupational structure. Thus, in a table where all the data are available, the rows add up to 100 percent. These "outflow" tables show the pattern of movement of the children out from the origin position of their parent(s). Table 13.1, based on 1962 and 1973 national data, is a good example. This table shows, for example, that in 1962, about 54 percent of sons whose fathers were in upper white-collar occupations were in similar kinds of occupations. This suggests quite a bit of occupational inheritance. Under conditions of perfect inheritance, the occupational distribution among the sons would be identical to that among the fathers. Table 13.2 is an example of a situation in which inheritance is at its maximum.

Figure 13.1 shows where to look on a mobility table for the extent of inheritance and the nature and amount of upward and downward mobility. If statuses of origin (parents) have no influence on statuses of destination (children), one would expect to find that the proportion of children from a given origin status who wind up in that status is exactly equal to the proportion of the parents who are in that status in the labor force. For example, if professionals made up 30 percent of the labor force, under conditions of no relationship between status of origin and status of destination, one would expect to find that only 30 percent of the sons of professionals are in that occupational category. Generally, however, sons are more likely to be in positions identical or similar to their fathers than in any others. One of the problems with mobility studies is that, up until about 1980, they tended to focus on intergenerational shifts among males and rarely examined the role of the mother's occupation or the attainment of female offspring. As we shall see, a fuller understanding of mobility and attainment requires such inclusion.

COMPARATIVE STUDIES OF MOBILITY

During the late 1950s, concerted attempts were made to compare social mobility rates among Western industrialized countries. Unfortunately, most of the analyses were done using extremely general occupational categories of nonmanual, manual, and farm. In different countries, specific occupations are not always classified into the same general category, and this creates problems of comparability between studies (Matras 1980; Goldthorpe 1985).

Most notable among the analyses was one made by Lipset and Zetterberg (1959). A total of nine countries were analyzed, including the United States. On the basis of their research, Lipset and Zetterberg concluded that (1) the rates of observed mobility in industrialized societies were quite similar, (2) the United States is not higher in upward mobility from manual occupations than all other industrialized nations, and (3) mobility into the elite from manual categories was higher in the United States than in the other nations studied.

TABLE 13.2   Example of Maximum-Inheritance Model

PARENT'S OCCUPATIONAL STATUS	OFFSPRING'S OCCUPATIONAL STATUS			PARENT'S PERCENTAGE TOTALS
	High	Medium	Low	
High	100%	0	0	10%
Medium	0	100%	0	60%
Low	0	0	100%	30%
Offspring's Percentage Totals	10%	60%	30%	

Summary of mobility measures: total; mobility = 0; structural = 0; circulation = 0.

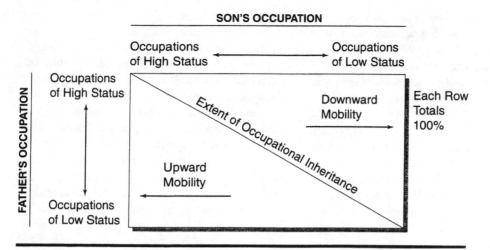

FIGURE 13.1 Where to Look in Reading a Standard Outflow Mobility Table

This study gave rise to increased interest in the apparent relationship between industrialization/development and mobility rates. Several explanatory versions of this relationship have appeared (Goldthorpe 1985). Essentially, Lipset and Zetterberg (1959) suggested that general social mobility will become increasingly similar in industrial countries because of shifts in the occupational structure. "The overall pattern of social mobility appears to be much the same in industrial societies of various Western countries" (p. 13). Rises in the proportion of urban occupations coupled with the decline of agricultural work, and the growth of service industries, white-collar occupations, and bureaucracy all provide impetus for greater social mobility. Specifically, the *industrialism thesis* contends that "industrialization, directly or indirectly, demolishes old barriers, opens new avenues for ascendance, and shifts the basis of status attainment from ascription to achievement. It, therefore, loosens the dependence of destinations on origins and generates a gradual openness in the mobility structure, in addition to transforming the occupational structure and promoting structural mobility" (Wong 1994, p. 122). According to this argument, industrialism has an "inner logic" that, when introduced into countries, overshadows the distinctive cultural and social

characteristics of industrial nations. The expectation is also that specific cultural elements will accompany industrialism, such as the greater significance of relevant qualifications over social background in obtaining occupational positions.

The argument that industrialization inevitably increases upward social mobility in a similar manner in all industrial countries has come under severe attack, however. In the United States, for instance, income inequality has increased as well as the proportion who are poor or near poor. Concerns about increased *downward* mobility have also intensified in this highly advanced nation. Moreover, as education becomes more important, lack of it gives those on the bottom a smaller chance of moving up.

In addition to the implications from U.S. trends, many recent studies also do not support the industrialism thesis. Simply put, industrial countries vary in their *rates* and *patterns* of mobility. Comparative studies suggest that *overall* observed mobility rates in western industrial nations are not that similar (e.g., Miller 1975; Grusky and Hauser 1984; Kurz and Muller 1987). Roughly, the same can be said for upward social mobility rates in industrialized nations; in fact, social mobility does not seem to have changed in many of such nations since World War II (Wong 1994). Mobility does not continuously increase with economic development (e.g., Erikson, Goldthorpe, and Portocarero 1983; Hazelrigg and Garnier 1976).

What this suggests is that the industrialism thesis is flawed because it ignores the central role of the often unique historical, cultural, and institutional context of countries in which mobility does or does not occur. The patterns of mobility vary between countries because of differences in their contexts. First of all, the process of industrialization does not follow the same route in all countries. Historical and political conditions help shape the occupational structure and mobility within the country (Hauser and Grusky 1988). Second, varying characteristics of educational institutions affect access to quality education and the connection between education and employment. Thus, the pathways to mobility vary between countries (Kerckhoff 1995). Think about this: Every society provides institutional pathways through which a citizen needs to move if he or she is to be mobile. These pathways differ not only in their structure but, because of the culture, also in terms of who is eligible to use them and when they can use them. Between one's origin and one's destination lies a patterned structure through which one must pass to be socially mobile. What did your parents have to go through to get where they are? How about your grandparents? The pathways to mobility for different generations vary to the extent that economic, social, political, and cultural structures also change between generations, creating new opportunities while eliminating or altering old ones.

Finally, it may be that any relationship found between industrialization and mobility depends, in large part, on the shape of the system of inequality, and these vary across countries. The greater the income inequality, the greater effect an individual's social origins have on his or her occupational destination. In other words, greater equality is linked to greater mobility (Tyree, Semyonov, and Hodge 1979). All this leads us to expect variations in social mobility among industrial countries.

In altering the industrialism hypothesis and trying to account for the differences in observed mobility between industrial nations, Featherman and his colleagues (1975) suggested that (1) although Western industrial societies may have similar amounts of *openness* ("social fluidity," "circulation mobility"), (2) they differ in their occupational structures through time, and thus the observed differences in mobility rates between countries are due primarily to historical and cultural variations in the occupational structure. This underscores the importance of the distinction between "structural" and "circulation" mobility. The former is generally thought of as mobility that results purely from changes in the occupational structure, whereas the latter is ordinarily interpreted as the mobility that results from other sources and is an index of the openness or "fluidity" of the society. This has been a crucial distinction in studies of mobility since the 1950s, but there is some argument whether it is possible, methodologically, to sustain such a distinction (Sobel 1983b). Indeed, the usage of a variety of terms among social scientists from various countries to describe "circulation" mobility has not helped consistency or communication among them.

Research generally supports the conclusion that circulation mobility has been quite consistent and constant in most industrial countries. For example, not much difference in openness or mobility has been found between Canada and the United States. There appears to be no major discernible trend in mobility at all in these countries (McRoberts and Selbee 1981). Research on Great Britain and the United States has not revealed any significant differences in openness or downward mobility between the countries, even given the suggested differences in values of the two societies (Kerckhoff, Campbell, and Winfield-Laird 1985). The comparative stability in the amount of openness or circulation in western capitalist societies has been attributed to its class structure. "For systems of class stratification, as ones essentially of differential advantage and power, must be regarded as possessing important self-maintaining properties. The general expectations would therefore be for continuing stability in relative rates [i.e., openness]" (Erikson, Goldthorpe, and Portocarero 1983, p. 339).

A number of studies also have found support for the conclusion that occupational-structure changes/composition are largely responsible for variations in mobility between countries (e.g., Grusky and Hauser 1984; Kerckhoff, Campbell, and Winfield-Laird 1985; Erikson, Goldthorpe, and Portocarero 1983). Kerckhoff and colleagues (1985), for example, found that the differences in mobility between Great Britain and the United States are due to historical differences in the occupational structures and career paths taken by people in each society. Specifically, the decline in farming and the rise in professional occupations have been more accentuated in the United States than in Britain, and the routes taken by Britons and Americans while pursuing their careers are different. Americans are more likely to begin their careers in professional occupations, whereas Britons, in part because of the availability of apprenticeships, are more likely to have crafts positions as their first jobs.

One of the principal changes in the U.S. occupational structure has been the decline in the number of those in agricultural occupations. This change in the *composition* of the occupational structure has increased mobility in the United States, since the farming occupations have been among those most likely to be passed on through generations (Kurz and Muller 1987). On the other hand, other changes in the occupational structure may slow mobility. Goldthorpe (1985) suggested that the trend in advanced industrial societies toward more high-status service occupations may increase inheritance and the stability of the class structure, since most mobility takes place in the middle of the class structure rather than at its extremes.

U.S. MOBILITY OVER TIME

The extent and future of mobility in the United States have been the subject of many debates extending back decades. Serious mobility research began in the 1940s, and even then there was concern about what the future held. Changes in mobility studies since the 1940s have been driven by changes in the data bases used and increases in the sophistication of techniques for analyzing them.

Estimate of Mobility Trends from World War II to the 1960s

One of the first attempts to arrive at some conclusions regarding post–World War II mobility trends using national sample data was carried out by Jackson and Crockett (1964). The authors compared data for intergenerational mobility between father and son collected in 1957 by the Survey Research Center at the University of Michigan with national data collected in 1945, 1947, and 1952 to determine trends in mobility from 1945 to 1957. The results suggested that greater mobility occurred in 1952 and 1957 than in 1947. There was scant evidence that the system of occupational inheritance [was] growing more rigid" (Jackson and Crockett 1964, p. 15). Some mobility would have occurred simply because of changes in the occupational structure between generations. Increases in the white-collar governmental sector after World War II, for example, even encouraged working-class and middle-class youths to leave high school or college to get jobs in the expanding economy (Shanahan, Miech, and Elder 1998).

In other words, between any two periods of time, some mobility is bound to occur if the occupational distributions in the two generations in question are different. The difference between that minimum amount of *expected* mobility and what *actually* occurs is often referred to as the amount of *circulation mobility*. As noted earlier, most consider this to be a better measure of the openness of a system of inequality than the total amount of mobility because it allegedly already has taken into account changes that have occurred because of alterations in the occupational structure. A greater proportion of the total mobility in 1947 appears to have been due to circulation than to structural conditions, whereas in 1952 and 1957, the reverse is the case.

Blau and Duncan (1967) added 1962 data to those used by Jackson and Crockett. Their data suggested that circulation increased between 1957 and 1962 and that the son's occupation was less dependent on that of the father. In other words, the system of inequality as measured by the amount of circulation appears to have been more open in 1962 than in the earlier years.

Some of the principal findings from the national study on intergenerational mobility by Blau and Duncan (1967) revealed some clear patterns:

1. Despite a good deal of mobility, especially of the short-range variety, occupational inheritance was higher than would be expected if no relationship existed between the father's status and the son's 1962 occupational status.

2. Upward mobility was much more prevalent than downward mobility, most of it being structurally induced.

3. The occupational categories that contained the greatest proportions of occupational inheritance and self-recruitment were those involving self-employment: independent professionals, proprietors, and farmers. The authors suggested that being an owner made it hard for the son to leave the occupation (inheritance) and also made it less likely that sons from other origins would enter that occupation (self-recruitment).

4. The highest rates of *inflow* into an occupational category from other categories occurred among the lower white-collar and lower blue-collar occupations. That is, they recruited individuals from a wide variety of occupational backgrounds.

5. The highest rates of *outflow* from an occupational category occurred among the two lowest white-collar, blue-collar, and farm groupings. That is, a greater proportion of these sons went to other occupations, suggesting that they had greater chances for mobility. In the salaried professions, on the other hand, just the opposite situation occurred. The sons were much less likely to outflow to other occupations, suggesting a high degree of inheritance.

6. An increasing proportion of men with non-farm/manual origins moved up into the white-collar occupations. But men who started their own careers in a blue-collar occupation were less likely to be mobile than those who began their careers as white-collar workers or farmers (pp. 28–41).

Current Mobility Patterns in the United States

Mobility in the United States, as in most industrial countries, tends to be greatest in the middle of the occupational hierarchy and limited at the extremes (Featherman and Hauser 1978; Grusky and Hauser 1984). The top and bottom of the occupational structure are fairly closed, suggesting "barriers to movement across class boundaries" (Featherman and Hauser 1978, p. 180). In contrast, mobility in the middle is more extensive. Men in upper blue-collar occupations are as likely to have come from or be on their way to any lower or higher occupation as their present occupation. "There is no evidence of 'class' boundaries limiting the chances of movement to or from the skilled manual occupations" (ibid.).

Featherman and Hauser's (1978) replication of Blau and Duncan's national study of American men reached a variety of conclusions about the openness and mobility in the U.S. occupational structure in the 1970s:

1. There was a great deal of movement both within and between generations. Well over half the sons moved out of the occupational strata of their fathers and out of the strata of their own first jobs.

2. Rates of mobility were "far larger" than would be suggested by transformation of the occupational structure alone. There was an increase in mobility from the son's first to current occupation, which is independent of changes in the composition of the occupational structure.

3. If there was a trend at all, it was toward greater mobility. But there was greater short- than long-distance mobility, and more mobility in the middle of the occupational structure than at the extremes. Upward mobility was more prevalent than downward mobility.

4. There was still a "moderate" correlation between occupational origins and destinations both within and between father's and son's generations, but there has been a decline in this correlation. "Thus, among American men a reduction of obstacles to occupational change appears to be a long-term and continuing tendency" (Featherman and Hauser 1978, p. 136). Background seems to have become less important in determining occupational position. This has been substantiated for the period from 1972 to 1985 as well. "Socioeconomic status has become less important for men's and women's occupational mobility since 1972" (Hout 1988, p. 1389). The decline in the association between an individual's social background and where he or she ends up occupationally appears to be linked to the rise in the proportion of workers who have higher education. This is the case for both men and women (Hout 1988).

5. Race, farm background, and paternal occupation were still important predictors of occupational status and mobility, but recent changes moderated their impact. On the one hand, the educational level of Blacks increased. Black fathers were more able to pass on their status to sons, and the growing "rationality" of the economy created pressures to reduce discrimination. On the other hand, discrimination did not appear to be any less significant than in the 1960s, racial differences in returns to human-capital investments still remained, and the likelihood of young Blacks being in the labor force was smaller in the 1970s than in the 1960s.

6. Stratification within the Black community became more visible and clear. Blacks became more differentiated with respect to socioeconomic status, creating more distinct classes and greater inequalities among them.

7. Overall, on balance, there appeared to be "declining status ascription and increasingly universalistic status allocation" (Featherman and Hauser 1978, p. 481).

With respect to the last point, results from the analysis of several national surveys conducted between 1972 and 1985 indicated that the openness of the U.S. occupational structure may have increased, whereas changes in the composition of the occupational structure may have slowed. This means that, overall, the extent of observed mobility remains unchanged because the increase in openness has been offset by a reduction in mobility resulting from changes in the occupational structure. In the 1980s, women were more likely to have had parental heads with similar occupational status than was the case even as recently as

1970. The same was true for men. For example, the share of men and women whose origins are upper middle class has grown, whereas those with farm backgrounds have declined in proportion. For most of the twentieth century, the extent of mobility in the United States was due primarily to changes in the occupational structure between generations. More recently, however, mobility shifts may be due especially to increases in openness and related factors.

Research on occupational and income mobility during the last part of the twentieth century suggests that it may be declining. Tracking trends from 1968 to 1986 within a national sample of almost 5,000 families suggests that income mobility has declined while the extent of income inequality has increased since 1980. Thus, individuals have less chance to improve their income positions than they did in the late 1960s (Veum 1992). Historically, upward mobility has been heavily attributed to shifts in the occupational structure. The influx of new jobs and restructuring of old jobs due to advances in information technologies such as the Internet have profound implications for mobility patterns now and in the future. This is also true for the further establishment and stability of women in the employed labor force, as mothers' occupations have independent effects on the positions of their children, especially those of their daughters (Khazzoom 1997). Changes in the extent of racial/ethnic discrimination also affect mobility patterns. For instance, between 1940 and 1990, the occupational disadvantages of being Japanese- or Chinese-American appears to have declined, especially in the white-collar sector (Sakamoto, Liu, and Tzeng 1998).

Mobility toward and at the Bottom

Evidence of growing numbers of poor people, rising income/earnings inequality, and speculation about a declining middle class have spurred questions about whether downward mobility has increased in the United States in recent years. Research suggests that in some respects it has, but that conclusions depend on whether such mobility is measured in absolute or relative terms. *Absolute downward mobility* refers to a downward shift in economic resources without a simultaneous change in an individual's position relative to others. For example, one's income may decline, but because the income of others is also declining or because those below are much poorer, one may still remain in the same place on the income ladder. *Relative downward mobility,* on the other hand, refers to an actual shift in position on the ladder, a switching of position with others. So, for example, one may start out in the third quintile in the income distribution, but then fall into the fourth because of declines in income. Evidence from large nationally representative samples suggest that absolute downward mobility increased during in the mid-1980s, but that relative downward mobility did not. Moreover, larger amounts of downward mobility came from the middle and lower quintiles than from the upper quintiles. The chances of falling into poverty are much greater for Blacks and those who are near poor (Rodgers 1995). They are also greater for women than for men. Together with evidence cited earlier about growing economic inequality, these trends fit the saying that the "rich are getting richer and poor getting poorer." While its degree varied, the actual risk of downward mobility increased for most demographic groups during the 1980s (Smith 1994).

Mobility at the bottom of the economic ladder has also become a growing concern as questions about the underclass and possible intergenerational transmission of poverty have arisen. To what extent do those born on the bottom move up and to what extent is poverty passed on to subsequent generations? Several recent studies have used data from the Panel Study of Income Dynamics (PSID), which has followed the economic fortunes of 5,000 families and their children since 1968. These data suggest that the chances of upward mobility of both White and Black children are reduced when raised in a poor family. Being from a Black family increases the negative effects of poverty. Generally, about 25 percent of Blacks who were raised in poor families stay poor in early adulthood, compared to about 10 percent of Whites who were raised poor. In other words,

most will move out of poverty, but a minority will be poor like their parents, and the chances of being poor increase significantly for those raised in families where the parents were poor most of the time (Corcoran 1995).

Children who are raised poor are significantly more likely to be poor when they are adults than children brought up in nonpoor families. Even if they move out of poverty, having come from a poor family negatively and significantly affects children's future education, working hours, earnings, and incomes. "Children's futures are clearly constrained by a lack of economic resources.... Being poor matters a lot" (Corcoran 1995, pp. 249 and 261). *Why* these effects occur has been a subject of debate. The mechanisms linking background to future poverty are multiple. Lack of economic resources may affect the economic futures of poor children through their negative effects on intellectual development, stress, job networking, and lifestyle choices (Wilson 1987). Children raised in lower-income families are less likely to complete their schooling and more likely to have children out of wedlock (Duncan et al. 1998)—two conditions that would seem to increase the chances of poverty. Not having a high school education, having fewer parental resources, being raised in a troubled family, and not feeling connected to school increase the chances for unemployment among young adults (Caspi et al. 1998). Unemployment, in turn, increases risks for poverty. Evidence also strongly suggests that employment opportunities and neighborhood conditions are important. The number and nature of economic opportunities in an area also affect poverty risks (Haynie and Gorman 1999). Poor neighborhoods then become socially isolated from nonpoor areas as economic and employment flight from them occurs (Wilson 1987).

STATUS ATTAINMENT: WHAT DETERMINES HOW FAR ONE GOES?

Most mobility studies have not provided us with a systematic picture of the *process* through which mobility occurs. That is, they do not lay out the mechanisms and pathways that explain the connection between the positions of parents and their adult children. Status-attainment studies attempt to identify the factors that are primarily responsible for this connection by focusing on *how* individual parental status affects the status of offspring. These studies provide us with another way to measure a society's openness. A society is considered open to the extent that the economic statuses of children are not dependent on those of their parents. It is the extent of this dependence and how it is maintained that has been the focus of status-attainment research.

The first large-scale set of national data specifically collected for the study of intergenerational mobility in the United States became available with the study of Occupational Changes in a Generation (OCG), later published by Blau and Duncan under the title *The American Occupational Structure*. The data were obtained as part of the Current Population Survey (CPS) of the Bureau of the Census in March 1962. The Bureau regularly carries out surveys of the population on selected issues. At this time, 35,000 households were contacted for participation in the data collection. The regular CPS interview was supplemented on this occasion with a leave-behind questionnaire that the adult male respondents in the household were asked to fill out. The questionnaire contained a number of items on socioeconomic background and familial status of the individual. Of the roughly 25,000 men in these dwelling units, 20,700 responded and formed the basic sample for the OCG study by Blau and Duncan. This sample represents about 45 million men between 20 and 64 years of age who were in the civilian, noninstitutionalized population in March 1962 (Blau and Duncan 1967, pp. 10–19). Thus, this study says nothing about changing economic conditions among women, youths, or the elderly. Nevertheless, the data were considered to be of unusual reliability and completeness because they were collected by trained individuals using established techniques and working for an institution that had been carrying out such surveys for decades.

The real innovativeness in *The American Occupational Structure* lies in its attempt to determine the relative effect of socioeconomic background on occupational attainment. To do this, Blau and Duncan made use of a statistical approach, known as *path analysis,* that would allow them to get at such determination. Path analysis is a statistical and diagrammatic technique that allows an investigator to analyze causal relationships by examining the relative impacts, direct and indirect, of given variables on others. This can be done while simultaneously taking into account the effect of other factors. For example, your father's occupational status may affect your own occupational position indirectly through its impact on your educational attainment, and/or it may have a direct impact on your social position. This effect may be independent of the effect of any other factors on your occupational situation.

Blau and Duncan's basic attainment model is presented in Figure 13.2. They are concerned with the relative role of socioeconomic origins in the determination of the son's occupational status. From the diagram, it can be observed that the greatest direct effects on the occupational status of the son in 1962 come from education and status of his first job. A father's education has an indirect effect on 1962 status through its effect on education, whereas a father's occupation has a direct as well as an indirect effect through its connections with the son's first job and education.

In summarizing the findings of Blau and Duncan, social origin, education, and first job account for less than 50 percent of the variation that occurs in 1962 occupational attainments. The main factor that affects the chances of individuals moving up are the socioeconomic levels from which they begin. The lower the position from which a person begins, argued Blau and Duncan, the greater the probability that he or she will be upwardly mobile, if only because there are more occupational categories above the individual than below. But as men get older and move through their careers, their social origins appear to have less effect on their attainment than past experience and career accomplishments.

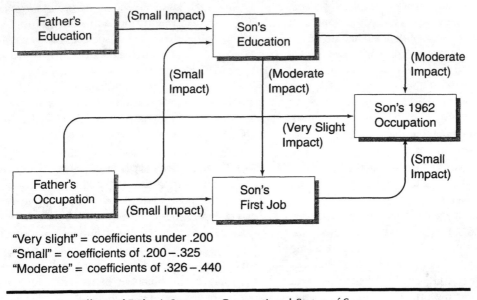

"Very slight" = coefficients under .200
"Small" = coefficients of .200 – .325
"Moderate" = coefficients of .326 – .440

FIGURE 13.2   Effects of Father's Status on Occupational Status of Son

Source: Based on Blau and Duncan 1967.

The Blau-Duncan findings also suggest that having a stable family life, having fewer siblings, and being the youngest or oldest male are positively related to occupational success. But those who come from large families *and* overcome obstacles are also likely to move up occupationally more readily than others who have not had such challenges.

Blau and Duncan concluded that there was no evidence of an increase in rigidity in the occupational structure; upward mobility seemed to have increased slightly since World War II, with no change in the dependence of the son's occupational status on that of his father. Moreover, evidence suggested that the role of education, which Blau and Duncan viewed as an achievement variable, had become increasingly important to occupational attainment. They suggested that this indicated an increase in the importance of universalistic factors in attainment.

In the past, some of the principal sources of mobility were differential fertility, immigration, and technological changes. Today, the main sources consist of (1) internal migration to areas of greater occupational opportunity; (2) continued differen-

tial fertility, which Blau and Duncan did not believe will be completely eliminated; and (3) technological improvements that have expanded occupations at the higher status levels and continually eroded those at the bottom. Like Porter (1967), they suggested that such improvement requires the expansion of a larger pool of trained personnel in the labor force.

Blau and Duncan concluded by indicating that increased industrialization and changes in the occupational structure have given the United States a higher rate of upward mobility from the manual and lower white-collar ranks than most other countries. However, despite the fact that the chances for an individual from the manual ranks to achieve upward mobility may be greater in the United States than elsewhere, the chances of such a person moving up into the highest nonmanual occupations is still less than 10 percent when structural factors are controlled (Hazelrigg 1974).

Blau and Duncan pointed out that the United States does not do as well compared with some other countries when it comes to the dependence of the son's occupational attainment on the father's. They also perceptively observe that *a high degree of mobility can be consistent with extensive inequality and can even help to perpetuate that inequality.* The possibility for mobility may make individuals more complacent about the inequality they observe. Mobility also means changes between generations. Thus, "although high rates of vertical mobility may preserve the status differences observable between *some* individuals, they undermine the status differences between the *same* families that are inherited from one generation to another" (Blau and Duncan 1967, p. 441, emphases in original).

The American Occupational Structure opened the door to a whole new way of examining the problem of the openness of the system of inequality, gave impetus to scores of studies, and made some valuable contributions to our understanding of movement in the occupational hierarchy, but it has its limitations. Since most of the basic ones relate to limitations in the status-attainment approach generally, comments on this matter will be deferred until after the discussion of more recent status-attainment research.

A replication of the March 1962 OCG study done in March 1973 suggested that "Americans today enjoy at least as much opportunity for socioeconomic mobility as in earlier periods of this century. For some, especially blacks in the labor force, opportunities seem to have expanded, even though large inequalities in opportunity persist" (Featherman 1977, p. 15).

Explanations of Status Attainment

The first OCG study by Blau and Duncan gave rise, as we saw, to a simple model of status attainment based on characteristics of the individual at different stages of the life cycle. Basically, the Blau-Duncan model relies on *structural* factors as explanatory variables. It is clear that this model does not consider social-psychological factors, such as aspirations and the influences of parents and peers, that may have a significant effect on attainment. That is, it does not lay out "the finer mechanisms through which status attainment takes place" (Haller and Portes 1973, p. 58).

To deal with the issue of the effect of varied social-psychological factors on educational and occupational attainment, Sewell and others developed what is known as the *Wisconsin model* of socioeconomic attainment (e.g., Sewell and Shah 1967; Sewell, Haller, and Ohlendorf 1970). The large volume of studies produced on this model grew out of an initial survey in 1957 of over 10,000 high school seniors in Wisconsin. Most of the early research was devoted to studying the influence of socioeconomic background and social-psychological factors on aspirations. The follow-up surveys were done in 1964 and in 1975, with a response rate among the original sample of about 90 percent.

Wisconsin Model. A basic version of the Wisconsin model of early occupational achievement is presented in Figure 13.3. Essentially, it shows that socioeconomic background (father's and mother's education, father's occupational status, and parental income) does not affect grades and is independent of academic ability. However, it does have a sizable ultimate effect on educational and occupational attainments through its influence on the mediating variables of significant others' influences and educational and occupational aspirations. Overall, the model explains about 57 percent of the variation in educational and about 40 percent of the variation in early occupational attainment for the men in the sample. The percentages are somewhat smaller for women (Sewell and Hauser 1976). The model has been applied to individuals with both rural and urban backgrounds, although it was first applied to a sample of farm residents and then later applied to groups from a variety of residential backgrounds.

The Wisconsin model is more effective in explaining the variation in educational and occupational attainment than the basic Blau-Duncan model. The earlier structural model accounts for 26 percent and 33 percent in educational and occupational attainment, respectively. It seems clear from the Wisconsin model that a variety of social-psychological factors play mediating roles linking socioeconomic background and ability to attainment (Haller and Portes 1973, p. 68).

Studies conducted after the development of the Wisconsin model and using national longitudinal

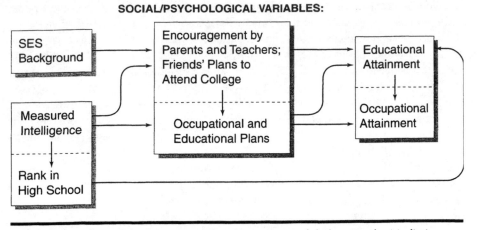

SOCIAL/PSYCHOLOGICAL VARIABLES:

FIGURE 13.3   A Simplified Version of the Wisconsin Model Showing the Mediating Role of Social-Psychological Factors in Individual Attainment

Source: Adapted from Sewell, Haller, and Ohlendorf 1970, p. 1023.

samples tended to support the general arguments of the model. Of the factors included in the model, education appears to be the most important factor in predicting occupational attainment, although it explains only a small percentage (9 to 11 percent) of the variation in occupational attainment (Alexander, Eckland, and Griffin 1975). And, in contrast to the model, it appears that social-psychological variables play less of role in accounting for educational attainment than do more objective factors such as "socioeconomic background, recorded ability, and school performance" (Wilson and Portes 1975, p. 354).

What is revealing in the other findings is that none of these models explains very much of the variations that exist among individuals in earnings and income, and what small proportion they do explain (under 20 percent) is due primarily to the effect of objective factors, such as SES, rather than to social-psychological variables.

The Role of Education in Attainment

The discovery that neither the Blau-Duncan nor the Wisconsin model of attainment accounts for very much of the variation in earnings and income has given rise to a variety of speculations about

what the really significant factors might be. The connection between education and economic achievement, as we have seen, has not been strong. These models leave almost half of the variation in occupational achievement and much more of the difference in earnings and income unexplained.

Still, most of those concerned with the extent of upward mobility have assumed the importance of education. But the level of its importance has been called into question. For one thing, level of education has been found to have less impact on attainment once one is in an organization, especially if one is trapped in a single-job ladder. Among nonmanual employees seeking mobility outside the organization where they presently work, having a higher education has been found to actually impede mobility. But among manual workers, education has the opposite effect. The negative effect of education among nonmanual workers may be due in part to the importance of on-the-job training and seniority returns in such white-collar positions. It may also be due to the increased importance of trust and predictability as qualities as one moves up the institution's hierarchy (Kanter 1977a; Jackall 1988). People in these occupations are not likely to find things any better outside the place where they work, and consequently, are less likely to move (DiPrete and Krecker 1991). It may also be the case that the specific characteristics necessary for many high-level professional/managerial positions within a given organization are unique and therefore not transferable to outside organizations. This would further inhibit mobility between occupations.

Education's effect also seems to vary across societies. First, education appears to have its greatest impact on occupational attainment in industrial countries, in large part because they are more likely than agrarian societies to be egalitarian and to stress achievement rather than ascription in their attainment process (Treiman and Ganzeboom 1990). Second, education appears to have its greatest impact when it provides specific skills for specific occupations or is tied to an apprenticeship program (Kurz and Muller 1987). The traditional argument for this has been that advances in technology and upgrading of the occupational structure have resulted in a need for greater skills and training that education is supposed to supply.

Collins (1971) challenged this conclusion, saying there is evidence that what is important about education is not the training it provides but the fact that it represents an introduction into a particular "status culture." Many individuals, argued Collins, are overeducated for their jobs, and those who are better educated do not necessarily perform better on their jobs than the less educated. In fact, Collins stated, U.S. schools generally are not very good at providing students with the vocational skills they need to be successful in the performance of their jobs. What is important about schools for early occupational achievement is that they teach the person a particular set of values and ways of acting and defining things. Employers then select those who would fit into the status culture of the elite and those who might be willing to serve under them because of their adherence to the prescriptions of a particular status culture. In this manner, schools can be used to control membership in economic institutions. Thus, what is important about schools for employment, argued Collins, is not their passing on of knowledge, but

the fact that in a variety of ways they instill in students certain kinds of status-cultural values. It is not known at this point whether the training effect of education on mobility is more important than its role in maintaining class positions across generations (Bielby 1981).

If the variables we have discussed, including education, do not fully explain earnings and income, what else does? Sex, race, labor market, industry, and economic sector of employment are involved. For example, sex segregation in occupation affects the chances for earning increases and joblessness. Working in a male-dominated occupation increases the likelihood for wage promotion for men, but also increases the odds that women will be pushed out of that job. Since male-typed occupations generally have higher earnings than female-typed jobs, access to such positions would seem to be necessary for women to increase their earnings significantly, but the pressures they encounter from resentful men only increase the probability that they will not last in these positions (Maume 1999). Mothers, then, disproportionately enter female-dominated occupations, which, in turn, raises the chances that their daughters will follow a similar path (Khazzoom 1997). Another suggestion is that factors associated with an individual's current experiences may be better predictors of earnings. These might include on-the-job training, job performance and satisfaction, and the nature of the job and labor markets (Sewell and Hauser 1976). The amount of time spent in the labor force also affects an individual's earnings (Spaeth 1976a). But as already noted, the length of time spent in a high-paying position depends in part on the pressures to which one is subjected.

In addition to these, networking and connections may play important roles in the explanation of earnings and income. Research suggests that individuals who get jobs through personal contacts are more likely to get wage increases and promotion opportunities than those who secure jobs without such contacts. By providing positive information and optimizing the chances of good matches between individuals and jobs, contacts can help create work environments for their acquaintances that are favorable for promotions and pay raises (Coverdill 1998).

Finally, some people just happen to be in the right spot at the appropriate time. For example, you happen to be in a community that has a greater range of jobs than others, or the weather may destroy your job in construction, or you happen to be in a city where a new plant locates (Jencks et al. 1973, p. 227). Some of these kinds of events may be appropriately labeled as luck, but others are factors that are systematically related to earnings but have not yet been incorporated into attainment models. The real job of the analyst, as Featherman stated, "is to reduce the size of the residual component toward the limits of 'luck's' imprint on the various occupational accomplishments of workers" (1977, p. 16).

Structures in the Process of Attainment

The notion that luck or being in the right place at the right time may play a role in attainment suggests that one's position in a broader social structure is significant for mobility. Most of the early research on the process of occupational and income attainment focused on characteristics of the individuals involved (i.e., their educations, parents, attitudes, etc.). In asking the question, What determines how far a person gets? especially when compared to their parents, U.S. sociology trained its eye almost solely on human capital factors and the peculiarities of people's backgrounds. This has been one of the primary deficiencies of that early research.

Especially since the mid-1980s, however, there has been an emphasis on structural factors in attainment. When one looks outside the individual for reasons for success or failure, one finds that structures in society and in organizations play a significant role in the chances for upward or downward movement. Moreover, while earlier research was concerned primarily with accounting for socioeconomic attainment *in general,* many post-1990 investigations examine the attainment process as it is played out within the structural context

of a given economic sector or organization. Attainment always takes place within a concrete organizational or economic context, and variations in the structural networks, hierarchies, and career pathways between organizations can help account for differences in attainment processes and outcomes. This latter realization has led to a focus on intragenerational career job mobility rather than on differences between parents and children.

How, specifically, is structure involved in the attainment process? At a broad level, shifts in the national occupational structure obviously create openings and closures in positions. They create new occupations and eliminate others. For example, there has been a lot of discussion of the United States moving rapidly from a manufacturing to a service-based economy, causing layoffs in one area and creating new openings in the rising service sector. Over the long run, occupations rise and fall in their dominance of a nation's employment structure. These national economic changes are in turn rooted in technology changes, international competition, and the movement of capital between and within nations. Attendant streamlining, downsizing, and simple shutdowns also affect the alternatives available for attainment.

So-called vacancy-driven models stress the fact "that mobility depends on the availability of empty positions and that the filling of jobs is interdependent. One person's move to a new job or out of a job system creates an opening to be filled" (Rosenfeld 1992). For example, historically, many immigrants have dominated certain types of lower status positions as natives have moved on to the greener pastures of more prestigious jobs. At the national level, attainment is also affected by legislative changes. Affirmative action and equal employment opportunity policies are aimed at broadening the opportunity structures of women and racial/ethnic minorities (ibid.).

Below the national level, attainment is also tied to the structure of opportunities within different economic sectors and organizations. Within large formal organizations of the core economic sector, as was noted earlier, jobs are more likely than in the peripheral sector to be part of a career ladder (i.e., an internal occupational hierarchy along which an individual can move). Frequently, the ladder may be multifaceted or have multiple branches, or an organization may have several job ladders of varying heights, widths, and connections. The relative location of a person in that structure affects the criteria needed and the chances for advancement. Upward mobility is generally slower if one is in a job that is close to the top of a ladder. The pathways to advancement can vary within the same structure (Diprete and Krecker 1991; Rosenfeld 1992). The presence of this treelike structure creates opportunities for differential attainment that are independent of the characteristics of individuals.

Some mobility is not vacancy driven, however. For example, in some unionized plants, one's time-in-grade or seniority affects economic advancement, and in colleges and universities, time-in-rank affects promotion up the professorial hierarchy (Rosenfeld 1992). Knowledge about and access to information about the various avenues to advancement within an organization also is important, and this may vary with one's position in it and the internal network of which one is a part. Being an insider, having connections, and being "in the know" affect one's chances for attainment, especially within an organization whose opportunity ladder is open solely or primarily only to current employees (Diprete and Krecker 1991).

Robert Jackall's intensive study of corporations reveals how critical social skills and personality characteristics are and how they can become more important and eventually displace hard work, education, and other achievement-based factors in moving up the corporate ladder. He found that "managers rarely speak of objective criteria for achieving success because once certain crucial points in one's career are passed, success and failure seem to have little to do with one's accomplishments" (Jackall 1988, p. 41). One manager observed that once a high administrative level is reached, "all have similar levels of ability, drive, competence, and so on. What happens is that people perceive in others *what they like*—operating styles, personalities, ability to get along. Now

these are all very subjective judgments" (p. 45; emphasis in original). Having the appropriate mentor and sponsor helps one's chances for upward mobility. Being in a structural location where one knows who is thinking and doing what enhances the probability that one can tailor oneself accordingly.

MOBILITY AND ATTAINMENT PROCESS AMONG AFRICAN AMERICANS

In their landmark study of U.S. men in the early 1960s, Blau and Duncan (1967) argued that Blacks generally start out from a lower position, but instead of moving up in a manner commensurate with their education and other human capital, they become involved in a vicious circle in which they are hindered at each step along the way in the attainment process. That is, their disadvantages are *cumulative*. They have a hard time getting a higher education, and when they do, the occupational returns for that education are less than those received by Whites. Knowledge of this fact may lower the incentive of Blacks to obtain such education, and thereby reinforce the negative stereotype of Blacks as unwilling to be educated. Although southerners and immigrants are disadvantaged, their problems are not of this cumulative nature.

The replication of this national study in the 1970s found that both Blacks and Whites have gained in educational attainment, but the gains in recent years have been greatest for Blacks and the economic returns to their educations have increased. Moreover, Blacks gained in occupational status relative to Whites. Recent changes have moderated the effects of racial barriers, according to Featherman and Hauser, and Black fathers who are in white-collar positions are able to a greater degree to pass on their occupational statuses to their sons.

Occupational inequality between Blacks and Whites, as measured by broad occupational categories, declined between 1950 and 1980. In the South, in contrast to the nation as a whole, the decline in occupational inequality began in the

1960s. It appears to have been governmental policies rather than economic growth that was linked to this decline (Fossett, Galle, and Kelly 1986). Declines in family income inequality since World War II, especially for vulnerable groups (e.g., female-headed families), are more closely related to the growth of social welfare programs than to upswings in the business cycle (Treas 1983).

Despite the positive tone of the preceding conclusions, the greater inheritance of occupational status among upper white-collar Black fathers and sons has helped to create greater economic inequality and more "visible" classes within the Black community (Featherman and Hauser 1978; Hout 1984). Blacks who moved up have been disproportionately drawn from more favored socioeconomic backgrounds, and those who had a privileged occupational position, especially in the public sector, were more likely to be able to hold onto it than individuals in manual positions. In other words, "class" factors became more important for Blacks' occupational attainment during the 1960s and 1970s (Hout 1984).

Research on eminent Black Americans listed in *Who's Who Among Black Americans* also has found that they are more likely to come from privileged backgrounds. Specifically, they are more likely than the average Black to have had parents who are professionals and are highly educated. Further back in their lineage, their ancestors were more likely to have been "free" Blacks with lighter skin (Mullins and Sites 1984). However, the paths to eminence and the occupations that characterize eminent Black Americans have differed historically from those that distinguish eminent White Americans (Lieberson and Carter 1979). Of course, an increase in the impact of class origins among Blacks does not necessarily mean that race has become *less* significant in their lives. Although this research may *suggest* that class is becoming more important than race in determining occupational attainment, Blacks do not perceive it this way. Data from national surveys conducted from the mid-1970s to the mid-1980s show no significant decline in the effects of race on feelings of despair. Blacks are significantly

more likely than Whites to feel that things are getting worse rather than better for the average person. In fact, the strength of the relationship between race and such feelings increased between 1980 and 1984 (Austin and Stack 1988).

While middle-class Blacks may be more able to retain their positions, Blacks who were in low-paid jobs were less likely than comparable Whites to be upwardly mobile (Pomer 1986). Movement from the peripheral to the core sector of the economy is especially difficult for Blacks. Mobility into the higher-paying core sector or into a higher status occupation may be hindered by residential segregation which limits access and opportunities to move up, especially in the private sector (Hirschman and Wong 1984; Hout 1986). If Blacks do move up, it is most likely to an adjacent category rather than to an upper nonmanual position. Blacks seldom advance to managerial positions, and in contrast to Whites, most of the movement into the "mainstream" is in the public rather than private sector.

The Black middle class has grown in recent decades. "In a period of slightly more than one hundred years (1865–1970), the Black middle class increased from a small group of 'free Negroes' to a sizable stratum of the Black population" (Durant and Louden 1986, p. 254). A variety of factors have been linked to this growth, including industrialization, urbanization, increased education and collective action, and occupational differentiation. However, much of the growth of the Black middle class can be attributed to the appreciable number who have assumed public or governmental white-collar jobs, rather than managerial or upper-level technical positions in the private sector (Collins 1983; Hout 1984). This makes the Black middle class more potentially vulnerable to shifts within government and its budget.

The instability in the position of Blacks who are in white-collar positions is further indicated by analyses of mobility in earnings using census data from 1967 to 1991 (Gittleman and Joyce 1995). Blacks, especially Black women, who are in the upper quintile of earnings are much less likely than Whites to maintain that position for at least one year. Part of the reason for this earnings instability is related to the fact that White men are more likely to occupy professional and managerial occupations, and Black men are more likely to be found in sales and clerical jobs, positions associated with greater fluctuations in earnings. In general, Blacks are less likely than Whites to be found in the upper-earnings quintile and more likely to be in the bottom quintile. When in the bottom, they are also more likely than Whites to stay there.

Thus, there is some debate about exactly how much progress there has been for Blacks as a whole. Blacks still lag significantly behind Whites in median family income, which has not improved relative to Whites since the 1960s. The poverty rate for Blacks is still three times the rate for Whites, and it has been that way for decades. Although there has been some occupational upgrading for Black men, it is in broad occupational categories. There are greater differences between the races when specific, narrower occupational categories are examined and mobility is more restricted (see Chapter 6).

Race and the Status-Attainment Process

Research has been done to determine if the models that have been developed to explain educational and occupational attainment apply to Blacks as well as they do to Whites. Since race has an effect on a variety of areas in U.S. life, it may be suspected that what applies to Whites does not apply to Blacks. Since race is an ascribed characteristic, a model based on achievement norms may not fit Blacks as well as Whites. Also, race affects mobility, and the relationship between many of the variables that are included in these standard models differ from one race to another. Finally, the nature of the socialization process in the two races may be different (Porter, 1974).

A study by Portes and Wilson (1976) suggested that the process of educational attainment does differ among Blacks. Analyzing a nationwide sample of boys who had been surveyed over a period of several years, and using a variant of the Wisconsin model of status attainment (described earlier), they found several differences between Blacks and Whites:

1. The variables in the model are better at explaining attainment among Whites than among Blacks, which suggests that factors not traditionally considered are more important for Blacks.
2. The more objective factors of socioeconomic background, mental ability, and academic performance are more important for White attainment, whereas among Blacks, the later and more subjective variables of self-esteem and educational aspirations are the significant ones for Blacks,
   a. There is a much stronger connection between mental ability and academic performance and between the latter and educational attainment among Whites than among Blacks. Among Blacks, there is no significant direct connection between academic performance and attainment.
   b. Conversely, the ties of mental ability to self-esteem and the ties of self-esteem to attainment are much stronger among Blacks than Whites.

In summarizing their findings, Portes and Wilson suggested that the results imply a distinction among Whites and Blacks as insiders and outsiders in the U.S. achievement system. In an open society, one would expect that performance and ability would be quite important, and they are for Whites. But for Blacks, educational attainment is more dependent on self-reliance and ambition. In a manner of speaking, then, while Blacks have had to rely on these qualities, Whites "have at their disposal an additional set of institutional 'machinery' which can, in effect, carry them along to higher levels of attainment" (Portes and Wilson 1976, p. 430).

Porter (1974) examined early occupational as well as educational achievement among Blacks and Whites and also found significant racial differences in the processes involved. His study of a large sample of males suggests that among Blacks, grades are largely a function of personality factors, such as conformity and ambition, whereas among Whites, both personality and intelligence play roles. As in the Portes and Wilson (1976) findings, subjective rather than objective conditions appear to play a greater part in the attainment process for Blacks. "It would appear that the official sanctions of the school system operate primarily with reference to the visible being of the pupil, and only secondarily, and on the condition that he is White, with reference to academic ability" (Porter 1974, p. 311). Another interesting finding of this study is that in contrast to the results among Whites, grades have no direct effect on either educational or occupational attainment.

Porter did note that there are similarities in the attainment process between the races. Among both, educational attainment is strongly affected by intelligence, and occupational attainment is more affected by educational achievement than by any other factor in the model. Despite these similarities, Porter stated that the main results are those that bring out the differences in the attainment process between the races.

Blacks themselves feel that their path to occupational attainment is made more difficult by the lack of decent available jobs for which they are qualified, the concentrated poverty of their neighborhoods, and their lack of social contacts in the inner city. They believe that luck, connections, education, help from those who have made it, and being from the right neighborhood make all the difference:

> "It's not where you go, it's the people; you got to know somebody to get you in."
>
> "Oh, white people got the best chance.... They got the top jobs, and in this city, man, you know, it's all who you know."
>
> "If you're from a nice neighborhood I believe it's easier for you to get a job and stuff.... The people from the Projects...we tend to think of them as being the lowest of the low in society."
>
> "You notice: your own people don't like to help you. Among blacks, I'll put it that way. Because, I got some people in my family...they say they'll help you but they won't." (Venkatesh 1994, pp. 171, 173)

PATTERNS OF MOBILITY AND ATTAINMENT AMONG WOMEN

The major national studies done on intergenerational mobility during the 1960s and 1970s concentrated on the occupational statuses of *men*. Thus, most of what we have been reviewing about social mobility has really concerned only the mobility of men. It is difficult to think of the results of national mobility studies as being representative of the entire mobility structure of the United States when at least half of the population is not represented in those studies. Part of the reason for the omission of women in these studies is that they are based on the assumption that women's positions are dependent on those of their husbands or fathers, and that to know the mobility patterns of men is, therefore, to know the patterns for the entire society. Thus, intergenerational mobility studies involving women most often will compare a woman's position with that of her father rather than her mother, or with her husband or brother(s). The latter is done in studies of marital mobility, as you will see. If the husband's position is higher than that of the wife's brother, then upward mobility through marriage is said to have occurred. This is the same bias that exists when one argues that a woman's class position can be measured by her father's or husband's position, which is an assumption that pervades much traditional stratification literature (Acker 1973).

The central problem with all this is that women are not considered as independent persons, some even unmarried, with their own occupational, educational, and income resources. From discussions earlier in this book, you know that sex and gender inequality exists along a variety of dimensions, and yet people's concepts (like class position) reflect a concern primarily for the attributes of males. The fact of sex inequality needs to be taken into fuller account in measures and studies of mobility (Acker 1973).

Evidence varies on the extent to which the socioeconomic position of women has improved. In *absolute* terms, there appears to have been improvement in the occupational, educational, and income attainments of women, but in relation to men, little change seems to have occurred since the late 1960s (Richards 1986). Women still tend to be concentrated in certain kinds of jobs, although there is some evidence that, especially since the 1970s, there has been a decline in occupational segregation between the sexes (Jacobs 1989). An examination of national data from 1910 to 1986 suggests that although the extent of such segregation remained fairly constant in the period from 1910 to 1970, since that time there has been a measurable decline, especially in nonfarm occupations. Jacobs suggested that part of the reason for the perceived lack of decline in desegregation during the first 70 years of this century relates to the decline of child and agricultural labor, both of which were among the most integrated kinds of work. Had these remained as large relative to other general occupational categories as they were at the turn of the century, desegregation would have been more obvious.

Other evidence, however, suggests that some traditionally "female" occupations—such as phone operators, servers, and maids/servants—also have declined in numbers over the last several decades, helping to account for any desegregation that has occurred (Beller 1984). Thus, structural shifts among more narrowly defined occupations also contribute to changes in sex segregation. Moreover, some researchers have suggested that the movement toward more openness in the broadly defined occupational structure is indicative of a long-term trend, but others believe that the movement of women into certain traditionally male occupations may be the first step toward a resegregation of women (Reskin 1988). At one time, for example, school teaching was a predominantly "male" occupation, but since early in this century it has increasingly become defined as a "female" occupation. In more recent years, this trend has occurred for other occupations as well, such as bank tellers and residential real estate brokers. This is important because, as you have seen, the earnings associated with an occupation are related to the proportion of women in it. A greater percentage of females in an occupation is associated with lower earnings.

What causes this shift of males out of an occupation, creating an opportunity for women to move into it? Several factors are involved. First, the decline in rewards attached to an occupation can motivate males to leave the occupation, especially if other more lucrative positions are open to them. Second, changes in the nature of the work in an occupation, such as the work becoming more monotonous, also can cause them to move to another occupation, Third, a lack of opportunity to advance or move up increases the probability of movement out of an occupation. Finally, the larger the supply of women available in the labor force, the more likely they are to move into these vacancies, eventually becoming the majority proportion within these occupations (Reskin 1988). The chances of the latter happening are enhanced by the fact that fewer numbers of occupations, especially male occupations, are open to women. The redefinition of an occupation as "female," coupled with the crowding of women into it, then fosters a decline in the wages of workers in that field (Bergmann 1974; Strober and Arnold 1987). "Is resegregation the inevitable outcome of occupational integration? The answer is probably yes as long as only a small number of traditionally male occupations become open to the large number of women who want and need better paying jobs" (Reskin 1988, p. 263).

What can be said about the occupational mobility of patterns of women? The intergenerational mobility of women is characterized by specific characteristics (Roos 1985). Men and women may come from the same status origins, but they tend to go to different destinations. Although there is a relationship between class of origin and class of destination among both men and women, in general women tend to move into clerical, low-status professional, and service occupations, whereas men go into professional and production occupations. This is the case not only in the United States but in many other industrial countries as well (Roos 1985). The limitations for women in occupational mobility are echoed in their earnings experiences, as well. Among those with salaries or wages, women are *more* likely than men to be and remain at the bottom of the earnings ladder, but are *less* likely than men to be or remain at the top (Gittleman and Joyce 1995).

The likelihood of working in a professional occupation is greatest for daughters from professional or managerial backgrounds, and lowest for those who have fathers who are in farm or production work. This suggests that most of the mobility is short range in nature. At the same time, however, women who have parents with service occupations are more likely to move into white-collar than blue-collar jobs. While parental occupations affect the attainment of their children, it is the mothers' occupations that appear to have more impact on the destination of their daughters (Khazzoom 1997)

Although it has not been extensively examined for men, mobility through marriage for women has been studied. This itself is a telling commentary on the manner in which women have been incorporated into mobility studies. *Marital mobility* refers to the mobility for the daughter that results from movement from the father's status to the occupational status of her husband. A woman's status is considered as being defined entirely in terms of the position of her husband and father. Studies using national data indicate that women who do not work but marry tend to marry men whose statuses are like those of their brothers; on the other hand, women who do work move into occupational statuses quite unlike those of their brothers (Tyree and Treas 1974). In other words, since the women who do marry adopt the statuses of their husbands, and since the patterns of mobility for the latter are similar to those of the brothers of these women, it is probable that they will attain statuses similar to those of their brothers, especially if they marry into the same social class. When these women are married but not working, their statuses are tied directly to the processes of mobility operant among males. If one is using the husband's occupation as the measure of status, women appear to have slightly greater mobility through their marriage than men have through their employment (Kurz and Muller 1987; Chase 1975).

Women who marry are more likely to cross major class boundaries, as from blue-collar origins to the white-collar status of their husbands. Chase suggested that the greater mobility of daughters who marry as compared with the intergenerational mobility of men may be due in part to two factors: (1) It is easier to obtain the requirements needed to be maritally mobile (such as attractiveness and charm) than it is for men to obtain the requirements to be occupationally mobile (such as skills and education) and (2) Sons are more likely to inherit the businesses of their fathers than are daughters, leaving the latter freer to marry higher or lower than their fathers' statuses (Chase 1975). Of course, these are only suggested reasons. It may very well be that the first is not accurate, and as far as the second is concerned, a son can always sell the business and marry whomever he pleases.

The occupational attainment of women who are employed, and thereby derive their statuses from their own work, is affected by a pattern of factors that is different from the pattern that affects the attainment path of men. Thus, the attainment process of employed women is quite different from that of married, nonemployed women, whose attainment path is directly tied to that of their husbands. The differences are largely due to the features of the structural context that women encounter when they move into the labor force—features that frequently involve curves, bumps, and walls not often experienced by men. Think of the road to attainment as akin to a maze, and some mazes are more complex and difficult than others. How successful one is in getting through it may depend partially on individual attributes, but it also depends heavily on the structure of the maze itself.

Obstructions in the Context of Mobility

To understand fully the process of mobility, it is important to remember that the mobility of groups and individuals always takes place within a given social and cultural context. Consider that mobility for men and women, like that for the races, takes place in a context in which (1) there are different expectations of each sex, (2) occupations are sex segregated to begin with, (3) internal labor markets and hierarchies exist within the organizations in which persons are employed, and (4) firms are differentiated in terms of formalization, complexity, size, market, and other characteristics. What this all means is that mobility does not take place in a vacuum. Rather, there is a particular texture in the paths to mobility that exist in different countries. The structuring of the private economy into different industrial sectors, for example, creates explicit barriers and avenues for career mobility (Tolbert 1982). For women, especially, part of this texture consists of obstacles and dead ends (DiPrete and Soule 1988).

For men, as well as for women, part of the texture is related to the autonomous nature of an occupation and/or the specialization of the education associated with it. Barriers to mobility appear to exist between the autonomous and less specialized jobs, on the one hand, and those that are less autonomous or require less specialized education, on the other. In a study of 20,000 men in the civilian labor force, Snipp (1985) found that the most difficult barriers to cross in the path to mobility are those that divide manual from nonmanual labor, professional from nonprofessional, and skilled crafts from semi- or unskilled labor, respectively. Similarly, for women there are also broad occupational divides that are difficult to cross. For example, it is harder for women than for men to move from the secondary labor market or lower rungs of the primary market into the well-paying, stable professional, managerial, and craft positions at the top of the primary labor market (Waddoups and Assane 1993).

The patterns of mobility and immobility being described are shaped in part by the expectations people have about categories of individuals, and, in the absence of knowledge about a person, external characteristics such as sex and/or race are used to provide clues to what might be expected (Berger et al. 1972, 1977). Traditional U.S. culture contains beliefs about the usual behavior and personality characteristics of each sex. These expectations help to generate and maintain sex segregation in occupations, which, in turn, reinforce expectations. Women, for example, are much less likely than men to be corporate executives, meaning that when someone below or outside the organization is being considered for a top executive position, most of those involved in making the decision will be men who have been socialized into having particular expectations about male and female candidates.

In her study of an industrial corporation, Kanter (1977a) found that at the top is an inner circle of individuals who have to be counted on to share a similar view of the organization and to behave in a manner consistent with that view. There are distinct pressures for homogeneity and conformity at the managerial level. A large part of the reason for this pressure to conform arises from the open nature of organizations and the managerial positions within them. Since position tasks are not well defined at that level and the organization operates in a "turbulent" environment with other organizations, the conclusion is that executives have to be able to trust each other and see each other's behavior as predictable. "Women were decidedly placed in the category of the incomprehensible and unpredictable" (Kanter 1977a, p. 58).

Consistent with this conclusion, additional research has found that middle-level managers *believe* that upwardly mobile men are more likely to be promoted because of greater support and sponsorship within the organization, and that men's future power and mobility would be greater because of this support and sponsorship. The managers also thought that promoted men would be considered to be more successful than women who had been promoted, even if their performances were not any better (Wiley and Eskilson 1983). What all this research suggests is that the external characteristic of sex is used as a criterion to conclude that it may be too much of a risk to have women and other "unpredictable" individuals within management. By continually recruiting men into those positions, the inequality in occupational positions between the sexes is perpetuated.

One of the difficult dilemmas for women's mobility concerns the fact that the hiring and promoting of women at given managerial levels may depend on the proportion of women already present in an organization at or below those levels. A recent study of managerial positions in 333 savings-and-loan associations suggests that the chances for hiring and promotion into a managerial position are increased as the proportion of women in or below that position goes up. They are also optimized when a solid proportion, though not a majority, of those in higher decision-making positions are also women. Thus, women appear to have to be present in relatively high percentages before women are hired or promoted in good numbers. But the question remains: "Although having women present in managerial positions is crucial to bringing more women into management, it remains unclear how women initially attain managerial positions" (Cohen, Broschak, and Haveman 1998, p. 723).

Women, of course, have traditionally been socialized into the same general beliefs about the sexes as men, and their beliefs can have an impact on the probability of their being upwardly mobile. For example, the willingness to move is an important factor in career mobility, but generally women are less willing to move than men. Research among white-collar employees in a federal agency, for example, found that regardless of their education and other factors, women express less desire to move (Markham et al. 1983). Part of the reason may be that women see more family conflict arising as a result of moving. Perhaps this sensitivity is due to the socialization among women to have the family as a central focus of their lives. A significant factor in the reluctance to move is that most men consider themselves to be the "primary providers," and most women do not. Women who *do* see themselves in these terms are just as willing to move as men in similar circumstances (Markham et al. 1983).

These self-definitions and expectations combine with occupational segregation and the internal market structure of organizations to limit mobility by women. When women are in a position that is part of an internal labor market, they benefit less from that position than men do, in large part because a majority of them do not make job changes within a firm but move to other employers. Thus, women do not participate as fully as men in the career ladders available in many organizations, and this contributes heavily to the wage differences between the sexes (Felmlee 1982). In any case, "women's" positions are less likely to be linked to apprenticeships and career ladders and more likely to be surrounded by "dead space"—that is, not connected to a distinct career-promotion ladder (Seidman 1978). Moreover, when women are in "female" white-collar positions, such as that of secretary, and perform admirably because of their accumulated but very specific job expertise, they may have less chance to be occupationally mobile within an organization (Kanter 1977a). Being promoted or not promoted is not always based on merit at the level of the concrete organization (Hartmann 1987). These obstacles in the attainment process for women may provide some of the reasons past research has shown that the career trajectories of women are relatively flat when compared to those of men.

In other words, the entry-level jobs and job families are structured, often even in large firms, to maintain sex segregation. Moreover, if a position is a dead end, it will have consequences on the behavior and demeanor of the individual in that position. "Opportunity structures shape behavior in such a way that they confirm their own prophecies. Those people set on high-mobility tracks tend to develop attitudes and values that impel them further along the track: work commitment, high aspirations, and upward orientations. Those set on low-mobility tracks tend to become indifferent, to give up, and thus to 'prove' that their initial placement was correct.... It is graphically clear how cycles of advantage and cycles of disadvantage are perpetuated in organizations and in society" (Kanter 1977a,

p. 158). Once in a low-status, "female" job, it is difficult to move out. This result only reconfirms the position as a "female" one and, therefore, one with certain characteristics. "It may be because the jobs are done by women that they are viewed as unskilled and are lower paid, not just that low-wage (low-skills) jobs are created and women are channeled into them" (Hartmann 1987a, p. 63).

Sex and the Process of Status Attainment

Some studies have suggested that the basic attainment process is similar for working males and females (Featherman and Hauser 1976; Treiman and Terrell 1975; McClendon 1976). Among both men and women, for example, education has been the most important factor of those included in models of occupational attainment. Socioeconomic background has a much weaker effect. This appears to be the case in most industrial countries. Also, the average occupational prestige of men and women is similar.

Despite their presence, these similarities mask important inadequacies and gender differences found within status-attainment studies. The gender-related inadequacies involve a focus on occupational prestige rather than other dimensions of occupational life such as power, earnings, and autonomy. Not only do these other areas reveal occupational inequalities between men and women not easily seen in studies of occupational prestige but, when used in models of occupational attainment, important differences also appear between the sexes in the factors that affect attainment. For example, Roos (1985) found in her study of 12 industrial countries that when "occupational wage hierarchy" is substituted for "occupational prestige" as the dependent variable, then differences in the effects of variables surface between men and women. Men receive better income returns on each of the determinants in the models. Another inadequacy is the exclusion of housework as as a form of occupation. Because housework is not formally defined as part of the labor force, a significant percentage of people, mostly women, are excluded

from studies of attainment. When one considers that housework contributes to the maintenance of society and capitalism, it appears obvious that it should be considered valuable work and incorporated into the occupational hierarchy in a meaningful and measurable way (Acker 1973). In other words, a class analysis that involves women should include housework as an occupation as well as other occupational differences among women (Eisenstein 1990). Attainment studies have also tended to neglect the contribution of the mother's occupation to the attainment of offspring, especially the daughter's. Research demonstrates that a mother's occupation is even more important than a father's in predicting a daughter's attainment (Rosenfeld 1978; Stevens and Boyd 1980).

While suffering from gender-related inadequacies, status-attainment research has uncovered significant differences in the attainment processes of men and women. As just indicated, women's attainment is more significantly affected by the mother's occupation. In addition, although education is a critical factor for attainment for both sexes, it is only one of several factors that are important for men, yet it is the only or by far the most significant factor in attainment for women (Roos 1985). For example, education is especially more important for females as a predictor of mobility from a secondary labor market position to one in the lower primary market. Women also are more significantly affected by household-related variables than are men. The presence of a child has a dampening effect on the upward mobility of women, but it has no similar effect for men (Waddoups and Assane 1993).

SOME OBSERVATIONS ON STUDIES OF STATUS ATTAINMENT

In recent years, the study of status attainment has played a dominant role in U.S. research on social stratification and mobility. Indeed, among many of those doing this research, the process of stratification has come to be defined largely in terms of status attainment.

There is no question that the research in this area has been remarkably coherent, consistent, and cumulative—a feat rarely achieved in sociology. Moreover, the statistical techniques that have been brought to bear on issues concerning mobility and achievement processes have become increasingly sophisticated in the last 30 years. Finally, the conclusions of these studies, which are often quite similar, are stabilized by the fact that data from a variety of national samples have been used in reaching them.

Yet the research discussed here and the orientation to inequality or stratification as status attainment have distinct limitations. First, *the study of status transmission is not coterminous with the study of stratification or inequality.* "Social stratification means the differentiation of a given population into hierarchically superposed classes. It is manifested in the existence of upper and lower social layers" (Sorokin 1959, p. 11). This element of stratification is missing from the status-transmission portrayal. The population could be similarly distributed among income categories over a period of time even in the absence of status transmission. If one were to follow only the attainment approach, one would wind up missing a great deal that is of interest to the student of stratification and inequality. There are several ways to view inequality and stratification, and status attainment is just one of these. Status attainment occurs *within* a system of inequality.

Second, *status-attainment models are inadequate explanations of economic inequality.* Status-attainment models help illuminate part of the process involved in bringing about varying levels of educational and occupational success. But they do much more poorly in explaining income distribution, which some feel to be the major component of the system of inequality. As indicated earlier, large amounts of the variations in socioeconomic attainment are left unexplained by these models. Part of their inadequacy as explanations may be due to the fact that, as Blau and Duncan themselves have confessed, attainment research "is not suited for the study of the problems posed by stratification theory" such as that of Marx or Durkheim (1967, p. 3). Yet, closer attention to these theories would surely make attainment researchers more sensitive to the social and cultural context in which attainment takes place.

Third, *status-attainment models have tended to ignore the effect of nonindividual factors on attainment.* Much of the unexplained variance in early models may be due to the operation of wider societal and institutional contexts that are not incorporated in these explanations. It seems evident that one cannot explain inequality or stratification by reference solely to characteristics of the individual or his or her background—even if some of these are ascribed and others achieved in nature. Characteristics of the career line, internal labor-market structure, organizational culture, sector of the economy, industry, and local supply and demand all affect the occupational positioning and mobility of individuals. All of these suggest the rich texturing of the context in which the attainment process occurs (Spilerman 1978). More scholars have effectively incorporated considerations of labor market, economic sector, organizational structure, race, sex, and region into their attainment models. The recent work on structural models is especially exciting because it broadens one's vision beyond the narrow notion that attainment is simply in the hands of the individual.

Finally, *the theoretical underpinnings of much status-attainment research have a conservative bent.* Occupational inequality is conceived in terms of positions graded on a continuum according to prestige, rather than in terms of discrete groups making up social classes. The attainment process itself is assumed to take place in an open and homogeneous market in which individuals compete freely. It is a society in which universalistic values and standards (e.g., ability, knowledge) have increasingly displaced the role of ascribed and other particularistic values (e.g., family ties, race, sex) in determining attainment (Horan 1978; Knottnerus 1987).

Although status-attainment research has been voluminous, more and more methodologically sophisticated, and contributed to an understanding of attainment, acceptance of its adequacy as an explanation for inequality rests in large part on acceptance of the theoretical assumptions it makes about society. Other sections of the text have indicated the weaknesses of the image of society on which much attainment research rests.

SUMMARY

This chapter has surveyed some of the research that has dealt with the trends in the nature of the openness of industrial societies, including the United States. These areas of research concern occupational mobility and status attainment.

After a review of some of the basic concepts developed early in the study of mobility, several of the basic problems in studying mobility were considered. Summaries of various studies of mobility were presented which, up until 1962, relied either on local data or research that had not been specifically designed for the study of mobility. Generally, the findings of mobility studies suggest that the trend in mobility has not been altogether uniform in U.S. society. Most of the mobility that has occurred in this century appears to have been brought about by changes in the occupational structure over time rather than through greater democracy and freedom in the society. The United States has more upward than downward mobility, but most of the upward mobility is of short distance. There does not appear to have been much significant change in the last 80 years in the extent to which the occupational status of the son is dependent on that of his father. Some broad socioeconomic advances have occurred for Blacks and women in recent years, but they still lag significantly behind White males.

The second major part of the chapter concerned status-attainment research, originally given its impetus by the research of Blau and Duncan. This area of investigation was extensively covered because it has dominated much of the stratification research over the last 30 years and has reshaped the study of mobility. Two basic models of status attainment surfaced: the Blau-Duncan model, which emphasizes the importance of structural factors for attainment, and the Wisconsin model, which incorporates social-psychological elements into its explanation. Both models explain occupational and educational attainment better than they account for differences in earnings and income. The effect of education is conditioned by the level of one's occupation and the society involved. Other factors of importance include economic and organizational opportunity structures and one's place in them. The process of attainment among African Americans and females varies from that found among White males.

Finally, although status-attainment research has made some valuable contributions, it has limitations, some of which were noted. Both mobility and attainment studies have suffered from this emphasis on males and measures based on male data. The weaknesses of status-attainment models also suggest that wider systemic factors are involved in the generation of inequality, as recognized by some of the theorists covered earlier. The social and economic structures in a particular society provide a context in which barriers and opportunities are created. The organization of these structures can help us understand why some are rich and others poor, or why some occupy positions of high status or power while others are stuck farther down the social ladder. The continued presence of these inequalities raises the possibility that many may consider them unjust. Chapter 14 explores the issue of legitimacy and perceived fairness in greater detail.

CRITICAL THINKING

1. The United States is often thought of as a land of opportunity, one in which there are few obstacles in the path of anyone who wants to move up. What do you think most accounts for this image?

2. Trace your own social mobility or that of your parents. What best explains the degree of attainment and its route?

3. Is the United States becoming a more open or closed society? Explain your answer.

WEB CONNECTIONS

Change in the occupational structure was the primary factor behind social mobility for most of the twentieth century. The third Industrial Revolution is characterized by the rapid growth of new, particular kinds of occupations. What occupations are growing the fastest? Which are declining in employment? What trends exist in wages for specific occupations? How do these vary by state? Search your state for trends in occupations and wages:

http://www.acinet.org/acinet/

CHAPTER 14

JUSTICE AND LEGITIMACY

ASSESSMENTS OF THE STRUCTURE OF INEQUALITY

The sense of justice is the stuff of human experience. Every day, and in all walks of life, justice matters play a part in human reflections, judgments, sentiments, and actions.
—Guillermina Jasso

Think about situations where you were rewarded differently from someone else. If the situations were important to you, undoubtedly you had feelings about whether such treatment was or was not justified. These feelings become issues and problems when you feel that your treatment was unjustified. What made the difference in whether you felt you were treated fairly or unfairly, or, in other words, why are some unequal distributions of rewards considered just while others are thought of as unjust?

Virtually every chapter in this book so far has provided evidence of extensive economic, political, gender, and racial inequality in U.S. society. There is no denying that this inequality is present, but is it unfair? It is difficult, if not impossible, to avoid the question of fairness in the presence of such pervasive inequality. The issue of fairness and justice, and how it is defined by individuals, is a legitimate topic of inquiry because of its strong connection with inequality: "The issues of social inequality and distributive justice are joined when individuals come to believe that they deserve what they get and get what they deserve" (Shepelak and

Alwin 1986). The study of distributive justice is also important because "the sense of justice is thought to be implicated in outcomes ranging from personal distress and divorce to revolution and international conflict" (Jasso 1999, p. 133).

Is it deserving that, when the average household income in 1995 was well under $40,000, Cal Ripken, Jr., made $5.4 million as shortstop for the Baltimore Orioles, that comedian/actor Jim Carrey made $29 million in income, that the average chief executive officer's total compensation was 419 times that of the average blue-collar worker, or that the top 20 percent hold over 44 percent of the wealth in the United States? What is fair? Who considers it fair? What determines whether individuals think the present distribution of resources is just? What criteria do people use before reaching a conclusion about the fairness of inequality? These are the empirical questions to be addressed in this chapter.

How people evaluate the inequality around them depends, in part, on what they think is primarily responsible for it, on the criteria they use when making their evaluative assessment about

NUTSHELL **14.1** _____

More Boom for Execs than Employees

ASSOCIATED PRESS

Washington—Top American corporate executives have seen their paychecks more than quadruple during the 1990s while factory workers' wage increases only slightly outpaced inflation, says a study by liberal advocacy groups.

Average worker pay rose from $22,952 a year in 1990 to $29,267 in 1998, up 28 percent compared with the 22.5 percent inflation rate, said the report released Sunday.

Meanwhile, average compensation packages for the top two executives at the nation's 365 biggest public companies—including manufacturing and other industries—rose from $1.8 million in 1990 to $10.6 million in 1998. That is equivalent to a 481 percent raise.

The study compared Labor Department statistics tracking wages of nonsupervisory workers in the manufacturing industry during the 1990s with trends in compensation packages for corporate executives as reported by *Business Week* magazine and other private sources.

"There's a big fairness problem here. While the headlines are saying the economy is doing so wonderfully, the benefits of that are not being spread around equitably," said Sarah Anderson, one of the report's authors.

"A Decade of Executive Excess: The 1990s" was a joint project of the Institute for Policy Studies in Washington and United for a Fair Economy, a Boston-based group that targets economic inequality.

A business critic of the report said it was flawed because it included stock options for executives, whose value can fluctuate depending on the market.

But he acknowledged there are differences in compensation.

"Obviously there is a considerable distinction between the lowest and the highest paid, and my reaction to that is, 'So what? It's a market-driven society,'" said Charles Peck, an executive compensation specialist at The Conference Board, a New York-based research and networking organization supported by the memberships of corporate executives.

The Conference Board keeps its own statistics on executive compensation. By its latest count of salaries and cash bonuses only, executive pay in the manufacturing industry averaged $783,000 in 1997.

The pay disparities may hurt morale and the spirit of teamwork at a company, said Chuck Collins, co-director of United for a Fair Economy. He also suggested that CEOs holding huge stock options have a financial incentive to base management decisions disproportionately on what will please investors in the short term rather than what's best for the company, workers or communities.

Source: The Daily Record, August 30, 1999, p. A2. Reprinted with permission of Associated Press.

---

the extent of inequality, and on the effectiveness of national ideologies and institutions in justifying extensive inequality. When individuals come to the conclusion that a given distribution of rewards is fair, then they also tend to believe that it is legitimate. Beliefs in the fairness and legitimacy of the structure of inequality in a society are two elements that contribute to its stability and continuity over time. Thus, when trying to account for its perpetuation, it is important to know how people feel about inequality and what

factors underlie its legitimacy. Believing that a given distribution is unfair and therefore illegitimate, however, does not necessarily mean that individuals will rise up against it by initiating riots or social movements. We will explore the conditions behind these reactions fully in the next chapter. Here, we are concerned only with individuals' attitudes toward the structure of inequality and the conditions that foster legitimation.

We begin with a discussion of how people feel about inequality, proceed to a survey of ideas

on what constitutes a just distribution of resources, and finish with an examination of factors
that contribute to the legitimation of inequality. In
essence, we are concerned with the principles
used to define justice and then the evaluation of
our present system of inequality using those principles. The next chapter will focus on "justice
consequences," the reaction to injustice in the
form of social movements (Jasso 1994).

U.S. ATTITUDES ABOUT THE DISTRIBUTION OF INCOME AND WEALTH

Americans often have ambivalent attitudes about
social and economic inequality. Their ambivalence is manifested in their sporadic anger, confusion, and inconsistent attitudes about these
matters (Sennett and Cobb 1973; Hochschild
1981). Lengthy telephone interviews with over
2,200 Americans confirm the operation of an "underdog" principle in reactions to equality and inequality (Kluegel and Smith 1986). As a group,
Blacks are more likely than Whites to consider
economic equality as unjust, to desire more equality, and to feel that income should be based more
on need than on skills. Women also are more
likely than men to see occupational inequality and
their own personal income as being unfair. Conversely, Whites with higher incomes are more
likely than others to endorse the present unequal
distribution of income, to believe that income
should be based more on skills than on needs, and
to be skeptical about the positive outcomes from a
more equal distribution.

Despite these differences in opinion, there is
still widespread support, even among underdogs,
for a system of inequality. A majority of adults believe that "people should be allowed to accumulate
as much wealth as they can even if some make millions while others live in poverty," and that inequalities in earnings are required to motivate
workers to take on extra responsibilities (Davis and
Smith 1996). A recent analysis of large national
samples in nine industrial countries, including the
United States, revealed that the United States was
among those favoring a higher degree of income

inequality between top and bottom occupations
(Kelley and Evans 1993). At the same time, virtually no one in these countries was in favor of a
completely egalitarian distribution of income.

How people feel about existing inequalities
depends on what they think brought them about.
Inequalities are viewed as justified or not, depending on their perceived sources. Being given an
equal chance and personal effort are perceived as
important for a just distribution. Almost 9 out of
10 adults believe that equality of opportunity
should be promoted rather than equality of economic outcomes, but almost half are not satisfied
with the opportunities for a poor person to move
up or with the mobility chances for the next generation. Most U.S. citizens believe that hard work
is more important than luck in getting ahead, and
that this is the way it *should be* (Davis and Smith
1996; Gallup 1997). Even a majority of Blacks
believe that inequality can be just in principle, especially if it is based more on skills than on need.
Only among the poor does there appear to be clear
support for need as a dominant criterion in determining income distribution (Kluegel and Smith
1986). When asked why they think Blacks are
worse off than Whites, about half of U.S. adults
attribute Blacks' lack of success to lack of motivation and effort, and less than half to discrimination
(Davis and Smith 1996).

The international survey of nine countries al-
luded to earlier confirmed that citizens feel that
those in the highest-ranking occupations should
be paid, on average, three to five times the salary
of those in the lowest-ranking positions (Kelley
and Evans 1993). More so than their citizen counterparts, older persons with higher education, incomes, and self-identified social classes favor
greater pay for individuals in high-ranking occupations. For example, a conservative, high-income
60-year-old man with a college education who
identifies with the upper class, and who is also a
supervising manager of his own company, feels
that those in high-prestige positions should be
paid seven times the minimum wage. In contrast,
an individual with the opposite characteristics believes that a person in that kind of occupation

should receive a salary of only three times the minimum wage. When it comes to the lowest-status jobs, however, the results are distinctly different. There is general consensus across groups about the appropriate wages for unskilled workers. Surprisingly, the single difference shows those with higher incomes favoring higher pay for those at the bottom. In essence, then, the only major disagreement among individuals revolved around the size and legitimacy of the salaries accorded high-prestige occupations.

Overall, a majority of Americans appear to support the idea of income inequality as being fair, but do not see the present system as necessarily equitable. This is corroborated by a Gallup poll which revealed that a solid majority of Americans believe that income and wealth should be more evenly distributed. Some 72 percent of those with incomes below $10,000 supported a more even distribution, but even among those with incomes above $40,000 (which admittedly includes a wide range of incomes), 45 percent felt it should be more evenly distributed (Gallup, 1986). A majority of those surveyed by the National Opinion Research Center (NORC) during the mid- to late 1980s also felt that the income differences in the United States were "too large" (Davis and Smith 1989). A 1996 NORC survey found that 63 percent of adults believed that inequality continues because it helps the rich and powerful. But they are seriously divided on whether they think the government should do something about it (Davis and Smith 1996). In sum, Americans' attitudes about inequality are complex and often contradictory.

WHAT IS A JUST DISTRIBUTION?

The question of what constitutes a just distribution of scarce and desired goods is an issue that has been wrestled with for centuries. There seem to be two broad principles used in such definitions, but each of these is more complex than at first appears. One basically argues that a just distribution exists when equal people are treated equally and unequal people are treated unequally.

It assumes that people (1) start out with different abilities and traits, (2) are free to realize those potentials, and (3) are therefore entitled to make different claims on scarce resources and rewards. This is what Hochschild (1981) called the "principle of differentiation" and it approximates what Ryan (1981) called the principle of "fair play." Given that individuals vary in their talents, abilities, and interests, it is predictable that they also will and should vary in their socioeconomic success, and that those with high levels of appropriate talents will assume higher positions in the hierarchy of inequality (Ryan 1981). If persons of *unequal* talent and ability are given *equal* rewards, then this must be justified (Hochschild 1981). While this position is consistent with a belief in meritocracy, one complication is that one's competencies and motivations may be due to luck related to biology or environment, factors over which one may have little control. So if people are not fully responsible for their competencies or motivations, a question can be raised as to whether they really *merit* what they get (Marshall, Swift, and Roberts 1997). Generally speaking, this position is consistent with conservative theories such as functionalism and human-capital theory, both of which imply that one should get out of a system what one puts into it. Findings from the international study just cited are broadly consistent with this view.

A second broad principle, the "principle of equality," argues that people are of "equal value and can make equal claims on society. Differences in treatment must be justified" (Hochschild 1981, p. 51). This conception approximates Ryan's (1981) notion of "fair shares" as a basis for a just distribution. People ought to have equal rights and equal access to society's resources in order to live decent lives. This principle is consistent with more radical, Marxian views of inequality and its roots, such as those that consider private property to be a major source of exploitation. Although there are a number of variations on these two principles, none of which are agreed upon by all, we cannot pursue them here. While these two conceptions appear to be incompatible, there is some evidence that people's perceptions of the fairness of inequality are affected by both of these criteria (i.e., on their personal assessment of both the distributive *outcome* of rewards as well as the *process* that led to it). Moreover, how they feel about the process is related to their feelings about the outcome, and vice versa (Törnblom and Vermunt 1999).

How do Americans define a just distribution of economic rewards in society? This partly depends on their characteristics and history, the criteria suggested by the society's dominant ideology, and their beliefs about the causes of economic inequality (Stolte 1987; Shepelak and Alwin 1986). With respect to the latter, Americans appear to give mixed messages when asked what they believe determines an individual's economic position. Data from national surveys during the mid- to late 1980s indicate that they are close to being split in half on whether they agree that when a person has a high position, it demonstrates

that the person has "special abilities or great accomplishments," or that "what one can achieve in life depends mainly upon one's family background." At the same time, a large majority believe that, in general, "one can live well in America" and that how far one gets in life depends "on the abilities one has and the education one acquires" (Davis and Smith 1989). The variations in the patterns of responses may be linked to variations in the wording of questions, but very likely also reflect the ambivalence of Americans about the system of inequality mentioned earlier.

The NORC survey asked respondents how important various factors were for "getting ahead in life." The response distributions were as shown in Table 14.1. The data in the table show clearly that the vast majority of Americans believe that individually achieved factors such as hard work, ambition, good education, and natural ability are critically important if a person wants to get ahead

TABLE 14.1 Perceived Importance of Various Factors in "Getting Ahead in Life" (National Sample)

	ESSENTIAL/ VERY IMPORTANT	FAIRLY IMPORTANT	NOT VERY IMPORTANT/ NOT IMPORTANT
Being from a wealthy family	20%	29%	51%
Having well-educated parents	39	41	20
Having a good education	84	15	0
Having ambition	88	11	0
Having natural ability	59	36	4
One's hard work	89	9	2
Knowing the right people	40	45	14
Having political connections	16	31	52
One's race	15	26	60
One's religion	15	14	71
One's sex	15	24	62
One's political beliefs	9	26	65
Region of country one comes from	7	15	78

Source: Davis and Smith 1989, pp. 490–493.

in life. A majority of individuals in all social classes also feel that intelligence and selfishness (i.e., personal ambition) increase as an individual goes up the class ladder (Jackman and Senter 1983). The sum of these results strongly suggests that individualism has been and continues to be a dominating influence in our perceptions of why people occupy unequal positions (Ritzman and Tomaskovic-Devey 1992). Most Americans subscribe to the dominant ideology that (1) opportunity for economic mobility is prevalent; (2) each individual is personally responsible for the extent of his or her own economic success; and (3) in general, therefore, the system of inequality is fair (Kluegel and Smith 1986). Structural factors—or those over which individuals have little control such as race, sex, being from a wealthy or poor family, and region of origin—are believed by most Americans to be quite unimportant in determining how far a person gets in life.

These and other findings indicate that Americans tend to underestimate the real effects of nonachievement factors such as race and sex on economic attainment, because as was demonstrated earlier, both have a significant impact on occupational and earnings attainment (Shepelak and Alwin 1986). Moreover, despite the strong belief by most Americans that education is very important in explaining occupational success, research suggests that it explains well under half of the variation in occupational attainment and that its tie to such attainment is much weaker than would be expected in a society in which merit is supposed to determine accomplishment (Krauze and Slomczynski 1985).

Not everyone, of course, is equally likely to subscribe to the belief that individuals are primarily responsible for where they wind up. For example, when it comes to explaining why some people are wealthy, African Americans, regardless of their incomes, and women are more likely than White males to cite structural reasons such as inheritance, the connection between political and economic power, and the ability of the rich to exploit the poor. They are also more likely to believe that structural factors, such as the lack of schooling provided by society and the low wages provided in some parts of the economy, are involved in explaining poverty (Kluegel and Smith 1986).

Other techniques have been used to uncover the criteria Americans believe actually *are* used versus those that *should be* used to determine income. When asked to judge what incomes certain kinds of hypothetical households received, respondents in an Indianapolis study, perhaps not unexpectedly, associated higher occupational status, higher education, being White, and being male in a single-person household with higher incomes, whereas those with larger families were believed to receive lower incomes (Shepelak and Alwin 1986). Another study presented hypothetical vignettes to a sample of 200 White adults (Jasso and Rossi 1977). The individuals in these vignettes varied in sex, marital status, number of children, educational attainment, occupation, and earnings. Respondents were asked if the fictitious person in each of a limited number of vignettes presented to them was (1) overpaid, (2) fairly paid, or (3) underpaid. There was a nine-point rating scale ranging from "extremely underpaid" to "fairly paid" to "extremely overpaid." The results revealed some interesting patterns. Single females were more likely than married females to be seen as being overpaid. Those with higher education and occupational status (especially males) and those with a greater number of children who are married and male were more likely than opposite groups to be viewed as underpaid.

These findings indicate that people use a mixture of achievement-related and unrelated criteria to make decisions about what is fair. While occupation and education are used to make judgments, so are sex and marital status. Most Americans, including African Americans and women, also apparently feel that income should be based more on skills than on level of need (Kluegel and Smith 1986). A direct implication of all these findings is that an equal distribution of income among the individuals in these vignettes would be considered unfair, although respondents were not in favor of the range of incomes that presently exists. When respondents were asked in the Jasso and Rossi study to attribute a fair income to each of the fictitious individuals, the responses ranged from just over $7,000 for a single female with seven years of education and a low-status job, to about $34,500 for a college-educated married couple with high-status professional jobs. This suggested fair range in earnings is much smaller than the range that actually exists in the labor market. The conclusion that most Americans believe that the range of incomes from bottom to top is too great is supported by other research as well (Davis and Smith 1989; Kluegel and Smith 1986; Alves and Rossi 1978; Rainwater 1974). Thus, Americans not only have identifiable opinions about the factors on which individuals' incomes should be based but also about the overall fairness of the current extent of economic inequality.

BASES FOR THE LEGITIMATION OF STRUCTURED INEQUALITY

The preceding studies indicate that most people in the United States believe that it is the individual more than anything else that determines upward mobility in the socioeconomic hierarchy. Most Americans subscribe to the dominant ideology mentioned earlier. Fitting this in with the theories of a just distribution, most people use the "principle of differentiation" in defining a just distribution. It is the *process* that must be seen as being just. The evidence also suggests that criteria over which the individual presumably has great control, such as education and skills, *should be* used more than other kinds of factors to determine income. These beliefs obviously fit into the dominant American ideology that if people invest in themselves, they can improve their economic fate in life. Yet, as mentioned earlier, the evidence suggests that there are obstacles to equal opportunity for certain categories of individuals, and that not everyone with the same kind of job and education earns the same amount of income.

The question, then, is how do individuals come to accept a belief system even though there is evidence that contradicts it? How is an ideology

internalized so that Americans come to believe that inequality is legitimate and justified?

In this section, various mechanisms through which the system of inequality in the United States is legitimated will be explored. These mechanisms exist on the microlevel of the *individual* in her or his everyday experiences as well as on the *institutional* macrolevel, working through the family, the education system, and other institutions. Let us begin at the level of the individual to see how people internalize the belief that inequality is fair.

Legitimation at the Level of the Individual

How do ideologies become internalized by people? This is a question addressed by Della Fave (1980), who tried to describe how individuals develop self-evaluations and judgments about the fairness of inequality. Interaction seems to be critical. To begin with, individuals are social beings—that is, they develop only in relationship with each other. As individuals grow and develop, they come into contact with greater numbers of people who react to them in a variety of ways. Individuals learn the expectations others have of them by noticing how others behave toward them. This combination of the expectations and reactions of others toward us makes up what Mead called the "generalized other" (Della Fave 1980). It is through the relationship with the generalized other that individuals develop a definition and image of themselves. Seeing how others react to us leads to the development of a particular self-image. We can see ourselves as others see us; we can view ourselves as an object, from the outside, as it were. By viewing ourselves as others see us, we come to a conclusion about our own worth and our contributions to society. A consistent self-image over time requires the social support of others. "A person who maintains a self-definition with no social support is mad; with minimum support, a pioneer; and with broad support, a lemming. Most of us are lemmings" (Huber 1988, p. 92).

The generalized other, rooted in social relationships, helps us understand why we evaluate *ourselves* as we do. How we evaluate the quality of *others* also depends on interaction. When individuals with different *amounts* of money or other resources *and* different *kinds* of noticeable nominal characteristics (e.g., race, sex, age) interact recurrently, each person draws associations between those characteristics, competence, and the differential amount of resources. Eventually, there develops a belief in the greater competence of those with more resources. One result is that better-off individuals can and are expected to present their opinions more forcefully and effectively, resulting in higher esteem for them and lower esteem for the less well-off. To the extent that the better-off tend to be male or White, beliefs in the greater quality of these types of people develop and are accepted by both parties in these interactions. "In effect, double dissimilar encounters [i.e., those in which individuals differ in resources and nominal characteristics] become beacons that continually broadcast support for status beliefs about the nominal distinction, encouraging and underpinning their diffusion and eventually their consensuality as well" (Ridgeway et al. 1998, p. 334).

Further strengthening of beliefs in the legitimacy of "who has how much" occurs because, as we have seen, people believe that hard work and ambition are critical and justifiable reasons for wealth. Thus, the wealthy are viewed as deserving of their high positions. This positive assessment of the wealthy influences not only individual images of them but people's own self-images.

But how does the individual reach the conclusion that those who are wealthy work harder, contribute more to society, and therefore deserve more than others? Briefly, Della Fave (1980) argued that individuals reach conclusions about the reasonableness of their beliefs from what they consider to be an "objective outside observer." In other words, it is from this observer that individuals develop ideas about what reality is and how it operates, and it is this observer whose judgments are internalized. It is the generalized other who fulfills the role of this observer, and it is the reactions of the generalized other to others that individuals internalize. Since a wide variety of people subscribe to the dominant ideology mentioned earlier, they react to the wealthy as being deserving. This appears to be an objective evaluation, and so they come to interpret them, others, and themselves accordingly. Those who are reacted to favorably or treated as if they were important by almost everyone, including other important people, develop a very positive self-image, whereas others develop self-evaluations that are not quite as positive. "It is from the generalized other that individuals form an evaluation of self and, thus, of the worth of their 'contributions.' It is upon these evaluations, in turn, that judgements of equity are made in accordance with the principle of distributive justice" (Della Fave 1980, p. 961).

Those who are successful also develop feelings of self-efficacy; that is, they believe that their own actions can bring about successful rewards. This is largely because of positive reactions to their success by others, which then encourages them to do more and reinforces their high self-efficacy. Viewing their own success as being a result of their own actions, they come to define it as legitimate and deserving (Stolte 1983).

Those who possess very positive self-evaluations, in turn, come to view their own high level of rewards as being deserved relative to others, whereas those with more negative self-images see themselves as being worthy of fewer rewards. In a large complex society, individuals generally have to piece together broad images of what others are like and what their contributions are on the basis of the limited information to which they have access. Thus, individuals make conclusions about the contributions of others based on the information that shows on the surface—namely, their wealth and income. Those with high incomes, in turn, can use their resources to manage the impressions that others have of them—that is, manipulate the interpretations of others in such a way that the latter develop a positive image of them (Goffman 1959). As was noted in Chapter 3, the demeanor of upper-class people can be tailored in such a way as to elicit deference and respect. Moreover, their ability to maintain high positions in educational, work, and other institutions reinforces the image of their greater contributions and worthiness for higher rewards. Those with greater amounts are viewed as making greater contributions, as deserving of their economic resources, given the widespread belief that rewards should be commensurate with contributions. Essentially, the process of legitimation in this case is circular: Those with greater rewards elicit greater respect and the feeling from others that they deserve what they have, which in turn reinforces the inequality found in the hierarchy of rewards (Della Fave 1980). A skeletal interpretation of this process is presented in Figure 14.1.

According to Della Fave (1980), the entire internalization and social process just described bears directly on the extent to which the system of inequality is legitimated. The greater the degree to which the distribution of self-evaluations in society matches the distribution of rewards, the more legitimate the system of inequality will be considered and the more stable the society's structure of inequality will be. Conversely, if the two sets of

distributions are not matched, then the stratification system is less likely to be defined as legitimate. This is consistent with Durkheim's views on the importance of the match between internal differences and rewards.

Several of the relationships suggested have been tested recently. Following Della Fave's theory, Shepelak (1987) tested relationships among income, self-evaluations, and the belief in individual responsibility for a person's position. Her interviews with over 300 Indianapolis residents revealed that those with higher incomes did indeed have more favorable self-evaluations than those with low incomes, and that those with better self-evaluations were more likely than others to attribute their incomes to their own effort. However, the latter explanations were not related either to family income or estimates of equity/fairness. Family income and self-appraisals were both found to be positively related to the feeling that an individual's income was fair.

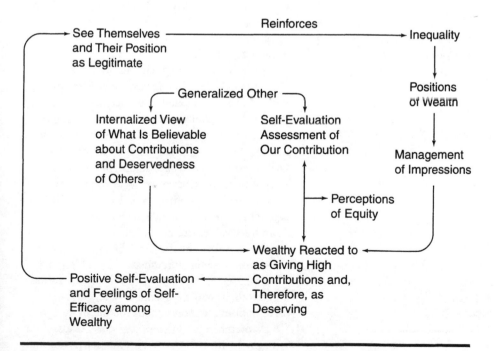

FIGURE 14.1 The Internalized Process of the Legitimation of Inequality

Source: Based on Della Fave 1980, pp. 955–958.

Conversely, those with low incomes were more likely to say that they were being underrewarded. In other words, contrary to Della Fave's self-evaluation theory, those with lower incomes do not feel that they deserve less than those above them. In fact, family income is more strongly linked to beliefs in the fairness of one's family income than are either self-evaluations or explanations of income level. "These findings fail to substantiate the view that disadvantaged persons believe they deserve less" (Shepelak 1987, p. 501). Rather, they provide support for those who found that income is inversely related to the belief that the system of inequality is legitimate (e.g., Robinson and Bell 1978). On the other hand, support was found for the conclusions that a person's income standing and explanation of present position do affect feelings of self-worth. Figure 14.2 shows the interrelationships found among self-evaluations, income, perceptions of fairness, and perceived causes of income.

In addition to the self-evaluation process just discussed, there are other bases of legitimacy that exist at the level of the everyday lives of individuals. Most people, perhaps especially those who have to scramble to eke out a living, are too wrapped up in their ordinary lives and personal troubles to give much thought to the broad public issues of legitimacy and stability. "What ordinary men are directly aware of and what they try to do are bounded by the private orbits in which they live; their visions and their powers are limited to the close-up scenes of job, family, neighborhood; in other milieux, they move vicariously and remain spectators" (Mills 1959, p. 3). They may not be happy with the way things are, but they are unsure of the structural sources of this vague discontent. The result is that more often than not they go along with the way things are and do not question the culture or social structure of the society, thereby lending legitimacy to social arrangements by default.

Some research studies show that the social activities of those in the working and lower classes are usually limited to those involving friends and relatives; exposure to a wide range of types of people and geographic areas is restricted. The value and belief system that develops out of involvement in this immediate environment is basically accommodative in nature, helping individuals to make sense out of their everyday concrete situation. Thus, it also tends to be parochial—tailored to explain or deal with the specific and immediate context in which these individuals live (Parkin 1971). As it concerns social inequality, part of the accommodation in this value system is to accept inequality but also to try to improve one's position within it. Thus, the value system generated in the local neighborhood does not ordinarily lead to a basic questioning of the system of inequality and its bases or to development of a radical ideology. Rather, people accept it in the abstract and then try to concretely adjust to it. So, "dominant values are not so much rejected or opposed as modified by the subordinate class as a result of their social circumstances and restricted opportunities" (Parkin 1971, p. 92). Marx further suggested, it will be recalled, that close-up involvement in the monotonous routine of everyday life by members of the working class leads them to begin to believe that their situation is normal and natural, and not to believe in or even to imagine an alternative situation.

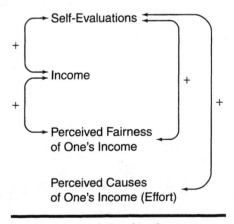

FIGURE 14.2 Relationships between Self-Evaluations, Income, and Fairness

Source: Based on Shepelak 1987, pp. 500–501.

Legitimation at the Cultural/Institutional Level

Although it is clear that self-evaluation and similar social-psychological processes are involved in legitimating social inequality, a society's culture and its social institutions are also directly implicated in the legitimation process. As in the case of self-evaluation's role, the basic question is: How do institutions and cultural values operate in ways that justify and maintain the hierarchy of social inequality?

It has been noted several times that Americans have ambivalent feelings about inequality. A large part of the reason for this ambivalence lies in the frequently inconsistent values that make up U.S. culture. At the abstract level, a core value in the culture is the belief in equal opportunity or fair play. But, in addition, Americans also tend to believe in competition, achievement, success, work or activity, efficiency, individual personality, freedom, nationalism, racism, humanitarianism, and morality (Williams 1970). Although these values are not all consistent with each other—for example, the belief in the sacredness of the individual versus the value of racism—most of these values help justify social and economic inequality in U.S. society. We have seen that differential rewards are more often believed to be the result of differential effort or work by individual personalities striving to achieve success in a context of free, open competition with others. To attack capitalism or the structure of inequality that has existed for generations would be, for many, not only unfair but also unpatriotic. So these values, by and large, push people in the direction of supporting the existing system, while other, though apparently fewer, values such as humanitarianism and moralism imply that inequality is inequitable.

The impact of values is often reflected in stereotypes that are held about different groups, and these stereotypes, in turn, often help to justify and sustain social inequalities. For example, images of what are appropriate attitudes and behavior for women have discouraged their movement into high corporate executive positions. As recently as 1989, male management students still believed that the qualities necessary to be a successful manager are more likely to be found in men than women. Consequently, these students were less likely to view women as being qualified for such positions. This is essentially the same belief as was held by male managers in the 1970s (Schein, Mueller, and Jacobson 1989). Part of the reason for this mistaken belief is probably the conviction that women are not as serious about their jobs and do not really work as hard as men at them.

Even when out in the labor force, as an increasing number of women are, traditional domestic stereotypes hold sway. Employed mothers are seen as being more masculine, less feminine, and less desirable than other kinds of mothers (Riedle 1991). Women who are physically attractive are also thought to be less qualified than unattractive ones for managerial positions, and, when they are in such positions, their performance is unjustifiably rated as being of less quality. Interestingly, attractiveness is considered a disadvantage for females in high positions, but it is considered an asset for them in clerical positions, a traditionally "female" occupation (Spencer and Taylor 1988). When in high positions that have been dominated by males historically, women are often pressured to adopt traditional feminine attitudes and behaviors, and if they don't, they suffer the consequences. "Women who do not wish to be classified…as deviant…must persist in playing the 'proper' role by following the interpersonal behavior pattern prescribed for them. Followed repeatedly, these patterns function as a means of control" (Henley and Freeman 1984, p. 475). In sum, images and stereotypes function to justify and maintain occupational inequality between men and women. Obviously, negative stereotypes of racial or ethnic minority groups perform a similar function. Perceiving Blacks, for example, as being less intelligent, less interested in education, and having less work incentive than Whites also serves to legitimize the economic and political inequalities that exist between the races. The power of these beliefs persists even when the evidence in each of these cases does not warrant such beliefs.

The beliefs and values that individuals endorse derive, in large part, from the broader institutional and cultural framework in which they are embedded. The task now is to describe how the system of inequality and the supporting values infiltrate the social institutions so that institutions foster activities and reinforce beliefs that legitimate inequality. How do institutions help to maintain the hierarchy of social inequality?

Before examining the roles of specific institutions, let us look at several ways in which dominant institutions influence behavior and attitudes, in general. Institutions consist of rules and structures that circumscribe what can and cannot be done. Moreover, these features of institutions help to define what is permissible and what is not, what is a legitimate issue or problem and what is not. Smith (1987) related how her research on mothering and education, which might help parents organize their collective interests in the schools, was controlled by the local school system. All research in the schools has to be cleared by the school board, and because of this, it has to be organized, proposed, and conducted in a manner that is consistent with the perspective of professional educators, not parents. *Professionalism* defines what is allowable and professionalism is defined by those most esteemed and dominant in the profession (generally White, higher status males). This creates limits on what information can be collected and what can be done with it.

The preceding example suggests that one of the tools used by institutions to legitimate social structure, including the system of inequality, is to frame the image of that structure and the processes associated with it in a particular way with the use of certain kinds of concepts and terms. Language can greatly influence the interpretations placed on issues such as poverty, welfare, and political participation. The terms used to describe what is defined as a social problem also can influence how people react to them. "Quiescent public acceptance of poverty as a fact of social life depends upon how it is defined, far more than upon its severity" (Edelman 1977, p. 7). Governments can affect the extent to which citizens interpret "pov-

erty" as legitimate by using particular symbols to describe it. To indicate that some people are "on welfare" to most Americans suggests something about the character of these individuals and their responsibility for their fate. Someone who is seen as a "welfare case" by an outsider is usually thought to be a person who does not work and probably does not want to work, one who is "living off" the rest of society. The term itself evokes an image quite different from the term *poor.*

When poverty is attributed glibly to "human nature" or to "economic laws," it allows people to justify denying help to the poor yet at the same time permits them to feel sorry for the poor. The result is that inequality is accepted and policies do not change (Edelman 1977). When arguments explaining the existence of inequality are couched in terms that cannot be tested empirically yet are emotionally powerful, it is difficult to argue against such reward differences. Referring to income as "rewards" or "earnings" plants the belief that the money is earned and thus deserved. Attributing the high rewards of a position to its "functional importance" to society helps to legitimize differential rewards. People have been socialized to react positively to the needs of society, the national interest, and earnings. Terms such as these encourage the acceptance and legitimation of "material sacrifices, constricted roles, political weakness, existing power hierarchies, and unfulfilled lives" (Edelman 1977, pp. 153–154).

Institutions of all types use language and symbols to create an imagery that legitimates the existing social reality. The use of certain terms to evoke images and thus to encourage the acceptance of inequalities between individuals applies not only to economic differences between rich and poor but also between men and women and Blacks and Whites. Because of the symbolic power of the concepts used by institutions and because of the intrusion of major institutions into most corners of their lives, people develop certain interpretations about society and other people, including those who are meritorious and deserving and those who are not. The images of the poor will be discussed more fully in Chapter 16.

The family, education, and religion all contain elements that encourage acceptance of inequality. Let us explore some of the ways in which each of these institutions fosters legitimation of social inequality.

Family.   The family is a principal instrument of socialization. It is within the domestic sphere that men and women learn much about how they should define themselves, their proper roles, and what they can expect from each other and society. Women are associated traditionally with an *expressive* role in the family; their primary responsibility is for nurturing and addressing the emotional needs of family members. In the urban setting of modern society, "the woman's fundamental status is that of her husband's wife, the mother of his children, and traditionally the person responsible for a complex of activities in connection with the management of the household, care of children, etc." (Parsons 1964b, p. 95). Women can, of course, choose to pursue a career instead, but if this occurred on a large scale, it would be necessary to bring about "profound alterations in the structure of the family" (Parsons 1964b, p. 96).

Men, on the other hand, have been expected to perform an *instrumental* role, which means that while the women's focus is on the internal life of the family, men's concerns are with adapting to the outside world, primarily in making a living to support the family. Functionalists such as Parsons have viewed this role differentiation as a source of complementarity and efficiency. Women have a central role in reproduction and, since this occurs in the domestic sphere, it is more efficient and more natural to have them be responsible for the expressive role in the family. The whole trend in social evolution, in this view, has been toward increased specialization and differentiation of function, which further legitimizes the role specialization of the two sexes.

Over generations, the continual socialization of men and women into these roles leads them eventually to be thought of as natural. The fact that this role differentiation has generally been thought of in the past as ideal by many Americans, and that most women have been content with the role indicates how powerful this ideology has been (Bem and Bem 1970). The balance that comes from the complementarity of these roles in the traditional functionalist view has integrative consequences for the society; it keeps society functioning smoothly. Of course, the behavior of others outside the family—such as nurses at the hospital when the child is born, babysitters, teachers, and relatives—further reinforces the gender-role distinctions considered appropriate for the sexes (Bernard 1981). The personality stereotypes of the sexes are consistent with their traditional roles. Men are still thought of favorably as being basically competitive, ambitious, independent, and logical, and women are well thought of for having good manners and being gentle, warm, softhearted, and affectionate (Werner and LaRussa 1985).

Although it may appear to be reasonable to view these personality traits and roles as merely complementary, as different but equal, the status and the power connected with each of them are quite different. As was pointed out earlier, capitalism and its values have shaped major institutions in modern society. This means that the social statuses attributed to families by individuals outside the family are based on what the occupational statuses of breadwinners are and how much income they bring home. As was noted in Chapter 4, the differences in status and power between the sexes are linked to the division of labor between them.

Education.   Schools perpetuate and legitimize inequality between the sexes, races, and classes through a variety of mechanisms. In general, it has been argued that one of the principal integrative functions of education is to have individuals perceive the educational system as a microcosm of the wider society in which their attainment is dependent on hard work and appropriate skills. The view is that, in education, individuals with varying abilities and levels of effort are channeled into appropriate levels of the occupational structure. The school appears as a forum in which students openly compete with each other and then are objectively evaluated by the experts. "The educational system fosters and reinforces the belief that economic success depends essentially on the possession of technical and cognitive skills—skills which it is organized to provide in an efficient, equitable, and unbiased manner on the basis of meritocratic principle" (Bowles and Gintis 1976, p. 103). But, Bowles and Gintis argued, the skills learned in school and IQ and test scores do not have a strong effect on an individual's economic success. Rather, according to this argument, schools are in the business of preparing students to be funneled into work roles at appropriate status levels.

At another level, various aspects of teacher-student relations encourage acceptance of an individual's traditional place in the structure of inequality. By teaching students about the nature of social reality, such as the values of the free market, intellectuals help to support the status quo. In Gramsci's (1971) phrase, intellectuals often have been "managers of legitimation." This includes members of the helping professions, such as social workers, psychiatrists, and teachers. Although educators often have encouraged happiness through adjustment to the status quo, those involved in these professions "have reinforced inequality by equating adjustment to existing social, economic, and political institutions with psychological health" (Edelman 1977, p. 152). People who deviate from their expected roles or who criticize the social structure are defined as "deviant" and are dealt with accordingly (Mills 1959).

Some of the teacher behaviors that encourage adjustment also reinforce traditional gender roles in U.S. society. Teachers in elementary schools pay more attention to males when they fight, suggesting that boys are more prone to aggression. At the same time, they pay more attention to the needs of girls by giving them more assistance than boys, thereby inadvertently encouraging their dependence on authority figures (Serbin et al. 1973; Fagot 1977). Since men are more likely to be in positions of authority (e.g., as principals in schools), children learn that it is normal for men rather than women to have power. Exposure to op-

posite situations appears to reduce the chances of children developing stereotypical views of gender roles (Paradiso and Wall 1986). What children read and how men and women are portrayed pictorially in textbooks also have an impact. When children act in a way that violates traditional sex-role expectations, they are usually ridiculed by their peers (Lamb, Easterbrooks, and Holden 1980).

Thorne's (1989) study in a California working-class elementary school further reveals the variety of ways in which traditional sex roles and inequalities are legitimated. Through participant observation research, she found that boys and girls frequently engage in "borderwork." This refers to "forms of cross-sex interaction which are based upon and reaffirm boundaries and asymmetries between girls' and boys' groups" (p. 76). Types of borderwork include various contests inside and outside the classroom in which the sexes are pitted against each other. Another form is chasing, in which boys and girls tease and try to elude each other on the playground. Invasions also occur in which members of one sex will "invade" the game being played by the other sex. These activities and what is said while each is going on reinforce and legitimize traditional ideas about what is appropriate for each sex. The dominance of boys in this informal world is demonstrated by (1) the greater playground space that they control, (2) the greater probability of invasion by boys in girls' games, and (3) the association of greater pollution (e.g., "cooties") with girls.

Class content is another avenue through which political and economic inequalities are legitimated. By and large, the information presented in classrooms and textbooks serves to reinforce a favorable interpretation of the United States and its history. Children have seldom been told in detail about unethical acts by national leaders or of the brutalization of such groups as American Indians. "None of this is very surprising.... Throughout history all children have been socialized to accept the dominant values and institutions of their society" (Kerbo 1983, p. 388).

Teacher expectations of Blacks and Whites and students from higher and lower classes also have been shown to be different. The images teachers have of lower status groups influence their expectations of them. Less is expected from them, which ultimately affects how well they do in school. Their lower performance only reinforces the initial negative image held by teachers, resulting in a self-fulfilling prophecy. Their lower performance also appears to justify their lower attainment, further strengthening the belief that attainment is linked to merit. The lower expectations by teachers of lower status individuals influence the teachers to place these students in lower noncollege-oriented tracks. Their placement in these tracks helps to ensure their lower educational attainment (Farley 1988).

Not only the curricula but also the social organization of schools at the secondary and university levels are different for those that primarily serve students who will enter relatively low-status positions after graduation, and those that have students who will enter elite positions. In the lesser junior colleges and lower tracks of high school, "students will be given more frequent assignments, have less choice in how to carry out those assignments, and will be subject to more detailed supervision by the teaching staff" (Hurn 1987, p. 331). This is in sharp contrast to the greater autonomy and flexibility permitted at more elite schools. The organization, rules, and curricula of each level of education are organized to prepare students for the tasks they will confront in the occupations they will likely enter. In this sense, education helps to keep the system of inequality intact by accommodating its students to the demands of the economy. Social reproduction explains more fully how the educational process works to maintain inequality from generation to generation (see Chapter 10).

What is important about all these mechanisms is that their effects are largely unrecognized, while most perceive that attainment is the result of individual effort and abilities. Schools are for learning, teachers are the objective experts, and students study and take valid tests, are judged on the basis of their performance, and are placed accordingly in the hierarchy of attainment. Where

students end up appears to be solely up to them. This reinforces the individualist ideology accounting for social inequality in the wider society.

Religion. French sociologist Emile Durkheim argued that the religious institution was functional for both the individual and society. For individuals, it helps them to deal with difficult problems, provides some answers to difficult questions, and makes their lives meaningful. For society, religion is integrative because its beliefs and rituals take individuals out of their secular lives and bring them together to form a community. Religion, for Durkheim, was primarily a *social institution* rather than a *personal psychological experience*. It is out of the social gathering of individuals that feelings of a superior force or power outside individuals first arises. Thus, Durkheim argued that the worship of supernatural forces in religious rituals is really an adoration of the powers in society. "In the divine, men realize to themselves the moral authority of society, the discipline beyond themselves to which they submit, which constrains their behavior even in spite of themselves, contradicts their impulses, rewards their compliance, and so renders them dependent and grateful for it" (Sahlins 1968, pp. 96–97).

Given this description, it should come as no surprise that images of the supernatural world often mirror the social structure of society. Swanson (1974) showed concretely in his study of nonwestern societies that a social hierarchy on earth is reflected in a social hierarchy among the supernatural. In societies in which older people occupied positions of importance, ancestors were a subject of worship, and in societies in which there was a great deal of social inequality, religion helped to legitimate the differences between the top and the bottom. A good example of this legitimation occurs in Hinduism in which the concepts of karma, dharma, and samsara combine to explain and justify the continuous inequality generation after generation. *Karma* indicates the belief that a person's present situation is the result of his or her actions in a previous life, and *dharma* refers to the duties and norms attached to each caste. Finally, *samsara* refers to the continual birth and rebirth of life. In other words, central beliefs in Hinduism absolve society or others from responsibility for social inequality. It is the result of individual actions (Turner, B. 1986).

Particular branches of Christianity also, of course, have legitimated people's beliefs about inequality. Protestantism, in general, which focuses on the individual relationship between each individual and God, stresses the importance of hard work and equality of opportunity in attaining success. Success is expected to be the result of self-denial and continuous effort, not the result of easy inheritance. This kind of spirit is what is embodied in Weber's concept of the "Protestant Ethic" and is especially associated with specific forms of Protestantism. Hard work and religious beliefs were intermingled by many famous preachers early in U.S. history. Cotton Mather, a charismatic Puritan preacher of the late seventeenth century, lectured that business and people's occupations were "callings" and not to be ignored. If individuals do not engage in their occupations, but rather remain idle (slothful), poverty will befall them. Riches are the result of industry, and poverty is the result of individual laziness. Those who are poor should expect no help from others since it is their own behavior that has resulted in their dismal situation. By engaging in business, people are doing what God intended: "Yea a *Calling* is not only our *Duty,* but also our *Safety.* Men will ordinarily fall into horrible *Snares,* and infinite *Sins,* if they have not a *Calling,* to be their preservative....If the Lord Jesus Christ might find thee, in thy *Store House,* in thy *Shop,* or in thy *Ship,* or in thy *Field,* or where thy *Business* lies, who knows, what *Blessings* He might bestow upon thee?" (cited in Rischin 1965, pp. 24, 26). It is only a short jump from this statement to the belief that those who are successful are so because of their own efforts and are among the favored of God, while those on the bottom do not work and are sinful.

Advocates of Dutch Calvinism justified slavery by viewing Blacks as sinners and slavery as a just condition for their sins and inferiority in the eyes of God. The legacy of these beliefs can be found in the contemporary dilemmas of inequality in South Africa (Turner, B. 1986; also see Chapters 6 and 8). In the United States, a slave catechism was used in many churches during the period of slavery to justify domination by masters, to encourage work, and to attribute lack of work to personal laziness. White pastors told Blacks that God created the masters over them and that the Bible tells them that they must obey their White masters (Fishel and Quarles 1967). There are also elements in Christianity that have been used to support continual subordination of women to men, including the biblical argument about the origins of woman out of man and the injunctions to obey one's husband in marriage.

Civil religion also uses religion to justify the "American way of life." It is a mixture of religious and political ideology in which the U.S. social structure and culture are seen as favored by God. God and Americanism go hand in hand in this ideology. This is a nation "under God" and its institutions are sanctified by the Almighty. At civil ceremonies and during certain public occasions, such as the opening of Congress, presidential inaugurations, and the pledge of allegiance, God is mentioned and the United States is his (her) benefactor. A recent study indicated that most elementary school children believe that the United States "has been placed on this earth for a special purpose," that it has a "chosen" status with God, and that it is successful because it is morally good (Smidt 1980). The "American way" that is so blessed incorporates the values of individualism, freedom, capitalism, and equality of opportunity, which make up a core part of the ideology supporting inequality. Preachers such as Pat Robertson and Jerry Falwell conjoin Christianity and Americanism in a manner that makes them not only mutually supportive but almost indistinguishable. In this ideology, to attack Americanism becomes tantamount to committing a serious sin. Americanism is supposed to be accepted, not criticized or undermined.

Karl Marx viewed religion under capitalism as having many of the effects on inequality just discussed. People are expected to put up with inequality; religion lulls them into a false sense of complacency. That is, it makes them *falsely conscious* of their real situation. It blinds them to the real causes of their predicament (i.e., class exploitation, not personal sin). In this way, socioeconomic inequality is seen as legitimate by those who blame only themselves or look forward to another life when conditions will be better for them.

Of course, Marx realized that historically, before capitalism, religion had been used to support the oppressed; even in our own time, religions have not always supported the status quo. Martin Luther King, Jr., and the Southern Leadership Christian Conference used religious ideas to try to improve conditions of Blacks in the United States, and Catholic bishops have fought on the side of the poor against many Latin American dictatorships (Light, Keller, and Calhoun 1989; Hehir 1981). Catholicism also has been a force for change in communist Eastern Europe (Parkin 1971). Despite these instances where religion has opposed inequality, historically it has been more closely associated with its legitimation and maintenance. This has been the case with each of the social institutions we have discussed. By and large, each has served to support the dominant value system as it pertains to inequality, and it is through each of them that individuals come to believe that the social inequality around them is legitimate.

SUMMARY

The principal focus of this chapter has been on examining the reactions to the fairness of social and economic inequality, the criteria that define such fairness, and to explore the factors that contribute to the legitimation and, therefore, the stability of inequality in the United States. Americans are clearly torn on the fairness issue. On the one hand, they believe that hard work, education, and similar personal investments are important for economic achievement and believe that they should be important. On the other hand, most feel that the extent of inequality is too great, but they do not think that full equality of income or wealth would

be fair either. Moreover, when asked what they think determines success, they tend to overestimate the significance of some factors and underestimate the impact of others, most notably race and sex. In their assessments of criteria to be used in determining a fair income, Americans tend to use a mixture of achievement and other factors (e.g., education, marital status, sex, occupational status).

The system of inequality itself is legitimated at the individual and institutional levels. Individuals develop interpretations of their own and others' rewards and contributions from the reactions of others to inequality. Their position in the rewards hierarchy affects their own self-evaluations and their appraisal of the fairness of their own incomes. At the same time, those with positive self-evaluations interpret their own incomes as being the result of their own efforts.

Through its culture and institutions, society helps to encourage traditional beliefs about the causes of inequality, thereby maintaining the structure of inequality. Generally, the values impressed on members and clients of those institutions are those of individualism and capitalism. Through the language and symbols used and their rules of knowledge, institutions define what is real and proper. In the case of the family and education, institutions shape beliefs and roles for those in different positions of the system of inequality and encourage a belief in the legitimacy of their positions. Religion also has used its resources on many occasions to legitimate the socioeconomic inequality that surrounds individuals.

At one point in the chapter, we noted conditions under which such inequality might be perceived as illegitimate. Illegitimacy is one of the factors motivating attempts to change the structure of inequality. The next three chapters deal more fully with concerted attempts to bring about such change. Chapter 15 deals with selected social movements that have tried to reduce social and economic inequality. Chapter 16 ends our discussion of inequality by examining formal government policies aimed at dealing with issues of economic inequality and poverty.

CRITICAL THINKING

1. What role, if any, should compassion play in determining the distribution of scarce resources? Should this issue even be a subject of debate? Why or why not?

2. Is it possible to develop a formula for the fair distribution of resources that is objective and generally agreed upon by most in society?

Explain your answer. If you agree that such a formula could be developed, what might go into such a formula?

3. How does the actual distribution of resources affect attitudes about the distribution of them?

WEB CONNECTIONS

Debates about the meaning of *justice, fairness,* and *equality* can be very contentious, especially when they concern the distribution of scarce resources such as income and wealth. Find out different opinions on this subject by reviewing a debate on "social equality and personal responsibility." What is equal opportunity, fairness, social justice, a "level playing field," equality of outcome, and so on? Read the discussion at the following website and think about where you stand on the issues:

http://bostonreview.mit.edu/dreader/series/equality.html

CHAPTER 15

SOCIAL INEQUALITY
AND SOCIAL MOVEMENTS

Thru this dread shape humanity betrayed,
plundered, profaned and disinherited,
cries protest to the judges of the world,
a protest that is also a prophecy.
—Edwin Markham

In societies where extensive social inequality not only exists but is also perceived as being unjust, it is not unusual for people to demonstrate their feelings against it. A variety of potential devices exist for redressing or reducing such inequality. Systems of inequality instigate social movements aimed at altering them, and conversely, the degree of ultimate success of social movements is measured in terms of their impacts on those systems. The extent to which either of these relationships is actualized, as you will see, depends on structural, cultural, and historical conditions in the society at the time. Economic shifts, prevalent ideologies, political policies, and unique historical events all impress themselves on the shapes of inequality and social movements.

Consistent with the multidimensional focus of treatment, this chapter will explore three social movements related to class, race, and gender that were explicitly aimed at reducing inequality and improving the life chances of the groups in question. The early labor movement of the latter part of the nineteenth century and the first decades of the twentieth century in the United States, the Civil Rights movement of the 1960s, and the women's movement of recent decades are examples of concerted efforts to change social and economic conditions for their constituencies. The purpose here is not to provide an exhaustive history of these movements, but rather to demonstrate systematically how each of them grew out of conditions relating to the structure of social inequality at the time, and how that structure affected the ebb and flow, goals, and tactics of those movements.

THE EARLY LABOR MOVEMENT

One of the first things to understand when examining any social movement is that the wider social, historical, and cultural context in which it takes place has an impact on the development, shape, and ultimate fate of the movement. Obviously, the poor conditions and deprivations experienced by industrial workers in the latter part of the nineteenth and early part of the twentieth centuries created dissatisfaction and feelings of hostility. Even though there was some improvement in wages after 1880, hours were long, wages were still low, and work conditions were dangerous. There were few, if any, protections against the hazards of chemicals, machinery, and inhalants from work in the mines and mills. Laborers on the railroads and in construction and logging industries also were exposed to extreme dangers. There was little concern for safety, and many of the wildcat strikes of this time were related to safety issues.

Writing of the period between 1865 and 1917, Asher (1986) observed that "industrial workers have been victimized by low wages, company stores, blacklisting, arbitrary dismissals, forced overtime, sexual exploitation, company spies, police brutality, and a host of other ills" (p. 115). Some of the dangers were inherent in the nature of the work and the technology used, and the fear of competition and concern for profit kept employers preoccupied with matters other than safety (Asher 1986). The early scientific-management movement among employers sought to organize, systematize, and thoroughly gain control of the workplace for management. In order to keep production and efficiency up in the early twentieth century, the pace of work in many plants was accelerated, stopwatches were used, and work was constantly checked by inspectors. This created further alienation among workers.

Living conditions in most instances also left much to be desired. Dubofsky (1975) described a typical immigrant residential area in Pittsburgh: "Situated in what is known as the Dump of Schoenville runs a narrow dirt road. Frequently strewn with tin cans and debris, it is bereft of trees and the glaring sun shines pitilessly down on hundreds of ragged, unkempt, and poorly fed children" (p. 23). The company towns and cramped urban ghettos made for dreary living conditions. In his study of "How the Other Half Lives," Riis (1890) described the conditions in which New York City workers lived. He found "an urban jungle of exploitation, family disintegration, crime, and human degradation" (quoted in Green 1980, p. 20). Even as late as the 1920s, living conditions for most workers were still poor. During these years, although some improvements had been made, work was hard, hours were long, and the level of wages left little money for leisure and recreational activities. In 1929, 42 percent of families had incomes below $1,500,

which was barely enough to keep a four-person family going (Zieger 1986).

Despite the awful circumstances of the lives of most industrial workers, however, more is needed to explain the development and continuation of the labor movement over time. Certainly, workers responded to negative changes in their workplaces and in the wider political economy. But as was discussed in Chapter 12, it takes more than deprivation to explain the development of collective action on the part of an aggrieved group. While exploitation and deprivation may have induced solidarity among workers, the strength of organized labor depends on other conditions, as well.

The growth of the labor movement was affected by a combination of external and internal factors. Externally, the strength of workers tended to be greater when there was a tight labor market; this gave them greater bargaining power. Strength also grew when economic opportunities were plentiful. The chances of a labor movement being successful also were enhanced when society allowed a variety of political and legal expressions and permitted greater access to resources (Jenkins 1983). For example, this occurred during the 1930s after Franklin Roosevelt's election and passage of the Wagner Act, which legalized the right to unionize. These events created alternate sources of power, and when the potential for political and economic power of labor were high, so was the solidarity of workers. The belief by workers that they would be spending a large part of their lives in their jobs and that they could make a political difference in society also increased their solidarity and the probability of a labor movement.

Sources of Control over Workers

The internal forces affecting the labor movement's shape and direction related heavily to disagreements among workers over membership, goals, and policy, as well as attempts used to break down cohesiveness among workers and thereby control them. Cohesiveness is a source of strength. Greater solidarity means greater organizational or collective power, and the relative strength of organization among opposing groups implicated in the situation affects the probability that a movement will develop (McAdam 1982). Employers who were more often better organized and had broader political resources on their side fought workers in many bloody battles in the latter part of the nineteenth and well into the twentieth century. Around the turn of the twentieth century, as now, it was in the economic interest of employers to minimize the solidarity among workers, thereby hindering the development of a labor movement. A variety of techniques were used to do this (Griffin, Wallace, and Rubin 1986). One of these was the use of largely unskilled immigrant laborers, many of whom, as machine tenders, replaced natives. Blacks and foreign labor also were used as strikebreakers. These moves on the part of employers created animosity against foreign laborers and weakened the cohesiveness of labor in general.

A second technique that created divisions within the ranks of labor involved the redesigning of the division of labor. For much of the nineteenth century, craftsworkers had held control over their work and occupied indispensable positions in the iron, steel, and machinery industries (Dubofsky 1975). Nevertheless, employers and their foremen controlled the workers through direct personal control, "intervening in the labor process often to exhort workers, bully and threaten them, reward good performance, hire and fire on the spot, favor loyal workers, and generally act as despots, benevolent or otherwise" (Edwards 1979, p. 19). The scientific-management movement further strengthened the power of supervisors over workers. It prescribed the dividing of tasks into their smallest, elemental components in order to increase efficiency and output. But in so doing, it also introduced extreme specialization and monotonous work on the shop floor. Tasks were divided into such small parts that even completely unskilled individuals could perform them.

While not universally implemented in industry, scientific management reflected an important perennial source of labor/management conflict—that is, the issue of who controls the work process.

Numerous early confrontations were over the question of who should direct the pace of work tasks (Dubofsky, 1975; Piven and Cloward 1977; Edwards 1979; Stephenson and Asher 1986). Through the use of scientific management, management was able to wrest control of production and the labor process from craftsworkers, who, until this point, had been the experts on how to accomplish given work tasks. All of this expropriation of control was done under the guise of being a "scientific" method for organizing work. Scientific management removed the planning and control aspects of the work process from the worker and placed it in the hands of the manager. Workers generally fought the use of scientific management.

The techniques for controlling the work process changed as capitalism perfected its technology. Improved manufacturing techniques such as the assembly line created technical controls. "*Technical control* involves designing machinery and planning the flow of work to minimize the problem of transforming labor power into labor as well as to maximize the purely physically based possibilities for achieving efficiencies" (Edwards 1979, p. 112). Later, control was achieved through the widespread implementation of bureaucratic structure, which builds control into formal sets of rules, positions, and authority hierarchies. Both technical and bureaucratic methods build control into the very fiber of the organization, replacing the personal control of the manager or foreman, which was often perceived as being arbitrary. The evolution of different forms of control can be legitimately viewed as attempts by industrialists to increase efficiency, production, and profit.

But the use of foreign and African American labor along with changes in the mechanisms of control were only two of the techniques used to weaken labor. Industrial management also used welfare capitalism to minimize solidarity among workers. Briefly, welfare capitalism included special savings plans and bonuses, homeownership aid programs, stock-purchasing options, and group insurance plans. Most significant among the programs offered were employee representation plans or work councils and company unions. The latter plans presumably gave workers a meaningful voice in the operation of the organization. Around World War I, the concept of "industrial democracy" had become quite popular. Clearly, these employee representation plans, while suggesting a democratic and more equal relationship between employer and employee, were aimed at reducing worker allegiance to outside unions and slowing their attempts to organize themselves (Brody 1980; Griffin, Wallace, and Rubin 1986).

There is some question as to whether the programs involved in this approach were primarily a conscious attempt by employers to reduce identification with other workers by making workers dependent on and loyal to industry, or rather an honest attempt to deal with the problems that attended changes in industrialization and to treat employees more humanely. The motivation was very likely a combination of paternalistic concern for workers, the belief that a more satisfied work force would increase productivity and efficiency, and a desire on the part of employers to control labor. The latter function, however, appears to have been the most important (Griffin, Wallace, and Rubin 1986; Brody 1980).

A variety of conditions contributed to the demise of welfare capitalism after the late 1920s. Many of the basic concerns of workers were still not being addressed, such as full control over the work process, protection against unemployment, higher wages, and a shorter work week. On top of these factors was the fact that welfare capitalism was expensive and only some large firms could afford the programs. Hence, it was not widespread among all industries. Finally, the Depression made it virtually impossible for firms to meet the idealized goals of welfare capitalism (Edwards 1979; Brody 1980).

Employers also fought the organized labor movement by fighting against closed or union shops, advocating open shops in their place. In the latter, employees need not be members of unions to remain employed. This push for open shops under the "American Plan" label was especially dominant during the first decade of this century. The

National Association of Manufacturers launched a campaign for open shops across industries, while other business-oriented groups (e.g., National Civic Foundation) argued that if unions were to exist and be acceptable, they had to be "responsible" in nature. In response to business attacks on union shops, some trade unions began to take in more unskilled workers as members (Green 1980). The conservative trade unionism of the American Federation of Labor (AFL) was preferable to the more militant and revolutionary approach of the International Workers of the World (IWW) (Griffin, Wallace, and Rubin 1986). The espousal of welfare capitalism and a conservative brand of labor organization helped create an appearance of employers as being reasonable and fair. But neither of these enhanced the ability of labor to organize effectively in its own interests.

Employers had, of course, other resources by which to resist encroachment by labor. Spies were employed to monitor labor activities; legal actions were encouraged against militant workers and organizations; and the power of police, state militia, and federal troops also were used to quell labor unrest. Some states had laws specifically outlawing unions that were considered to be revolutionary or that openly advocated the taking over of industries by workers (syndicalism). Leaders of such unions could be and were put in prison or deported (Perlman and Taft 1935; Griffin, Wallace, and Rubin 1986). The informal political alliance between business and government was reflected in the frequent use of police or military might in putting down worker protests.

In the late nineteenth century, workers often had the support of local officials, so industries had to get help from state and federal sources (Dubofsky 1975; Green 1980). In numerous strike actions between 1890 and 1920, state militia and federal troops were used against workers. The 1892 steel plant conflict at Homestead, Pennsylvania, and the Pullman railroad boycott of 1894 are only two instances in which soldiers were used against strikers. In Lawrence, Massachusetts, in 1912, the American Woolen mill employed roughly 40,000, about half the city's population. About half of the employees were young women and most were foreign born. But when a group of young Polish women were given reduced wages for no explicit reason, a strike was organized and spread to other mills. In this case, too, police and militia were used against strikers, but after a couple of months, the workers in the "Bread and Roses" strike, as it was called, won wage gains (Green 1980). In 1914, militia in Colorado waged a violent attack on coal miners, shooting strikers and burning their families out of homes. Their violence across the southern part of the state reminded some of the tactics that had been used in the earlier Indian Wars (Zieger 1986). Many other labor-employer confrontations occurred during this period. Throughout World War I up to 1920, large strikes by rail, meatpacking, and steel workers occurred. In 1919 alone, there were 3,600 strikes (Zieger 1986). But in most cases, employers emerged as the victors (Piven and Cloward 1977; Brody 1980).

In the last years of the nineteenth century and the early years of the twentieth century, workers simply did not have the political or organizational power to be consistently successful against industrial owners. "Whatever force workers mounted against their bosses, whatever their determination and their unity, they could not withstand the legal and military power of the state, and that power was regularly used against them" (Piven and Cloward 1977, p. 102). The only effective legal control on the contract imposed by the employer at the turn of the century was the condition of the labor market. As long as employers had government, the press, and the market behind them and a large number of immigrant workers available, there was little that could get employers to voluntarily improve their contracts with workers (Ginzberg and Berman 1963). All of the preceding discussion demonstrates that changing technological conditions, population composition, and the differential availability of political and economic resources to labor and management decisively affected the development of the labor movement. Access to resources had an especially significant

impact on the effectiveness of countermovements and countertactics by each side in the conflict (Griffin, Wallace, and Rubin 1986).

Internal Divisions in the Labor Movement

The particular directions taken by the labor movement have been explained in a variety of ways, but not altogether successfully (cf., Laslett 1987). The varying images of the roles of unions, industrial changes, and social and cultural heterogeneity within the working class and disagreements on the goals of unions all helped to shape the differentiation within the movement. An early approach of the 1880s emphasized the educational function of unions. These organizations were seen as educators of immigrants, proponents of public schools, and often supporters of the socialization of private industry. Thus, in this approach, unions were not seen as being preoccupied with wages and job conditions alone, but with broader issues. The actions and goals of several early unions (Knights of Labor, IWW, Congress of Industrial Organizations [CIO]) make that clear. Another approach to understanding unions saw them as organizations created to buffer the effect of the ill fit between humans who desired to be free and the controls inherent in modern mechanization. The Marxian approach viewed unions as being rooted in class struggle over control of the means of production.

A final and most influential view of labor unions in early America was to view them as tools for increasing the economic benefits of workers. Perlman (1928) argued that in surveying all the changes that have taken place in the economy and technology, workers came to the conclusion that they cannot operate independently as separate entrepreneurs. Rather, Perlman argued, they became reconciled to their positions as employees in businesses owned by others and realized there was not a great deal they could do to change the way things were. Given this situation, workers could hardly be expected to be revolutionary; they were only willing to fight for better wages and job conditions. It should be remembered that Perlman presented his theory before the Great Depression had occurred and before development of the CIO. He also does not appear to give much credit to the imagination and ambition of workers (Laslett 1987).

There is no question that some of these emphases were reflected in the internal structure of the organized labor movement of the early twentieth century. The forms the labor movement took in the United States were also conditioned by industrial changes. In the waning decades of the nineteenth century, the social organization of the economy was undergoing rapid change, and these changes had implications for both employer and employee. For example, the period beginning with the late 1880s was one in which economic enterprises dramatically increased in size and frequently merged with each other. In other words, it was a period in which economic power became more consolidated and concentrated (Edwards 1979). Even though in most of the nineteenth-century factories authority was decentralized among foremen and various craftsworkers, industrialization brought in its wake a more simplified, detailed division of labor, increasing the need for less skilled laborers.

Machines often fomented dissatisfaction among skilled craftsworkers and encouraged antagonism between the unskilled industrial workers who could do simple work and operate basic machines, and those who were skilled craftsworkers before machines became dominant (Stephenson and Asher 1986). Machines rapidly took the place of workers, and control over the workplace more frequently fell into the hands of owners and their foremen. "For more and more wage earners, the power over their working lives receded far off into distant central offices and into the hands of men probably unknown to them" (Brody 1980, p. 8). These shifts in technology helped to drive wedges between unskilled and skilled workers, thereby stimulating the different directions in which the organized labor movement would go.

Along with technological changes, productivity rose rapidly, but so did the demand for labor. Immigrants flooded into the United States from a variety of countries. Consequently, the late nineteenth century was also a period in which the size of company workforces increased. The industrial working class grew significantly, but it was composed of individuals from sharply contrasting social and cultural backgrounds. The industrial working class for much of the latter half of the nineteenth century was a conglomeration of native-born craftsworkers, some farmers who had left the land to come to the cities of New York and New England, skilled immigrants from Britain and western Europe, Irish who came to the United States after the potato famine in their native land, and Chinese who became employed primarily in the railroad industry.

After 1880, immigrants from eastern and southern Europe joined the ranks of the less skilled in industry and became an increasingly large part of the industrial working class (Aronowitz 1973). As the demand for labor grew and these immigrants flooded into the country to take lower positions in the mines, mills, and factories, the labor force in the North was almost as segregated by nationality in 1900 as the southern market was by race (Green 1980). Moreover, as the century came to an end, the proportion of women and African Americans involved in industry also increased. In 1900, almost a quarter of all women were in the labor force. The point of all this is that the heterogeneous nature of the working class at this time created divisions that often hindered the solidarity of workers when conflict arose with their employers.

This heterogeneity was used by employers to minimize worker cohesion. Businesses consciously recruited large numbers of unskilled immigrants who served as an available labor supply; this was used to regulate employment and possibly even wages. The employment of ethnically diverse workers stirred antiforeign sentiments among natives, which discouraged the organization of all workers. Blacks, Mexicans, and ethnic Whites also were used as strikebreakers, again discouraging unification among workers.

The racial and ethnic differences within the working class meant language, skill, and religious differences as well, making control of working-class militancy easier. So these internal divisions had direct implications for both the working class and its employers. Some labor leaders had no wish at all to bring non-Whites into the organized labor movement, but rather were primarily interested in advancing the interests of White, skilled craftsworkers. Exclusionary practices, including explicit policies prohibiting admission of non-Whites, were not uncommon among many AFL unions (Green 1980). This was to be a bitter source of antagonism within the labor movement. Samuel Gompers, who founded the American Federation of Labor in 1881, was against the inclusion of non-White, nonskilled workers. In 1905, Gompers proclaimed to a group of union members in Minneapolis that "caucasians" were "not going to let their standard of living be destroyed by negroes, Chinamen, Japs, or any others" (quoted in Green 1980, p. 46). The miscellaneous category of "others" referred to people from what were considered at that time the less desirable regions of Europe, such as the Slavic countries and Italy. Keep in mind that ideas about the biological inferiority of different groups were still circulating at this time (see Chapter 6).

In contrast to the American Federation of Labor, which sought to unionize skilled White craftsworkers, other organizers felt that it was crucial to organize all industrial workers. Among those groups that supported the organization of all workers, some had socialist or communist leanings. The Knights of Labor, briefly popular in the 1880s, was among those groups that argued that all workers should be included in the organized labor movement. Rather than advocating the homogeneous composition found in the trade and crafts unions of the AFL, the Knights preferred mixed groupings of workers. The Socialist Party of America, founded in 1901 and under the leadership of the charismatic Eugene Debs, also favored an organizational umbrella that would cover the mass of workers in industry. A few years later, the Industrial Workers of the World, and several decades later, the Congress of Industrial Organizations also actively sought the membership of Blacks and all industrial workers.

As their views about the compositions of labor organizations varied, so did labor leaders' views on the appropriate goals for the labor movement. The goals of the Knights of Labor were broad and involved the reorganization of the industrial order to create a more just society. These utopian goals were eschewed by the newer AFL trade unions that sought more immediate narrow rewards for their members, such as higher wages and better working conditions. This "pure-and-simple" or "business" unionism was more consistent with native American values according to some interpreters. A large part of the reason for this orientation, argued Lipset (1971), is related to the openness of the class structure, and the values of materialism, egalitarianism, and individual opportunity. Individuals in this context see themselves more as individuals than as members of a class, and see social change as resulting more from individual efforts than from mass organization or social structure. The American values of work, social and geographic mobility, comfort, and common sense also lie behind the belief that individuals do and should determine their own economic fates (Dunlop 1987).

The AFL's trade unionism has aimed at working within the present economic system rather than trying to change it. The emphasis on increasing labor's power has been for the purpose of more effective collective bargaining than for political reasons. Early AFL leaders felt that government should not interfere in labor matters. It should be up to labor to chart its own course and make its own gains (Brody 1971). Gompers's "voluntarism" perspective underscored the belief that labor should not solicit aid from the government for those goals it can accomplish by itself (Green 1980). Paradoxically, this stance helped to create a bond between the AFL and establishment forces, fostering increased cooperation between the union, management, and the government (Rogin 1971; Brody 1980).

In this interpretation, because of cultural and other differences, U.S. workers are not as interested as their European counterparts in a basic change *of* the economic system as much as they are in changing their individual positions *within* the system. "Most men and women live in a real world," wrote Dubofsky (1975), "a world of simple, everyday happenings, small pleasures and recurrent sufferings, which shape their attitudes as much as abstract principles" (p. 48). The trade unions, with their narrow orientation, help to sustain the job consciousness of U.S. workers. Similarly, Brody (1980) also concluded that in the waning years of the nineteenth century, the labor movement was (1) practical rather than utopian or theoretical, (2) nonrevolutionary with narrow material interests, and (3) impatient with intellectuals and academicians who had theories about the direction the labor movement should pursue.

Despite the narrow orientation of many workers, however, one should not conclude that there has been no revolutionary fervor or concerns within labor. "Such an approach has always been unfair, especially during the heyday of the IWW between 1905 and 1917, and in the early years of the history of the CIO. It was especially untrue during the period of the Knights of Labor ...which...upheld producer's and consumer's cooperation, equal pay for women, and a 'proper share of the wealth that they (the workers) create'" (quoted in Laslett 1987, p. 362). Organized labor has not been a uniform homogeneous mass.

As suggested earlier, differences in races, cultures, goals, and organizing principles have created fissures in the house of labor. There has been a consistent thread of concern among many workers since the nineteenth century over who controls and directs their work. Part of the battle that has been waged between labor and management has involved such issues. "In fact, American workers have waged a running battle over the ways in which their daily work and the human relations at work were organized over the nineteenth century, and in the process they have raised issues which go far beyond the confines of 'wage and job consciousness' or 'bread and butter' unionism, into which historians have long tried to compress the experiences and aspirations of American workers" (Montgomery 1983, p. 389).

Just prior to World War I, then, organized labor contained several different types of organizations and orientations. The trade-union wing, exemplified by the AFL, was solidly on its way but did not incorporate most unskilled and semi-skilled industrial workers. The Socialists had political influence on many workers even though the latter's trade-union orientation remained intact. The IWW organized those left out by the more conservative AFL affiliates, was active and militant, and was led by the imposing Big Bill Haywood (Brody 1980).

The Russian Revolution, America's involvement in World War I, and the accompanying patriotic fervor that swept the nation legitimated political and coercive attacks on Socialist organizations and the IWW. As a result, the power of the Left in organized labor declined. "The labor hopes of the American left, hitherto bright, died in World War I and its aftermath" (Brody 1980, p. 41). In the patriotic context of the postwar period, organized labor, in general, was a victim of attacks from industry. The "American Plan" of business proclaimed the consistency of the open shop with U.S. values. In this hostile atmosphere, the AFL became more cooperative with industry and government. With the restrictive immigration laws of the 1920s reducing the inflow of unskilled labor from culturally undesirable countries, industry's source of fresh workers was weakened. By the late 1920s, labor unrest had calmed down even though the benefits of welfare capitalism did not include all industrial workers. Moreover, the cost of living was increasing, erasing many of the gains that had been made by some workers (Zieger 1986).

From the Depression to the Present

On the whole, the 1920s and the early 1930s were not kind to U.S. workers. "The symbol of the twenties is gold...the twenties were, indeed, golden, but only for a privileged segment of the American population. For the great mass of people...—workers and their families—the appropriate symbol may be nickel or copper or perhaps even tin, but certainly not gold" (Bernstein 1960, p. 47). Bernstein labeled the 1920 to 1933 period as "the lean years" for the worker (ibid.). A litany of the problems for workers would include the stagnation of the union movement during the period (union membership fell from 5 million in 1920 to 3.5 million in 1929) and the absence of any effective industrywide collective-bargaining tools. Employers could hire who they wanted and workers had little recourse in the matter. Immigration slowed during the 1920s, which meant that it was no longer as easy for native workers to move up occupationally. Older workers found it more and more difficult to hold on to their jobs, as farm migrants and women increasingly entered the urban labor force. Mechanization displaced workers. Between 1920 and 1929, it is estimated that about one-third of those displaced by machines in the manufacturing, coal mining, and railways industries remained unemployed (Bernstein 1960). Moreover, the shift to more mechanized professional positions did not help many workers, who did not have the qualifications for such positions. Income inequality was also extensive in the society. The combined incomes of the top 0.1 percent of families were as great as those of the bottom 42 percent of the population. Within the working class there were also divisions in wages based on regional, ethnic, racial, skill, union membership, sex, and residential differences. Irish, Italian, Jewish, African American, and Mexican workers were generally worse off than native White workers (Bernstein 1960).

The effects of the Great Depression on employment were disastrous. In the middle of 1930, almost 4.5 million were without jobs. Shanty areas cropped up in and around cities, places of makeshift residences sometimes called "Hoovervilles." Hunger also rose dramatically. By early 1931, there were an estimated 8.3 million unemployed, but the number was to rise even further to 13.6 million by the end of that year, and to 15 million by early 1933. At that time, about one-third of all wage/salary workers were completely out of work. Many others were only working on a part-time basis (Bernstein 1960).

Needless to say, the Depression in the early 1930s changed political dynamics inside and outside the labor movement. The AFL had successfully cultivated close relationships with industrial management and government forces. It stressed union-management harmony and fought against leftist elements in the labor movement. The Depression made many workers and unions realize the need for state help and intervention. It spurred questions among the unemployed about the ability of the present economic and political systems to deal with catastrophic problems, especially as it became clear over the bitter years of the 1930s that it was not the lack of individual efforts but rather broader social forces that were behind much of the misery being experienced (Piven and Cloward 1977). At the same time, however, the vast majority of citizens still had faith in the U.S. system and did not see socialism or communism as a viable alternative. Nor did they think of themselves as a full-fledged working class fighting capitalism (Aronowitz 1973; Zieger 1986).

In the early part of the twentieth century, labor had received little help from the federal government, especially during the Republican administrations of the 1920s. This was a difficult time for government because in the past it had actively supported industry, even to the point of using federal troops against workers. Hoover had favored the voluntaristic and self-help approach to solving economic problems, but because of the continuing difficulties faced by labor during the Depression, there was also pressure for the federal government to step in and help solve the problems faced by average families. The massive problems caused by the Depression revealed "the primitive character of public assistance in America" (Zieger 1986). At the same time, the recently elected Roosevelt was viewed by workers as being more sympathetic to labor's cause. In essence, government had to carry on a balancing act between business and labor during the 1930s.

The feeling on the part of many workers that they had a more sympathetic president emboldened them to drive for more gains, but especially for the right to unionize without reprisals from

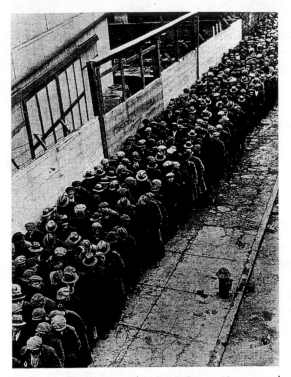

By the early 1930s, as the Great Depression moved on, an estimated 15 million people—about one-third of all workers—were unemployed. The bread-line in New York stretched a long way.

management. The workers were told by labor leaders that President Roosevelt wanted them to join unions. Labor was on the march, and union membership grew dramatically during the late 1930s.

While workers sought government support in the early 1930s, the AFL was against governmental unemployment and welfare programs as a means to improve the conditions of workers. Rather, they tried to rely on deliberations with employers as a means to keep earnings up to a decent level (Zieger 1986).

Given the conservative orientation of the dominant AFL, many still unorganized workers had to continue to fight for unionization and often fought against the approaches advocated by the AFL. Workers were pitted against mainstream

unions which tried to appease and mollify increasingly militant workers (Piven and Cloward 1977). The Depression had helped to destroy belief in the existing relationship between labor and management and to legitimate a move for the greater structural protection afforded by unionizing (Brody 1980). During the 1930s, labor became "uncommonly militant" (Zieger 1986). In this period, hundreds of sit-down strikes occurred. In 1937 alone, there were almost 500, involving approximately 400,000 workers (Piven and Cloward 1977).

Several critical events strengthened labor's hand during the 1930s, in addition to the political-administration changes that had occurred. One was the rising prospect of war in Europe. U.S. companies that had armament contracts with European countries could not afford major labor unrest to disrupt production. A second event was the passage of the Wagner Act in 1935, which legalized the right of workers to organize and bargain collectively under the protection of the National Labor Relations Board, which could monitor business compliance with the law. This law, bitterly fought by business, resulted in a rapid upsurge in union membership. In the mid- and late 1930s, union membership tripled, reaching about 9 million in 1939 (Zieger 1986). A third event that increased the power of labor was the creation of the CIO in 1935. The Congress of Industrial Organizations unionized many of the previously unorganized mass-production industrial workers. Unlike the AFL, it aimed at being a union for all workers. Its leader, John L. Lewis, also realized that the CIO had to recruit skeptical Blacks to prevent their being used as strikebreakers. In 1937, the CIO had about 4 million members. The New Deal and events during the 1930s left in their wake a triumvirate of power: big government, big business, and big labor. During and after World War II, union membership was still high and growing, and unions were an effective force for improving working conditions for their members.

Despite this growth in union power, the ideological tide had already begun to shift against organized labor by the end of the 1930s. The recession of 1938–1939, which led to a weakening of federal recovery programs, factionalism within the CIO (which many suspected had communist leanings), the growing patriotism during the early years of World War II, and the impatience of many with the increased militancy of workers immediately after the war strengthened conservative forces against unions (Zieger 1986). The increased bureaucratization and job consciousness of unions over the years and the routinization of formal contracts and the "rule of law" in industry also helped to institutionalize labor-industry conflict. Employers were more willing to buy off workers with higher wages than to relinquish control of the production process (Brody 1980; Zieger 1986). The Taft-Hartley Act of 1947 renewed many of the powers that had been lost to business in the Wagner Act. It also curbed the power of unions to strike, required an anti-Communist pledge from workers, and redefined labor's rights in much narrower terms (Piven and Cloward 1977; Zieger 1986).

The increased conservatism and narrowness of unions meant that workers often fought against the wishes of union leadership. The interests of workers and those of the union leadership did not always coincide. This internal division within the labor movement has continued. Although union membership generally grew during the 1950s and 1960s, and more public employees initiated unionization drives, differences of opinion within the labor community surfaced over Vietnam and the Civil Rights and women's movements of the 1960s. In the conservative 1980s and early 1990s, unions were again under attack, membership declined, and union leadership appeared weaker than in the earlier heyday of organized labor.

The lack of national unity among unions, rapid employment growth in new areas coupled with higher unemployment in traditional occupations, and a hostile political climate have certainly contributed to the decline of union power (Western 1993). But elements internal to labor unions themselves have also contributed to their decline. Publicized corruption, ethnic and gender bias within unions, and a lack of union democracy for rank-and-file workers have weakened their moral

authority (Kallick 1994). Unions have yet to fully accommodate the large number of immigrants and the growth in the numbers of women and ethnic groups (especially Hispanics) within the house of labor (DeFreitas 1993; Gooding and Reeve 1993). The face of labor has changed; to maximize their power, unions must successfully handle their heterogeneity. The splintering within unions is reminiscent of the labor movement of the 1920s. Perhaps the movement has come full circle and will again mobilize its constituencies to restore labor's power.

THE CIVIL RIGHTS MOVEMENT

Although it often discriminated against both Blacks and women, the labor movement was driven by concerns over inequities in political and economic power, and historical, cultural, and social conditions shaped its development and form. In general terms, the same can be said of the Civil Rights movement of the mid-1950s and 1960s. Although an indisputable specific date for its beginning cannot be given, there is general agreement that it began in the period between 1953 and 1955 during which the historic *Brown* v. *Board of Education* Supreme Court decision was made, and systematic bus boycotts had occurred in Baton Rouge, Louisiana, and Montgomery, Alabama. The nonviolent movement extended into the mid-1960s up to the point when other more radical, Black-power elements were becoming increasingly important.

As is the case of the labor movement, there had been many instances of protest by African Americans against Whites before the Civil Rights movement. Revolts by slaves against their masters, the underground railroad, the massive growth of the National Association for the Advancement of Colored People (NAACP) membership to almost half a million during World War II, the demands that led Roosevelt to establish a Fair Employment Practices Committee, and A. Philip Randolph's political activity in Washington and before Congress in the 1940s all provide evidence of racial protest and a push for racial equality before the Civil Rights movement (Morris 1984).

Thus, the movements of the 1950s and 1960s did not just suddenly appear out of nowhere. Public activism in movements waxes and wanes as social, economic, and political circumstances in the surrounding environment change. Consequently, what may appear to be the beginning of a social movement may only be a resurgence of activism that had been kept in abeyance because of lack of opportunity structures in the social context (Taylor 1989a). As was found in the labor movement's history, particular historical, political, economic, and social conditions created a context in which effective mass protest could be initiated, and the Civil Rights movement could be nurtured. The actual battle for racial justice predates, then, the so-called modern Civil Rights movement.

In the late nineteenth and early twentieth centuries, African Americans had few resources with which to launch a massive Civil Rights campaign. First of all, racist ideologies discouraged support from Whites. Second, most African Americans were fully but exploitively integrated into the southern economic and political structure. There were few economic opportunities open to them and Jim Crow laws kept them in their assigned place. In other words, the social context offered few political and economic opportunities or alternatives. Third, the federal government did little to alleviate the oppressive conditions under which Blacks lived. Earlier, national leaders had written into the Constitution that Black men, who were unfree, were to be considered only three-fifths persons. Now Congress stood by as Blacks were disenfranchised and violently treated in the South.

The North and the federal government did little while Black subjugation and White supremacy were being systematically institutionalized in the South. This structured inequality was especially evident in the political realm. Blacks were effectively prevented from voting through the use of various devices, including poll taxes, tests of literacy and "good character," grandfather requirements, and primaries limited to Whites. Laws in the South prohibited the integration of Blacks and Whites in schools, hospitals, motels, places of recreation, and even funeral homes and cemeteries. These Jim Crow laws made it legal to spend less public money on Black than on White institutions (Sitkoff 1981).

The Changing Context of Racial Inequality

After World War I, it was clear that changing economic and political conditions would strengthen the power position of African Americans in the United States. Among these economic changes was a decline in the centrality of agriculture in the southern economy coupled with increasing industrialization of the urban South. This agrarian decline was fostered, in part, by declines in immigration and agricultural exports during the war. Accompanying the decline in immigration was an increase in the demand by northern industry for laborers from the South. Both "King Cotton" and industry needed workers, but changing circumstances created a shift in demand from agriculture to industry. Before and after World War I, there was massive African American migration to the North and to cities to seek employment in industries (Piven and Cloward 1977; Sitkoff 1981; McAdam 1982). Southern agriculture suffered again during the Great Depression of the early 1930s. An overproduction of cotton due to decreased demand led to a drastic decline in its price, which spelled disaster for many southern farmers. In Mississippi, at that time perhaps the greatest stronghold of White supremacy, farmers lost their land at about twice the national rate (Bloom 1987). Later, during the 1940s, as mechanization also became more and more essential in agriculture, some farmers left agriculture behind, and the average size of landholdings increased. This meant that more Black as well as White farm workers were economically displaced and needed to seek employment in the industries of northern and southern cities (Piven and Cloward 1977). Southern agriculture also had to diversify its products to feed the soldiers in military camps during World War II (Bloom 1987). All of these circumstances served to shake up the foundations of the traditional economy in the South.

The changed geographic and economic base of Blacks helped to develop their voting power and the indigenous institutional bases needed for the Civil Rights movement (McAdam 1982). The city provided greater opportunities for Blacks to get organized, to receive more education, and to lay the basis for an expanded Black middle class. The growth of these basic strengths within the Black community was important in the genesis of the Civil Rights movement. There is good evidence that, despite the importance of external resources to the movement, its origins and development can be traced to reliance on institutions indigenous to the Black community (Oberschall 1973; McAdam 1982; Morris 1984; Jenkins and Eckert 1986).

However, some have suggested that professional organizations gave impetus to the Civil Rights movements (McCarthy and Zald 1973). These organizations, in contrast to "mass-based" organizations, have outside leaders, have a full-time staff on salary, have significant outside benefactors, and play the role of "speaking for" aggrieved groups. Despite the argument that the origins of the movement can be traced to these organizations, evidence suggests otherwise. Jenkins and Eckert (1986) traced the involvement and support of indigenous and professional organizations over an approximately 30-year period (the late 1940s to 1980). Their conclusions were clear enough: "Professional SMOs [social movement organizations] were not the model actors at any point in the civil rights movement. Nor did they initiate the challenge, their efforts coming on the heels of indigenous actions.... The challenge was initiated by the grassroots groups, especially the churches and student groups" (1986, p. 819).

African American colleges, churches, and civic and fraternal institutions provided not only economic resources but also the communication network and most of the leaders needed to organize the movement. Martin Luther King, Jr., for example, was influential as a movement leader not only because of his charisma but also, crucially, because of the personal and organizational backing he received. The influence of the Southern Christian Leadership Conference during most of the movement's career suggests the relevance of religious institutions. Local colleges also provided most of the students who, early in the 1960s, were involved in the civil disobedience actions that helped bring about legislative changes.

External support of protests generally comes after the protests themselves. These additional resources are a *product* rather than a *cause* of protest (McAdam 1982). The patronage that did come later from outsiders appears to have been given less out of feelings of conscience and injustice than out of concern to keep the movement moderate and weaken the radical element—that is, to exercise some control over the direction of the movement (Jenkins and Eckert 1986). The nonviolent sit-ins of college students and others in the South in the early 1960s, for example, brought much financial and other support from outside, northern groups. The violent protests later in the 1960s in northern and western cities, on the other hand, produced a White backlash, partly because of the violence, but also because of the switch in focus of problems from the rural South to the urban ghettos of the North.

The economic and attending geographic shifts that were occurring in the South, then, provided African Americans with the opportunity to "construct the occupational and institutional foundation from which to mount resistance to White oppression" (Piven and Cloward 1977, p. 205). It has been argued that the southern agricultural power structure benefited most from the traditional racist structure in the South. In this view, the southern agricultural elite (i.e., large plantation owners) had the most to lose from desegregation and equality for African Americans, for they relied on the cheap, accessible African American labor source. On the other hand, cities and businesses stood to suffer from the racial unrest caused by segregationist laws (Bloom 1987). Business growth and investment in Little Rock, Arkansas, were seriously damaged, for example, after the school desegregation confrontations in the late 1950s. With the growth of industries, cities gradually became more influential politically than agrarian areas (Bloom 1987). Consequently, changing economic and social conditions created a split in the "Solid South" between the interests of business and agriculture.

In addition to the shrinking role of agriculture and the expanding presence of industry, the increased stridence and militancy of the reaction against African American protests for equality also helped to isolate the South, especially the Deep South, from the rest of the nation. Thus, changes and reactions to them not only created deeper divisions within the South itself but also served to increasingly alienate the South from the remainder of the country. In other words, Bloom argued, the traditional social and political structure was grounded in a particular kind of economy. A weakening in the basis of that agricultural economy threatened the survival of sociopolitical arrangements that primarily benefited the rich landowner and discriminated against African Americans. "Racial patterns and racial consciousness have as their foundation particular class structures, and they develop and change as these structures themselves change." At the same time, however, "class structure may set the parameters of racial action, but it cannot reduce race to class" (Bloom 1987, p. 3).

This last point is very important. Class and economic factors were implicated in the shifting allegiances to racial inequality. However, *racist ideology* was still an underlying element in accounting for not only social and economic inequality in the South but also reactions to Black attempts to eliminate it. Recall that in the latter part of the nineteenth and well into the twentieth centuries, there were a variety of established racial ideologies justifying unequal treatment of Blacks. Beliefs about the inferiority of Blacks go back even further than that to the early founding of the United States (see Chapter 6). The continued significance of racism itself was manifested in the support given by lower-class as well as upper-class White Southerners to the discriminatory treatment of Blacks. Upper-class White Southerners who had vested local economic interests fought the hardest against voting rights for Blacks because to afford this right would have been tantamount to surrendering power to them.

Although the voting regulations effectively eliminated many lower-class Whites as well as Blacks from voting, the former went along with their upper-class brethren in supporting the laws. The southern aristocracy played on racist images of Blacks and used the image of competition between Blacks and Whites as a means to obtain the support of lower-class Whites (Piven and Cloward 1977). In addition, not only southern agricultural aristocrats but also local town and city business people fought against those who pushed for integration into local restaurants, motels, and so on. In essence, both economic factors and racism played roles in the dynamics of racial inequality and reactions to it.

Other social and cultural events gave strength to the Black effort to confront racial inequality. During the 1920s, the Harlem Renaissance encouraged Blacks to take pride in themselves and their cultural and literary heritage. In addition, the Civil Rights activists of the late 1920s and 1930s often fought alongside White radical unionists who were pushing the New Deal policies (Sitkoff 1981). Radical union leaders, it will be recalled, wanted to include not only Whites and skilled workers but also Blacks and unskilled industrial workers, as well. Both radical unions and Black organizations, however, were often labeled as being infiltrated by Communists. This would become a familiar theme again after World War II, especially with the rise of McCarthyism.

In addition to the changes in the U.S. economy and social-cultural factors that strengthened Black unity, other historical events and conditions also helped to lay the groundwork for the Civil Rights movement that was to come in the 1950s. Political circumstances were weakening the South's grip on Blacks and providing the latter with resources that could be used in their battle against racism. Migration to the North not only meant a greater probability of voting but also led to Blacks holding political office in several major cities (Sitkoff 1981; Bloom 1987). "Estimates of voting strength in 1948 saw Blacks holding the balance of power in sixteen states with a total of 278 electoral votes, compared to 127 electoral votes controlled by the South"

(Bloom 1987, p. 76). Politicians with presidential aspirations became increasingly concerned about potential Black political defections and, as a result, often courted the Black vote.

Despite this courtship, governmental policies continued to underrepresent the interests of Blacks. But they also, perhaps inadvertently, strengthened the position of Blacks. As you saw in the history of the early labor movement, the New Deal's policies had an impact on the fate of the labor movement. Similarly, the public works programs of the New Deal provided Blacks with an alternate source of income outside the relatively narrow range of private positions open to them. Having another source of income, which meant less dependence, created a source of power with which to fight oppression (Piven and Cloward 1971, 1982; Bloom 1987). This federal source of work and the increased demand for labor in industry helped to drive wages up—wages that dominant agricultural groups were increasingly hesitant to pay (Bloom 1987). Federal loans also became available as a substitute for local ones, again making Blacks less dependent on local White funding institutions.

World War II brought further changes to the situation of Blacks. Unionization of Blacks was less difficult than had been the case only a decade earlier. Employment conditions had improved, especially with the wartime economy. But national unity was the preferred emphasis and most Blacks did not favor protest in these circumstances (Sitkoff 1981). Despite continued demands by Black groups, any serious attempts to deal with racial problems took a back seat to dealing with the Axis powers. Although the war brought some positive changes, Blacks were still much worse off than Whites politically and economically, and discrimination was still prevalent.

After the war, several political events occurred that affected efforts for racial equality. The international situation was such that the United States became more involved with a larger number of countries, including some with non-White populations. This change, coupled with the racist overtones of Nazism, against which we had fought, meant that continued racial inequality at

home could prove to be an embarrassment. Harry Truman, in running for the presidency in 1948, had to present a platform that showed a strong desire for civil rights if he was to defeat opponents who also were courting the vote of those Blacks who had migrated to the cities of the North. In doing so, however, he alienated democrats from the Deep South who went on to present their own State's Rights Party candidate. He also ordered the desegregation of the military. The economic and political context had shifted to the extent that Truman was advised to court Blacks even at the risk of turning away southern democrats (Piven and Cloward 1977).

A final political element in the late 1940s that affected Civil Rights efforts came out of the developing "Cold War" with the former Soviet Union. "Red-baiting" was fashionable, and Civil Rights groups and leaders were not immune to accusations of being Communist. White supremacists argued that Communists were behind the movement for Black equality. It will be recalled that similar accusations had been made about unions and their leadership when they also pushed for greater economic and political power. McCarthyism frightened Blacks, and the majority of Black leaders took a gradual and calm approach. "The NAACP became less a protest organization and more an agency of litigation and lobbying after World War II" (Sitkoff 1981, p. 18).

All of the conditions discussed thus far composed the context in which the Supreme Court made its momentous *Brown* v. *Board of Education* decision in 1954. To summarize, several changes had occurred since World War I that changed the social context and the political and economic position of Blacks:

1. The basis of the South's economy had shifted from agriculture to industry, weakening the economic status of the traditional southern upper class. This change led to economic and political splits within the southern upper class. The interests of industrial leaders in the maintenance of Jim Crow laws were simply not as strong nor as necessary as they were for the agricultural elite. The South's social and political structure was

becoming increasingly out of step with other mac-rochanges occurring in the region and the nation.

2. The decline in agriculture and the growth of industry in the nation as a whole opened up new economic opportunities for African Americans, and, for those who moved to cities and to the North, new political/power bases as well. This served to build up institutions within the African American community. In addition, it created a "cognitive liberation" for African Americans, a new understanding of their situation and the potentiality for change (McAdam 1982). The combination of increased internal solidarity within the African American community and being tied to the White economic power structure in an exploitative relationship created a situation favorable to the mobilization of African Americans (Oberschall 1973).

3. Racism continued to provide a backdrop against which economic changes and battles for equality were fought.

4. Political policies brought on by the Depression, the Nazism of World War II, and the growing Black voting bloc were moving in the direction of being helpful for Blacks. Moreover, in the 1950s, growing awareness of independence movements by oppressed non-White groups against colonial powers gave encouragement to Civil Rights forces in the United States. For example, in the late 1940s, India had achieved independence from England, and several African nations had achieved independence from their colonial masters in the late 1950s and early 1960s. These events suggested to the U.S government that it might make geopolitical sense for the state not to appear racist. The liberation struggles abroad also heartened many Black leaders who became convinced that change was possible (Rollins 1986).

As stated at the beginning of this section, the date on which the Civil Rights movement formally began is debatable. Some tie its start to the 1953 bus boycott in Baton Rouge, Louisiana. Others associate it with Rosa Parks's refusal to give her bus seat to a White man and the Montgomery bus boycott that followed in 1955. In any case, the mid-1950s is generally agreed to mark the start of the movement, and no single event was any more consequential than the Supreme Court's decision of 1954. To suggest the specific dynamics involved in the process, following is a sketchy history of the movement from that point to the mid-1960s when it began to disintegrate into various factions.

A Brief History

The *Brown* v. *Board of Education* decision was a true watershed in the effort for civil rights. It declared segregation in education to be unconstitutional. In concluding his argument, Chief Justice Earl Warren stated simply, "We conclude that in the field of public education the doctrine of 'separate but equal' has no place. Separate educational facilities are inherently unequal" (quoted in Sitkoff 1981, p. 22). This decision had a powerful effect on both Blacks and southern Whites. The Black movement for equality was given a boost, but at the same time a White countermovement was established to fight these advances. While Blacks were jubilant about the decision, the South's White elite were not about to accept it without a fight. Many said unequivocally that they would not comply with the law in this case. "The prospect of desegregating public schools was fundamentally appalling to the average White Southerner. The thought of young 'niggers' mixing in school with little White children jarred the sensibilities of Southern Whites, whether poor farmers or highly placed government officials" (Morris 1984, p. 27). Even though the decision by the Court to segregate had been unanimous, it had not come to this decision easily. In order to get the unanimous ruling, Warren had to agree on a policy of gradual implementation of the desegregation policy. The qualification of gradualism left room for southern dissenters to fight enforcement, and it led to frustration on the part of Blacks who wished speedy implementation of the law.

President Eisenhower demonstrated no strong endorsement of the decision, nor did he actively move to have it enforced. He did not really believe that one could effectively legislate on such moral-laden matters (Sitkoff 1981). Before the decision had been made, he had tried to soften Warren's position by alluding to the basic goodness of the South's people: "These are not bad people. All they are concerned about is to see that their sweet little girls are not required to sit in school alongside some big overgrown Negroes" (quoted in Bloom 1987, p. 106). Eisenhower, then, was not an active supporter of civil rights, but later Black protests and militant White reactions to those actions would force him to intervene.

As mentioned, reaction from the southern White power structure to the Court's decision was immediate and strong. There was no strong push on the part of the government for swift implementation of the law; the dominance by conservative elements of the major political parties in Congress meant no rapid enforcement would be forthcoming. The FBI's J. Edgar Hoover still saw racial unrest as being Communist inspired (Bloom 1987). In the South, White churches and the press generally opposed the ruling, and local White Citizens' Councils were set up to fight desegregation (Sitkoff 1981). In 1956, the membership in these Councils approached 250,000 (Piven and Cloward 1977).

In the mid-1950s, notable bus boycotts by Blacks occurred in Baton Rouge, Montgomery, and Tallahassee. Perhaps the most famous of these was initiated by Rosa Parks in Montgomery in December of 1955. Mrs. Parks, who was an active NAACP participant and had been put off the bus previously for refusing to move to the back, had gotten on a crowded bus and refused to surrender her seat to a White male adult. At the next bus stop, Mrs. Parks was taken off the bus and arrested for violating the local bus ordinance (Sitkoff 1981). News of her arrest spread, and a bus boycott was organized by a group of local Black leaders. Assuming that it would be best to appoint an outsider as its leader, they appointed a hesitant, young, middle-class, nonviolent, and intellectually sophisticated Black minister to lead the boycott.

The Reverend Martin Luther King, Jr. was well educated, a newcomer to the area, and had attended theological school in the North. He was stunned by the blatant racism that seemed to be so out of place in a period when Blacks had become more educated and urbanized (Sitkoff 1981). Given his background and training, King assumed initially that Whites would respect logic and listen to reason, but he was wrong. "He now realized that the matter was one of power, not reason, that 'no one gives up his privileges without strong resistance'" (Sitkoff 1981, p. 51). Under his new organization, dubbed the Montgomery Improvement Association, King led a nonviolent boycott of the bus system. Local Black churches provided sites for meetings and arranged for alternative modes of transportation. The boycott went on for over a year, and during that time, White resistance had tried a range of tactics to bring it to an end. Legal tactics such as arrests and jailings for minor or fictitious infractions of local laws were used. Economic sanctions also were tried; some deeply involved in the boycott lost their jobs. Finally, violent tactics were used: Many beatings occurred, and four Black churches and the homes of King, his associate Ralph Abernathy, and another supporter were bombed. In the last analysis, however, the nonviolent boycott prevailed and the U.S. Supreme Court declared Alabama's bus segregation laws unconstitutional.

The nonviolent, long-suffering, patient approach of the boycott contrasted in the national media with the harsh White reaction. Many outside the South were appalled at the tactics used by the White resistance. In contrast, King's "neo-Gandhian persuasion" seemed reasonable and acceptable as a means for obtaining equal rights. Above all, it was nonviolent and embraced the Christian beliefs of turning the other cheek and not condemning individual racists. It blamed the system of segregation rather than the individuals who enforced it (King 1958; Sitkoff 1981). As a result of the boycott, King and his approach to injustice gained worldwide attention. Out of the boycott, other Civil Rights groups were organized, most notably the Southern Christian leadership Conference (SCLC) under King's leadership.

A familiar pattern of Black/White confrontation began to develop as a result of the early boycotts. Basically, the sequence would begin with nonviolent Black protests, followed by a militant White response, which in turn often led to federal intervention. It did not take long for Black leaders to figure out how to get the attention of federal officials who had been unreliable and largely unresponsive in the past in enforcing rights that were theirs under the Constitution.

Another prominent illustration of Black/White confrontation occurred a couple of years after Mrs. Parks's historic bus ride. In late 1957, Governor Orval Faubus of Arkansas called in National Guard troops to prevent Black students from entering the all-White Central High School in Little Rock. Ignoring another federal court order, troops would still not let these students in the next day. After threats of White mob violence, Eisenhower was forced to act by federalizing National Guard troops and bringing in paratroopers to guarantee safe admission for the students. The troops remained for the rest of the year.

The violent repressive tactics of Whites against nonviolent protestors angered many in the Black community and made them not altogether happy with King's patient, nonmilitant approach. This was especially the case as hostile White resistance intensified during the late 1950s and early 1960s. However, many young college-educated Blacks had had their resolve stiffened by the growing number of successes from King's approach. Beside boycotts and marches, additional nonviolent tactics were used. Among these was the sit-in, which also had been used effectively in the past in union strikes.

In the early 1960s, sit-ins were held throughout the South as a way of protesting segregation of public facilities. Similar protests were held in northern cities to demonstrate sympathetic support of the Civil Rights protestors. These protests involved thousands of individuals, many of them college students. One of the most famous of the sit-ins occurred in early February 1960 in Greensboro, North Carolina. Four Black students sat down at a Woolworth's lunch counter and asked for coffee and donuts. When refused, they kept their seats until the store closed. The next day,

more students did the same thing, but White officials remained implacable, and it was only after repeated sit-ins that Greensboro allowed such service six months later. This sit-in inspired similar protests throughout the South and afforded a means by which college students could become meaningfully involved in the Civil Rights movement. Adults also joined in these protests. Within one and one-half years of the Greensboro sit-in, demonstrations had been carried out in over 100 cities and towns in all the southern states (Blumberg 1984). Not only sit-ins at lunch counters, but sleep-ins in the lobbies of motels, swim-ins at pools, play-ins at recreational areas, kneel-ins at churches, and read-ins at libraries followed. Boycotts also were carried out against merchants who refused desegregation (Sitkoff 1981). Local White reactions were often swift and violent. Floggings, kickings, pistol whippings, dog attacks, jailings, and even acid throwings were among the repressive means used against the protestors. But still the sit-ins continued.

One of the results of these demonstrations was that they showed southerners the depth of Black feelings about these matters. They were also powerful in bringing to the attention of the nation the injustice of widespread legal segregation practices. Largely as a result of the active concern of Black college youths, their impatience with years of waiting, and the seemingly futile legal maneuverings of the more conservative approaches in the Civil Rights movement as typified by the NAACP, other, more militant types of organizations (such as the Student Nonviolent Coordinating Committee [SNCC]) began appearing in the early 1960s (Blumberg 1984; Sitkoff 1981).

In 1961, the Congress of Racial Equality (CORE), which had been founded in 1942 and had advocated direct nonviolent means of protest, organized a "freedom ride" from Washington, DC, to New Orleans to see if states and municipalities were complying with the federal law against discrimination in interstate bus terminals. These rides went into the Deep South where White resistance was strongest. As in other peaceful protests, these too evoked violent White resistance. Beatings and deaths of protestors, for example, took place in several Alabama cities, including Birmingham and Montgomery. Again, much of the violence was broadcast through the media.

It was only when waves of public sympathy came that the federal government acted to protect the protestors and enforce the law. When there was no publicity, little was done; violations of the law were left unpunished. It became clear to protestors that they apparently had to elicit a violent response to receive public attention and sympathy, and to trigger the government to act. When the White resistance reacted with legal nonviolent measures, such publicity and sympathy was not as likely, nor as a result, was governmental intervention. Barkan (1984) suggested that had Whites used these means more often, the results may have been different. Examining the confrontations in Montgomery, Selma, Birmingham, Albany (Georgia), and Danville (Virginia), he concluded that in those cities where legal means such as arrests, high bails, court proceedings, and injunctions had been used, protestors were less successful (see also Sitkoff 1981).

Federal officials were always reluctant to intervene in Civil Rights protests. Many of the reasons were political in nature. Both major political parties were still concerned with alienating the power structure and White voters of the Deep South. As in the 1930s, when the federal administration was trying to balance allegiances between labor and business, the government in the 1950s and early 1960s did not want to antagonize either Blacks or Whites. The result was a lot of fence-sitting, and many acts of violence against legitimate protests evoked no response from Washington (Piven and Cloward 1977; Sitkoff 1981).

One of the most brutal reactions to the nonviolent demonstrations of King and the SCLC occurred in Birmingham in the spring of 1963. Sit-ins, marches, and similar techniques had been used to protest local segregation. After these had been going on for a time, the local police commissioner, Eugene "Bull" Connor, came down violently on the protestors. His violent response was seen by millions on television. Officials used

dogs, high-pressure hoses, cattle prods, clubs, and even a police tank to beat down the protestors. President Kennedy and his brother, Robert, who had wanted "cooling-down" periods by Blacks and a more gradual approach to desegregation, sent federal representatives to help reach a compromise between King and local officials. But the protestors would not back down. Finally, the SCLC obtained desegregation of some public facilities, a promise of nondiscriminatory hiring, and the formation of a biracial committee in Birmingham (Sitkoff 1981). The local reaction to the agreement was not completely positive. Bombings resulted, causing some Blacks to again question King's nonviolent approach.

As successful protests became more frequent, more working-class Blacks were drawn into the movement. Greater competition among the major Black organizations (SCLC, SNCC, CORE, NAACP) occurred with each group vying for the dominant position. They sponsored massive demonstrations throughout the country. A national March on Washington was made in August 1963, sponsored by numerous Civil Rights, union, and church organizations and involving well over 200,000 individuals. During the summer of 1964, hundreds of individuals worked in Mississippi to increase voter registration, and three workers were brutally murdered. The government asked workers to remain calm, but this request only deepened their distrust of administration policies and motives. Riots broke out in several cities. President Kennedy began to press for a Civil Rights law in 1963, and shortly thereafter the Civil Rights and Voting Rights Acts were passed under President Johnson. This national legislative response to the basic problems of Blacks, particularly in the South, helped to delegitimize the need for protest, especially in the eyes of northern Whites.

But despite the passage of these laws, as has already been suggested, several other changes had occurred that helped alter the nature of the Black movement from the nonviolent protest tactics of King to cries for "Black Power" and Black "liberation." First, the slow, compromising approach of the federal government to the problems experienced by

Blacks on a day-to-day basis, coupled with the patient nonviolent method of King, convinced some in the Civil Rights movement of the need for more drastic action on their own behalf. The consistently violent reactions by Whites to the nonviolent protests of Blacks over the years widened the gap between factions within the Civil Rights movement in the early 1960s.

Second, the focus of the Civil Rights movement had been on the South, but the migration of many Blacks into the cities of the North and West led to a shift in goal emphasis within the movement. The problems of Black city dwellers became the focus: poverty, employment, housing, poor schools, and so on. The Civil Rights movement has been interpreted by some as largely a movement by and for middle-class individuals, while the focus of the Black movement on problems of city residents appeared to demonstrate a greater concern for the Black working and lower classes (Oberschall 1973; Blumberg 1984; Bloom 1987). In total, the shift in the movement was from an emphasis on integration, political and so-

cial rights, and nonviolence to one on Black separatism, economic needs, and more militant tactics (Blumberg 1984; Bloom 1987; Schaefer 1988). Different segments stressed the importance of cultural and Black nationalism, while others spoke of Black power, Despite their dissimilarities, all of these more militant perspectives betrayed a basic distrust of White institutions, the need for Blacks to develop their own institutions or identities, and the need for stronger reactions to discrimination against Blacks. Stokely Carmichael's statement about the need for Black power suggests the feelings that some were having: "Power is the only thing respected in this world, and we must get it at any cost" (in Sitkoff 1981, p. 214).

Violent riots occurred during these "long hot summers" in many major cities, including Chicago, Cleveland, Milwaukee, Dayton, San Francisco, Detroit, Newark, New Haven, Boston, Buffalo, and others. During 1967 alone, there were 150 such outbreaks (Sitkoff 1981). Certainly with this turn of events, it was clear that by the mid-1960s, while the Black push for equality was

Marches were commonly used by the Civil Rights Movement in the 1960s as a way to convey a message of the need for racial equality.

continuing, the nonviolent Civil Rights movement phase had passed.

Since the late 1960s, changes have occurred that have altered the speed and vibrancy of the movement to reduce racial inequality. Over the last couple of decades, shifts in the economy, greater political conservatism and complacency, the rise of Hispanics and concerns about new immigrants, and growing economic inequality outside and inside the Black community have softened the national focus on Blacks' living conditions and created divisions among Blacks themselves. There have even been attempts to eliminate policies originally aimed at equalizing opportunities for all groups. The ongoing assault on Affirmative Action is, in large part, a reflection of fears about competition for jobs and beliefs that changes have largely rectified abuses against Blacks, thus rendering Affirmative Action unnecessary. Despite the fact that Affirmative Action appears to have benefited women more than Blacks and that Blacks continue to be worse off than Whites on many socioeconomic and life-chance measures, the broad-based, national sense of urgency to the plight of Blacks appears to have been muted in recent years. Again, this demonstrates how much the health of movements is dependent on changes in the wider society.

THE WOMEN'S MOVEMENT

In both the Civil Rights and earlier labor movements, women had been victims of discrimination. Women needed their own movement to advance their interests. Like the Civil Rights movement, the women's movement has had an uneven history. Its unevenness is reflected in the fact that some scholars suggest that there were two or three separate such movements in history, yet others suggest that a single women's movement went through several phases. Freeman (1975b), for example, stated that "sometime during the 1920s, feminism died in the United States" (p. 448). But as is the case in the other movements, the push for political, economic, and other rights for women never completely "died." Rather, during the natural history of the

women's movement, there were times when the movement was widely and publicly active, while in other times, those in the movement were retrenching and the movement was, so to speak, being held in suspension or in abeyance (Taylor 1989a). The point is that what may appear to be separate women's movements can be viewed as distinct phases of one movement. As was the case with the other movements we have surveyed, internal conditions interacted with external circumstances to determine the nature of the movement. Many of those conditions were related to structures of economic, racial, and sexual inequality in the society, as you will see.

The women's movement in the United States began in the late 1700s and early 1800s and has continued, although not always actively and publicly, to this day (Hole and Levine 1975; Chafe 1977; Snyder 1979). Throughout its history, feminism has incorporated two seemingly paradoxical general goals. One is the belief that since women are, in most respects, the *same* as men in their potential and abilities, they are deserving of the *same* rights as men. The other is the belief that since women are *different* from men, they deserve special protections. At different times and by different groups, each of these positions has been emphasized. Women's rights, then, are defined according to which of these two sets of beliefs and goals is stressed (Cott 1986). For example, in the nineteenth and early twentieth centuries, women argued that they were entitled to the same options and opportunities as men, and that such equal opportunity would allow society to benefit from the unique contributions of both sexes. Harriet Burton Laidlaw, an early suffragist, distilled both these beliefs in her statement that to the extent that women were like men, they ought to have the same rights, but to the extent that they were unlike men, they alone should represent themselves. This bifurcation of beliefs and goals was reflected in the specific goals set by various women's organizations throughout the movement's history. It will be recalled that interpretations of justice and fairness are often based on beliefs about the fundamental differences and similarities between individuals (see Chapter 14).

The earliest organized efforts by women involved attempts to increase their educational rights and to fight for the abolition of slavery, and it was during involvement in the abolitionist movement of the 1830s that some women became acutely aware of their own low political status. As proved to be the case with their involvement in other historical movements, women were not given significant status or voice in the abolitionist movement. Indeed, while this movement was fighting for an end to slavery, women were being prevented from joining some abolitionist organizations and were being muzzled in their attempt to speak in public on the issues. Women had to create their own antislavery organizations because they were being excluded from many of the men's organizations (Hole and Levine 1975). It will be recalled that women had a similar experience in the early labor union movement. While demanding rights and social justice for workers, many unions were at the same time barring women from membership. In those cases where women were members, few held leadership positions.

In 1840, a world antislavery meeting was held in London. Men at the meeting, including so-called radicals, were shocked to see women present, and so had them put in galleries where they could not participate effectively in the meeting. Later in 1867, Sojourner Truth, a crusader for both women's and African Americans' rights, wrote of the neglect of women's rights among those who advocated such fights for African Americans: "There is a great stir about colored men getting their rights, but not a word about colored women; and if colored men get their rights and not colored women theirs, you see the colored men will be masters over the women, and it will be just as bad as it was before" (quoted in Ferree and Hess 1985, p. 32). Time and again, it became clear to many women that they would have to have their own organizations and movement if their rights were ever to be granted (Hole and Levine 1975; Snyder 1979).

Two of the women who had attended the antislavery convention in London were Elizabeth Cady Stanton and Lucretia Mott. Convinced of the need for an organization exclusively for women's rights, these women organized a meeting that was held in Seneca Falls, New York, in July of 1848. About 300 men and women attended, including Frederick Douglass and Susan B. Anthony. The attendees approved a "Declaration of Sentiments" based loosely on the wording of the Declaration of Independence. Among other things, this document argued for the basic equality of men and women and stressed that historically men had dominated over women in religious institutions, employment opportunities, and family and political life. Included among the declarations made was a demand for the right to vote. Although this latter demand has been said to signal the beginning of the suffrage movement, most of the women at the Seneca Falls meeting were more concerned with issues in their immediate experience: control of property and earnings, rights over children, rights to divorce, and so forth. From 1848 to the Civil War, women's conventions were held almost every year in different cities of the East and Midwest (Hole and Levine 1975).

The Early Social Context and Directions

The social environment within which women were advocating greater freedoms and rights was not hospitable. Not only was this reflected in women's imposed marginal status in male abolitionist and labor organizations but also in the reactions within other dominant institutions. Religious institutions and the media railed against the embryonic women's movement. It was as if a natural and supernatural order were being violated by the attempts to gain women rights equal to those of men. In order to spread the word, women had to rely on some abolitionist papers and their own journals. Late in the nineteenth century, Stanton and others produced *The Woman's Bible,* a systematic critique to demonstrate that the traditional Bible was a major source of the subjugation of women.

The early formation of the movement also was affected by the forces of early industrialization. Not being allowed to learn skills, women who needed to work were relegated to either household or low-paying work (Huber 1982). Women who were from the middle or upper class, on the other hand, were not expected to work but rather to appear and act as "ladies." "The nineteenth-century concept of a lady was that of a fragile, idle, pure creature, submissive and subservient to her husband and to domestic needs. Her worth was based on her decorative value, a quality that embraced her beauty, her character, and her temperament. She was certainly not a paid employee" (Fox and Hesse-Biber 1984, p. 19). Not only working-class women but also Black women especially were not in a social and economic position to live up to the ideals of this image. They had to work, and in places and ways that did not foster an image of them as "ladies." If a woman was lacking in the qualities expected of a "lady," it "meant a woman was unnatural, unfeminine, and thus a species of a different—if not lower—female order.... Women who worked outside the home, or whose race had a history of sexual exploitation, were outside the realm of 'womanhood' and its prerogatives" (Giddings 1984, pp. 48–49). Thus, race as well as class circumstances divided women.

This class division among women had an impact on the membership and goals of the early women's organizations. It was largely middle- and upper-class women who initiated the early movement and who fashioned its goals to fit their problems and desires, such as the desire for education in the professions and civil service and property and voting rights. At the same time, they pushed for lower numbers of hours for female factory workers (Huber 1982). Although the latter appeared as a form of protection for women, it also was seen by many men as a way to minimize work competition from women. This suggests, as discussed earlier, the varying emphases on women as being different as well as the same as men. A desire for protection implies that women are different and more vulnerable than men, whereas the desire on the part of some women for equal employment opportunities implies that they are the equals of men. In sum, the religious and cultural milieu, along with the conditions of industrialization and slavery, helped to shape the form of the early women's movement as well as reactions to it. As you will see later, the 1980s did not afford the movement a hospitable environment either and for some of the same basic reasons.

After the Civil War, when the Fourteenth and Fifteenth Amendments on Black rights were being debated, women were told that attempts to include women in these amendments would only diffuse the focus that was being placed on rights for Blacks alone. The incorporation of women as well as men into the amendments, they were told, would only hinder their passage (Hole and Levine 1975; Snyder 1979). The thrust for a separate women's movement accelerated, and basically two strands developed. One, under Elizabeth Cady Stanton and Susan B. Anthony, formed the National Woman Suffrage Association. It emphasized a variety of rights for women and viewed the vote as a means to obtaining them. The other, exemplified by the American Woman Suffrage Association under Lucy Stone and others, focused only on the vote. Eventually, the emphasis on the vote won out in the movement and the two organizations merged into the National American Woman Suffrage Association (Hole and Levine 1975). "By the decade beginning in 1910 the demand for woman suffrage was a capacious umbrella under which a large diversity of beliefs and organizations could shelter, or...an expansive platform on which they could all comfortably, if temporarily, stand" (Cott 1986, p. 52). It is during this period that the term *feminism* came on to the public scene. It would have been unthinkable to use such a term during the "woman movement" of the nineteenth century. Feminism suggested a radical change in all relations with men and also attracted smaller numbers of followers than the earlier "woman movement" (Cott 1987).

Two of the most militantly active groups pushing for the enfranchisement of women were the Congressional Union and the group derived from it, the National Woman's Party (NWP). Both were at the forefront of the movement between 1910 and 1920. Their intellectual leaders, Alice Paul and Lucy Burns, were both highly educated, militant, and single minded in their pursuit of enfranchisement. By all accounts, Paul was a highly charismatic and enthusiastic individual who was an ardent advocate of single-issue politics (Cott 1987). Apparently, she also practiced a dictatorial style of leadership in the National Woman's Party, which drove some women from the group (Taylor 1989a). The militance of the Party was evident in mass protests, picketing and marches on Wilson's White House, hunger strikes, and even jailings (Hole and Levine 1975; Cott 1987).

The NWP was viewed as having a single objective and any diversion from its pursuit was considered harmful. The rigid adherence to this philosophy resulted in insensitivity to the unique goals and problems of subgroups within the female population. "Only women holding culturally hegemonic values and positions—that is, in the United States, women who are White, heterosexual, middle class, politically midstream—have the privilege (or deception) of seeing their condition as that of 'woman,' glossing over their other characteristics," observed Cott perceptively (1986, p. 58). For example, some Blacks felt that the NWP was basically racist and did not care about the rights of Blacks. Most suffragist groups of the time were imbued with the racism of the broader culture and did little to combat it. Black women's concerns were considered by Paul to be racial rather than feminist problems (Cott 1987).

In 1919, shortly before the passage of the Nineteenth Amendment enfranchising women, Walter White, leader of the NAACP, remarked about the NWP and its leadership: "If they could get the Suffrage Amendment through without enfranchising colored women, they would do it in a moment" (quoted in Cott 1987, p. 69). Just as women had been marginalized in the abolitionist movement by those fighting for Black rights, the specific problems of Blacks were now being put aside to focus on those of women only. In the same vein, some educated women were fighting for the same right to vote that "drunken male immigrant layabouts" possessed. This implied a kind of elitism among some segments of the suffrage movement (Ferree and Hess 1985). But it also reflected a class and race elitism present in the

wider society in the early 1900s, a division whose implications for the suffrage movement were not fully understood by its leaders. Those in the movement "profoundly misread the degree to which ethnic, class, and family allegiances undermined the prospect of sex-based political behavior" (Chafe 1977, p. 118).

In April of 1917, the United States entered World War I, but not all groups championed this. The Socialist Party condemned it, while the moderate suffragists in the National American Woman Suffrage Association (NAWSA) took a patriotic stance and endorsed it. The militant National Woman's Party, on the other hand, took no official stand on the war, or on socialism for that matter. The two women's organizations just mentioned were substantially different from each other. The NAWSA was as moderate and nonmilitant in its tactics as the NWP was radical. It was disgusted by the militant and unseemly activities of the NWP (Cott 1987). In a period when anti-Russian and antisocialist feelings were running strong in much of the nation, the alignment of militant feminists with socialists and pacifists alienated the nonaligned NWP from the rest of the country. Antisuffrage groups cropped up attempting to link the "dangers" of socialism, communism, and feminism.

After the enfranchisement of women was accomplished in 1920, the movement for women's rights changed drastically. One interpretation is that "the woman's movement virtually died in 1920 and, with the exception of a few organizations, feminism was to lie dormant for forty years" (Hole and Levine 1975, p. 446). Rather than completely dying, the movement became fractured internally, in large part because the attainment of the franchise had meant different things to different organizations and individuals. In essence, some women saw enfranchisement as an end in itself, while others viewed it as a means to reach more important goals, such as an equal rights amendment (ERA) for women.

The latter was now the goal of the National Woman's Party, while the more conservative National American Woman Suffrage Association fought against the ERA, formed the League of Women Voters, and worked for the active citizenship of women. The idea of universalistic legislation covering women's rights also was opposed by the Women's Bureau of the Department of Labor and a number of voluntary women's organizations. They feared that the legalization of equality with men would remove the shelters women received under the protectionist legislation of the 1920s, which limited women's involvement in the labor force. Some of the motivation on the part of the government for passing protective legislation was concern over the declining fertility rate early in the twentieth century. Officials feared that too drastic a decline would have harmful effects on the size of the defense forces and on the growth of the economy. It was believed that encouraging women to remain at home might stem the tide toward a lower birth rate.

At the bottom of everything, what divided women was the question of the priority of women's maternal roles compared to their employment opportunities. Protectionist legislation was interpreted by its adherents as conserving the maternal role of women (Huber 1982). Those pressing for an ERA, on the other hand, expressed an interest in the full potentiality of women, not merely their roles in the family. In a real sense, this difference of opinion on ERA resurrected the old question about the natures of men and women. Those who were in favor of the ERA were saying that women and men were basically the same, whereas those opposed to it and in support of protective legislation were saying that the two groups were basically different. Although both groups believed that sex inequality existed, the first group saw it as unnecessary and undesirable, yet the second saw it as a given and, therefore, women needed protection. This division in position was duplicated in England (Cott 1986).

The movement also was splintered by the multiple ties of many women to other social movements. Once the Nineteenth Amendment had passed, many women moved on to other causes, such as temperance, birth control, union organizing, and poverty (Ferree and Hess 1985). Black

women and working women had concerns other than those held by middle- or upper-class, educated women, and some eventually formed their own organizations. Black women, for example, did not put the passage of the ERA and goals of the birth control movement anywhere near the top of their agenda: "For them, racial concerns overwhelmed those of sex" (Giddings 1984, p. 183). Lynching was a problem that hit much closer to home for them.

Given the class, cultural, employment, racial, and other differences among women, it should be expected that there would be significant fissures within the women's movement. Another source of division among women in the 1920s was a cultural phenomenon of the time. Some women became caught up in the flapper movement of the 1920s and sought to improve their positions through the statuses attained by dress and lifestyle (Snyder 1979). With the defection of many women in different directions, some of the more militant organizations such as the National Woman's Party became increasingly isolated. In sum, whatever mass base existed in the women's movement in 1920 dwindled because of (1) internal divisions, (2) the accomplishment of suffrage, and (3) the growing diversity in the lives of women (Taylor 1989a).

Whether or not significant divisions in a movement can be minimized or made to appear invisible or unimportant depends on the style and message of leadership in the movement, the definition of feminism at the time, and the presence of widespread cultural and social unrest in the society. When the style of leadership is liberal and the interpretation of feminism is broad, the presence of multifaceted rebellion can forge effective though often only temporary alliances among factions. Groups can then fight for the same thing even though it is for different reasons (Cott 1986).

From Limbo to Resurgence

From 1945 to the 1960s, the women's movement was in limbo. In the years immediately after World War II, the social and cultural environment was not hospitable to protest from any minority group.

This chapter has mentioned the "anti-Red" climate and the narrow and frightening jingoism of McCarthyism in another context. At the same time, the "feminine mystique" perception of the perfect woman was dominant. This woman was expected to be married, have children, be a helpmate to her husband and his career, and to be happy in her domestic life. In other words, it was a conservative cultural period—one that sanctified the traditional male/female lifestyles. Women who protested or sought "masculine" roles were considered not only unstable and possibly neurotic but also deviant (Rupp 1985; Taylor 1989a). Thus, even if some women wanted to protest, there were few effective avenues through which to do so, and their protests would not have had the support of the federal government. The media ridiculed feminism and reinforced traditional husband/wife roles (Taylor 1989a). It will be recalled that during this postwar expansion period, social inequality, in general, was an issue that was minimized.

Adding to the inhospitality of the social and cultural context, support for feminism also dwindled and extant women's groups had little mass power. The Women's Bureau of the Department of Labor had little influence and was anti-EPA anyway, and the National Woman's Party had been reduced to a relatively small number of faithful followers. None of these groups made much progress during this period, although they kept the movement for women's rights alive.

The National Woman's Party's role in this respect has been examined in detail. Most of the women still present in this organization after World War II were White, middle or upper class, employed, well educated, unmarried, and over 50 years of age (Rupp 1985; Taylor 1989a). In other words, it was a very homogeneous group composed of women who had the time, resources, and interest to keep feminist issues alive. A variety of factors held this group together as a cohesive unit:

1. Considering their age, most of the women had gone through similar experiences in the fight for suffrage, and this common participation was a source of identification.

2. All had identified with the "feminist" label despite hostile opposition from the traditional and dominant culture. That is, they had survived some difficult times together.

3. Most were highly, sometimes fanatically, committed to feminist activities and to the cause of the organization.

4. The members had developed deep and enduring friendship networks. They were personally committed to each other.

5. The many shared activities, living accommodations, and meetings at the Alva Belmont House, their national headquarters in Washington, DC, helped fuse them into a unified group (Rupp 1985).

With respect to the last factor, it should be pointed out that social arrangements in the Alva Belmont House, with its own set of hired cooks and servants, suggested the privileges of class. Moreover, the high and almost exclusive commitment demanded of members and their need to travel to meetings in various cities made it difficult for working-class women or those with major family obligations to become involved (Rupp 1985).

In light of its persistence through the difficult climate of the postwar period, the National Woman's Party served as an abeyance organization for the women's movement. It provided tactics, social networks, and an identity to spur the resurgence of the movement in the 1960s. The National Organization for Women (NOW), which was founded in 1966, used many of the tactics of the NWP, such as political pressure and lobbying. The NWP activists kept pressure on the government, helping to bring about President Kennedy's decision to form a Presidential Commission on the Status of Women, and to include "sex" in Title VII of the 1964 Civil Rights Act. Some NWP members also were instrumental in the founding of NOW and became openly active in the 1960s. Finally, the NWP became a source of identification for 1960s feminists who could define it as part of the history of their struggle for equal rights. As such, it helped to give the later movement a "collective identity" (Taylor 1989a). The NWP, then, served as a link between the past and the present in the women's movement, and its internal solidarity allowed it to serve as a source for the upsurge in feminist activity in the 1960s.

Although the 1945 to 1960 period was not marked by significant advances in the women's movement, several other social, cultural, and economic changes were occurring that created the opportunity structure necessary for a later resurgence in the 1960s. External conditions provide the social context in which a movement can either prosper or wither. "Feminism does not have a story discrete from the rest of historical process" (Cott 1986, p. 60). In the period after World War II, the number of educational degrees given to women was increasing, as was women's participation in the labor force. Opportunities to work, coupled with a trend toward smaller families and a desire for more consumer goods on the part of families who could go on the installment plan, encouraged more women to enter the market. More children were moving on to attend college, which further increased the need in most families for added income. The contours of the female labor force changed from one that had been primarily composed of single women in 1940 to one that consisted mainly of married women and mothers in 1950. But women also experienced significant job segregation following their removal from jobs after the war and the return of more men to the labor force (Freeman 1975a; Huber 1982). Nevertheless, successful participation in traditionally male positions during the war convinced many women that they could do the same jobs as men in most cases. Moreover, their increasing participation in the labor market was at odds with the vision of the perfect family in which the wife/mother stays at home to perform domestic and wifely chores.

In other words, by the time the 1960s arrived, women were more educated, had more earnings, and many had had significant labor-force experience. Women's labor-force experiences brought them face to face with their limited occupational opportunities. This is important because continuous labor-force experience appears to have a posi-

tive impact on feminist attitudes (Plutzer 1988). Added to this was the fact that the Civil Rights movement was peaking in the early 1960s and ideas about equality and personal intimacy were becoming more popular. The "sexual revolution" of the mid-1960s, which encouraged control of one's own body and tolerance of different sexual practices, also was consistent with feminist goals (Chafe 1977). All these events and conditions made the context ripe for a resurgence of the women's movement.

It should be kept in mind that this resurgence took place at a time and at the partial expense of the Civil Rights movement. Despite the occurrence of all the racial incidents in the South during this time, sudden concern was deflected from racial issues and focused on the problems of women, especially, it appeared, those of White middle-class women. The concerns that Betty Friedan expressed in *The Feminine Mystique,* those of the bored suburban housewife, seemed far removed from the real everyday problems of Black women. The issues posed clearly described a kind of woman unfamiliar to the average Black woman. Many Black women considered White women to be just another part of the White enemy, and considered their own problems to be both more serious and qualitatively different from those of White women. Further souring feelings between Black and White women was the fact that the women's movement was seen as having benefitted from the earlier and heavily paid for efforts of the Civil Rights movement (Giddings 1984).

In 1961, after pleas from Esther Petersen of the Labor Department's Women's Bureau, President Kennedy created the President's Commission on the Status of Women, which, although of short duration, was able to thoroughly document the poor status of women relative to men in the United States. The Commission saw no reason, however, to endorse an equal rights amendment because it thought that such protection was already afforded by the Fourteenth Amendment. One of the most significant outcomes of the Commission's work was the proliferation of state-level commissions on the status of women. One consequence of these commissions was the sharing of information and the generation of a network of activists who were cognizant of the problems faced by women and were convinced of the urgency of change (Freeman 1975a; Ferree and Hess 1985).

It was at a June 1966 meeting of such state commissions in Washington, DC, that the National Organization for Women was created, largely because of the belief that the Equal Employment Opportunity Commission, which had developed out of the Civil Rights Act of 1964 and was supposed to deal with sex discrimination, was doing little about the problems of women in the labor market. Race and sex again appeared to be working at cross purposes. NOW's early emphasis on equal rights, which was attractive to many middle- and upper-class women, turned off Black women and those who were members of unions (Giddings 1984). Conversely, when NOW leaders desired membership in the Leadership Conference on Civil Rights, they were denied with the argument that women's problems did not constitute a Civil Rights issue (Ferree and Hess 1985).

The Civil Rights movement and the newly resurgent women's movement of the 1960s intertwined race and sex issues in other ways as well. Experience in Civil Rights activities provided many women with knowledge about tactics and organizing problems and gave them a sense of their own capabilities. At the same time, however, their participation made it clear, as it had been made clear to women involved in the abolitionist movement, that they needed to develop their own organizations and movement. Women, Black and White, were not accorded high status in the Civil Rights movement, especially in the later Black Power stage. This is despite the fact that, though largely unrecognized, Black women had performed many varied leadership roles in the Civil Rights movement (Barnett 1993). As in society at large, women were treated largely as tools or sex objects. Stokely Carmichael's notorious statement captures one of the dominant feelings about the role of women: "The only position for women in SNCC is prone" (quoted in Freeman 1975b, p. 450).

Black men in the movement often thought of White women as conquests. "Women were sexual conquests, supportive workers behind the scenes, effective organizers on a local level; only in these secondary roles were they welcome in the cause. When women questioned their limited power within the movement, and ultimately in the society, they were ridiculed, abused, and excluded" (Ferree and Hess 1985, p. 47). The perception by many young Black leaders and most Whites who identified with them was that it was the Black male who suffered most from discrimination and poverty because his self-esteem, his "manhood" was being attacked (Ferree and Hess 1985).

Young women's experiences in the student New Left movement also left much to be desired. While the movement preached fewer restrictions on sexuality, the men generally treated the movement women as objects available for the taking. Women did not have positions of power in the New Left. This male arrogance was in sharp contrast to the conditions in the Old Left earlier in this century. In that movement, women were accorded a more important place and the movement supported women who needed child care. It was also ideologically committed to the equality of women, something missing in the New Left (Flacks 1971; Ferree and Hess 1985).

The experiences of many younger women in both the Black Power and New Left movements helped motivate them to create a network of feminists committed to their own unique cause. Thus, another less formal branch of the women's network developed alongside the more centralized and national-level organizations of the women's movement. This strand consisted of more locally based informal groupings composed primarily of younger women. These groups arose all over, in Chicago, Toronto, Detroit, Seattle, Gainesville, and other places. They were not well organized, nor were they intended to be, and they had no central leadership. While the formal national organizations stressed legislation and lobbying as routes to women's rights, the younger, less formal, and more radical strand emphasized the importance of education, consciousness raising, and "rapping" as means to personal power and women's liberation.

The diversity hinted at should suggest the level of richness and depth of the current women's movement. But its complexity, broadness of constituency, and decentralized organization is only one of the ways in which it differs from earlier active abolitionist and suffrage phases of the women's movement. A second difference lies in the fact that its development during the 1960s was more in tune with broader changes in the society at large, as well as more in touch with the real experiences of many women. The cultural contexts during the suffrage and abolitionist movements, it will be recalled, were much more hostile to a woman's movement for equal rights or liberation. Third, in contrast to the earlier active phases of the movement, the goals became much more diverse. The suffrage movement concentrated on a single issue—the vote (Chafe 1977). Similarly, the abolitionist movement concentrated on a single problem—slavery. As you have seen, feminist organizations are attacking a variety of separate problems. Finally, there appears to be more of a concern for the actual transcendence of sex roles rather than a simple concern for equal treatment of men and women under the law.

Its diversity, depth, structural flexibility, relatively broad base of adherents, and institutionalized organization make it likely that the present movement will remain active far longer than the earlier suffrage movement. It has "a momentum of its own, almost independent of the generating conditions that gave rise to it" (Taylor 1989b, p. 484). At the same time, the political, economic, and social conditions of the 1980s generated a strong antifeminist countermovement. By the end of the 1970s, many average citizens had been told by the media that women had reached their goals. In 1980, Republicans dropped advocacy of the ERA from their platform after 40 years of supporting it. The New Right began to flower in the late 1970s and has consistently attacked the feminist agenda. This movement is composed of professionals, ministers, and politicians who subscribe to a combination of funda-

mentalist religious dogma and conservative politics antagonistic to feminism. It has appealed to traditional American labels as a way of discrediting the women's movement. *Family, pro-life,* and *Moral Majority* are only some of the buzzwords used to strengthen the countermovement (Taylor 1989b). The acquired immune deficiency syndrome (AIDS) epidemic has probably also reinforced those antifeminists who link together sin, homosexuality, free sex, and feminism. Although the efforts of countermovement organizations have whittled away at changes advocated and instituted at the urging of those in the women's movement, their efforts also have strengthened the resolve of many radical feminists (Taylor 1989b).

At this time, the vast majority of Americans appear to support many of the specific ideas associated with the equality of men and women, even though for most, women's rights is an issue of only moderate importance. There is also some ambivalence in general support for women, reflecting deeper debates about the underlying basic similarity and differences between the sexes. For example, a large majority of Americans think that it is fine for women, like men, to work full time outside the home after they marry, but a similar majority is against this once there is a young child in the home (Davis and Smith 1994).

Race and class divisions reveal further differences in opinions about feminism. Black males tend to be more traditional than White males in their ideas about sex roles, especially when it comes to believing that women's place is in the home and the belief that women are not emotionally equipped for active political life. On the other hand, there appear to be few differences among Black and White women in their support of feminism. Finally, among Black males and females, the middle class is more traditional than the working class (Ransford and Miller 1983).

Although Blacks and working-class women have been recruited and attempts have been made to integrate issues of concern to them, the women's movement has traditionally been a White middle-class one and complete integration of these groups has not yet occurred (Ferree and

Hess 1985; Taylor 1989b). The diversity within the movement with respect to race, class, specific goals, and assumptions about the nature of men and women has provided a source of strength. But under the pressures of a countermovement against feminism, these divisions could widen and splinter the movement. What can be a source of strength can also be a source of damaging division. At this point, the future is still open.

INEQUALITY, CONTEXT, AND SOCIAL MOVEMENTS: A SYNTHESIS

In this brief section, and instead of a summary, I will use the preceding discussions on the labor, Civil Rights, and women's movements to distill some more general observations about the implications of social inequality for social movements. The focus here will be on the effects of external economic, political, cultural, and social environmental factors on the development and internal structure of social movements. Because the principal concern of this book is social inequality, particular attention will be paid to the interactions among race, class, and sex outside and inside these social movements.

It is a given that in each case, the social movements centered on deep and systematic grievances on the part of labor, women, or Blacks. It would seem that there would be little reason for a movement to spring up or for one to develop, were it not for the presence of some perceived injustice or serious problem. Movements do seem to develop when there is a widespread sensitivity to or awareness of injustice (Chafe 1977; Taylor 1989b). Each of the movements, but especially those in the 1960s, can be viewed as movements aimed at inequality. But as has been noted before, such grievance is not sufficient for either the development or continuance of a social movement.

Both the surrounding *structure of opportunities* and *cultural context* affect the probability of a movement developing and flowering over time. Both affect the amount of power that aggrieved groups can develop. With respect to the structure of opportunities, it is not enough to say that social unrest or upheaval generates social movements.

World wars, for example, certainly periods of drastic change in society, often have had a muffling effect on movements. It is the potential economic and political opportunities created by such events, however, rather than the events themselves, that are related to the appearance of social movements. The same can be said of industrialization, which created new opportunities for many individuals. For example, in the early labor movement, it is clear that a tighter labor market created more favorable opportunities for labor, providing it with more bargaining power than it might have had otherwise. Economic expansion and the increased movement of women into the labor force provided them with new opportunities, gave them greater awareness of occupational discrimination, and helped to restructure their images of what was possible for them. It also gave them a greater potential for economic independence. Each of these was important in generating the women's movement. In the case of the Civil Rights movement, massive industrialization created new occupational opportunities for freed Blacks, allowing them to build up a more independent and resource-laden set of social institutions that could serve as a basis for a social movement.

Political opportunities also play a role in creating an environment conducive to social movements. Certainly, at the most fundamental level, a formally democratic political structure is supposed to tolerate dissent, freedom to organize, and peaceful protest. In addition, any political situation favorable to the aggrieved creates another political opportunity. For example, the perception on the part of many of those in the labor movement that President Roosevelt was sympathetic with their cause provided them with a resource that strengthened their cause. The Wagner Act, the Nineteenth Amendment, and the Civil Rights Act of 1964 all provided political avenues that could be used by aggrieved groups to organize and protest.

Moreover, the political vulnerability of those in power also provided those who perceived themselves as victims (i.e., workers, Blacks, women) with a political trump card to use in organizing. It has been pointed out in the case of each movement, for example, that presidents often acted in support of a minority's cause despite occasional personal feelings to the contrary because of fear of alienating a potentially powerful voting bloc. Roosevelt had to weigh the relative benefits of supporting business against unions and workers. Truman and Eisenhower had to worry about supporting southern politicians against a growing Black voting bloc. Kennedy had to deal with pressure from women's groups and, consequently, created a Presidential Commission to examine discrimination against women.

Finally, social movements themselves often offer opportunities to be used in the genesis of new movements. Many of the younger women active in the current women's movement got much of their tactical and organizational training by working in the Civil Rights movement, and women active in the suffrage movement were also frequently active in the union movement. In sum, the existence of both economic and political structural opportunities creates a social context in which social movements can grow.

The cultural context also affects the life and structure of a social movement. You have seen how a variety of societal values and ideologies have been reflected in the character of labor, women's, and Civil Rights movements. Individualism and antisocialism undergirded several of the goals of the mainstream strand of the early labor movement. The AFL's business unionism, with its emphasis on the accomplishment of narrow, material, economic goals for union members as opposed to goals emphasizing the restructuring of capitalism, is an example of these values at work. A fundamental belief in capitalism on the part of most workers affected what they believed the labor movement should be all about. At the same time, however, the important strain of socialist and communist thinking among a minority of workers helped to diversify the internal structure of the labor movement. The cultural heterogeneity of immigrants who entered the labor force and the anti-Communist feelings following World War I and the Russian Revolution also were factors determining the future direction of the labor movement. These values, along with racism, also affected the composition of the

women's suffrage movement, as did the "flapper" values of the 1920s.

Racist, sexist, and class values and their intersection deeply influenced membership in each movement, creating internal divisions and pressures toward homogeneous organizations. In the early labor movement, both Blacks and women were frequently not wanted by unions. When women were permitted into unions, they seldom were permitted to occupy positions of power. Unskilled immigrants also were not invited to join the craft unions of more skilled workers. Women often were seen as potential competitors in the labor force by men. Blacks were used as strikebreakers by employers in factories made up of White workers. In the Civil Rights movement, middle-class Blacks dominated, leaving many immediate working-class concerns for the later development of Black Power in the cities. Women often were used as tools in Civil Rights and Black Power organizations. Earlier, they had been shunned by male abolitionist organizations. Whites as well were discouraged from being part of the Black Power movement of the mid-1960s. With respect to the women's movement, early suffrage organizations often had little use for immigrant or working-class women. Their composition and goals also reflected the racism of the time. Many Black women found themselves in an uncomfortable position in the 1960s feminist movement primarily made up of college-educated, White, middle-class women. Working-class women also did not make up a large part of that movement.

What all this indicates is that prevailing social norms with respect to race, sex, and class impress themselves on the internal dynamics and structure of social movements at the same time that they are related to the structural opportunities afforded each of these groups. The diversity of a movement's membership affects not only its stability but also the diversity and depth of the goals it seeks and the tactics it uses. As we have seen in the histories of each of the three movements covered, there often has been a tendency to develop homogeneous organizations within the movement by barring individuals with undesirable racial, sexual, or class characteristics.

In some cases, the structure of opportunities and the prevailing cultural context are both supportive of minority protests. Such was the case in the 1960s with the women's movements. But in other cases, the structure may provide an amenable setting, but the trend in cultural values is against the minority and its protest. Many of the feelings and dominant ideologies after each war, for example, worked against a movement opening up and expanding. In these instances, a movement is often held in abeyance, squelched, or denied birth. Clearly, the interaction of the structure and culture in a society affect the favorableness of the environment for given social movements. In a culturally hostile setting, countermovements are especially important. In the conservative 1980s and early 1990s, for example, countermovements influenced by fundamentalist religious beliefs and political conservatism offered a serious threat to liberating movements such as feminism. The survival of a movement depends on both its structural strength relative to opposing groups and the cultural values dominant at the time.

In addition to structural opportunities and cultural milieu, the resources available to a group affect the development of a movement. One of the most influential recent theories of social movements, resource mobilization, proposes that access to resources is the most critical factor in the development of movements (Jenkins and Perrow 1977;

Jenkins 1983). Resources are of all types and include leadership, organization, money, skills, communication networks, space, and time. Of course, whether an aggrieved group can obtain such resources also depends on the structure of opportunities and the cultural milieu just mentioned. The early Civil Rights movements could rely largely on an indigenous set of religious and educational institutions for many of the resources it needed to develop. Later, as the movement gained strength, the nonviolent nature of the protests, which was consistent with prevailing values, also attracted resources from outside groups. The early suffragists depended on resources from more wealthy donors and supporters among the middle and upper classes of women. In the case of the labor, women's, and Civil Rights movements, effective leadership was also a valuable resource that helped organize and strengthen each movement.

Finally, the presence of opportunities, resources, and a favorable cultural milieu foster the development of power and a sense of a *cognitive liberation* in which groups of aggrieved individuals redefine their situation and their potential for successful solutions (McAdam 1982). On the other hand, when groups have few opportunities, no resources, and the culture is adverse, the chances of a new revolutionary consciousness and a successful social movement are slim, indeed.

CRITICAL THINKING

1. In addition to those covered in the chapter, what other movements have developed that are fundamentally about issues of inequality? How are they different from and similar to the movements already discussed?

2. What kinds of new inequalities are developing over which movements might develop?

What conditions might maximize or minimize the chances for these movements?

3. What conditions would need to be present for a movement to eliminate all socioeconomic inequalities between groups (i.e., a movement that cuts across all class, ethnic, racial, and gender lines)? Is such a movement even possible? Why or why not?

WEB CONNECTIONS

With the decline in union membership in recent years, the labor movement has been under siege.

The number of strikes has declined drastically over the last several decades. The power of labor is not as evident as it was 50 years ago. To find out what issues are of concern to labor, visit the AFL-CIO's home page on the Internet. Consider that this is a union source, but think about the information provided on executive pay trends, the reasons people join unions, safety and health on the job, and issues for the working family. What issues seem to be of importance to workers? Visit the union's home page:

http://www.aflcio.org/home.htm

CHAPTER 16

ADDRESSING INEQUALITY AND POVERTY

PROGRAMS AND REFORMS

The ongoing similarities between welfare reform at the closure of the twentieth century and the previous half a millennium are striking. Both the "menace" of welfare and its "cures" have not really changed. Welfare policy...still lies in the shadow of the sturdy beggar.
—Joel F. Handler

One of the greatest pains to human nature is the pain of a new idea.
—Walter Bagehot

The previous chapter was concerned with social movements on the part of groups who are in disadvantaged positions in the system of economic and political inequality. Those movements were sometimes informal and sporadic and sometimes formal and continuous attempts to rectify the poor situations experienced by the groups in question. This closing chapter (1) analyzes and assesses recent major governmental programs aimed at alleviating poverty and inequality, (2) describes proposed welfare reform alternatives, and (3) reviews current state welfare policies and their initial success.

The first parts of this book established the extensiveness of inequality and its personal and social impact in U.S. society. They also demonstrated that the problems of those on the bottom are often tied to inequality and wider social conditions. Yet, traditionally and significantly, governmental programs have focused their attention on poverty rather than the broader and more difficult issue of *inequality*. By focusing on the poor alone, attention has been deflected away from the systemic nature of the poverty problem and toward the conclusion that poverty is an isolated problem generated within a specific segment of the population. The notion that poverty is fostered by a system of social inequality has not been enthusiastically embraced in policy circles. It has been more consistent with the belief in individualism to conclude that the problems of those on the bottom— be they the poor, minority groups, or women—are peculiar to them. Consequently, the programs suggested to alleviate their troubles have focused on them rather than on the broader society. The belief has been that it is not society but rather particular groups within it that have a problem. In sum, *U.S. policy has been more concerned with addressing the poverty of individuals than the social inequality of society.*

ADDRESSING THE PROBLEM OF INEQUALITY

Although little attention has been given to programs that directly address reducing social inequality, a few major attempts should be mentioned. Among these is the federal tax system, which ostensibly, is supposed to be "progressive" and thereby lessen the differences in incomes among *economic* strata. In this sense, its concern is with income differences between the rich and the poor. The effectiveness of taxes in this regard will be addressed shortly. A second approach involves programs that can be lumped under the general category of "affirmative action." Does the supposedly progressive tax system reduce poverty or redistribute income from the rich to the poor? Do government programs reduce poverty? When one incorporates the effect of taxes, but not the effect of transfer programs, on the poverty rate, one finds that 20.1 percent of the population was poor in 1997, virtually identical to the pretax poverty

rate. Thus, the tax system has not served to redistribute income in a manner that reduces poverty, nor has it served to reduce the amount of income concentration in the United States. Table 16.1 shows what the poverty rate was in 1997 using income before and after taxes, before and after government benefits as measures. The first definition is the one used to compute the official poverty rate. What is immediately noticeable about these figures is that when the market value of various governmental cash and noncash benefits is added to income, the poverty rate declines to 10.0 percent. The concentration of income and differences in income shares are also lower when these programs are considered. Without such transfers, the poverty rate is about 10 percentage points higher whether considering private income before or after taxes. This suggests that the government's transfer programs have helped to reduce the official poverty rate. The decline in poverty in Canada and its rise in the United States during the 1980s appears to be due to the expansion of transfer programs in

TABLE 16.1   Poverty Rates and Income Inequality under Four Definitions of Income: 1997

INCOME MEASURE*	POVERTY RATE	INDEX OF INCOME CONCENTRATION	PERCENT OF INCOME RECEIVED BY	
			Lowest Quintile	Highest Quintile
Pretax income	13.3	.448	3.6	49.3
Pretax private income	20.3	.513	0.9	54.0
Posttax private income	20.1	.487	1.2	50.6
Posttax income + all transfers	10.0	.403	4.8	45.6

Source: U.S. Bureau of the Census, *Money Income in the United States: 1995.* Current Pop. Reports, Series P60, No. 200, September 1996, Table E; and U.S. Bureau of the Census, *Poverty in the United States: 1997.* Current Pop. Reports, Series P60, No. 201, September 1998, Table E.

*Note: "Pretax income" is before-tax income from all sources but excluding capital gains; "pretax private income" is before-tax income from only private sources plus capital gains and health insurance supplements to salary or wages; "posttax private income" is after-tax income from private sources only; "posttax income + all transfers" is after-tax income plus the value of means-tested government cash and noncash transfers.

Canada and their contraction in the United States, further suggesting the impact of such programs on poverty (Hanratty and Blank 1992).

Affirmative Action Programs

Like taxes, affirmative action is also aimed at reducing inequality between groups. Overall, affirmative action programs can be viewed "as a conscious effort to increase the representation of women and other designated groups in particular organizations, occupations, programs, and a wide range of activities" (Orlans and O'Neill 1992, p. 7). Most notably, affirmative action attempts have been associated with improving the socioeconomic chances and conditions of racial and ethnic minorities, especially African Americans. In this sense, in contrast to taxes, affirmative action aims at redressing racial and gender inequities.

The general argument for such programs is rooted in the unique historical experiences of African Americans in this country. In contrast to other ethnic groups and women, African Americans came as the property of others rather than as free individuals. While others were free to engage in the pursuit of property, "Blacks had to cease being property before they could begin to acquire it" (Hamilton 1992, p. 14). Because of their distinctive skin color, African Americans could not as easily disavow or hide their ethnic background and melt into the landscape. Finally, in contrast to the discrimination experiences of many White ethnic immigrants, the discrimination faced by African Americans was virtually comprehensive and widespread until the mid-1960s (Jencks 1992).

These unique conditions and history implied that a special set of programs was needed to address the problem of racial inequality. There have been two general approaches and meanings to affirmative action. The first, dominant until the late 1960s, stresses the prejudice and lack of opportunity that some minorities have experienced, and therefore aims at implementing "equality of opportunity" to improve the status of minorities vis-à-vis the majority. This approach is consistent with the American belief in individualism and the definition of fairness as equal opportunity. A good example of this approach is found in the policy of the Equal Employment Opportunity Commission (EEOC) created in 1965 to foster nondiscrimination in employment.

The second approach, more significant since the Nixon presidency, stresses the importance of continuing and ingrained institutional racism as the principal source of racial inequality, and therefore aims at implementing equal group representation or "equality of results" to improve minority status. This approach is more reflective of the idea that fairness means equality of result or conditions and, in the view of some, minority preference (Graham 1992). The Office of Federal Contract Compliance, which monitors the active hiring of minorities, is an example of a program built on this approach.

Affirmative action programs have been a focus of controversy, especially since the 1970s. Those who support them argue that past wrongs and continued discrimination against minorities warrant such policies, even though they may be temporary. As Supreme Court Judge Harry Blackmun argued, "In order to get beyond racism, we must first take account of race" (Orlans and O'Neill 1992, p. 8). Proponents have also argued that such programs have been effective in reducing racial discrepancies. Increased compliance by employers and increased enrollments in colleges by minorities during the 1970s are cited as illustrations of the success of such programs, but other results are more mixed (Taylor and Liss 1992; Jencks 1992).

The arguments against affirmative action have centered on beliefs and some evidence that such programs may reduce work and training incentives, and reinforce stereotypes that Whites have of minorities (Loury 1992). Policies that appear to give special preference to particular groups (race-specific programs) rather than the same preference to all individuals (universalistic programs) are especially distasteful to many Americans. They feel like Frederick Douglass did after the Civil War—that "promoting an image of blacks as privileged wards of the state" will only help to sustain stereotypical beliefs that Blacks do not have what it takes to make it on their own (Lipset 1992, p. 73). The psychological fallout for Blacks from these programs is also damaging, because they encourage the conclusion among those who benefit that they did not *earn* their success (Jencks 1992). There is also the issue of whether Civil Rights laws have become so broadly defined that *every* kind of group and type of person is encouraged to think of themselves as a victim of rights violation and is entitled to pursue legal action. In a word, the critics say these broad interpretations create a sense of unwarranted victimization.

The problem with many of these criticisms of affirmative action programs is that they are built on existing prejudicial views about minorities that are left unquestioned. For example, the concern that these programs reinforce stereotypes of minorities would not be necessary if such stereotypes were addressed as problems and attacked. Moreover, the worry that Blacks, women, and other beneficiaries of affirmative action might not be seen as having *earned* their success is due in large part to a lack of understanding of barriers to success over which these groups have little if any control. These complaints may say more about those who have these perceptions than it does about the individuals against whom discrimination has been directed.

Plous (1996) has recently listed and countered many of the myths about affirmative action; several of her observations are as follows:

Myth #1: We need color-blind policies, not those aimed at only particular groups. Plous has argued that such policies would leave advantages long held by dominant groups unchanged. Some groups would continue to have an initial advantage in economic competition.

Myth #2: Affirmative action has not been successful. Evidence from governmental studies on employment and contract gains for women and minorities suggests otherwise.

Myth #3: Average citizens want to eliminate all affirmative action. Most citizens continue to support some forms of affirmative action, want to keep many of the programs, and want to see only some of them changed.

Myth #4: Affirmative action programs harm many White workers. Given the differences in the sizes of Black and White populations, even if every unemployed Black replaced a White employee, less than 2 percent of White workers would be displaced. The principal causes of job displacement are factory closings, downsizing, and technological changes.

Myth #5: Affirmative action damages the self-esteem of its beneficiaries because they suspect they obtained their positions under false pretenses. In fact, most employed Blacks and women do not question their own abilities, and the employment may actually raise their self-esteem.

Myth #6: Affirmative action results in the hiring of unqualified candidates. Most supporters of these programs do not endorse the hiring of unqualified applicants. Indeed, the most accepted form of affirmative action is that which allows the hiring of a minority person from among a pool of at least roughly comparable candidates. The hiring of unqualified persons is illegal under federal affirmative action regulations.

Additional myths about affirmative action exist, and many continue because they give solace or support to privileged groups and the status quo. Programs like affirmative action that have attempted to reduce social and economic inequality have generally been controversial because they dredge up old arguments about helping individuals versus groups, providing equal opportunity versus equal results, and showing color blindness rather than color preference. In periods of general economic recession, we can expect this controversy to intensify. Given this controversy and the dominance of U.S. values like individualism and equal opportunity, it should not be surprising that U.S. policies have aimed at helping the poor rather than reducing inequality. To many, inequality is both necessary and inevitable; it is poverty that is the problem that needs to be addressed.

THE CONUNDRUM OF DEFINING POVERTY

The statistics on poverty, its definition, and the characteristics of income-maintenance programs are riddled with hidden assumptions and social values that have affected approaches to understanding and grappling with poverty. We begin with the thorny issue of defining *poverty*, then proceed with an analysis of the social values and orientations and myths that have affected the approach to poverty in the United States. From there, we review the statistics on the extent of poverty among various groups and survey some of the major programs that have been at the heart of the U.S. income-maintenance system.

Defining poverty is basically a political act, and how it is defined depends largely on one's values. Some have defined it *broadly,* while others have given it a *narrow* definition. Some use *pretransfer* income levels, while others use *posttransfer* levels to measure the extent of poverty. Finally, some believe that poverty is an *absolute* condition, while others are convinced that poverty level should be defined in *relative* terms. The definition one chooses powerfully and directly affects the rate of poverty and, ultimately, the kinds of policies prescribed to confront the problem. For a variety of reasons, as will become apparent, no one definition or set of programs has proven to be completely acceptable. A large portion of the reason for this is that the values that underlie these definitions frequently are in conflict (Ellwood 1988).

Broad and Narrow Definitions of Poverty

Several persons have suggested that poverty is a multidimensional phenomenon and should be defined in broad terms. Consequently, from this point of view, simple economic definitions are inadequate because they do not capture all of what it means to be poor. Low income and minimal consumption level are important aspects of being poor, but poverty also has other class, status, and party implications. According to some, assets, basic services, self-respect, educational opportunities, and political participation must all be considered if one is to have a well-rounded conception of poverty (Miller and Roby 1970; Valentine 1968). By this definition, a variety of resources would have to be incorporated in the definition of poverty. Unfortunately, broad concepts of poverty have been difficult to measure because of the multiple dimensions in them and because there are disagreements about how best to measure each of them.

Consequently, the measures used have virtually always been narrowly economic in nature. Attempts were made as far back as the turn of the century to assess the minimum level of income needed for a family to "subsist," and, at a higher level, to live "decently" (Rainwater 1974, Ch. 3). Despite the relatively long history of concern with adequate levels of income and economic resources, there is still no consensus on what measure of income should be used or what level ought to be used to define poverty. And, of course, conclusions about the extent of poverty are determined in large part by the measures and levels we accept.

A number of problems even face investigators who wish to use only income as the measure of poverty. Should they use gross or disposable cash income? Moreover, *current* income does not always accurately indicate what one's *future* income will be, especially if one is early in a career. Nor does it reflect *past* income and expenditures adequately. "A family's yearly income may be unusually high or low relative to its normal level, depending upon factors such as spells of unemployment, labor force participation choices of family members, windfall gains or losses, and illness. Income variations due to such causes are particularly important among low-income groups" (Plotnick and Skidmore 1975, p. 35; see also Miller and Roby 1970; Mirer 1974).

Absolute and Relative Definitions of Poverty

The absolute approach to defining poverty is characterized by determining a specific level of income that serves as a threshold separating the poor from the nonpoor. A poverty income line is determined and anyone falling below that line is considered poor. To establish a minimum level of required income, a list of basic needs is usually composed (e.g., food, fuel, shelter, clothing, transportation) and then it is asked how much it would cost to satisfy minimum needs in each of these areas. On this basis, a budget is developed that constitutes the basic income threshold separating the poor from the nonpoor. One of the problems with determining the absolute minimum necessary to live above the poverty level is that what is defined as a "necessity" varies from time to time and group to group. What may be one person's luxury is another person's necessity.

One of the consequences of using an absolute measure of poverty is that nothing is being said about the distribution or range of income in the society. This is the perspective that U.S. policy has taken. A threshold can be set without concern for the extent of income inequality. When using this measure, *poverty* and *inequality* are really different issues. Under certain conditions, for example, absolute poverty might disappear but extensive income inequality remains (Morris and Williamson 1986).

In contrast, relative measures of poverty are tied to how the rest of the society (i.e., the nonpoor) are doing in terms of income. The assumption is that poverty is relative to the social and economic context in which people live. Thus, a relative definition of poverty is linked to the broader system of income inequality in society. Poverty and inequality are not considered to be discrete problems, and relative poverty can only disappear if income inequality is reduced or eliminated.

A frequently used form of the relative measure is to define the poor as those who have only 50 percent of the household median income in the country. If poverty is defined in relation to the median, the decline of poverty is dependent on what happens in the overall distribution of income—that is, to income inequality. The 50 percent level is frequently picked because in 1967 it defined the same families as poor that were defined as poor by the official standard of the government. However, in recent times, the rises in the median income have outstripped the poverty threshold set by the government, meaning that a measure that defines poverty as 50 percent of the median income is significantly higher than the official poverty threshold. In 1965, the official poverty threshold was 46 percent of the median income for a four-person family, whereas by 1995, it had dropped to 31 percent (U.S. Bureau of the Census, September 1996). In other words, if the relative measure were used officially, many more would be defined as poor.

Pretransfer and Posttransfer Definitions

Once a decision has been made about the relative/absolute issue, it still has to be determined if the level of income for a family or individual is to incorporate all sources of income or to include only income from private sources. Using a *pretransfer* measure for determining income levels means that only income obtained from private sources such as earnings, private pensions or gifts, and alimony or child support are included. That is, a pretransfer poverty measure of this kind includes only those individuals and families whose incomes do not reach a given threshold before government economic aid is considered. A *posttransfer* measure of poverty, in contrast, includes income from any source, private or public, in determining an individual's poverty status. So if one wanted to get some idea as to how effective the government's cash-assistance programs are in reducing the poverty rate, one would compare the rate of poverty under the pretransfer measure with the rate under the posttransfer measure.

When it comes to incorporating the effect of government transfers on a family's income, some have argued that all government transfers such as food stamps and medical assistance should be considered. This *adjusted-income* measure is argued by many to give a more complete and accurate reading of a family's actual economic situation. It is suggested that if the value of food stamps and the like were incorporated into the family's income, many fewer families would be considered poor (Haveman 1987; Danziger and Gottschalk 1983; Smeeding 1982).

On the other hand, several other decisions would have to be made if it was decided to include the value of such nonincome or in-kind government transfers in the determination of family income. First, one would have to decide which in-kind benefits should be included. Does one include private as well as public in-kind transfers, such as exchanges, gifts, and services from private individuals in addition to such governmental transfers? (Haveman 1987). Should only those transfers that are aimed primarily at the poor (e.g., food stamps and Medicaid) be included, or should *all* noncash transfers (e.g., Medicare, educational benefits, housing, government loans at low interest rates, depreciation allowances, etc.) be included? In-kind benefits from welfare programs go disproportionately to the poor, but when all government in-kind transfers are considered, the value of the amount received goes up with increasing income (Haveman 1987). In other words, the nonpoor benefit more from government policies than the poor. The nonpoor receive at least 50 percent of all government in-kind benefits, and over 25 percent of those who are poor receive no in-kind transfers from the government (Rodgers 1982). What this means is that if all governmental benefits were included, even the incomes of the nonpoor would be inflated.

Second, one also has to develop a method by which the value of an in-kind transfer is determined. One method might be to find out how much an individual would have to pay for a certain item on the open market were it to be purchased (i.e., market value), while another would be to determine the value of the transfer to the given recipient by finding out how much the person would be willing to pay for it (i.e., recipient value). A third method of determining value would be to determine how much a person or family actually spent on the given good before such goods were given by the government (i.e., poverty-budget-share value) ("Poverty in the United States" 1984).

Once the value of an in-kind benefit has been determined, however, one still has to consider whether the recipient's economic level has been raised because of it (see Chapter 2). "A $5,000 Medicaid payment to cover the costs of surgery, for example, merely increases the family's resources by the same amount as the family's needs were increased by the costs of surgery: the net effect on a family's ability to meet its basic needs is virtually unchanged" (Duncan 1984, p. 36). A family's standard of living is not increased because its members have some of their medical expenses paid for by the government. In this light, if poverty is defined in terms of the family's ability to meet basic needs, then the addition of certain in-kind benefits may not actually improve its economic situation.

The Official Measure of Poverty

The official government definition of poverty is based on a formulation developed by the Social Security Administration (SSA) in 1965, which was then formally adopted by the government in 1969. In this definition, total family income refers to posttransfer *cash income before taxes*. It does not include capital gains or losses. The poverty threshold was determined by using the Department of Agriculture's 1961 Economy Food Plan, which reflects the different consumption needs of families of different sizes and composition, with heads of different sex and age, and place of residence. This food plan, in turn, had been developed using the Department of Agriculture's 1955 survey of food consumption, which revealed that families of three or more persons spent about one-third of their incomes on food. A family was then defined as poor if it spent more than one-third of its income while following the economy food plan. The poverty level, consequently, was set as being equal to three times the cost of the food plan. In the early 1960s, for example, it was estimated that the minimal diet would cost $1,000. Thus, the poverty level was set at $3,000 in 1964. In 1997, the average poverty threshold for a family of four was $16,400. Every year, the level is adjusted according to changes in the Consumer Price Index. Adjustments are also made for differences in the size, composition, and residences of families. The poverty thresholds for farm families are slightly lower than those for non-farm families to allow for in-kind income, primarily in the form of food grown on the farm. In the table that appears later in the chapter, this conception of poverty is referred to as the "official definition" of poverty.

Problems with the Official Measure. One of the major sources of debate about the official poverty measure is that it does not include the noncash transfers to the poor (just discussed) even though expenditures on programs such as food stamps, Medicaid, subsidized housing, and school lunches more than doubled in the period from 1970 to 1986 (Sawhill 1988).

There are also problems with the measure of income used. First, there appears to be little question that individuals' net or disposable incomes are a better measure of the economic resources available to them than their incomes before taxes (Sawhill 1988). Yet the Bureau of the Census continues to use pretax income in its official measure of poverty. If taxes are not considered, the official measure is too broad a definition, and if corporate profits, capital gains or losses, nonmoney income (such as rent and do-it-yourself production), and employer and government nonincome benefits of various kinds are not incorporated, it is too narrow a definition (Plotnick and Skidmore 1975; Danziger and Plotnick 1977). In addition to not including the goods and services a family receives from others, it does not include the value of the services a family provides for itself, such as child care and housework (Duncan 1984). The latter point suggests that *consumption* or *actual expenditures* is a more accurate measure of a family's economic position than is current income.

Second, its use of current instead of permanent income creates difficulties in assessing the "true levels of well-being" of families at the proposed poverty level (Plotnick and Skidmore 1975, p. 35). Assessing a family's economic status by using its income at one point does not allow us to distinguish those who have consistent levels of income from those whose incomes have fluctuated from year to year. Moreover, by using the one-year snapshot as the unit for determining how many are and who is poor, the official measure does not permit distinctions to be made between those who are poor only for a short time from those who are more "persistently poor." This distinction is important because these groups have different characteristics, which means that the programs that may prove effective in reducing their poverty would probably differ. Those who are poor only for a brief period are not significantly different in their characteristics from the rest of the population, while those who are poor for long periods are different from the majority in major ways. They tend to be "heavily concentrated" among Black and female-headed households. Those from rural areas and the South are also disproportionately represented among the "persistently poor" (Duncan 1984).

Third, the use of the 33 percent formula to arrive at the poverty threshold assumes that the Department of Agriculture's costing method and food plan apply to all families of a given type. This may not be the case at all. Given the differences in sizes and age distributions of families, and therefore varying demands or needs among them, it is unrealistic to assume that one-third of the budgets of all these families is spent on food. Perhaps most importantly, the official formula was based on an emergency, temporary budget, not on food budgets actually observed among families under ordinary circumstances (Duncan 1984; Haveman 1987).

Fourth, establishing a given threshold tells us nothing about how far below that threshold given percentages of the poor really are. Certainly, knowing how impoverished the poor are is an important dimension of their predicament. Finally, many have argued that poverty ought to be defined in terms of changes in the standard of living, so that as the standards go up, the level that is designated as the poverty threshold also goes up. While the official poverty rate fluctuates with the Consumer Price Index, it does not take into account rises in income standards (Haveman 1987). It ignores the fact that these same individuals compare their incomes to those around them. Poverty in this sense is a relative matter, not an absolute one.

LEVELS OF AND TRENDS IN POVERTY

As the discussion thus far should make evident, what conclusions are drawn about the extent of and trends in poverty depend on the definition adopted. Since giving only information on the extent of official poverty would present a misleading picture of the amount of poverty, three definitions are used in discussing poverty after 1958: the official measure, a relative measure, and the adjusted-income measure.

Poverty before 1959

Before poverty in the contemporary United States is discussed, some note should be made of poverty as it existed earlier. Even though the concern for the poor was increasing during the latter half of the nineteenth century, there was little information about the actual extent of poverty at the time. Jacob Riis estimated that between 20 and 30 percent of the population of New York lived in poverty near the end of the nineteenth century; Spahr also suggested that the number of poor was quite large (Bremner 1956). Using a minimum decency standard, Hartley (1969) estimated that the proportion of the population in poverty was about 45 percent in 1870 and 35 percent in 1910, indicating a general decrease in the intervening decades. Using another minimum-decency standard, Ornati (1966) put the proportion of the population in poverty in the mid-1930s at around 45 percent. With the exception of 1944, poverty in the 1940s appears to have been near the 30 percent mark, and in the early 1950s, it was between 22 and 29 percent of the population (Hartley 1969; Ornati 1966; Weinstein and Smolensky 1978).

Poverty from 1959 to the Present

Poverty data based on the official government definition were first collected for 1959. Using that measure, the poverty rate fell significantly from 22 to 12 percent between 1959 and 1969 (see Figure 16.1). During that decade, the number of children and adults who were poor dropped from 39.4 million to 24.1 million. Between 1970 and 1979,

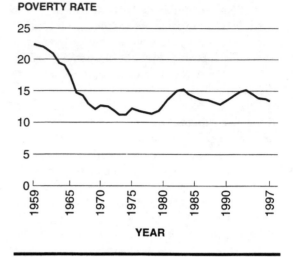

POVERTY RATE

YEAR

FIGURE 16.1   U.S. Official Poverty Rates: 1959–1997

Source: U.S. Bureau of the Census, *Poverty in the United States: 1997.* Current Pop. Reports, Series P60, No. 201, September 1998, p. C-2.

the number of poor people vacillated between 23 and 26 million. The poverty rate for those years varied between 11.1 and 12.6 percent. However, from 1980 to 1983, the poverty population increased by 44 percent, going from 26 million in 1979 to 35.3 million in 1983. After 1983, the poverty rate fell but rose again in 1990 and continued to rise through 1993. After that, it fell so that in 1997 the poverty rate was 13.3 percent, meaning that over 35.5 million were poor. This rate, however, is above what it was a decade after the War on Poverty in the mid-1960s. At the same time, it is significantly lower than the 22.4 percent poverty rate of 1959 (U.S. Bureau of the Census, February 1989).

The relative stagnation in the decline in the official poverty rate during the 1970s appears to have been due to a variety of factors. First, there had been a rise in the proportion of families headed by females, and a greater percentage of these family types were poor. Second, the 1970s witnessed high inflation and recession. These conditions have more negative consequences for those in lower income than high-income groups. Higher unemployment in the latter part of the

1970s and early 1980s also had negative effects on the incomes of workers. Third, there has been a growing inequality in earnings in the last few decades. This inequality helped increase the poverty rate for those below the median (Sawhill 1988).

In comparing Blacks and Whites, the poverty rate for both groups is about 60 percent of what it was in 1959. At the same time, however, the 1997 poverty rate for Blacks was still over three times that of non-Hispanic Whites, even though non-Hispanic Whites compose almost half of all poor.

Among families, the poverty rates of those with female householders has also decreased since 1959. In 1959, almost 43 percent of such families were poor, compared to 31.6 percent in 1997. However, the percentage of poor who live in families with female householders has increased dramatically since 1959. In 1959, 23 percent of all poor families were headed by female householders, compared to 55 percent in 1997. This trend is especially visible among Blacks. In 1959, about 24 percent of the Black poor resided in families with female householders, whereas in 1997, the figure was 62 percent. It is these kinds of trends that suggest to many that a "feminization" of poverty has been occurring.

With respect to age trends, declines in poverty rates have been especially noticeable among older Americans. The 1997 poverty rate for those 65 years of age or older was 10.5 percent, compared to 35.2 in 1959. This decline occurred for both Blacks and Whites, although the rate for older Whites has decreased farther. In sharp contrast, poverty rates among children have increased since 1980. In 1997, about 20 percent of all those under age 18 were poor, and 40 percent of all poor were under age 18 (U.S. Bureau of the Census, September 1998c).

Trends under Different Definitions of Poverty.
We noted earlier in this chapter that the definition of poverty one chooses has a significant impact on one's perception of the extent of poverty. This becomes clear when we examine different measures of poverty and the varying poverty rates associated with them. *Pretransfer poverty measures,* it will be recalled, do not take into account

any program interventions on the part of the government. If one wants to find out how fluctuations in the operation of the economy alone affect the poverty rate, a pretransfer measure is what should be used.

Overall, pretransfer measures of poverty show little progress in poverty-rate reduction in the last several decades. In 1965, the pretransfer poverty rate was over 21 percent. In 1979, the poverty rate when no government cash transfers were included in a person's income was still 19.5 percent, and in 1997, 21 percent (U.S. Bureau of the Census, September 1998c). Thus, when only pretransfer, pretax income is considered, the poverty rate has not changed significantly since the mid-1960s. This calls into question the ability of the present economy and economic growth to bring about significant reductions in the poverty rates on their own. What does seem to have an effect on the level of poverty is the unemployment rate. When full-employment conditions prevail and the labor market is tight, poverty declines. In this light, one should keep in mind that the poor in the labor market tend to be among the most unskilled and least educated and are members of the secondary labor market. Consequently, they are the most likely to be affected by changes in the employment conditions in the economy since they are among the first to be laid off and the least likely to find other jobs. The effect of fluctuations in employment conditions on these persons is even more magnified because earnings make up a greater proportion of their total incomes than is the case among the nonpoor. Hence, their economic situation is highly sensitive to shifts in the market (Plotnick and Skidmore 1975, pp. 117–119). The recent rise in unemployment of white-collar workers since the late 1980s has further intensified upward pressure on the poverty rate.

PERCEPTIONS OF THE POOR

The preceding data indicate that poverty in the United States continues. What one suggests as a means to reduce or eliminate poverty is heavily conditioned not only by the definition of poverty one chooses but also by the images one holds concerning the causes of poverty and the characteristics of the poor. Consequently, if we are to understand U.S. policy reactions to poverty, we must first understand the cultural and historical bases for them.

Most of the images of the poor and the causes of poverty that have dominated U.S. history have focused in one way or another on alleged weaknesses among the poor themselves. "Rogues, beggars, vaga-bonds...commonly are of no civil society or corporation, nor of any particular Church: and are as rotten legges, and armes, that droppe from the body" (Hill 1964, pp. 227–228). This focus on the individual's characteristics as the basic cause of poverty emerged in fourteenth-century Europe with the rise of industrialism, the new freed wage-laborer, and the growth of international commerce. The massive economic changes occurring on the continent during this period—in addition to famines, widespread diseases, and war—generated a large number of paupers and beggars. Something had to be done to deal with these individuals. At the same time, the process of industrialization required the ready availability of workers.

As the dominant source of relief and welfare moved progressively out of the hands of the church and private charity and into the hands of public institutions and officials, a clear distinction between the "deserving" and "undeserving" poor developed in the latter part of the fifteenth century. Women who were pregnant, individuals who were seriously ill, and the elderly were among those who were considered worthy of help. Individuals who could but did not work were considered undeserving of assistance. The principle of "less eligibility" was used—that is, the idea that any relief given not be great enough to discourage work. The amount of relief was not expected to be higher than the wages of the lowest worker in the community (Dolgoff and Feldstein 1984).

The Elizabethan Poor Law of 1601 distinguished among the "able-bodied poor," the "impotent poor," and "dependent children." The former were required to work; refusal to do so would mean punishment, and nonpoor citizens were forbidden to aid them. Those classified as being "impotent"—such as the disabled, deaf, blind, elderly, and mothers with small children—were given either "in-door relief" (placed in an institution or almshouse) or given "outdoor relief" (allowed to stay in their own homes but given relief such as food, clothing, or other needed goods). "Dependent children" who could not be supported by their families were farmed out as apprentices, taught trades, and expected to serve in this capacity until early adulthood (Zastrow 1982). To be eligible for aid, the poor person was expected to have been a stable member of the community and without family support.

The distinction between the deserving and undeserving poor found in the Elizabethan Poor Law became deeply ingrained in the approaches taken to the poor and welfare in Britain and the United States and have remained so to this day. In early America, poverty was becoming a serious problem. Before the Civil War, upheavals in the economy, sickness, immigration, and demographic changes generated large numbers of poor individuals. Specifically, the decline of home manufacture of goods, unemployment, the rise of low-wage labor, the seasonality of much work, and crop failures were among the economic changes responsible for poverty. Growing population pressure on the land, the changing age structure of the population, and increasing immigration also led to increased poverty levels (Katz 1986).

Reaction to the poverty problem was heavily influenced by the English reaction. Relief was considered a public responsibility. It was to be locally administered and controlled; it was not to be given to those who had families who could support them, and those who could work were expected to do so (Katz 1986). Even then, however, many believed that any relief would discourage the motivation to work and weaken character. Efforts were placed then, as now, on seeking out and eliminating the "able-bodied" from the relief rolls. The Quincy Report, a 1821 Massachusetts study of poverty and welfare, made the by-now familiar distinction between the impotent poor and the able poor. The "poorhouse," an early attempt to take care of the poor, aimed at (1) eliminating the undeserving from help by requiring work and banning alcohol for residents and (2) encouraging children and the deserving able poor by stressing work education and discipline in the hopes that such treatment would set them on the path out of poverty. The goal was to transform the character and behavior of its residents (Katz 1986).

The poorhouses did not work out very well. The conflict in goals that plagues many current welfare programs was already present in the early poorhouse program. A concern for order, cost, routine, and custody overcame the initial goal of reforming the individuals in them. Many became rundown and the care given became less than adequate. Officers of the poorhouses were often found to be guilty of graft. Inmates had greater and greater control over their behavior in the poorhouse; discipline was not enforced nor was useful work found for most inmates (Katz 1986).

Cultural Values and the Poor

Historically, perceptions of the poor have been conditioned by the cultural context. A number of U.S. values have had a significant impact on our views of the poor. Among the most central of these are (1) individualism/autonomy and (2) the belief in work, intertwined with its moral character. The roots of these values go back several centuries and originated in intellectual and religious events in Europe.

Individualism/Autonomy. The image of the quintessential pioneer as someone who was an island unto himself or herself, a singular and stalwart rock against the rigors of frontier life, has captivated the idea of what true Americans should be like. Despite the fact that most early Americans traveled and lived in groups, the idea of the rugged individual has had great appeal (Boorstin 1967). Basic to this ideal image of the heroic American are several components:

1. This person is physically and psychologically independent; he or she needs no help from others.

2. Individual achievement is sought despite difficult obstacles.

3. Achievement under even difficult circumstances means that anyone can succeed if he or she tries hard enough.

4. Those who do not make it either lack the ability or are lazy and therefore immoral. In any case, they do not have what it takes to succeed.

5. The possibility of material gain is needed to motivate people (Dolgoff and Feldstein 1984).

These components suggest the scenario that being poor or rich is largely a result of "contest mobility" in which the best win and the worst fail. Clearly in this view, individuals who are poor either do not have the personal qualities necessary to succeed or do not put forth enough effort. Moreover, being poor and on welfare indicates dependency, and therefore flies in the face of the ideal autonomous person.

The Enlightenment of the eighteenth century and Adam Smith's economic theories also provided intellectual support to the centrality of the autonomous individual. It was believed that intelligent individuals, equipped with modern knowledge, could do almost anything for themselves as well as society. Smith's economic theories stressed a laissez-faire approach to economic affairs. Free individuals, unencumbered by governmental and other regulations, seeking their own goals would create the most efficient and productive society. Governmental interference in the form of any aid was believed to violate the intricate processes of freely working, "natural systems." "The 'inefficient poor' like inefficient businesses, were to die off through natural selection" (Tropman 1989, p. 137).

Thomas Malthus, the principal architect of early population theory, also did not favor outside relief for the destitute because "natural positive checks" (poverty, pestilence, hunger, etc.) were thought necessary to encourage the growth of self-restraint and self-reliance, especially in chilbearing. One of the myths that was derived from this belief, of which we will speak later, was that the poor have more children to obtain more welfare (Bell 1987).

The Moral Character of Work.

"God helps those who help themselves" goes the old saying. The belief that individuals are responsible for their own destinies can be traced back to religious doctrines that meshed with a society having a large frontier to be explored, conquered, and populated by a motley collection of individuals who had emigrated from Europe largely in the nineteenth century. One of these religious strands was Calvinism, which Miller (1977) has called "the most individualistic development out of the most individualistic wing of the most individualistic part of the Judeo-Christian heritage" (p. 3). Calvinism is a puritanical, grim religion that stresses the importance of the individual and his or her own work as an indication of whether he or she is among the "elected."

The Calvinism of England, in particular, emphasized the importance of individual responsibility, discipline, and an ascetic lifestyle. Under this doctrine, work is considered crucial to a meaningful life. Idleness is not only a sin but a social evil as well. People who become poor do so because they lack character. Since they are not successful, it is a sign that they are not among God's elect. Calvin even was against free almsgiving to those he considered idle and lazy (Dolgoff and Feldstein 1984).

The Puritan minister Cotton Mather (1663 to 1728) confirmed the religious importance of work in his exhortations about the importance of having "a calling." Every man should have an occupation through which he contributes to society, argued Mather, otherwise he cannot expect anything from society. "How can a man Reasonably look for the *Help of other men,* if he be not in some *Calling* Helpful to *other men?*" wrote the minister. When men do not put forth their efforts, what happens? "By *Slothfulness* men bring upon themselves...Poverty...Misery...all sorts of Confusion.... On the other Side...a *Diligent* man is very rarely an *Indigent* man" (Rischin 1965, pp. 24–28; emphases in original). It would be easy to see why those in positions of wealth and

power might subscribe to these views, since they not only justify the wealth of those at the top but also locate the source of poverty in a lack of effort by the poor individual.

Although the explicitly religious character of many of these pronouncements has become less evident, the hold of the essential ideas continues strong. Individual work still dominates much of our thinking about what it takes to succeed, and the dominant American belief system continues to place the "individual" on a pedestal (see Williams 1970; Miller 1977). To place the reason for economic success or failure on the individual is (1) to exonerate society and others from playing a role in the creation of poverty, and, just as important, (2) to isolate the poor from the rest of society and to foster a "them versus us" imagery of the population. The further perception, though inaccurate, of most of the poor as Black intensifies the belief that the poor are qualitatively different in character from the rest of the population.

Moreover, the work ethic, referring to work in the marketplace (not housework, for example), dominates much of the rationale in current welfare policies. The thrust is on getting able-bodied people to work outside the home so that they will not take advantage of welfare benefits. Only the deserving poor should receive help. The notion that those without jobs, especially during times of relative prosperity, are to blame for their own economic troubles goes back deep in our history. As Bremner (1956) noted in his analysis of reactions to poverty during the nineteenth century, "In normal times Americans were accustomed to think of unemployment as exclusively the problem of the inefficient and indolent. Conservatives stuck to this view even in depression years." It was also believed that the presence and fear of poverty served as incentives to work and to use one's abilities to the fullest (Bremner 1956, pp. 16–17).

The beliefs in individualism, work, and its moral character influence present-day images of the poor and welfare. This is not to say that other values are not also implicated in current images. A sense of community and compassion (humanitarianism), the beliefs in achievement and success as upward mobility, and the belief that the family is supposed to play a crucial role in maintaining its members are all additional values that have helped to shape our perceptions of the poor and what is to be done with them. The focus here has been on individualism and the work ethic because, more often than not, these values have been most salient in those perceptions and have informed those responsible for crafting welfare policies.

Myths about the Poor

Values and beliefs often distort social reality by suggesting that most of the poor have characteristics that they, in fact, do not possess. Blacks are often believed to make up the bulk of those who are poor and on welfare, but, in fact, Whites comprised two-thirds of the poor in 1997. Given their beliefs about work and their images about those on welfare, some people assume that the majority of those receiving aid are able-bodied, middle-aged men who are too lazy to work. In fact, about 49 percent of the poor are either below 18 or over 65 years old. Of the remainder, there are also those nonaged who are disabled in some way and families in which no husband is present. Thus, the majority are not able-bodied, middle-aged men. But women who receive aid are now considered part of the "able-bodied poor." They are viewed as the new paupers of poverty. That is, they are considered a danger to society if they do not work and are also considered to be perfectly capable of working.

There are other misconceptions about the poor that reinforce the belief that they are undeserving. One is that they have a significantly greater number of children than the nonpoor. This is plainly not the case. There is only a slight difference in the average size of poor and nonpoor families. In 1991, the average size of U.S. families in general was 3.17, whereas that of poor families was 3.52, about a third of a person larger. Nor is there any good evidence that poor mothers have children, including illegitimate ones, to increase their benefits. Yet a majority of Americans apparently believe that the presence of welfare encourages young women to have children and

discourages those who get pregnant from marrying the fathers (Davis and Smith 1989). The assumption that people have children to get more support from the government simply does not hold up when the evidence is examined (Morris and Williamson 1986).

First, in general, benefits from Aid to Families with Dependent Children (AFDC) tended to be quite low. In 1993, for example, the average monthly AFDC payment per family was $381. Second, over four-fifths of unmarried mothers on AFDC in recent years have had only one child (Bell 1987). Moreover, evidence indicates that illegitimacy rates tend to be *lower* in states with higher welfare benefits (Ellwood and Bane 1984). Finally, given the small size of the extra amount recipients receive each month for each additional child makes it highly unlikely that economic motivation is the reason for their having children.

When one considers that in 1999 even families with incomes under $36,000 spent well over $100,000 to raise a child to age 18, receiving under $100 per month for each child hardly makes it economically worthwhile to have large numbers of children (Children's Defense Fund 1999; Zastrow 1982). In European countries, in fact, which generally have much higher benefits for children than the United States, there have been concerns over the *declining* birth rates in recent years (Bell 1987). This again suggests that benefit levels are not a major cause of birth rates.

Another image of those on welfare is that they are usually guilty of fraud and cheating. But in fact, only an extremely small percentage cheat and then, in almost all cases, only a small amount of money is involved. More prevalent and more serious than cheating by recipients are the honest mistakes and errors made by public officials when determining eligibility for and level of public aid (Zastrow 1982; Bell 1987). In addition, recent exposures of pervasive fraud by building contractors and others who profit from the government's housing program, extensive overcharging by contractors charged with cleaning up polluted areas, and overcharging and similar behaviors by health-care providers strongly suggest that if fraud is a

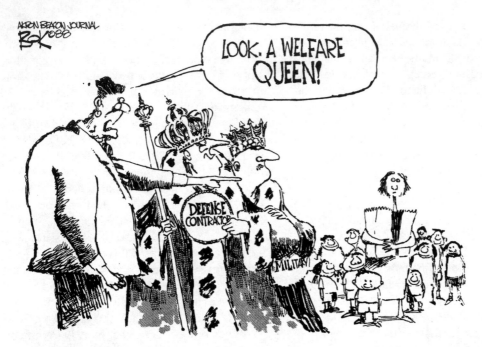

Our images of the poor and those on welfare often are distorted by stereotypes. Many of those who are not poor but who receive a great deal of help from the government are not seen in this same negative light.

problem in poverty programs, the poor are not its primary source.

When considering the deservedness of those who receive welfare and who they are, one should remember that many nonpoor also receive governmental welfare, although one usually does not think of middle-class or wealthy persons or corporations as receiving such aid. For this reason, it has been called *phantom welfare* (Huff and Johnson 1993). Direct cash and credit subsidies, tax exemptions and deductions, subsidized or reduced-cost services, and various trade restrictions are among the assistance programs provided to businesses. In total, the estimated cost of these benefits has been put at $150 to 200 billion per year (ibid.). Not only businesses but also nonpoor persons receive heavy amounts of aid:

(1) in 1989 the government spent more for the medical care of well-off seniors than it did on Head Start, job training and WIC (Women, Infants,

Children's Program] combined. (2) Counting the mortgage-interest and other homeownership tax breaks, the government spends more than four times as much on middle- and upper-income families as it does to house the poor. In fact, it spends more just on those with incomes above $75,000 than on the poor. (3) If one counts a broad range of federal spending and tax programs, an average upper-income person will get more than a typical poor person. (Waldman 1992, p. 56)

Despite these benefits, all of the evidence discussed here and other findings suggest that the view of the poor as "undeserving" and "disreputable" with "flawed character" is still with most people. In addition to blaming the poor for their own conditions, people often view the poor as being content with their conditions "The image is that of the 'noble savage'—uninhibited, enjoying nature, unfettered by the responsibilities of middle-class life" (Riessman 1965, p. 40). The condition of poverty has even been considered good fortune in disguise, since those who are in that state luckily have to work hard to succeed and are not exposed to the temptations of wealth. Because they have to earn their living the hard way, they become "athletes trained for the contest, with sinews braced, indomitable wills, resolved to do or die" (Carnegie 1901). It is unlikely that many today would look on poverty as a blessing, and needless to say, this romantic view is largely inaccurate; few of the poor ever move up to the top rungs of the occupational ladder in their lifetimes, as we noted in Chapter 13.

The Poor and Incentive to Work. Perhaps the most consequential perception of the poor involves their attachment to work and the work ethic. As mentioned earlier, the value of work is deeply ingrained in U.S. culture, as is the belief that most people can succeed if they try hard enough. These beliefs force us to raise some important questions about the poor. First, are people poor primarily because they do not work? Second, do the poor believe in the work ethic or do they prefer not to work? With respect to the first question, census data indicate that a significant proportion of the poor work, many of them full time. In 1997, 42 percent of poor individuals over 16 years of age worked during the year, and about one-quarter of these did so full time, year-round. Fully 64 percent of the incomes of poor two-parent families come from earnings, while 23 percent is derived from welfare programs. In 1995, 2.4 million poor adults worked full time year-round, and over 1 million more worked part time, year-round. Yet they are still poor, and low wages are an important part of the reason. The 1996 legislation to raise the minimum wage to $5.15 per hour still gave a family of three only 87 percent of the income they needed to reach the poverty threshold. Among poor female-headed families with children, the patterns are different. While over half obtain income from earnings, only 29 percent of their income comes from earnings. Welfare is the source for over half their income (Schiller 1998).

On the question of a work ethic among the poor, most poor adults who do not work cite, in order of frequency, family reasons, school, illness, and inability to find work as reasons for not working (U.S. Bureau of the Census, September 1998c). "It's an interesting phenomenon," stated Patrick McGrath, director of a county Department of Human Services in Ohio, "A lot of our people do work and are still eligible for assistance. It's a myth that our people are lazy and don't work" (Brett 1989). Of those poor who did not work at all in the United States in 1991, over half were either ill, disabled, retired, or going to school. Roughly another third were not working because they were keeping house. When one considers that a majority of the poor are old, children, or disabled, the image that these figures conjure up for the poor as a whole is not one of laziness.

What these data indicate is that many poor individuals work, but despite their efforts, they remain poor. Because of the importance of earnings as a source of income for most families, it is important that programs be designed with work incentives in mind. Both the poor and the nonpoor respond to such incentives (Danziger, Haveman, and Plotnick, 1986). Most Americans want to work. When asked if they would continue to work even if they had enough money to live on comfortably for the rest of their lives, a vast majority of Americans say they would continue to work (Davis and Smith 1989). Given that work is a hub around which many Americans' most cherished values revolve, these findings should not be surprising. Work is a major source of self-esteem and identity. "In America, this hold on the psyche is true even for those only marginally employable and thus barely sharing in the economic, social, and psychic rewards of work.... [And] paid, employed work is a central identifier of the self. The characteristic used as a person's overall social identification and evaluation is his or her general occupational status" (Gamst 1995, pp. 5 and 13). As a result, those few who are able-bodied but do not work frequently suffer in more ways than one from their lack of employment (Weiss and Riesman 1966; James 1972). A large number of studies have found that there is virtually no difference between the poor and nonpoor in their desire to work (Goodwin 1983; Kaplan and Tausky 1972, 1974; Smith 1974; Davidson and Gaitz 1974; Morris and Williamson 1986).

A study of the federally identified "hard-core unemployed" in New England revealed that a large majority (over 75 percent) gave wanting "to make a living and support my family" as a reason for wanting a job. A similar proportion said that they would work even if they did not need the money. One simple reason is that it is boring not to work. As one respondent said, "Sure I'd work. It's too boring doin' nothing. I've been out of work before and you get tired of doin' nothin'. Even if I was retired, I'd work at something" (Kaplan and Tausky 1974, p. 193). Another respondent to a study on the chronically unemployed expressed a similar view about work and welfare: "It's a feeling of independence. If I'm on welfare my kids won't want to work. There's too many people on welfare. You go up there [to the welfare office] and can't even get in the door. Healthy people who are able to work should" (Kaplan and Tausky 1972, p. 475). In part for these reasons, many who are poor do not participate in any welfare programs at all. Statistics suggest that less than 50 percent of those who are eligible for food stamps actually participate in the program, and only about half of the elderly who are eligible participate in the Supplemental Security Income (SSI) program designed for them (Duncan 1984; see also Rodgers 1982; Morris and Williamson 1986). These results contradict the prevalent stereotype that the poor do not want to work, though they do not mean that the poor are psychologically committed to the kinds of menial jobs they are likely to get.

POVERTY PROGRAMS

Historically, there have been different kinds of attempts to address the problem of poverty. Some of the earliest were private and local in nature, whereas many of the contemporary programs involve different levels of governmental participation. The extent to which government should be directly involved in solving this problem has been a source of controversy. The most stringent view—the *residual,* or conservative view—holds that social welfare aid should only be given to the poor when their families and their involvement in the private economy have not been able to lift them out of poverty. In this sense, welfare is only to provide a "residual" function, coming in only after other more traditional, nongovernmental sources of help have been exhausted. As this function implies, social welfare expenditures and programs are expected to be kept to a minimum and only those who demonstrate indisputably that they are in need are considered eligible for welfare help. Even then, benefits will be low and short term so as to provide a work incentive. Poverty is viewed as being caused primarily by individual defects and character flaws, rather than by wider social or cultural conditions. The result is that there is a social stigma for those seeking welfare under these circumstances. This also helps keep aid to the desired minimum. Up until the New Deal, this approach to welfare dominated the U.S. welfare system (Zastrow 1982; Bell 1987).

The second view of social welfare—the *institutional,* or liberal perspective—has basically the opposite characteristics from the residual approach. Specifically, it assumes that social welfare programs are an integral part of the institutional structure of modern society, and that like other institutions, they play a vital role in dealing with many of the problems generated by society's social structure and events, such as aging, which are largely inevitable. Since these problems are largely beyond their control, people should be able to expect help without stigmas being attached to such aid. Beginning with the New Deal in the 1930s, an institutional element was formally introduced on a broad scale into the general income-maintenance system of the United States. The result is that the present system is largely a mixture of both approaches.

A third view of social welfare programs interprets them differently than either conservatives or liberals. Instead of being considered either an unnecessary burden on government or as an integral and humane part of it, this more radical perspective views social welfare programs as a means of controlling the working class and the poor. Social welfare programs expand when there is rising unrest among these groups and contract when these groups are calm (Piven and Cloward 1971). This pacifying function of welfare is closely related to the uneven operation of the capitalist economy. Oversupplies of labor lead to increases in government-sponsored programs. At the same time, however, the work requirements and benefit levels of welfare programs are stringent enough to ensure the availability of a cheap labor force to employers.

A Profile of Some Major Programs

Current U.S. income-maintenance programs can be divided into two general parts: social insurance and public assistance. Both parts include cash and in-kind benefits. *Social insurance* is aimed at replacing income lost because of death, unemployment, disability, or retirement. Most of the social insurance programs were developed under the Social Security Act of 1935; they include old-age insurance, survivors' insurance, disability insurance, unemployment insurance, and, in many cases, worker's compensation. Medicare is also a social insurance program. These programs are financed by the insured through payroll taxes, by the employer, and by the government. Eligibility for participation depends on the extent of a person's prior work history. As long as individuals satisfy certain basic requirements, they are automatically eligible for these programs. There is little stigma attached to participation in these programs because individuals are thought of as deserving of such benefits. These programs are most illustrative of the "institutional" perspective on welfare.

Public-assistance programs, which have been more "residual" in the assumptions built into them, are "means-tested" programs that aim at temporarily assisting poor individuals and families. These make up what most people think of as "welfare." The major programs included in the public-assistance category are Temporary Assistance to Needy Families (TANF replaced Aid to Families with Dependent Children (AFDC)), Supplemental

Security Income (SSI), Food Stamps, and Medicaid. In addition, local general assistance and housing also are included under this category. Public-assistance programs are financed by general revenues, and instead of individuals being automatic participants upon the satisfaction of basic requirements, persons wishing to receive welfare (i.e., public assistance) must prove that their income is low enough to justify their receiving aid (Lynn 1977; Sawhill 1988). Thus, there tends to be more of a stigma attached to applying for and receiving welfare than is the case, for example, when one receives social security income in the mail. However, the stigma appears to be largely attached to recipients by others rather than one held by the recipients themselves (Morris and Williamson 1986).

Table 16.2 indicates number of recipients and federal amounts for the major social insurance and public-assistance programs in 1998. Let's take a closer look at some of the major social insurance and public-assistance programs.

Social Security Programs

Social security is by far the most expensive of the income maintenance programs. In 1998, mandatory outlays exceeded $376 billion and the program served 42 million beneficiaries. Social security provides monthly benefits to eligible retired and disabled workers, as well as to their spouses, children, and survivors. Retirement benefits make up most of these expenses. To receive full benefits at retirement when age 65 or older, the person must have worked for a specified period of time (10 years) and paid social security taxes out of his or her paycheck. The government taxes earnings up to a certain limit. In 1997, taxes had to be paid on the first $65,400 of one's earnings. The level of benefits received depends on the presence of a spouse and young or disabled children.

Although most of the benefits from the social security retirement program go to nonpoor recipients, millions are protected from falling into poverty because of the program. Despite this benefit, social security has become a source of contention

TABLE 16.2 Number of Recipients and Federal Expenditures for Major Social Insurance and Public Assistance Programs: 1998 and 2000

PROGRAM	NO. OF RECIPIENTS (IN MILLIONS) (1998)	FEDERAL MANDATORY EXPENDITURES (IN BILLIONS)	
		1998	*2000 (est.)*
Social Insurance			
Social security (total)	42	$376	$408
Social security (retirement & survivors)	37	$329	
Social security (disability)	6	$ 48	
Medicare	40	$190	$217
Public Assistance			
Temporary Assistance for Needy Families[a]		$ 19	$ 17
Supplemental Security Income	6	$ 26	$ 29
Food stamps	20[b]	$ 25	$ 22
Medicaid	33	$100	$115

Source: Budget of the United States Government, Fiscal Year 2000 (Washington, DC: U.S. Government Printing Office, 1999).

Note: Numbers of recipients are rounded to the nearest million and expenditures to the nearest billion.

[a]This program, TANF, replaced Aid to Families with Dependent Children (AFDC) under the 1996 welfare reform law. Different states call it by different names, however.

[b]Per month.

between younger and older generations. As its costs have gone up due to an aging population and a comparatively smaller base of workers to support it, younger workers resent the program's immediate cost to them and worry whether it will be able to support them when they retire. "I'm going to pay the highest payroll taxes of any group in American history, and get the lowest benefits. That's the best-case scenario.... The worst case is that the system will be flat-out broke when it's time for me to retire," said Jon Cowan, a 27-year-old self-employed activist who expected to pay over 12 percent of his 1993 $35,000 income in social security taxes (Green 1993, p. A2). When the huge bubble of baby-boomers retires in the next decade or two, there will be a larger number of people to be supported by a smaller number of workers.

In addition to the retirement program of social security, *survivors' and disability insurance*

are also a part of social security. Under the first, a worker's surviving dependents receive cash benefits. These survivors can include children under age 18, spouses who have a child in their care who is under 16 years of age, dependent parents of the deceased, and disabled unmarried children of any age. Disability insurance provides protection against the loss of family income resulting from a "breadwinner" being disabled. An individual is considered disabled if he or she is incapable, because of severe mental and/or physical impairments, of working for at least a year or is expected to die as a result of those impairments. In 1998, $48 billion was spent on disability costs (see Table 16.2).

In 1965, *Medicare* was added to the social security package. Its purpose is to provide hospital and medical insurance to people age 65 or older and those who are disabled but covered by social security. The hospital component (Part A) helps to pay for inpatient care and some follow-up care, while the voluntary medical insurance component (Part B) takes care of many of the expenses derived from doctor's care and related medical services. Part B is optional and paid for by a combination of individual premium payments and general revenues. Payment under Medicare is made directly to the care provider. At the present time, Medicare does not pay for all medical services. For example, it does not cover custodial or routine dental care, nor does it pay for long-term nursing home care. The latter has been an issue of increasing concern, especially as the number of elderly increases. However, Medicare does cover hospice care for terminally ill patients with a life expectancy of six months or less. In 1998, federal government expenditures for Medicare were over $190 billion.

Public-Assistance Programs.   The programs that we have been discussing are largely based on the assumption that their beneficiaries have contributed both to the financial support of those programs and to the society through their years of employment. Thus, the benefits are interpreted more as a right than as a handout; that is, they are viewed as deserved. In contrast, public-assistance programs are controversial in large part because they are not always seen as serving the truly deserving. It is with these programs that questions about fraud, laziness, and deservedness arise most often. Groups that traditionally have been the most vulnerable to poverty conditions are most likely to receive welfare. These include women, children, Blacks, Hispanics, and the elderly.

Under the public-assistance umbrella have been the AFDC (now TANF), Food Stamps, Medicaid, and SSI programs (see Table 16.2). All of them are *means tested;* that is, individuals are required to prove that their level of need is such that they require help. Most of them involve at least two levels of government in their administration or funding. The federal government has given states wide latitude in determining eligibility criteria. The form of benefit also varies. The benefits

from the TANF and SSI programs come in the form of cash assistance, while those from Food Stamps and Medicaid come in the form of in-kind benefits (e.g., checks are not sent to the beneficiaries; rather it is goods or services that are provided). Let us look briefly at each of these major programs.

Largely because of its cost and the controversy surrounding it, Aid to Families with Dependent Children was replaced in 1996 with block grants to states (TANF), which could then exercise greater control over the manner in which funds are spent. The professed purpose of AFDC was to provide financial support for poor families with children who did not have parental support and for families with children who needed emergency support. The program was a combined federal/state effort, with each state determining what constitutes "needy" and a "suitable home," as well as the level of payment. Consequently, a great deal of variation existed between states. In many states, the standard of need was set below the official poverty level, making even many of those who were poor ineligible for aid (Levitan 1985). Benefit levels differed across states, but, on average, the benefits brought the family up only to 75 percent of the poverty level. In every state, however, recipients were required to register for employment and training and pass income and assets tests to prove their eligibility. Federal payments for AFDC in 1996 were over $16 billion, and in 1998, the expenditures for its replacement, the Temporary Assistance for Needy Families (TANF) program were $19 billion.

A large part of the controversy over AFDC, and now TANF, concerned the fact that it was the most expensive of the cash public-assistance programs. Another reason focused on the profile of the typical recipient. Table 16.3 presents the socioeconomic characteristics of AFDC mothers in the summer of 1993. Compared to their non-AFDC counterparts, AFDC mothers are younger, more likely to be Black or Hispanic, less educated, more likely to be unemployed, and have a much lower income. The changing racial and marital-status composition of the beneficiary group tended

TABLE 16.3   AFDC Mothers versus Non-AFDC Mothers, by Socioeconomic Characteristics: Summer 1993

	AFDC MOTHERS	NON-AFDC MOTHERS
Mean age	30	34
Race		
White	55%	82%
Black	39%	13%
Hispanic Origin		
Hispanic	21%	11%
Non-Hispanic	79%	89%
Marital Status		
Currently married	30%	79%
Widowed or divorced	23%	13%
Never married	48%	8%
Educational Attainment		
Less than high school	44%	15%
High school graduate	38%	40%
At least some college	19%	45%
Employment Status		
Worked all or some weeks	13%	68%
No job last month	87%	32%
Monthly Family Income		
Less than $500	36%	3%
$500–$999	36%	7%
$1,000–$1,449	13%	10%
$1,500 or over	15%	80%

Source: U.S. Bureau of the Census, *Statistical Brief: Mothers Who Receive AFDC Payments* (Washington, DC: U.S. Government Printing Office, March 1995).

Note: *All percentages rounded to nearest whole.

to increase dissatisfaction with the program on the part of taxpayers (Morris and Williamson 1986). Also speeding the program's demise were convictions that it encouraged the breakup of families and discouraged individuals from working. The new TANF program places a heavy emphasis on the need to work and the amount of time over which a person can receive benefits. The stated aim is to move abled-bodied individuals off welfare as soon as possible.

Supplemental Security Income (SSI) is another cash-benefit welfare program aimed at people who are in financial need, and who are either 65 years of age or older, blind, or disabled. Implemented in 1974, it replaced federally reimbursed programs being run by the state to help the elderly, blind, and disabled. It is a federal means-tested program, and to be eligible, individuals have to satisfy basic income and assets limitations. There is no work requirement attached to eligibility. In 1998, over 6 million persons received SSI payments. In any given month, average benefits ranged from $242 for elderly adults to $430 for blind and disabled children

The programs just examined—AFDC, TANF, and SSI—are cash-assistance programs. In addition to these types of programs, welfare also includes a variety of in-kind programs. Included are several food programs aimed at helping the needy. Among these are the Supplemental Food Program for Women, Infants, and Children (WIC) and Food Stamps. In 1998, WIC served 7.4 million participants each month at a yearly cost of just under $4 billion. In 2000, they were expected to serve 7.5 million people at a cost of $4.1 billion (*Budget of the United States* 1999).

The *food stamp program* is much larger, consequently, it is one of the major in-kind public-assistance programs offered by the federal government. Although such a program operated during the period from 1939 to 1943, it was not reinstituted again until the early 1960s. Although some experts would have preferred increases in cash benefits to a food stamp program, the program has grown significantly since its reintroduction in the 1960s. In 1998, about $17 billion in food stamps were allotted and during any given month there were 20 million recipients. This is a decline since March 1994, when 28 million received stamps. Still, only about 60 percent of those eligible sign up to receive them. In 2000, it is expected that the monthly benefit to the 20 million recipients will average $75 (*Budget of the United States* 1999).

The profile of households who receive food stamps has shifted since the early 1990s. There has been a decline in the households with children

TABLE 16.4   Profile of Food-Stamp Participants: 1998

TOTAL # OF PARTICIPANTS: 19,969,000	
Sex	
Female	60%*
Male	40%
Age	
Under 18	53%
18–59	39%
60 or older	8%
Race/Ethnicity	
Non-Hispanic White	40%
African American	36%
Hispanic	18%
Other	5%
Average Monthly Gross Income	$584
Average Household Size	2.4 persons
% Households with Earned Income	26%
% Households with Unearned Income	79%
% Households with No Income	9%

Source: Castner and Anderson 1999.

*All percentages rounded to nearest whole.

who receive stamps, but an increase in households with elderly or disabled members. Still, in 1998, over 58 percent of households receiving food stamps had children. A majority of recipients are children and just over 8 percent are individuals 60 years of age or older. Under half are non-Hispanic Whites, and over one-third are African American. The average gross monthly incomes of recipient households was low, averaging $584 in 1998. A full profile is provided in Table 16.4.

Although the value of food stamps is raised each year to keep up with rising food prices, the average benefit requires a family to exercise great care if anything close to a nutritionally adequate diet is to be kept. Obviously, to eat nutritiously with this level of benefit requires not only planning skills and discipline but also access to low-cost stores and places to store food adequately.

Unfortunately, the latter two are not as likely to be available to the poor as to others (Levitan 1985).

For a person under 60 years old to be eligible to participate in the program, a household's disposable assets must be below $2,000 in value. Gross income must be below 130 percent of the official poverty threshold, and net income below 100 percent of that line (U.S. Bureau of the Census 1989). How much an individual or family receives depends on the size of the family as well as the level of income and resources.

Food stamps have obviously been an important potential source of nutrition for many poor families. But there is no guarantee that families will use the stamps to purchase the most nutritious foods, nor is there any rigorous monitoring to make sure that unscrupulous storeowners do not take advantage of food stamp recipients. Although the stamps may enable families to eat more, it does not necessarily mean that they will eat better (Morris and Williamson 1986). The program also has been criticized for fostering a stigma among those who use them, causing them to "parade dependency in stores and wherever a purchase is made" (Dolgoff and Feldstein 1984, p. 199).

Medicaid is another in-kind program aimed at providing financial assistance to states to pay for the medical care of those on public assistance, children, pregnant women, and the elderly who meet basic economic requirements. It is different from Medicare in a number of ways. First, it is a selective program, whereas Medicare is a universal program. This means that applicants have to satisfy certain economic requirements before they can receive the service; that is, the program is means tested. In contrast, everyone in a particular age category is qualified to receive basic Medicare benefits, regardless of income. Second, Medicaid is a federal- and state-administered program, whereas Medicare is nationally administered. Finally, at least on paper, Medicaid covers all kinds of services, whereas Medicare is more restrictive in coverage (Dolgoff and Feldstein 1984).

To participate in the Medicaid program, states are required to cover several groups of eligible people, including some low-income elderly, women, and children, and disabled individuals. They must also provide hospital care, nursing-home care, and physician services. Medicaid covers about one-fourth of all children and two-thirds of nursing-home residents. The elderly and disabled compose less than one-third of beneficiaries, but they account for almost two-thirds of its costs. Finally, Medicaid serves at least half the adults with AIDS, and about 90 percent of children with AIDS.

In 1998, federal expenditures for the 33 million who received Medicaid services were over $100 billion.

There seems to be fairly widespread agreement that programs such as Medicare and Medicaid have made it possible for more people to get needed medical care. More people have used more health services than before the inception of these programs (Rodgers 1986; Morris and Williamson 1986). Despite these salutary trends, however, problems still remain. Variations between states in their coverage rules and the optional facilities/services available create inequalities among individuals who are equally in need of medical care. Finally, the availability of Medicaid has not erased the differences in the care of the poor and nonpoor discussed earlier in the text. Many physicians still hesitate to take Medicaid patients (Morris and Williamson 1986).

In this section, we have discussed several of the major programs aimed at alleviating the problems associated with low income. Although the typical person on public assistance may be more likely to be poor, of minority status, unemployed, and poorly educated than those not receiving aid, it should be kept in mind that many who are poor or minority do not receive aid. In 1990, during a typical month, only 53 percent of the poor participated in a public-assistance program, less than one-third of Blacks did so, and only a quarter of Hispanics participated. About one out of five persons with less than a high school education were involved, and 24 percent of the unemployed were on assistance. Finally, 37 percent of female householders received public assistance at this time (U.S. Bureau of the Census, November 1994).

Before we leave this discussion of income-maintenance programs, it should be pointed out that there are additional programs that have not been mentioned and that make the government's involvement in poverty even more complicated. These include unemployment insurance, workers compensation, housing and energy assistance, locally administered general cash assistance, and employment and training programs. The latter especially have taken various forms, and criticisms of them maintain that they have included too heavy an emphasis on public-service jobs, too little focus on the poor alone, and that they have had, at best, only a modest effect on reducing poverty (Schiller 1998). A full evaluation of the effect of employment and training programs on reducing long-term poverty still needs to be done.

FLAWS IN RECENT PROGRAMS

Equity

Part of the problem with recent programs is that they are not equitable across groups or states. Granting states greater control is only likely to accelerate these discrepancies. Certain groups are also more likely to benefit from government maintenance programs. Those over age 65 are more likely to be lifted out of poverty by these programs than other groups (Danziger, Haveman, and Plotnick 1986). Male-headed families that are just as poor as female-headed families are often left out of the benefit picture. The presence of an adult male in the family is frequently taken as proof that the family can fend for itself. Historically, AFDC was meant primarily for families without a father. Up to 1988, a number of states still did not have AFDC coverage for unemployed fathers. The hidden assumption is that such a person could and should be working and supporting his family.

At the same time, however, poor female heads of families are at a unique disadvantage for several reasons. The difficulties faced by women in these circumstances have generally not been taken into account by programs, resulting in inequitable treatment. First, when a family splits up, women usually end up raising any children of the marriage, women suffer more economically, and the economic costs of raising children have increased while the average benefit levels have decreased. Second, women who work are more likely than men to be poor at every level of labor-market involvement. A large part of the reason relates to the obstacles encountered by women in the market. Another concerns the lack of good-paying jobs for which the poorly educated are qualified. "If I could get a job before two years, I'd be off AFDC quicker than you can imagine," contends 20-year-old Kristin Nichols in reaction to the new work requirements in the welfare reform bill. But "nobody wants me, because I don't have a high school education.... They tell you you can find a good job. And to them, a good job is any job. You can get one of them and you're still going to be poor" (Golden 1996, p. A9). These problems are not considered when program rules require that eligible recipients either work or search for employment. Third, programs have not provided adequate child care for women with children. Each of these problems places women in a more vulnerable position and makes it less likely that they can escape poverty. If a definition of equity is that equal cases should be treated equally, and unequal cases unequally, then clearly there is inequitable treatment here.

The main point of these examples is that since welfare programs cover certain categories of individuals better than others, there are bound to be inequities. Some of the poor will be covered, while others who do not fit the category (e.g., age, sex, place of residence, etc.) but are equally poor will not be accorded benefits. Two-parent families, single individuals, and couples without children who are not of retirement age are among those slighted by current categorical programs, even though some may be just as poor as female-headed families or elderly individuals (Bell 1987).

There are also geographical inequities in benefits. Some states have much higher benefit levels than others, and since states are given a certain amount of flexibility within federal guidelines, some states offer more services and benefits than others. Since a disproportionate number of poor Black women have been living in the South, which generally has lower benefits, it means that this group has suffered inordinately because of geographical inequities (Pearce 1984).

An interesting side issue to these variations in benefit levels is that the states with below-average benefits had a greater influx of migrants than the states with higher benefits. States in the South have had lower benefits than those in the Midwest and Northeast, and the migration patterns just cited indicate that it is the possibility of finding a job rather than seeking higher welfare benefits that attracts many of the poor to the South (Pearce 1984).

Adequacy

None of the public-assistance programs has a standard benefit level that will enable a recipient to live comfortably. When one considers the stringency of the requirements for most of these programs, it is obvious that the vast majority of those receiving aid are quite poor. Many of those who are eligible have incomes that fall well below the poverty threshold. The poor are not getting rich off these programs. Recall that the average monthly gross income of food-stamps households is $584, and that they receive an average of $165 per month in food stamps. These figures confirm the general low levels of recent programs. Even in the late 1960s and early 1970s, when the real value of benefits had not yet eroded to the extent that it has today, those who were poor but did work often did not receive enough benefits to raise them above the poverty line (Plotnick and Skidmore 1975). Since the 1970s, the value of public-assistance benefits in real terms has not even kept pace with inflation. Between 1965 and 1978, the size of the benefits from government transfers was growing at a faster rate than real income in the society, but after 1978, this growth stopped (Greenstein 1985; Danziger and Gottschalk 1985; Danziger, Haveman, and Plotnick 1986). This trend was exacerbated by federal cutbacks in the early 1980s. These revisions in the welfare system were based on several assumptions and goals.

First, there was the belief on the part of some conservative thinkers that the number of poor had been drastically reduced and only a small number of the poor still were without any help. But an unfortunate side effect of welfare, according to him, was that it has made people dependent on the government, and the task should be to get them off welfare. Work disincentives should be removed from programs and individuals who are able should be required to work. These same worries over the poor's "dependency" on welfare and lack of working were also major incentives for the later reforms enacted by the Congress in 1996. The same kind of draconian logic, however, has not been applied to those in the middle and upper class who benefit from the phantom welfare system discussed earlier.

A second belief of the Reagan administration was that waste and fraud were prevalent in the welfare system and there was a need to eliminate it in part by making sure that only the "truly needy" were eligible for benefits. Making requirements more stringent and benefits lower, however, has only encouraged fraud among welfare recipients. Since the benefits received by a typical poor family do not come close to putting them at the poverty income level, they are often forced to find income elsewhere, such as in the underground economy, from relatives or friends, and so on. Most of this is not reported, since to do so would lower their meager benefits even more. Evidence from case studies in Chicago and New York indicates that, like the rest of us, those on welfare feel their primary obligation is to support their families, and that they are forced to do so through the use of unreported income because of deficiencies in the program. "Welfare mothers are not miracle workers. Like everyone else, they must pay for clothing, laundry, cleaning supplies, school supplies, transportation, furniture, appliances, and so on" (Jencks 1992, pp. 207–208).

Third, there was a conviction that welfare breeds dependency and encourages the breakup of families—that is, a belief that poverty programs, especially those from the Great Society's War on Poverty, make the poverty problem worse. "In 1964, the famous War on Poverty was declared and a funny thing happened," Reagan said in 1986. "Poverty as measured by dependency stopped shrinking and then actually began to grow worse. I guess you could say poverty won the war" (quoted in Kosterlitz 1986, p. 2926). The issues of work disincentive and family-composition effects are major topics of the debate on current welfare policy, and these will be addressed more fully later.

Fourth, the conservative administration had faith in the power of voluntarism as a solution to poverty, a belief that goes back to the fourteenth century. This approach emphasizes the critical roles of private individuals, voluntary agencies, and religious organizations in providing many of the services and goods (e.g., food, jobs, shelters) required by the truly needy (Burghardt and Fabricant 1987). This, of course, reflected a broader desire of the administration to reduce the federal government's involvement in many social problems and a belief that the private sector could accomplish most tasks more efficiently than government. Historically, however, voluntarism has never been able to effectively handle the miseries associated with widespread poverty (Katz 1986). As we have seen, in the early 1980s, official poverty increased, as did homelessness and hunger. Closely related to this attempt to divest the federal government of its role in welfare has been the effort to decentralize the programs or shift more responsibility onto local and state governments. The trend toward such a shift continued with the 1996 Personal Responsibility and Work Opportunity Act. It remains to be seen whether states will be able to support programs fully with less federal help.

While the preceding attitudes and assumptions permeated the Reagan administration's beliefs about welfare, others have argued that the cuts were really deliberately directed against the poor and unemployed. Piven and Cloward (1987) contended that one major function of welfare is protection from market exploitation. That is, if potential workers have an alternate source of income, they do not have to work for any meager wage offered them. They argued, however, that employers have a vested interest in having a surplus army of laborers available to work at low wages. This increases their profits, and, Piven and Cloward suggested, employers are the group the administration was most interested in pleasing. They suggested that the tax revisions, recent investment and depreciation allowances for corporations, and the cutbacks in welfare are all aimed at aiding business at the expense of others.

A final piece of evidence on the inadequacy of the U.S. assistance programs comes from a comparative study of 15 affluent industrialized nations. Kenworthy found that social welfare in the United States was less effective in lifting individuals out of poverty, and a principal reason was the low levels of benefits (1999).

Conflicts in Goals

Another basic problem with recent income-maintenance approaches is that the proposed goals of these programs conflict with each other (Schiller 1998). Obviously, any government wants to hold down costs, to be viewed as efficient, to balance its budget, if only for political reasons. One of the ostensible goals of income-maintenance programs is to reduce the necessary cost as much as possible. A second goal is to provide a minimum income provision to those who are in need and worthy. A third goal, consistent with the work ethic, is to encourage individuals to work rather than to be on welfare. Unfortunately, these goals are generally incompatible; that is, not all of them can be accomplished to the maximum because one's advance is at the expense of the others.

For example, let's say that we are "liberal" and, out of humanitarian feelings, desire to raise the poverty threshold or in some other way try to ensure that no one falls below a certain minimum. From the statistics given, we are aware of the low benefits associated with welfare programs. After all, recent evidence also has indicated that if we

Public housing has been thought to be an effective way to provide shelter for the poor, but high-rise buildings like the one above in Chicago have been, at best, a mixed blessing. Many of the apartments are now boarded up, evidenced by the darkened windows in the building above. High drug and crime rates have plagued these areas. Experiments with low-rise buildings occupied with a mix of those on welfare and the working poor have, so far, had mediocre success, as some of the same problems have been visited upon them.

examine the average benefits for each of the many income-maintenance programs, only three (two under social security and Iowa's temporary total disability benefit) would put the recipient above the poverty line (Bell 1987). So we are feeling generous and decide to raise the minimum income floor. One of the decisions we have to make, of course, is how far up we want to put it. If we put it too high, perhaps we would end up encouraging dependency on welfare because we would be making it too comfortable. In addition, the cost to the taxpayer may be prohibitive. Consequently, the desire to raise the minimum conflicts with work incentives and cost goals.

If, on the other hand, we wish to minimize costs, it means lowering benefits or reducing other related services. If we lower the benefits too far, they may then be inadequate to sustain a minimal standard of living. In trying to reduce costs, we might lower the benefit-reduction rate for earnings obtained by recipients; that is, we may want either to tax those earnings more or reduce their benefits in a way commensurate with their additional income from earnings. For example, we might want to reduce their benefits 67 cents for every dollar earned, or perhaps 100 percent—a dollar reduction for every dollar earned beyond some small amount, such as $30 a month. But in trying to reduce costs by increasing benefit reductions as individuals earn more money, we may inadvertently lower the incentive to work.

Theoretically, by raising the tax on working for welfare recipients, one would discourage them from working, while lowering the cost of working to the recipient would increase the motivation to work ("Measuring the Effects" 1985). Often those on cash-assistance programs have been caught in this dilemma, the "notch" as it is sometimes called. Specifically, they may be able to get a job or a raise in pay, but in doing so they may become ineligible for given kinds of aid such as food stamps or even Medicaid. If the value of the aid to them is greater than the increase in salary, should they take the raise or not? Rationally, evidence suggests it makes economic sense to choose wel-

fare over work if the benefits are greater than wages (Bane and Ellwood 1994). So in trying to lower costs, we may frustrate our ability to reach the goals of having an adequate benefit and a program that encourages rather than discourages work.

Finally, suppose we wish to increase the work incentive of those on welfare. We might do this by lowering the rate at which earnings are taxed and not lowering any benefits. This might help to increase the income levels of recipients, but it also would increase the costs of the program. But perhaps we do not have to be concerned about encouraging the work incentive for all of the poor, certainly not the elderly, disabled, children, or blind. Thus, for some groups, we might want to emphasize maximizing the minimum income and downplay work incentives since they do not apply to some individuals. But for other groups, such as the nonaged healthy poor, we might want to encourage work incentives. But in doing that, we may raise the short-term costs of the program. In any case, for any given program, the three goals of low cost, adequacy, and work incentive have been found to be incompatible.

Work Incentive, Family Structure, and Welfare Effectiveness

Even though the flaws just noted are important, the most troubling and damning accusations about welfare concern its supposed tendency to sap work incentive, destroy families, and create long-term dependency. How justified and accurate are these accusations? In *Losing Ground*, Murray (1984) presented a conservative critique of the effectiveness of welfare programs. He argued that welfare programs have (1) helped to increase pretransfer, or what he called "latent" poverty; (2) created work disincentives and encouraged individuals to drop out of the labor force; and (3) undermined traditional family structure by fostering the disintegration of married arrangements and the growth of female-headed households and illegitimacy. Welfare afforded them the opportunity to survive without working, with minimal pain. These programs made "it profitable for the poor to behave in the short term in ways that were destructive in the long term" (Murray 1984, p. 9). "As people became less inclined to take low-paying jobs, hold onto them, and use them to get out of poverty, they became dependent on government assistance." In effect, welfare programs made the situation for the poor worse by "emasculating the work ethic and creating 'work disincentives'" (Murray, 1982, p. 11). Murray went on to say that welfare benefits also have had a destructive impact on the family by encouraging the breakup of two-parent families and promoting the growth of female-headed families and illegitimacy.

What are we to make of Murray's arguments? On the last point, there does not appear to be any firm evidence to support the claim that welfare benefits encourage families to have illegitimate children. Most studies find no relationship between benefits and out-of-wedlock births (Winegarden 1974; Fechter and Greenfield, 1973; Ellwood and Bane 1984). The most thorough statistical study of the relationship between welfare benefits, family dissolution, and illegitimacy was conducted by Ellwood and Bane (1984). They found no evidence of welfare benefits having an impact on the fertility rates of unmarried women. They also found little support for the belief that welfare promotes divorce or separation of intact families. In his hypothetical example of what a father would do in deciding whether to marry or not, Murray (1982) used Pennsylvania data, a state in which benefits have increased twice as fast as the rest of the nation. In other words, it is a state with higher-than-average benefits. In most states, it was *not* more profitable to go on welfare than to be employed (Greenstein 1985). It should be pointed out, however, that there was evidence in the Ellwood and Bane study that young single mothers were more likely to set up independent households in states with high benefits, instead of living with parents or relatives. But it should also be mentioned that in most states, pregnant single women do not qualify for benefits unless they live

independently. Those single mothers in states with lower benefits were more inclined to live with their parents.

Murray specifically linked high benefit levels with high rates of female-headed households. Given this position, we would expect those states with higher benefits to have higher rates of such households, but this is not the case. Increases in female-headed households have occurred everywhere (Greenstein 1985). States with high levels of benefits have about the same proportion of female-headed households as those with low benefit levels (O'Hare 1987).

In sum, there does not appear to be a close relationship between family composition and benefit levels; they do not seem to change together. Welfare is not the most important cause of the increase in female-headed families (Sawhill 1988). In recent years, benefits have been cut, yet changes in family structure have continued to occur. Moreover, the growth of female-headed households has been higher than the growth in the number of families on welfare (Ellwood and Summers 1986). Between 1975 and 1985, the number of single-parent families went up 42 percent, but the number of families on AFDC stayed about the same. If welfare caused families to break up, one would think that the number of AFDC families would have gone up as the number of single-parent families increased. But it didn't. Moreover, while welfare benefits have declined in real value, the number of female-headed families has accelerated in recent years. If high welfare benefits increase the dissolution of families, why did the numbers of these single-parent families continue to grow in the face of the declining value of benefits (O'Hare 1987)?

Benefit levels are not a major factor in the breakup of families or illegitimacy rates (Danziger, Haveman, and Plotnick 1986; Ellwood and Summers 1986; Wilson 1987). Instead, the reasons for the basic changes in family composition we are discussing are tied to changing attitudes about families and divorce during the late 1960s, as well as to broader events in the economy (Ellwood and

Summers 1986; Sawhill 1988). Specifically, it has been suggested that the factor most responsible for the increase in family dissolution (separation, divorce) among Whites is the greater availability of employment opportunities for women, which can make them economically independent and allow them to escape oppressive marriages. Among young Black women, on the other hand, the reluctance to marry initially or remarry later is tied to the problems of employment encountered by Black men (Wilson 1987; Ellwood and Summers 1986).

The problem of Black joblessness, in turn, appears to have little to do with welfare. Rather, it is deeply related to macroeconomic changes: (1) the shift from the production of goods to services, (2) the movement of jobs out of the central city to other regions in the country, (3) the decline in demand for particular kinds of unskilled labor, (4) a growing mismatch between the work skills of Blacks and the types of job opportunities available because of the decline of entry-level positions in the central city, and (5) the inadequacy of ghetto schools in preparing their students for economic opportunities (Wilson 1987).

Work Disincentives, Dependency, and the Effectiveness of Transfers

There is clear evidence that welfare programs reduce poverty rates in virtually all affluent democratic countries, including the United States. A recent analysis of the effects of such programs in 15 of these nations demonstrated a reduction in both absolute and relative poverty over a 30-year period (Kenworthy 1999). Nevertheless, Murray (1984) intimated that in a general and perverse way, welfare alters the attitudes and behavior of rational individuals in a manner that discourages them from working. In doing so, it pushes unemployment up, thereby increasing pretransfer poverty rates. If this is the case, then welfare programs may be more of a cause than a consequence of poverty (Murray 1984). He pointed out that, during the 1950s and early 1960s, official

poverty was declining at a time when income-maintenance programs were growing at only a low rate, but that during the hey-day of the Great Society programs in the late 1960s, not only were benefits increasing but pretransfer poverty was increasing at the same time. He stated specifically that the pretransfer poverty rate increased between 1968 and 1980 and that Black employment decreased during roughly the same period, indicating that increases in welfare programs led to less Black employment, which in turn led to higher pretransfer poverty rates.

Other evidence suggests that pretransfer poverty was decreasing when benefits were rising between 1965 and 1968, but it also increased for a few years after that up to the early 1970s, when benefits also were rising. Thus, during a period in which benefits were rising, the pretransfer poverty decreased and then increased. Moreover, the real value of cash benefits was about the same in 1977 as it was in 1983, yet pretransfer poverty rates increased significantly.

These data suggest that increases in benefits are not a major cause of pretransfer poverty. Instead, pretransfer poverty is sensitive to changes in the economy and unemployment rates. From 1965 to 1969, unemployment was relatively low and pretransfer poverty dropped. After that, unemployment rose, as did pretransfer poverty. When the growth of transfers stalled and unemployment continued to rise, the official poverty rate also began to rise (Danziger and Gottschalk 1985). It is widely accepted that poor economic and employment conditions are a principal—if not *the* principal—cause of the poverty rate (e.g., Greenstein 1985; Danziger, Haveman, and Plotnick 1986; Ellwood and Summers 1986; Kosterlitz 1986; Wilson 1987; Sawhill 1988).

During the very late 1960s and 1970s, the economy weakened, inflation increased, and unemployment rose. In addition, the real value of benefits began to decline in the early 1970s. Under the conditions of a weakened economy and the declining real value of benefits, those who were protected by social insurance saw their poverty rates decline while the rates of others increased (Danziger and Gottschalk 1985). Although welfare benefits, in general, do reduce the poverty rate, cash social insurance such as social security have been the most effective programs in lifting individuals out of poverty, followed by in-kind transfers and cash public assistance (Danziger, Haveman, and Plotnick 1986; see also Sawhill 1988; Schiller 1989). Thus, persons over age 65 are most likely to be helped by government programs. In contrast, those who were on AFDC, such as younger women, have not been as effectively aided. By 1980, the combined real value of AFDC and food stamps had declined 16 percent from its 1972 value; by 1984, their value was only 4 percent above what it had been in 1960, and 22 percent below what it had reached in 1972 (Danziger and Gottschalk 1985). In the mid-1970s, low-income individuals also were given an incentive to work in the form of the Earned Income Tax Credit (EITC). This allowed low-income workers to claim a tax credit of 10 percent of their earned income up to $5,000, giving them a maximum benefit of $500 (Levitan 1985). In 1993, this was expanded to include childless families.

One would think that if Murray is correct about the relationship between welfare benefits and employment, that with the combined work incentive of the EITC and the decreased value of benefits since the early 1970s, unemployment would be down and employment would be up. Instead, unemployment rose during the 1970s (Greenstein 1985; Wilson 1987). This suggests strongly that broader economic conditions are more closely related to employment rates than are welfare benefits. While high benefit levels combined with high benefit-reduction rates if one works may have some disincentive effects, these effects appear to be small. While having perhaps a modest negative effect, welfare does not appear to be a very significant cause of either the labor supply or the number of hours worked (Danziger, Haveman, and Plotnick 1986; Sawhill 1988).

The alleged attractiveness of welfare is supposed to discourage people from working as well as increase dependency on government programs. Does it? Are those on welfare likely to be on it for a long time? Recent analyses indicate that the welfare population is very dynamic, with individuals moving in and out constantly for shorter and longer periods. The statistics on these matters are quite complex, and the conclusions reached depend heavily on how one looks at them. As an analogy, imagine that we are trying to find out who uses the services in a hospital and for how long. If we took our observations in the admitting room, we would notice that many people come and go, and are in the hospital for only short times. However, when we go upstairs to view those individuals who are in beds, we find that the vast majority are there for a much longer period of time. So, *at any given time,* we are more than likely to find those people there. In sum, the view from the admitting room suggests a very dynamic group who use the facilities for a short time, whereas that from bed usage suggests a more stable, long-term group of patients (Bane and Ellwood 1994). The same is true of welfare recipients. This analogy helps account for the disagreements about whether those on welfare are dependent on it for long periods of time or not. Let's look at the data.

Information gathered from 5,000 families over a 21-year period indicates that almost half of those beginning a *spell* of consecutive years on AFDC will be on less than two years (as in the hospital admitting room), whereas *at any given time,* almost half of those on welfare are in spells that will last at least 10 years (as in hospital bed usage) (Bane and Ellwood 1994). Keep in mind that during the year(s) on welfare, most individuals go on and off it for different amounts of time. The length of a beginning spell on welfare is longer for Blacks, high school dropouts, never-marrieds, the disabled, and those with no recent employment experience. On average, the first spells for these groups will last 5 to 6 years. The higher rates for Blacks appear to be linked, in part, to their lower education, single status, and bigger families. The effect of race itself is not great

(Bane and Ellwood 1994). Once on welfare, teenage women with a child and with less than a high school education, who have never been married, have no significant work experience, and who are members of a minority are more likely than other groups to be on it for a long period. But even for this group, only one-third, at most, will be welfare recipients for 10 years (Handler 1995).

Many of those who are considered "dependent" on welfare are actually those who move on and off it, never being quite able to leave it permanently for one reason or another. Only about 15 percent are constantly on welfare for 5 years (Handler 1995). The longer a person is off welfare, the less likely he or she is to return. Scattered over their lifetimes, less than one-quarter will be on welfare for a total of 10 or more years, whereas about a half will be on welfare a total of less than 3 years during their lives. "The overall picture is that one group receives welfare for short periods of time and never return. A middle group cycles on and off, some for short periods and others for longer periods, but again, not for five *continuous* years. And a third, but quite small group stays on welfare for long periods of time" (Handler 1995, p. 49). Most are not on welfare continuously for long periods: "Welfare does not typically become a permanent way of life in which recipients make few efforts to escape and remain on welfare for generations" (Bane and Ellwood 1994, p. 42). The vast majority (80 percent) of daughters of mothers who received at least 25 percent of their families' average income from welfare for long periods do not themselves become dependent. Generational welfare, for most, simply does not exist (Handler 1995).

In sum, what this tangle of evidence seems to indicate is that economic conditions are closely related to employment, which in turn significantly affects the pretransfer poverty rate. Welfare and social insurance benefits reduce the poverty levels created by these economic conditions, and the reductions are reflected in lower posttransfer poverty rates. Cutbacks in welfare and social insurance programs increase rather than decrease poverty,

and in recent years, reductions in the real value of benefits have led to higher official poverty rates. Although high benefit levels may have small disincentive effects, it is economic conditions that are most directly and powerfully related to employment rates. For most, neither is motivation to work destroyed nor dependency over long periods created by the welfare system.

REFORM IN PUBLIC ASSISTANCE

We have reached the conclusion that income-maintenance programs have helped to reduce poverty. Cash-transfer programs such as social security and AFDC have helped to stabilize conditions for individuals and society when economic circumstances are difficult. In spite of their documented deficiencies, food stamps and the school lunch program create opportunities for better nutrition and health for millions of children and adults, and AFDC has helped to send generations of poor children to school on a regular basis (Bell 1987). Despite these effects, however, continued complaints about the system have led to suggestions for alternative income-maintenance programs.

Many scholars have offered proposals to reform the income-maintenance system, especially its public-assistance component. Most of these emphasize the importance of economic growth and the promotion of recipient self-sufficiency through the availability of stable, meaningful jobs (Danziger, Haveman, and Plotnick 1986; Ellwood and Summers 1986; Morris and Williamson 1986; Solomon 1987; Sawhill 1988; Ellwood 1988). Most agree that public-assistance programs have sometimes encouraged dependency and done little to provide a long-term solution even though they provide short-term help with the problems associated with poverty. Thus, some explicitly label their proposals "nonwelfare" programs because they attempt to remove many of the stigmatizing, dependency, disincentive features often associated with public assistance. For those who can work, it is crucial that self-sufficiency be promoted and work incentive maximized (e.g., Levitan 1985; Danziger and Gottschalk 1985; Morris and Williamson 1986; Schiller 1989). Most scholars recognize that there are different kinds of poor people and that diverse strategies and programs will be needed to address the unique problems of each group.

David Ellwood, for example, who served as a welfare advisor to President Clinton, has argued that since different kinds of individuals and families are poor for different reasons, different programs need to be tailored for each kind. Two-parent families, single-parent families, and ghetto families face unique difficulties whose causes must be addressed to curb poverty among all of them. Some 44 percent of the poor two-parent families have a parent who works full time. Especially for them, low wages are a major cause of poverty. Even when working full time, their wages are not enough to bring them up to the poverty level. This should not be: "People who work shouldn't be poor. Those who are playing by the rules should not lose the game" (Bane and Ellwood 1994, p. 143). About one-third of these families contain parents who are unemployed, and about one-fourth of two-parent poor families are retired.

It is the two-parent family that is most helped by the "trickle-down" effect of economic fluctuations. When the economy is booming, these families do better; but when there are economic downturns, their incomes suffer accordingly. For this group, Ellwood has recommended (1) a program that would ensure coverage of basic medical needs; (2) making work attractive either through spurring economic growth/production or through raising the minimum wage or the earned income tax credit; (3) providing transitional help for those who are in temporary need of help, such as training, job-search assistance, support for short-term disabled and unemployed; and (4) developing a small jobs program for those who simply cannot find employment.

Single-parent families make up the second type of poor families requiring help. Ellwood focuses primarily on female-headed families in this case. Like the two-parent families, the causes of poverty lie partially in employment problems. But what makes the causes of their poverty distinctive from the first group is that (1) their poverty is often linked to the fact that the single parent is performing dual roles as nurturant and provider and (2) the present welfare system encourages dependency by, in essence, requesting female heads to either work *or* be on welfare. If they work full time, they may neglect their children; but if they go on welfare, they become dependent. Neither of these is an attractive choice.

Ellwood argues that single parents cannot be expected to do nurturing and work full time. According to Ellwood's proposal, the other parent (usually the father) should be required to provide support. He suggests that perhaps 25 percent of the absent parent's income could be used for support of two children. Instead of trying to hunt down the father or force payment, Ellwood recommends that such payments be deducted from earnings checks by employers in the same way as social security money is currently collected. If the amount collected was not enough for child support because of the father's low wages, the federal government could make up the difference. Ellwood views this as a kind of unemployment insurance for children. This support money could provide the female head with a basis on which to build for her future independence. To this proposal for child support, Ellwood would add the medical, work, transitional, and job features mentioned in the two-parent program.

The third and final poor family group covered by Ellwood's plan is the ghetto poor. As pointed out by him, it is this group that fixes in the imagination of most people when they think about welfare recipients. This is the group known as the "underclass," a group discussed earlier in the book. The list of their problems is long and serious: Families are frequently broken; economic resources are low; individuals are concentrated and isolated from other groups; education is poor; economic opportunities are few and disappearing; deviance is prevalent; welfare is a source of dependency; and discrimination makes life even more difficult. In the face of these monumental difficulties, Ellwood considers Charles Murray's suggestion to "cut off the lifeline" ridiculous.

As he does for the other groups, Ellwood recommends medical, work, transitional, and jobs components. But given the qualitative differences in the problems faced by the ghetto poor, he also argues for improved education. This could come in the form of better preschool programs, a school/job co-op program, employment training programs, or even extending the length of the school year. Given the flight of industry, manufacturing, and the middle class from the central city, Ellwood proposes an experimental jobs program for the ghetto in an attempt to generate jobs. Finally, he advocates attempts to empower these residents who often feel powerless, to find ways to teach and promote the value of personal responsibility, and to speed integration with other groups in society. Each of the latter would be attempts to deal with some of the unique causes of poverty in the ghetto.

While acknowledging these internal differences among the poor, there is also the realization that administrative complexities, duplications, and waste must be significantly reduced. The hope is that greater efficiency and specific program categories can go together harmoniously. Another feature that many reform proposals have in common is a suggestion for a more meaningful child-support/allowance program. These vary in form from the more traditional recommendation of increasing benefits according to the number of children, to implementing more child-care facilities and support, to providing an across-the-board children's allowance as applied in some European countries. Although a more aggressive redistribution of wealth and income is recommended by a few, those same individuals recognize the reluctance with which most Americans would accept such a proposal.

In some ways, these proposals have elements in common with welfare programs found in many European countries. First, those programs are generally characterized by universal rather than means-tested criteria; in other words, programs often apply to everyone regardless of family status or income. Second, European programs also usually contain some kind of child-allowance benefit. Third, two-parent as well as one-parent families are under the umbrella of assistance. Cash assistance goes to all the poor, regardless of the nature of their families (Rodgers 1986).

In contrast to European programs, the United States has not had a single, basic cash program for all poor families. Rather, in the public-assistance sphere, the emphasis for help has been on single-parent, primarily female-headed, families. Moreover, we have had no universal child-care assistance program. Nor do we have a national program of health care (Rodgers 1986). It is often tempting to suggest that the United States copy the programs of some of its European neighbors, but it must be remembered that in every case those countries are smaller and tend to be less heterogeneous than the United States. This makes it unlikely that such programs could be transplanted effectively without significant alterations. What is useful on a small scale can often prove to be unwieldly or unworkable on a large scale.

Despite the daunting task of reforming the welfare system, the Congress passed a welfare-reform package in 1996. At first glance, changes brought about by the Personal Responsibility and Work Opportunity Act of 1996, as its title suggests, are based on many of the same assumptions of past programs: individual characteristics are responsible for poverty, policymakers have to get tough with those on welfare to save them, people need to be pushed off welfare into work, welfare creates dependency, and single mothers form the core of those on public assistance. The 1996 act is designed to reform the welfare system through an emphasis on making welfare recipients less dependent on public aid by pressuring them to find and accept work in the marketplace. Consistent with past policy and welfare recipients, the provisions of the law assume that those on welfare need to be pushed into work, that, if given the chance, they would prefer to remain dependent on welfare. But in contrast to past legislation, it does not guarantee public aid to a poor person. Among the act's provisions are the following:

1. Able-bodied adults are required to work after two years of aid or lose benefits.
2. Aid is limited to five years over a person's lifetime.
3. Block grants are given to states that can devise their own programs (Aid to Families with Dependent Children [AFDC] is eliminated).
4. Future legal immigrants are ineligible for benefits in their first five years.
5. Spending on food stamps is lowered by about $24 billion over a six-year period, and guarantees of cash assistance for children are eliminated.
6. Medicaid coverage is continued for people on welfare and for one year after leaving it if they are working.
7. Encouragement is given for teenage mothers to identify fathers of their children, stay in school, and live at home with parents.

Proponents hail the new package as a reflection of American values of work and independence and as a way of forcing those on welfare to be "responsible." Critics claim that it creates few, if any, jobs in which welfare recipients can work and will push more than a million more children into poverty. In many ways, the new legislation appears to have many of the same flaws that have plagued past policies.

President Clinton also signed into law a raise in the minimum wage to $5.15. Although many believe that good wages and earned income tax credits are a better way to remove people from poverty than welfare programs, this wage increase alone will not raise most poor families out of poverty. If one worked full time, 40 hours a week, 52 weeks a year, minimum wage earnings would still total $10,712, well below what is needed to raise an average poor family above the poverty line. Inadequacy has been a traditional weakness

of American welfare programs, and, as suggested, some critics fear that more children will be thrown into poverty by the 1996 changes. We shall see.

State Welfare Policies

The block grants resulting from the welfare reforms of 1996 were aimed at giving states more leeway in shaping their own programs and encouraging individuals to reduce their assumed dependency on welfare by becoming employed as soon as possible. Consequently, by July 1997, every state had devised its own mixture of programs and requirements that fall within federal guidelines (National Governors' Association 1999). Some states impose lifetime limits of 60 months on assistance, while others have shorter limits. Some require individuals to be working before two years of aid are over, while others hold to the two-year limit. States also vary on how they treat interstate immigrants, assistance to drug felons, available transitional child care, and the existence of caps on total assistance amounts.

A central feature of these reforms is the Temporary Assistance for Needy Families (TANF) program, which replaced AFDC. Thus, it is likely to be one of the more controversial dimensions of welfare reform. In Wisconsin, one of the first states to experiment with extensive welfare reform, the W-2 (Wisconsin Works) program replaced AFDC. Individuals participating in W-2 are "guided to the best available immediate job opportunity." In the event individuals do not find jobs, they are given subsidized or community employment, or are required to enter a work training program. The aim is to remove individuals from welfare rolls as soon as possible. After two years, they are on their own, and can only be in the program for a total of 5 years over their lifetimes. To provide transitional support while in employment or training, Wisconsin has provided job centers, some child support, emergency loans to keep them working, transportation assistance, and health care (Medicaid) (Department of Workforce Development 1999). The programs of all the states emphasize self-sufficiency as a goal and impose limits and punishments for those who violate them.

Surveys conducted since the mid-1990s indicate that national welfare caseloads have fallen by close to 40 percent (Meyer 1999; Tweedie, Reichert, and O'Connor 1999). However, there is disagreement about the reasons for this decline. Some have pointed to the reformed state welfare programs as the principal cause (Rector 1997; Meyer 1999), while others have argued that the good economy has also been a main reason for declines in welfare participation (Schott, Greenstein, and Primus 1999). Undoubtedly, both of these factors have played a role in reducing the number of welfare recipients.

The reduction in welfare rolls is only one potential indicator of the success of welfare reform, however. Simply getting people off the rolls does not necessarily mean that they are now self-sufficient or out of poverty. It tells us nothing about the wages and stability of individuals' jobs, if they are employed at all. Nor does it tell us what has happened to children who are part of families no longer on TANF. Finally, it does not provide certainty that those who leave will not be back on welfare within a year or two after their exit. A fuller measure of the success of welfare reform needs to consider the effects in each of these areas.

The likelihood that a former welfare recipient will stay off welfare depends on a variety of factors. A national study of 1,268 young women who had received AFDC were followed over a 14-year period to find out who was most and least likely to leave welfare permanently (Sandefur and Cook 1998). The general findings indicate that the longer one is on welfare, the less likely one is to leave it. More specifically, women are less likely than other welfare recipients to get off welfare rolls permanently if they do not have a high school diploma, have two or more children, live in a rural area, have no available employment, are unmarried, are of a minority, and have not had recent work experience. But even if welfare reform is successful in getting some of these women off

welfare, their long-term prospects for better lives are bleak, given the few options that are likely to be available to those with little education, no spouse, several children, little work experience, and living in an area of high unemployment (ibid.).

Many states have begun to track what happens to welfare recipients after they leave welfare. It appears that one-half to two-thirds of them find jobs of one kind or another, but most of these jobs have wages between $5.50 and $7.00 per hour, not enough to lift a family out of poverty. Much of this employment is in companies that tend to be unstable and have weak records of developing jobs. Thus, individuals who leave welfare for work tend to get low-paying, low-status positions similar to near-poor women who have not received welfare recently. It is still too early to conclude that their prospects will brighten or how many will become permanently self-sufficient (Tweedie, Reichert, and O'Connor 1999; Withorn 1999; Loprest 1999). Close to a third of those who leave welfare do not find jobs, and little is known what happens to them. The poorest of female-headed families actually sunk deeper into poverty between 1995 and 1997, caused primarily by reductions in governmental assistance. This is especially disturbing because it has occurred in the context of a strong economy (Center on Budget and Policy Priorities, 1999). About one-third of those who left welfare after 1995 were back on it in 1997 (Loprest 1999). Granted, most of the studies upon which these conclusions have been based were conducted only one to three years after initiation of the 1996 welfare reforms, so these results can be considered tentative. But they are nonetheless disturbing if the primary goal of these reforms is to create self-sufficient families who can live at a level of decency above poverty. Even in Wisconsin, where the number of those receiving welfare dropped by 67 percent between 1986 and 1997, the number of poor declined by only 12 percent and the number of "extremely poor" (those with incomes less than half the poverty line) increased threefold in the same period (Moore and Selkowe 1999). Nationwide, in the one-year period between 1996 and 1997, 426,000 more children were living in extreme poverty. This increase has been linked to the weakening in the safety net provided by cash- and food-assistance programs (Children's Defense Fund 1999).

Beyond its impact on welfare recipients, welfare reform has had implications for governmental agencies and local economies. It has increased the stresses and demands on local agencies that try to implement required changes and speed the removal of clients from their rolls (Withorn 1999). The full implications of a significant increase of former welfare recipients into the labor force are not yet clear. If they do find jobs, their entrance may drive down wages and push present employees in low-wage jobs into poverty. If they cannot all find jobs, public-sector positions may need to be created to accommodate them, but this may cost more than is desirable. Finally, if they cannot find any kind of jobs, individuals who have left welfare may have to burden those who cannot afford to support them or they may resort to efforts to get money in the underground economy. Any or some mixture of these consequences could occur (Leete and Bania 1998).

The focus on work as the principal way out of poverty assumes the existence of plentiful, well-paying jobs. But as you have already seen, several recent economic trends appear to threaten this scenario: recent downsizing, more temporary work, increased automation and robotization, the decline of unionized manufacturing jobs, and movement by corporations into lower-wage, often foreign, labor markets. If good jobs are the key, how can they be maintained or created, given these trends? Gans (1995) has suggested several possibilities: (1) the government may have to increase and stabilize the number of public-works jobs; (2) in the long run, some capital-intensive jobs may be able to be converted back to more labor-intensive jobs; and (3) greater democratization in the workplace might generate greater productivity, lower prices, and

higher demand, ultimately leading to the creation of more jobs. But simply having *more* jobs is not enough, since many women who, through concerted effort, take the job route out of welfare wind up returning because of continued low wages, lack of adequate training, lack of medical coverage, and child-care difficulties. Because of these inadequacies surrounding the current work solution, "work among poor women should be viewed as the *problem* rather than the solution" (Harris 1996, p. 424). While it is still too soon to guess welfare reform's full effects over the long run, they are likely to be significant.

Suggestions for Reducing Inequality

Historically, the focus of welfare discussions and programs has been on the reduction of poverty rather than inequality. Poverty and inequality have been viewed as separate issues by most people primarily because the former has been interpreted as an *individual* phenomenon while the latter is generally seen as a characteristic of *social* structure. Poverty has widely been considered a problem that must be confronted, while few have called for a full-fledged assault on social and economic inequality. Yet poverty and inequality are interlinked because poverty is basically a problem rooted in economic and inequality processes in U.S. society.

How can we explain the reluctance to view poverty in terms of economic inequality? Why isn't inequality defined as a major problem by most of the public?

Since social services and programs that arise from policies do not originate with the poor, they rarely call for fundamental changes in the economic and/or political conditions in the society. Rather, the emphasis is on working within present economic and political arrangements, thereby maintaining the status quo.

The continued persistence of poverty has suggested to some that the poor may serve basic functions for the society, and particular nonpoor groups within it. Indeed, having an "undeserving" poor population serves many functions for the rest of us:

1. It justifies their poor treatment, makes us feel superior, and provides us with a convenient scapegoat for societal problems.
2. Conceiving the poor as a separate group creates a whole battery of jobs for those who are not poor, including a wide variety of "helping" professional positions.
3. The undeserving label justifies pushing the poor out of the legitimate labor market and provides an easily available group of laborers to do work in the informal and illegal economy, and to serve as a surplus army to hire when nonpoor workers balk at working under poor conditions.
4. Our labeling and hostile treatment of the poor serves to reinforce and legitimate our own lives and institutions.
5. Their violation of mainstream values helps to remind us of those values, thereby constantly reaffirming them.
6. Blaming the poor for their own problems relieves others and social institutions of any blame for their situation.
7. The poor's lowly position and their label as undeserving weakens their political power and strengthens that of higher classes.
8. Labeling the poor as undeserving permits the agencies that deal with them to treat them in a way that reinforces and reproduces the stigma associated with poverty (Gans 1995).

By indicating these and other basic functions performed by the poor in U.S. society, Gans implied that poor people are not an *isolated* group who are poor because of their lack of integration into the mainstream of society, but rather are an *integral* part of the society. Alternative poverty programs that have been suggested vary in the extent to which their recommendations focus on the uniqueness and isolated nature of the poor, or on the nature of their integration into society. Those that stress the former tend to believe that the root causes of poverty lie in the flawed characters and characteristics of the poor themselves, whereas those in the latter camp are more likely to see social structures and processes as forces that create a poor population

Those who see the operation of wider social forces in the generation of poverty and inequality also tend to argue that broader-based policies and programs must be implemented to address these problems. For more than a decade, William Julius Wilson has stressed that for any program to be fully accepted by the public it must be seen as benefiting everyone, not just particular groups. "I am convinced," wrote Wilson in 1987, "that, in the last few years of the twentieth century, the problems of the truly disadvantaged in the United States will have to be attacked primarily through universal programs that enjoy the support and commitment of a broad constituency" (1987, p. 120).

Most recently, Wilson has again stressed the crucial importance of a universally agreed-upon approach and a broad-based coalition to reduce the gap dividing the privileged and underprivileged (1999). Part of the problem with programs like affirmative action is that they are seen as preferential, privileging some groups over others. Consequently, they are viewed as unfair and unacceptable by many. Some of this is due to the language used in labeling the program and inferred by those who interpret it. Affirmative action, for example, is linked, in the minds of many, with "quotas" and "preferential treatment." Instead of focusing on numbers, Wilson proposes, we ought to relabel our efforts as "affirmative opportunity" since "it echoes the phrase *equal opportunity,* which connotes a principle that most Americans still support, while avoiding connotations now associated (fairly or not) with the idea of affirmative action—connotations such as quotas, lowering standards, and reverse discrimination, which most Americans detest" (Wilson 1999, p. 111). Perhaps most fundamentally, Wilson believes that racial, ethnic, and other groups need to deemphasize how they are *different* from one another, and emphasize and act on the values, goals, and destinies that they have in *common*. Organized coalitions of different groups that focus on problems that they all share are more likely to be effective: "In the final analysis, unless groups of ordinary citizens embrace the need for mutual political cooperation, they stand little chance of generating the political muscle needed to ease their economic and social burdens" (Wilson 1999, p. 123). Since we are all part of one society, economic events and inequality have implications for all of our lives.

Perhaps the most controversial and recent proposal to address broad-based inequality in the United States has been put forward by Ackermann and Alstott (1999). Their argument recalls Oliver and Shapiro's demonstration that inequality develops over generations as the structure of opportunities allows some groups to prosper and pass on their prosperity to future generations, while others are left to languish and struggle, leaving little to their children (1995). In this way, inequality becomes fixed and individuals from different groups but in the same generation start out their lives with unequal amounts of advantages.

Briefly, Ackerman and Alstott suggest that the most direct way to address economic inequality between individuals is to grant every young adult a "stake" so they can begin their adult lives on a more equal level. Specifically, they suggest a one-time stake of $80,000 for young adults to use as they wish to develop their futures. Individuals take responsibility for the success or failure of their choices, and in old age they would have an obligation to repay the stake if they are able to do so. To fund the $80,000 stakes for beginning adults, a tax of 2 percent on all wealth would need to be levied. Ackerman and Alstott believe this is fair, since "every American has an obligation to contribute to a fair starting point for all" (1999, p. 5). Like Wilson, they imply the importance of stressing that all citizens are in the American en-

terprise together, and thus we have to work together to reach a more just society. Existing programs of the welfare state have been too divisive, and we need a plan that will invigorate common values. A "stakeholder society" will do that, say Ackerman and Alstott. They believe that beneficiaries of their proposed policy "will locate themselves in a much larger national project devoted to the proposition that all men are created equal. By invoking this American ideal in their own case, they link themselves not only to all others in the past who have taken steps to realize this fundamental principle but also to all those who will do so in the future" (1999, p. 7).

Attempts at reform have frequently gotten hung up because of the difficulty of trying to balance conservative and liberal approaches, trying to be tough but compassionate at the same time. Suggestions aim at helping those who need help but also at encouraging individual responsibility. American values encourage us to be generous but to encourage others to realize that there is no "free lunch." Both society and the individual have obligations. "Any successful social policy must strike a balance between collective compassion and individual responsibility," wrote Christopher Jencks (1992, p. 87). Historically, the reform pendulum has swung between these two kinds of themes.

Recent federal suggestions have mirrored some of the preceding state efforts, but have also incorporated elements of compassion. The Family and Medical Leave Act of 1993 requires those who employ at least 50 workers to provide three months of unpaid leave per year for child care or medical reasons. But only about half of the private labor force is covered, along with government workers (Landers 1993). Suggestions have also been made to increase the Earned Income Tax Credit (EITC) to low-income families. Last, the 1996 Kennedy-Kassebaum health plan allows currently insured individuals to take their insurance with them if they change employers, and minimizes the chances of anyone being denied health insurance because of a preexisting condition. All of these efforts reflect a concern for compassion, but as you have seen, many of the aspects of current policy mirror a harsher, tougher view of those on welfare. Humanity as well as inhumanity have been mixed into our recipes for welfare. As yet, the recipe is not perfected.

SUMMARY

This chapter has discussed approaches and programs aimed at addressing problems associated with inequality and poverty. Affirmative action and taxes aim at reducing income, racial, and gender inequality, but since these are controversial, more federal programs have been focused on the reduction of poverty. There is no question that the measurement of poverty is laden with political implications. Depending on what is included under the category of economic resources, poverty rates may be higher or lower. The controversies surrounding the definition and measurement of poverty alone make the topic a political "hot potato."

Adding to this controversy are people's images of the poor, especially those on public assistance (welfare). The traditional values of individualism, independence, hard work, material success, and others encourage a negative attitude toward those who are not economically successful. At the same time, humanitarian and community values encourage people to take care of those who are less fortunate than themselves. Believing that virtually all people can make it if they try hard, but at the same time knowing from historical events such as the Depression, plant closings, and market declines that not everything about their economic fates is in their hands to control has resulted in a somewhat bifurcated approach to income-maintenance programs for the needy. There are elements of both a residual and institutional approach in this system.

In one category, social insurance programs such as social security retirement, disability, and Medicare insurance provide universal coverage with a minimum of stigma to a wide variety of individuals who fall into a particular demographic category. There is no means-testing or demeaning administrative process suggesting that these recipients are receiving welfare. They are considered individuals who have contributed to both these programs and society and are, therefore, deserving of such aid. In the other category of public assistance are those who are poor but not elderly and/or disabled. Individuals with these characteristics—often women who head their own households, children, and members of minorities—must provide proof that they are indigent. They must prove that they are deserving of benefits from food stamps, Medicaid, and similar programs.

Problems of inequity, inadequacy, and goal conflict have permeated public assistance programs for the poor. In addition, questions about how they affect work incentive, family composition, and effectiveness have also generated heated debate. By and large, it does not appear that the present system has had major effects on either work incentive or family composition. Nor has it created massive dependency. Rather, broader economic conditions are related to both employment possibilities and the rise of single-parent families, especially among Blacks. The present programs, despite their deficiencies, have reduced poverty.

Alternative proposals attempt to grapple with the problems of adequacy, employment, work incentives, and so on. Many have suggested economic growth and full employment as the key to the puzzle of poverty. This would mean greater self-sufficiency for everyone. Indeed, the welfare reform act of 1996 focuses on pushing individuals into the labor force. But this leaves some pessimistic, and the initial follow-ups on those leaving state welfare are decidedly mixed. In many cases, policies have deepened poverty, at least in the short run. More time is needed, however, to fully assess state reform's full impact.

As difficult as poverty may be to understand, we still have not confronted the even thornier issue of economic inequality. A focus on inequality unavoidably involves all of us, since we all live out our lives within its structure. The suggestions of Wilson, Ackermann, and Alstott, as improbable as they may seem, are based realistically on a recognition that any effective policy to reduce inequality must incorporate groups from every strata, not just the poor. In one way or another, we need to reach across the widening gaps that separate us. If inequality continues to grow as it has in recent years, we may be forced to address this topic. The real question is whether poverty, let alone inequality, can be eliminated within a democratic capitalist society. This brings us back to some of the core questions with which we began this book.

If poverty is generated not merely by differences among individuals, but by conditions that are part of a capitalist economy, such as unemployment and the pressure for profit and lower wages, then a permanent solution, as Morris and Williamson suggested, is very unlikely unless fundamental changes in the political economy occur. Are inequality and poverty inevitable? Given the present social structure, the answer is probably *yes*. Are inequality and poverty desirable? It depends. Although it is a serious problem for those who must suffer with it, poverty appears to be functional for others. It helps maintain the attractiveness of low wages and menial jobs, especially when coupled with low benefits from programs. At the same time, it provides employment for many middle-class professionals. As to the immediate future of inequality and poverty, the fact that income and wealth inequality has increased in recent years, despite the presence of income-maintenance programs, suggests that either (1) we do not really consider inequality to be a major problem, (2) we do not really know what causes it to fluctuate, and/or (3) some find inequality beneficial.

Evidence strongly suggests that what happens in the economy has a major impact on both inequality and poverty. At the dawn of the twenty-first century, many organizations are streamlining and downsizing in an effort to maintain profits in the face of intensified domestic and foreign competition. While executives and shareholders frequently reap the economic benefits of these leaner and more efficient organizational structures, the attendant layoffs have led many in the middle class to fall near or into poverty. These shifts have also exacerbated the poor financial conditions of those already on the bottom and are also likely to cause further tensions among racial/ethnic groups and between the sexes. In sum, the rewards and punishments of recent economic changes are clearly and unequally divided. The combination of the economic trends and their varied effects on different groups, together with our reluctance to address the problem of inequality and to recognize its social roots, are not good omens. The signs do not look good for a systematic reduction of social inequality in the near future

CRITICAL THINKING

1. Why have policymakers tended to focus on poverty rather than inequality as an economic problem? Why has poverty been so difficult to define and measure?

2. Can the conflicting goals of welfare policy ever be reconciled to produce an effective welfare policy? Explain your answer.

3. What specific data on welfare help to eliminate the negative stereotype of the "welfare mother"? Is simply having the facts enough to eliminate this stereotype? Explain your answer.

4. Given what has been suggested in this chapter, what do you think should be the cornerstone features of any effective antipoverty plan?

WEB CONNECTIONS _____

This chapter has focused on the sources, characteristics, and flaws in the current welfare system, and has also considered recent state reforms in public assistance. Find out the characteristics of the welfare system in your own state, and evaluate the effects of your state's welfare program compared to other states. What has happened to former welfare recipients since leaving the program? Investigate the comparisons at:

http.//www.welfareinfo.org

http//www.nga.org/CBP/Activities/
WelfareReform.asp

GLOSSARY OF BASIC TERMS

absolute downward mobility a downward shift in economic resources without a simultaneous change in an individual's position relative to others.

anomic division of labor an abnormal condition in which the rules of relationships among those in the production process and limits in the marketplace are unclear.

assimilationist theory an explanation of race relations that views minority groups as being on a one-way road to blending in with the rest of society.

berdaches in traditional Navajo society, persons who were men anatomically, but were considered to be in a third gender and intersexed.

burakumin a minority outcaste group in Japan distinguished and discriminated against on the basis of the impurity of their occupations and place of residence.

capitalism an economic system based on private ownership, competition, and open markets.

caste system a closed social ranking system dividing categories of individuals in which position is ascribed and which is legitimated by cultural and/or religious institutions.

chronic illness health problems that continue over a long period of time.

circulation of elites Pareto's argument that as conditions change, those most competent to rule move into positions of power while the incompetent move into the governed class.

circulation mobility mobility that reflects the cultural and social openness of a society.

class defined variously as individuals or groups who (1) occupy the same position on hierarchies of occupational prestige, income, and education; or (2) are in the same relation to the system of production; or (3) are in the same relation to the system of production and are also class conscious.

class consciousness the full awareness within a group of its class position and relationship with other classes, along with action based on this awareness.

closed society a society in which little social mobility occurs and position is entirely dependent on the position into which one is born.

competitive race relations a set of relationships between races most often found in industrial systems and characterized by competition and aggressive rather than accommodative behavior.

core economic sector the section of the private economy occupied by large, capital-intensive, highly productive firms with large sometimes international markets (also called **monopoly sector**).

crises of overproduction the inability of capitalism to sell all that it produces, largely because of the inconsistency between low, impoverished wages and advanced technology.

cross-gender the situation of one sex regularly performing and acting in a manner socially and culturally expected of a different sex.

cultural capital a group's cultural values, experiences, knowledge, and skills passed on from one generation to the next.

dependency theory the argument that countries are interlinked through economic and political ties that perpetuate development or underdevelopment.

derivations Pareto's term for justifications or reasons people give for their behavior.

drift hypothesis in the study of the relationship between mental illness and social class, the argument that illness causes one's downward mobility through the class system.

dual economy the view of the economy as being split between large, economically powerful, monopolistic firms on the one hand, and small, less stable, local, poorer economic organizations on the other.

embourgeoisement the taking on by the working class of middle-class cultural and social characteristics.

estate system a fairly rigid system of ranking based primarily on land ownership, and usually sanctioned by the state and religion.

ethnic group a group distinguished on the basis of its native cultural and linguistic characteristics.

Eugenics Movement an early twentieth-century movement concerned with heredity and mating as means for the perfection of a race.

forced division of labor an abnormal condition in which the distribution of accorded positions and occupations is inconsistent with the distribution of talents and skills among individuals.

functionalist theory of stratification the argument that stratification is a necessary device for motivating talented people to perform the society's most difficult and important tasks, and that it arises from scarcity of talent and the differential social necessity of tasks.

gender a set of attitudinal, role, and behavior expectations, which are socially and culturally defined, associated with each sex.

habitus Bourdieu's term for a system of stable dispositions to view the world in a particular way.

health maintenance organization (HMO) a health organization that provides a variety of core services to individuals for a fixed monthly premium.

hermaphrodites individuals who lack an enzyme at birth that would allow them to develop male genitals and are, consequently, defined as females even though male features later begin to develop.

human capital the investments one makes in oneself (i.e., education, acquisition of skills, and experience).

hyperghettoization the extreme concentration of underprivileged groups in the inner city.

hypersegregation the isolation, clustering, and heavy concentration of Blacks in given geographic areas, especially the center of the city.

income deficit how far below the poverty level one's income falls.

Index of Income Concentration a measure of how far the actual distribution of income is from perfect equality (also called **Gini coefficient**).

Index of Social Position Hollingshead's two-factor measure of class position based on occupational prestige and education.

Index of Status Characteristics Warner's quantitative measure of class position based on dwelling area, occupation, house type, and source of income.

individual-level analysis a focus on individuals or individual actions in the analysis of relationships between variables.

industrialism thesis the argument that, regardless of the country, industrialization breaks down barriers to social mobility and results in an emphasis on achievement rather than ascription as a basis for vertical mobility.

inflow table an intergenerational mobility table showing the degree to which those with different occupational backgrounds move into the same occupational category.

in-kind benefits noncash outlays given to recipients of government programs, such as food stamps, medical assistance, and job training.

inner circle a network of leaders from large corporations who serve as top officers at more than one firm, who are politically active, and who serve the interests of the capitalist class as a whole.

inner/outer orientation a view of the environment as hospitable, fruitful, and freely giving (inner) or as one in which the environment is alien, hostile and must be conquered (outer).

institutional view of social welfare belief that since poverty is often beyond the control of individuals, and one of government's legitimate roles is to help those in need, welfare should be available to help people out of poverty.

intergenerational mobility a change in economic or social hierarchical position between generations.

internal colonialism a situation in which a minority group is culturally, socially, and politically dominated as if it were a colony of the majority group.

intragenerational mobility vertical economic or social movement within one's own lifetime.

jati the complex system of local castes found in Indian villages.

labor power the mental and physical capacities exercised by individuals when they produce something of use.

law of need Lenski's argument that individuals are willing to share goods to the extent that such sharing is necessary for their own survival.

law of power Lenski's view that beyond that necessary for one's survival, power determines the distribution of rewards in a society.

legitimation process the means and manner by which social inequality is explained and justified.

marital mobility vertical social mobility that occurs because of one's marriage.

mass society a society in which the vast majority of the population is unorganized, largely powerless, and manipulated by those at the distant top.

means of production the material (e.g., machines) and nonmaterial (e.g., lectures) techniques used to produce goods and services in an economy.

microinequities everyday ways in which, because of their social ranking, individuals are ignored, put down, highlighted, or demeaned.

mobility ratio the percentage of offsprings of employed parents who are in a given occupation, divided by the percentage of the labor force that is in that category.

mode of production the particular type of economic system in a society, including its means of production (e.g., technology) and social/authority relations among workers and between workers and owners. Capitalism and feudalism are two modes of production.

necessary labor   the labor needed to reproduce workers and their replacements.

net worth   one's wealth minus one's debts.

open society   a society in which social mobility and opportunity is available to all.

origin myths   in this context, the view of the world's origin as being due to either masculine or feminine forces.

outflow table   a mobility table showing the between-generation movement of individuals out of a given occupational category into a variety of others.

party   an association aimed at or specifically organized for gaining political power in an organization or society (Weber)

paternalistic race relations   a system of somewhat stable established relationships most likely to be found in complex agricultural systems in which relationships between races are dictated by a recognized social code and in which members of the dominant race treats members of the subordinated race as if they were children.

path analysis   a statistical technique used to uncover the nature and strength of causal connections within a set of variables.

patriarchy   a complex of structured interrelationships in which men dominate women.

peripheral economic sector   part of the private economy occupied by small, local, labor-intensive, less productive, and less stable economic organizations (also called **competitive sector**).

phantom welfare   government cash, tax, and in-kind programs and policies that largely benefit the non-poor.

pluralism   the view stressing that power is distributed throughout society among various groups rather than concentrated.

political action committee (PAC)   a group that organizes around a broad or narrow common interest to influence political policy in its favor.

posttransfer poverty   having an income below the official poverty level, even when government benefits are taken into account.

power elite   a small group or set of groups that dominate the political process and masses in a society.

prestige   the social ranking accorded a position or occupation; a synonym for status honor.

pretransfer poverty   having an income below the official poverty level, not taking into account any kind of government assistance.

primary labor market   the labor market associated with jobs that are stable, good paying, and unionized; have good working conditions; and in which there is an internal job structure through which one can move.

principle of differentiation   the belief that it is fair that those with unequal talents should receive unequal rewards.

principle of equality   the belief that since all people are ultimately of equal value, they should therefore receive equal consideration or treatment.

proletarianization   the conversion of white-collar and middle-class occupations into occupations with traditional working-class characteristics (i.e., boring, routine, etc.).

public assistance   cash and in-kind government programs for the poor that are means tested (i.e., require that an individual prove his or her eligibility) and to which there is a social stigma attached.

race-specific programs   programs of government aid that target particular racial groups for help.

rationalization   the increasing bureaucratic, technological, and impersonal character of the modern world (Weber).

relations of production   the nature of relationships among workers, between workers and managers/supervisors, and between owners and nonowners in an economic system.

relative downward mobility   a shift in one's position on the economic ladder to a lower position and involving a switch in place with another person or group.

relative income   the distance an income is from the middle of the income distribution.

residual view of social welfare   the belief that since poverty is caused by personal flaws, welfare programs should be minimal, with low benefits and strict eligibility requirements to discourage use of them.

residues   Pareto's term for manifestations of underlying basic human propensities or basic drives.

ruling class   the broad Marxian view that the upper class, or an active arm of it generally dominates the political process in society to protect its interests.

scientific management   a system of control used by management in which labor tasks are simplified and standardized by being broken down into their smallest elements.

secondary labor market the labor market associated with poor, unstable, low-paying, and often dead-end jobs.

sex stratification the degree to which access to valued resources is restricted because of sex.

slave system a system of inequality based on ownership of human beings.

social causation thesis in the study of the relationship between mental illness and social class, the argument that social class position is causally related to the probability of mental illness.

Social Darwinism a social philosophy stressing perfection of society through a natural, unfettered process of survival of the fittest.

social insurance government programs, such as social security, for which individuals who have worked for a certain period of time are automatically eligible and seen as deserving of aid.

social-level analysis a focus on examining relationships between group, aggregate, or societal characteristics rather than those between individuals.

social reproduction the process by which structural conditions reproduce themselves.

social stratification a condition in which the ranking system among groups or categories of individuals is firmly established, resulting in a set of social layers separated by impermeable boundaries.

socioeconomic status a person's position on several continuous social and economic hierarchies, such as education, income, occupation, and wealth.

stages of capitalism capitalism's movement through phases of cooperation, manufacture, and modern industry (Marx).

status the ranking of individuals and groups on the basis of *social* and evaluated characteristics; contrasts with class, which is largely an *economic* ranking.

status attainment the study of the factors and processes that account for the educational, occupational, and economic attainment of individuals.

strategic elites individuals who serve fundamental coordinating functions that have significant relevance for a whole society.

street crime crimes listed by the FBI's Crime Index, including burglary, larceny-theft, motor vehicle theft, arson, murder, forcible rape, robbery, and aggravated assault.

structural mobility mobility that is due to shifts in the occupational distribution or changes in technology.

suite crime a synonym for **white-collar crime.**

surplus labor labor time that is left over after socially necessary labor has been subtracted from the total labor time spent on the job. It produces profit for the employer.

transgendered referring to individuals who deviate from traditional gender binaries of Western society and who sometimes define themselves as belonging to a third gender.

underclass a small, urban, largely unemployed, chronically poor, welfare-dependent group of individuals living in impoverished neighborhoods and whose children often wind up in the same position.

vacancy-driven mobility mobility that depends on the availability and distribution of open positions.

varna a major ritual caste in India, such as the Brahmins.

welfare capitalism special benefits used by management to minimize solidarity among workers.

white-collar crime crimes committed by individuals of high status or corporations using their powerful positions and generally involving violations of trust and extensive victimization.

whitening the social process by which individuals can change their racial classification because of their education, occupation, or high-class position.

Wisconsin model a model of status attainment that stresses the impact of social-psychological as well as structural factors on attainment.

world system theory the perspective that all countries are part of an international division of labor driven by international capitalism in which some countries become dominant over others.

REFERENCES

Aaronson, Daniel, and Daniel G. Sullivan. 1998. "The Decline of Job Security in the 1990s: Displacement, Anxiety, and Their Effect on Wage Growth." *Economic Perspectives* 22:17–43.

Aberle, D. F., A. K. Cohen, A. D. Davis, M. J. Levy, and F. X. Sutton. 1950. "The Functional Prerequisites of a Society." *Ethics* 60:100–11.

Abrahamson, Mark. 1973. "Functionalism and the Functional Theory of Stratification: An Empirical Assessment." *American Journal of Sociology* 78:1236–46.

Abramson, Jill, and Thomas Petzinger, Jr. June 11, 1992a. "Big Political Donors Find Ways Around Watergate Reforms." *The Wall Street Journal,* pp. A1, A6.

Abramson, Jill, and Thomas Petzinger, Jr. June 11, 1992b. "How Big Money Has Leached Back into Campaigns." *The Wall Street Journal,* p. A6.

Acker, Joan. 1973. "Women and Social Stratification: A Case of Intellectual Sexism." *American Journal of Sociology* 78:936–45.

Acker, Joan. 1988. "Class, Gender, and the Relations of Distribution." *Signs: Journal of Women in Culture and Society* 13:473–97.

Ackerman, Bruce, and Ann Alstott. 1999. *The Stakeholder Society.* New Haven: Yale University Press.

Adams, Bert N. 1975. *The Family: A Sociological Interpretation.* Skokie, IL: Rand McNally.

Adams, Charles Francis, ed. 1969. *The Works of John Adams,* vol. IX. Freeport, NY: Books for Libraries Press.

Adler, Patricia A., and Peter Adler. 1998. *Peer Power.* New Brunswick, NJ: Rutgers University Press.

Agnello, T. J. 1973. "Aging and the Sense of Political Powerlessness." *Public Opinion Quarterly* 37:251–59.

Aho, C. Michael. January 1993. "America and the Pacific Century: Trade Conflict or Cooperation?" *International Affairs* 69:19–37.

Aldrich, Howard, and Jane Weiss. 1981. "Differentiation within the United States Capitalist Class: Workforce Size and Income Differences." *American Sociological Review* 46:279–90.

Alexander, Herbert E. 1992. "The PAC Phenomenon." Pp. ix–xv in *Almanac of Federal PACs: 1992,* edited by E. Zuckerman. Washington, D.C.: Amward.

Alexander, Karl L., and Bruce K. Eckland. 1974. "Sex Differences in the Educational Attainment Process." *American Sociological Review* 39:668–82.

Alexander, Karl L., Bruce K. Eckland, and Larry J. Griffin. 1975. "The Wisconsin Model of Socioeconomic Achievement: A Replication." *American Journal of Sociology* 81:324–42.

Allan, Emilie Andersen, and Darrell J. Steffensmeier. 1989. "Youth, Underemployment, and Property Crime: Differential Effects of Job Availability and Job Quality on Juvenile and Young Adult Arrest Rates." *American Sociological Review* 54:107–23.

Allen, Michael Patrick. 1987. *The Founding Fortunes: A New Anatomy of the Super-Rich Families in America.* New York: Truman Talley Books.

Allen, Robert L. 1969. *Black Awakening in Capitalist America.* Garden City, NY: Anchor.

Almond, Gabriel A. September 1991. "Capitalism and Democracy." *PS: Political Science & Politics* 24:467–74.

Almond, Gabriel A., and Sidney Verba. 1963. *The Civic Culture: Political Attitudes and Democracy in Five Nations.* Princeton, NJ: Princeton University Press.

Almquist, Elizabeth McTaggart. 1984. "Race and Ethnicity in the Lives of Minority Women." Pp. 423–53 in *Women: A Feminist Perspective,* edited by J. Freeman. Palo Alto, CA: Mayfield.

Alves, W. M., and P. H. Rossi. 1978. "Who Should Get What? Fairness Judgments of the Distribution of Earnings." *American Journal of Sociology* 84:541–65.

Alwin, Duane F. 1974. "College Effects on Educational and Occupational Attainments." *American Sociological Review* 39:210–23.

American Civil Liberties Union. 1997. "Antidiscrimination Laws Protect Equal Rights for Gays and Lesbians." Pp. 143–51 in *Gay Rights,* edited by T. L. Roleff. San Diego: Greenhaven.

Andersen, Margaret L. 1993. *Thinking about Women.* New York: Macmillan.

Andersen, Margaret L. 1997. *Thinking about Women.* Boston: Allyn and Bacon.

Andreas, Peter. 1994. "The Making of Amerexico." *World Policy Journal* XI:45–56.

Andrews, Frank M., and Stephen B. Withey. 1976. *Social Indicators of Well-Being.* New York: Plenum.

Angell, Robert. 1962. "Preferences for Moral Norms in Three Problem Areas." *American Journal of Sociology* 67:650–60.

Anheier, Helmut K., Jurgen Gerhards, and Frank P. Romo. 1995. "Forms of Capital and Social Structure in Cultural Fields: Examining Bourdieu's Social Topography." *American Journal of Sociology* 100:859–903.

Ansberry, Clare. November 29, 1988. "Dumping the Poor: Despite Federal Law, Hospitals Still Reject Sick Who Can't Pay." *The Wall Street Journal,* pp. A1, A4.

Anson, Ofra, and Jon Anson. 1987. "Women's Health and Labour Force Status: An Enquiry Using a Multi-Point Measure of Labor Force Participation." *Social Science & Medicine* 25:57–63.

Appalachian Regional Commission. 1985. *Appalachia: Twenty Years of Progress.* Washington, D.C.: Author.

Archer, M. S., and S. Giner. 1971. "Social Stratification in Europe." In *Contemporary Europe: Class, Status and Power,* edited by M. S. Archer and S. Giner. New York: St. Martin's Press.

Aristotle, "Justice." Pp. 16–27 in *Justice: Selected Readings,* edited by J. Feinberg and H. Gross. Encino, CA: Dickenson Publishing.

Aronowitz, Stanley. 1973. *False Promises: The Shaping of American Working Class Consciousness.* New York: McGraw-Hill.

Asher, Robert. 1986. "Industrial Safety and Labor Relations in the United States, 1865–1917." Pp. 115–30 in *Life and Labor: Dimensions of American Working-Class History,* edited by C. Stephenson and R. Asher. Albany, NY: State University of New York Press.

Atkinson, Glen. 1998. "Regional Integration in the Emerging Global Economy: The Case of NAFTA." *The Social Science Journal* 35:159–68.

Austin, Roy L., and Steven Stack. 1988. "Race, Class, and Opportunity: Changing Realities and Perceptions." *The Sociological Quarterly* 29:357–69.

Awanohara, Susumu, and Shim Jae Hoon. May 14, 1992. "Melting Pot Boils Over." *Far Eastern Economic Review,* pp. 10–11.

Bachrach, Peter, and Morton S. Baratz. 1962. "Two Faces of Power." *American Political Science Review* 56:947–52.

Bagehot, Walter. Quote from *The Oxford Dictionary of Quotations,* 3rd ed. Oxford: Oxford University Press, p. 29.

Bailey, J. Michael. 1996. "Gender Identity." Pp. 71–93 in *The Lives of Lesbians, Gays, and Bisexuals,* edited by R. C. Savin-Williams and K. M. Cohen. Fort Worth, TX: Harcourt Brace.

Baltzell, E. Digby. 1958. *Philadelphia Gentleman: The Making of a National Upper Class.* Glencoe, IL: The Free Press.

Bane, Mary Jo. 1985. "Household Composition and Poverty: Which Comes First?" Albany, NY: New York State Department of Social Services.

Bane, Mary Jo, and David T. Ellwood. 1994. *Welfare Realities.* Cambridge, MA: Harvard University Press.

Banyard, Victoria L. 1999. "Childhood Maltreatment and the Mental Health of Low-Income Women." *American Journal of Orthopsychiatry* 69:161–71.

Banyard, Victoria L., and Sandra A. Graham-Bermann. 1998. "Surviving Poverty: Stress and Coping in the Lives of Housed and Homeless Mothers." *American Journal of Orthopsychiatry* 68:479–89.

Barar, Paul, and Paul Sweezy. 1966. *Monopoly Capital.* New York: Monthly Review Press.

Barkan, Steven E. 1984. "Legal Control of the Southern Civil Rights Movement." *American Sociological Review* 49:552–65.

Barlow, Hugh D. 1987. *Introduction to Criminology.* Boston: Little, Brown.

Barnett, Bernice McNair. 1993. "Invisible Southern Black Women Leaders in the Civil Rights Movement." *Gender & Society* 7:162–82.

Baron, James N., and William T. Bielby. 1984. "The Organization of Work in a Segmented Economy." *American Sociological Review* 49:454–73.

Barone, Michael, and Grant Ujifusa. 1997. *The Almanac of American Politics 1998.* Washington, D.C.: National Journal.

Barrera, Mario. 1979. *Race and Class in the Southwest: A Theory of Racial Inequality.* Notre Dame, IN: University of Notre Dame Press.

Barringer, Felicity. January 11, 1990. "The Dress for Success: A Second Time Around." *The New York Times,* p. A18.

Bassett, Mary T., and Nancy Krieger. 1986. "Social Class and Black–White Differences in Breast Cancer Survival." *American Journal of Public Health* 76:1400–03.

Bassi, Laurie J., and Orley Ashenfelter. 1986. "The Effect of Direct Job Creation and Training Programs on Low-Skilled Workers." Pp. 133–51 in *Fighting Poverty: What Works and What Doesn't,* edited by S. H. Danziger and D. H. Weinberg. Cambridge, MA: Harvard University Press.

Batteau, Allen. 1984. "The Sacrifice of Nature: A Study in the Social Production of Consciousness." Pp. 94–106 in *Cultural Adaptation to Mountain Environments,* edited by P. D. Beaver and B. L. Purrington. Athens, GA: The University of Georgia Press.

Bauer, John, and Andrew Mason. December 1992. "The Distribution of Income and Wealth in Japan." *The Review of Income and Wealth* 38:403–28.

Beaver, Patricia D. 1984. "Appalachian Cultural Adaptations: An Overview." Pp. 73–93 in *Cultural Adaptation to Mountain Environments,* edited by P. D. Beaver and B. L. Purrington. Athens, GA: The University of Georgia Press.

Beck, E. M., Patrick M. Horan, and Charles M. Tolbert, II. 1980. "Industrial Segmentation and Labor Market Discrimination." *Social Problems* 28:113–30.

Becker, Gary S. 1971. *The Economics of Discrimination.* Chicago: University of Chicago Press.

Becker, Howard S. 1963. *Outsiders.* New York: The Free Press.

Bedau, H. A. 1964. "Death Sentences in New Jersey." *Rutgers Law Review* 19:1–55.

Beeghley, Leonard. 1983. *Living Poorly in America.* New York: Praeger.

Bell, Winifred. 1987. *Contemporary Social Welfare.* New York: Macmillan.

Bellas, Marcia L. 1994. "Comparable Worth in Academia: The Effects of Faculty Salaries of the Sex Composition and Labor-Market Conditions of Academic Disciplines." *American Sociological Review* 59:807–21.

Beller, Andrea H. 1984. "Trends in Occupational Segregation by Sex and Race. 1960–1981." Pp. 11–26 in *Sex Segregation in the Workplace: Trends, Explanations, Remedies,* edited by B. F. Reskin. Washington, D.C.: National Academy Press.

Bem, Sandra L., and Daryl J. Bem. 1970. "Case Study of a Nonconscious Ideology: Training the Woman to Know Her Place." Pp. 89–99 in *Beliefs, Attitudes and Human Affairs,* edited by D. J. Bem. Belmont, CA: Brooks/Cole.

Benokraitis, Nijole V., and Joe R. Feagin. 1986. *Modern Sexism.* Englewood Cliffs, NJ: Prentice Hall.

Bensman, Joseph. 1972. "Status Communities in an Urban Society: The Musical Community." Pp. 113–30 in *Status Communities in Modern Society,* edited by H. R. Stub. Hinsdale, IL: Dryden.

Benson, Michael L., and Esteban Walker. 1988. "Sentencing the White-Collar Offender." *American Sociological Review* 53:294–302.

Benston, Margaret. 1969. "The Political Economy of Women's Liberation." *Monthly Review* 21:15–16.

Berger, J., P. Cohen, and M. Zelditch, Jr. 1972. "Status Characteristics and Social Interaction." *American Sociological Review* 37:241–55.

Berger, J., M. H. Fisek, R. Z. Norman, and M. Zelditeh, Jr. 1977. *Status Characteristics and Social Interaction: An Expectation States Approach.* New York: Elsevier.

Bergmann, Barbara R. 1974. "Occupational Segregation, Wages and Profits When Employers Discriminate by Race or Sex." *Eastern Economic Journal* 1:103–10.

Berk, Richard A., Kenneth J. Lenihan, and Peter H. Rossi. 1980. "Crime and Poverty: Some Experimental Evidence from Ex-Offenders." *American Sociological Review* 45:766–86.

Berki, S. E. 1980. "HMO Enrollment: Who Joins What and Why, A Review of the Literature." *Milbank Memorial Fund Quarterly/Health and Society* 58:588–632.

Berkowitz, Edward D. 1984."Changing the Meaning of Welfare Reform." Pp. 23–42 in *Maintaining the Safety Net: Income Redistribution Programs in the Reagan Administration,* edited by J. C. Weicher. Washington, D.C.: American Enterprise Institute for Public Policy Research.

Berle, Adolf. 1959. *Power without Property.* New York: Harcourt Brace Jovanovich.

Bernard, Jessie. 1972. *The Sex Game.* New York: Atheneum.

Bernard, Jessie. 1981. *The Female World.* New York: The Free Press.

Bernhardt, Annette, Martina Morris, and Mark S. Handcock. 1995. "Women's Gains or Men's Losses? A Closer Look at the Shrinking Gender Gap in Earnings." *American Journal of Sociology* 101:302–28.

Bernstein, Aaron. February 26, 1996. "Is America Becoming More of a Class Society?" *Business Week* 55:86–96.

Bernstein, Irving. 1960. *The Lean Years: A History of the American Worker 1920–1933.* Boston: Houghton Mifflin.

Berreman, Gerald D. 1960. "Caste in India and the United States." *American Journal of Sociology* 66 120–27.

Berreman, Gerald D. 1972. "Race, Caste, and Other Invidious Distinctions in Social Stratification." *Race* 13:385–414. Reprinted on pp. 21–39 in *Majority & Minority: The Dynamics of Race and Ethnicity in American Life,* edited by N. R. Yetman. Boston: Allyn and Bacon, 1985.

Bersani, Carl A., and Huey-Tsyh Chen. 1988. "Sociological Perspectives in Family Violence." Pp. 57–86 in *Handbook of Family Violence,* edited by V. B. Van Hasselt, R. L. Morrison, A. S. Bellack, and M. Hersen. New York: Plenum.

Bibb, Robert, and William H. Form. 1977. "The Effects of Industrial, Occupational, and Sex Stratification on Wages in Blue-Collar Markets." *Social Forces* 55:974–96.

Bielby, Denise D., and William T. Bielby. 1988. "She Works Hard for the Money: Household Responsibilities and the Allocation of Work Effort." *American Journal of Sociology* 93:1031–59.

Bielby, William T. 1981. "Models of Status Attainment." Pp. 3–26 in *Research in Social Stratification and Mobility,* edited by D. J. Treiman and R. V. Robinson. Greenwich, CT: JAI Press.

Bielby, William T., and James N. Baron. 1984. "A Woman's Place Is with Other Women: Sex Segregation within Organizations." Pp. 27–55 in *Sex Segregation in the Workplace,* edited by B. F. Reskin. Washington D.C.: National Academy Press.

Bielby, William T., and James N. Baron. 1986. "Men and Women at Work: Sex Segregation and Statistical Discrimination." *American Journal of Sociology* 91:759–99.

"Bigotry in the Military," August 30, 1999. *New York Times,* p. A22.

Biller, Henry B., and Richard S. Solomon. 1986. *Child Maltreatment and Paternal Deprivation.* Lexington, MA: Lexington Books.

Billings, Dwight. 1974. "Culture and Poverty in Appalachia: A Theoretical Discussion and Empirical Analysis." *Social Forces* 53:315–24.

Bingham, Richard D., Roy E. Green, and Sammis B. White, eds. 1987. *The Homeless in Contemporary Society.* Newbury Park, CA: Sage.

Blackwell, James E. 1985. *The Black Community: Diversity and Unity.* New York: Harper & Row.

Blau, Francine D. 1978. "The Data on Women Workers, Past, Present, and Future." Pp. 29–62 in *Women Working,* edited by A. H. Stromberg and S. Harkess. Palo Alto, CA: Mayfield.

Blau, Francine D. 1984. "Occupational Segregation and Labor Market Discrimination." Pp. 117–43 in *Sex Segregation in the Workplace,* edited by B. F. Reskin. Washington, D.C.: National Academy Press.

Blau, Francine D., and Marianne A. Ferber. 1986. *The Economics of Women, Men, and Work.* Englewood Cliffs, NJ: Prentice Hall.

Blau, Francine D., and Carol L. Jusenius. 1976. "Economists' Approaches to Sex Segregation in the Labor Market: An Appraisal." *Signs: Journal of Women in Culture and Society* 1:181–99.

Blau, Judith R., and Peter M. Blau. 1982. "The Cost of Inequality: Metropolitan Structure and Violent Crime." *American Sociological Review* 47:114–29.

Blau, Peter M., and Otis Dudley Duncan. 1967. *The American Occupational Structure.* New York: John Wiley & Sons.

Blauner, Robert. 1964. *Alienation and Freedom: The Factory Worker and His Industry.* Chicago: University of Chicago Press.

Blauner, Robert. 1972. *Racial Oppression in America.* New York: Harper & Row.

Blendon, Robert J., Linda H. Aiken, Howard E. Freeman, and Christopher R. Corey. 1989. "Access to Medical Care for Black and White Americans: A Matter of Continuing Concern." *Journal of the American Medical Association* 261:278–81.

Block, Fred. 1977. "The Ruling Class Does Not Rule: Notes on the Marxist Theory of the State." *Socialist Revolution* 7:6–28.

Bloom, Allan, trans. 1968. *The Republic of Plato.* New York: Basic Books.

Bloom, Jack M. 1987. *Class, Race & the Civil Rights Movement.* Bloomington, IN: Indiana University Press.

Bluestone, Barry. 1977. "The Characteristics of Marginal Industries." Pp. 97–102 in *Problems in Political Economy: An Urban Perspective,* edited by D. M. Gordon. Lexington, MA: D. C. Heath.

Blumberg, Paul. 1980. *Inequality in an Age of Decline.* New York: Oxford University Press.

Blumberg, Rae Lesser. 1978. *Stratification: Socioeconomic and Sexual Inequality.* Dubuque, IA: William C. Brown.

Blumberg, Rae Lesser. 1984. "A General Theory of Gender Stratification." Pp. 23–101 in *Sociological Theory,* edited by R. Collins. San Francisco, CA: Jossey-Bass.

Blumberg, Rhoda Lois. 1984. *Civil Rights: The 1960s Freedom Struggle.* Boston: Twayne.

Bollen, Kenneth A. 1983. "World System Position, Dependency and Democracy." *American Sociological Review* 48:468–79.

Bonacich, Edna. 1976. "Advanced Capitalism and Black/White Relations in the United States: A Split Labor Market Interpretation." *American Sociological Review* 41:34–51.

Bonacich, Edna. 1980. "Class Approaches to Ethnicity and Race." *Insurgent Sociologist* 10(2).

Bonacich, Edna. 1985. "Class Approaches to Ethnicity and Race." Pp. 62–77 in *Majority and Minority: The Dynamics of Race and Ethnicity in American Life,* edited by N. R. Yetman. Boston: Allyn and Bacon.

Boorstin, Daniel J. 1967. *The Americans.* New York: Vintage.

Bornschier, Volker, and Thanh-Huyen Ballmer-Cao. 1979. "Income Inequality: A Cross-National Study of the Relationship between MNC-Penetration, Dimensions of the Power Structure and Income Distribution." *American Sociological Review* 44:487–506.

Bositis, David A. 1996. "Blacks and the 1996 Elections: A Preliminary Analysis." Washington, D.C.: Joint Center for Political and Economic Studies.

Bottomore, Tom B. 1964. *Elites and Society.* Baltimore: Penguin.

Bottomore, Tom B. 1966. *Classes in Modern Society.* New York: Pantheon.

Bottomore, Tom B., and Maximilien Rubel, eds. 1956. *Karl Marx: Selected Writings in Sociology and Social Philosophy.* New York: McGraw-Hill.

Bourdieu, Pierre. 1977a. "Cultural Reproduction and Social Reproduction." Pp. 487–510 in *Power and Ideology in Education,* edited by J. Karabel and A. H. Halsey. New York: Oxford University Press.

Bourdieu, Pierre. 1977b. *Outline of a Theory of Practice.* Cambridge: Cambridge University Press.

Bourdieu, Pierre. 1990. *The Logic of Practice.* Stanford, CA: Stanford University Press.

Bourdieu, Pierre, and Loic J. C. Wacquant. 1992. *An Invitation to Reflexive Sociology.* Cambridge, MA: Polity Press.

Bowles, Samuel, and Herbert Gintis. 1976. *Schooling in Capitalist America.* New York: Basic Books.

Box, Steven. 1983. *Power, Crime, and Mystification.* London: Tavistock.

Braithwaite, John. 1981. "The Myth of Social Class and Criminality Reconsidered." *American Sociological Review* 46:36–57.

Braverman, Harry. 1974. *Labor and Monopoly Capital.* New York: Monthly Review Press.

Bremner, Robert H. 1956. *From the Depths: The Discovery of Poverty in the United States.* New York: New York University Press.

Brenner, R. 1977. "The Origins of Capitalist Development: A Critique of Neo-Smithian Marxism." *New Left Review* 104:25–92.

Brett, Regina. February 5, 1989. "Myths Disguise Extent, Severity of Problem." *Akron Beacon Journal,* p. A7.

Brett, Regina. June 8, 1999. "Cliques Draw Clear Lines." *Akron Beacon Journal,* pp. A1, A6.

Brewer, Rose M. 1988. "Black Women in Poverty: Some Comments on Female-Headed Families." *Signs: Journal of Women in Culture and Society* 13:331–39.

Brickman, P., R. Folger, E. Goode, and Y. Schul. 1981. "Microjustice and Macrojustice." Pp. 173–202 in *The Justice Motive in Social Behavior,* edited by M. J. Lerner and C. S. Lerner. New York: Plenum.

Britt, David W., and Omer Galle. 1974. "Structural Antecedents of the Shape of Strikes: A Comparative Analysis." *American Sociological Review* 39:642–51.

Brody, David, ed. 1971. *The American Labor Movement.* New York: Harper & Row.

Brody, David. 1980. *Workers in Industrial America: Essays on the Twentieth Century Struggle.* New York: Oxford University Press.

Brooke, James. October 13, 1998. "Gay Man Dies from Attack, Fanning Outrage and Debate." *New York Times,* pp. A1, A17.

Brooks, John. 1979. *Showing Off in America.* Boston: Little, Brown.

Brown, B. Bradford, and Mary Jane Lohr. 1987. "Peer-Group Affiliation and Adolescent Self-Esteem: An Integration of Ego-Identity and Symbolic-Interaction Theories." *Journal of Personality and Social Psychology* 52:47–55.

Brown, Diane Robinson, and Lawrence E. Gary. 1988. "Unemployment and Psychological Distress among Black American Women." *Sociological Focus* 21:209–21.

Brown, Erika, Doug Donovan, Joanne Gordon, and Peter Newcomb. July 1999. "The World's Working Rich: United States." *Forbes,* pp. 206–12.

Brown, James S., and Harry K. Schwarzweller. 1970. "The Appalachian Family." Pp. 85–97 in *Change in Rural Appalachia: Implications for Action Programs,* edited by J. D. Photiadis and H. K. Schwarzweller. Philadelphia: University of Pennsylvania Press.

Brown, Judith K. 1975. "Iroquois Women: An Ethnohistoric Note." In *Toward an Anthropology of Women,* edited by R. R. Reiter. New York: Monthly Review Press.

Brown, Timothy C. 1997. "The Fourth Member of NAFTA: The U.S.-Mexico Border." *Annals of the American Academy of Political and Social Science* 550:105–21.

Brownstein, Ronald, and Nina Easton. 1982. *Reagan's Ruling Class.* Washington, D.C.: Presidential Accountability Group.

Buchanan, J. L., and S. Cretin. 1986. "Risk Selection of Families Electing HMO Membership." *Medical Care* 24:39–51.

Buckley, Walter. 1958. "Social Stratification and the Functional Theory of Social Differentiation." *American Sociological Review* 23:369–75.

Budget of the United States Government Fiscal Year 2000. 1999. Washington, D.C.: U.S. Government Printing Office.

Burghardt, Steve, and Michael Fabricant. 1987. *Working Under the Safety Net: Policy and Practice with the New American Poor.* Newbury Park, CA: Sage.

Burke, Peter, and Austin Turk. 1975. "Factors Affecting Postarrest Dispositions: A Model for Analysis." *Social Problems* 22:313–32.

Burnham, Linda. 1985. "Has Poverty Been Feminized in Black America?" *Black Scholar* 16:14–16.

Burr, Jeffrey A., John T. Hartman, and Donald W. Matteson. 1999. "Black Suicide in the U.S. Metropolitan Areas: An Examination of the Racial Inequality and Social Integration-Regulation Hypotheses." *Social Forces* 77:1049–81.

Burris, Val. 1988. "New Directions in Class Analysis." *Critical Sociology* 15:57–66.

Button, James W., Barbara A. Rienzo, and Kenneth D. Wald. 1997. *Private Lives, Public Conflicts.* Washington, D.C.: Congressional Quarterly Press.

Cain, Glen G. 1976 December. "The Challenge of Segmented Labor Market Theories to Orthodox Theory." *Journal of Economic Literature*: 1215–57.

Cairns, Robert B., and Beverley D. Cairns. 1994. *Lifelines and Risks: Pathways of Youth in Our Time.* Cambridge: Cambridge University Press.

Campaign Financing Monitoring Project, Common Cause. 1974. *1972 Federal Campaign Finances Interest Groups and Political Parties.* Washington D.C.: Common Cause.

Cannon, Lynn Weber. 1984. "The Trends in Class Identification among Black Americans from 1952 to 1978." *Social Science Quarterly* 65:112–26.

Cantor, David, and Kenneth C. Land. 1985. "Unemployment and Crime Rates in the Post-World War II United States: A Theoretical and Empirical Analysis." *American Sociological Review* 50: 317–32.

Cantor, Muriel G. 1987. "Popular Culture and the Portrayal of Women: Content and Control." Pp. 190–214 in *Analyzing Gender,* edited by Beth B. Hess and Myra Marx Ferree. Newbury Park, CA: Sage.

Caplan, Pat, ed. 1987. *The Cultural Construction of Sexuality.* London: Tavistock.

Carawan, Guy, and Candie Carawan. 1975. *Voices from the Mountains.* New York: Knopf.

Carliner, Michael S. 1987. "Homelessness: A Housing Problem?" Pp. 119–28 in *The Homeless in Contemporary Society,* edited by R. D. Bingham, R. E. Green, and S. B. White. Newbury Park, CA: Sage.

Carlson, Lewis H., and George A. Colburn. 1972. *In Their Place: White America Defines Her Minorities 1850–1950.* New York: John Wiley & Sons.

Carmichael, Stokely, and Charles V. Hamilton. 1967. *Black Power.* New York: Vintage.

Carnegie, Andrew. 1901. *Gospel of Wealth and Other Essays.* Cambridge, MA: Belknap Press of Harvard University Press, 1962.

Carr, Barry. 1999. "Globalization from Below: Labour and Internationalism under NAFTA." *International Social Science Journal* 51:49–59.

Casanave, N. A., and M. A. Straus. 1979. "Race, Class, Network Embeddedness and Family Violence: A Search for Potent Support Systems." *Journal of Comparative Family Studies* 10:281–99.

Cash, Thomas F., and Patricia E. Henry. 1995. "Women's Body Images: The Results of a National Survey in the U.S.A." *Sex Roles* 33:19–28.

Casper, Lynne M., and Loretta E. Bass. 1998. *Voting and Registration in the Election of November 1996.* Current Population Reports, Series P20, No. 504. Washington, D.C.: U.S. Government Printing Office.

Casper, Lynne M., Sara S. McLanahan, and Irwin Garfinkel. 1994. "The Gender-Poverty Gap: What We Can Learn from Other Countries." *American Sociological Review* 59:594–605.

Caspi, Avshalom, Terrie E. Moffitt, Bradley E. Entner Wright, and Phil A. Silva. 1998. "Early Failure in the Labor Market: Childhood and Adolescent Predictors of Unemployment in the Transition to Adulthood." *American Sociological Review* 63:424–51.

Castner, Laura, and Jacquelyn Anderson. 1999. *Characteristics of Food Stamp Households: Fiscal Year 1998.* Washington, D.C.: U.S. Department of Agriculture.

Catalano, Ralph, and David Dooley. 1983. "Health Effects of Economic Instability: A Test of Economic Stress Hypothesis." *Journal of Health and Social Behavior* 24:46–60.

Caudill, Harry M. 1962. *Night Comes to the Cumberlands: A Biography of a Depressed Area.* Boston: Little, Brown.

Cauthen, Kenneth. 1987. *The Passion for Equality.* Totowa, NJ: Rowman & Littlefield.

Center on Budget and Policy Priorities. 1999. *Average Incomes of Very Poor Families Fell during Early Years of Welfare Reform, Study Says.* Washington, D.C.: Author.

Center for Mental Health Services and National Institution of Mental Health. 1992. *Mental Health, United States, 1992.* Ronald W. Manderscheid and Mary Anne Sonnenschein, eds. DHHS Pub. No. (SMA) 92–1942. Washington, D.C.: U.S. Government Printing Office.

Chafe, William H. 1977. *Women and Equality: Changing Patterns in American Culture.* New York: Oxford University Press.

Chafetz, Janet Saltzman. 1984. *Sex and Advantage: A Comparative, Macro-Structural Theory of Sex Stratification.* Totowa, NJ: Rowman & Allanheld.

Chafetz, Janet Saltzman. 1988. *Feminist Sociology: An Overview of Contemporary Theories.* Itasca, IL: F. E. Peacock.

Chagnon, Napoleon A. 1977. *Yanomamo: The Fierce People.* New York: Holt, Rinehart and Winston.

Chakravarti, Anand. 1983. "Some Aspects of Inequality in Rural India: A Sociological Perspective." Pp. 129–81 in *Equality and Inequality: Theory and Practice,* edited by A. Beteille. Delhi: Oxford University Press.

Chambliss, William J. 1969. *Crime and the Legal Process.* New York: McGraw-Hill.

Charles, Maria. 1992. "Cross-National Variation in Occupational Sex Segregation." *American Sociological Review* 57:483.

Chase, Ivan D. 1975. "A Comparison of Men's and Women's Intergenerational Mobility in the United States." *American Sociological Review* 40:483–505.

Chase-Dunn, Christopher. 1975. "The Effects of International Economic Dependence on Development and Inequality: A Cross-National Study." *American Sociological Review* 40:720–38.

Children's Defense Fund. August 22, 1999. *Extreme Child Poverty Rises by More than 400,000 in One Year, New Analysis Shows.* Washington, D.C.: Author.

Chinoy, Ely. 1955. "Social Mobility Trends in the United States." *American Sociological Review* 20:180–86.

Chira, Susan. February 12, 1992. "Bias against Girls Is Found Rife in Schools, with Lasting Damage." *The New York Times,* pp. A1, B6.

Chiricos, T. G. 1987. "Rates of Crime and Unemployment: An Analysis of Aggregate Research Evidence." *Social Problems* 34:187–212.

Chiricos, T. G., P. D. Jackson, and G. P. Waldo. 1972. "Inequality in the Imposition of a Criminal Label." *Social Problems* 19:553–72.

Chiricos, T. G., and G. P. Waldo. 1975. "Socioeconomic Status and Criminal Sentencing: An Empirical Assessment of a Conflict Proposition." *American Sociological Review* 40:753–72.

Chirot, Daniel, and Thomas D. Hall. 1982. "World-System Theory." Pp. 81–106 in *Annual Review of Sociology,* vol. 8, edited by R. H. Turner and J. F. Short, Jr. Palo Alto, CA: Annual Reviews.

Cigler, Allan J., and Burdett A. Loomis, eds. 1995. *Interest Group Politics.* Washington, D.C.: Congressional Quarterly.

Cimini, Michael H. 1996. "Major Work Stoppages in 1995." *Compensation and Working Conditions.* Washington, D.C.: U.S. Government Printing Office.

Clancy, Tom. 1993. Quoted in *Newsweek,* July 12, 1993, p. 15.

Clark, Ramsey. 1970. *Crime in America.* New York: Simon & Schuster.

Clark, Terry N. 1968. *Community Structure and Decision Making: Comparative Analysis.* Corte Madera, CA: Chandler & Sharp.

Clarke, Stevens H., and Gary G. Koch. 1976. "The Influence of Income and Other Factors on Whether Criminal Defendants Go to Prison." *Law and Society Review* 11:57–92.

Clawson, Dan, Alan Neustadt, and James Bearden. 1986. "The Logic of Business Unity: Corporate Contributions to the 1980 Congressional Elections." *American Sociological Review* 51:797–811.

Cleary, Paul D., and David Mechanic. 1983. "Sex Differences in Psychological Distress among Married People." *Journal of Health and Social Behavior* 24:111–21.

Clinard, Marshall B. 1946. "Criminological Theories of Violations of Wartime Regulations." *American Sociological Review* 11:258–70.

Cockerham, William C., Gerhard Kunz, Guenther Leuschen, and Joe L. Spaeth. 1986. "Symptoms, Social Stratification and Self-Responsibility for Health in the United States and West Germany." *Social Science & Medicine* 22:1263–71.

Cockerham, William C., Guenther Leuschen, Gerhard Kunz, and Joe L. Spaeth. 1986. "Social Stratification and Self-Management of Health." *Journal of Health and Social Behavior* 27:1–14.

Cohen, Albert K., and Harold M. Hodges, Jr. 1963. "Characteristics of the Lower-Blue-Collar Classes." *Social Problems* 10:303–34.

Cohen, Lisa E., Joseph P. Broschak, and Heather A. Haveman. 1998. "And Then There Were More? The Effect of Organizational Sex Composition on the Hiring and Promotion of Managers." *American Sociological Review* 63:711–727.

Coleman, James S. 1982. *The Asymmetric Society.* Syracuse, NY: Syracuse University Press.

Coleman, Richard P., and Lee Rainwater. 1978. *Social Standing in America.* New York: Basic Books.

Collier, Jane Fishburne, and Sylvai Junko Yanagisako, eds. 1987. *Gender and Kinship: Essays toward a Unified Analysis.* Stanford, CA: Stanford University Press.

Collins, Randall. 1971. "Functional and Conflict Theories of Educational Stratification." *American Sociological Review* 36:1002–19.

Collins, Randall. 1975. *Conflict Sociology: Toward an Explanatory Science.* New York: Academic Press.

Collins, Randall, ed. 1984. *Sociological Theory 1984.* San Francisco: Jossey-Bass.

Collins, Randall. 1986. *Weberian Sociological Theory.* Cambridge and New York: Cambridge University Press.

Collins, Randall. 1988. *Theoretical Sociology.* New York: Harcourt Brace Jovanovich.

Collins, Sharon. 1983. "The Making of the Black Middle Class." *Social Problems* 30:369–81.

Collins, Sharon. 1993. "Blacks on the Bubble." *The Sociological Quarterly* 34:429–47.

Connolly, William E. 1969. *The Bias of Pluralism.* New York: Lieber-Atherton.

Cookson, Peter W., Jr., and Caroline Hodges Persell. 1985. *Preparing for Power: America's Elite Boarding Schools.* New York: Basic Books.

Coontz, Stephanie, and Peta Henderson, eds. 1986. *Women's Work, Men's Property: The Origins of Gender and Class.* London: Verso.

Corcoran, M. 1995. "Rags to Rags: Poverty and Mobility in the United States." Pp. 237–67 in *Annual Review of Sociology,* edited by J. Hagan and K. S. Cook. Palo Alto, CA: Annual Reviews.

Corcoran, Mary, and Greg J. Duncan. 1979. "Work History, Labor Force Attachment, and Earnings Differences between the Races and Sexes." *Journal of Human Resources* 14:3–20.

Coreil, Jeannine, and Patricia A. Marshall. 1982. "Locus of Illness Control: A Cross Cultural Study." *Human Organizations* 41:131–38.

Coser, Lewis A. 1967. *Continuities in the Study of Social Conflict.* New York: The Free Press.

Coser, Lewis A. 1971. *Masters of Sociological Thought.* New York: Harcourt Brace Jovanovich.

Cott, Nancy F. 1986. "Feminist Theory and Feminist Movements: The Past Before Us." Pp. 49–62 in *What Is Feminism?* edited by J. Mitchell and A. Oakley. New York: Pantheon.

Cott, Nancy F. 1987. *The Grounding of Modern Feminism.* New Haven, CT: Yale University Press.

Counts, George S. 1925. "The Social Status of Occupations: A Problem in Vocational Guidance." *School Review* 33:16–27.

Coverdill, James E. 1988. "The Dual Economy and Size Differences in Earnings." *Social Forces* 66:970–93.

Coverdill, James E. 1998. "Personal Contacts and Post-Hire Job Outcomes: Theoretical and Empirical Notes on the Significance of Matching Methods." *Research in Social Stratification and Mobility* 16:247–69.

Cox, Oliver C. 1942. "The Modern Caste School of Race Relations." *Social Forces* 21:218–26.

Cox, Oliver C. 1945. "Race and Caste: A Distinction." *American Journal of Sociology* 50:360–68.

Cox, Oliver C. 1948. *Caste, Class and Race.* New York: Monthly Review Press.

Cox, Oliver C. 1959. *The Foundations of Capitalism.* New York: Philosophical Library.

Cox, Oliver C. 1964. *Capitalism as a System.* New York: Monthly Review Press.

Cox, Oliver C. 1976. *Race Relations: Elements and Social Dynamics.* Detroit: Wayne State University Press.

Crandall, N. Fredric, and Marc J. Wallace, Jr. 1998. *Work & Rewards in the Virtual Workplace.* New York: American Management Association.

Crompton, Rosemary, and Gareth Jones. 1984. *White Collar Proletariat: Deskilling and Gender in Clerical Work.* Philadelphia: Temple University Press.

Crutchfield, Robert D. 1995. "Ethnicity, Labor Markets, and Crime." Pp. 194–211 in *Ethnicity, Race, and Crime,* edited by D. F. Hawkins. Albany: State University of New York Press.

Cuber, John F., and William F. Kenkel. 1954. *Social Stratification in the United States.* New York: Appleton-Century-Crofts.

Cunningham, Frank. 1975–1976. "Pluralism and Class Struggle." *Science and Society* 39:385–416.

Curran, Debra A. 1983. "Judicial Discretion and Defendant's Sex." *Criminology* 21:41–58.

Currie, Elliott, and Jerome H. Skolnick. 1988. *America's Problems: Social Issues and Public Policy.* Glenview, IL: Scott, Foresman.

Dahl, Robert A. 1982. *Dilemmas of Pluralist Democracy.* New Haven, CT: Yale University Press.

Dahrendorf, Ralf. 1958a. "Out of Utopia: Toward a Reorientation of Sociological Analysis." *American Journal of Sociology* 64:115–27.

Dahrendorf, Ralf. 1958b. "Toward a Theory of Social Conflict." *Journal of Conflict Resolution* 2:170–83.

Dahrendorf, Ralf. 1959. *Class and Class Conflict in Industrial Society.* Stanford, CA: Stanford University Press.

Dahrendorf, Ralf. 1970. "On the Origin of Inequality Among Men." Pp. 3–30 in *The Logic of Social Hierarchies,* edited by E. O. Laumann, P. M. Siegel, and R. W. Hodge. Chicago: Markham.

Danigelis, Nicholas L. 1978. "Black Political Participation in the United States." *American Sociological Review* 43:756–71.

Danziger, Sheldon, and Peter Gottschalk. 1983. "The Measurement of Poverty: Implications for Antipoverty Policy." *American Behavioral Scientist* 26:739–56.

Danziger, Sheldon, and Peter Gottschalk. May–June 1985. "The Poverty of Losing Ground." *Challenge,* pp. 32–38.

Danziger, Sheldon, and Peter Gottschalk. 1986. "Work, Poverty, and the Working Poor: A Multifaceted Problem." *Monthly Labor Review* 109:17–21.

Danziger, Sheldon H., Robert H. Haveman, and Robert D. Plotnick. 1986. "Antipoverty Policy: Effects on the Poor and the Nonpoor." Pp. 50–77 in *Fighting Poverty: What Works and What Doesn't,* edited by S. H. Danziger and D. H. Weinberg. Cambridge, MA: Harvard University Press.

Danziger, Sheldon, and Robert Plotnick. November 1977. "Poverty Today: Does It Persist or Has It Been Eliminated?" Paper prepared for the Center for the Study of Democratic Institutions, Santa Barbara, CA.

Danziger, Sheldon, and David Wheeler. 1975. "The Economics of Crime: Punishment or Income Distribution." *Review of Social Economy* 33:113–31.

Darling, Sharon. 1984. "Illiteracy: An Everyday Problem for Millions." *Appalachia* 18:22–23.

Daro, Deborah. 1988. *Confronting Child Abuse: Research for Effective Program Design.* New York: The Free Press.

Das, Man Singh, and F. Gene Acuff. 1970. "The Caste Controversy in Comparative Perspective: India and the United States." *International Journal of Comparative Sociology* 11:48–54.

D'Augelli, Anthony R. 1998. "Developmental Implications of Victimization of Lesbian, Gay, and Bisexual Youths." Pp. 187–210 in *Stigma and Sexual Orientation,* edited by G. M. Herek. Thousand Oaks, CA: Sage.

Davidson, Chandler, and Charles M. Gaitz. 1974. "Are the Poor Different? A Comparison of Work Behavior and Attitude among the Urban Poor and Nonpoor." *Social Problems* 22:229–45.

Davies, James C. 1969. "The J-Curve of Rising and Declining Satisfactions as a Cause of Some Great Revolutions and a Contained Rebellion." In *Vio-*

lence in America: Historical and Comparative Perspectives, edited by H. D. Graham and T. R. Gurr. Washington, D.C.: National Commission on the Causes and Prevention of Violence.

Davies, James C. 1971. "Introduction." Pp. 3–9 in *When Men Revolt and Why,* edited by J. C. Davies. New York: The Free Press.

Davis, Allison, Burleigh B. Gardner, and Mary R. Gardner. 1941. *Deep South.* Chicago: University of Chicago Press.

Davis, Angela. 1981. *Women, Race and Class.* New York: Random House.

Davis, James Allan, and Tom W. Smith. 1989. *General Social Surveys, 1972–1989.* Principal Investigator, James A. Davis; Director and Co-Principal Investigator, Tom W. Smith. NORC ed. Chicago: National Opinion Research Center, producer; Storrs, CT: The Roper Center for Public Opinion Research, University of Connecticut, distributor.

Davis, James Allan, and Tom W. Smith. 1994. *General Social Surveys, 1972–1994.* Principal Investigator, James A. Davis; Director and Co-Principal Investigator, Tom W. Smith. NORC ed. Chicago: National Opinion Research Center, producer; 1994: Storrs, CT: The Roper Center for Public Opinion Research, University of Connecticut, distributor.

Davis, James Allan, and Tom W. Smith. 1996. *General Social Surveys, 1972–1996.* Principal Investigator, James A. Davis; Co-Principal Investigator, Tom W. Smith. NORC ed. Chicago: National Opinion Research Center, producer; Storrs, CT: The Roper Center for Public Opinion Research, University of Connecticut, distributor.

Davis, John A. 1974. "Justification for No Obligation: View of Black Males Toward Crime and the Criminal Law." *Issues in Criminology* 9:69–87.

Davis, Karen. 1997. "Uninsured in an Era of Managed Care." *Health Services Research* 31:641–49.

Davis, Kingsley. 1948–1949. *Human Society.* New York: Macmillan.

Davis, Kingsley. 1953. "Reply to Tumin." *American Sociological Review* 18:394–97.

Davis, Kingsley, and Wilbert E. Moore. 1945. "Some Principles of Stratification." *American Sociological Review* 10:242–49.

Davis, Mike. 1992a. *City of Quartz.* New York: Vintage.

Davis, Mike. June 1, 1992b. "In L.A., Burning All Illusions." *The Nation:* 743–46.

Davis, Mike. Summer 1992c. "The L.A. Inferno." *Socialist Review:* 57–80.

Daymont, Thomas N. 1977. "Black-White Differences in Labor Market Allocation Processes in the Late 1960's." Madison, WI: Center for Demography and Ecology Working Paper No. 77–21, University of Wisconsin.

de Tocqueville, Alexis. 1969. Quoted in *Democracy in America,* edited by J. P. Mayer. New York: Doubleday.

DeFreitas, Gregory. 1993. "Unionization among Racial and Ethnic Minorities." *Industrial and Labor Relations Review* 46:284–301.

Della Fave, Richard. 1980. "The Meek Shall Not Inherit the Earth: Self-Evaluation and the Legitimacy of Stratification." *American Sociological Review* 45:955–71.

Department of Workforce Development. June 22, 1999. *Wisconsin Works Overview.* Madison, WI: Author.

Devine, Joel A., Joseph F. Sheley, and M. Dwayne Smith. 1988. "Macroeconomic and Social-Control Policy Influences on Crime Rate Changes. 1948–1985." *American Sociological Review* 53:407–20.

DeVos, George A., and Hiroshi Wagatsuma, eds. 1966. *Japan's Invisible Race: Caste in Culture and Personality.* Berkeley: University of California Press.

DeVos, George A., and William O. Wetherall. 1983. *Japan's Minorities: Burakumin, Koreans, Ainu and Okinawans.* London: Minority Rights Group.

d'Houtaud A., and Mark G. Field. 1984. "The Image of Health: Variations in Perception by Social Class in a French Population." *Sociology of Health and Illness* 6:30–59.

"Did Milken Get Off Too Lightly?" May 7, 1990. *U.S. News and World Report,* pp. 22–24.

Dionne, E. J., Jr. April 18, 1989. "Poor Paying More for Their Shelter." *New York Times,* p. A18.

DiPlacido, Joanne. 1998. "Minority Stress among Lesbians, Gay Men, and Bisexuals." Pp. 138–59 in *Stigma and Sexual Orientation,* edited by G. M. Herek. Thousand Oaks, CA: Sage.

DiPrete, Thomas, and Margaret L. Krecker. 1991. "Occupational Linkages and Job Mobility within and across Organizations." Pp. 91–131 in *Research in Social Stratification and Mobility,* vol. 10, edited by R. Althauser and M. Wallace. Greenwich, CT: JAI Press.

DiPrete, Thomas A., and Whitman T. Soule. 1988. "Gender and Promotion in Segmented Job Ladder Systems." *American Sociological Review* 53:26–40.

Dixon, Jo, Cynthia Gordon, and Tasnim Khomusi. 1995. "Sexual Symmetry in Psychiatric Diagnosis." *Social Problems* 42:429–46.

Dobash, R. E., and R. P. Dobash. 1979. *Violence against Wives: A Case against Patriarchy.* New York: The Free Press.

Dobratz, Betty A., and Stephanie L. Shanks-Meile. 1997. *White Power, White Pride.* New York: Twayne.

Doeringer, Peter B., and Michael J. Piori. 1971. *Internal Labor Markets and Manpower Analysis.* Lexington, MA: D. C. Heath.

Dohrenwend, Bruce P. 1975. "Sociocultural and Social-Psychological Factors in the Genesis of Mental Disorders." *Journal of Health and Social Behavior* 16:365–92.

Dolbeare, Kenneth M., and Murray J. Edelman. 1971. *American Politics.* Lexington, MA: D. C. Heath.

Dolgoff, Ralph, and Donald Feldstein. 1984. *Understanding Social Welfare.* New York: Longman.

Dollard, John. 1957. *Caste and Class in a Southern Town.* Garden City, NY: Doubleday.

Domhoff, G. William. 1971. *The Higher Circles.* New York: Vintage.

Domhoff, G. William. 1998. *Who Rules America?* Mountain View, CA: Mayfield.

Dooley, C. David, and Ralph Catalano. 1980. "Economic Changes as a Cause of Behavioral Disorder." *Psychological Bulletin* 87:450–68.

Dougherty, Regina, Everett C. Ladd, David Wilber, and Lynn Zayachkiwsky, eds. 1997. *America at the Polls 1996.* Storrs, CT: Roper Center.

Downs, Hugh. June 30, 1996. "The Complete Medical Checkup: What You Need to Know." *Parade,* pp. 1–5.

Dublin, Thomas. 1979. *Women at Work.* New York: Columbia University Press.

Dubofsky, Melvyn. 1975. *Industrialism and the American Workers, 1865–1920.* Arlington Heights, IL: AHM Publishing.

DuBois, W. E. B. 1969. *An ABC of Color.* New York: International Publishers.

DuBois, W. E. B. 1973. *The Philadelphia Negro.* Millwood, NY: Kraus-Thompson.

Duke, James T. 1976. *Conflict and Power in Social Life.* Provo, UT: Brigham Young University Press.

Dumont, Louis. 1970. *Homo Hierarchicus,* trans. M. Sainsbury. Chicago: University of Chicago Press.

Dumont, Louis, and D. Pocock, eds. 1961. *Contributions to Indian Sociology,* vol. 5. The Hague: Mouton.

Duncan, Cynthia M., ed. 1992. *Rural Poverty in America.* New York: Auburn House.

Duncan, Greg J. 1984. *Years of Poverty, Years of Plenty: The Changing Economic Fortunes of American Workers and Families.* Ann Arbor, MI: Institute for Social Research, University of Michigan.

Duncan, Greg J., Jeanne Brooks-Gunn, W. Jean Yeung, and Judith R. Smith. 1998. "How Much Does Childhood Poverty Affect the Life Chances of Children?" *American Sociological Review* 63:406–423.

Duncan, Otis Dudley. 1961. "A Socioeconomic Index for All Occupations." Chapter 6 in *Occupations and Social Status,* edited by Albert J. Reiss, Jr. New York: The Free Press.

Dunlop, John T. 1987. "The Development of Labor Organization: A Theoretical Framework." Pp. 12–22 in *Theories of the Labor Movement,* edited by S.

Larson and B. Nissen. Detroit: Wayne State University Press.

Durant, Thomas J., Jr., and Joyce S. Louden. 1986. "The Black Middle Class in America: Historical and Contemporary Perspectives." *Phylon* 47:253–63.

Durkheim, Emile. 1933. *The Division of Labor in Society.* New York: The Free Press.

Dutton, Diana B. 1978. "Explaining the Low Use of Health Services by the Poor: Costs, Attitudes or Delivery Systems?" *American Sociological Review* 43:348–68.

Dye, Thomas R. 1995. *Who's Running America? The Conservative Years.* Englewood Cliffs, NJ: Prentice Hall.

Eakins, Barbara W., and R. Gene Eakins. 1978. *Sex Differences in Human Communication.* Boston: Houghton Mifflin.

Eckert, Penelope. 1989. *Jocks & Burnouts.* New York: Teachers College Press.

"The Economic Crisis of Urban America." May 18, 1992. *Business Week,* pp. 38–43.

Edelhertz, Herbert. 1970. *The Nature, Impact and Prosecution of White-Collar Crime.* Washington, D.C.: National Institute of Law Enforcement Assistance Administration, U.S. Department of Justice.

Edelman, Murray, 1977. *Political Language: Words That Succeed and Policies That Fail.* New York: Academic Press.

Eder, Donna. 1995. *School Talk: Gender and Adolescent School Culture.* New Brunswick, NJ: Rutgers University Press.

Edsall, Thomas Byrne. 1984. *The New Politics of Inequality.* New York: W. W. Norton.

Edwards, Alba M. 1943. *Comparative Occupations Statistics for the United States.* Washington, D.C.: U.S. Government Printing Office.

Edwards, Richard. 1979. *Contested Terrain: The Transformation of the Workplace in the Twentieth Century.* New York: Basic Books.

Ehrenreich, Barbara. September 7, 1986. "Heading for a Two-Tier Society." *Akron Beacon Journal,* p. F1.

Ehrenreich, Barbara, and Deirdre English. 1981. "The Sexual Politics of Sickness." Pp. 327–50 in *The Sociology of Health and Illness: Critical Perspectives.* New York: St. Martin's Press.

Ehrlich, Isaac. 1973. "Participation in Illegitimate Activities: A Theoretical and Empirical Investigation." *Journal of Political Economy* 81:521–65.

Eisenstein, Zillah. 1977/1990. "Constructing a Theory of Capitalist Patriarchy and Socialist Feminism." *Insurgent Sociologist* 7(1977):3–17. Reprinted on pp. 114–45 in *Women, Class, and the Feminist Imagination: A Socialist-Feminist Reader,* edited by K. V. Hansen and I. J. Philipson. Philadelphia: Temple University Press.

Eisenstein, Zillah. 1981. *The Radical Future of Liberal Feminism.* New York: Longman.

Eisinger, Peter. June 1996. "Toward a National Hunger Count." *Social Service Review*, pp. 214–32.

Eisler, Benita, ed. 1977. *The Lowell Offering.* Philadelphia: J. B. Lippincott.

Eismeier, Theodore J., and Philip H. Pollock III. 1986. "Strategy and Choice in Congressional Elections: The Role of Political Action Committees. *American Journal of Political Science* 30:197–213.

Elder, Glen H., and Jeffrey K. Liker. 1982. "Hard Times in Women's Lives: Historical Influences across Forty Years." *American Journal of Sociology* 88:241–69.

Elkins, Stanley. 1959. *Slavery: A Problem in American Institutional and Intellectual Life.* Chicago: University of Chicago Press.

Eller, Ronald D. 1982. *Miners, Millhands, and Mountaineers: Industrialization of the Appalachian South, 1880–1930.* Knoxville, TN: University of Tennessee Press.

Ellwood, David T. 1988. *Poor Support: Poverty in the American Family.* New York: Basic Books.

Ellwood, David T., and Mary Jo Bane. 1984. "The Impact of AFDC on Family Structure and Living Arrangements." Working paper prepared for the U.S. Department of Health and Human Services under grant no. 92A–82.

Ellwood, David T., and Lawrence H. Summers. 1986. "Poverty in America: Is Welfare the Answer or the Problem?" Pp. 78–105 in *Fighting Poverty: What Works and What Doesn't,* edited by S. H. Danziger and D. H. Weinberg. Cambridge, MA: Harvard University Press.

Engels, Frederick. 1973. "The Origin of the Family, Private Property and the State." Pp. 204–334 in *Karl Marx and Frederick Engels: Selected Works.* Moscow: Progress Publishers.

England, Paula. 1984. "Socioeconomic Explanations of Job Segregation." Pp. 28–46 in *Comparable Worth and Wage Discrimination,* edited by H. Remick. Philadelphia: Temple University Press.

England, Paula, and Dana Dunn. 1985. "Why Men Dominate." *The Women's Review of Books* 2:14–15.

England, Paula, and George Farkas. 1986. *Households, Employment, and Gender: A Social, Economic and Demographic View.* New York: Aldine.

England, Paula, George Farkas, Barbara Kilbourne, and Thomas Dou. 1988. "Explaining Occupational Sex Segregation and Wages: Findings from a Model with Fixed Effects." *American Sociological Review* 53:544–58.

Erikson, Kai T. 1976. *Everything in Its Path.* New York: Simon & Schuster.

Erikson, Robert, John H. Goldthorpe, and Lucienne Portocarero. 1983. "Intergenerational Class Mobility and the Convergence Thesis: England, France, and Sweden." *British Journal of Sociology* 34:303–43.

Erlanger, Howard S. 1974. "Social Class and Corporal Punishment in Childrearing: A Reassessment." *American Sociological Review* 39:68–85.

Espenshade, Thomas J. 1995. "Unauthorized Immigration to the United States." Pp. 195–216 in *Annual Review of Sociology,* vol. 21, edited by J. Hagan and K. S. Cook. Palo Alto, CA: Annual Reviews.

"Executive Pay." April 19, 1999. *Business Week,* pp. 72–90.

Fagot, Beverly I. 1977. "Consequences of Moderate Cross-Gender Behavior in Preschool Children." *Child Development* 48:902–07.

Faller, Kathleen Coulborn, and Marjorie Ziefert. 1981. "Causes of Child Abuse and Neglect." Pp. 32–51 in *Social Work with Abused and Neglected Children,* edited by K. C. Faller. New York: The Free Press.

Fallers, Lloyd A. 1966. "Review Symposium." *American Sociological Review* 31:718–19.

Faludi, Susan. 1991. *Backlash: The Undeclared War against American Women.* New York: Crown.

Fanon, Frantz. 1963. *The Wretched of the Earth.* New York: Grove Press.

Faris, R. E. L., and H. W. Dunham. 1939. *Mental Disorders in Urban Areas: An Ecological Study of Schizophrenia and Other Psychoses.* Chicago: University of Chicago.

Farley, John E. 1988. *Majority-Minority Relations.* Englewood Cliffs, NJ: Prentice Hall.

Farrell, Ronald A. 1971. "Class Linkages of Legal Treatment of Homosexuals." *Criminology* 9:49–68.

Fatsis, Stefan. November 22, 1990. "Milken Gets 10 Years in Wall Street Scandal." *Akron Beacon Journal,* pp. A1 and A13.

Featherman, David L. 1977. "Has Opportunity Declined in America?" Institute for Research on Poverty Discussion Paper No. 437–77. Madison, WI: University of Wisconsin.

Featherman, David L., and Robert M. Hauser. 1976. "Sexual Inequalities and Socioeconomic Achievement in the U.S.: 1962–1973." *American Sociological Review* 41:462–83.

Featherman David L., and Robert M. Hauser. 1978. *Opportunity and Change.* New York: Academic Press.

Featherman, David L., F. Lancaster Jones, and Robert M. Hauser. 1975. "Assumptions of Social Mobility Research in the U.S.: The Case of Occupational Status." *Social Science Research* 4:329–60.

Fechter, A., and S. Greenfield. 1973. "Welfare and Illegitimacy: An Economic Model and Some Preliminary Results." Working Paper No. 963–37, Urban Institute, Washington, D.C.

Feldstein, Stanley, ed. 1972. *The Poisoned Tongue: A Documentary History of American Racism and Prejudice.* New York: William Morrow.

Felmlee, Diane H. 1982. "Women's Job Mobility Processes within and between Employers." *American Sociological Review* 43:142–51.

Fenton, Steve. 1984. *Durkheim and Modern Sociology.* Cambridge: Cambridge University Press.

Ferraro, Kenneth F., and Melissa M. Farmer. 1996. "Double Jeopardy to Health Hypothesis for African Americans: Analysis and Critique." *Journal of Health and Social Behavior* 37:27–43.

Ferree, Myra Marx, and Beth B. Hess. 1985. *Controversy and Coalition: The New Feminist Movement.* Boston: Twayne.

Fiala, Robert, and Gary LaFree. 1988. "Cross-National Determinants of Child Homicide." *American Sociological Review* 53:432–45.

Firestone, Shulamith. 1970. *The Dialectic of Sex: The Case for Feminist Revolution.* New York: William Morrow.

Fishel, Leslie, Jr., and Benjamin Quarles. 1967. *The Negro American: A Documentary History.* Glenview, IL: Scott, Foresman.

Fitzgerald, F. Scott. 1925. *The Great Gatsby.* New York: Scribner's.

Flacks, Richard. 1971. *Youth and Social Change.* Chicago: Markham.

Flanagan, Timothy J., and Katherine M. Jamieson, eds. 1988. *Sourcebook of Criminal Justice Statistics— 1987.* U.S. Department of Justice, Bureau of Justice Statistics. Washington, D.C.: U.S. Government Printing Office.

Flanagan, Timothy J., and Kathleen Maguire, eds. 1990. *Sourcebook of Criminal Justice Statistics— 1989.* U.S. Department of Justice Bureau of Justice Statistics. Washington, D.C.: U.S. Government Printing Office.

Foner, Philip S. 1979. *Women and the American Labor Movement,* vol. 1. New York: The Free Press.

Form, M. H., and G. P. Stone. 1957. "Urbanism, Anonymity, and Status Symbolism." *American Journal of Sociology* 62:504–14.

Form, William. 1983. "Sociological Research and the American Working Class." *The Sociological Quarterly* 24:163–84.

Form, William H., and Joan Huber. 1971. "Income, Race, and the Ideology of Political Efficacy." *Journal of Politics* 33:659–88.

Form, William, and Joan Rytina. 1969. "Ideological Beliefs on the Distribution of Power in the United States." *American Sociological Review* 34:19–31.

Fossett, Mark A., Omer R. Galle, and William R. Kelly. 1986. "Racial Occupational Inequality. 1940– 1980: National and Regional Trends." *American Sociological Review* 51:421–29.

Foster, George M. 1973. *Traditional Societies in Technological Change,* 2nd ed. New York: Harper & Row.

Fox, Mary Frank, and Sharlene Hesse-Biber. 1984. *Women at Work.* Palo Alto, CA: Mayfield.

Frank, Andre Gunder. 1969. *Latin America: Underdevelopment or Revolution.* New York: Monthly Review Press.

Franklin, John Hope. 1980. *From Slavery to Freedom: A History of Negro Americans.* New York: Knopf.

Frazier, E. Franklin. 1937. "Negro Harlem: An Ecological Study." *American Journal of Sociology* 43:72–88.

Frazier, E. Franklin. 1957. *Race and Culture Contacts in the Modern World.* Westport, CT: Greenwood Press.

Fredrickson, George M. 1971. *The Black Image in the White Mind: The Debate on Afro-American Character and Destiny, 1817–1914.* New York: Harper & Row.

Fredrickson, George M. 1981. *White Supremacy: A Comparative Study in American and South African History.* New York: Oxford University Press.

Freeborn, D., and C. Pope. 1982. "Health Status, Utilization, and Satisfaction among Enrollees in Three Types of Private Health Insurance Plans." *The Group Health Journal* 3:4–11.

Freeman, Jo, ed. 1975a. *Women: A Feminist Perspective.* Palo Alto, CA: Mayfield.

Freeman, Jo. 1975b. "The Women's Liberation Movement: Its Origins, Structures, Impact, and Ideas." Pp. 448–60 in *Women: A Feminist Perspective,* edited by J. Freeman. Palo Alto, CA: Mayfield.

Freeman, Richard B. 1989. "The Relation of Criminal Activity to Black Youth Employment." *Review of Black Political Economy* 16:99–107.

Freire, Paulo. 1986. *Pedagogy of the Oppressed.* New York: Continuum.

Freitag, Peter J. 1975. "The Cabinet and Big Business: A Study of Interlocks." *Social Problems* 23:137–52.

Fusfeld, Daniel R. 1972. "The Rise of the Corporate State in America." *Journal of Economic Issues* 6:1–22.

Fussell, Paul. 1983. *Class.* New York: Summit Books.

Gagne, Patricia, and Richard Tewksbury. 1998. "Conformity Pressures and Gender Resistance among Transgendered Individuals." *Social Problems* 45:81–101.

Galbraith, John Kenneth. 1952. *American Capitalism: The Concept of Countervailing Power.* Boston: Houghton Mifflin.

Galinsky, Ellen, and James T. Bond. 1996. "Work and Family: The Experiences of Mothers and Fathers in the U.S. Labor Force." Pp. 79–103 in *The American Woman 1996–97,* edited by C. Costello and B. K. Krimgold. New York: W. W. Norton.

Galle, Omer R., Candace Hinson Wiswell, and Jeffrey A. Burr. 1985. "Racial Mix and Industrial Productivity." *American Sociological Review* 50:20–33.

Gallup, George, Jr. 1985. "Mood of the Nation." *The Gallup Report* 243:22–24.

Gallup, George, Jr. 1986. *The Gallup Poll: Public Opinion 1985.* Wilmington, DE: Scholarly Resources.

Gallup, George, Jr. 1988. *The Gallup Poll: Public Opinion 1987.* Wilmington, DE: Scholarly Resources.

Gallup, George, Jr. 1989. *The Gallup Poll: Public Opinion 1988.* Wilmington, DE: Scholarly Resources.

Gallup, George, Jr. 1994. *The Gallup Poll: Public Opinion 1993.* Wilmington, DE: Scholarly Resources.

Gallup, George, Jr. 1995. *The Gallup Poll: Public Opinion 1994.* Wilmington, DE: Scholarly Resources.

Gallup, George, Jr. 1996. *The Gallup Poll: Public Opinion 1995.* Wilmington, DE: Scholarly Resources.

Gallup, George, Jr. 1997. *The Gallup Poll: Public Opinion 1997.* Wilmington, DE: Scholarly Resources.

The Gallup Report. January/February 1987. Report No. 256–57, p. 14.

Gamboa, Glenn. July 14, 1996. "Unions Step Up Bridgestone Pressure." *Akron Beacon Journal,* pp. B1–B2.

Gamst, Frederick, ed. 1995. *Meanings of Work.* Albany: State University of New York Press.

Gans, Herbert J. 1968. *More Equality.* New York: Vintage.

Gans, Herbert J. 1972. "Positive Functions of Poverty." *American Journal of Sociology* 78:275–89.

Gans, Herbert J., ed. 1974. "The Equality Revolution." Pp. 7–35 in *More Equality,* edited by H. J. Gans. New York: Vintage.

Gans, Herbert J. 1995. *The War against the Poor.* New York: Basic Books.

Garbarino, Merwyn S. 1976. *American Indian Heritage.* Boston: Little, Brown.

Garfinkel, Irwin. 1978. "Income Support Policy: Where We've Come From and Where We Should Be Going." Institute for Research on Poverty Discussion Paper No. 490–78. Madison, WI: University of Wisconsin.

Garfinkel, S. A., W. E. Schlenger, K. R. McLeroy, F. A. Bryan, Jr., B. J. G. York, G. H. Dunteman, and A. S. Friedlob. 1986. "Choice of Payment Plan in the Medicare Capitation Demonstration." *Medical Care* 24:628–40.

Garson, Barbara. 1988. *The Electronic Sweatshop.* New York: Simon & Schuster.

Gaventa, John. 1980. *Power and Powerlessness: Quiescence and Rebellion in an Appalachian Valley.* Urbana: University of Illinois Press.

Gaventa, John. 1984. "Land Ownership, Power, and Powerlessness in the Appalachian Highlands." Pp. 142–55 in *Cultural Adaptation to Mountain Environments,* edited by P. D Beaver and B. L. Purington. Athens: University of Georgia Press.

Geis, Gilbert. 1967. "The Heavy Electrical Equipment Antitrust Cases of 1961." Pp. 139–50 in *Criminal Behavior Systems,* edited by M. Clinard and R. Quinney. New York: Holt, Rinehart and Winston.

Geis, Gilbert. 1974. "Upperworld Crime." Pp. 114–37 in *Crime Perspectives on Criminal Behavior,* edited by A. S. Blumberg. New York: Knopf.

Gelles, Richard J., and Claire Pedrick Cornell. 1985 and 1990. *Intimate Violence in Families.* Beverly Hills, CA: Sage.

Gelman, David, and Patrick Rogers. April 12, 1993. "Mixed Messages." *Newsweek,* pp. 28–29.

Gerson, Kathleen. 1985. *Hard Choices: How Women Decide about Work, Career, and Motherhood.* Berkeley: University of California Press.

Gerson, Kathleen. 1987. "Emerging Social Divisions among Women: Implications for Welfare State Politics." *Politics and Society* 15:213–21.

Gerson, Kathleen. 1998. "Gender and the Future of the Family." Pp. 11–21 in *Challenges for Work and Family in the Twenty-First Century,* edited by D. Vannoy and P. J. Dubeck. New York: Aldine de Gruyter.

Gerth, Hans H., and C. Wright Mills, eds. 1962. *From Max Weber: Essays in Sociology.* New York: Oxford University Press.

Giddens, Anthony. 1973. *The Class Structure of the Advanced Societies.* New York: Harper & Row.

Giddens, Anthony. 1978. *Emile Durkheim.* New York: Penguin.

Giddens, Anthony. 1982. *Sociology: A Brief but Critical Introduction.* New York: Harcourt Brace Jovanovich.

Giddings, Paula. 1984. *When and Where I Enter: The Impact of Black Women on Race and Sex in America.* New York: Bantam.

Gil, D. G. 1971. "Violence against Children." *Journal of Marriage and the Family* 33:637–48.

Gil, D. G. 1975. "Unraveling Child Abuse." *American Journal of Orthopsychiatry* 45:346–56.

Gilbert, Dennis, and Joseph A. Kahl. 1993. *The American Class Structure.* 2nd ed. Chicago: Dorsey.

Gilliam, Franklin D., Jr. 1986. "Black America: Divided by Class. *Public Opinion* 9:53–60.

Gillison, Gilliam. 1980. "Images of Nature in Gimi Thought." Pp. 143–73 in *Nature, Culture and Gender,* edited by C. MacCormack and M. Strathem. Cambridge: Cambridge University Press.

Ginzberg, Eli, and Hyman Berman. 1963. *The American Worker in the Twentieth Century.* New York: The Free Press.

Giovannoni, Jeanne M., and Andrew Billingsley. 1970. "Child Neglect among the Poor: A Study of Parental Adequacy in Three Ethnic Groups." *Child Welfare* 49:196–204.

"Girl Watching." November 2, 1992. *Fortune,* p. 146.

Giroux, Henry A. 1983. *Theory & Resistance in Education: A Pedagogy for the Opposition.* South Hadley, MA: Bergin & Garvey.

Gittleman, Maury, and Mary Joyce. September 1995. "Earnings Mobility in the United States, 1967–91. *Monthly Labor Review,* pp. 3–11.

Gladstone, Rick. May 9, 1988. "Despite Crash, Executive Salaries Keep Rising." *Wooster Daily Record,* p. B4.

Glasgow, Douglas G. 1987. "The Black Underclass in Perspective." Pp. 129–144 in *The State of Black America 1987.* New York: National Urban League.

Glenn, Evelyn Nakano, and Roslyn L. Feldberg. 1977. "Degraded and Deskilled: The Proletarianization of Clerical Work." *Social Problems* 25:52–64.

Goffman, Erving. 1959. *The Presentation of Self in Everyday Life.* Garden City, NY: Doubleday.

Goffman, Erving. 1967. *Interaction Ritual.* Garden City, NY: Anchor Books, Doubleday.

Gold, David A., Clarence Y. H. Lo, and Erik Olin Wright. 1975. "Recent Developments in the Marxist Theories of the Capitalist State." *Monthly Review* 27(Oct.):29–43 and 27(Nov.):36–51.

Goldberg, Steven. 1973. *The Inevitability of Patriarchy.* New York: Morrow.

Golden, Tim. August 1, 1996. "People on Welfare, Too, Find a Lot to Criticize." *New York Times,* p. A9.

Goldhamer, Herbert. 1968. "Social Mobility." *International Encyclopedia of the Social Sciences* 14:429–38.

Goldman, Robert, and Ann Tickameyer. 1984. "Status Attainment and the Commodity Form: Stratification in Historical Perspective." *American Sociological Review* 49:196–209.

Goldthorpe, John H. 1964. "Social Stratification in Industrial Society." Pp. 97–122 in *Development of Industrial Society,* edited by P. Halmos under the auspices of *The Sociological Review,* Monograph No. 8. Reprinted on pp. 452–65 in *Structured Social Inequality,* edited by C. S. Heller. 1969. New York: Macmillan.

Goldthorpe, John H. 1985. "On Economic Development and Social Mobility." *British Journal of Sociology* 36:549–73.

Gonsiorek, John C. 1996. "Mental Health and Sexual Orientation." Pp. 462–78 in *The Lives of Lesbians, Gays, and Bisexuals,* edited by R. C. Savin-Williams and K. M. Cohen. Fort Worth, TX: Harcourt Brace.

Good, David H., and Maureen A. Pirog-Good. 1987. "A Simultaneous Probit Model of Crime and Employment for Black and White Teenage Males." *Review of Black Political Economy* 16:109–27.

Goode, Erica. June 1, 1999. "For Good Health, It Helps to Be Rich and Important." *New York Times.*

Gooding, Cheryl, and Pat Reeve. 1993. "The Fruits of Our Labor: Women in the Labor Movement." *Social Policy* 23:56–64.

Goodman, William C., and Timothy D. Consedine. 1999. "Job Growth Slows during Crises Overseas." *Monthly Labor Review* 122:3–23.

Goodwin, Leonard. 1971. *A Study of the Work Orientations of Welfare Recipients Participating in the Work Incentive Program.* Washington, D.C.: The Brookings Institution.

Goodwin, Leonard. 1983. *Causes and Cures of Welfare: New Evidence on the Social Psychology of the Poor.* Lexington, MA: Lexington Books.

Gordon, David M. 1972. *Theories of Poverty and Underemployment.* Lexington, MA: D. C. Heath.

Gordon, David M. 1973. "Class and the Economics of Crime." Warner Modular Publication Reprint No. 350. Andover, MA: Warner Modular Publications.

Gordon, Milton M. 1949. "Social Class in American Sociology." *American Journal of Sociology* 55:262–68.

Gossett, Thomas F. 1963. *Race: The History of an Idea in America.* Dallas, TX: Southern Methodist University Press.

Gottesman, Irving I., Peter McGuffin, and Anne E. Farmer. 1987. "Clinical Genetics as Clues to the 'Real' Genetics of Schizophrenia." Pp. 39–63 in *Special Report: Schizophrenia 1987,* edited by D. Shore. Rockville, MD: U.S. Department of Health and Human Services.

Grabb, Edward G. 1984. *Social Inequality: Classical and Contemporary Theorists.* Toronto: Holt, Rinehart and Winston of Canada.

Graham, Hugh Davis. 1992. "The Origins of Affirmative Action: Civil Rights and the Regulatory State." *The Annals of the American Academy of Political and Social Science* 523:50–62.

Gramlich, Edward M. 1986. "The Main Themes." Pp. 341–47 in *Fighting Poverty. What Works and What Doesn't,* edited by S. H. Danziger and D. H. Weinberg. Cambridge, MA: Harvard University Press.

Gramsci, Antonio. 1971. *Selections from the Prison Notebooks.* London: Lawrence and Wishart.

Grandjean, Burke D. 1975. "An Economic Analysis of the Davis-Moore Theory of Stratification." *Social Forces* 53:543–52.

Grant, Madison. 1926. *The Passing of the Great Race.* New York: Scribner's.

Green, Charles. April 11, 1992. "Bush Endorses Drastic Wisconsin Welfare Reforms." *Akron Beacon Journal,* p. A4.

Green, Charles. April 18, 1993. "Social Security Creates Age Gap." *Akron Beacon Journal,* p. A2.

Green, Gordon, John Coder, and Paul Ryscavage. March 1992. "International Comparisons of Earnings Inequality for Men in the 1980s." *The Review of Income and Wealth* 38:1–15.

Green, James R. 1980. *The World of the Worker: Labor in Twentieth-Century America.* New York: Hill and Wang.

Greenlick, M. R. 1984. "An Investigation of Selection Bias in an HMO Enrollment Experiment." *The Group Health Journal* 5:22–30.

Greenstein, Robert. March 1985. "Losing Faith in 'Losing Ground.'" *The New Republic* 25:12–17.

Grenzke, Janet M. 1989. "PACs and the Congressional Supermarket: The Currency Is Complex." *American Journal of Political Science* 33:1–24.

Griffin, Larry J., Michael E. Wallace, and Beth A. Rubin. 1986. "Capitalist Resistance to the Organization of Labor Before the New Deal: Why? How? Success?" *American Sociological Review* 51:147–67.

Gross, David J., Lisa Alecxih, Mary Jo Gibson, John Corea, Craig Caplan, and Normandy Brangan. *Health Services Research* 34:241–54.

Gross, Jane. March 27, 1989. "What Medical Care the Poor Can Have: Lists Are Drawn Up." *New York Times,* pp. A1, A12.

Grubb, W. Norton, and Robert H. Wilson. June 1992. "Trends in Wage and Salary Inequality, 1967–88." *Monthly Labor Review* 115:23–39.

Grusky, David B., and Robert M. Hauser. 1984. "Comparative Social Mobility Revisited: Models of Convergence and Divergence in 16 Countries." *American Sociological Review* 49:19–38.

Guest, Robert. July 9, 1992. "A Tale of Two Sisters." *Far Eastern Economic Review* 155:28–29.

Gurney, Joan Neff, and Kathleen J. Tierney. 1982. "Relative Deprivation and Social Movements: A Critical Look at Twenty Years of Theory and Research." *Sociological Quarterly* 23:33–47.

Gusfield, Joseph R. 1962. "Mass Society and Extremist Politics." *American Sociological Review* 27:19–30.

Hacker, Helen. 1951. "Women as a Minority Group." *Social Forces* 30:60–69.

Haddock, Geoffrey, and Mark P. Zanna. 1998. "Authoritarianism, Values, and the Favorability and Structure of Antigay Attitudes." Pp. 82–107 in *Stigma and Sexual Orientation,* edited by G. M. Herek. Thousand Oaks, CA: Sage.

Hagan, John, A. R. Gillis, and John Simpson. 1985. "The Class Structure of Gender and Delinquency: Toward a Power-Control Theory of Common Delinquent Behavior." *American Journal of Sociology* 90:1151–78.

Hagan, John, John Simpson, and A. R. Gillis. 1987. "Class in the Household: A Power-Control Theory of Gender and Delinquency." *American Journal of Sociology* 92:788–816.

Hagen, Everett E. 1962. *On the Theory of Social Change.* Homewood, IL: Dorsey.

Hall, Edwin L., and Albert A. Simkus. 1975. "Inequality in the Types of Sentences Received by Native Americans and Whites." *Criminology* 13:199–222.

Haller, Archibald O., and Alejandro Portes. 1973. "Status Attainment Processes." *Sociology of Education* 46:51–91.

Hamilton, Charles V. 1992. "Affirmative Action and the Clash of Experiential Realities." *The Annals of the American Academy of Political and Social Science* 523: 10–18.

Hamilton, Richard F. 1966. "The Marginal Middle Class: A Reconsideration." *American Sociological Review* 31:192–93.

Hammett, Paula. January 1999. "Teaching Tools for Evaluating World Wide Web Resources." *Teaching Sociology,* pp. 31–36.

Hampton, Robert L. 1987. *Violence in the Black Family: Correlates and Consequences.* Lexington, MA: Lexington Books.

Handler, Joel F. 1995. *The Poverty of Welfare Reform.* New Haven, CT: Yale University Press.

Hanratty, Maria J., and Rebecca M. Blank. 1992. "Down and Out in North America: Recent Trends in Poverty Rates in the United States and Canada." *Quarterly Journal of Economics* 107:233–54.

Hansen, Karen V., and Ilene J. Philipson, eds. 1990. *Women, Class, and Feminist Imagination: A Socialist-Feminist Reader.* Philadelphia: Temple University Press.

"The Hard Choices Facing Low-Income American Families." June 1987. *Consumer Reports,* pp. 375–78.

Haring, Marilyn H., William A. Stock, and Morris A. Okun. 1984. "A Research Synthesis of Gender and Social Class as Correlates of Subjective Well-Being." *Human Relations* 37:645–57.

Harkey, John, David L. Miles, and William A. Rushing. 1976. "The Relation between Social Class and Functional Status: A New Look at the Drift Hypothesis." *Journal of Health and Social Behavior* 17:194–204.

Harris, Kathleen Mullan. 1996. "Life after Welfare: Women, Work and Repeat Dependency." *American Sociological Review* 61:407–26.

Harris, Olivia. 1980. "The Power of Signs: Gender, Culture and the Wild in the Bolivian Andes." Pp. 70–94 in *Nature, Culture and Gender,* edited by C. MacCormack and M. Strathem. Cambridge: Cambridge University Press.

Harris Survey. August 21, 1967. *Newsweek,* p. 19.

Hart, C. W. M., and Arnold R. Pilling. 1966. *The Tiwi of North Australia.* New York: Holt, Rinehart and Winston.

Hartley, W. B. 1969. *Estimation of the Incidence of Poverty in the United States, 1870–1914.* Ph.D. dissertation, University of Wisconsin, Madison.

Hartmann, Heidi. 1976/1990. "Capitalism, Patriarchy, and Job Segregation by Sex." *Signs: A Journal of Women in Culture and Society* 1:137–69. Reprinted in *Women, Class, and the Feminist Imagination: A Socialist-Feminist Reader,* edited by K. V. Hansen and I. J. Philipson. Philadelphia: Temple University Press.

Hartmann, Heidi. 1981. "The Unhappy Marriage of Marxism and Feminism." Pp. 15–29 in *Women and Revolution,* edited by L. Sargent. Boston: South End Press.

Hartmann, Heidi. 1987. "Internal Labor Markets and Gender: A Case Study of Promotion." Pp. 59–92 in *Gender in the Workplace,* edited by C. Brown and J. A. Pechman. Washington, D.C.: Brookings Institution.

Hauchler, Ingomar, and Paul M. Kennedy, eds. 1994. *Global Trends: The World Almanac of Development and Peace.* New York: Continuum.

Haug, Marie. 1972. "Social-Class Measurement: A Methodological Critique," Pp. 429–51 in *Issues in Social Inequality,* edited by Gerald W. Thielbar and Saul D. Feldman. Boston: Little, Brown.

Hauser, Robert M., and David B. Grusky. 1988. "Cross-National Variation in Occupational Distribution, Relative Mobility Chances, and Intergenerational Shifts in Occupational Distributions." *American Sociological Review* 53:723–41.

Haveman, Robert H. 1977. "Poverty Income Distribution and Social Policy: The Last Decade and the Next." *Public Policy* 25:3–24.

Haveman, Robert H. 1987. *Poverty Policy and Poverty Research: The Great Society and the Social Sciences.* Madison, WI: University of Wisconsin Press.

Hawley, Amos. 1963. "Community Power and Urban Renewal Success." *American Journal of Sociology* 68:422–31.

Haynes, Norris. 1995. "How Skewed Is the Bell Curve?" *Journal of Black Psychology* 21:275–92.

Haynie, Dana L., and Bridget K. Gorman. 1999. "A Gendered Context of Opportunity: Determinants of Poverty across Urban and Rural Labor Markets." *Sociological Quarterly* 40:177–97.

Hayward, Mark D., Amy M. Pienta, and Diane K. McLaughlin. 1997. "Inequality in Men's Mortality: The Socioeconomic Status Gradient and Geographic Context." *Journal of Health and Social Behavior* 38:313–30.

Hazelrigg, Lawrence E. 1972. "Class, Property, and Authority: Dahrendorf's Critique of Marx's Theory of Class." *Social Forces* 50:473–87.

Hazelrigg, Lawrence E. 1974. "Cross-National Comparisons of Father-to-Son Occupational Mobility." Pp. 469–93 in *Social Stratification: A Reader,* edited by J. Lopreato and L. S. Lewis. New York: Harper & Row.

Hazelrigg, Lawrence E., and Maurice A. Garnier. 1976. "Occupational Mobility in Industrial Societies: A Comparative Analysis of Differential Access to Occupational Ranks in Seventeen Countries." *American Sociologic Review* 41:498–511.

Hehir, J. Bryan. April 10, 1981. "The Bishops Speak on El Salvador." *Commonwealth,* pp. 199, 223.

Heller, Celia S., ed. 1969. *Structured Social Inequality.* New York: Macmillan.

Henderson, A. M., and Talcott Parsons, trans. 1947. *Max Weber: The Theory of Social and Economic Organization.* New York: The Free Press.

Henley, Nancy, and Jo Freeman. 1984. "The Sexual Politics of Interpersonal Behavior." Pp. 465–77 in *Women: A Feminist Perspective,* edited by J. Freeman. Palo Alto, CA: Mayfield.

Herdt, Gilbert. 1997. *Same Sex, Different Cultures.* Boulder, CO: Westview Press.

Herek, Gregory M., and Kevin T. Berrill, eds. 1992. *Hate Crimes.* Newbury Park, CA: Sage.

Herman, M. W. 1972. "The Poor: Their Medical Needs and the Health Services Available to Them." *Annals of the American Academy of Political and Social Science* 399:12–21.

Herrnstein, Richard J., and Charles Murray. 1994. *The Bell Curve: Intelligence and Class Structure in American Life.* New York: The Free Press.

Hershey, William. June 16, 1993. "Temporary Workers Growing in Numbers." *Akron Beacon Journal,* p. B7.

Hertzler, J. O. 1952. "Some Tendencies toward a Closed Class System in the United States." *Social Forces* 30:313–23.

Herz, Diane E., and Barbara H. Wootten. 1996. "Women in the Workforce: An Overview." Pp. 44–78 in *The American Woman 1996–97,* edited by C. Costello and B. K. Krimgold. New York: W. W. Norton.

Hess, Robert D., and Judith V. Torney. 1968. *The Development of the Political Attitudes in Children.* New York: Anchor Books.

Hewitt, Christopher. 1995. "The Socioeconomic Position of Gay Men: A Review of the Evidence." *American Journal of Economics and Sociology* 54:461–79.

Hibbard, Judith H., and Clyde R. Pope. 1987. "Employment Characteristics and Health Status among Men and Women." *Women & Health* 12:85–102.

Hicks, Alexander M., Roger Friedland, and Edwin D. Johnson. 1978. "Class Power and State Policy." *American Sociological Review* 43:302–15.

Higley, John, and Given Moore. 1981. "Elite Integration in the United States and Australia." *American Political Science Review* 75:581–97.

Higley, Stephen Richard. 1995. *Privilege, Power, and Place.* Lanham, MD: Rowman & Littlefield.

Hill, Christopher. 1964. *Puritanism and Revolution.* New York: Schocken Books.

Hine, Lewis W. 1977. *America & Lewis Hine.* New York: Aperture.

Hinkle, Roscoe C., Jr., and Gisela J. Hinkle. 1965. *The Development of Modern Sociology.* New York: Random House.

Hirschman, Charles, and Morrison G. Wong. 1984. "Socioeconomic Gains of Asian Americans, Blacks, and Hispanics: 1960–1976." *American Journal of Sociology* 90:584–606.

Hirschman, Charles, and Ellen Kraly. 1988. "Immigrants, Minorities, and Earnings in the United States in 1950." *Ethnic and Racial Studies* 11:332–65.

Hoch, Charles. 1987. "A Brief History of the Homeless Problem in the United States." Pp. 16–32 in *The Homeless in Contemporary Society,* edited by R. D. Bingham, R. E. Green, and S. B. White. Newbury Park, CA: Sage.

Hochschild, Jennifer. 1981. *What's Fair: American Beliefs about Distributive Justice.* Cambridge, MA: Harvard University Press.

Hodge, Robert W., and Paul M. Siegel. 1968. "The Measurement of Social Class." Pp. 316–326 in *International Encyclopedia of the Social Sciences* 15:316–25.

Hodge, Robert W., Paul Siegel, and Peter H. Rossi. 1964. "Occupational Prestige in the United States. 1925–1963." *American Journal of Sociology* 70:286–302.

Hodge, Robert W., and Donald J. Treiman. 1968. "Class Identification in the United States." *American Journal of Sociology* 73:535–42.

Hodson, Randy. 1984. "Companies, Industries, and the Measurement of Economic Segmentation." *American Sociological Review* 49:335–48.

Hodson, Randy, and Robert L. Kaufman. 1982. "Economic Dualism: A Critical Review." *American Sociological Review* 47:727–39.

Hoffman, Donna L., and Thomas P. Novak. 1998. "Bridging the Racial Divide on the Internet." *Science* 280:390–91.

Hole, Judith, and Ellen Levine. 1975. "The First Feminists." Pp. 436–47 in *Women: A Feminist Perspective,* edited by J. Freeman. Palo Alto, CA: Mayfield.

Hollingshead, August B., and Fredrick Redlich. 1958. *Social Class and Mental Illness.* New York: John Wiley & Sons.

Hollingsworth, J. Rogers. 1981. "Inequality in Levels of Health in England and Wales: 1891–1971." *Journal of Health and Social Behavior* 22:268–83.

hooks, bell. 1981. *Ain't I a Woman: Black Women and Feminism.* Boston: South End Press.

Hope, Marjorie, and James Young. 1986. *The Faces of Homelessness.* Lexington, MA: Lexington Books.

Horan, Patrick M. 1978. "Is Status Attainment Research Atheoretical?" *American Sociological Review* 43:534–41.

Horrigan, M. W., and S. E. Haugen. 1988. "The Declining Middle-Class Thesis: A Sensitivity Analysis." *Monthly Labor Review* 111:3–13.

Hotaling, G. T., and D. B. Sugerman. 1984. "An Identification of Risk Factors." In *Domestic Violence Surveillance System Feasibility Study, Phase 1 Report.* Rockville, MD: Westat.

Hout, Michael. 1984. "Occupational Mobility of Black Men: 1962 to 1973." *American Sociological Review* 49:308–22.

Hout, Michael. 1986. "Opportunity and the Minority Middle Class: A Comparison of Blacks in the United States and Catholics in Northern Ireland." *American Sociological Review* 51:214–23.

Hout, Michael. 1988. "More Universalism, Less Structural Mobility: The American Occupational Structure in the 1980s." *American Journal of Sociology* 93:1358–1400.

Huaco, George A. 1963. "A Logical Analysis of the Davis-Moore Theory of Stratification." *American Sociological Review* 28:801–04.

Huber, Joan. 1982. "Toward a Sociotechnological Theory of the Women's Movement." Pp. 24–38 in *Women and Work: Problems and Perspectives,* edited by R. Kahn-Hut, A. K. Daniels, and R. Colvard. New York: Oxford University Press.

Huber, Joan. 1988. "From Sugar and Spice to Professor." Pp. 92–101 in *Down to Earth Sociology: Introductory Readings,* edited by J. M. Henslin. New York: The Free Press.

Huber, Joan. 1989. "A Theory of Gender Stratification." Pp. 110–119 in *Feminist Frontiers II: Rethinking Sex, Gender, and Society,* edited by L. Richardson and V. Taylor. New York: Random House.

Huber, Joan, and William H. Form. 1973. *Income and Ideology: An Analysis of the American Political Formula.* New York: The Free Press.

Huff, Daniel D., and David A. Johnson. 1993. "Phantom Welfare: Public Relief for Corporate America." *Social Work* 38:311–16.

Hughes, Michael, and Melvin E. Thomas. 1998. "The Continuing Significance of Race Revisited: A Study of Race, Class, and Quality of Life in America, 1972 to 1996." *American Sociological Review* 63:785–95.

Humphrey, Ronald, and Howard Schuman. 1984. "The Portrayal of Blacks in Magazine Advertisements: 1950–1982." *Public Opinion Quarterly* 48:551–63.

Hunter, Herbert M., and Sameer Y. Abraham, eds. 1987. *Race, Class, and the World System: The Sociology of Oliver C. Cox.* New York: Monthly Review Press.

Hurn, Christopher. 1987. "Theories of Schooling and Society: The Functional and Radical Paradigms." Pp. 322–333 in *Introducing Sociology,* edited by R. T. Schaefer and R. P. Lamm. New York: McGraw-Hill.

Imershein, Allen W., Philip C. Rond, III, and Mary P. Mathis. 1992. "Restructuring Patterns of Elite Dominance and the Formation of State Policy in Health Care." *American Journal of Sociology* 97:970–93.

Inkeles, Alex, and David H. Smith. 1974. *Becoming Modern: Individual Change in Six Developing Countries*. Cambridge, MA: Harvard University Press.

International Bank for Reconstruction and Development/The World Bank. 1992. *World Development Report 1992*. New York: Oxford University Press.

Irwin, John. 1985. *The Jail: Managing the Underclass in American Society*. Berkeley: University of California Press.

Iyer, Pica. June 1, 1992. "Goneril's Lament." *The New Republic*: 12.

Jackall, Robert. 1988. *Moral Mazes: The World of Corporate Managers*. New York: Oxford.

Jackman, Mary R., and Robert W. Jackman. 1983. *Class Awareness in the United States*. Berkeley: University of California Press.

Jackman, Mary R., and Mary Scheuer Senter. 1983. "Different, Therefore Unequal: Beliefs about Trait Differences between Groups of Unequal Status." Pp. 309–35 in *Research in Social Stratification and Mobility: A Research Annual*, edited by D. J. Treiman and R. V. Robinson. Greenwich, CT: JAI Press.

Jackman, Robert W. 1975. *Politics and Social Equality: A Comparative Analysis*. New York: John Wiley & Sons.

Jackson, Elton F., and Harry J. Crockett, Jr. 1964. "Occupational Mobility in the United States: A Point Estimate and Trend Comparison." *American Sociological Review* 29:5–15.

Jacobs, Jerry A. 1989. "Long-Term Trends in Occupational Segregation by Sex." *American Journal of Sociology* 95:160–73.

Jacobson, Sharon, and Arnold H. Grossman. 1996. "Older Lesbians and Gay Men: Old Myths, New Images, and Future Directions." Pp. 345–73 in *The Lives of Lesbians, Gays, and Bisexuals*, edited by R. C. Savin-Williams and K. M. Cohen. Fort Worth, TX: Harcourt Brace.

James, Dorothy Buckton. 1972. *Poverty, Politics, and Change*. Englewood Cliffs, NJ: Prentice Hall.

Jasso, Guillermina. 1994. "Assessing Individual and Group Differences in the Sense of Justice." *Social Science Research* 23:368–406.

Jasso, Guillermina. 1999. "How Much Injustice Is There in the World? Two New Justice Indexes." *American Sociological Review* 64:133–68.

Jasso, Guillermina, and Peter Rossi. 1977. "Distributive Justice and Earned Income." *American Sociological Review* 42:639–51.

Jefferson, Alphine W. 1993. "Contemporary Diaspora and the Future." Pp. 102–18 in *Africana Studies*, edited by M. Azevedo. Durham, NC: Carolina.

Jencks, Christopher. 1992. *Rethinking Social Policy*. New York: HarperCollins.

Jencks, Christopher, Marshall Smith, Henry Acland, Mary Jo Bane, David Cohen, Herbert Gintis, Barbara Heyns, and Stephen Michelson. 1973. *Inequality: A Reassessment of the Effect of Family and Schooling in America*. New York: Colophon Books.

Jenkins, J. Craig. 1983. "Resource Mobilization Theory and the Study of Social Movements." Pp. 527–53 in *Annual Review of Sociology*, edited by R. H. Turner and J. F. Short, Jr. Palo Alto, CA: Annual Reviews.

Jenkins, J. Craig, and Craig M. Eckert. 1986. "Channeling Black Insurgency: Elite Patronage and Professional Social Movement Organizations in the Development of the Black Movement." *American Sociological Review* 51:812–29.

Jenkins, J. Craig, and Charles Perrow. 1977. "Insurgency of the Powerless: Farm Worker Movements (1946–1972)." *American Sociological Review* 42:249–68.

Johnson, Cathryn. 1994. "Gender, Legitimate Authority, and Leader-Subordinate Conversations." *American Sociological Review* 59:122–35.

Johnson, Harry A., ed. 1976. *Ethnic American Minorities*. New York: R. R. Bowker.

Joint Center for Political and Economic Studies. 1990. *Black Elected Officials: A National Roster*. Washington, D.C.: Author.

Joint Center for Political Studies. 1989. *Black Elected Officials: A National Roster*. Washington, D.C.: Author.

Jones, Woodrow, Jr., and K. Robert Keiser. 1987. "Issue Visibility and the Effects of PAC Money." *Social Science Quarterly* 68:170–76.

Judis, John B. January 21, 1990. "Pulling U.S. Strings: Japanese Money Buys Influence." *Akron Beacon Journal*, pp. E1, E4.

Judson, C. J., J. J. Pandell, J. B. Owens, J. L. McIntosh, and D. L. Matchullat. 1969. "A Study of the California Penalty Jury in First Degree Murder Cases." *Stanford Law Review* 21:1297–1431.

Kaelble, Hartmut. 1981. *Historical Research on Social Mobility: Western Europe and the USA in the Nineteenth and Twentieth Centuries*. New York: Columbia University Press.

Kahl, Joseph A. 1957. *The American Class Structure*. New York: Holt, Rinehart and Winston.

Kaiser, S. 1985. *The Social Psychology of Clothing and Personal Adornment*. New York: Macmillan.

Kallick, David. 1994. "Toward a New Unionism." *Social Policy* 25:2–6.

Kamerman, Sheila B. 1980. *Parenting in an Unresponsive Society: Managing Work and Family Life*. New York: The Free Press.

Kane, Joseph Nathan. 1974. *Facts about the Presidents,* 3rd ed. New York: H. W. Wilson.

Kanter, Rosabeth Moss. 1977a. *Men and Women of the Corporation.* New York: Basic Books.

Kanter, Rosabeth Moss. 1977b. "Some Effects of Proportions on Group Life: Skewed Sex Ratios and Responses to Token Women." *American Journal of Sociology* 82:965–90.

Kaplan, H. Roy, and Curt Tausky. 1972. "Work and the Welfare Cadillac: The Function of and Commitment to Work among the Hardcore Unemployed." *Social Problems* 19:469–83.

Kaplan, H. Roy, and Curt Tausky. 1974. "The Meaning of Work among the Hardcore Unemployed." *Pacific Sociological Review* 17:185–98.

Kasarda, John D. 1989. "Urban Industrial Transition and the Underclass." *Annals of the American Academy of Political and Social Science* 501:26–47.

Katz, Michael B. 1986. *In the Shadow of the Poorhouse: A Social History of Welfare in America.* New York: Basic Books.

Kaufman, Bruce E. 1982. "The Determinants of Strikes in the United States: 1900–1977." *Industrial and Labor Relations Review* 35:473–90.

Kaufman, Robert L., and Thomas N. Daymont. 1981. "Racial Discrimination and the Social Organization of Industries." *Social Science Research* 10:225–55.

Kawachi, Ichiro, and Bruce P. Kennedy. 1999. "Income Inequality and Health: Pathways and Mechanisms." *Health Services Research* 34:215–27.

Keller, Suzanne. 1969. "Beyond the Ruling Class-Strategic Elites." Pp. 520–24 in *Structured Social Inequality,* edited by C. S. Heller. New York: Macmillan.

Keller, Suzanne. 1987. "Social Differentiation and Social Stratification: The Special Case of Gender." Pp. 329–49 in *Structured Social Inequality,* edited by Celia S. Heller. New York: Macmillan.

Kelley, Jonathan, and M. D. R. Evans. 1993. "The Legitimation of Inequaiity: Occupational Earnings in Nine Nations." *American Journal of Sociology* 99:75–125.

Kemper, Theodore D. 1976. "Marxist and Functionalist Theories in the Study of Stratification: Common Elements That Lead to a Test." *Social Forces* 54:559–78.

Kenkel, William F. 1952. *An Experimental Analysis of Social Stratification in Columbus, Ohio.* Unpublished Ph.D. dissertation, Ohio State University, Columbus.

Kennelly, Ivy. 1999. "That Single-Mother Element': How White Employers Typify Black Women." *Gender & Society* 13:168–92.

Kennickell, Arthur B., and Martha Starr-McCluer. 1994. "Changes in Family Finances from 1989 to 1992: Evidence from the Survey of Consumer Finances." *Federal Reserve Bulletin* 80:861–82.

Kenworthy, Lane. 1999. "Do Social-Welfare Policies Reduce Poverty? A Cross-National Assessment." *Social Forces* 77:1119–39.

Kephart, William M. 1950. "Status After Death." *American Sociological Review* 15:635–43.

Kerbo, Harold R. 1983. *Social Stratification and Inequality: Class Conflict in the United States.* New York: McGraw-Hill.

Kerbo, Harold R., and L. Richard Della Fave. 1979. "The Empirical Side of the Power Elite Debate: An Assessment and Critique of Recent Research." *The Sociological Quarterly* 20:5–22.

Kerckhoff, Alan C. 1995. "Institutional Arrangements and Stratification Processes of Industrial Societies." Pp. 323–47 in *Annual Review of Sociology,* edited by J. Hagan and K. S. Cook. Palo Alto, CA: Annual Reviews.

Kerckhoff, Alan C., Richard T. Campbell, and Idee Winfield-Laird. 1985. "Social Mobility in Great Britain and the United States." *American Journal of Sociology* 91:281–301.

Kessler, Denis, and Edward N. Wolff. September 1991. "A Comparative Analysis of Household Wealth Patterns in France and the United States." *The Review of Income and Wealth* 37:249–66.

Kessler, Ronald C. 1982. "A Disaggregation of the Relationship between Socioeconomic Status and Psychological Distress." *American Sociological Review* 47:752–64.

Kessler, Ronald C., and Paul D. Cleary. 1980. "Social Class and Psychological Distress." *American Sociological Review* 45:463–78.

Kessler, Ronald C., and Jane D. McLeod. 1984. "Sex Differences in Vulnerability to Undesirable Life Events." *American Sociological Review* 49:620–31.

Kessler, Ronald C., and James A. McRae, Jr. 1983. "Trends in the Relationship between Sex and Attempted Suicide." *Journal of Health and Social Behavior* 24:98–110.

Kessler-Harris, Alice. 1989. "Women, Work, and the Social Order." Pp. 191–203 in *Feminist Frontiers II: Rethinking Sex, Gender, and Society,* edited by L. Richardson and V. Taylor. New York: Random House.

Khazzoom, Aziza. 1997. "The Impact of Mothers' Occupations on Children's Occupational Destinations." *Research in Stratification and Mobility* 15:57–89.

Kilborn, Peter T. April 22, 1993. "Finding a Way: The Quest of Derrick, 19." *New York Times,* pp. A1, A14.

Killian, Lewis M. 1984. "Organization, Rationality and Spontaneity in the Civil Rights Movement." *American Sociological Review* 49:770–83.

King, Deborah K. 1988. "Multiple Jeopardy, Multiple Consciousness: The Context of a Black Feminist Ideology." *Signs* 14:42–72.

King, Martin Luther. 1958. *Stride toward Freedom.* New York: Harper & Row.

Kinney, David A. 1993. "From Nerds to Normals: The Recovery of Identity among Adolescents from Middle School to High School." *Sociology of Education* 66:21–40.

Kite, Mary E., and Bernard E. Whitley, Jr. 1998. "Do Heterosexual Women and Men Differ in Their Attitudes toward Homosexuality?" Pp. 39–61 in *Stigma and Sexual Orientation,* edited by G. M. Herek. Thousand Oaks, CA: Sage.

Kleck, Gary. 1981. "Racial Discrimination in Criminal Sentencing: A Critical Evaluation of the Evidence with Additional Evidence on the Death Penalty." *American Sociological Review* 46:783–805.

Kleck, Gary. 1982. "On the Use of Self-Report Data to Determine the Class Distribution of Criminal and Delinquent Behavior." *American Sociological Review* 47:427–33.

Klein, Ethel. 1984. *Gender Politics.* Cambridge, MA: Harvard University Press.

Klerman, Gerald L., and Myrna M. Weissman. 1989. "Increasing Rates of Depression." *Journal of the American Medical Association* 261:2229–35.

Kluegel, James R., and Eliot R. Smith. 1986. *Beliefs about Inequality: Americans' Views of What Is and What Ought to Be.* New York: Aldine de Gruyter.

Knottnerus, J. David. 1987. "Status Attainment Research and Its Image of Society." *American Sociological Review* 52:113–21.

Koch, Donald W. 1969. "Income Distribution and Political Structure in Seventeenth Century Salem, Massachusetts." *Essex Institute Historical Collections* 105:54–63.

Koegel, Paul, M. Audrey Burnam, and Jim Baumohl. 1996. "The Causes of Homelessness." Pp. 24–33 in *Homelessness in America,* edited by J. Baumohl. Phoenix, AZ: Oryx Press.

Kohn, Melvin L. 1969. *Class and Conformity.* Homewood, IL: Dorsey.

Kohn, Melvin. 1976a. "The Interaction of Social Class and Other Factors in the Etiology of Schizophrenia." *American Journal of Psychiatry* 133:177–80.

Kohn, Melvin. 1976b. "Occupational Structure and Alienation." *American Journal of Sociology* 82:111–30.

Kohn, Melvin L., and Carmi Schooler. 1982. "Job Conditions and Personality: A Longitudinal Assessment of Their Reciprocal Effects." *American Journal of Sociology* 87:1257–86.

Kolenda, Pauline. 1978. *Caste in Contemporary India.* Prospect Heights, IL: Waveland Press.

Korpi, Walter. 1974. "Conflict, Power, and Relative Deprivation." *American Political Science Review* 68:1569–78.

Kosterlitz, Julie. December 6, 1986. "Reexamining Welfare." *National Journal,* pp. 2926–31.

Kosters, Marvin H., and Murray N. Ross. 1988. "A Shrinking Middle Class." *The Public Interest* 90:3–27.

Kotlowitz, Alex. 1991. *There Are No Children Here.* New York: Doubleday.

Kposowa, Augustine J., Kevin D. Breault, and Beatrice M. Harrison. 1995. "Reassessing the Structural Covariates of Violent and Property Crimes in the USA: A County Level Analysis." *British Journal of Sociology* 46:79–105.

Kramer, Ronald C. 1984. "Corporate Criminality: The Development of an Idea." In *Corporations as Criminals,* edited by E. Hoshstedler. Beverly Hills, CA: Sage.

Krauze, Tadeusz, and Kazimierz M. Slomczynski. 1985. "How Far to Meritocracy? Empirical Tests of a Controversial Thesis." *Social Forces* 63:623–42.

Kriesberg, Louis. 1979. *Social Inequality.* Englewood Cliffs, NJ: Prentice Hall.

Kromm, Jane E. 1994. "The Feminization of Madness in Visual Representation." *Feminist Studies* 20:507–35.

Krotz, Joanna L. July/August 1999. "Getting Even." *Working Woman,* pp. 42–50.

Kruttschnitt, Candace, and Donald E. Green. 1984. "The Sex-Sanctioning Issue: Is It History?" *American Sociological Review* 49:541–51.

Kumar, Awadhesh. 1982. "The Conditions of Social Mobility in Caste-System." *Indian Journal of Social Research* 23:120–25.

Kurz, Karin, and Walter Muller. 1987. "Class Mobility in the Industrial World." Pp. 417–42 in *Annual Review of Sociology,* vol. 13, edited by W. R. Scott and J. F. Short, Jr. Palo Alto, CA: Annual Reviews.

Kuznets, Simon. 1963. "Quantitative Aspects of the Economic Growth of Nations, VIII: The Distribution of Income by Size." *Economic Development and Cultural Change* 11:1–80.

Labich, Kenneth. March 8, 1993. "The New Unemployed." *Fortune,* pp. 40–49.

Lachman, Margie E., and Suzanne L. Weaver. 1998. "The Sense of Control as a Moderator of Social Class Differences in Health and Well-Being." *Journal of Personality and Social Psychology* 74:763–73.

LaFree, Gary D. 1980. "The Effect of Sexual Stratification by Race on Official Reactions to Rape." *American Sociological Review* 45:842–54.

LaFree, Gary. 1995. "Race and Crime Trends in the United States: 1946–1990." Pp. 169–93 in *Ethnic-*

ity, Race, and Crime, edited by D. F. Hawkins. Albany: State University of New York Press.

Lamb, Michael E., M. Ann Easterbrooks, and George W. Holden. 1980. "Reinforcement and Punishment among Preschoolers: Characteristics, Effects, and Correleates." *Child Development* 51:1230–36.

Landers, Susan. March 1993. "Family Leave Ushers in New Era." *NASW News* 38:1, 8.

Langeland, Willie, and Christina Hartgers. 1998. "Child Sexual and Physical Abuse and Alcoholism: A Review." *Journal of Studies on Alcohol* 59:336–48.

Lannoy, Richard. 1975. *The Speaking Tree: A Study of Indian Culture and Society.* New York: Oxford University Press.

Lapham, Lewis H. 1988. *Money and Class in America.* New York: Weidenfeld & Nicolson.

Laslett, John H. M. 1987. "The American Tradition of Labor Theory and Its Relevance to the Contemporary Working Class." Pp. 359–78 in *Theories of the Labor Movement,* edited by S. Larson and B. Nissen. Detroit: Wayne State University Press.

Lasswell, Thomas E. 1965. *Class and Stratum.* Boston: Houghton Mifflin.

Laumann, Edward O., John H. Gagnon, Robert T. Michael, and Stuart Michaels. 1994. *The Social Organization of Sexuality.* Chicago: University of Chicago Press.

Leacock, Eleanor. 1986. "Women, Power and Authority." Pp. 107–35 in *Visibility and Power: Essays on Women in Society and Development,* edited by L. Dube, E. Leacock, and S. Ardener. Delhi: Oxford University Press.

Leete, Laura, and Neil Bania. 1998. "The Impact of Welfare Reform on Local Labor Markets." *Journal of Policy Analysis and Management* 18:50–76.

Leftwich, Richard H. 1977. "Personal Income and Marginal Productivity." Pp. 78–81 in *Problems in Political Economy: An Urban Perspective,* edited by D. M. Gordon. Lexington, MA: D. C. Heath.

Lehmann, Jennifer M. 1995. "The Question of Caste in Modern Society: Durkheim's Contradictory Theories of Race, Class, and Sex." *American Sociological Review* 60:566–85.

Lemon, James T., and Gary B. Nash. 1968. "The Distribution of Wealth in the Eighteenth Century America: A Century of Change in Chester County, Pennsylvania, 1693–1802." *Journal of Social History* 2:1–24.

Lengermann, Patricia Madoo, and Jill Niebrugge-Brantley. 1988. "Contemporary Feminist Theory." Pp. 282–325 in *Contemporary Sociological Theory,* edited by George Ritzer. New York: Knopf.

Lenski, Gerhard. 1966. *Power and Privilege.* New York: McGraw-Hill.

Lenski, Gerhard. 1988. "Rethinking Macrosociological Theory." *American Sociological Review* 53:163–71.

Lenski, Gerhard, and Jean Lenski. 1982. *Human Societies: An Introduction to Macrosociology.* New York: McGraw-Hill.

Levine, Steven B. 1980. "The Rise of American Boarding Schools and the Development of a National Upper Class." *Social Problems* 28:63–94.

Levinger, George. 1966. "Marital Dissatisfaction among Divorce Applicants." *American Journal of Orthopsychiatry* 36:803–07.

Levinson, David. 1988. "Family Violence in Cross-Cultural Perspective." Pp. 435–55 in *Handbook of Family Violence,* edited by V. B. Van Hasselt, R. L. Morrison, A. S. Bellack, and M. Hersen. New York: Plenum.

Levitan, Sar A. 1985. *Programs in Aid of the Poor.* Baltimore: Johns Hopkins University Press.

Levy, Frank, and Richard J. Murnane. 1992. "U.S. Earnings Levels and Earnings Inequality: A Review of Recent Trends and Proposed Explanations." *Journal of Economic Literature* 30:1333–81.

Lewis, Helen. 1974. "Fatalism or the Coal Industry." P. 222 in *Appalachia: Its People, Heritage, and Problems,* edited by Frank S. Riddel. Dubuque, IA: Kendall/Hunt.

Lichter, Daniel T. 1988. "Racial Differences in Underemployment in American Cities." *American Journal of Sociology* 93:771–92.

Lichter, Daniel T., and David J. Eggebeen. March 1993. "Rich Kids, Poor Kids: Changing Income Inequality among American Children." *Social Forces* 71:761–80.

Lieberson, Stanley, and Donna K. Carter. 1979. "Making It in America: Differences between Eminent Blacks and White Ethnic Groups." *American Sociological Review* 44:347–66.

Liebow, Elliot. 1967. *Tally's Corner.* Boston: Little, Brown.

Light, Donald, Susanne Keller, and Craig Calhoun. 1989. *Sociology.* New York: Knopf.

Lindblom, Charles E. 1977. *Politics and Markets.* New York: Basic Books.

Lindert, Peter, and Jeffrey G. Williamson. 1976. "Three Centuries of American Inequality." Institute for Research on Poverty Discussion Paper No. 333–76. Madison: University of Wisconsin, Madison.

Link, Bruce G., Bruce P. Dohrenwend, and Andrew E. Skodol. 1986. "Socio-Economic Status and Schizophrenia: Noisome Occupational Characteristics as a Risk Factor." *American Sociological Review* 242–58.

Link, Bruce G., Jo Phelan, Michaeline Bresnahan, Ann Stueve, Robert Moore, and Ezra Susser. 1995. "Lifetime and Five-Year Prevalence of Homelessness in the United States: New Evidence on an Old Debate." *American Journal of Orthopsychiatry* 65:347–54.

Link, Bruce G., Jo C. Phelan, Ann Stueve, Robert E. Moore, Michaeline Bresnahan, and Elmer L. Struening. 1996. "Public Attitudes and Beliefs about Homeless People." Pp. 143–48 in *Homelessness in America,* edited by J. Baumohl. Phoenix, AZ: Oryx Press.

Lipman, Joanne. April 14, 1993. "The Nanny Trap: The Dark Side of Child Care Is How Poorly Workers Are Sometimes Treated." *Wall Street Journal,* pp. A1, A8.

Lipset, Seymour Martin. 1971. "Trade Unionism and the American Social Order." Pp. 7–29 in *The American Labor Movement,* edited by D. Brody. New York: Harper & Row.

Lipset, Seymour Martin. 1992. "Equal Chances versus Equal Results." *The Annals of the American Academy of Political and Social Science* 523:63–74.

Lipset, Seymour Martin, and Reinhard Bendix. 1959. *Social Mobility in Industrial Society.* Berkeley: University of California Press.

Lipset, Seymour Martin, and Hans L. Zetterberg. 1959. "Social Mobility in Industrial Societies." Pp. 11–75 in *Social Mobility in Industrial Society,* edited by S. M. Lipset and R. Bendix. Berkeley: University of California Press.

Lo, Jeannie. 1990. *Office Ladies, Factory Women: Life and Work at a Japanese Company.* Armonk, NY: M. E. Sharpe.

Loewenstein, Gaither. 1985. "The New Underclass: A Contemporary Sociological Dilemma." *Sociological Quarterly* 26:35–48.

Loftin, Colin, and Robert H. Hill. 1974. "Regional Subculture and Homicide: An Examination of the Gastil-Hackney Thesis." *American Sociological Review* 39:714–24.

Long, J. Scott, and Mary Frank Fox. 1995. "Scientific Careers: Universalism and Particularism." Pp. 45–71 in *Annual Review of Sociology 1995,* edited by J. Hagan and K. S. Cook. Palo Alto, CA: Annual Reviews.

Lopreato, Joseph. 1965. *Vilfredo Pareto: Selections from his Treatise.* New York: Thomas Y. Crowell.

Lopreato, Joseph, and Lawrence E. Hazelrigg. 1972. *Class, Conflict, and Mobility.* Corte Madera, CA: Chandler & Sharp.

Lopreato, Joseph, and Lionel S. Lewis. 1963. "An Analysis of Variables in the Functional Theory of Stratification." *Sociological Quarterly* 4:301–10.

Lopreato, Joseph, and Lionel S. Lewis, eds. 1974. *Social Stratification: A Reader.* New York: Harper & Row.

Loprest, Pamela. 1999. *Families Who Left Welfare: Who Are They and How Are They Doing?* Washington, D.C.: The Urban Institute.

Lorber, Judith. 1996. "Beyond the Binaries: Depolarizing the Categories of Sex. Sexuality, and Gender." *Sociological Inquiry* 66:143–59.

Loring, Marti, and Brian Powell. 1988. "Gender, Race, and DSM-III: A Study of the Objectivity of Psychiatric Behavior," *Journal of Health and Social Behavior.* 29:1–22.

Loury, Glenn C. 1992. "Incentive Effects of Affirmative Action." *The Annals of the American Academy of Political and Social Science* 523:19–29.

Low, Jason, and Peter Sherrard. 1999. "Portrayal of Women in Sexuality and Marriage and Family Textbooks: A Content Analysis of Photographs from the 1970s to the 1990s." *Sex Roles* 40:309–18.

Lowe, Marian, and Ruth Hubbard, eds. 1983. *Women's Nature: Rationalizations of Inequality.* New York: Pergamon.

Luft, H. S. 1983. "Health Maintenance Organizations." Pp. 318–51 in *Handbook of Health, Health Care, and the Health Professions,* edited by D. Mechanic. New York: The Free Press.

Luibheid, Eithne. 1998. "'Looking Like a Lesbian': The Organization of Sexual Monitoring at the United States-Mexican Border." *Journal of the History of Sexuality* 8:477–506.

Lurie, Alison. 1987. "Fashion and Status." Pp. 124–30 in *The Social World,* 3rd ed., edited by Ian Robertson. New York: Worth Publishers.

Lurie, Nancy Oestreich. 1982. "The American Indian: Historical Background." Pp. 131–44 in *Majority & Minority: The Dynamics of Race and Ethnicity in American Life,* 3rd ed., edited by N. R. Yetman and C. H. Steele. Boston: Allyn and Bacon.

Lyman, Rick. February 24, 1999. "Man Guilty of Murder in Texas Dragging Death." *New York Times,* pp. A1, A12.

Lynn, Laurence E., Jr. 1977. "A Decade of Policy Developments in the Income-Maintenance System." Pp. 55–117 in *A Decade of Federal Antipoverty Programs,* edited by R. H. Haveman. New York: Academic Press.

Lystad, M. H. 1975. "Violence at Home: A Review of the Literature." *American Journal of Orthopsychiatry* 45:328–45.

MacCormack, Carol P. 1980. "Nature, Culture and Gender: A Critique." Pp. 1–24 in *Nature, Culture and Gender,* edited by C. MacCormack and M. Strathern. Cambridge: Cambridge University Press.

MacCormack, Carol, and Marilyn Strathern, eds. 1980. *Nature, Culture and Gender.* Cambridge: Cambridge University Press.

MacIver, Robert M. 1964. *Power Transformed.* New York: Random House.

MacLeod, Jay. 1987. *Ain't No Makin' It: Leveled Aspirations in a Low-Income Neighborhood.* Boulder, CO: Westview.

Madon, Stephanie. 1997. "What Do People Believe about Gay Males? A Study of Stereotype Content and Strength." *Sex Roles* 37:663–85.

Maguire, Kathleen, and Ann L. Pastore. 1995. *Sourcebook of Criminal Justice Statistics—1994*. U.S. Department of Justice, Bureau of Justice Statistics. Washington, D.C.: U.S. Government Printing Office.

Maguire, Kathleen, and Ann L. Pastore, eds. 1997. *Sourcebook of Criminal Justice Statistics 1996*. Washington, D.C.: U.S. Department of Justice.

Main, Jackson T. 1976. "The Distribution of Property in Colonial Connecticut." Pp. 54–104 in *The Human Dimensions of Nation Making*, edited by Martin James Kirby. Madison, WI: The State Historical Society.

Makinson, Larry, and Joshua Goldstein. 1994. *Open Secrets: The Encyclopedia of Congressional Money and Politics*. Washington, D.C.: Congressional Quarterly.

Manderscheid, Ronald W., and Sally A. Barrett, eds. 1987. *Mental Health, United States, 1987*. Washington, D.C.: U.S. Government Printing Office.

Manderscheid, Ronald W., and Mary Anne Sonnenschein, eds. 1992. *Mental Health, United States, 1992*. Washington, D.C.: U.S. Department of Health and Human Services.

Manley, John F. 1983. "Neo-Pluralism: A Class Analysis of Pluralism I and Pluralism II." *American Political Science Review* 77:368–83.

Marden, Charles F., and Gladys Meyer. 1973. *Minorities in American Society*. New York: Van Nostrand.

Mare, Robert D. 1982. "Socioeconomic Effects on Child Mortality in the United States." *American Journal of Public Health* 72:539–47.

Mare, Robert D., and Meei-Shenn Tzeng. 1989. "Fathers' Ages and the Social Stratification of Sons." *American Journal of Sociology* 95:108–31.

Marger, Martin. 1997. *Race and Ethnic Relations*. Belmont, CA: Wadsworth.

Margolin, Gayla, Linda Gorin Sibner, and Lisa Gleberman. 1988. "Wife Battering." Pp. 89–117 in *Handbook of Family Violence*, edited by V. B. Van Hasselt, R. L. Morrison, A. S. Bellack, and M. Hersen. New York: Plenum.

Markham, Edwin. 1958. "The Man with the Hoe." Reprinted in *One Hundred and One Famous Poems*, compiled by R. J. Cook. Chicago: Reilly & Lee. (poem is out of print).

Markham, William T., Patrick O. Macken, Charles M. Bonjean, and Judy Corder. 1983. "A Note on Sex, Geographic Mobility, and Career Advancement." *Social Forces* 61:1138–46.

Markham, William T., and Joseph H. Pleck. 1986. "Sex and Willingness to Move for Occupational Advancement: Some National Results." *The Sociological Quarterly* 27:121–43.

Marshall, Gordon, Adam Swift, and Stephen Roberts. 1997. *Against the Odds? Social Class and Social Justice in Industrial Societies*. New York: Oxford University Press.

Marshall, Ray, and Beth Paulin. 1987. "Employment and Earnings of Women: Historical Perspective." Pp. 1–36 in *Working Women: Past, Present, Future*, edited by K. S. Koziara, M. H. Moskow, and L. D. Tanner. Washington, D.C.: Bureau of National Affairs.

Martin, M. Kay, and Barbara Voorhies. 1975. *Female of the Species*. New York: Columbia.

Martyna, W. 1978. "What Does 'He' Mean? Use of the Generic Masculine." *Journal of Communication* 28:131–38.

Marx, Karl. 1967. *Capital*, vol. I. New York: International Publishers.

Marx, Karl, and Federick Engels. 1969 and 1970. *Selected Works*, vols. 1, 2, 3. Moscow: Progress Publishers.

Massey, Douglas S. 1995. Review of the Bell Curve. *American Journal of Sociology* 101:747–53.

Massey, Douglas S., and Nancy A. Denton. 1993. *American Apartheid*. Cambridge, MA: Harvard University Press.

Matras, Judah. 1975. *Social Inequality, Stratification, and Mobility*. Englewood Cliffs, NJ: Prentice Hall.

Matras, Judah. 1980. "Comparative Social Mobility." Pp. 401–31 in *Annual Review of Sociology*, vol. 6, edited by A. Inkeles, N. J. Smelser, and R. H. Turner. Palo Alto, CA: Annual Reviews.

Matthaei, Julie A. 1982. *An Economic History of Women in America*. New York: Schocken Books.

Matthews, Donald R. 1954. "United States Senators and the Class Structure." *Public Opinion Quarterly* 18:5–22. Reprinted on pp. 331–342 in *Social Stratification: A Reader*, edited by J. Lopreato and L. S. Lewis. New York: Harper & Row.

Maume, David J. Jr., 1999. "Occupational Segregation and the Career Mobility of White Men and Women." *Social Forces* 77:1433–59.

Mayer, Kurt B. 1972. "The Changing Shape of the American Class Structure." Pp. 62–69 in *Status Communities in Modern Society*, edited by Holger R. Stub. Hinsdale, IL: Dryden.

Mayer, Kurt B., and Walter Buckley. 1970. *Class & Society*. New York: Random House.

McAdam, Doug. 1982. *Political Process and the Development of Black Insurgency. 1930–1970*. Chicago: University of Chicago Press.

McAdam, Doug. 1983. "Tactical Innovation and the Pace of Insurgency." *American Sociological Review* 48:735–54.

McAneny, Leslie. 1994. "Ethnic Minorities View the Media's View of Them." *The Gallup Poll Monthly* 346:31–41.

McCarthy, John D., and Mayer N. Zald. 1973. *The Trend of Social Movements in America: Professionalization and Resource Mobilization*. Morristown, NJ: General Learning Press.

McCarthy, John D., and Mayer N. Zald. 1977. "Resource Mobilization and Social Movements: A Partial Theory." *American Journal of Sociology* 82:1212–14.

McClelland, David C. 1961. *The Achieving Society.* New York: The Free Press.

McClendon, McKee J. 1976. "The Occupational Status Attainment Processes of Males and Females." *American Sociological Review* 41:52–64.

McCloskey, Laura Ann. 1996. "Socioeconomic and Coercive Power within the Family." *Gender & Society* 10:449–63.

McDonough, Peggy, David R. Williams, James S. House, and Greg J. Duncan. 1999. "Gender and the Socioeconomic Gradient in Mortality." *Journal of Health and Social Behavior* 40:17–31.

McFate, Katherine. 1985. "Defining the Underclass: A Contemporary Sociological Dilemma." *The Sociological Quarterly* 26:35–38.

McFate, Katherine. June 1987. "Defining the Underclass." *Focus,* pp. 8–12.

McIntosh, Peggy. 1988. "White Privilege and Male Privilege: A Personal Account of Coming to See Correspondences through Work in Women's Studies." Center for Research on Women Working Paper No. 189. Wellesley, MA: Wellesley College.

McKissack Fredrick L. Jr., June 1998. "Cyberghetto: Blacks Are Falling through the Net." *The Progressive,* pp. 20–22.

McRoberts, Hugh A., and Kevin Selbee. 1981. "Trends in Occupational Mobility in Canada and the United States: A Comparison." *American Sociological Review* 46:406–21.

Mead, Margaret. 1963. *Sex and Temperament in Three Primitive Societies.* New York: William Morrow.

"Measuring the Effects of the Reagan Welfare Changes on the Work Effort and Well-Being of Single Parents." Spring 1985. *Focus,* pp. 1–8.

Meiksins, Peter F. 1988. "A Critique of Wright's Theory of Contradictory Class Locations," *Critical Sociology* 15:73–82.

Meisel, James H., ed. 1965. *Pareto & Mosca.* Englewood Cliffs, NJ: Prentice Hall.

Melchionno, Rick. Spring 1999. "The Changing Temporary Work Force." *Occupational Outlook Quarterly,* pp. 25–32.

Memmi, Albert. 1965. *The Colonizer and the Colonized.* New York: Orion.

Merten, Don E. 1997. "The Meaning of Meanness: Popularity, Competition, and Conflict among Junior High School Girls." *Sociology of Education* 70:175–91.

Messner, Steven F. 1980. "Income Inequality and Murder Rates: Some Cross-National Findings." *Comparative Social Research* 3:185–98.

Messner, Steven F. 1989. "Economic Discrimination and Societal Homicide Rates: Further Evidence on the Cost of Inequality." *American Sociological Review* 54:597–611.

Messner, Steven F., and Richard Rosenfeld. 1994. *Crime and the American Dream.* Belmont, CA: Wadsworth.

Meyer, Ilan H., and Laura Dean. 1998. "Internalized Homophobia, Intimacy, and Sexual Behavior among Gay and Bisexual Men." Pp. 160–86 in *Stigma and Sexual Orientation,* edited by G. M. Herek. Thousand Oaks, CA: Sage.

Meyer, Jack A. Summer 1999. "Assessing Welfare Reform: Work Pays." *The Public Interest,* pp. 113–20.

Meyers, Marcia Clark. 1979. "Presbyterian Home Missions in Appalachia, A Feminine Enterprise." M. Div. Thesis, Princeton Theological Seminary.

Meyerson, Harold. May 25, 1992. "Fractured City." *The New Republic,* pp. 23–25.

Michalowski, Raymond J. 1985. *Order, Law, and Crime.* New York: Random House.

Miech, Richard A., Avshalom Caspi, Terrie E. Moffitt, Bradley R. Entner Wright, and Phil A. Silva. 1999. "Low Socioeconomic Status and Mental Disorders: A Longitudinal Study of Selection and Causation during Young Adulthood." *American Journal of Sociology* 104:1096–1131.

Miles-Doan, Rebecca. 1998. "Violence between Spouses and Intimates: Does Neighborhood Context Matter?" *Social Forces* 77:623–45.

Miliband, Ralph. 1977. *Marxism and Politics.* New York: Oxford University Press.

Miller, Casey, and Kate Swift. 1993. "Women and Names." Pp. 77–84 in *Experiencing Race, Class, and Gender in the United States,* edited by Virginia Cyrus. Mountain View, CA: Mayfield.

Miller, S. M. 1963. *Max Weber: Selections from His Work.* New York: Thomas Y. Crowell.

Miller, S. M. 1975. "Comparative Social Mobility." Reprinted in part on pp. 79–112 in *Social Mobility,* edited by A. P. M. Coxon and C. L. Jones. Baltimore: Penguin.

Miller, S. M., and Pamela Roby. 1970. *The Future of Inequality.* New York: Basic Books.

Miller, William Lee. 1977. *Welfare and Values in America: A Review of Attitudes toward Welfare and Welfare Policies in Light of American History and Culture.* Durham, NC: Welfare Policy Project, Institute of Policy Sciences and Public Affairs of Duke University, The Ford Foundation.

Mills, C. Wright. 1951. *White Collar.* New York: Oxford University Press.

Mills, C. Wright. 1956. *The Power Elite.* New York: Oxford University Press.

Mills, C. Wright. 1959. *The Sociological Imagination.* New York: Oxford University Press.

Mills, C. Wright. 1962. *The Marxists*. New York: Dell.

Milner, Murray, Jr. 1987. "Theories of Inequality: An Overview and a Strategy for Synthesis." *Social Forces* 65:1053–84.

Milner, Murray, Jr. 1994. *Status and Sacredness*. New York: Oxford University Press.

Mincer, Jacob, and Solomon Polachek. 1974. "Family Investments in Human Capital: Earnings of Women." *Journal of Political Economy* 82:76–110.

Miniter, Richard. July 1999. "The False Promise of Slave Redemption." *Atlantic Monthly*, pp. 63–70.

Mintz, Beth. 1975. "The President's Cabinet, 1897–1972: A Contribution to the Power Structure Debate." *Insurgent Sociologist* 5:131–48.

Mirer, Thad W. 1974. "Aspects of the Variability of Family Income." In *Five Thousand American Families: Patterns of Economic Progress,* vol. 2, edited by J. N. Morgan et al. Ann Arbor, MI: Institute for Social Research.

Mirowsky, John, and Catherine E. Ross. 1983. "Paranoia and the Structure of Powerlessness." *American Sociological Review* 48:228–39.

Mirowsky, John, and Catherine E. Ross. 1986. "Social Patterns of Distress." Pp. 23–45 in *Annual Review of Sociology,* vol. 12, edited by R. H. Turner and J. F. Short, Jr. Palo Alto, CA: Annual Reviews.

Mirowsky, John, and Catherine E. Ross. 1995. "Sex Differences in Distress: Real or Artifact?" *American Sociological Review* 60:449–68.

Mishel, Lawrence, and Gary Burtless. 1995. *Recent Wage Trends: The Implications for Low Wage Workers*. Washington, D.C.: Economic Policy Institute.

Mitzman, Arthur. 1971. *The Iron Cage: An Historical Interpretation of Max Weber*. New York: Grosset & Dunlap.

"Mixed Messages." April 12, 1993. *Newsweek*, pp. 28–29.

Montgomery, David. 1983. "The Past and Future of Workers' Control." Pp. 389–405 in *Workers' Struggles, Past and Present: A "Radical America" Reader,* edited by James Green. Philadelphia: Temple University Press.

Moore, Thomas S., and Vicky Selkowe. 1999. *The Growing Crisis among Wisconsin's Poorest Families: A Comparison of Welfare Caseload Declines and Trends in the State's Poverty Population—1986–1997*. Milwaukee: Institute for Wisconsin's Future.

Moore, Wilbert E. 1970. "But Some Are More Equal than Others." Pp. 143–48 in *The Logic of Social Hierarchies,* edited by E. O. Laumann, P. M. Siegel, and R. W. Hodge. Skokie, IL: Markham.

Morris, Aldon D. 1984. *The Origins of the Civil Rights Movement: Black Communities Organizing for Change*. New York: The Free Press.

Morris, Michael, and John B. Williamson. 1986. *Poverty and Public Policy: An Analysis of Federal Intervention Efforts*. New York: Greenwood Press.

Mukhopadhyay, Carol C., and Patricia Higgins. 1988. "Anthropological Studies of Women's Status Revisited: 1977–1987." Pp. 461–95 in *Annual Review of Anthropology,* vol. 17, edited by B. J. Siegel, A. R. Beals, and S. A. Tyler. Palo Alto, CA: Annual Reviews.

Muller, Edward. 1988. "Democracy, Economic Development, and Income Inequality." *American Sociological Review* 53:50–68.

Mullins, Elizabeth I., and Paul Sites. 1984. "The Origins of Contemporary Eminent Black Americans: A Three-Generation Analysis of Social Origins." *American Sociological Review* 49:672–85.

Murray, Charles. Summer 1982. "The Two Wars against Poverty: Economic Growth and the Great Society." *The Public Interest,* pp. 3–16.

Murray, Charles. 1984. *Losing Ground: American Social Policy 1950–1980*. New York: Basic Books.

Murray, Charles. 1985. "Have the Poor Been 'Losing Ground'?" *Political Science Quarterly* 100:427–45.

Murray, Charles. Summer 1986. "No, Welfare Isn't Really the Problem." *The Public Interest,* pp. 3–11.

Murray, Stephen O. 1996. *American Gay*. Chicago: University of Chicago Press.

Myrdal, Gunnar. 1944. *An American Dilemma: The Negro Problem and Modern Democracy*. New York: Harper and Brothers.

Nagel, S. S. 1969. *The Legal Process from a Behavioral Perspective*. Homewood, IL: Dorsey.

Nagel, S. S., and L. J. Weitzman. 1971. "Women as Litigants." *Hastings Law Journal* 23:171–98.

Nasar, Sylvia. August 16, 1992. "The Rich Get Richer, But Never the Same Way Twice." *New York Times,* p. E3.

National Center for Health Statistics. 1988. *Vital Statistics of the United States. 1986,* Vol. II, Mortality, Part B. DHHS Pub. No. (PHS) 88–1114. Public Health Service. Washington, D.C.: U.S. Government Printing Office.

National Center for Health Statistics. 1992. *Health United States 1991*. Hyattsville, MD: Public Health Service.

National Center for Health Statistics. 1998. *Health, United States, 1998 with Socioeconomic Status and Health Chartbook*. Hyattsville, MD: National Center for Health Statistics.

National Coalition for the Homeless. February 1999. "Who Is Homeless?" *NCH Fact Sheet #5*. Washington, D.C.: Author.

National Governors' Association Center for Best Practices. 1999. *Round Two Summary of Selected Elements of State Programs for Temporary Assistance for Needy Families.* Washington, D.C.: National Governors' Association.

National Telecommunications and Information Administration. 1999. *Falling through the Net: Defining the Digital Divide.* Washington, D.C.: U.S. Government Printing Office.

Neft, Naomi, and Ann D. Levine. 1997. *Where Women Stand.* New York: Random House.

"Nest-Egg Planning for the Not-So-Average Joe." July 21, 1997. *Business Week,* pp. 78–84.

Newman, Donald J. 1958. "White-Collar Crime: An Overview and Analysis." *Law and Contemporary Problems* 23:735–53.

Newman, Katherine S. 1989. *Falling from Grace.* New York: Vintage.

Newman, Katherine S. 1993. *Declining Fortunes.* New York: Basic Books.

Newport, Frank. July 1998. "Americans Remain More Likely to Believe Sexual Orientation Due to Environment, Not Genetics." *The Gallup Poll Monthy,* pp. 14–16.

Nicholson, Linda J. 1984. "Making Our Marx." *The Women's Review of Books* 1:8–9.

Nielsen, Francois. 1994. "Income Inequality and Industrial Development: Dualism Revisited." *American Sociological Review* 59:654–77.

Nielsen, Francois. 1995. Review of the Bell Curve. *Social Forces* 74:337–41.

Nielsen, Francois, and Arthur S. Alderson. 1995. "Income Inequality, Development, and Dualism: Results from an Unbalanced Cross-National Panel." *American Sociological Review* 60:674–701.

Nilson, Linda Burzotta. 1974. "The Occupational and Sex Related Components of Social Standing." Ph.D. Dissertation, Madison: University of Wisconsin.

Nisbet, Robert A. 1966. *The Sociological Tradition.* New York: Basic Books.

Noel, Donald L. 1968. "A Theory of the Origin of Ethnic Stratification." *Social Problems* 16:157–72. Reprinted on pp. 109–20 in *Majority and Minority: The Dynamics of Race and Ethnicity in American Life,* edited by N. R. Yetman. 1985. Boston: Allyn and Bacon.

Noland, Cheryl. July 2, 1993. "Tries to Play by the Rules, But Is Beaten by the System." *The Canton Repository,* p. A-5.

Northrup, Herbert R. 1985. "The Coal Mines." Pp. 159–71 in *Blacks in Appalachia,* edited by W. H. Turner and E. J. Cabbell. Lexington, KY: University Press of Kentucky.

Nozick, Robert. 1977. "Distributive Justice." Pp. 120–28 in *Justice: Selected Readings,* edited by J. Feinberg and H. Gross. Encino, CA: Dickenson Publishing.

Oberschall, Anthony. 1973. *Social Conflict and Social Movements.* Englewood Cliffs, NJ: Prentice Hall.

O'Connor, James. 1973. *The Fiscal Crisis of the State.* New York: St. Martin's Press.

Offe, Claus. 1973. "Class Rule and the Political System: On the Selectiveness of Political Institutions." Mimeographed paper. A Translation of Chapter 3 of *Strukturprobleme des Kapitaliistischen Staates.* Frankfurt: Suhrkamp.

Offe, Claus. 1975. "The Theory of the Capitalist State and the Problem of Policy Formation." In *Stress and Contradiction in Modern Capitalism,* edited by L. Lindberg et al. Lexington, MA: D. C. Heath.

O'Hare, William P. 1987. *America's Welfare Population: Who Gets What?* Publication No. 13. Washington, D.C.: Population Reference Bureau.

Okun, Arthur. 1975. *Equality and Efficiency: The Big Tradeoff.* Washington, D.C.: Brookings Institution.

Oliver, Thomas R. 1991. "Health Care Market Reform in Congress: The Uncertain Path from Proposal to Policy." *Political Science Quarterly* 106:453–77.

Oliver, Melvin, and Thomas Shapiro. 1995. *Black Wealth and White Wealth: A New Perspective on Racial Inequality.* New York: Routledge.

Ollman, Bertell. 1968. "Marx's Use of Class." *American Journal of Sociology* 73:573–80.

Ollman, Bertell. 1987. "How to Study Class Consciousness and Why We Should." *The Insurgent Sociologist* 14:57–96.

Olsen, Marvin E. 1970a. *Power of Societies.* New York: Macmillan.

Olsen, Marvin E. 1970b. "Social and Political Participation of Blacks." *American Sociological Review* 35: 682–97.

Olzak, Susan, Suzanne Shanahan, and Elizabeth H. McEneaney. 1996. "Poverty, Segregation, and Race Riots: 1960 to 1993." *American Sociological Review* 61:590–613.

Omi, Michael, and Howard Winant. 1986. *Racial Formation in the United States: From the 1960s to the 1980s.* New York: Routledge, Kegan and Paul.

Orlans, Harold, and June O'Neill. 1992. "Preface." *The Annals of the American Academy of Political and Social Science* 523:7–9.

Ornati, Oscar. 1966. *Poverty Amid Affluence.* New York: The Twentieth Century Fund.

Ortner, Sherry B. 1974. "Is Female to Male as Nature Is to Culture?" Pp. 67–87 in *Woman, Culture & Society,* edited by M. Z. Rosaldo and L. Lamphere. Stanford, CA: Stanford University Press.

Ortner, Sherry B., and Harriet Whitehead, eds. 1981. *Sexual Meanings: The Cultural Construction of Gender and Sexuality.* Cambridge: Cambridge University Press.

Ossowski, Stanislaw. 1963. *Class Structure in the Social Consciousness.* New York: The Free Press.

Osterman, Paul. 1975. "An Empirical Study of Labor Market Segmentation." *Industrial and Labor Relations Review* 28:508–23.

Ostrander, Susan. 1984. *Women of the Upper Class.* Philadelphia: Temple University Press.

O'Sullivan, Katherine, and William J. Wilson. 1988. "Race and Ethnicity." Pp. 223–242 in *Handbook of Sociology,* edited by N. J. Smelser. Newbury Park, CA: Sage.

Otto, Luther B., and David L. Featherman. 1975. "Social Structural and Psychological Antecedents of Self-Estrangement and Powerlessness." *American Sociological Review* 40:701–19.

Page, Charles H. 1969. *Class and American Sociology: From Ward to Ross.* New York: Schocken Books.

Paradiso, Louis V., and Shauvan M. Wall. 1986. "Children's Perceptions of Male and Female Principals and Teachers." *Sex Roles* 14:1–7.

Parcel, Toby L., and Charles W. Mueller. 1983. *Ascriptions and Labor Markets: Race and Sex Differences in Earnings.* New York: Academic Press.

Parcel, Toby L., and Marie B. Sickmeier. 1988. "One Firm, Two Labor Markets: The Case of McDonald's in the Fast-Food Industry." *Sociological Quarterly* 29:29–46.

Parenti, Michael. 1970. "Power and Pluralism: A View from the Bottom." *The Journal of Politics* 32:501–30.

Parkin, Frank. 1971. *Class Inequality and Political Order.* New York: Praeger.

Parkin, Frank. 1979. *Marxism and Class Theory: A Bourgeois Critique.* London: Tavistock.

Parlee, Mary Brown. 1979. "Conversational Politics." *Psychology Today* 12:48–91.

Parsons, Talcott. 1964a. "A Revised Analytical Approach to the Theory of Social Stratification." Reprinted on pp. 386–439 in *Essays in Sociological Theory,* rev. ed., by T. Parsons. 1964. New York: The Free Press.

Parsons, Talcott. 1964b. *Essays in Sociological Theory,* rev. ed. New York: The Free Press.

Parsons, Talcott, and Robert F. Bales. 1955. *Family, Socialization and Interaction Process.* New York: The Free Press.

Paternoster, Raymond. 1984. "Prosecutorial Discretion in Requesting the Death Penalty: A Case of Victim-Based Racial Discrimination." *Law & Society Review* 18:437–78.

Pavalko, Eliza K., and Brad Smith. 1999. "The Rhythm of Work: Health Effects of Women's Work Dynamics." *Social Forces* 77:1141–62.

Pearce, Diana M. 1984. "Farewell to Alms: Women's Fare Under Welfare." Pp. 502–515 in *Women: A Feminist Perspective,* edited by J. Freeman. Palo Alto, CA: Mayfield.

Pearlin, L. I., E. G. Menaghan, M. A. Lieberman, and J. T. Mullan. 1981. "The Stress Process." *Journal of Health and Social Behavior* 22:337–56.

Pearlin, Leonard I. 1975. "Status Inequality and Stress in Marriage." *American Sociological Review* 40:344–57.

Pease, John, William H. Form, and Joan Huber Rytina. 1970. "Ideological Currents in American Stratification Literature." *The American Sociologist* 5:127–37.

Perlman, Selig. 1923. *A History of Trade Unionism in the United States.* New York: Macmillan.

Perlman, Selig. 1928. *A Theory of the Labor Movement.* New York: Macmillan.

Perlman, Selig, and Philip Taft. 1935. *History of Labor in the United States, 1896–1932. Volume IV: Labor Movements.* New York: Macmillan.

Perrone, Luca. 1983. "Positional Power and Propensity to Strike." *Politics and Society* 12:231–61.

Person, James E., Jr. 1993. *Statistical Forecasts of the United States.* Detroit: Gale Research.

Pessen, Edward. 1973. *Riches, Class and Power Before the Civil War.* Lexington MA: D. C. Heath.

Pettigrew, Thomas F. 1985. "New Black-White Patterns: How Best to Conceptualize Them." Pp. 329–46 in *Annual Review of Sociology,* edited by R. H. Turner and J. F. Short, Jr. Palo Alto, CA: Annual Reviews.

Phelan, Jo, Bruce G. Link, Robert E. Moore, and Ann Stueve. 1997. "The Stigma of Homelessness: The Impact of the Label 'Homeless' on Attitudes toward Poor Persons." *Social Psychology Quarterly* 60:323–37.

Phelps, Linda. 1981. "Patriarchy and Capitalism." Pp. 161–73 in *Building Feminist Theory: Essays from Quest.* New York: Longman.

Philipson, Ilene J., and Karen V. Hansen. 1990. "Women, Class, and the Feminist Imagination: An Introduction." Pp. 3–40 in *Women, Class, and the Feminist Imagination: A Socialist-Feminist Reader,* edited by K. V. Hansen and I. J. Philipson. Philadelphia: Temple University Press.

Physician Task Force on Hunger in America. 1985. *Hunger in America: The Growing Epidemic.* Middletown, CT: Wesleyan University Press.

Pierini, David. June 2, 1992. "Doubts Raised about Welfare Reform Plan." *Kalamazoo Gazette,* p. C1.

Piori, Michael J. 1977. "The Dual Labor Market: Theory and Implications." Pp. 93–97 in *Problems in Political Economy: An Urban Perspective,* edited by D. M. Gordon. Lexington, MA: D. C. Heath.

Piven, Frances Fox, and Richard A. Cloward. 1971. *Regulating the Poor: The Functions of Public Welfare.* New York: Random House.

Piven, Frances Fox, and Richard A. Cloward. 1977. *Poor People's Movements: Why They Succeed, How They Fail.* New York: Pantheon.

Piven, Frances Fox, and Richard A. Cloward. 1982. *The New Class War.* New York: Pantheon.

Piven, Frances Fox, and Richard A. Cloward. 1987. "The Historical Sources of the Contemporary Relief Debate." Pp. 3–43 in *The Mean Season: The Attack on the Welfare State,* edited by F. Block, R. A. Cloward, B. Ehrenreich, and F. F. Piven. New York: Pantheon.

Plotnick, Robert. 1977. "Welfare Expenditures and the Poor: The 1965–1976 Experience and Future Expectations." Institute for Research on Poverty Discussion Paper No. 443–77. Madison: University of Wisconsin.

Plotnick, Robert D., and Felicity Skidmore. 1975. *Progress against Poverty: A Review of the 1964–1974 Decade.* New York: Academic Press.

Plous, S. 1996. "The Affirmative Action Debate: What's Fair in Policy and Programs?" *Journal of Social Issues* 52:25–31.

Plutzer, Eric. 1988. "Work Life, Family Life, and Women's Support of Feminism." *American Sociological Review* 53:640–49.

Pomer, Marshall I. 1986. "Labor Market Structure, Intragenerational Mobility, and Discrimination: Black Male Advancement Out of Low-Paying Occupations. 1962–1973." *American Sociological Review* 51:650–59.

Pope, Charles. January 9, 1999. "New Congress Is Older, More Politically Seasoned." *Congressional Quarterly Weekly,* pp. 60–63.

Porter, James N. 1974. "Race, Socialization, and Mobility in Educational and Early Occupational Attainment." *American Sociological Review* 39:303–16.

Porter, John. 1965. *The Vertical Mosaic: An Analysis of Social Class and Power in Canada.* Toronto: University of Toronto.

Porter, John. April 1967. "The Future of Upward Mobility." Lecture, Ohio Valley Sociological Association Meeting.

Portes, Alejandro, Kenneth L. Wilson. 1976. "Black-White Differences in Educational Attainment." *American Sociological Review* 41:414–31.

Poulantzas, Nico. 1973. *Political Power and Social Classes.* London: New Left Books.

"Poverty in the United States: Where Do We Stand Now?" Winter 1984. *Focus.* Madison: Institute for Research on Poverty, University of Wisconsin.

Powell, G. Bingham, Jr. 1986. "American Voter Turnout in Comparative Perspective." *American Political Science Review* 80:17–43.

Powers, Charles H. 1987. *Vilfredo Pareto.* Beverly Hills, CA: Sage.

Praeger, Jeffrey. 1987. "The Meaning of Difference: A Response to Michael Banton." *Ethnic and Racial Studies* 10:469–72.

Presser, Harriet B. 1998. "Toward a 24 Hour Economy: The U.S. Experience and Implications for the Family." Pp. 39–47 in *Challenges for Work and Family in the Twenty-First Century,* edited by D. Vannoy and P. J. Dubeck. New York: Aldine de Gruyter.

Presthus, Robert. 1962. *The Organizational Society.* New York: Vintage Books.

Prewitt, Kenneth, and Alan Stone. 1973. *The Ruling Elites.* New York: Harper & Row.

"Pricey Sneakers in Inner City Help Set Nation's Fashion Trend." December 1, 1988. *The Wall Street Journal,* pp. A1, A6.

Public Citizen. 1999. *NAFTA at Five: School of Real Life Results.* http://www.citizen.org/pctrade/nafta/reports/5years.htm

Quinney, Richard. 1970. *The Social Reality of Crime.* Boston: Little, Brown.

Quinney, Richard. 1974. *Criminology: Analysis and Critique of Crime in the United States.* Boston: Little, Brown.

Raabe, Phyllis Hutton. 1998. "Being a Part-Time Manager: One Way to Combine Family and Career." Pp. 81–91 in *Challenges for Work and Family in the Twenty-First Century,* edited by D. Vannoy and P. J. Dubeck. New York: Aldine de Gruyter.

Radelet, Michael L. 1981. "Racial Characteristics and the Imposition of the Death Penalty." *American Sociological Review* 46:918–27.

Radzinowicz, L. 1971. "Economic Conditions and Crime." In *The Criminal in Society,* edited by L. Radzinowicz and M. Wolfgang. New York: Basic Books.

Rainwater, Lee. 1974. *What Money Buys.* New York: Basic Books.

Ransdell, Eric. April 26, 1993. "South Africa on the Brink." *U.S. News and World Report* 114:43–44.

Ransford, H. Edward, and Jon Miller. 1983. "Race, Sex and Feminist Outlooks." *American Sociological Review* 48:46–59.

Record, Wilson. 1987. "White Sociologists and Black Studies." Paper presented at the Annual Meeting of the American Sociological Association, New Orleans.

"Record Number of Women, Blacks in Congress." November 12, 1988. *Congressional Quarterly* 46:3293–95.

Rector, Robert. March–April 1997. "Wisconsin's Welfare Miracle." *Policy Review,* No. 82.

Redburn, F. Stevens, and Terry F. Buss. 1986. *Responding to America's Homeless: Public Policy Alternatives.* New York: Praeger.

Redmond, Sonjia Parker. 1988. "An Analysis of the General Well-Being of Blacks and Whites: Results of a National Study." *Journal of Sociology and Social Welfare* 15:57–71.

Reich, Michael. 1977. "The Economics of Racism." Pp. 183–88 in *Problems in Political Economy: An Urban Perspective,* edited by D. M. Gordon. Lexington, MA: D. C. Heath.

Reich, Michael, David M. Gordon, and Richard C. Edwards. 1977. "A Theory of Labor Market Segmentation." Pp. 108–13 in *Problems in Political Economy: An Urban Perspective,* edited by D. M. Gordon. Lexington, MA: D. C. Heath.

Reid, Pamela Trotman. 1984. "Feminism versus Minority Group Identity: Not for Black Woman Only." *Sex Roles* 10:247–55.

Reid, Sue Titus. 1988. *Crime and Criminology.* New York: Holt, Rinehart and Winston.

Reiss, Albert J., Jr., ed. 1961. *Occupations and Social Status.* New York: The Free Press.

Reissman, Leonard. 1959. *Class in American Society.* Glencoe, IL: The Free Press.

Reskin, Barbara F. 1984. "Introduction." Pp. 1–7 in *Sex Segregation in the Workplace: Trends, Explanations, Remedies,* edited by B. F. Reskin. Washington, D.C.: National Academy Press.

Reskin, Barbara F. 1988. "Occupational Resegregation." Pp. 258–63 in *The American Woman 1988–89: A Status Report,* edited by Sara E. Rix. New York: W. W. Norton.

Richards, Robert K. 1986. "The Declining Status of Women…Revisited." *Sociological Focus* 19:315–32.

Richardson, Laurel. 1987. *The Dynamics of Sex and Gender: A Sociological Perspective.* New York: Harper & Row.

Richmond, Anthony H. September/December 1990. "Race Relations and Immigration: A Comparative Perspective." *International Journal of Comparative Sociology* 31:156–76.

Ridgeway, Cecilia L., Elizabeth Heger Boyle, Kathy J. Kuipers, and Dawn T. Robinson. 1998. "How Do Status Beliefs Develop? The Role of Resources and Interactional Experience." *American Sociological Review* 63:331–50.

Riedle, Joan E. 1991. "Exploring the Subcategories of Stereotypes: Not All Mothers Are the Same." *Sex Roles* 24:711–22.

Ries, Paula, and Anne J. Stone, eds. 1993. *The American Woman 1992–93: A Status Report.* New York: W. W. Norton.

Riesman, David, with Reuel Denney and Nathan Glazer. 1950. *The Lonely Crowd.* New Haven, CT: Yale University Press.

Riessman, Frank. 1965. "The Strengths of the Poor." Pp. 40–47 in *New Perspectives on Poverty,* edited by A. B. Shostak and W. Gomberg. Englewood Cliffs, NJ: Prentice Hall.

Riis, Jacob. 1890. *How the Other Half Lives.* Williamstown, MA: Corner House. 1972.

Rischin, Moses, ed. 1965. *The American Gospel of Success.* New York: Quadrangle/The New York Times Books.

Ritzer, George. 1988. *Contemporary Sociological Theory.* New York: Knopf.

Ritzman, Rosemary, and Donald Tomaskovic-Devey. 1992. "Life Chances and Support for Equality and Equity as Normative and Counternormative Distribution Rules." *Social Forces* 70:745–63.

Roach, Jack L., Llewelyn Gross, and Orville Gurrslin. 1969. *Social Stratification in the United States.* Englewood Cliffs, NJ: Prentice Hall.

Robert, Stephanie A. 1998. "Community-Level Socioeconomic Status Effects on Adult Health." *Journal of Health and Social Behavior* 39:18–37.

Robey, John S. 1999. "Civil Society and NAFTA: Initial Results." *Annals of the American Academy of Political and Social Science* 565:113–125.

Robinson, Robert, and Wendell Bell. 1978. "Equality, Success and Social Justice in England and the United States." *American Sociological Review* 43:125–43.

Robinson, Robert, and Jonathan Kelley. 1979. "Class as Conceived by Marx and Dahrendorf: Effects on Income Inequality, Class Consciousness, and Class Conflict in the United States and Great Britain." *American Sociological Review* 44:38–58.

Rodgers, Harrell R., Jr. 1982. *The Cost of Human Neglect: America's Welfare Failure.* Armonk, NY: M. E. Sharpe.

Rodgers, Harrell R., Jr. 1986. *Poor Women, Poor Families: The Economic Plight of America's Female-Headed Households.* Armonk, NY: M. E. Sharpe.

Rodgers, Joan R. 1995. "An Empirical Study of Intergenerational Transmission of Poverty in the United States." *Social Science Quarterly* 76:178–94.

Rodriguez, Richard. 1982. *Hunger of Memory: The Education of Richard Rodriguez.* New York: Bantam Books.

Rogin, Michael. 1971. "Voluntarism: The Political Functions of an Anti-Political Doctrine." Pp. 100–18 in *The American Labor Movement,* edited by D. Brody. New York: Harper & Row.

Rohter, Larry. April 29, 1993. "Era of Female Combat Pilots Opens With Shrugs and Glee." *New York Times,* pp. A1, A12.

Rollins, Judith. 1986. "Part of a Whole: The Interdependence of the Civil Rights Movement and Other Social Movements." *Phylon* 47:61–70.

Romero, Mary. 1992. *Maid in the USA.* London: Routledge.

Roos, Patricia A. 1985. *Gender & Work: A Comparative Analysis of Industrial Societies*. Albany: State University of New York Press.

Roos, Patricia A., and Barbara F. Reskin. 1984. "Institutional Factors Contributing to Sex Segregation in the Workplace." Pp. 235–60 in *Sex Segregation in the Workplace: Trends, Explanations, Remedies*. Washington, D.C.: National Academy Press.

Roosevelt, Franklin Delano. 1966. "Second Inaugural Address." In *Poverty in the Affluent Society*, edited by H. H. Meissner. New York: Harper & Row.

Ropers, Richard H. 1988. *The Invisible Homeless: A New Urban Ecology*. New York: Insight Books.

Rose, Arnold M. 1968. *The Power Structure*. New York: Oxford University Press.

Rosencranz, Mary Lou. 1962. "Clothing Symbolism." *Journalism of Home Economics* 54:18–22.

Rosenfeld, Rachel A. 1978. "Women's Intergenerational Occupational Mobility." *American Sociological Review* 43:36–46.

Rosenfeld, Rachel A. 1992. "Job Mobility and Career Processes." Pp. 39–61 in *Annual Review of Sociology*, vol. 18, edited by J. Blake and J. Hagan. Palo Alto, CA: Annual Reviews.

Rosenfield, Sarah. 1989. "The Effects of Women's Employment: Personal Control and Sex Differences in Mental Health." *Journal of Health and Social Behavior* 30:77–91.

Ross, Irwin. 1980. "How Lawless Are Big Companies?" *Fortune* 102:57.

Rossi, Peter. 1989. *Without Shelter: Homelessness in the 1980s*. New York: Priority Press.

Rossi, Peter H., and James D. Wright. 1989. "The Urban Homeless: A Portrait of Urban Dislocation." *Annals of the American Academy of Political and Social Sciences* 501:132–42.

Rossides, Daniel W. 1976. *The American Class System: An Introduction to Social Stratification*. Boston: Houghton Mifflin.

Rostow, W. W. 1960. *The Stages of Economic Growth*. Cambridge: Cambridge University Press.

Roth, Guenther, and Claus Wittich, eds. 1968. *Max Weber: Economy and Society*. 3 vols. New York: Bedminster Press.

Rothman, Barbara Katz. 1984. "Women, Health, and Medicine." Pp. 70–80 in *Women: A Feminist Perspective*, edited by J. Freeman. Palo Alto, CA: Mayfield.

Rowley, Anthony. December 6, 1990. "Unmentioned Underclass." *Far Eastern Economic Review* 150:36–37.

Rubenstein, William B. 1996. "Lesbians, Gay Men, and the Law." Pp. 331–43 in *The Lives of Lesbians, Gays, and Bisexuals*, edited by R. C. Savin-Williams and K. M. Cohen. Fort Worth, TX: Harcourt Brace.

Rubin, Alissa J. May 1, 1993. "Special Interests Stampede to Be Heard on Overhaul." *Congressional Quarterly* 51:1081–1084.

Rubin, Beth A. 1986. "Class Struggle American Style: Unions, Strikes and Wages." *American Sociological Review* 51:618–31.

Rubin, Lillian Breslow. 1976. *Worlds of Pain: Life in the Working-Class Family*. New York: Basic Books.

Rubinson, Richard. 1976. "The World Economy and the Distribution of Income within States: A Cross-National Study." *American Sociological Review* 41:638–59.

Rubinson, Richard, and Dan Quinlan. 1977. "Democracy and Social Inequality: A Reanalysis." *American Sociological Review* 42:611–23.

Rupp, Leila J. 1985. "The Women's Community in the National Women's Party, 1945 to the 1960's." *Signs: Journal of Women in Culture and Society* 10:715–40.

Rushing, William A. 1978. "Status Resources, Societal Reactions, and Type of Mental Hospital Admission." *American Sociological Review* 43:521–33.

Ryan, William. 1981. *Equality*. New York: Random House.

Rytina, Joan H., William H. Form, and John Pease. 1975. "Income and Stratification Ideology: Beliefs about the American Opportunity Structure." *American Journal of Sociology* 75:703–16.

Sacks, Karen. 1975. "Engels Revisited: Women, the Organization of Production, and Private Property." Pp. 211–34 in *Toward an Anthropology of Women*, edited by R. R. Reiter. New York: Monthly Review Press.

Safran, Claire. August 1992. "The New Faces of Poverty." *Redbook* 179:84–87.

Sahlins, Marshall D. 1968. *Tribesmen*. Englewood Cliffs, NJ: Prentice Hall.

Sakamoto, Arthur, Jeng Liu, and Jessie M. Tzeng. 1998. "The Declining Significance of Race Among Chinese and Japanese American Men." *Research in Social Stratification and Mobility* 16:225–46.

Salant, Jonathan D. 1998. "Introduction." Pp. vii–xvii in *Federal PACs Directory 1998–1999*. Washington, D.C.: Congressional Quarterly.

Sampson, Robert J. 1986. "Effects of Socioeconomic Context on Official Reaction to Juvenile Delinquency." *American Sociological Review* 51:876–85.

Sampson, Robert J., and William Julius Wilson. 1995. "Toward a Theory of Race, Crime, and Urban Inequality." Pp. 37–54 in *Crime and Inequality*, edited by J. Hagan and R. D. Peterson. Stanford: Stanford University Press.

San Marco, Louise R. 1979. *Differential Sentencing Patterns among Criminal Homicide Offenders in*

Harris County, Texas. Ph.D. Dissertation, Sam Houston State University.

Sanday, Peggy Reeves. 1981. *Female Power and Male Dominance: On the Origins of Sexual Inequality.* Cambridge: Cambridge University Press.

Sandefur, Gary D., and Steven T. Cook. 1998. "Permanent Exits from Public Assistance: The Impact of Duration, Family, and Work." *Social Forces* 77:763–86.

Sanders, Scott Russell. 1993. "The Men We Carry in Our Minds." Pp. 67–69 in *Experiencing Race, Class, and Gender in the United States,* edited by Virginia Cyrus. Mountain View, CA: Mayfield.

Sanderson, Stephen K. 1988. *Macrosociology: An Introduction to Human Societies.* New York: Harper & Row.

Sandler, Bernice R. 1986. "The Campus Climate Revisited: Chilly for Women Faculty, Administrators, and Graduate Students." Washington, D.C.: Association of American Colleges.

Savin-Williams, R. C., and R. G. Rodriguez. 1993. "A Developmental, Clinical Perspective on Lesbian, Gay Male, and Bisexual Youths." Pp. 77–101 in *Adolescent Sexuality,* edited by T. P. Gullotta, G. R. Adams, and R. Montemayor. Newbury Park, CA: Sage.

Savin-Williams, Ritch C. 1996. "Dating and Romantic Relationships Among Gay, Lesbian, and Bisexual Youths." Pp. 166–80 in *The Lives of Lesbians, Gays, and Bisexuals,* edited by R. C. Savin-Williams and K. M. Cohen. Fort Worth, TX: Harcourt Brace.

Savin Williams, Ritch C., and Kenneth M. Cohen. 1996. "Psychosocial Outcomes of Verbal and Physical Abuse among Lesbian, Gay, and Bisexual Youths." Pp. 181–200 in *The Lives of Lesbians, Gays, and Bisexuals,* edited by R. C. Savin-Williams and K. M. Cohen. Fort Worth, TX: Harcourt Brace.

Sawhill, Isabel V. 1988. "Poverty in the U.S.: Why Is It So Persistent?" *Journal of Economic Literature* 26:1073–1119.

Schaefer, Richard T. 1987. "Racial Prejudice in a Capitalist State: What Has Happened to the American Creed?" Pp. 162–168 in *Introducing Sociology: A Collection of Readings,* edited by R. T. Schaefer and R. P. Lamm. New York: McGraw-Hill.

Schaefer, Richard T. 1988. *Racial and Ethnic Groups.* Glenview, IL: Scott, Foresman.

Schaefer, Richard T. 1996. *Racial and Ethnic Groups.* New York: HarperCollins.

Schein, Virginia, Ruediger Mueller, and Carolyn Jacobson. 1989. "The Relationship between Sex Role Stereotypes and Requisite Management Characteristics among College Students." *Sex Roles* 20:103–10.

Schellenberg, E. Glenn, Jessie Hirt, and Alan Sears. 1999. "Attitudes towards Homosexuals among Students at a Canadian University." *Sex Roles* 40:139–52.

Schiller, Bradley R. 1998. *The Economics of Poverty and Discrimination.* Englewood Cliffs, NJ: Prentice Hall.

Schlegel, Alice, ed. 1977. *Sexual Stratification: A Cross-Cultural View.* New York: Columbia University Press.

Schmittroth, Linda, ed. 1994. *Statistical Record of Children.* Detroit: Gale Research.

Schneider, William. July 1992. "The Suburban Century Begins." *The Atlantic Monthly,* pp. 33–44.

Schott, Liz, Robert Greenstein, and Wendell Primus. 1999. *The Determinants of Welfare Caseload Decline: A Brief Rejoinder.* Washington, D.C.: Center on Budget and Policy Priorities.

Schur, Edwin H. 1969. *Our Criminal Society.* Englewood Cliffs, NJ: Prentice Hall.

Schuttinga, J. A., M. Falik, and B. Steinwald. 1985. "Health Plan Selection in the Federal Employees Health Benefits Program." *Journal of Health Politics, Policy and Law* 10:119–39.

Schwarz, John E., and Thomas J. Volgy. 1992. *The Forgotten Americans.* New York: W. W. Norton.

Schwartz, Michael, ed. 1987. *The Structure of Power in America.* New York: Holmes & Meier.

Schwartz, William B., Joseph P. Newhouse, and Albert P. Williams. 1985. "Is the Teaching Hospital an Endangered Species?" *The New England Journal of Medicine* 313:157–62.

Scully, Diana, and Pauline Bart. 1981. "A Funny Thing Happened on the Way to the Orifice: Women in Gynecology Textbooks." Pp. 350–55 in *The Sociology of Health and Illness: Critical Perspectives,* edited by P. Conrad and R. Kern. New York: St. Martin's Press.

Seabrook, Jeremy. September 11, 1992. "Land of Broken Toys." *New Statesman and Society* 5:16–17.

Secombe, Wally. 1973. "The Housewife and Her Labour Under Capitalism." *New Left Review* 83:19.

Sedgwick, Eve Kosofsky. 1998. "What's Queer?" Pp. 183–87 in *Gender Inequality,* edited by J. Lorber. Los Angeles: Roxbury.

Segal, Troy. May 18, 1992. "The Riots: 'Just as Much about Class as about Race.'" *Business Week,* p. 47.

Seider, Maynard S. 1974. "American Big Business Ideology: A Content Analysis of Executive Speeches." *American Sociological Review* 39: 802–15.

Seidman, Ann. 1978. *Working Women: A Study of Women in Paid Jobs.* Boulder, CO: Westview Press.

Select Committee on Hunger. 1992. *Hunger in America: Who Cares?* Series 102–28. Washington, D.C.: U.S. Government Printing Office.

Sell, Ralph R., and Michael P. Johnson. 1977. "Income and Occupational Differences between Men and Women in the United States." *Sociology and Social Research* 62:1–20.

Sennett, Richard, and Jonathan Cobb. 1973. *The Hidden Injuries of Class.* New York: Vintage.

Serbin, Lisa A., K. Daniel O'Leary, Ronald N. Kent, and Illene J. Tonick. 1973. "A Comparison of Teacher Response to the Preacademic and Problems Behaviors of Boys and Girls." *Child Development* 44:796–804.

Sewell, William H., Archibald O. Haller, and George W. Ohlendorf. 1970. "The Educational and Early Occupational Status Attainment Process: Replication and Revision." *American Sociological Review* 35:1014–27.

Sewell, William H., and Robert M. Hauser. 1972. "Causes and Consequences of Higher Education: Models of the Status Attainment Access." *American Journal of Agricultural Economics* 54:851–61.

Sewell, William H., and Robert M. Hauser. 1976. "Recent Developments in the Wisconsin Study of Social and Psychological Factors in Socioeconomic Achievement." Center for Demography Working Paper No. 76–11. Madison: University of Wisconsin.

Sewell, William H., and Vimal Shah. 1967. "Socioeconomic Status, Intelligence, and the Attainment of Higher Education." *Sociology of Education* 40:1–23.

Shanahan, Michael J., Richard A. Miech, and Glen H. Elder, Jr. 1998. "Changing Pathways to Attainment in Men's Lives: Historical Patterns of School, Work, and Social Class." *Social Forces* 77:231–56.

Shapiro, Henry D. 1978. *Appalachia on Our Mind.* Chapel Hill: University of North Carolina Press.

Shen, Ce, and John B. Williamson. 1997. "Child Mortality, Women's Status, Economic Dependency, and State Strength: A Cross-National Study of Less Developed Countries." *Social Forces* 76:667–94.

Shepelak, Norma J. 1987. "The Role of Self-Explanations and Self-Evaluations in Legitimating Inequality." *American Sociological Review* 52:495–503.

Shepelak, Norma J., and Duane Alwin. 1986. Beliefs about Inequality and Perceptions of Distributive Justice." *American Sociological Review* 51:30–46.

Sherman, Lawrence W. 1987. "Deviant Organizations." Pp. 52–62 in *Corporate and Governmental Deviance,* edited by M. D. Ermann and R. J. Lundman. New York: Oxford.

Sherrod, Drury, and Peter M. Nardi. 1998. "Homophobia in the Courtroom." Pp. 24–38 in *Stigma and Sexual Orientation,* edited by G. M. Herek. Thousand Oaks, CA: Sage.

Shihadeh, Edward S., and Nicole Flynn. 1996. "Segregation and Crime: The Effect of Black Social Isolation on the Rates of Black Urban Violence." *Social Forces* 74:1325–52.

Shils, Edward A. 1970. "Deference," Pp. 420–28 in *The Logic of Social Hierarchies,* edited by Edward O. Laumann, Paul M. Siegel, and Robert W. Hodge. Chicago: Markham.

Shinkman, Ron. July 5, 1999. "Nine Health Plans Drop Medicare Markets." *Modern Healthcare,* p. 3.

Shinn, Marybeth, and Beth C. Weitzman. 1996. "Homeless Families Are Different." Pp. 109–22 in *Homelessness in America,* edited by J. Baumohl. Phoenix, AZ: Oryx Press.

Shortell, Stephen M. 1984. "Factors Associated with the Use of Health Services." Pp. 49–88 in *Introduction to Health Services,* edited by S. J. Williams and P. R. Torrens. New York: John Wiley & Sons.

Simkus, Albert A. 1981. "Comparative Stratification and Mobility." *International Journal of Comparative Sociology* 22:213–36.

Simon, Angela. 1998. "The Relationship between Stereotypes of and Attitudes toward Lesbians and Gays." Pp. 62–81 in *Stigma and Sexual Orientation,* edited by G. M. Herek. Thousand Oaks, CA: Sage.

Simon, David R., and D. Stanley Eitzen. 1993. *Elite Deviance.* Boston: Allyn and Bacon.

Simon, R. J., and Navin Sharma. 1979. *The Female Defendant in Washington, D.C.: 1974 and 1975.* Washington, D.C.: INSLAW.

Simpson, George Eaton, and J. Milton Yinger. 1965. *Racial and Cultural Minorities.* New York: Harper & Row.

Singleton, Judy. 1998. "The Impact of Family Caregiving to the Elderly on the American Workplace: Who Is Affected and What Is Being Done?" Pp. 201–214 in *Challenges for Work and Family in the Twenty-First Century,* edited by D. Vannoy and P. J. Dubeck. New York: Aldine de Gruyter.

Sitkoff, Harvard. 1981. *The Struggle for Black Equality. 1954–1980.* New York: Hill and Wang.

Sivaramayya, B. 1983. "Equality and Inequality: The Legal Framework." Pp. 28–70 in *Equality and Inequality: Theory and Practice,* edited by A. Beteille. Delhi: Oxford University Press.

Skeels, Jack W. 1982. "The Economic and Organizational Basis of Early United States Strikes. 1900–1948." *Industrial and Labor Relations Review* 35:491–503.

Skocpol, Theda. 1988. "An 'Uppity Generation' and the Revitalization of Macroscopic Sociology." Pp. 145–59 in *Sociological Lives,* edited by M. W. Riley. Newbury Park, CA: Sage.

Slater, Courtenay M., and Cornelia J. Strawser, eds. 1998. *Business Statistics of the United States.* Washington, D.C.: Bernan Press.

Slesinger, Doris P., Richard C. Tessler, and David Mechanic. 1975. *The Effects of Social Class on the Utilization of Preventive Medical Services in Contrasting Health Care Programs.* Research and Analytic Report No. 1. Madison, WI: Center for Medical Sociology and Health Services Research, University of Wisconsin.

Sloane, David Charles. 1991. *The Last Great Necessity: Cemeteries in American History.* Baltimore: Johns Hopkins University.

Smeeding, Timothy. 1982. "The Antipoverty Effects of In-Kind Transfers." *Policy Studies Journal* 10:491–521.

Smeeding, Timothy M. January–February 1992. "Why the U.S. Antipoverty System Doesn't Work Very Well." *Challenge* 35:30–35.

Smidt, Corwin. 1980. "Civil Religious Orientations among Elementary School Children." *Sociological Analysis* 41:24–40.

Smith, Dorothy E. 1987. *The Everyday World as Problematic: A Feminist Sociology.* Boston: Northeastern University Press.

Smith, James D. 1987. "Recent Trends in the Distribution of Wealth in the U.S.: Data, Research Problems, and Prospects." Pp. 72–89 in *International Comparisons of the Distribution of Household Wealth,* edited by Edward D. Wolff. Oxford: Clarendon Press.

Smith, Kevin B., and Robert A. Bylund. 1983. "Cognitive Maps of Class, Racial, and Appalachian Inequalities among Rural Appalachians." *Rural Sociology* 48:253–70.

Smith, Mapheus. 1943. "An Empirical Scale of Prestige Status of Occupations." *American Sociological Review* 8:185–92.

Smith, Patricia K. 1994. "Downward Mobility: Is It a Growing Problem?" *American Journal of Economics and Sociology* 53:57–72.

Smith, Robert J. Winter 1987. "Gender Inequality in Contemporary Japan." *Journal of Japanese Studies* 13:1–25.

Smith, Vernon K. 1974. *Welfare Work Incentives: The Earnings Exemption and Its Impact Upon AFDC Employment, Earnings, and Program Costs.* Lansing, MI: Michigan Department of Social Services.

"Sniping at the Milken Deal." May 7, 1990. *Newsweek,* p. 48.

Snipp, C. Matthew. 1985. "Occupational Mobility and Social Class: Insights from Men's Career Mobility." *American Sociological Review* 50:475–93.

Snyder, David. 1975. "Institutional Setting and Industrial Conflict: Comparative Analyses of France, Italy, and the United States." *American Sociological Review* 40:259–78.

Snyder, David, and Charles Tilly. 1972. "Hardship and Collective Violence in France, 1830–1960." *American Sociological Review* 37:520–32.

Snyder, David, and Charles Tilly. 1974. "On Debating and Falsifying Theories of Collective Violence." *American Sociological Review* 39:610–13.

Snyder, Eloise C., ed. 1979. *The Study of Women: Enlarging Perspectives of Social Reality.* New York: Harper & Row.

Sobel, Michael E. 1983a. "Lifestyle Differentiation and Stratification in Contemporary U.S. Society." Pp. 115–44 in *Research in Social Stratification and Mobility,* vol. 2, edited by Donald W. Treiman and Robert V. Robinson. Greenwich, CT: JAI Press.

Sobel, Michael E. 1983b. "Structural Mobility, Circulation Mobility and the Analysis of Occupational Mobility: A Conceptual Mismatch." *American Sociological Review* 48:721–27.

Society for Hospital Social Work Directors. March–April 1989. "1988 Hospital Closings Continue at Record Pace." *Social Work Administration* 15:21–22.

Sokoloff, Natalie, J. 1988. "Evaluating Gains and Losses by Black and White Women and Men in the Professions. 1960–1980." *Social Problems* 35:36–49.

Solomon, Barbara Bryant. 1987. "Social Welfare Reform." Pp. 113–27 in *The State of Black America 1987.* Washington, D.C.: National Urban League.

Solon, Gary. June 1992. "Intergenerational Income Mobility in the United States." *The American Economic Review* 82:383–408.

Soltow, Lee. 1975. *Men and Wealth in the United States.* New Haven, CT: Yale University Press.

Sontag, Susan. 1973. "The Third World of Women." *Partisan Review* 60:201–03.

Sorokin, Pitirim. 1959. *Social and Cultural Mobility.* New York: The Free Press. With the exception of the last chapter, originally published as *Social Mobility.* New York: Harper & Row. 1927.

Spaeth, Joe L. 1976a. "Cognitive Complexity: A Dimension Underlying the Socioeconomic Achievement Process." In *Schooling and Achievement in American Society,* edited by W. H. Sewell, R. M. Hauser, and D. L. Featherman. New York: Academic Press.

Spain, Daphne. 1992. *Gendered Spaces.* Chapel Hill: The University of North Carolina Press.

Spain, Daphne. April 21–24, 1993. "Built to Last: Public Housing as an Urban Gendered Space." Paper presented at the Urban Affairs Association, Indianapolis.

Spector, Malcolm, and John I. Kitsuse. 1977. *Constructing Social Problems.* Menlo Park, CA: Cummings Publishing.

Spencer, Barbara, and G. Stephen Taylor. 1988. "Effects of Facial Attractiveness and Gender on Causal Attributions of Managerial Performance." *Sex Roles* 19:273–85.

Spilerman, Seymour. 1978. "Careers, Labor Market Structure, and Socioeconomic Achievement." *American Journal of Sociology* 83:551–93.

Srole, Leo, Thomas S. Langner, Stanley T. Michael, Marvin K. Opler, and Thomas A. C. Rennie. 1962. *Mental Illness in the Metropolis*. New York: McGraw-Hill. Reprinted in part on pp. 404–12 in *Social Stratification in the United States* by J. L. Roach, L. Gross, and O. Gursslin. Englewood Cliffs, NJ: Prentice Hall.

Stack, Steven, and Delores Zimmerman. 1982. "The Effect of World Economy on Income Inequality: A Reassessment." *The Sociological Quarterly* 23:345–58.

Stanley, Thomas J., and William D. Danko. 1996. *The Millionaire Next Door*. Atlanta, GA: Longstreet Press.

Staples, Clifford L., Michael L. Schwalbe, and Viktor Gecas. 1984. "Social Class, Occupational Conditions, and Efficacy-Based Self-Esteem." *Sociological Perspectives* 27:85–109.

Stark, Evan, and Anne Flitcraft. 1988. "Violence among Intimates: An Epidemiological Review." Pp. 293–317 in *Handbook of Family Violence*, edited by V. B. Van Hasselt, R. L. Morrison, A. S. Bellack, and M. Hersen. New York: Plenum.

Stark, Louisa. 1987. "A Century of Alcohol and Homelessness: Demographics and Stereotypes." *Alcohol Health & Research World* 2:8–13.

Starr, Raymond H., Jr. 1988. "Physical Abuse of Children." Pp. 119–55 in *Handbook of Family Violence*, edited by V. B. Van Hasselt, R. L. Morrison, A. S. Bellack, and M. Hersen. New York: Plenum.

Steffensmeier, Darrell, and Chris Hebert. 1999. "Women and Men Policymakers: Does the Judge's Gender Affect the Sentencing of Criminal Defendants?" *Social Forces* 77:1163–96.

Stefl, Mary E. 1987. "The New Homeless: A National Perspective." Pp. 46–63 in *The Homeless in Contemporary Society*, edited by R. D. Bingham, R. E. Green and S. B. White. Newbury Park, CA: Sage.

Steil, Janice M. 1984. "Marital Relationships and Mental Health: The Psychic Costs of Inequality." Pp. 113–23 in *Women: A Feminist Perspective*, edited by J. Freeman. Palo Alto, CA: Mayfield.

Steinitz, Victoria, and Ellen R. Solomon. 1986. *Starting Out: Class and Community in the Lives of Working-Class Youth*. Philadelphia: Temple University Press.

Stephenson, Charles, and Robert Asher, eds. 1986. *Life and Labor: Dimensions of American Working-Class History*. Albany, NY: State University of New York Press.

Stern, Philip M. 1988. *The Best Congress Money Can Buy*. New York: Pantheon.

Stevens, Gillian, and Monica Boyd. 1980. "The Importance of Mother Labor Force Participation and Intergenerational Mobility of Women." *Social Forces* 59:186–92.

Stolte, John F. 1983. "The Legitimation of Structural Inequality: Reformulation and Test of the Self-Evaluation Argument." *American Sociological Review* 48:331–42.

Stolte, John F. 1987. "The Formation of Justice Norms." *American Sociological Review* 52:774–84.

Stone, Gregory P. 1962. "Appearance and the Self." Pp. 86–118 in *Human Behavior and Social Processes*, edited by Arnold M. Rose. Boston: Houghton Mifflin.

Strathern, Marilyn. 1980. "No Nature, No Culture: The Hagen Case." Pp. 174–222 in *Nature, Culture and Gender*, edited by C. MacCormack and M. Strathern. Cambridge: Cambridge University Press.

Straus, Murray A., and Richard J. Gelles. 1990. *Physical Violence in American Families*. New Brunswick, NJ: Transaction.

Straus, Murray A., Richard J. Gelles, and Suzanne K. Steinmetz. 1980. *Behind Closed Doors: Violence in the American Family*. Garden City, NY: Anchor Press.

Strauss, Anselm L. 1971. *The Contexts of Social Mobility*. Chicago: Aldine.

Strober, Myra, and Carolyn L. Arnold. 1987. "The Dynamics of Occupational Segregation among Bank Tellers." In *Gender in the Workplace*, edited by C. Brown and J. Pechman. Washington, D.C.: The Brookings Institution.

"Study Shows Shift to Lower-Pay Jobs." September 2, 1988. *Akron Beacon Journal*.

Sturm, James L. 1977. *Investing in the United States, 1798–1893*. New York: Arno Press.

"Suddenly, Health-Care Players Are Ready to Talk." December 28, 1992. *Business Week*, pp. 36–37.

Sullivan, Gerard. 1983. "Uneven Development and National Income Inequality in Third World Countries: A Cross-National Study of the Effects of External Economic Dependency." *Sociological Perspectives* 26:201–31.

Susser, Merwyn, Kim Hopper, and Judith Richman. 1983. "Society, Culture, and Health." Pp. 23–49 in *Handbook of Health, Health Care, and the Health Professions*, edited by D. Mechanic. New York: The Free Press.

Sutherland, Edwin H. 1949. *White Collar Crime*. New York: Dryden.

Swafford, M. 1978. "Sex Differences in Soviet Earnings." *American Sociological Review* 43:657–73.

Swanson, Guy E. 1974. *The Birth of the Gods*. Ann Arbor, MI: University of Michigan.

Swardson, Roger. March/April 1993. "Greetings from the Electronic Plantation." *Utne Reader,* pp. 88–93.

Sweeney, Richard. 1993. *Out of Place: Homelessness in America.* New York: HarperCollins.

Szafran, Robert F. 1982. "What Kinds of Firms Hire and Promote Women and Blacks? A Review of the Literature." *The Sociological Quarterly* 23:171–90.

Szymanski, Albert. 1976. "Racial Discrimination and White Gain." *American Sociological Review* 41:403–14.

Szymanski, Albert. 1978. *The Capitalist State and the Politics of Class.* Cambridge, MA: Winthrop.

Tabb, William K. September 4–11, 1970. "Black Americans: Internal Colony or Marginal Working Class." Paper presented at the Seventh World Congress of Sociology of the International Sociological Association, Varna, Bulgaria.

Taeuber, Cynthia. 1996. *Statistical Handbook on Women in America.* Phoenix: Oryx Press.

Takagi, Masayuki. July–September 1991. "A Living Legacy of Discrimination." *Japan Quarterly* 38:283–90.

Tausig, Mark, and Rudy Fenwick. 1999. "Recession and Well-Being." *Journal of Health and Social Behavior* 40:1–16."

Taylor, Verta. 1989a. "Social Movement Continuity: The Women's Movement in Abeyance." *American Sociological Review* 54:761–75.

Taylor, Verta. 1989b. "The Future of Feminism: A Social Movement Analysis." Pp. 473–90 in *Feminist Frontiers II: Rethinking Sex, Gender, and Society,* edited by L. Richardson and V. Taylor. New York: Random House.

Taylor, William L., and Susan M. Liss. 1992. "Affirmative Action in the 1990s: Staying the Course." *The Annals of the American Academy of Political and Social Science* 523:30–37.

Teachman, Jay D., Karen A. Polonko, and John Scanzoni. 1987. "Demography of the Family." Pp. 3–36 in *Handbook of Marriage and the Family,* edited by Marvin B. Sussman and Suzanne K. Steinmetz. New York: Plenum.

Tessler, R., and D. Mechanic. 1975. "Factors Affecting the Choice between Prepaid Group Practice and Alternative Insurance Programs." *Milbank Memorial Fund Quarterly/Health and Society* 53:149–72.

Thoits, Peggy A. 1983. "Multiple Identities and Psychological Well-Being: A Reformulation and Test of the Social Isolation Hypothesis." *American Sociological Review* 48:174–87.

Thomas, Melvin E., and Michael Hughes. 1986. "The Continuing Significance of Race: A Study of Race, Class, and Quality of Life in America. 1972–1985." *American Sociological Review* 51:830–41.

Thompson, James D. 1967. *Organizations in Action.* New York: McGraw-Hill.

Thompson, William E. 1991. "Hanging Tongues: A Sociological Encounter with the Assembly Line." Pp. 225–34 in *Down to Earth Sociology,* edited by James M. Henslin. New York: The Free Press.

Thornberry, T. P. 1973. "Race, Socioeconomic Status and Sentencing in the Juvenile Justice System." *Journal of Criminal Law and Criminology* 64:90–98.

Thornberry, Terrence P., and R. L. Christenson. 1984. "Unemployment and Criminal Involvement: An Investigation of Reciprocal Causal Structures." *American Sociological Review* 49:398–411.

Thorne, Barrie. 1989. "Girls and Boys Together...But Mostly Apart: Gender Arrangements in Elementary Schools." Pp. 73–84 in *Feminist Frontiers II: Rethinking Sex, Gender, and Society,* edited by L. Richardson and V. Taylor. New York: Random House.

Thurow, Lester C. 1969. *Poverty and Discrimination.* Washington, D.C.: The Brookings Institution.

Thurow, Lester C. 1975. *Generating Inequality.* New York: Basic Books.

Thurow, Lester. 1985. "Medicine versus Economics." *The New England Journal of Medicine* 313:611–14.

Thurow, Lester C. June 1999. "Building Wealth." *Atlantic Monthly,* pp. 57–69.

Tienda, Marta, and Ding-Tzann Lii. 1987. "Minority Concentration and Earnings Inequality: Blacks, Hispanics, and Asians Compared." *American Journal of Sociology* 93:141–65.

Tiffany, Lawrence, Yakov Avichai, ad Geoffrey Peters. 1975. "A Statistical Analysis of Sentencing in Federal Courts." *Journal of Legal Studies* 4:369.

Tilly, Charles. 1998. *Durable Inequality.* Berkeley: University of California Press.

Tittle, Charles R., and Wayne J. Villemez. 1977. "Social Class and Criminality." *Social Forces* 56:474–502.

Tittle, Charles R., Wayne J. Villemez, and Douglas A. Smith. 1978. "The Myth of Social Class and Criminality: An Empirical Assessment of the Empirical Evidence." *American Sociological Review* 43: 643–56.

Tolbert, Charles M., II. 1982. Industrial Segmentation and Men's Career Mobility." *American Sociological Review* 47:457–77.

"The Top 500 Women-Owned Businesses." June 1999. *Working Woman,* pp. 35–65.

Törnblom, Kjell Y., and Riel Vermunt. 1999. "An Integrative Perspective on Social Justice: Distributive and Procedural Fairness Evaluations of Positive and Negative Outcome Allocations." *Social Justice Research* 12:39–64.

Tracy, Joseph S. 1986. "An Investigation into the Determinants of U.S. Strike Activity." *American Economic Review* 76:423–36.

Treas, Judith. 1983. "Trickle Down or Transfers? Postwar Determinants of Family Income Inequality." *American Sociological Review* 48:546–59.

Treiman, D. J., and H. I. Hartmann, eds. 1981. *Women, Work, and Wages: Equal Pay for Jobs of Equal Value.* Washington, D.C.: National Academy Press.

Treiman, Donald J., and Harry B. G. Ganzeboom. 1990. "Cross-National Comparative Status Attainment Research." Pp. 105–27 in *Research in Social Stratification and Mobility,* vol. 9, edited by A. L. Kalleberg. Greenwich, CT: JAI Press.

Treiman, Donald J., Heidi I. Hartmann, and Patricia A. Roos. 1984. "Assessing Pay Discrimination Using National Data." Pp. 137–54 in *Comparable Worth and Wage Discrimination,* edited by H. Remick. Philadelphia: Temple University Press.

Treiman, Donald, and Kermit Terrell. 1975. "Sex and the Process of Status Attainment: A Comparison of Working Women and Men." *American Sociological Review* 40:174–200.

Tropman, John E. 1989. *American Values & Social Welfare: Cultural Contradictions in the Welfare State.* Englewood Cliffs NJ: Prentice Hall.

Tumin, Melvin M. 1953. "Some Principles of Stratification: A Critical Analysis." *American Sociological Review* 18:387–94.

Turk, Austin T. 1969. *Criminality and Legal Order.* Chicago: Rand McNally.

Turner, Bryan S. 1986. *Equality.* New York: Methuen.

Turner, Jonathan H. 1986. *The Structure of Sociological Theory.* Chicago: Dorsey.

Turner, Jonathan, and Leonard Beeghley. 1981. *The Emergence of Sociology Theory.* Homewood, IL: Dorsey.

Turner, Jonathan H., Leonard Beeghley, and Charles H. Powers. 1989. *The Emergence of Sociological Theory.* Chicago: Dorsey.

Turner, Jonathan H., Royce Singleton, Jr., and David Musick. 1984. *Oppression: A Socio-History of Black-White Relations in America.* Chicago: Nelson-Hall.

Turner, Jonathan H., and Charles E. Starnes. 1976. *Inequality: Privilege and Poverty in America.* Pacific Palisades, CA: Goodyear.

Turner, R. Jay, and John W. Gartrell. 1978. "Social Factors in Psychiatric Outcome: Toward the Resolution of Interpretive Controversies." *American Sociological Review* 43:368–82.

Turner, R. Jay, and Samuel Noh. 1983. "Class and Psychological Vulnerability among Women: The Significance of Social Support and Personal Control." *Journal of Health and Social Behavior* 24:2–15.

Turner, R. Jay, and Morton O. Wagenfeld. 1967. "Occupational Mobility and Schizophrenia: Assessment of the Social Causation and Social Selection Hypotheses." *American Sociological Review* 32:104–13.

Turner, Ralph H., ed. 1967. *Robert E. Park: On Social Control and Collective Behavior.* Chicago: Phoenix Books.

Turner, Richard. May 17, 1999. "The $25 Million Secret." *Newsweek,* p. 35.

Turner, William H. 1986. "The Black Ethnographer 'At Home' in Harlem: A Commentary and Research Response to Stephenson and Greer." *Human Organization* 45:279–92.

Tweedie, Jack, Dana Reichert, and Matt O'Connor. 1999. *Tracking Recipients After They Leave Welfare.* Washington, D.C.: National Conference of State Legislatures.

Tyree, Andrea, Moshe Semyonov, and Robert W. Hodge. 1979. "Gaps and Glissandos: Inequality, Economic Development, and Social Mobility in 24 Countries." *American Sociological Review* 44:410–24.

Tyree, Andrea, and Judith Treas. 1974. "The Occupational and Marital Mobility of Women." *American Sociological Review* 39:293–302.

U.S. Bureau of the Census. 1979. *The Social and Economic Status of the Black Population in the United States: An Historical View, 1790–1978.* Current Population Reports, Series P-21, No. 80. Washington, D.C.: U.S. Government Printing Office.

U.S. Bureau of the Census. 1987. *Money Income and Poverty Status of Families and Persons in the United States: 1986.* Current Population Reports, Series P-60, No. 157.

U.S. Bureau of the Census. August 1987. *Male-Female Differences in Work Experience, Occupation, and Earnings: 1984.* Current Population Reports, Series P-70, No. 10. Washington, D.C.: U.S. Government Printing Office.

U.S. Bureau of the Census. 1988. *Statistical Abstract of the United States 1988.* Washington, D.C.: U.S. Government Printing Office.

U.S. Bureau of the Census. 1989. *Statistical Abstract of the United States 1989.* Washington, D.C.: U.S. Government Printing Office.

U.S. Bureau of the Census. February 1989. *Poverty in the United States 1987.* Current Population Reports, Series P-60, No. 163. Washington, D.C.: U.S. Government Printing Office.

U.S. Bureau of the Census. 1990. *Statistical Abstract of the United States 1990.* Washington, D.C.: U.S. Government Printing Office.

U.S. Bureau of the Census. September 1990. *Money Income and Poverty Status in the United States 1989.* Current Population Reports, Series P-60. No. 168. Washington, D.C.: U.S. Government Printing Office.

U.S. Bureau of the Census. March 1992. *Workers with Low Earnings: 1964 to 1990.* Current Population

Reports, Series P-60, No. 178. Washington, D.C.: U.S. Government Printing Office.

U.S. Bureau of the Census. August 1992a. *Money Income of Households, Families, and Persons in the United States: 1991.* Current Population Reports, Series P-60, No. 180. Washington, D.C.: U.S. Government Printing Office.

U.S. Bureau of the Census. August 1992b. *Poverty in the United States: 1991.* Current Population Reports, Series P-60, No. 181. Washington, D.C.: U.S. Government Printing Office.

U.S. Bureau of the Census. August 1992c. *Measuring the Effects of Benefits and Taxes on Income and Poverty: 1979 to 1991.* Current Population Reports, Series P-60, No. 182-RD. Washington, D.C.: U.S. Government Printing Office.

U.S. Bureau of the Census. November 1992. *1990 Census of Population: General Population Characteristics United States.* Washington, D.C.: U.S. Government Printing Office.

U.S. Bureau of the Census. September 1993. *Poverty in the United States 1992.* Washington, D.C.: U.S. Government Printing Office.

U.S. Bureau of the Census. January 1994. *Household Wealth and Asset Ownership: 1991.* Current Population Reports, Series P70, No. 34. Washington, D.C.: U.S. Government Printing Office.

U.S. Bureau of the Census. November 1994. *Statistical Brief: Participants in Assistance Programs.* Washington, D.C.: U.S. Government Printing Office.

U.S. Bureau of the Census. 1995. *Statistical Abstract of the United States 1995.* Washington, D.C.: U.S. Government Printing Office.

U.S. Bureau of the Census. 1996. *Asset Ownership of Households: 1993.* [Online]. <www.census.gov/ftp/pub/hhes/wealth/wlth93f.html>

U.S. Bureau of the Census. April 1996. *Income, Poverty, and Valuation of Noncash Benefits: 1994.* Current Population Reports, Series P60, No. 189. Washington, D.C.: U.S. Government Printing Office.

U.S. Bureau of the Census. September 1996. *Money Income in the United States: 1995.* Current Population Reports, Series P-60, No. 193. Washington, D.C.: U.S. Government Printing Office.

U.S. Bureau of the Census. 1998a. *Statistical Abstract of the United States 1998.* Washington, D.C.: U.S. Government Printing Office..

U.S. Bureau of the Census. 1998b. *Measuring 50 Years of Economic Change.* Current Population Reports, Series P60, No. 203. Washington, D.C.: U.S. Government Printing Office.

U.S. Bureau of the Census. September 1998a. *Health Insurance Coverage: 1997.* Current Population Reports, Series P60, No. 202. Washington, D.C.: U.S. Government Printing Office.

U.S. Bureau of the Census. September 1998b. *Money Income in the United States: 1997.* Current Population Reports, Series P60, No. 200. Washington, D.C.: U.S. Government Printing Office.

U.S. Bureau of the Census. September 1998c. *Poverty in the United States: 1997.* Current Population Reports, Series P60, No. 201. Washington, D.C.: U.S. Government Printing Office.

U.S. Bureau of the Census. October 1999. *Health Insurance Coverage.* Current Population Reports, Series P-60, No. 208. Washington, D.C.: U.S. Government Printing Office.

U.S. Census Office. 1903. *Statistical Atlas of the United States, 1900.* Washington, D.C.: U.S. Government Printing Office.

U.S. Conference of Mayors. 1998. *A Status Report on Hunger and Homelessness in America's Cities: 1998.* Washington, D.C.: Author.

U.S. Department of Commerce and Labor, Bureau of Statistics. 1911. *Statistical Abstract of the United States 1911.* Washington, D.C.: U.S. Government Printing Office.

U.S. Department of Education. March 1990. *Faculty in Higher Education Institutions, 1988.* Washington, D.C.: U.S. Government Printing Office.

U.S. Department of Justice. 1976. *Capital Punishment 1975.* National Prisoner Statistics Bulletin, Law Enforcement Assistance Administration, National Criminal Justice Information and Statistics Service.

U.S. Department of Justice. 1998. *Uniform Crime Reports for the United States 1997.* Washington, D.C.: Federal Bureau of Investigation.

U.S. Department of Labor. January 1996. *Employment and Earnings.* Washington, D.C.: Government Printing Office.

U.S. Department of Labor. January 1999. *Employment & Earnings.* Washington, D.C.: U.S. Government Printing Office.

U.S. Department of Labor. April 1999. *Highlights of Women's Earnings in 1998.* Report 928. Washington, D.C.: U.S. Government Printing Office.

U.S. Department of Labor, Bureau of Labor Statistics. March 1982. *Analysis of Work Stoppages, 1980.* Bulletin 2120. Washington, D.C.: U.S. Government Printing Office.

U.S. Department of Labor, Bureau of Labor Statistics. June 1985. *Handbook of Labor Statistics, Bulletin 2217.* Washington, D.C.: U.S. Government Printing Office.

U.S. Department of Labor, Bureau of Labor Statistics. January 1989. *Employment and Earnings.* Washington, D.C.: U.S. Government Printing Office.

U.S. Department of Labor, Bureau of Labor Statistics. March 1989. *Monthly Labor Review.* Washington, D.C.: U.S. Government Printing Office.

U.S. Department of Labor, Bureau of Labor Statistics. June 1989. *Current Wage Developments.* Washington, D.C.: U.S. Government Printing Office.

U.S. Department of Labor, Bureau of Labor Statistics. Spring 1998. *The 1996–2006 Job Outlook in Brief.* Washington, D.C.: U.S. Government Printing Office.

U.S. Department of Labor, Women's Bureau. 1947. *Women's Occupations through Seven Decades.* Washington, D.C.: U.S. Government Printing Office.

Uchitelle, Louis, and N. R. Kleinfield. March 3, 1996. "The Downsizing of America: A National Heartache." *New York Times.*

Ulbrich, Patricia M., George J. Warheit, and Rick S. Zimmerman. 1989. "Race, Socioeconomic Status, and Psychological Distress: An Examination of Differential Vulnerability." *Journal of Health and Social Behavior* 30:131–46.

Umberson, Debra. 1993. "Sociodemographic Position, World Views, and Psychological Distress." *Social Science Quarterly* 74:575–89.

United Nations. 1991. *The World's Women 1970–1990: Trends and Statistics.* New York: United Nations.

United Nations. 1995. *The World's Women 1995: Trends and Statistics.* New York: United Nations.

United Nations. 1998. *Human Development Report 1998.* New York: Oxford University Press.

Urgent Relief for the Homeless Act. February 4, 1987. *Hearing before the Subcommittee on Housing and Community Development of the Committee on Banking, Finance and Urban Affairs, House of Representatives.* Serial No. 100–3. Washington, D.C.: U.S. Government Printing Office.

Useem, Michael. 1978. "The Inner Group of the American Capitalist Class." *Social Problems* 25:225–40.

Useem, Michael. 1979. "The Social Organization of the American Business Elite and Participation of Corporation Directors in the Governance of American Institutions." *American Sociological Review* 44:553–72.

Useem, Michael. 1980. "Which Business Leaders Help Govern?" Pp. 199–225 in *Power Structure Research,* edited by G. W. Domhoff. Beverly Hills, CA: Sage.

Useem, Michael. 1984. *The Inner Circle: Large Corporations and the Rise of Business Political Activity in the U.S. and U.K.* New York: Oxford University Press.

Valentine, Charles A. 1968. *Culture and Poverty.* Chicago: University of Chicago Press.

van den Berghe, Pierre L. 1967. *Race and Racism: A Comparative Perspective.* New York: John Wiley & Sons.

van den Berghe, Pierre L. 1985. "Review of J. S. Chafetz's Sex and Advantage." *American Journal of Sociology* 90:1350.

Van Hasselt, Vincent B., Randall L. Morrison, Alan S. Bellack, and Michel Hersen, eds. 1988. *Handbook of Family Violence.* New York: Plenum.

Vanneman, Reeve, and Lynn Weber Cannon. 1987. *The American Perception of Class.* Philadelphia: Temple University Press.

Vanneman, Reeve, and Fred C. Pampel. 1977. "The American Perception of Class and Status." *American Sociological Review* 42:422–37.

Veblen, Thorstein. 1953. *The Theory of the Leisure Class.* New York: The New American Library.

Venkatesh, Sudhir Alladi. 1994. "Getting Ahead: Social Mobility among the Urban Poor." *Sociological Perspectives* 37:157–82.

Verba, Sidney, and Norman H. Nie. 1972. *Participation in America: Political Democracy and Social Equality.* New York: Harper & Row.

Verba, Sidney, and Gary R. Orren. 1985. *Equality in America: The View from the Top.* Cambridge, MA: Harvard University Press.

Verbrugge, Lois M. 1983. "Multiple Roles and Physical Health of Women and Men." *Journal of Health and Social Behavior* 24:16–30.

Verbrugge, Lois M. 1999. "Pathways of Health and Death." Pp. 377–94 in *Health, Illness, and Healing,* edited by K. Charmaz and D. A. Paterniti. Los Angeles: Roxbury.

Veum, Jonathan R. December 1992. "Accounting for Income Mobility Changes in the United States." *Social Science Quarterly* 73:773–85.

Vogel, David. 1987. "Political Science and the Study of Corporate Power: A Dissent from the New Conventional Wisdom." *British Journal of Political Science* 17:385–405.

Vogel, Lise. 1983. *Marxism and the Oppression of Women.* New Brunswick, NJ: Rutgers University Press.

Vogeler, Ingolf. 1975. "American Peasantry." *Anthropological Quarterly* 48:223–35.

Volgy, Thomas J., John E. Schwarz, and Lawrence E. Imwalle. 1996. "In Search of Economic Well-Being: Worker Power and the Effects of Productivity, Inflation, Unemployment and Global Trade on Wages in Ten Wealthy Countries." *American Journal of Political Science* 40:1233–52.

Wacquant, Lois J. D., and William Julius Wilson. 1989. "The Cost of Racial and Class Exclusion in the Inner City." *Annals of the American Academy of Political and Social Science* 501:8–25.

Waddoups, Jeffrey, and Djeto Assane. 1993. "Mobility and Gender in a Segmented Labor Market: A Closer Look." *American Journal of Economics and Sociology* 52:399–411.

Wade, Peter. 1993. *Blackness and Race Mixture.* Baltimore: Johns Hopkins University Press.

Waegel, William B. 1984. "How Police Justify the Use of Deadly Force." *Social Problems* 32:144–55.

Waldman, Steven. August 10, 1992. "Benefits 'R' Us." *Newsweek,* pp. 56–58.

Wallace, Michael, Larry J. Griffin, and Beth A. Rubin. 1989. "The Positional Power of American Labor, 1963–1977." *American Sociological Review* 54:197–214.

Wallace, Michael, and Arne L. Kalleberg. 1981. "Economic Organization, Occupations, and Labor Force Consequences: Toward a Specification of Dual Economy Theory." Pp. 77–117 in *Sociological Perspectives on Labor Markets,* edited by I. Berg. New York: Academic Press.

Wallerstein, I. 1974. *The Modern World-System: Capitalist and the Origins of the European World-Economy in the Sixteenth Century.* New York: Academic.

Wallerstein, I. 1979. *The Capitalist World-Economy.* Cambridge: Cambridge University Press.

Walton, Anthony. January 1999. "Technology versus African-Americans." *Atlantic Monthly,* pp. 14–18.

Ward, Kathryn B. 1993. "Reconceptualizing World System Theory to Include Women." Pp. 43–68 in *Theory on Gender/Feminism on Theory,* edited by Paula England. New York: Aldine de Gruyter.

Warner, W. Lloyd, with Marchia Meeker and Kenneth Eells. 1960. *Social Class in America.* New York: Harper & Row.

Wasilewski, Edward, Jr. 1996. "Bargaining Outlook for 1996." *Compensation and Working Conditions.* Washington, D.C.: U.S. Government Printing Office.

Waters, Mary C., and Karl Eschbach. 1995. "Immigration and Ethnic and Racial Inequality in the United States." Pp. 419–46 in *Annual Review of Sociology,* edited by J. Hagan and K. S. Cook. Palo Alto, CA: Annual Reviews.

Weber, Max. 1964. *The Theory of Social and Economic Organization,* edited by Talcott Parsons. New York: The Free Press.

Webster, Murray, Jr., and James E. Driskell, Jr. 1983. "Beauty as Status." *American Journal of Sociology* 89:140–65.

Weede, Erich. 1982. "The Effects of Democracy and Socialist Strength on the Size Distribution of Income." *American Sociological Review* 23:151–65.

Weinstein, Michael M., and Eugene Smolensky. 1978. "Poverty." *Dictionary of American Economic History.*

Weiss, Gregory L., and Lynne E. Lonnquist. 1994. *The Sociology of Health, Healing, and Illness.* Englewood Cliffs, NJ: Prentice Hall.

Weiss, Michael J. 1988. *The Clustering of America.* New York: Harper & Row.

Weiss, Robert S., and David Riesman. 1966. "Work and Automation: Problems and Prospects." Pp. 553–618 in *Contemporary Social Problems,* edited by R. K. Merton and R. A. Nisbet. New York: Harcourt Brace Jovanovich.

Welch, Susan, and Michael W. Combs. 1985. "Intraracial Differences in Attitudes of Blacks: Class Cleavage or Consensus." *Phylon* 46:91–97.

Welch, Susan, John Gruhl, and Cassia Spohn. 1984. "Dismissal, Conviction, and Incarceration of Hispanic Defendants: A Comparison with Anglos and Blacks." *Social Science Quarterly* 65:257–64.

Welch, W. P. 1985. "Regression toward the Mean in Medical Care Costs." *Medical Care* 23:1234–41.

"The Well-Heeled: Pricey Sneakers in Inner City Help Set Nation's Fashion Trend." December 1, 1988. *Wall Street Journal,* pp. A1 and A6.

Weller, Jack E. 1965. *Yesterday's People: Life in Contemporary Appalachia.* Lexington: University of Kentucky Press.

Werner, Paul D., and Georgina Williams LaRussa. 1985. "Persistence and Change in Sex-Role Stereotypes." *Sex Roles* 12:1089–1100.

Wertz, Richard W., and Dorothy C. Wertz. 1981. "Notes on the Decline of Midwives and the Rise of Medical Obstetricians." Pp. 165–83 in *The Sociology of Health and Illness: Critical Perspectives,* edited by P. Conrad and R. Kern. New York: St. Martin's Press.

Western, Bruce. 1993. "Postwar Unionization in Eighteen Advanced Capitalist Countries." *American Sociological Review* 58:266–82.

Western, Mark, and Erik Olin Wright. 1994. "The Permeability of Class Boundaries to Intergenerational Mobility among Men in the United States, Canada, Norway and Sweden." *American Sociological Review* 59:606–29.

Wheaton, B. 1978. "The Sociogenesis of Psychological Disorder: Reexamining the Causal Issues with Longitudinal Data." *American Sociological Review* 43:383–403.

Wheaton, B. 1980. "The Sociogenesis of Psychological Disorder: An Attributional Theory." *Journal of Health and Social Behavior* 21:100–24.

Wheaton, B. 1983. "Stress, Personal Coping Resources, and Psychiatric Symptoms: An Investigation of Interactive Models." *Journal of Health and Social Behavior* 24:208–29.

Wheeler, Stanton, David Weisburd, and Nancy Bode. 1982. "Sentencing the White-Collar Offender: Rhetoric and Reality." *American Sociological Review* 47:641–59.

Whisnant, David E. 1983. *All That Is Native & Fine: The Politics of Culture in an American Region.* Chapel Hill: University of North Carolina Press.

Whitt, J. Allen. 1980. "Can Capitalists Organize Themselves?" Pp. 97–113 in *Power Structure Research,* edited by G. W. Domhoff. Beverly Hills, CA: Sage.

Wilensky, Gail R., and Louis F. Rossiter. 1986. "Patient Self-Selection in HMOS." *Health Affairs* 4:66–80.

Wilensky, Harold L. 1972. "Word Careers, and Social Integration." Pp. 79–92 in *Status Communities in Modern Society,* edited by Holger R. Stub. Hinsdale, IL: Dryden.

Wiley, Mary Glenn, and Arlene Eskilson. 1983. "Scaling the Corporate Ladder: Sex Differences in Expectations for Performance, Power and Mobility." *Social Psychology Quarterly* 46:351–9.

Wilhite, Allen, and John Theilmann. 1986. "Women, Blacks, and PAC Discrimination." *Social Science Quarterly* 67:283–96.

Williams, David R., and Chiquita Collins. 1995. "U.S. Socioeconomic and Racial Differences in Health: Patterns and Explanations." Pp. 349–86 in *Annual Review of Sociology 1995,* edited by J. Hagan and K. S. Cook. Palo Alto, CA: Annual Reviews.

Williams, Kirk R. 1984. "Economic Sources of Homicide: Reestimating the Effects of Poverty and Inequality." *American Sociological Review* 49:283–89.

Williams, Kirk R., and Robert L. Flewelling. 1988. "The Social Production of Criminal Homicide: A Comparative Study of Disaggregated Rates in American Cities." *American Sociological Review* 53:421–31.

Williams, Robin M., Jr. 1970. *American Society: A Sociological Interpretation.* New York: Knopf.

Williams, Ted. May 8, 1987. "On the Reservation: America's Apartheid." *National Review,* pp. 28–30.

Willie, Charles Vert. 1979. *The Caste and Class Controversy.* Bayside, NY: General Hall.

Willis, Angela Gonzalez, Gordon B. Willis, Alisa Male, Marilyn Henderson, and Ronald W. Manderscheid. 1998. "Mental Illness and Disability in the U.S. Adult Household Population." Pp. 113–18 in *Mental Health, United States, 1998,* edited by R. W. Manderscheid and M. J. Henderson. Washington, D.C.: Center for Medical Health Services.

Wilson, Kenneth L., and Alejandro Portes. 1975. "The Educational Attainment Process: Results from a National Sample." *American Journal of Sociology* 81:343–63.

Wilson, William J. September 14–19, 1970. "Race Relations Models and Explanations of Ghetto Behavior." Paper presented at the Seventh World Congress of Sociology of the International Sociological Association, Varna, Bulgaria.

Wilson, William J. 1978. *The Declining Significance of Race: Blacks and Changing American Institutions.* Chicago: University of Chicago Press.

Wilson, William Julius. 1982. "The Declining Significance of Race-Revisited but Not Revised."

Pp. 399–405 in *Majority & Minority: The Dynamics of Race and Ethnicity in American Life,* edited by N. R. Yetman and C. H. Steele. Boston: Allyn and Bacon.

Wilson, William Julius. 1987. *The Truly Disadvantaged: The Inner City, the Underclass, and Public Policy.* Chicago: University of Chicago Press.

Wilson, William Julius. 1999. *The Bridge Over the Racial Divide.* Berkeley: University of California Press.

Winegarden, C. R. 1974. "The Fertility of AFDC Women: An Economic Analysis." *Journal of Economics and Business* 26:159–66.

Withorn, Ann. 1999. *Worrying about Welfare Reform: Community-Based Agencies Respond.* Boston: Academics Working Group on Poverty.

Wolf, Naomi. 1991. *The Beauty Myth: How Images of Beauty Are Used against Women.* New York: Morrow.

Wolf, Wendy C. 1976. "Occupational Attainments of Married Women: Do Career Contingencies Matter?" Madison, WI: Center for Demography and Ecology Working Paper No. 76–3, University of Wisconsin.

Wolff, Edward N. May 1992. "Changing Inequality of Wealth." *American Economic Review* 82:552–58.

Wolff, Edward N. 1995. "How the Pie Is Sliced." *The American Prospect* 22:58–64.

Wolinsky, F. D. 1980. "The Performance of Health Maintenance Organizations: An Analytic Review." *Millbank Memorial Fund Quarterly* 58:537–87.

"Women-Owned Businesses Employ More People than the Fortune 500." April 20, 1993. *Akron Beacon Journal,* p. D6.

Wong, Raymond Sin-Kwok. 1994. "Postwar Mobility Trends in Advanced Industrial Societies." Pp. 121–44 in *Research in Social Stratification and Mobility,* edited by R. Althauser and M. Wallace. Greenwich, CT: JAI Press.

The World Bank. 1999. *World Development Report: Knowledge for Development 1998/99.* Oxford: Oxford University Press.

Wright, Erik Olin. 1976. "Class Boundaries in Advanced Capitalist Societies." *New Left Review* 98:3–41.

Wright, Erik Olin. 1977. "Class Structure and Occupation: A Research Note." Institute for Research on Poverty Discussion Paper No. 415–77. Madison: University of Wisconsin-Madison.

Wright, Erik Olin. 1978. "Race, Class, and Income Inequality." *American Journal of Sociology* 83:1368–97.

Wright, Erik Olin, Janeen Baxter, and Gunn Elisabeth Birkelund. 1995. "The Gender Gap in Workplace Authority in Seven Nations." *American Sociological Review* 60:407–35.

Wright, Erik Olin, and Donmoon Cho. 1992. "The Relative Permeability of Class Boundaries to Cross-

Class Friendships: A Comparative Study of the United States, Canada, Sweden, and Norway." *American Sociological Review* 57:85–102.

Wright, Erik Olin, and Bill Martin. 1987. "The Transformation of the American Class Structure. 1960–1980." *American Journal of Sociology* 93:1–29.

Wright, Erik Olin, and Luca Perrone. 1977. "Marxist Class Categories and Income Inequality." *American Sociological Review* 42:32–55.

Wright, Erik Olin, and Joachim Singelmann. 1982. "Proletarianization in the Changing American Class Structure." Pp. S176–S209 in *Marxist Inquiries: Studies of Labor, Class, and States,* edited by M. Burawoy and T. Skocpol. Chicago: University of Chicago Press.

Wright, James D., and Julie A. Lam. 1987. "Homeless and the Low-Income Housing Supply." *Social Policy* 17:48–53.

Wrong, Dennis H. 1959. "The Functional Theory of Stratification: Some Neglected Considerations." *American Sociological Review* 24:772–82.

Wrong, Dennis H. 1972. "Social Inequality without Social Stratification." Pp. 69–79 in *Status Communities in Modern Society,* edited by H. R. Stub. Hinsdale, IL: Dryden.

Yanagisako, Sylvia Junko, and Jane Fishburne Collier. 1987. "Toward a Unified Analysis of Gender and Kinship." Pp. 14–50 in *Gender and Kinship: Essays Toward a Unified Analysis,* edited by J. F. Collier and S. J. Yanagisako. Stanford, CA: Stanford University Press.

Yang, Alan S. 1997. "Attitudes toward Homosexuality." *Public Opinion Quarterly* 61:477–507.

Yeuell, H. Davis. 1985. *Moving Mountains: A History of Presbyterian and Reformed Faith at Work in Appalachia.* Amesville, OH: Coalition for Appalachian Ministry.

Yllo, K. 1983. "Sexual Equality and Violence against Wives in American States." *Journal of Comparative Family Studies* 14:67–86.

Yllo, K. 1984. "The Status of Women, Marital Equality and Violence against Wives." *Journal of Family Issues* 5:307–20.

Zaldivar, R. A. February 15, 1993a. "Is There a Cure for U.S. Health Care?" *Akron Beacon Journal,* pp. D1, D5.

Zaldivar, R. A. February 26, 1993b. "New Tax May Aid Health Care." *Akron Beacon Journal,* pp. A1, A4.

Zastrow, Charles. 1982. *Introduction to Social Welfare Institutions: Social Problems, Services and Current Issues.* Homewood, IL: Dorsey.

Zeitlin, Irving. 1968. *Ideology and the Development of Sociological Theory.* Englewood Cliffs, NJ: Prentice Hall.

Zeitlin, Maurice, ed. 1977. *American Society, Inc.* Skokie, IL: Rand McNally.

Zieger, Robert H. 1986. *American Workers, American Unions, 1920–1985.* Baltimore: The Johns Hopkins University Press.

Zigler, Edward, and Susan Muenchow. 1983. "Infant Day Care and Infant-Care Leaves." *American Psychologist* 38:91–94.

Zimmerman, Don H., and Candace West. 1975. "Sex Roles, Interruptions and Silences in Conversation." Pp. 105–29 in *Language and Sex: Difference and Dominance,* edited by B. Thorne and N. Henley. Rowley, MA: Newbury House.

Zingraff, Rhonda, and Michael D. Schulman. 1984. "Social Bases of Class Consciousness: A Study of Southern Textile Workers with a Comparison by Race." *Social Forces* 63:98–116.

Zipp, John F. 1994. "Government Employment and Black-White Earnings Inequality, 1980–1990." *Social Problems* 41:363–82.

Zuckerman, Alan. 1977. "The Concept 'Political Elite': Lessons from Mosca and Pareto." *The Journal of Politics* 39:324–44.